Titles in the Series

J. Błażewicz, K. Ecker, B. Plateau and D. Trystram (Eds.)
Handbook on Parallel and Distributed Processing
ISBN 978-3-540-66441-3

H.H. Adelsberger, Kinshuk, J.M. Pawlowski and D. Sampson (Eds.)
Handbook on Information Technologies for Education and Training
ISBN 978-3-540-74154-1, 2nd Edition

C.W. Holsapple (Ed.)
Handbook on Knowledge Management 1 Knowledge Matters
ISBN 978-3-540-43527-3
Handbook on Knowledge Management 2 Knowledge Directions
ISBN 978-3-540-43848-9

J. Błażewicz, W. Kubiak, I. Morzy and M. Rusinkiewicz (Eds.)
Handbook on Data Management in Information Systems
ISBN 978-3-540-43893-9

P. Bernus, P. Nemes and G. Schmidt (Eds.)
Handbook on Enterprise Architecture
ISBN 978-3-540-00343-4

S. Staab and R. Studer (Eds.)
Handbook on Ontologies
ISBN 978-3-540-70999-2, 2nd Edition

S.O. Kimbrough and D.J. Wu (Eds.)
Formal Modelling in Electronic Commerce
ISBN 978-3-540-21431-1

P. Bernus, K. Merlins and G. Schmidt (Eds.)
Handbook on Architectures of Information Systems
ISBN 978-3-540-25472-0, 2nd Edition

S. Kirn, O. Herzog, P. Lockemann and O. Spaniol (Eds.)
Multiagent Engineering
ISBN 978-3-540-31406-6

J. Błażewicz, K. Ecker, E. Pesch, G. Schmidt and J. Weglarz (Eds.)
Handbook on Scheduling
ISBN 978-3-540-28046-0

F. Burstein and C.W. Holsapple (Eds.)
Handbook on Decision Support Systems 1
ISBN 978-3-540-48712-8

F. Burstein and C.W. Holsapple (Eds.)
Handbook on Decision Support Systems 2
ISBN 978-3-540-48715-9

D. Seese, Ch. Weinhardt and F. Schlottmann (Eds.)
Handbook on Information Technology in Finance
ISBN 978-3-540-49486-7

T.C. Edwin Cheng and Tsan-Ming Choi (Eds.)
Innovative Quick Response Programs in Logistics and Supply Chain Management
ISBN 978-3-642-04312-3

J. vom Brocke and M. Rosemann (Eds.)
Handbook on Business Process Management 1
ISBN 978-3-642-00415-5
Handbook on Business Process Management 2
ISBN 978-3-642-01981-4

T.-M. Choi and T.C. Edwin Cheng
Supply Chain Coordination under Uncertainty
ISBN 978-3-642-19256-2

C. Schwindt and J. Zimmermann
Handbook on Project Management and Scheduling Vol.1
ISBN 978-3-319-05442-1
Handbook on Project Management and Scheduling Vol.2
978-3-319-05914-3

R. Bisdorff, L. Dias, P. Meyer, V. Mousseau and M. Pirlot (Eds.)
Evaluation and Decision Models with Multiple Criteria
ISBN 978-3-662-46815-9

More information about this series at http://www.springer.com/series/3795

International Handbooks on Information Systems

Series Editors

Peter Bernus, Jacek Błażewicz, Günter Schmidt, Michael J. Shaw

Raymond Bisdorff • Luis C. Dias • Patrick Meyer •
Vincent Mousseau • Marc Pirlot
Editors

Evaluation and Decision Models with Multiple Criteria

Case Studies

Springer

Editors
Raymond Bisdorff
Faculty of Science, Technology and Communication
Computer Science and Communications Research Unit
University of Luxembourg
Luxembourg

Luis C. Dias
Faculty of Economics
University of Coimbra
Coimbra, Portugal

Patrick Meyer
Télécom Bretagne
Brest Cedex, France

Vincent Mousseau
Ecole Centrale Paris
Châtenay-Malabry Cedex
France

Marc Pirlot
Faculté Polytechnique
Université de Mons
Mons, Belgium

International Handbooks on Information Systems
ISBN 978-3-662-46815-9 ISBN 978-3-662-46816-6 (eBook)
DOI 10.1007/978-3-662-46816-6

Library of Congress Control Number: 2015942695

Springer Heidelberg New York Dordrecht London

Printed on acid-free paper

Springer-Verlag GmbH Berlin Heidelberg is part of Springer Science+Business Media (www.springer.com)

Preface

The elaboration of this Handbook has a long and colorful history. The initial call for contributions goes back to Spring 2008. It was sent to colleagues we knew were engaged in applications of Multiple Criteria Decision Aiding (MCDA); the aim of the initial book project being to emphasize methodological issues and, in particular, appropriate application of existing procedures for modelling and aggregating preferences in view of aiding decision.

The book project emerged as an initiative of the *Decision Deck Project*[1] and was positively supported by COST Action IC0602 *Algorithmic Decision Theory*.[2] An early contact with Springer offered the opportunity to publish a Handbook on MCDA Applications in their "International Series." From the simple editing of a collection of individual papers, as planned in the beginning and aligning a list of MCDA applications, we shifted hence to an ambitious comprehensive Springer Handbook editing project, including furthermore a methodological part.

This move revealed more demanding and time consuming than anticipated. We succeeded in convincing the authors of the Evaluation and Decision Models book series (D. Bouyssou, T. Marchant, P. Perny, M. Pirlot, A. Tsoukiàs, and P. Vincke) to provide the required methodological part. It became also later opportune to add a chapter about XMCDA, a data standard to encode MCDA data in XML, and one about *diviz*, a software workbench to support the analyst in the decision aid process, both developed in the context of the Decision Deck Project.

Finally, we are in the position to present this Handbook to the reader. We would like to address here our apologies to our contributors for the resulting very long editing time, a time span which can explain why some references cited by the earliest contributors in this Handbook might not be the most recent. We acknowledge and take full responsibility for this inconvenience. However, we are convinced that this project became much richer. The book showcases a large variety of MCDA applications, within a coherent framework provided by the methodological chapters

---

[1] http://www.decision-deck.org.

[2] http://www.cost-ic0602.org/.

and the comments accompanying each case study. The chapters describing XMCDA and *diviz* invite the reader to experiment with MCDA methods, and perhaps develop new variants, using data from these case studies or other cases the reader might face. Every time the lessons and tools presented in this book contribute to the use of MCDA in classrooms or in real-world problems, we will feel our objective has been accomplished.

Acknowledgements The editors are thankful to all the chapter contributors for sharing some of their experience in applying MCDA, as well as the authors of the methodological chapters. We would also like to express our gratitude to the many reviewers invited to read and comment on initial drafts of the chapters, thus contributing to improve their organization and clarity.

This project would not have been possible without the support of the Decision Deck Consortium, the COST ACTION IC0602 "Algorithmic Decision Theory" and the GDRI Algodec. Also, Springer, by providing us the ambitious opportunity to edit a Handbook, contributed much to the actual content the reader will discover hereafter.

Luxembourg, Luxembourg — Raymond Bisdorff
Coimbra, Portugal — Luis C. Dias
Brest, France — Patrick Meyer
Paris, France — Vincent Mousseau
Mons, Belgium — Marc Pirlot
July 2014

Contents

About the Editors

Raymond Bisdorff holds a degree in Business Administration from the University of Liège, Belgium (1975), a Ph.D. in Operations Research (supervisor Prof. B. Roy) from the Université Paris Dauphine (1981) and a Ph.D. in Management Sciences from the University of Liège, Belgium (2002). He is since 2003 full professor of Applied Mathematics and Computer Science at the University of Luxembourg, where he teaches courses on algorithmic decision theory, multiple criteria decision aiding, computational statistics and discrete mathematics. He served the international OR community as president of ORBEL—the Belgian OR society (2008–2010), vice president of EURO—the Association of European OR Societies (1997–2000) and vice president of IFORS—the International Federation of OR Societies (2005–2007). His main research interest is focused on outranking based decision aiding algorithms for selecting, ranking, sorting or rating, and clustering with multiple incommensurable performance criteria. His major articles appeared in EJOR, Computers & OR, 4OR, and JMCDA.

Luis C. Dias obtained a degree in Informatics Engineering from the School of Science and Technology at the University of Coimbra in 1992, a Ph.D. in Management by the University of Coimbra in 2001, and a Habilitation degree in Decision Aiding Science in 2013 in the same university. He is currently a tenured assistant professor at FEUC (School of Economics at the University of Coimbra), which he joined in 1992, where he has been teaching courses on decision analysis, operations research, informatics, and related areas. He is also a researcher at the INESC Coimbra R&D Institute, a member of the coordination board of U.Coimbra's Energy for Sustainability Initiative. His research interests include multicriteria decision analysis, performance assessment, group decision and negotiation support, decision support systems, and applications in the areas of energy and environment. His publications include over 50 articles in peer-reviewed international journals.

Patrick Meyer obtained a degree in Mathematics from the University of Liège in 1999, a Ph.D. in Mathematics and Engineering Sciences jointly from the University of Luxembourg and the Faculty of Engineering of Mons in 2007 and, in 2013, a Habilitation degree in Computer Science from the Université Paris Dauphine. He is currently associate professor at Télécom Bretagne, where he teaches courses on operational research, multicriteria decision aiding (MCDA), and algorithmics. He is a researcher in the Lab-STICC CNRS Laboratory (UMR 6285), where he is also co-responsible of the DECIDE research team. His research interests include the modeling of the MCDA process and the development of tools to support it, group decision making and applications of MCDA to real world decision problems, as well as its promotion in other research domains, as, e.g., economics. Moreover, he is the author or co-author of 23 scientific publications.

Vincent Mousseau obtained a degree in Computer Science (1989) and a Ph.D. (1993) from Université Paris Dauphine. He received habilitation from Université Paris Dauphine in 2003. He was assistant professor at Université Paris Dauphine (1994–2008), and is now full professor at Ecole Centrale Paris (2008–). He heads the research team on "Decision Aid for Production/Distribution Systems" in the Industrial engineering laboratory (Ecole Centrale Paris). He is president of the Decision Deck Consortium. His research interests include Multiple Criteria Decision Aid, Preference Modelling and Elicitation, Group Decision Making, and Spatial Decision Making. He authored or co-authored more than 50 scientific publications.

Marc Pirlot holds a degree in Mathematics from Université Libre de Bruxelles and a Ph.D. in Mathematics from Université de Mons-Hainaut (1981). He has been teaching operations research, statistics, and decision analysis at the Faculty of Engineering, University of Mons, since 1989. He served as president of ORBEL, the Belgian OR society (1996–1998) and as principal editor of its journal *JORBEL* (1992–2002). He is the author or co-author of over 80 scientific publications and 3 books, which mainly focus on multicriteria decision analysis, preference modelling, multi-objective optimization, and metaheuristics. He has also been involved in applied research projects with the industry and the public sector.

Contributors

Mohamed Ali Aloulou
LAMSADE, Université Paris Dauphine, Paris, France

Gabriela Fernández Barberis
Department of Quantitative Methods, San Pablo - CEU University, Madrid, Spain

Sébastien Bigaret
Institut Mines-Télécom, Télécom Bretagne, UMR CNRS 6285 Lab-STICC, Technopôle Brest-Iroise CS 83818, 29238 Brest Cedex 3, France

Raymond Bisdorff
Faculty of Science, Technology and Communication, Computer Science and Communications Research Unit, University of Luxembourg, Luxembourg

Denis Bouyssou
CNRS LAMSADE & Université Paris Dauphine, Paris, France

Oliver Braun
Department of Quantitative Methods for Business and Management, Trier University of Applied Sciences, Birkenfeld, Germany

Pierre Bulens
Laborelec, Linkebeek, Belgium

Salem Chakhar
Portsmouth Business School, University of Portsmouth, Portland Building, Portland Street, Portsmouth, PO1 3AH, UK

Eric Chojnacki
IRSN - Institut de Radioprotection et de Sûreté Nucléaire, Centre d'études de Cadarache, Saint Paul Lez Durance, France

Alberto Colorni
Dipartimento Design, Politecnico di Milano, Milano, Italy

Sébastien Damart
Département d'administration économique et sociale, Université de Rouen, Rouen, France

Luis C. Dias
Faculty of Economics, University of Coimbra, Coimbra, Portugal

Michael Doumpos
Department of Production Engineering and Management, Financial Engineering Laboratory, Technical University of Crete, Chania, Greece

Léon Duvivier
Business Development, Laborelec, Linkebeek, Belgium

María Carmen Escribano
Department of Quantitative Methods, San Pablo - CEU University, Madrid, Spain

José Rui Figueira
CEG-IST Instituto Superior Técnico, Universidade de Lisboa, A. Rovisco Pais 1, 1049-001 Lisbon, Portugal

Coralie Goffin
Sustainable Process Technologies, Laborelec, Linkebeek, Belgium

Sylvie Guerrand
SNCF, Saint-Etienne-du-Rouvray, France

Serge Haddad
Laboratoire Spécification et Vérification, École Normale Supérieure de Cachan, Cachan, France

Pierre Louis Kunsch
CoDE Department, Université libre de Bruxelles (ULB), Brussels, Belgium

Alessandro Luè
Poliedra, Milano, Italy
Dipartimento Design, Politecnico di Milano, Milano, Italy

Thierry Marchant
Department of Data analysis, Ghent University, Gent, Belgium

Catherine Mercat-Rommens
IRSN - Institut de Radioprotection et de Sûreté Nucléaire, Centre d'études de Cadarache, Saint Paul Lez Durance, France

Stéphane Aimé Metchebon Takougang
Université de Mons, Faculté Polytechnique, Mons, Belgium
Institut Supérieur d'Informatique et de Gestion, Ouagadougou, Burkina Faso

Patrick Meyer
Institut Mines-Télécom, Télécom Bretagne, UMR CNRS 6285 Lab-STICC, Technopôle Brest-Iroise CS 83818, 29238 Brest Cedex 3, France

Lynda Mokdad
LACL, Faculté des Sciences et Technologies, Université Paris XII, Créteil, France

Florent Montignac
CEA, LITEN, Grenoble, France

Vincent Mousseau
Laboratoire Géne Industriel, Ecole Centrale Paris, Grande Voie des Vignes, 92295 Châtenay-Malabry Cedex, France

Pascal Oberti
Université di Corsica Pasquale Paoli - CNRS UMR 6240 LISA, Corte, France

Meltem Öztürk
Lamsade - Université Paris IX Dauphine, Paris, France

Christophe Paoli
Department of Computer Engineering, Galatasaray University, Istanbul, Turkey

Marc Pirlot
Université de Mons, Faculté Polytechnique, Mons, Belgium

Herimandimbiniaina Ralijaona
AGETIPA, Bâtiment Le Colisée, Ampasanimalo, Antananarivo, Madagascar

Benjamin Rousval
LAMSADE, Université Paris Dauphine, Paris, France

Carlos A. Silva
IN+ Center for Innovation Technology and Policy Research (IST), MIT Portugal Program, Sustainable Energy Systems, Technical University of Lisbon, Lisbon, Portugal

Blaise Some
Université de Ouagadoudou, Laboratoire LANIBIO, Ouagadougou, Burkina Faso

Marco Spohn
Department of Quantitative Methods for Business and Management, Trier University of Applied Sciences, Birkenfeld, Germany

Jacques Teghem
Université de Mons, Faculté Polytechnique, Mons, Belgium

Tommi Tervonen
Erasmus University Rotterdam, Rotterdam, Netherlands

Miguel Trigueiros Covas
Portugal Telecom, MIT Portugal Program, Sustainable Energy Systems, Lisboa, Portugal

Alexis Tsoukiàs
CNRS - LAMSADE, UMR 7243 Université Paris Dauphine, Paris, France

Berthold Ulungu
Université de Mons, Faculté Polytechnique, Mons, Belgium
Institut Supérieur des Techniques Appliquées de Kinshasa, Kinshasa, DR Congo

Mathieu Vander Straeten
CoDE Department, Université libre de Bruxelles (ULB), Brussels, Belgium

Philippe Vincke
Université libre de Bruxelles, Ecole Polytechnique, Campus de la Plaine, CP210/01, boulevard du Triomphe, 1050 Bruxelles, Belgium

Samuel Yonkeu
Institut Supérieur d'Informatique et de Gestion, Ouagadougou, Burkina Faso

Samir Youcef
LAMSADE Université Paris Dauphine, Paris, France

Constantin Zopounidis
Department of Production Engineering and Management, Financial Engineering Laboratory, Technical University of Crete, Chania, Greece

Chapter 1
Introduction

Raymond Bisdorff, Luis C. Dias, Patrick Meyer, Vincent Mousseau, and Marc Pirlot

Abstract This introductory chapter explains, first, the strategy guiding the editing of the MCDA application case studies. The second section illustrates the overall organization of the handbook into three parts: a concise methodological introduction to the concepts of decision aiding, preference modelling and recommendation building; the main part with 15 case studies of MCDA applications; and a short third part devoted to support tools for the MCDA process. The chapter ends with listing some highlights of the book content.

1.1 The Editing Strategy

Our main goal with this book was to illustrate the rich diversity of aspects which is typical of multiple criteria decision problems. Decision aiding is a *process*. As such, it involves a series of actors (decision maker(s), stakeholders, experts, analysts, etc.); interaction and feedback play a crucial role. The activity of modelling the problem

R. Bisdorff (✉)
Faculty of Science, Technology and Communication, Computer Science and Communications Research Unit, University of Luxembourg, Luxembourg
e-mail: raymond.bisdorff@uni.lu

L.C. Dias
Faculty of Economics, University of Coimbra, Coimbra, Portugal
e-mail: lmcdias@fe.uc.pt

P. Meyer
Institut Mines-Télécom, Télécom Bretagne, UMR CNRS 6285 Lab-STICC, Technopôle Brest-Iroise CS 83818, 29238 Brest Cedex 3, France
e-mail: patrick.meyer@telecom-bretagne.eu

V. Mousseau
Laboratoire Génie Industriel, Ecole Centrale Paris, Grande Voie des Vignes, 92295 Châtenay-Malabry Cedex, France
e-mail: vincent.mousseau@ecp.fr

M. Pirlot
Université de Mons, Faculté Polytechnique, Mons, Belgium
e-mail: marc.pirlot@umons.ac.be

R. Bisdorff et al. (eds.), *Evaluation and Decision Models with Multiple Criteria*, International Handbooks on Information Systems,
DOI 10.1007/978-3-662-46816-6_1

and the decision maker's preferences is more important and time consuming than the more technical part consisting in choosing and applying a method for aggregating the decision maker's (DM's) preferences. Formulating a recommendation to the DM is also a delicate part of the process.

In line with our desire to illustrate the complexity of the decision aiding process, we addressed the interested contributors the following guidelines for writing their application.

- The context of the case should be described: what is the decision problem, the decision maker(s), the stakeholders, the analysts, the alternatives, the criteria, the performances of the alternatives, … ?
- What have been the difficulties in the process of identifying or constructing these elements?
- Which method(s) has (have) been used ? How have the parameters of these methods been set?
- How did the decision aiding process evolve (main steps, feedback loops, branching, abandoned branches, …)?
- Recommendation, decision.
- Comments on the case and on the decision aiding process.

The proposed framework underlies a way of conceiving a decision aiding process that is quite general. A wide range of applications fit in the model that is described in a formal way in the methodological part of this book (see Chap. 2). The study of decision aiding processes is a research domain in itself, in which there is still much work to be done. In particular, a detailed and operational description of this sort of process is required in view of building computerized decision aiding systems that could help analysts to monitor such processes.

The 15 applications presented in Part II of this book describe examples of decision aiding processes. In view of emphasizing their salient features, we decided to add an individual editors' commentary to each application chapter. A common line of critical reviewing guidelines was therefore developed. The eventually chosen template for structuring our comments identifies five major aspects: application context, problem structuring, performance evaluation modelling, decision aiding process, tangibility and practical impact of results.

1. Context of the decision aid application

    - How does this application fit into the "big picture" of the book, and MCDA in general?
    - What was the objective of the decision aid intervention?
    - (Possibly:) Other objectives: e.g., had authors the objective of trying a novel method?
    - Who was the decision aid addressee?
    - What actors participated directly or indirectly?
    - Who acted as analyst and what was his role?
    - What phases can be identified and what was the time span of the decision aid process?

2. Problem structuring
   - (Possibly:) Use of problem structuring methods.
   - Type of result sought (problem statement[1]).
   - How was the set of alternatives defined ? Global characteristics of this set.
   - How was the set of evaluation criteria defined? Global characteristics of this set.
   - (Possibly:) Modelling of uncertainties.
3. Performance evaluation
   - MCDA model choice for aggregating criteria.
   - Elicitation process.
   - (Possibly:) How divergence among actors was addressed (aggregation, discussion, ...)
4. Process-related aspects
   - Client-analyst interaction.
   - Reiterations.
   - Interactions between phases.
   - Sensitivity/robustness analysis.
5. Results
   - Tangible results: artifacts
   - Intangible results: knowledge, relationship among actors
   - Impact relatively to the objective of the decision process
6. Other remarks
   - Methodology aspects (questionable aspects, success factors, what else might have been tried).
   - Relevance of this application.

We hope that the case studies of MCDA applications may thus contribute to validate the general framework and permit to deepen the analysis of decision aiding processes, as a step towards the implementation of decision aiding monitoring systems.

1.2 Organization of the Handbook

The Handbook is divided into three, unequal parts. A first methodological part, consisting of three chapters, gives insight into respectively the concepts and issues of a decision aid approach, the problem of constructing an aggregated perspective with multiple preference dimensions, and the building of convincing decision aid recommendations. The second and by far the main part consists of 15 chapters devoted to present and discuss selected MCDA applications that will be introduced in detail hereafter in Sect. 1.2.2. Each application is followed by a short commentary. The last part, which describes tools to support the MCDA process, first presents the

[1]In some of the contributed chapters of this book, the authors use the french word *problématique* when they refer to the problem statement.

XMCDA data standard, before detailing the *diviz* software platform to design and execute MCDA methods.

1.2.1 Theoretical Background

Besides aiming to contribute to the analysis of decision aiding processes, this book also aims at shedding some light on multicriteria decision methods, i.e. methods that aggregate the decision maker's preferences on the different criteria in an overall preference. Such methods make the necessary trade-offs between conflicting objectives, and yield a model of the decision maker's overall preference. A bunch of methods have been proposed since the 1950s. Some of them are inserted in elaborated methodologies, and all of them use more or less complex mathematical procedures (for panoramas of such procedures, see e.g. Vincke, 1992; Roy and Bouyssou, 1993; Pomerol and Barba-Romero, 2000; Belton and Stewart, 2002; Ishizaka and Nemery, 2013).

The choice of an aggregation method is an issue in MCDA. Several papers in the literature deal with the selection of the most appropriate MCDA method depending on the decision problem, the type of data available, etc. (see e.g. Ozernoy, 1987, 1992; Hobbs et al., 1992; Guitouni and Martel, 1998; Polatidis et al., 2006). Why such a diversity of methods? Is there a best one? Some authors—and most proponents of such methods—support this idea. Also, in applications, many analysts systematically use a particular method or a family of variants of a method. Our *credo* is different. We believe that some methods are better suited for some contexts and other for some other contexts. For instance, certain methods can naturally deal with qualitative evaluations. The logic underlying the aggregation of the criteria values in some methods may be more easily understandable by some decision makers than by some others. Or these may be more inclined to answer certain types of questions than other types. The logical analysis of the aggregation methods allows to produce a precise view of the strengths and weaknesses of the various models. It is possible, for instance, to determine which kind of preferences can be represented by a given method (through an axiomatic analysis of the methods or the preferences). Alternatively, the properties of the methods can be established, which allows to compare them and select one in a more informed way. Hence, in our view, the analyst should master several methods and be able to choose the most appropriate one in a given context.

Chapter 3 in Part I, entitled *Modelling preferences*, browses a picture of the main logic at work in usual aggregation procedures. More precisely, it characterizes the families of preferences that can be represented by some general types of models. This chapter does not provide a description of all aggregation methods used throughout the book. Instead, it analyzes general frameworks, into which most particular methods do belong. These frameworks allow to better understand the logic of aggregation implemented in the methods. Analysts can benefit from such a knowledge for improving the way they question decision makers about their preferences. Or, even better, to design methods that maximize the information yielded by each answer to well-chosen questions (*active learning*). In the applications we can see how the general aggregation principles were used and it may also be interesting to question the choice made by the analyst in charge. We observe that in some applications, several aggregation methods were used for the same decision problem, leading to decision recommendations that are likely to be more convincing.

A third methodological issue is the subject of the last chapter (Chap. 4) in Part I. This chapter is entitled *Building recommendations*. It deals with the last part of the decision aiding process. It uses the model of the decision maker's preferences that was built during the aggregation phase to derive a recommendation addressed to the decision maker. Such a conclusion is by no means a decision, the latter pertaining to the exclusive responsibility of the decision maker. The recommendation gathers the conclusions that appear sufficiently well-established to be valid independently on the remaining uncertainties about the decision maker's preferences (*robust conclusions*). Less robust conclusions can be part of the recommendation but these should be accompanied with appropriate comments. The main source of the difficulty in formulating recommendations is that the decision maker's preferences may not be always fully determined and they are not, in general, perfectly reflected in the aggregation model. Chapter 4 reviews the different problem statements contexts (choosing, sorting, ranking) and specifies, in each case, a certain number of ideas that can be used to derive reasonably well-established recommendations.

1.2.2 Case Studies of MCDA Applications

The applications collected in Part II of this book span multiple countries, multiple fields, and multiple types of problems. In geographical terms, most applications occurred in Europe, with Belgium, France, and Greece represented in more than one case. The exceptions are two applications in African countries, coauthored by African and European authors. In terms of type of problem statement, the book presents choice, ranking, and classification problems. Nine out of the 15 applications intend to eventually select the best alternative, although many of them perform a ranking or a classification of the alternatives as a modelling option. One classification method, ELECTRE TRI, is the aggregation approach used more often in this set of applications, but other approaches such as additive value aggregation (Chaps. 14 and 17), AHP (Chap. 18), and PROMETHEE (Chap. 19), among others, are also represented in the book. Table 1.1 provides a summary of the applications chapters, indicating these and other characteristics of each application.

The first chapters have diversified application domains, but share a common goal: to select the most preferred alternative. The chosen modelling options are however diverse. Chapter 5, by R. Bisdorff, addresses a problem of a decision by a jury intending to select a winner in a posters competition. It describes how the process unfolded and further (re-)analyzes the problem using a different approach. Chakhar et al.'s Chap. 6 presents a framework to evaluate webservices that need to be assembled for a particular purpose. Although the ultimate goal is to select one composition of services, it proceeds to classify the possible compositions according

Table 1.1 Applications in this book

Application	Field of application	Country	Goal	Problem statement	Method	Client type	Decision maker(s)	Decision support system
Chapter 5 choosing the best poster in a conference	Jury decisions	Greece	Analysis of a problem	Choice	Condorcet method and RUBIS	Scientific association	Jury members	An existing software
Chapter 6 composite web service selection	Internet services	France	Framework	Choice (by sorting)	ELECTRE TRI	Consumer	An individual	A prototype was developed
Chapter 7 site selection for a kindergarten	Education	Spain	Analysis of a problem	Choice (by ranking)	SMAA-III	Corporation	Group of decision makers	An existing software
Chapter 8 choosing a cooling system for a power plant	Energy/environment	Belgium	Proof of concept (ex-post)	Choice (by ranking)	Weighted sum and ELECTRE II	Competence centre	Group of experts	Not mentioned
Chapter 9 localization of wind farm projects	Energy/environment	France	Proof of concept	Choice (by ranking)	ELECTRE III	Public administration	Group of stakeholders	A SDSS was developed
Chapter 10 assessment of data centers environmental sustainability	Energy/environment	Portugal	Framework	Sorting	ELECTRE TRI	Corporation	Group of experts	An existing software

Chapter 11 cost valuation of a nuclear-fuel repository	Energy/environment	Belgium	Analysis of a problem	Choice (determining a value)	fuzzy inference	Public administration	Group of experts	A DSS was developed
Chapter 12 Assessing the response to land degradation risk	Energy/environment	Burkina Faso	Framework	Sorting	ELECTRE TRI	(Public administration)	An expert	A SDSS was developed
Chapter 13 Post-accident nuclear risk evaluation	Energy/environment	France	Analysis of a problem	Sorting	ELECTRE TRI	Public administration	Group of stakeholders	A SDSS was developed
Chapter 14 hazardous material transport	Energy/environment, transportation	Italy	Proof of concept	Choice (by ranking)	Weighted sum	Public administration	Group of experts	SDSS (custom adapted)
Chapter 15 rural road maintenance	Transportation	Madagascar	Proof of concept	Sorting	ELECTRE TRI	Public administration	Group of stakeholders	A DSS was developed
Chapter 16 evaluation of comfort	Transportation	France	Proof of concept	Sorting	ELECTRE TRI	State-owned company	Group of experts	Not mentioned

(continued)

Table 1.1 (continued)

Application	Field of application	Country	Goal	Problem statement	Method	Client type	Decision maker(s)	Decision support system
Chapter 17 evaluating hydrogen storage systems for future vehicles	Transportation	European Union (sponsor)	Proof of concept	Choice (by ranking)	MACBETH	(Several corporations)	Group of experts	An existing software
Chapter 18 personal financial planning	Finance	Germany (authors)	Framework	Choice	Optimization and AHP	(Generic)	An individual	A DSS was developed
Chapter 19 bank rating	Finance	Greece	Analysis of a problem	Rating/scoring	PROMETHEE	Corporation	Group of experts	A DSS was developed

to quality of service classes. Chapter 7, by T. Tervonen et al., addresses the choice of one location among several candidate sites for a kindergarten, but approaches the problem using a ranking method.

Chapters 8–14 address applications related with the energy/environment field, which is clearly in this book, as it is probably in practice, the most popular application area for MCDA. Problems concerning the environment typically gather multiple actors in the decision process and involve evaluating many criteria that are not easy to convert into a single performance measure. The work "Choosing a Cooling System for a Power Plant in Belgium" by M. Pirlot et al. intended to demonstrate the usefulness of MCDA to an industrial client by examining *a posteriori* a decision it had faced concerning a technology choice. In their Chap. 9, Oberti and Paoli provide an account of a decision process open to the general public that addressed a siting problem. Chapter 10, by M. Covas et al., addresses the assessment of environmental impacts of the data centers that underlie most common Internet and telecommunications services available today, proposing a classification framework.

Chapters 11–14 address a particular concern in applications dealing with the environment/energy field: risk. Kunsch and Vander Straeten's Chap. 11 focuses on costs, namely on the problem of estimating the costs of a project by aggregating the opinions of different experts, the main concern being the risk of budget overrun. In Chap. 12, S. Metchebon et al. make an assessment of risks of land degradation, using a classification method to assign geographical locations to risk classes. Mercat-Rommens et al. also use a method to classify risks, in the event of an accident, for different geographical locations in their Chap. 13. Their work considers not only risks to the environment and human health, but also risks for economic activities. Finally, the Chap. 14, by A. Luè and A. Colorni, considers the choice of routes for transportation of hazardous materials, taking into account the risk of accidents. Chapters 12–14 (and also Chap. 9) have in common the development of Spatial Decision Support Systems (SDSS), based on extending the capabilities of Geographical Information Systems (GIS) to deal with MCDA problems.

A. Luè and A. Colorni's chapter, together with the next three chapters, address transportation-related issues. In Chap. 15, A. Tsoukiàs and H. Ralijaona provide an account of their involvement in a project to classify roads with regards to their maintenance needs. Öztürk et al.'s Chap. 16 also addresses a classification problem, aiming at assigning potential future railways rolling stock to comfort classes. The Chap. 17, by F. Montignac et al., concerns a technology choice problem for future vehicles, which was addressed as a ranking problem.

The two final applications in this book are related with the field of finance (Chap. 11 is also loosely related to this field). Chapter 18, by O. Braun and M. Spohn focuses on the perspective of an individual, offering a portfolio optimization framework for planning personal finances. Chapter 19, by M. Doumpos and C. Zopounidis, concerns the perspective of a central bank who must rate commercial banks. Although rating is usually considered as a sorting problem, in this case a ranking method was used to derive a global performance value for each bank being evaluated.

There are a few aspects shared by many of the applications in these chapters that deserve some reflection. Although the set of contributed chapters cannot be interpreted as an accurate representation of the panorama of all MCDA applications throughout the world, these shared aspects will match what happens in many situations. The main aspect (not depicted in Table 1.1 because it applies to most chapters with very few exceptions) is the importance attributed to problem structuring. By going through these cases the reader will be able to appreciate the effort required to define the set of alternatives to be evaluated and the set of evaluation criteria, besides other discussions concerning the actors involved and the problem statement to be adopted. In many cases, most of the value of the analysis concerns this stage: after the problem structuring stage the following steps can be sometimes relatively easy.

The type of client commissioning the application varies. In some cases it is a publicly or a privately owned company, but in most cases it was some type of public administration entity (a regional administration, an agency, or other). Indeed, this type of "client" is the one most likely to value the added transparency brought by conducting an explicit MCDA analysis. Another concern of public administration (also shared by private organizations) is the need to involve many parties in decision processes. Indeed, most of the applications deal with multi-actor situations, involving a group of decision makers, or a group of experts, or a group of stakeholders potentially affected by a decision, including the general public. As demonstrated in these chapters, MCDA can be an excellent instrument to gather the interested parties and to model their potentially different concerns, in a joint problem-solving activity. Nevertheless, true decision makers did not intervene much in most of the applications. Perhaps due to the nature of the client—often a public administration—the expression of priorities and preferences is delegated to experts and/or to stakeholders, rather than the person or a group of persons who have the authority to decide.

Another peculiar aspect emerging from this set of applications is that in many cases they are described as a proof of concept, a pilot study, or a demonstration project (all labeled as proof of concept in Table 1.1). In these cases, as the authors explain, the MCDA intervention was conducted to prove its value to the client. MCDA was applied on a no-problem (as in the case of an ex-post evaluation) or a small-scale problem, so that it would be approved and legitimated to be applied on a larger scale. Fortunately, in most cases, this demonstration was deemed successful.

Under the heading "Goal" in Table 1.1, the reader will see that some case studies are labeled "Framework". By this expression, we mean that the decision models involved are designed for a generic decision problem in a specific domain of application. In general, the proposed approach is illustrated on real data and expert evaluations, but the decision aiding process may be incomplete (e.g. there may be no definite decision maker). In contrast, the label "Analysis of a problem" refers to an actual decision aiding process for a specific instance of a decision problem and with a well-identified decision maker.

In most applications, there were tangible outcomes besides the answer to the initial problem statement. It is generally accepted that a factor that contributes to the popularity of MCDA is the availability of software. Indeed, the use of some software is reported in most of the applications in this book. It is noteworthy however that in some cases the software itself was developed on purpose for the particular application, thus remaining as a tangible tool on the hands of the client for the reiterated use of the models and knowledge developed during the intervention. In some cases, as already mentioned, the development consisted in building a SDSS, using a GIS as a starting basis.

Finally, maybe the biggest testimony of success in many of these applications, is the fact that the chapter is coauthored not only by MCDA analysts but also by someone from the client organization. This is not only an indication of approval, but also a sign that MCDA know-how was passed onto the client organization, which might now be able to conduct further analyzes without MCDA expertise from outside.

1.2.3 MCDA Process Support Tools

The third and final part of the book consists of two chapters. First, Chap. 20, which describes XMCDA, a proposal for an MCDA data standard, and second, Chap. 21, which presents the *diviz* environment for multi-criteria decision analysis. Why these chapters? It was stated in the outset that the project of this book grew up in the framework of the Decision Deck Consortium, a gathering of researchers which aims at making publicly available software tools that allow to deal with multi-criteria decision problems. The collaborative development effort of the consortium gave birth to various initiatives, among which a quite impressive set of web-services, which allow to access to elementary MCDA resources (aggregation algorithms, data treatment and visualization components, ...) in a unified manner. These calculation elements all speak a common language, namely XMCDA. This XML-based encoding standard for MCDA data and concepts, which is presented thoroughly in Chap. 20, allows to make these web-services interoperable. Consequently very naturally, the need for a tool to combine these calculation elements in complex workflows appeared. Chapter 21 presents the *diviz* workbench, which facilitates the construction of such calculation sequences via a very intuitive graphical user interface. This chapter also illustrates, on a didactic example, how *diviz* can be used to support a decision aiding process. The idea is to suggest that the reader could play the role of the analyst in all the case studies for which the evaluation and preferential data are available. In view of allowing for this, we asked the authors to make the data used in their application available to the reader (whenever this was possible). The reader can consequently reproduce the analyzes performed in the cases, test other hypotheses, apply other methods they may wish to try, or follow other methodologies. This also means that the cases, together with the *diviz* software, can be used for teaching purposes, e.g. for training students to act as analysts. What is particular to decision aiding, indeed, is the fact that numerical data is not enough to describe a problem. The context and sufficient information on the goals and preferences of the decision maker must be specified before a meaningful sequence of treatments can be proposed in view of "solving the problem". In most of the cases described in this book, a teacher can find enough material to design an exercise for training students to play the analyst's role in a realistic simulated decision aiding process. As such, *diviz* provides an adequate environment to support the students in their analyzes of the case and their experimentation with several methods.

1.3 Highlights

To summarize, this book may be useful:

- for studying the decision aiding process: the book contains the description of 15 cases of decision aiding processes in various domains of application and with contrasted characteristics. These case studies are commented within a decision aiding process framework that is described in the three initial methodological chapters. This corpus of case studies provides a basis for deepening a scientific analysis of the decision aiding process.
- for experimenting with a variety of MCDA methods in the realistic decision aiding situations described in the case studies. The *diviz* software platform provides a common framework for such an experimentation.
- for training students for the role of analyst by involving them in simulated decision aiding processes inspired from a case study. Again, the *diviz* platform is a suitable tool for supporting this training.
- for providing decision analysts with examples of decision aiding processes in which they could find inspiration for their own practice.

We trust the reader will find in the descriptions of the applications and the adjoined commentaries motivation and lessons useful to apply MCDA in all types of organizations, possibly using the tools described in the third part of this book. We are sure new lessons will emerge. And, who knows, the reader may share such lessons in a future book like this one.

References

Belton, V., & Stewart, T. (2002). *Muliple criteria decision analysis: An integrated approach.* Dordrecht: Kluwer Academic.

Guitouni, A., & Martel, J. -M. (1998). Tentative guidelines to help choosing an appropriate {MCDA} method. *European Journal of Operational Research, 109*(2), 501–521.

Hobbs, B., Chankong, V., Hamadeh, W., & Stakhiv, E. (1992). Does choice of multicriteria method matter? An experiment in water resources planning. *Water Resources Research, 28*(7), 1767–1779.

Ishizaka, A., & Nemery, P. (2013). *Multi-criteria decision analysis: methods and software*. New York: Wiley.

Ozernoy, V. (1987). A framework for choosing the most appropriate discrete alternative multiple criteria decision-making method in decision support systems and expert systems. In Y. Sawaragi, K. Inoue, & H. Nakayama (Eds.), *Toward Interactive and Intelligent Decision Support Systems: Proceedings of the Seventh International Conference on Multiple Criteria Decision Making*. Lecture Notes in Economics and Mathematical Systems (Vol. 2, pp. 56–64), Kyoto, Japan. New York: Springer.

Ozernoy, V. (1992). Choosing the best multiple criteria decision-making method. *INFOR, 30*(2), 159–171.

Polatidis, H., Haralambopoulos, D. A., Munda, G., & Vreeker, R. (2006). Selecting an appropriate multi-criteria decision analysis technique for renewable energy planning. *Energy Sources, Part B: Economics, Planning, and Policy, 1*(2), 181–193.

Pomerol, J., & Barba-Romero, S. (2000). *Multicriterion decision making in management*. Series in Operation Research. Dordrecht: Kluwer Academic.

Roy, B., & Bouyssou, D. (1993). *Aide Multicritère à la Décision: Méthodes et Cas*. Paris: Economica.

Vincke, P. (1992). *Multicriteria decision-aid*. New York: Wiley.

Part I
Theoretical Background

Chapter 2
Aiding to Decide: Concepts and Issues

Denis Bouyssou, Thierry Marchant, Marc Pirlot, Alexis Tsoukiàs, and Philippe Vincke

Abstract This chapter is about the decision aiding process. In professional contexts, there are cases of decision problems which require using formal processes and methods. In the first part of the chapter, we identify and describe the essential steps of a decision aiding process. In the second part, we discuss four practical questions that have to be tackled by an analyst in charge of a decision aiding process.

2.1 Introduction

What should I do now? It is sure that you have asked yourself more than once such a question. We all face problem situations in which we need to think before acting. It is also sure that several times it happens that you address such a question to somebody else or that somebody else asks you *what to do now?* It is this precise situation we are interested in: when somebody asks somebody else some help in order to decide (a decision aiding situation). However, we need to be more precise.

First of all we are not interested in any type of decision aiding. Putting aside intuitive and friendly advising activities which occur in our everyday life, we are interested in the professional dimension of such an activity and more specifically

D. Bouyssou • A. Tsoukiàs (✉)
CNRS-LAMSADE UMR 7243, Université Paris Dauphine, Place du Maréchal de Lattre de Tassigny, 75775 Paris Cedex 16, France
e-mail: bouyssou@lamsade.dauphine.fr; tsoukias@lamsade.dauphine.fr

T. Marchant
Department of Data analysis, Ghent University, H. Dunantlaan 1, 9000 Gent, Belgium
e-mail: Thierry.Marchant@UGent.be

M. Pirlot
Université de Mons, Faculté Polytechnique, Mons, Belgium
e-mail: marc.pirlot@umons.ac.be

P. Vincke
Ecole Polytechnique, Université libre de Bruxelles, Campus de la Plaine, CP210/01, boulevard du Triomphe, 1050 Bruxelles, Belgium
e-mail: Philippe.Vincke@ulb.ac.be

R. Bisdorff et al. (eds.), *Evaluation and Decision Models with Multiple Criteria*, International Handbooks on Information Systems,
DOI 10.1007/978-3-662-46816-6_2

when formal tools and languages are adopted, introducing some form of rationality (just to be distinguished from psychotherapists and lawyers, to mention two decision aiding professions who do not use such formal tools and languages). We are interested in the profession of "decision analyst".

Does it always make sense to use such formal tools and languages in order to help somebody deciding? Of course not and we are all aware that both, intuitive support as well as other professional approaches, can be very useful and successful. However, there are situations where a formal analysis is requested, needed, preferred, imposed and such situations are the ones we are interested in. We are not going to analyse when such situations occur (it is out of the scope of this chapter), but rather focus on what happens when such a demand arises. Why are we focussing on such a subject?

1. Despite the decision analyst profession being almost a century old, there is very little analysis of what makes this profession specific. In other terms, it rarely happened that the activities of decision aiding have been the subject of scientific investigation. It seems as if the fact of using rational tools prevents from conducting a rational analysis of this activity. We would like to contribute in filling such a gap.
2. Professions are based on guidelines. Practical guidelines which novice practitioners use in order to fill the lack of experience. Decision Analysis is surely a craft (see Rivett 1994), but is increasingly becoming a profession which needs such guidelines (see for instance the discussion about ethical guidelines in Gass 2009). We try to introduce some basis for such guidelines here.
3. Decision Analysis has been most of the time taught as if the students were going to become on their turn researchers in Decision Analysis. It turns out that most of these students are going to become practitioners. We need to structure our teaching following how decision analytic tools and methodologies are used in practice. We try to contribute in this direction.

The following chapter is basically divided in two large sections. In the first one we analyse the concept of decision aiding process and the cognitive artifacts produced within it. The second section tries to provide some answers to practical questions of the type:

- how to formulate a decision problem?
- what is a problem statement?
- how to structure the information provided by different stakeholders, criteria and scenarios?
- how to choose a decision analytic method?

2.2 The Decision Aiding Process

Aiding somebody (or a more complex entity such as an organisation, a committee or any other informal setting of actors with some decision power) is a rather complicated issue although addressed routinely in informal and/or professional way. Psychologists, lawyers, family counsellors, priests, friends, the family, consultants, experts, trusted accountants, all qualify as potential advisors for somebody who feels to be in trouble (independently if really she is in trouble) and is asking: "what should I do now?"

Keeping our discussion informal, trying to help somebody involved in some process for which she feels in difficulty in order to decide what to do next, implies aiding her (who asks for advice) and yourself (as an advisor) to understand issues such as:

- what is exactly the problem?
- who else is affected by that problem?
- why is this a problem?
- how "serious" is this problem?
- what resources (including time) do we have?
- what do we know about that problem?
- what is important in that problem as far as who asked the advice is concerned?
- what is possible? feasible? preferable?

The reader will note that some of these questions are not necessarily the ones you may ask yourself if you are in some trouble. For instance you know your values and preferences and you are not going to ask yourself to understand them, while you have to do so if you advise somebody who naturally will have different values. We can thus consider two different settings.

- One where somebody "decides" for herself and we can imagine a sequence of mental activities allowing her (and we thus call her a decision maker) to reach a conclusion: we call such setting a *decision process*.
- Another where we can imagine a discussion, a sequence of interactions between two entities which we will identify as the "client" (who demands for advice) and the "analyst" (who provides the advice) aiming at aiding the client to go further in some decision process she is involved: we call that a *decision aiding process*.

There is one critical observation to make at this point. In a decision process we assume that who is involved in that process (individual or collective entity, human or artificial) is going to make a decision. We can thus allow ourselves to call this entity a decision maker. In a decision aiding process we can not make a similar hypothesis. The analyst makes no decisions at all and the client's concern is not necessarily a decision. She might be interested in understanding, in describing, in arguing, in justifying, in discussing, in convincing etc. and the advice she looks for needs to be appropriate for that scope.

Decision processes have been accepted as a subject of scientific investigation in economy, computer science, cognitive sciences, sociology, organisation studies and there is a large literature around this subject (see Barthelemy et al. 2002; Bell et al. 1988; Dean and Sharfman 1996; Elbanna 2006; Huber 1991; Humphreys et al. 1983; Kahneman and Tversky 2000; Mintzberg et al. 1976; Moscarola 1984; Nutt 1984, 1993; Simon 1954; Svenson 1979, 1996; Teisman 2000; Vlek 1984).

Decision Aiding Processes instead have been very little studied in the literature (if not as reports of real world case studies, but see also Schrenk 1969). Professional bodies such as lawyers, therapists and councilors have manuals for conducting, assessing and validating such processes in their respective professional areas, but there is nothing similar for decision analysts. Roy (1993, 1994) adopt this term as a different approach in decision analysis, while Brown (1989, 2005) follows a more profession oriented analysis of this concept. Bouyssou et al. (2006) and Tsoukiàs (2007) suggest a different perspective which is discussed here.

The basic idea is that the decision aiding process can be on the one hand a subject of scientific investigation and on the other hand it can be used as a basis in order to help decision analysts in conducting their activities. Under such a perspective a decision aiding process can be seen as a sequence of cognitive artifacts produced through the interactions between the client and the analyst. Such artifacts summarise the information modelled through the process and can be used as a checklist by the analyst while conducting the process itself. The four cognitive artifacts suggested by Tsoukiàs (2007) are the following ones:

- a representation of the problem situation;
- a problem formulation;
- an evaluation model;
- a final recommendation.

The reader will note that not all such artifacts are produced in all decision aiding processes. Aiding somebody to decide could be just help her to understand the problem situation where she is involved or arrive to formulate a decision problem without necessarily elaborating an evaluation model and/or a recommendation. Besides, in real decision aiding processes such artifacts are not constructed linearly. In the following we present more in detail the above mentioned artifacts.

2.2.1 The Problem Situation

A representation of the problem situation is the result of an effort aimed at replying to questions of the type:

- who has a problem?
- why is this a problem?
- who decides on this problem?

- what is the commitment of the client on this problem?
- who is going to pay for the consequences of a decision?

The construction of such an artifact allows, on the one hand, the client to better understand his position within the decision process for which she asked the decision support and, on the other hand, the analyst to better understand his role within this decision process.

From a formal point of view a representation of the problem situation is a triplet:

$$\mathscr{P} = \langle \mathscr{A}, \mathscr{O}, \mathscr{S} \rangle$$

where:

- $\mathscr{A}$ is the set of participants to the decision process;
- $\mathscr{O}$ is the set of stakes each participant brings within the decision process;
- $\mathscr{S}$ is the set of resources the participants commit on their stakes and the other participants' stakes.

Such a representation is not fixed once for all within the decision aiding process, but usually will evolve. Actually, one of the reasons for which such a representation is constructed is to help clarify the misunderstandings during the client—analyst interaction and therefore improve the communication between these two actors. It can also turn useful when both the two actors have to establish whether their efforts are legitimated with respect to the decision process.

2.2.2 The Problem Formulation

For a given representation of the problem situation the analyst might propose to the client one or more "problem formulations". This is a crucial point of the decision aiding process. The representation of the problem situation has a descriptive (at the best explicative) objective. The construction of the problem formulation introduces what can be called a model of rationality. A problem formulation reduces the reality of the decision process, within which the client is involved, to a formal and abstract problem. The result is that one or more of the client's concerns are transformed into formal problems on which we can apply a method (already existing, adapted from an existing one or created ad-hoc) of the type studied in decision theory.

From a formal point of view a problem formulation is a triplet:

$$\Gamma = \langle \mathbb{A}, V, \Pi \rangle$$

where:

- $\mathbb{A}$: is the set of potential actions the client may undertake within the problem situation as represented in $\mathscr{P}$;
- V: is the set of points of view under which the potential actions are expected to be observed, analysed, evaluated, compared, including different scenarios for the future;
- Π: is the problem statement, the type of application to perform on the set A, an anticipation of what the client expects (the reader can see more details on this point in Bana e Costa (1996), Ostanello (1990), Roy and Bouyssou (1993), for a detailed example see Stamelos and Tsoukiàs 2003).

Obtaining the client's consensus on a problem formulation has, as a consequence, the gain of insight, since instead of having an "ambiguous" description of the problem we have an abstract and formal problem. Several decision aiding approaches will stop here (for examples see Rosenhead 1989), considering that formulating (and understanding) a problem is sufficient to act upon, thus limiting decision aiding at helping to formulate problems, the solution being a personal issue of the client. Other approaches instead will consider the problem formulation as given (as suggested in many Operational Research and Decision Analysis textbooks, see Williams 1990). Within a constructive approach the problem formulation is one among the artifacts of the decision aiding process, the one used in order to construct the evaluation model.

2.2.3 The Evaluation Model

With this term we indicate what the decision aiding models traditionally are, as conceived through any operational research, decision theory or artificial intelligence method. Classic decision theoretic approaches will focus their attention on the construction of this model and consider the problem formulation as given.

An evaluation model is an n-uplet:

$$\mathscr{M} = \langle A, \{D, \mathscr{E}\}, H, \mathscr{U}, \mathscr{R} \rangle$$

where:

- A is the set of alternatives on which the model applies. Formally it establishes the universe of discourse (including the domain) of all relations and functions which are going to be used in order to describe the client's problem.
- D is the set of dimensions (attributes) under which the elements of A are observed, described, measured etc. The set D might be endowed with different structuring properties. Formally D is a set of functions such that each element of A is mapped to a co-domain which we call a "scale".

- $\mathscr{E}$ is the set of scales associated to each element of D. Formally each element of $\mathscr{E}$ is the co-domain of some element within D ($\forall i\ \forall d \in D,\ d_i : A \rightarrow E_i \in \mathscr{E}$).
- H is the set of criteria under which each element of A is evaluated in order to take into account the client's preferences. Formally a criterion is a preference relation, that is a binary relation on A (a subset of $A \times A$) or a function representing the criterion.
- $\mathscr{U}$ is a set of uncertainty structures and/or epistemic states applied on D and/or H. Depending on the language adopted, $\mathscr{U}$ collects all uncertainty distributions or the beliefs expressed by the client which can be associated to the relations and functions applied on A, besides possible scenarios to which uncertainty can be related.
- $\mathscr{R}$ is a set of operators such that the information available on A, through D and H can be synthesised to a more concise evaluation. Formally $\mathscr{R}$ is a set of operators such that it is possible to obtain a global relation and/or function on A, possibly allowing to infer a final recommendation.

The reader can observe that a large part of the existing decision aiding models and methods (see e.g. Belton and Stewart 2002) can be represented trough the above description (from traditional optimisation procedures to multiple criteria decision making methods and artificial intelligence tools). Besides, such a description allows to draw the attention of the reader to a number of important remarks:

1. It is easy to understand that working with only one or more evaluation dimensions, a single or multiple criteria or that using a combinatorial optimisation algorithm or some other method is the result of some modelling activity where as analysts we convince ourselves and our clients that this is the correct way to proceed. What is important is not to choose the method before the problem has been formulated and the evaluation model constructed, but to show that this is the natural consequence of the decision aiding process as conducted up to that moment.
2. The technical choices (typology of the measurement scales, different preference models, different aggregation operators) are not neutral. Even in the case where the client has been able to formulate his problem clearly and he is convinced about it (possibly using one of the techniques aiding in formulating problems), the choice of a certain technique, procedure, operator can have important consequences which are not discussed at the moment where the problem has been formulated (for a critical discussion see Bouyssou et al. 2000). Characterising such techniques, procedures and operators is therefore crucial since it allows to control their applicability to the problem as has been formulated during the decision aiding process.
3. The evaluation models are subject to validation processes, namely (see Landry et al. 1983):
   - conceptual validation (verify the suitability of the concepts used);
   - logical validation (verify the logical consistency of the model);

- experimental validation (verify the results using experimental data);
- operational validation (verify the implementation and use of the model in everyday life).

2.2.4 The Final Recommendation

The final recommendation represents the return to reality for the decision aiding process. Usually the evaluation model will produce a result, let's call it Φ. The final recommendation should translate such a result from the abstract and formal language in which Φ is formulated to the current language of the client and the decision process in which she is involved. Some elements are very important in constructing this artifact:

- the analyst has to be sure that the model is formally correct;
- the client has to be confident that the model represents her preferences, that she understands it and that she should be able to use its conclusions (the client should feel as the "owner"' of the results, besides being satisfied of them);
- the recommendation should be "legitimated" with respect to the decision process for which the decision aiding has been asked (Landry et al., 1996).

We should pay some attention to this last observation. The decision aiding process is an activity which introduces a certain distance between the participants on the one hand and the reality of the decision process and its organisational dimension on the other hand. Returning back to reality requires to check whether the results are legitimated. We should check whether such results are accepted or not by the participants to the decision process and understand the reasons for their position (such reasons can be completely independent from the decision process itself). Being able to put in practice the final recommendation definitely depends on such legitimation. No legitimation means no implementation.

2.3 Some Practical Questions

In the following we are going to address a number of practical questions an analyst has to answer while involved in a decision aiding process. We will keep the presentation to a rather informal shape although we are discussing formal concepts.

2.3.1 What Is the Problem?

The client you are working with does not have a single problem. There are many problems she is facing depending on her activities and her position within a certain organisational context (possibly a context involving multiple organisations). Typically she will be involved in several decision processes. If she asks for some advice or help that will concern at least one (if not more than one) of such decision processes. There are two "steps" to follow trying to understand "what is the problem".

1. The first step consists in getting an insight of the one or several decision processes in which the client is involved and more precisely the one for which the aid is requested. If there is a problem then there is a process within which the problem appears. A decision process implies other participants who carry on their own concerns and commitments of resources in order to handle such concerns. These need to be understood.
2. The second step consists in understanding why this problem is perceived as such by the client: why is it a problem and why does she need an external advice in order to handle it? Only at that point it is possible to start formulating a decision problem to work with. *Establishing a production plan is a problem for your client's organisation because actually they need a production plan, but it becomes a problem for you as analyst because your client does not know how to handle the combinatorial explosion of all possible single production actions that are presently used.*

Not all decision aiding activities end stating a formal decision problem. A frank discussion with the client or a post-it session with a group of clients can be sufficient and much more effective than many mathematical or formal exercises. However, there are cases where we need to go further than simply understanding the problem situation and we have to formulate a formal decision problem. In doing so we need to establish three types of information.

1. On what are we deciding? A formal decision problem needs to fix a set of objects on which to apply a decision procedure. The question is: how is this set constructed? It could be an enumeration of objects. It could result from combining "portfolios" of single actions or options, thus obtaining complex sequences, plans or actions. It could result from combining the values of different attributes or continuous decision variables. We call such a set "alternatives". Where does this information come from? Certainly we need to ask the client, however, the analysis of the problem situation should be the starting point. Typically some of the client's concerns can be translated in terms of potential decisions and thus in potential actions. Then it should be understood if such actions can stand alone (thus obtaining an enumeration of objects) or if they have to be combined among them. Moreover it should be understood whether such actions could be described under different points of view.
2. What do we know or should we know about the alternatives? There are three different potential sources of information and/or knowledge to be considered. First, different descriptive dimensions (attributes) of the alternatives. Then different opinions of relevant stakeholders involved in the decision process. Finally different scenarios and/or states of the world under which the problem

could evolve. We call all these different assessment dimensions “points of view”. Where does this information come from? Some of the client’s concerns can be the source of such points of view. At the same time the analysis of the resources committed (or requested) by the client in order to handle the decision problem can be a hint in order to construct such a set of points of view.

3. How the client’s problem translates in terms of formal decision problem? Since we work with formal models we need at a certain point to establish a formal decision problem: in other terms we need to establish how the set of alternatives is going to be manipulated in order to obtain something which could be considered useful for the client as far as her problem is concerned. We call that a “problem statement”.

2.3.2 *What Is a Problem Statement?*

At this point we already have a set of potential alternatives. The problem is what are we going to do with such a set? From a formal point of view we need to establish how the client’s decision problem will become an application on the set of potential alternatives.

It is easy to observe that we can take different “decisions”. Consider a set of alternatives being candidates (persons). We may be looking for *THE* candidate (to recruit for some position) or to rank the candidates from the worst to best or to classify them in good, acceptable and unacceptable candidates or even to separate them in the ones fitting a scientific scholarship from the ones fitting a humanities scholarship. Several times the concept of “deciding” is associated to the one of “choosing”, but this is rather limited with respect to the large variety of problem situations in which our clients happen to be. We need a more broad concept of “decision problem” in order to be able to take into account such different situations.

Technically speaking we can generalise the concept of decision problem as an “appropriate partitioning” of the set of alternatives (see Colorni and Tsoukiàs, 2013). In other terms a “decision” results in constructing a set of equivalence classes of alternatives having some desirable properties. Going back to the candidates example if we are looking for *THE* candidate this implies partitioning the alternatives in two classes: the choice element and all the others. Instead if we are ranking the candidates we are constructing a number of equivalence classes (unknown; maximum as much as the candidates) to be ranked from the worst to the best.

There are two possible ways to characterise the partitioning of the set of alternatives.

1. The first concerns the possibility to have ordered classes (on one or more dimensions) or not.
2. The second concerns the use of external information (with respect to the set of alternatives) in order to define the classes or not; in other terms whether the classes are defined using information about the alternatives only or are

pre-established with respect to some external source of information (profiles, standards, references etc.).

Combining these two partitioning characteristics we obtain the four basic problem statements which we claim cover all possible formal decision problems:

- ranking (ordered equivalence classes not predefined);
- rating (ordered predefined equivalence classes);
- clustering (unordered equivalence classes not predefined);
- assigning (unordered predefined equivalence classes).

There are two special cases for all the above problem statements:

- the case where the equivalence classes are only two, one being the complement of the other;
- the case where the cardinality of one or more equivalence classes is fixed.

Example 2.1 Let's go back to the candidate's case.

- Ordering the candidates from the best to the worst is a ranking problem statement. The specific case where only two classes are requested, the first being as small as possible will be called a choice problem statement.
- Separating the candidates to the ones to be accepted with no further inquiry, from the ones to be rejected with no further inquiry, from the ones to be further interviewed respecting the school's standards is a rating problem statement.
- Grouping the candidates in similar anatomic characteristics is a clustering problem statement.
- Identifying the candidates fitting the scientific scholarships programme as well as the ones fitting the humanities scholarships programme is an assigning problem statement.

How do we choose a problem statement? Of course it depends on what the client specifies as her problem. Usually decision makers understand the difference between the problem statements and are able to provide reasonable information about it. On the other hand this is a typical case where the trial and error approach works fine. An unappropriate problem statement will immediately generate information the client will realise being useless. The problem statement will be refined through feedback.

2.3.3 *Stakeholders, Criteria, Uncertainties*

As already mentioned in Sect. 2.3.1 we generally assume the existence of three different types of information concerning the alternatives:

- the opinions and judgements that relevant stakeholders (including the client) have about these objects (or parts of them);
- features of the alternatives on several different attributes;

- possible scenarios and states of the nature under which the information concerning the alternatives may be different.

The raw information comes under sentences of the type:

- stakeholder α likes alternative x;
- stakeholders α and β prefer x to y;
- the client does not like z especially if combined with w;
- the opinion of stakeholder α counts more than the opinion of stakeholder β;
- the value of x on attribute a_1 is k;
- the value of y on attribute a_2 is more or less m;
- the value of z on attribute a_3 is $\langle$*linguistic_variable*$\rangle$ (such as fat, young, intelligent, not better specified);
- attributes a_1 and a_2 are more important than attributes a_3 and a_4;
- under scenario n_1 alternative x is unacceptable;
- under scenario n_2 alternative y is better than alternative z;
- scenario n_1 is more likely to occur than scenario n_2; etc.

From a formal point of view opinions, attributes and scenarios are all different dimensions on which we assess the alternatives. We can summarise the possible information under three types of sentences:

- alternative x on dimension d_j is k (k being more or less precise and/or well defined);
- alternative x is before (after, very near) alternative y on dimension d_j (ordering information);
- dimension(s) d_j is "more important" than dimension(s) d_i;
- as well as all possible combinations and conditional sentences that can be constructed (such as *"stakeholders α and β have a positive opinion about x on attribute a_1 and a negative one on attribute a_2, but only under scenario n_1; in case of scenario n_2 then opinions split in opposite directions"*).

The issue is what do we do with such information. What we really need in order to elaborate some recommendation for the client is to transform all that in terms of preferences (and/or constraints), possibly in an homogeneous way which should allow us to elaborate them and return something of the type: "taking into account the information and your preferences the winner is …". There are three steps to undertake in order to do so.

1. First we need to understand if all this information really matters for the client. Does the opinion of a certain stakeholder or the value of an attribute matter for the client's decision? A typical way to check that, is to consider hypothetic alternatives which are identical, but for one dimension and then ask the client if this difference would be sufficient to take a decision. If yes, then this dimension some way matters, if not, then it is irrelevant.
2. Then we need to transform all relevant information in some homogeneous preferential information. The first basic step here is to obtain for each single dimension an ordering relation reflecting the client's preferences and values. *If x*

is red and y is yellow we need to know than the client prefers red things to yellow things. If a certain stakeholder considers differently two alternatives we need to know how this concerns the client's preferences. And so on. The second basic step is to check whether it is possible to associate to such an ordering relation some more rich information in terms of "distances": *if x is before y which is before z on a certain dimension, can we tell something about the distance between x and y and between y and z? Can we compare such distances?* The third basic step is to understand whether the orderings on each dimension (possibly the more rich ones) can be compared to orderings on other dimensions: *if x is better than y on dimension* d_1 *can we compare this preference with the preference of y against x obtained on dimensions* d_2 *and* d_3*? If we know the distance between x and y on dimension* d_1 *can this be compared to the distance of z and w on dimension* d_2*?*

3. The last step consists in checking dependencies among the preferential statements of the client. *The typical example in this case is the situation where if we order at the restaurant meat we prefer red wine to white wine, but if we order fish we prefer white wine to red wine.* If such conditional statements exist and if preferential independence does not occur then we need to take that into account on how to proceed further when we will have to manipulate this information in order to obtain the final recommendation.

How do we obtain such information? There is abundant literature on this subject (see Blum et al. 2004; Dias and Mousseau 2006; Ha and Haddawy 2003; Haddaway et al. 2003; Hüllermeier and Brinker 2008; Hüllermeier et al. 2008; Jacquet-Lagrèze and Siskos 1982; Jacquet-Lagrèze and Siskos 2001; Salo and Hamalainen 1992, 2001; Sandholm and Boutilier 2006; Wang 1994). Basically there are three possible approaches in order to do so:

- direct protocols (see von Winterfeldt and Edwards 1986);
- undirect protocols (see Bana e Costa and Vansnick 1994; Saaty 1980);
- learning from examples (see Fürnkranz and Hüllermeier 2010; Greco et al. 2008).

A final remark the reader should consider is the following. There is always a certain distance between the intuitive way the client expresses her preferential information and the formal way in which this is considered within a model. The client is not necessarily aware of the formal consequences a certain statement has: *when she claims that a certain dimension is more important than another one she implicitly assumes that these two dimensions have comparable preference orderings and if she tries to quantify such an importance she implicitly establishes a quantitative way to compare such orderings. However, if we submit to her such consequences it is not sure that she will agree. It is extremely important to be very clear on such aspects of the modelling process.*

2.3.4 How to Choose a Method?

The problem of choosing an appropriate method in order to elaborate the preferential information obtained from the client is an old one and already studied in the literature (see Balestra and Tsoukiàs 1990; Guitouni and Martel 1998; Ouerdane 2009; Ozernoy 1992). In the following we are going to adopt an approach introduced in Ouerdane (2009) based on the idea that the choice of a method should allow to reinforce the arguments under which the recommendation suggested can be accepted by the client and be legitimated within her decision process, besides being formally correct.

In order to understand how the process works we need to fix which are the "primitives" on which our model is based. With such a term we intend the elementary information which cannot be derived from other preferential information. Our starting point thus are the preferential sentences the client uses in order to communicate her values and constraints.

Recent literature (Bouyssou et al., 2006; Marchant, 2003) suggests that such primitives are only the comparisons among alternatives either on single attributes or on bundles of attributes. With that in mind we are now ready to suggest the main guidelines under which classify the methods (and thus choose them).One parenthesis has been [added/deleted] to balance the delimiters. Please check that this was done correctly, and amend if necessary.

1. A first major distinction, (obtained from establishing the appropriate problem statement) is whether the comparisons among alternatives express preferences (asymmetric comparisons) or similarities (symmetric comparisons). Ordering problem statements (such as rating and ranking) are based on preferences, while not ordering problem statements (such as clustering and assigning) are based on similarities. There are of course special cases where asymmetric relations are used in order to make similarity comparisons, but the basic idea remains the distinction previously introduced.
2. A second major distinction, obtained from elaborating the preferential statements of the client, concerns how the preferences on each single dimension and among the different dimensions should be considered. As already mentioned in Sect. 2.3.3 we need to know whether the preferences expressed on each dimension are purely ordinal or not (the distances among the alternatives are considered or not) and how such preferences compare among the different dimensions. At this point we should pay attention to the fact that often among the preferential statements provided by the client we get sentences concerning the "importance" of the different attributes. Although this is useful information it should be noted that this is not a primitive information and should be double checked using the comparison of vectors of values of the attributes in order to validate such statements. Further on we need to establish any dependencies among the preferences expressed on the different dimensions.

3. A third major distinction concerns the possibility to use explicitly "negative preferential statements" which should be considered independently from the "positive ones". The idea here is that there are cases where the client needs to express negative judgements and values which are not complementary to the positive ones (such as a veto on a specific dimension). Under the perspective where the model elaborated is expected to be used in order to construct the arguments for which a certain recommendation is acceptable it might be important to have a clear distinction between the positive arguments supporting the recommendation and the negative ones against it.

The above three dimensions cover practically the whole area of possible methods that can be used in a decision aiding process.

2.4 Conclusions

What do we have at the end of the day? Let's try to summarise the important issues we discussed in this chapter.

There are situations where it is requested to provide decision support using formal tools and languages. We defined the activities occurring in such a setting as a decision aiding process. This can be scientifically investigated, analysed, decomposed and represented under the form of checklists, practical guidelines and teaching modules. We do not want to reduce the importance of the craft dimension of aiding somebody to decide, but focus on the potential of structuring this type of activities.

There is no single way to state a decision problem and this is extremely important when we try to construct a formal model of our client's problem situation. We have introduced a simple classification of formal problem statements which we claim covers the whole range of methods and tools used in our profession.

Despite decision aiding being a rather complex process, a thorough analysis of the formal structures used in order to provide some advice reveals that we use few, simple and relatively easy to manipulate tools: ordered structures and sets, elementary measuring principles and basic epistemic concepts about beliefs and uncertainties are sufficient along with the algorithmic aspects of the methods adopted. Of course these combine in more complex objects (the decision analysis protocols and methods), but the elementary bricks are simple.

Where do we go from here? This is just a small introduction on how the complex knowledge about decision aiding using formal tools and languages can be structured. Hopefully further investigation, analysis of real world experiences and discussion will provide deeper insight about this exciting profession.

References

Balestra, G., & Tsoukiàs, A. (1990). Multi-criteria analysis expert knowledge represented by artificial intelligence formalisms. *Journal of Operational Research Society, 41*, 419–430.

Bana e Costa, C. (1996). Les problématiques de l'aide à la décision : vers l'enrichissement de la trilogie choix-tri-rangement. *RAIRO/ Recherche Opérationnelle, 30*(2), 191–216.

Bana e Costa, C., & Vansnick, J. (1994). MACBETH – An interactive path towards the construction of cardinal value fonctions. *International Transactions in Operational Research, 1*, 489–500.

Barthelemy, J., Bisdorff, R., & Coppin, G. (2002). Human centered processes and decision support systems. *European Journal of Operational Research, 136*, 233–252.

Bell, D., Raiffa, H., & Tversky, A. (Eds.) (1988). *Decision making: descriptive, normative, and prescriptive interactions*. Cambridge: Cambridge University Press.

Belton, V., & Stewart, T. (2002). *Muliple criteria decision analysis: An integrated approach*. Dordrecht: Kluwer Academic.

Blum, A., Jackson, J., Sandholm, T., & Zinkevich, M. (2004). Preference elicitation and query learning. *Journal of Machine Learning Research, 5*, 649–667.

Bouyssou, D., Marchant, T., Pirlot, M., Perny, P., Tsoukiàs, A., & Vincke, P. (2000). *Evaluation and decision models: A critical perspective*. Dordrecht: Kluwer Academic.

Bouyssou, D., Marchant, T., Pirlot, M., Perny, P., Tsoukiàs, A., & Vincke, P. (2006). *Evaluation and decision models with multiple criteria: Stepping stones for the analyst*. International Series in Operations Research and Management Science (vol. 86, 1st ed.). Boston: Springer. ISBN 0-387-31098-3.

Brown, R. (1989). Toward a prescriptive science and technology of decision aiding. *Annals of Operations Research, 19*, 467–483.

Brown, R. (2005). The operation was a success but the patient died: Aider priorities influence decision aid usefulness. *Interfaces, 36*, 511–521.

Colorni, A., & Tsoukiàs, A. (2013). What is a decision problem? Preliminary Statements, Proceedings of ADT 2013, LNAI 8176, Springer Verlag, Berlin, 139–153.

Dean, J., & Sharfman, M. (1996). Does decision process matter? A study of strategic decision-making effectiveness. *Academy of Management Journal, 39*, 368–396.

Dias, L. C., & Mousseau, V. (2006 April). Inferring ELECTRE's veto-related parameters from outranking examples. *European Journal of Operational Research, 170*(1), 172–191.

Elbanna, S. (2006). Strategic decision-making: Process perspectives. *International Journal of Management Reviews, 8*, 1–20.

Fürnkranz, J., & Hüllermeier, E. (2010). *Preference learning*. Berlin: Springer.

Gass, S. (2009). Ethical guidelines and codes in operations research. *Omega, 37*, 1044–1050.

Greco, S., Mousseau, V., & Slowinski, R. (2008 December). Ordinal regression revisited: Multiple criteria ranking using a set of additive value functions. *European Journal of Operational Research, 191*(2), 415–435.

Guitouni, A., & Martel, J. (1998 September). Tentative guidelines to help choosing an appropriate MCDA method. *European Journal of Operational Research, 109*(2), 501–521.

Ha, V., & Haddawy, P. (2003). Similarity of personal preferences: Theoretical foundations and empirical analysis. *Artificial Intelligence, 146*, 149–173.

Haddaway, P., Ha, V., Restificar, A., Geisler, B., & Miyamoto, J. (2003). Preference elicitation via theory refinement. *Journal of Machine Learning Research, 4*, 317–337.

Huber, G. (1991). Organizational learning: The contributing processes and the literatures. *Organization Science, 2*, 88–115.

Hüllermeier, E., & Brinker, K. (2008). Learning valued preference structures for solving classification problems. *Fuzzy Sets and Systems, 159*, 2337–2352.

Hüllermeier, E., Fürnkranz, J., Cheng, W., & Brinker, K. (2008). Label ranking by learning pairwise preferences. *Artificial Intelligence, 172*, 1897–1917.

Humphreys, P., Svenson, O., & Vári, A. (1983). *Analysis and aiding decision processes*. Amsterdam: North-Holland.

Jacquet-Lagrèze, E., & Siskos, Y. (1982). Assessing a set of additive utility functions for multicriteria decision making: the UTA method. *European Journal of Operational Research, 10*, 151–164.

Jacquet-Lagrèze, E., & Siskos, Y. (2001 April). Preference disaggregation: 20 years of MCDA experience. *European Journal of Operational Research, 130*(2), 233–245.

Kahneman, D., & Tversky, A. (2000). *Choice, values, frames*. Cambridge: Cambridge University Press.

Landry, M., Banville, C., & Oral, M. (1996). Model legitimisation in operational research. *European Journal of Operational Research, 92*, 443–457.

Landry, M., Malouin, J., & Oral, M. (1983). Model validation in operations research. *European Journal of Operational Research, 14*, 207–220.

Marchant, T. (2003). Towards a theory of MCDM: stepping away from social choice theory. *Mathematical Social Sciences, 45*, 343–363.

Mintzberg, H., Raisinghani, D., & Théoret, A. (1976). The structure of unstructured decision processes. *Administrative Science Quarterly, 21*, 246–272.

Moscarola, J. (1984). Organizational decision processes and ORASA intervention. In R. Tomlinson & I. Kiss (Eds.), *Rethinking the process of operational research and systems analysis* (pp. 169–186). Oxford: Pergamon Press.

Nutt, P. (1984). Types of organizational decision processes. *Administrative Science Quarterly, 19*, 414–450.

Nutt, P. (1993). The formulation processes and tactics used in organizational decision making. *Organization Science, 4*, 226–251.

Ostanello, A. (1990). Action evaluation and action structuring - Different decision aid situations reviewed through two actual cases. In C. Bana e Costa (Ed.), *Readings in multiple criteria decision aid* (pp. 36–57). Berlin: Springer.

Ouerdane, W. (2009). *Multiple Criteria Decision Aiding: a dialectical perspective*. PhD thesis, Université Paris-Dauphine.

Ozernoy, V. (1992). Choosing the best multiple criteria decision-making method. *Information Systems and Operational Research, 30*(2), 159–171.

Rivett, P. (1994). *The craft of decision modelling*. New York: Wiley.

Rosenhead, J. (1989). *Rational analysis of a problematic world*. New York: Wiley. 2nd revised edition in 2001.

Roy, B. (1993). Decision science or decision-aid science? *European Journal of Operational Research, 66*, 184–203.

Roy, B. (1994). On operational research and decision aid. *European Journal of Operational Research, 73*, 23–26.

Roy, B., & Bouyssou, D. (1993). *Aide Multicritère à la Décision : Méthodes et Cas*. Paris: Economica.

Saaty, T. (1980). *The analytic hierarchy process, planning, priority setting, resource allocation*. New York: McGraw-Hill.

Salo, A., & Hamalainen, R. (1992). Preference assessment by imprecise ratio statements. *Operations Research, 40*(6), 1053–1061.

Salo, A., & Hamalainen, R. (2001 November). Preference ratio in multiattribute evaluation (PRIME) - elicitation and decision procedures under incomplete information. *IEEE Transactions on Systems, Man and Cybernetics: Part A, 31*(6), 533–545.

Sandholm, T., & Boutilier, C. (2006). Preference elicitation in combinatorial auctions. In P.Cramton, Y. Shoham, & R. Steinberg (Eds.), *Combinatorial auctions* (pp. 233–264). Boston: MIT Press.

Schrenk, L. (1969). Aiding the decision maker - a decision process model. *Ergonomics, 12*, 543–557.

Simon, H. (1954). A behavioral model of rational choice. *Quarterly Journal of Economics, 69*, 99–118.

Stamelos, I., & Tsoukiàs, A. (2003). Software evaluation problem situations. *European Journal of Operational Research, 145*, 273–286 (2003)

Svenson, O. (1979). Process description of decision making. *Organizational Behavior and Human Performance, 23*, 86–112.

Svenson, O. (1996). Decision making and the search for fundamental psychological regularities: what can we learn from a process perspective? *Organisational Behaviour and Human Decision Processes, 65*, 252–267.

Teisman, G. (2000). Models for research into decision-making processes: On phases, streams and decision-making rounds. *Public Administration: Journal of the Royal Institute of Public Administration, 78*, 937–956.

Tsoukiàs, A. (2007). On the concept of decision aiding process. *Annals of Operations Research, 154*, 3–27.

Vlek, C. (1984). What constitutes a good decision?: A panel discussion among Ward Edwards, István Kiss, Giandomenico Majone and Masanao Toda. *Acta Psychologica, 56*, 5–27.

von Winterfeldt, D., & Edwards, W. (1986). *Decision analysis and behavorial research.* Cambridge: Cambridge University Press.

Wang, J. (1994). Artificial neural networks versus natural neural networks: a connectionist paradigm for preference assessment. *Decision Support Systems, 11*, 415–429.

Williams, H. (1990). *Model building in mathematical programming* (3rd ed.). New York: Wiley.

Chapter 3
Modelling Preferences

Denis Bouyssou, Thierry Marchant, Marc Pirlot, Alexis Tsoukiàs, and Philippe Vincke

Abstract This chapter deals with a crucial step in the decision aiding process: the aggregation of the alternatives' performances on each criterion in order to faithfully model the overall preference of the decision maker. The approach we follow is that of conjoint measurement, which aims at determining under which conditions a preference can be represented in a particular aggregation model. This approach is first illustrated with the classical additive value function model. Then, we describe two broad families of preference models, which constitute a framework encompassing many aggregation models used in practice. The aggregation rules that fit with the second family of models rely on the aggregation of preference differences. Among this family we find, in particular, models for the outranking relations (concordance relations with vetoes) that are used in several case studies in this book.

D. Bouyssou • A. Tsoukiàs
CNRS-LAMSADE UMR 7243, Université Paris Dauphine, Place du Maréchal de Lattre de Tassigny, 75775 Paris Cedex 16, France
e-mail: bouyssou@lamsade.dauphine.fr; tsoukias@lamsade.dauphine.fr

T. Marchant (✉)
Department of Data analysis, Ghent University, H. Dunantlaan 1, 9000 Gent, Belgium
e-mail: Thierry.Marchant@UGent.be

M. Pirlot
Université de Mons, Faculté Polytechnique, Mons, Belgium
e-mail: marc.pirlot@umons.ac.be

P. Vincke
Université libre de Bruxelles, Ecole Polytechnique, Campus de la Plaine, CP210/01, boulevard du Triomphe, 1050 Bruxelles, Belgium
e-mail: Philippe.Vincke@ulb.ac.be

R. Bisdorff et al. (eds.), *Evaluation and Decision Models with Multiple Criteria*, International Handbooks on Information Systems,
DOI 10.1007/978-3-662-46816-6_3

3.1 Introduction

In this chapter, we address a very peculiar point in a particular step of the decision aiding process as it has been described in Chap. 2. We try to deal in a general way with the operation of aggregating descriptions on various dimensions into a global object, called *preference*, that synthesises all relevant features of the alternatives and incorporates the preference of the client in a given problem situation $\mathcal{P}$. To this end, we follow the tradition of *conjoint measurement theory*, first developed in Economics by Debreu (1960) and in Psychology by Luce and Tukey (1964), and then adopted in decision analysis by Edwards (1971) and Raiffa (1969). It provides us with families of models that decompose the preference into elements related to the description of the alternatives along the various dimensions. Besides these families of models, conjoint measurement theory provides us with very powerful tools: the axiomatic characterizations of these models. The characterisations take the following form: if a preference satisfies some conditions (called axioms), then it admits a description within a particular model. Characterising a model amounts to finding the properties of all the preferences that fit into the model.

Knowing the axioms characterizing a model can help the analyst to determine whether that model is adequate in the given problem situation. He can for instance ask the client how he feels the preference behaves in the situations evoked in the axioms. Depending on the answers, he can then decide to work further with that model or to reject it and examine another one. A deep understanding of a model can also help the analyst to elicit the parameters involved in that model.

Another possible framework for the analysis of aggregation techniques is *social choice theory* (see Chapter 5 in Bouyssou et al. 2006). In spite of the interest of this framework, we will not present it here because of size constraints.

Before analysing very general and abstract families of models, we will start with a somewhat easier section (Sect. 3.2), focussing on a specific and well-known model: the additive value function model. This will give us the opportunity to introduce some notation, to define many concepts and to discuss many aspects of conjoint measurement theory.

In Sects. 3.3 and 3.4, we will mainly analyse two types of models. In the first one, the comparison of two alternatives results from the comparison of the description of each of them on the various dimensions. In the second type of models, for each pair of alternatives and each dimension, the differences of preference between these alternative on that dimension is assessed and the model makes the balance between all these differences in order to determine which of the two alternatives is the preferred one. Each type of model has its own logic and suggests a corresponding strategy of elicitation. Section 3.5 is devoted to concordance relations.

3.2 The Additive Value Function Model

Suppose that, within a certain problem formulation, we have started to build an evaluation model: we have determined a set of alternatives A and n dimensions that can describe all the aspects relevant to the decision problem at hand. We shall assume that the set of functions g_i used to describe the alternatives on each dimension is exhaustive, so that any alternative a can be identified with the vector $(g_1(a), \ldots, g_i(a), \ldots, g_n(a))$. We may work with the set of vectors representing the alternatives instead of the alternatives themselves. These vectors form a subset $\{(g_1(a), \ldots, g_n(a)),\ a \in A\}$ of the Cartesian product $X = X_1 \times X_2 \times \ldots X_i \times \ldots X_n$ of the various scales. We assume further that each vector of X corresponds to an alternative and that the client's preferences, denoted by $\succsim$, is a relation on the whole[1] set X. Hence, any alternative will be identified with a vector $x = (x_1, \ldots, x_n)$ of X where $x_1, \ldots, x_i, \ldots, x_n$ denote the evaluations of the alternative x on the n criteria. And any vector $x = (x_1, \ldots, x_n)$ of X represents an alternative.

Conjoint measurement theory studies the links that may exist—depending on the properties of $\succsim$—between any pair (x, y) of vectors of X and the fact that $x \succsim y$ or not.

In the most popular model of this theory, it can be determined that x is preferred to y by comparing the values that a function u, defined on X, assigns to x and y; u is called a *multi-attribute value function* (MAV function). A very particular case for u, but also by far the most frequent in practice, is when u decomposes into a sum of n functions u_i each of a single variable, i.e. $u(x) = u(x_1, \ldots, x_n) = \sum_{i=1}^{n} u_i(x_i)$. The main model of conjoint measurement—called *additive value function model*—thus deals with preferences on X such that for all $x, y \in X$:

$$x \succsim y \Leftrightarrow u(x) = \sum_{i=1}^{n} u_i(x_i) \geq u(y) = \sum_{i=1}^{n} u_i(y_i), \tag{3.1}$$

where u_i is a function from X_i into $\mathbb{R}$ for all i. In this representation, the relative importance of the criteria is reflected in the magnitude of the functions u_i.

There is an alternative way of representing the same model, which makes more explicit the importance of the criteria:

$$x \succsim y \Leftrightarrow v(x) = \sum_{i=1}^{n} k_i v_i(x_i) \geq v(y) = \sum_{i=1}^{n} k_i v_i(y_i), \tag{3.2}$$

[1] This postulates the extension to all the Cartesian product X of the preference relation that is perceived on $\overline{g}(A) = \{(g_1(a), \ldots, g_n(a)),\ a \in A\}$. In practice, such an extension could force the client to compare alternatives that appear artificial or unrealistic to him. Despite possible unwanted practical consequences and provided that the range X_i is not unrealistic, we consider that the extension of $\succsim$ to X is not an outrageous assumption.

in which k_i are nonnegative "weighting factors" summing up to 1. Representations (3.1) and (3.2) are perfectly equivalent; indeed, it suffices to set $u_i = kv_i$ to find that any relation representable in (3.1) is also representable in (3.2). Depending on the context, one or another formulation of the model may offer an advantage.

3.2.1 *Additive Value Function and Conjoint Measurement*

The above model, in either of its forms (3.1) or (3.2), will be referred to as the *additive value function model*; u is called an additive MAV function. Conjoint measurement theory is concerned with establishing conditions on $\succsim$ under which a representation according to model (3.1) (or (3.2)) exists. Conditions of uniqueness of the representation are also looked for.

Why is this interesting? Clearly, if we have reasons to believe that a preference might obey model (3.1), we can try to determine the preference—which is usually not known explicitly—by constructing the functions u_i; alternatively, for eliciting model (3.2), we should construct the functions v_i and estimate the coefficients k_i. Each model suggests a strategy (or several ones) for eliciting preferences that are representable in the model. Of course, not all preferences satisfy model (3.1); we shall not specify here the necessary and sufficient conditions but just mention the following two important and obvious requirements on the preference:

- $\succsim$ must be a weak order, i.e. a transitive and complete preference, in other words a complete ranking, possibly with ties. This is clearly a necessary requirement since model (3.1) exactly says that the order $\succsim$ on X is obtained by transporting the natural order on $\mathbb{R}$ onto X by means of the function u.
- $\succsim$ must satisfy (strong) preference independence. The decomposition of u into a sum of functions each of a single variable reveals that if $x \succsim y$ while x and y have received the same assessment on dimension i, then, if we change that common level into another level still keeping it common, the transformed x and y will compare in the same way as before. More formally, let x and y be such that $x_i = y_i = a_i$; let x' be equal to x except that $x'_i = b_i \neq x_i$ and let y' be equal to y except that $y'_i = b_i \neq y_i$, then:

$$x \succsim y \Leftrightarrow x' \succsim y'$$

since

$$u_i(a_i) + \sum_{j \neq i} u_j(x_j) \geq u_i(a_i) + \sum_{j \neq i} u_j(y_j) \quad \Leftrightarrow$$

$$u_i(b_i) + \sum_{j \neq i} u_j(x_j) \geq u_i(b_i) + \sum_{j \neq i} u_j(y_j)$$

The independence property of the preference has far-reaching consequences; it allows in particular for ceteris paribus reasoning, i.e. comparing alternatives the evaluations of which differ only on a few attributes without specifying the common level of their evaluations on the remaining attributes; the independence property guarantees that the result of such a comparison is not altered when changing the common level on the attributes that do not discriminate the alternatives. We shall further discuss this property below in Sect. 3.2.5.

The two conditions stated above are not sufficient for ensuring that $\succsim$ satisfies (3.1). In case the evaluation space X is infinite, various sets of sufficient conditions have been provided in the literature; they are often categorised in two branches, the algebraic and the topological theories, respectively (see e.g. Fishburn, 1970, ch. 5). We give a schematic outline of the algebraic approach in Sect. 3.2.6. In case the set of possible levels X_i on each dimension is finite, the situation is rather unpleasant: the sufficient conditions (Fishburn, 1970, ch. 4) are quite complex and not very insightful. We therefore do not present them.

3.2.2 *Uniqueness Issues*

If the model is to be used in order to elicit preferences through the construction of functions u_i, it may also be important to know whether these u_i are uniquely determined. If they are not and provided we find a way of eliciting them independently of one another, at the end, it will remain to make sure that the obtained versions of the u_i's are compatible, i.e. that they can be used directly in (3.1).

Actually, the u_i's are not unique. For a preference $\succsim$ that fits in the additive value model, there is a family of value functions u that both

- decompose additively as $u(x) = \sum_{i=1}^{n} u_i(x_i)$
- and represent the preference i.e. satisfy $x \succsim y \Leftrightarrow u(x) \geq u(y)$.

Suppose indeed that we start with a particular representation of $\succsim$, $u(x) = \sum_{i=1}^{n} u_i(x_i)$ and we transform u_i into u'_i by a *positive affine transformation*

$$u'_i = \alpha u_i + \beta_i, \tag{3.3}$$

with $\alpha > 0$ and β_i a real number (that may vary with i). By using u'_i instead of u_i in the additive model, we get

$$u'(x) = \sum_{i=1}^{n} u'_i(x_i) = \alpha \sum_{i=1}^{n} u_i(x_i) + \sum_{i=1}^{n} \beta_i = \alpha u(x) + \sum_{i=1}^{n} \beta_i.$$

Clearly, u' is an alternative representation of the preference $\succsim$ since $x \succsim y \Leftrightarrow u(x) \geq u(y) \Leftrightarrow u'(x) \geq u'(y)$. So, the u_i's to be used in an additive representation are at best determined up to a positive affine transformation.

In case X is infinite, it is possible to prove that the u_i's are actually unique up to a positive affine transformation (with the same α and possibly different β). This requires the use of a non-necessary condition ensuring that each set X_i is sufficiently rich (see Sect. 3.2.6 for more details).

Assuming that the u_i's are determined up to a positive affine transformation, we shall briefly explain in Sect. 3.2.4 how we can take advantage of this to construct an additive representation of the preference.

3.2.3 Marginal Preferences Within the Additive Value Model

Under the hypothesis that $\succsim$ fits with model (3.1), the model suggests that functions u_i could be elicited. Going one step further, it is readily seen that $u_i(x_i)$ must be compatible with the marginal preference relation $\succsim_i$ defined as:

$$x_i \succsim_i y_i \Leftrightarrow \forall\ a_{-i} \in X_i, (x_i, a_{-i}) \succsim (y_i, a_{-i}), \tag{3.4}$$

where (x_i, a_{-i}) represents an alternative that has x_i as ith component while the other components are those of vector a. So, (x_i, a_{-i}) and (y_i, a_{-i}) are two alternatives that may only differ on attribute i; they have common evaluations a_j on all attributes j but for $j = i$. If the client states $(x_i, a_{-i}) \succsim (y_i, a_{-i})$, this means, in terms of the marginal preference relation $\succsim_i$, that $x_i \succsim_i y_i$ and it translates in model (3.1) into:

$$u_i(x_i) + \sum_{j \neq i} u_j(a_j) \geq u_i(y_i) + \sum_{j \neq i} u_j(a_j),$$

from which we deduce $u_i(x_i) \geq u_i(y_i)$. Thus, for all levels x_i, y_i in X_i, we have $x_i \succsim_i y_i$ iff $u_i(x_i) \geq u_i(y_i)$. Therefore, in model (3.1), the function u_i interprets as a numerical representation of the marginal preference $\succsim_i$, which is a weak order.

The fact that the marginal preference is a weak order has strong links with the independence property of the preference $\succsim$ (see Sect. 3.3.5). There remains however a difficulty; the u_i functions that we need for using in the additive representation of the preference are not just *any* numerical representation of the marginal preference relations $\succsim_i$. Among the whole set of possible representations of the weak order $\succsim_i$, we have to select the right one (determined up to a positive affine transformation), the one that is needed for a representation of the global preference in the additive model.

Example 3.1 (Buying a Sports Car) Let us consider an example extensively discussed in chapter 6 of Bouyssou et al. (2000). We recall briefly the context. A student, Thierry, who is also passionate about sports cars but earns little money, assesses fourteen cars among which he considers to buy one, on the five dimensions that are of importance to him, namely cost, acceleration, pick up, brakes and

Table 3.1 Ranges of the five dimensions in the "Buying a sports car example"

Attribute	i	X_i	Unit	To be
Cost	1	[13; 21]	1,000 €	Minimised
Acceleration	2	[28; 31]	Second	Minimised
Pick up	3	[34; 42]	Second	Minimised
Brakes	4	[1; 3]	Qualitative	Maximised
Roadholding	5	[1; 4]	Qualitative	Maximised

roadholding. Assume that his preference fits with the additive value model (3.1) and let us help Thierry to build a value function u that represents his preference according with the additive model.

We first settle the ranges X_i in which the attributes will reasonably vary (in view of the evaluations of the fourteen selected cars). These ranges are shown in Table 3.1. The evaluations on the first three attributes are expressed in "physical" units (thousands of €, and, twice, seconds, respectively); the latter two belong to a qualitative scale. On the first three attributes scales, the less is the better, while on the latter two, the more is the better. What is the relationship between the evaluations and the value function u? There are two main features that we want to emphasise:

- the information contained in the evaluations is transferred to the value function through the marginal preferences;
- the marginal preferences—which are weak orders in the additive model (3.1)—cannot be identified with the natural ordering of the evaluations although these weak orders are not unrelated.

Take for example the cost attribute. Clearly, a car, say x, that costs 15,000 € is not preferred over a car y that costs 14,000 € if both cars are tied on all other dimensions. And the conclusion will be the same when comparing the former car with any other one that costs less and has the same evaluations on all other attributes. More formally, the car x can be described by the vector $(15, a_2, a_3, a_4, a_5)$ and y by $(14, a_2, a_3, a_4, a_5)$; the first dimension of these vectors represent the cost (in thousands of €) and a_i, for $i = 2, \ldots, 5$, designates any level on the other attributes. The car y is certainly at least as preferred as x ($y \succsim x$) since y is cheaper than x and all other evaluations are identical for both cars. It is a typical case in which "ceteris paribus" reasoning applies; the property of the preference we use here is *weak preference independence* (see Definition 3.1, p. 45); it is implied by strong preference independence which is a necessary condition for a preference being represented in the additive value model (3.1).

The fact that car y is preferred over x, independently of the value of a_j, can be translated into a statement involving the marginal preference $\succsim_1$ on the Cost attribute, namely $14 \succsim_1 15$. For all pairs of costs x_1, y_1 in the range 13; 21, we would similarly have $y_1 \succsim_1 x_1$ as soon as $x_1 \geq y_1$. But $x_1 > y_1$ does not necessarily implies $y_1 \succsim_1 x_1$ because a small difference between x_1 and y_1 could be considered as negligible with respect to the imprecision in the evaluation of the costs.

3.2.4 Leaning on the Additive Value Model for Eliciting Preferences

The additive value model suggests a general strategy for the elicitation of a preference that fits with the model. We assume here that the conditions of uniqueness of the additive representation are fulfilled (see Sect. 3.2.2). The strategy consists in eliciting the functions u_i, relying upon the fact that the u_i's are numerical representations of the marginal preferences. The main problem is to find among the many representations of the marginal preferences, the essentially unique ones that can be summed up and yield an additive representation u of the preference. This can be done in many different ways, which have been well-studied (see, e.g., Fishburn, 1967; Keeney and Raiffa, 1976; von Winterfeldt and Edwards, 1986). For the reader's convenience, we briefly illustrate the method of *standard sequences* on the example of ranking sports cars evoked in the previous section; we refer the reader to Bouyssou et al. (2000, ch. 6) for more detail and for the illustration of other elicitation methods applied to the same example.

We start with considering two hypothetical cars that differ only on cost and acceleration attributes, their performance levels on the other dimensions being tied. We assume that the two cars differ in cost by a noticeable amount, say for instance $1,000$ €; we locate an interval of cost of that amplitude, for example, in the middle of the cost range, say $[16,500; 17,500]$ €. Then we fix a value of the acceleration, also in the middle of the acceleration range, say, 29.5 s in the middle of $[28; 31]$. We ask the client to consider a car costing $16,500$ € and accelerating in 29.5 s, the evaluations on the other dimensions being fixed at an arbitrary (say mid-range) value. We ask the client to assess a value x_2 of the acceleration such that he would be indifferent between the cars $(16.5; 29.5)$ and the car $(17.5; x_2)$. This question amounts to determining which improvement on the performance on the acceleration attribute (starting from a value of 29.5 s) would be worth a cost increase of $1,000$ € (starting from $16,500$ €), all other performance levels remaining constant. Since the client is supposed to be fond of sports cars, he could say for instance that $x_2 = 29.2$ s, which would result in the following indifference judgement: $(16.5; 29.5) \sim (17.5; 29.2)$. In view of the hypothesis that the client's preference fits into the additive value model, this indifference judgement can be translated into the following equality:

$$u_1(16.5) + u_2(29.5) + \sum_{j=3}^{5} u_j(x_j) = u_1(17.5) + u_2(29.2) + \sum_{j=3}^{5} u_j(x_j) \qquad (3.5)$$

Since the performance of both cars on attributes $j = 3, 4, 5$ are equal, the corresponding terms of the sum cancel and we are left with $u_1(16.5) + u_2(29.5) = u_1(17.5) + u_2(29.2)$ or:

$$u_1(16.5) - u_1(17.5) = u_2(29.2) - u_2(29.5). \qquad (3.6)$$

The second question to the client uses his answer to the first question; we ask him to assess the value x_2 of the acceleration that would leave him indifferent between the two cars (16.5; 29.2) and (17.5; x_2). Suppose the answer is $x_2 = 28.9$; we would then infer that:

$$u_1(16.5) - u_1(17.5) = u_2(28.9) - u_2(29.2). \tag{3.7}$$

Note that the lefthand side has remained unchanged: we always ask for acceleration intervals that are considered as equivalent to the same cost interval.

The next question asks for a value x_2 such that $(16.5; 28.9) \sim (17.5; x_2)$ and so on. We may imagine that the sequence of answers could be e.g.: 29.5; 29.2; 28.9; 28.7; 28.5; 28.3; 28.1. In view of (3.6), this amounts to saying that this sequence of levels on the marginal value scale of the acceleration attribute are equally spaced and that all differences of value between consecutive pairs of levels in the list are worth the same difference of cost, namely a difference of 1,000€ placed between 16,500 and 17,500€. In other words, the client values 1,000€ an improvement of

0.3 s w.r.t. a performance level of 29.5 s or 29.2 s
0.2 s w.r.t. a performance level of 28.9 s, 28.7 s, 28.5 s or 28.3 s

on the acceleration attribute. He thus praises more improvements in the lower range of the scale. Similar questions are asked for the upper half of the range of the acceleration attribute, i.e. from 29.5 to 31 s. We ask the client to assess x_2 such that he would be indifferent between (16.5; x_2) and (17.5; 29.5). Assume the client's answer is $x_2 = 30.0$. Then we go on asking for x_2 such that $(16.5; x_2) \sim (17.5; 30.0)$ and suppose we get $x_2 = 31$. From all these answers, one understands that the client values in the same way a gain in acceleration performance of 1 s between 31 and 30 and a gain of 0.2 s between e.g. between 28.9 and 28.7, a ratio of 1 to 5.

What can we do with this piece of information? We can build a piecewise linear approximation of the function u_2 (defined on the range going from 28 to 31 s). Using an arbitrary unit length on the vertical axis [the unit length represents 1,000€ or more precisely the difference $u_1(16.5) - u_1(17.5)$], we get the function u_2 represented on Fig. 3.1; it is in fact a linear interpolation of nine points the first coordinate of which correspond to the answers made by the client to seven indifference judgments; the second coordinate of these points have just to be equally spaced (by one unit length). The position of the origin is arbitrary. We have extrapolated the line from 28.1 to 28 (thinner piece of line). Note that the function u_2 is decreasing since smaller is better with the measure chosen for evaluating the acceleration.

For determining u_3, u_4 and u_5, we search successively, in the same way as for acceleration, for intervals on the pick up, brakes and roadholding scales that would compensate exactly the cost interval (16.5; 17.5) in terms of preference.

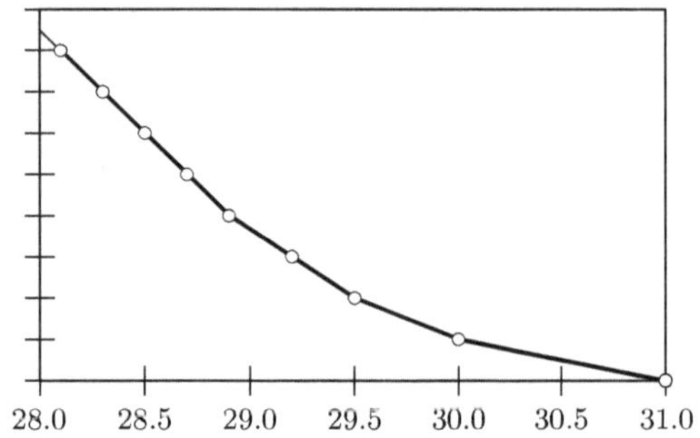

Fig. 3.1 Piecewise linear interpolation of the marginal value function u_2 on the acceleration attribute

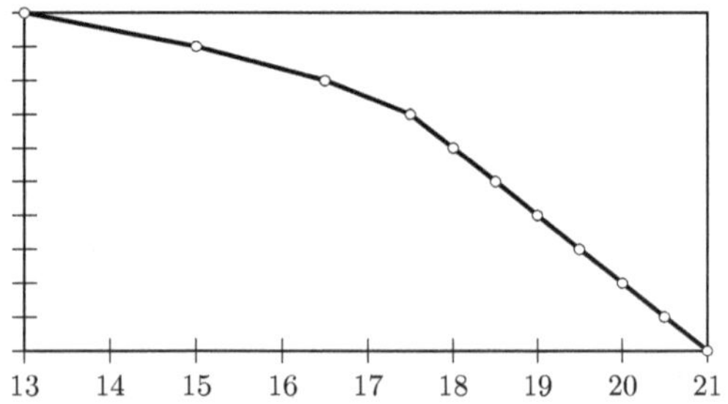

Fig. 3.2 Piecewise linear interpolation of the marginal value function u_2 on the cost attribute

Finally, we have to do the same recoding for the cost itself. We fix an interval for instance on the acceleration scale, say [29.2; 29.5]. We already know the answer to one question: (17.5; 29.2) is indifferent with $(x_1, 29.5)$ when $x_1 = 16.5$. We then ask the client, which level x_1 on the cost scale would leave him indifferent between (16.5; 29.2) and $(x_1, 29.5)$. A cost lower than 16,500€ is expected and we use it in the next question, and so on. We might end up for instance with the curve shown on Fig. 3.2. Looking at that curves indicates that the client is inclined to pay more for the same improvement on the acceleration attribute for a car priced in the lower part of the cost range than in the upper part. Plausibly, with a limited budget as a student, Thierry can reasonably spend up to 17,500€ on buying a car; paying more would imply restrictions on other expenses.

Suppose we have built that way piecewise linear approximations of u_1 to u_5. If we have chosen the same unit on all vertical axes to represent intervals equivalent to $u_1(16.5) - u_1(17.5)$, it only remains to add up these functions to obtain a piecewise linear approximation of u; ranking in turn the alternatives according with their decreasing value of u [formula (3.1)] yields the preference $\succsim$ (or an approximation of it). For the sake of illustration, we show in Table 3.2 the additive value function[2] computed for the five best cars among the 14 cars selected as alternatives by Thierry.

[2]In reality, these values have been determined by means of another elicitation method; details are provided in Bouyssou et al. (2000, ch. 6).

Table 3.2 Ranking of the cars in decreasing order of the value function u

Cars	Value u	Rank
Peugeot 309/16	0.85	1
Nissan Sunny	0.75	2
Honda Civic	0.66	3
Peugeot 309	0.65	4
Renault 19	0.61	5

3.2.5 Independence and Marginal Preferences

We have seen in Sect. 3.2.3 how it is possible to use the preference relation $\succsim$ in order to define a preference relation on a single dimension (i.e., on the set X_i). We now extend this concept of marginal preferences to subsets of dimensions. We denote by N the set of integers $\{1, 2, \ldots, n\}$. For any nonempty subset J of N, x_J is the product set $\prod_{i \in J} X_i$ and we define the *marginal relation* $\succsim_J$ induced on X_J by $\succsim$ letting, for all $x_J, y_J \in X_J$:

$$x_J \succsim_J y_J \Leftrightarrow (x_J, z_{-J}) \succsim (y_J, z_{-J}), \text{ for all } z_{-J} \in X_{-J},$$

with asymmetric (resp. symmetric) part $\succ_J$ (resp. $\sim_J$). When $J = \{i\}$, we often abuse notation and write $\succsim_i$ instead of $\succsim_{\{i\}}$ (see the Definition (3.4) of $\succsim_i$ on p. 40). Note that if $\succsim$ is reflexive (resp. transitive), the same will be true for $\succsim_J$. This is clearly not true for completeness however.

Definition 3.1 (Independence) Consider a binary relation $\succsim$ on a set $X = \prod_{i=1}^n X_i$ and let $J \subseteq N$ be a nonempty subset of dimensions. We say that $\succsim$ is independent for J if, for all $x_J, y_J \in X_J$,

$$[(x_J, z_{-J}) \succsim (y_J, z_{-J}), \text{ for some } z_{-J} \in X_{-J}] \Rightarrow x_J \succsim_J y_J.$$

If $\succsim$ is independent for all nonempty subsets of N, we say that $\succsim$ is *independent* (or strongly independent). If $\succsim$ is independent for all subsets containing a single dimension, we say that $\succsim$ is *weakly independent.*

In view of (3.1), it is clear that the additive value model will require that $\succsim$ is independent. This crucial condition says that common evaluations on some dimensions do not influence preference. Whereas independence implies weak independence, it is well-know that the converse is not true (Wakker, 1989).

Independence, or at least weak independence, is an almost universally accepted hypothesis in multiple criteria decision making. It cannot be overemphasised that it is possible to find examples in which it is inadequate. Yet, many authors (Keeney, 1992; Roy, 1996; von Winterfeldt and Edwards, 1986) have argued that such failures of independence were almost always due to a poor structuring of dimensions.

When $\succsim$ is a weak order and is weakly independent, marginal preferences are also weak orders and combine in a *monotonic* manner with the preference $\succsim$. For instance, if an alternative is preferred to another on all dimensions, then the former should be globally preferred to the latter. This monotonicity property of the preference with respect to the marginal preferences has strong links with the idea of *dominance*.

It should however be kept in mind that preferences that are not weak orders may show different behaviours. For more general preferences, the marginal preferences may no longer be the adequate tool on which to lean for eliciting the preference. This will be strongly emphasised and analysed in the generalisations of the additive value model discussed in Sects. 3.3, 3.4, and 3.5.

3.2.6 The Additive Value Model in the "Rich" Case

The purpose of the rest of Sect. 3.2 is to present the conditions under which a preference relation on a product set may be represented by the additive value function model (3.1) and how such a model can be assessed. Some limitations of this approach will also be discussed. We begin here with the case that most closely resembles the measurement of physical dimensions such as length.

When the structure of X is supposed to be "adequately rich", conjoint measurement is an adaptation of the process that is used for the measurement of physical extensive quantities such as length. The basic idea of this type of measurement (called *extensive measurement*, see Krantz et al., 1971, ch. 3) consists in comparing the object to be measured to a standard object that can be replicated while the length of the chains of replicas is an integer number of times that of the standard "unit" object. What will be measured here is the "length" of preference intervals on a dimension using a preference interval on another dimension as a standard.

3.2.6.1 The Case of Two Dimensions

Consider first the two dimension case, where the relation $\succsim$ is defined on a set $X = X_1 \times X_2$. In Sect. 3.2.1, p. 38, we already identified necessary conditions for a relation to be representable in the additive value model, namely, we have to assume that $\succsim$ is an *independent weak order*. In such a case, $\succsim_1$ and $\succsim_2$ are weak orders, as stated in Sect. 3.2.5. Consider two levels $x_1^0, x_1^1 \in X_1$ on the first dimension such that $x_1^1 \succ_1 x_1^0$, i.e. x_1^1 is preferable to x_1^0. Note that we will have to exclude the case in which all levels on the first dimension would be marginally indifferent in order to be able to find such levels.

Choose any $x_2^0 \in X_2$. The, arbitrarily chosen, element $(x_1^0, x_2^0) \in X$ will be our "reference point". The basic idea is to use this reference point and the "unit" on the first dimension given by the reference preference interval $[x_1^0, x_1^1]$ to build a standard sequence on the preference intervals on the second dimension. Hence, we are looking for an element $x_2^1 \in X_2$ that would be such that:

$$(x_1^0, x_2^1) \sim (x_1^1, x_2^0). \tag{3.8}$$

Clearly this will require the structure of X_2 to be adequately "rich" so as to find the level $x_2^1 \in X_2$ such that the reference preference interval on the first dimension $[x_1^0, x_1^1]$ is exactly matched by a preference interval of the same "length" on the second dimension $[x_2^0, x_2^1]$. Technically, this calls for a solvability assumption or, more restrictively, for the supposition that X_2 has a (topological) structure that is close to that of an interval of $\mathbb{R}$ and that $\succsim$ is "somehow" continuous.

If such a level x_2^1 can be found, model (3.1) implies:

$$\begin{aligned} u_1(x_1^0) + u_2(x_2^1) &= u_1(x_1^1) + u_2(x_2^0) \text{ so that} \\ u_2(x_2^1) - u_2(x_2^0) &= u_1(x_1^1) - u_1(x_1^0). \end{aligned} \tag{3.9}$$

Let us fix the origin of measurement letting: $u_1(x_1^0) = u_2(x_2^0) = 0$, and our unit of measurement letting: $u_1(x_1^1) = 1$ so that $u_1(x_1^1) - u_1(x_1^0) = 1$. Using (3.9), we therefore obtain $u_2(x_2^1) = 1$. We have therefore found an interval between levels on the second dimension ($[x_2^0, x_2^1]$) that exactly matches our reference interval on the first dimension ($[x_1^0, x_1^1]$). We may proceed to build our standard sequence on the second dimension (see Fig. 3.3) asking for levels $x_2^2, x_2^3, \ldots$ such that:

$$\begin{aligned} &(x_1^0, x_2^2) \sim (x_1^1, x_2^1), \\ &(x_1^0, x_2^3) \sim (x_1^1, x_2^2), \\ &\ldots \\ &(x_1^0, x_2^k) \sim (x_1^1, x_2^{k-1}). \end{aligned}$$

As above, using (3.1) leads to:

$$\begin{aligned} u_2(x_2^2) - u_2(x_2^1) &= u_1(x_1^1) - u_1(x_1^0), \\ u_2(x_2^3) - u_2(x_2^2) &= u_1(x_1^1) - u_1(x_1^0), \\ &\ldots \\ u_2(x_2^k) - u_2(x_2^{k-1}) &= u_1(x_1^1) - u_1(x_1^0), \end{aligned}$$

so that:

$$u_2(x_2^2) = 2, u_2(x_2^3) = 3, \ldots, u_2(x_2^k) = k.$$

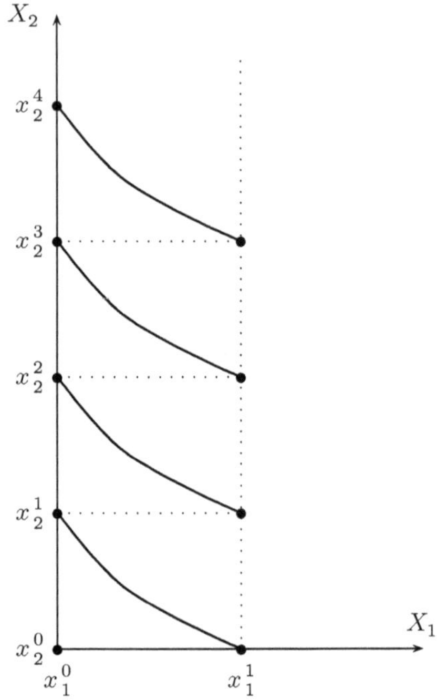

Fig. 3.3 Building a standard sequence on X_2

This process of building a standard sequence of the second dimension therefore leads to defining u_2 on a number of, carefully, selected elements of X_2. Suppose now that there is a level $y_2 \in X_2$ that can never be "reached" by our standard sequence, i.e. such that $y_2 \succ_2 x_2^k$, even for very large k. This is clearly not compatible with an additive representation as in (3.1). We therefore need to exclude this case by imposing a specific condition, called *Archimedean* because it mimics the property of the real numbers saying that for any positive real numbers x, y it is true that $nx > y$ for some integer n, i.e. y, no matter how large, may always be exceeded by taking any x, no matter how small, and adding it with itself and repeating the operation a sufficient number of times.

Now that a standard sequence is built on the second dimension, we may use any part of it to build a standard sequence on the first dimension. This will require finding levels $x_1^2, x_1^3, \ldots \in X_1$ such that (see Fig. 3.4): $(x_1^2, x_2^0) \sim (x_1^1, x_2^1)$, $(x_1^3, x_2^0) \sim (x_1^2, x_2^1)$, $\ldots (x_1^k, x_2^0) \sim (x_1^{k-1}, x_2^1)$. Using (3.1) leads to:

$$u_1(x_1^2) - u_1(x_1^1) = u_2(x_2^1) - u_2(x_2^0),$$

$$u_1(x_1^3) - u_1(x_1^2) = u_2(x_2^1) - u_2(x_2^0),$$

$$\ldots$$

$$u_1(x_1^k) - u_1(x_1^{k-1}) = u_2(x_2^1) - u_2(x_2^0),$$

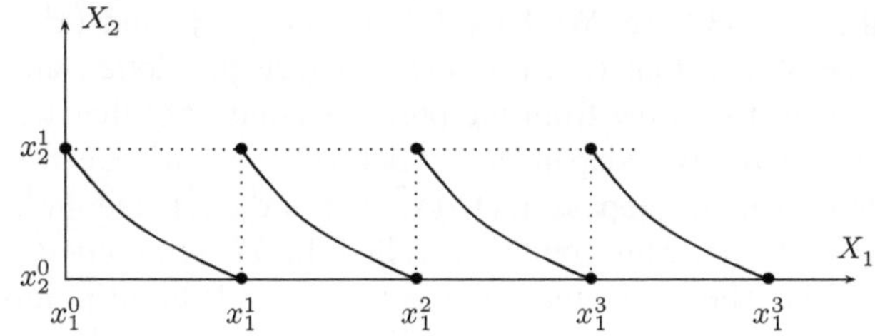

Fig. 3.4 Building a standard sequence on X_1

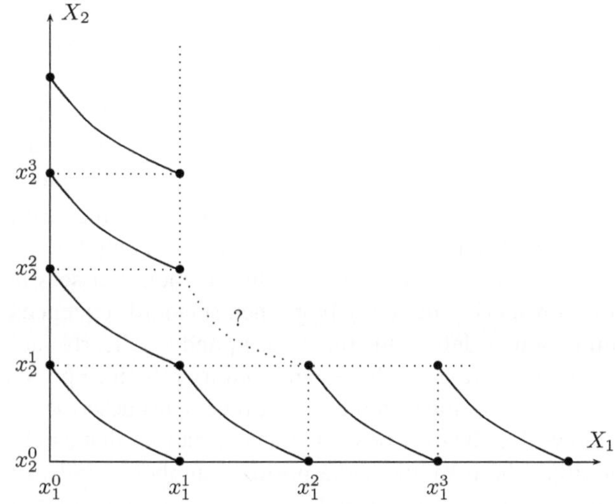

Fig. 3.5 The grid

so that: $u_1(x_1^2) = 2, u_1(x_1^3) = 3, \ldots, u_1(x_1^k) = k$. As was the case for the second dimension, the construction of such a sequence will require the structure of X_1 to be adequately rich, which calls for a solvability assumption. An Archimedean condition will also be needed in order to be sure that all levels of X_1 can be reached by the sequence.

We have defined a "grid" in X (see Fig. 3.5) and we have $u_1(x_1^k) = k$ and $u_2(x_2^k) = k$ for all elements of this grid. Intuitively such numerical assignments seem to define an adequate additive value function on the grid. We have to prove that this intuition is correct. Let us first verify that, for all integers $\alpha, \beta, \gamma, \delta$:

$$\alpha + \beta = \gamma + \delta = \epsilon \Rightarrow (x_1^\alpha, x_2^\beta) \sim (x_1^\gamma, x_2^\delta). \tag{3.10}$$

When $\epsilon = 1$, (3.10) holds by construction because we have: $(x_1^0, x_2^1) \sim (x_1^1, x_2^0)$. When $\epsilon = 2$, we know that $(x_1^0, x_2^2) \sim (x_1^1, x_2^1)$ and $(x_1^2, x_2^0) \sim (x_1^1, x_2^1)$ and the claim is proved using the transitivity of $\sim$.

Consider the $\epsilon = 3$ case. We have $(x_1^0, x_2^3) \sim (x_1^1, x_2^2)$ and $(x_1^0, x_2^3) \sim (x_1^1, x_2^2)$. It remains to be shown that $(x_1^2, x_2^1) \sim (x_1^1, x_2^2)$ (see the dotted arc in Fig. 3.5). This does not seem to follow from the previous conditions that we more or less explicitly used: transitivity, independence, "richness", Archimedean. Indeed, it does not. Hence, we have to suppose that: $(x_1^2, x_2^0) \sim (x_1^0, x_2^2)$ and $(x_1^0, x_2^1) \sim (x_1^1, x_2^0)$ imply $(x_1^2, x_2^1) \sim (x_1^1, x_2^2)$. This condition, called the *Thomsen condition*, is clearly necessary for (3.1). The above reasoning easily extends to all points on the grid, using weak ordering, independence and the Thomsen condition. Hence, (3.10) holds on the grid.

It remains to show that:

$$\epsilon = \alpha + \beta > \epsilon' = \gamma + \delta \Rightarrow (x_1^\alpha, x_2^\beta) \succ (x_1^\gamma, x_2^\delta). \tag{3.11}$$

Using transitivity, it is sufficient to show that (3.11) holds when $\epsilon = \epsilon' + 1$. By construction, we know that $(x_1^1, x_2^0) \succ (x_1^0, x_2^0)$. Using independence this implies that $(x_1^1, x_2^k) \succ (x_1^0, x_2^k)$. Using (3.10) we have $(x_1^1, x_2^k) \sim (x_1^{k+1}, x_2^0)$ and $(x_1^0, x_2^k) \sim (x_1^k, x_2^0)$. Therefore we have $(x_1^{k+1}, x_2^0) \succ (x_1^k, x_2^0)$, the desired conclusion.

Hence, we have built an additive value function of a suitably chosen grid (see Fig. 3.6). The logic of the assessment procedure is then to assess more and more points somehow considering more finely grained standard sequences. Going to the limit then unambiguously defines the functions u_1 and u_2. Clearly such u_1 and u_2 are intimately related. Once we have chosen an arbitrary reference point (x_1^0, x_2^0) and a level x_1^1 defining the unit of measurement, the process just described entirely defines u_1 and u_2. It follows that the only possible transformations that can be applied to u_1 and u_2 is to multiply both by the same positive number α and to add to both a, possibly different, constant. This is usually summarised saying that u_1 and u_2 define interval scales with a common unit.

Fig. 3.6 The entire grid

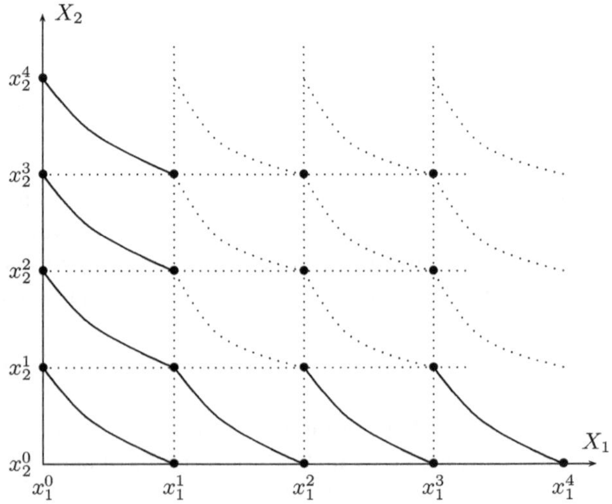

The above reasoning is a rough sketch of the proof of the existence of an additive value function when $n = 2$, as well as a sketch of how it could be assessed. Careful readers will want to refer to Fishburn (1970, ch. 5), Krantz et al. (1971, ch. 6) and Wakker (1989, ch. 3).

It is worth emphasising that the assessment technique using standard sequences outlined above makes no use of the vague notion of the "importance" of the various dimensions. The "importance" is captured here in the lengths of the preference intervals on the various dimensions.

A common but critical mistake is to confuse the additive value function model (3.1) with a weighted average and to try to assess weights asking whether a dimension is "more important" than another. This makes no sense.

3.2.6.2 The Case of More Than Two Dimensions

The good news is that the process is exactly the same when there are more than two dimensions. With one surprise: the Thomsen condition is no longer needed to prove that the standard sequences defined on each dimension lead to an adequate value function on the grid. A heuristic explanation of this strange result is that, when $n = 2$, there is no difference between independence and weak independence. This is no more true when $n \geq 3$ and assuming independence is much stronger than just assuming weak independence.

We use below the "algebraic approach" (Krantz, 1964; Krantz et al., 1971; Luce and Tukey, 1964). A more restrictive approach using a topological structure on X is given in Debreu (1960), Fishburn (1970, ch. 5) and Wakker (1989, ch. 3). We formalise below the conditions informally introduced in the preceding section. The reader not interested in the precise statement of the results or, better, having already written down his own statement, may skip this section.

Definition 3.2 (Thomsen Condition) Let $\succsim$ be a binary relation on a set $X = X_1 \times X_2$. It is said to satisfy the Thomsen condition if

$$(x_1, x_2) \sim (y_1, y_2) \text{ and } (y_1, z_2) \sim (z_1, x_2) \Rightarrow (x_1, z_2) \sim (z_1, y_2),$$

for all $x_1, y_1, z_1 \in X_1$ and all $x_2, y_2, z_2 \in X_2$.

Figure 3.7 shows how the Thomsen condition uses two "indifference curves" (i.e. curves linking points that are indifferent) to place a constraint on a third one. This was needed above to prove that an additive value function existed on our grid. Remember that the Thomsen condition is only needed when $n = 2$; hence, we only stated it in this case.

Definition 3.3 (Standard Sequences) A standard sequence on dimension $i \in N$ is a set $\{a_i^k : a_i^k \in X_i, k \in K\}$ where K is a set of consecutive integers (positive or negative, finite or infinite) such that there are $x_{-i}, y_{-i} \in X_{-i}$ satisfying $Not[x_{-i} \sim_{-i} y_{-i}]$ and $(a_i^k, x_{-i}) \sim (a_i^{k+1}, y_{-i})$, for all $k \in K$.

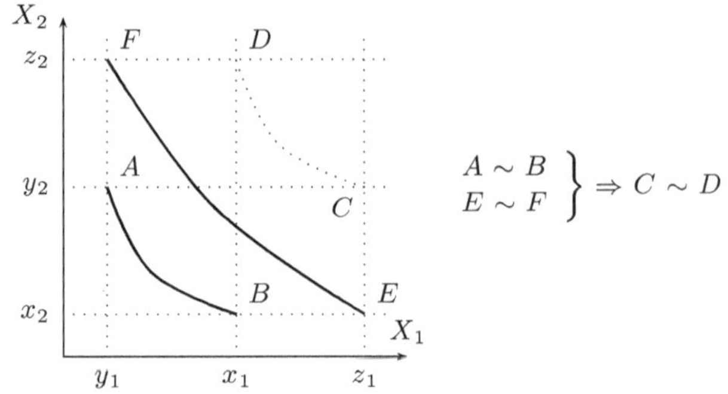

Fig. 3.7 The Thomsen condition

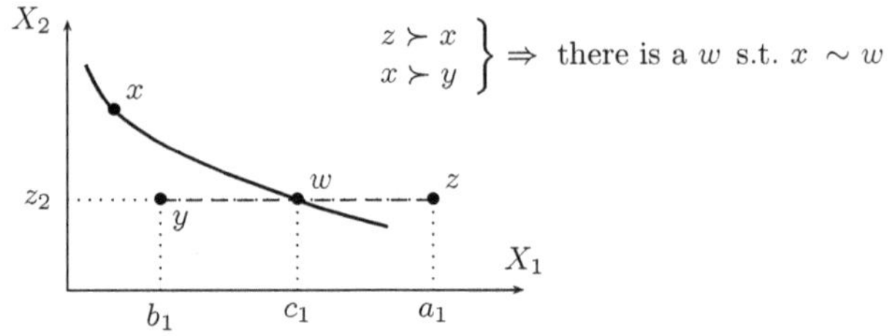

Fig. 3.8 Restricted solvability on X_1

A standard sequence on dimension $i \in N$ is said to be *strictly bounded* if there are $b_i, c_i \in X_i$ such that $b_i \succ_i a_i^k \succ_i c_i$, for all $k \in K$. It is then clear that, when model (3.1) holds, any strictly bounded standard sequence must be finite.

Definition 3.4 (Archimedean) For all $i \in N$, any strictly bounded standard sequence on $i \in N$ is finite.

The following condition rules out the case in which a standard sequence cannot be built because all levels are indifferent.

Definition 3.5 (Essentiality) Let $\succsim$ be a binary relation on a set $X = X_1 \times X_2 \times \cdots \times X_n$. dimension $i \in N$ is said to be essential if $(x_i, a_{-i}) \succ (y_i, a_{-i})$, for some $x_i, y_i \in X_i$ and some $a_{-i} \in X_{-i}$.

Definition 3.6 (Restricted Solvability) Let $\succsim$ be a binary relation on a set $X = X_1 \times X_2 \times \cdots \times X_n$. Restricted solvability is said to hold with respect to dimension $i \in N$ if, for all $x \in X$, all $z_{-i} \in X_{-i}$ and all $a_i, b_i \in X_i$, $[(a_i, z_{-i}) \succsim x \succsim (b_i, z_{-i})] \Rightarrow [x \sim (c_i, z_{-i})$, for some $c_i \in X_i]$.

Restricted solvability is illustrated in Fig. 3.8 in the case where $n = 2$. It says that, given any $x \in X$, if it is possible find two levels $a_i, b_i \in X_i$ such that when combined with a certain level $z_{-i} \in X_{-i}$ on the other dimensions, (a_i, z_{-i}) is preferred to x and x is preferred to (b_i, z_{-i}), it should be possible to find a level c_i, between a_i and b_i, such that (c_i, z_{-i}) is exactly indifferent to x.

We are now in position to state the central results concerning model (3.1). Proofs may be found in Krantz et al. (1971, ch. 6) and Wakker (1991).

Theorem 3.1 (Additive Value Function When $n = 2$**)** *Let* $\succsim$ *be a binary relation on a set* $X = X_1 \times X_2$*. If restricted solvability holds on all dimensions and each dimension is essential then* $\succsim$ *has a representation in model (3.1) if and only if* $\succsim$ *is an independent weak order satisfying the Thomsen and the Archimedean conditions.*

Furthermore in this representation, u_1 *and* u_2 *are interval scales with a common unit, i.e. if* u_1, u_2 *and* w_1, w_2 *are two pairs of functions satisfying (3.1), there are real numbers* α, β_1, β_2 *with* $\alpha > 0$ *such that, for all* $x_1 \in X_1$ *and all* $x_2 \in X_2$

$$u_1(x_1) = \alpha w_1(x_1) + \beta_1 \text{ and } u_2(x_2) = \alpha w_2(x_2) + \beta_2.$$

When $n \geq 3$ and at least three dimensions are essential, the above result simplifies in that the Thomsen condition can now be omitted.

Theorem 3.2 (Additive Value Function When $n \geq 3$**)** *Let* $\succsim$ *be a binary relation on a set* $X = X_1 \times X_2 \times \ldots \times X_n$ *with* $n \geq 3$*. If restricted solvability holds on all dimensions and at least three dimensions are essential then* $\succsim$ *has a representation in (3.1) if and only if* $\succsim$ *is an independent weak order satisfying the Archimedean condition. Furthermore in this representation* $u_1, u_2, \ldots, u_n$ *are interval scales with a common unit.*

3.2.6.3 Implementation: Standard Sequences and Beyond

The assessment procedure based on standard sequences is, as we have seen, rather demanding; hence, it seems to be seldom used in the practice of decision analysis (Keeney and Raiffa, 1976). Many other simplified assessment procedures have been proposed that are less firmly grounded in theory. These procedures include *(1) direct rating* techniques in which values of u_i are directly assessed with reference to two arbitrarily chosen points; *(2)* procedures based on *bisection*, the decision-maker being asked to assess a point that is "half way", in terms of preference, two reference points, *(3)* procedures trying to build *standard sequences* on each dimension in terms of "preference differences." An excellent overview of these techniques may be found in von Winterfeldt and Edwards (1986, ch. 7).

3.2.7 Insufficiency of Additive Conjoint Measurement

We now present two examples showing that there are preferences that are both reasonable and do not satisfy the hypotheses for an additive representation. We also present an example that can be represented within the additive value function model but also in a more specific model than (3.1), with special u_i functions.

Example 3.2 A solution of a Flexible Constraint Satisfaction Problem is assessed by a vector of n numbers that represent the degree to which each of the n constraints are satisfied; the satisfaction degree is usually modelled as a number between 0 and 1. For instance, in certain scheduling problems (Dubois et al., 1995; Dubois and Fortemps, 1999), there may be an ideal range of time between the end of some tasks and the starting of some other ones; if more (or less) time elapses, then the schedule is less satisfactory; for each constraint of that type, the degree of satisfaction is equal to 1 if the corresponding slack time lies in the ideal range; it decreases outside this range and, outside a larger interval corresponding to the admissible delays between the end of a task and the beginning of another, the degree of satisfaction reaches 0. Usually, one considers that the scale on which the satisfaction degrees are assessed is ordinal and the same for all constraints: one may meaningfully compare satisfaction degrees (saying for instance that one is larger than the other), but the difference between two degrees cannot be compared meaningfully to another difference; moreover, the satisfaction degrees of two different constraints are commensurate: it is meaningful to say that a constraint is satisfied at a higher level than another one. A solution to such a scheduling problem is an assignment of a starting time to each task; comparing two solutions amounts to comparing their associated vectors of satisfaction degrees. Usually in practice, a solution is evaluated by its weakest aspect, i.e. the lowest degree of satisfaction it attains on the set of constraints. In other words, vectors of satisfaction can be compared using the "min-score"; for $x = (x_1, \dots, x_n)$ and $y = (y_1, \dots, y_n)$, where x_i and y_i respectively denote the degrees of satisfaction of constraint i by the two alternatives to be compared, one has:

$$x \succsim y \Leftrightarrow \min(x_1, \dots, x_n) \geq \min(y_1, \dots, y_n) \tag{3.12}$$

Clearly, the relation comparing the vectors of satisfaction degrees can be viewed as a relation $\succsim$ on the product set $X = [0, 1]^n$. It is defined by means of the "min"-score instead of an additive value function as in model (3.1). One can not exclude *a priori* that the relation defined by (3.12) could also be represented in model (3.1). This is however not the case, since this relation does not satisfy one of the necessary conditions stated above, namely the strong independence property: we can indeed transform an indifference into a strict preference by changing the common level of satisfaction that is achieved by two alternatives on the same constraint. This is shown by the following example. Suppose there are two constraints ($n = 2$) and $x = (0.6, 0.5)$, $y = (0.6, 0.7)$; one has $x \succ y$, but lowering for instance to 0.3 the common satisfaction level yields $x' \sim y'$ (with $x' = (0.3, 0.5)$ and $y' = (0.3, 0.7)$). It should be clear from this example that there are simple and well-motivated procedures the additive value function model is not able to encompass.

Example 3.3 The other necessary condition for model (3.1), namely transitivity, may also fail to be satisfied by some reasonable preferences. Let us just recall R. D. Luce's famous example (Luce, 1956) of the cup of coffee: a person who likes coffee is indifferent between two cups of coffee that differ by the addition of one grain of sugar; he normally would not be indifferent between a cup with no sugar and a cup containing one thousand grains of sugar; he would definitely prefer the latter or the former. A long sequence of indifferent alternatives may thus result in preference, contrary to the hypothesis of the additive value model, in which preferences are weak orders, hence transitive.[3]

Example 3.4 Assume $g_i(a)$ is a number. The PROMETHEE II method (Brans and Vincke, 1985) starts with comparing alternatives, in a pairwise manner, with respect to each attribute i. The intensity $S_i(a,b)$ of the preference of a over b on attribute i is a nondecreasing function P_i of the difference $g_i(a) - g_i(b)$:

$$S_i(a,b) = P_i(g_i(a) - g_i(b)). \tag{3.13}$$

When the difference $g_i(a) - g_i(b)$ is negative, it is assumed that $S_i(a,b) = 0$. The global intensity of the preference of a over b is described by means of a weighted sum of the S_i functions:

$$S(a,b) = \sum_{i=1}^{n} w_i S_i(a,b), \tag{3.14}$$

where w_i is the weight associated with attribute i. In a further step, the alternatives are evaluated by their "net flow" defined by:

$$\Phi(a) = \sum_{b \in \mathcal{A}} S(a,b) - S(b,a). \tag{3.15}$$

This score is then used to determine that a is preferred over b if $\Phi(a) \geq \Phi(b)$. This is the customary presentation of PROMETHEE II (see e.g. Vincke, 1992, p. 74).

By using Eq. (3.15), it is easy to rewrite $\Phi(a)$ as follows:

$$\Phi(a) = \sum_{i=1}^{n} w_i \sum_{b \in \mathcal{A}} [S_i(a,b) - S_i(b,a)]. \tag{3.16}$$

The latter formula can be seen as defining an additive value model in which the marginal value functions u_i have the particular form:

$$u_i(g_i(a)) = \sum_{b \in \mathcal{A}} [S_i(a,b) - S_i(b,a)]. \tag{3.17}$$

The computation of function u_i that models the influence of criterion i depends on the other alternatives (thereby violating a property called "independence of irrelevant alternatives" (Arrow, 1951)). Equation (3.17) suggests that constructing

[3] For further discussion of the transitivity of preference issue, mainly in the context of decision under risk, the reader could see Fishburn (1991a). For counter-arguments against considering intransitive preferences, see (Luce, 2000, section 2.2).

the preference can go through modelling for each dimension the value of any echelon $g_i(a)$ as the sum of its "advantages" and "disadvantages", respectively coded by $S_i(a,b)$ and $S_i(b,a)$. Model (3.1) makes no suggestion of intuitively interpretable concepts that would suggest that u_i could be viewed as a superposition (through a sum) of more elementary elements.

In the following sections, we present more general conjoint measurement models (providing more general representations of the preference); the proposed models all induce concepts that can support the construction or elicitation process.

3.3 A First Line of Generalisation: Models Based on Marginal Traces or Preferences

In this section we discuss a generalisation of the additive value function model while preserving the possibility of using the fundamental construction tool suggested by the model, namely marginal preferences that are weak orders represented by the functions u_i in (3.1). Interestingly, the generalised model admits a full characterisation through fairly simple and intuitive axioms, which was not the case with model (3.1) as we have just seen.

3.3.1 Decomposable Preferences

The so-called decomposable model has been introduced in Krantz et al. (1971, ch. 7) as a natural generalisation of model (3.1). The preference $\succsim$ is supposed to be a weak order and can thus be represented by a rule of the type

$$x \succsim y \Leftrightarrow u(x) \geq u(y) \tag{3.18}$$

with u, a real-valued function defined on X. Instead of specifying u as a sum of functions u_i of the variables x_i, u is just supposed to be decomposable in the form

$$u(x) = U(u_1(x_1), \ldots, u_n(x_n)) \tag{3.19}$$

where u_i is a function from X_i to $\mathbb{R}$ (the set of real numbers) and U is increasing in all its arguments.

The interesting point with this model is that it admits an intuitively appealing characterisation. The basic axiom for characterising the above decomposable model (with increasing U) is the weak independence condition (see Definition 3.1).

For preferences that are weak orders, it is possible to prove that the weak independence property is equivalent to the fact that the marginal preferences $\succsim_i$ are weak orders (Proposition 6.1 in Bouyssou et al. 2006). Moreover, it is easy to see that u_i in (3.19) is necessarily a numerical representation of $\succsim_i$, i.e. $x_i \succsim_i y_i$ iff $u_i(x_i) \geq u_i(y_i)$. This is an important result since it opens the door to the elicitation of the u_i's by questioning in terms of the marginal preferences $\succsim_i$ like was done in the additive utility model.

The following theorem states a simple and important characterisation of the decomposable model. This result was first proved in Krantz et al. (1971, ch. 7).

Theorem 3.3 (Representation in the Decomposable Model) *A preference relation $\succsim$ on X admits a representation in the decomposable model:*

$$x \succsim y \Leftrightarrow U(u_1(x_1), \ldots, u_n(x_n)) \geq U(u_i(y_1), \ldots, u_i(y_n))$$

with U increasing in all its arguments iff $\succsim$ is a weak order and satisfies weak independence.

If one intended to apply this model, one would go through specifying the type of function U, possibly by verifying further conditions on the preference that impose that U belongs to some parameterised family of functions (e.g. polynomials of bounded degree). Although decomposable preferences form a large family of preferences, it is not large enough to encompass all useful cases. A major restriction is that not all preferences may be assumed to be weak orders, as illustrated in Example 3.3 by the example of the cups of coffee.

3.3.2 *Insufficiency of Marginal Analysis: Marginal Traces*

In the decomposable model, the preference may be reconstructed on the basis of the marginal preferences $\succsim_i$ since it is represented by a function of the u_i's, themselves representing $\succsim_i$ (at least in the strict decomposable model).

This is no longer the case when $\succsim$ is not a weak order because the relation $\succsim_i$ on X_i is not very discriminating.

Example 3.5 To fix the ideas, suppose a decision-maker has preferences that can be represented by $a \succsim b$ iff $\sum_{i=1}^n u_i(a_i) \geq \sum_{i=1}^n u_i(b_i) - \delta$ for some positive and real δ. The reason for adding δ is that the decision-maker considers that small differences between $\sum_{i=1}^n u_i(a_i)$ and $\sum_{i=1}^n u_i(b_i)$ are not significant. In particular, $a \succ b$ iff $\sum_{i=1}^n u_i(a_i) > \sum_{i=1}^n u_i(b_i) + \delta$. Suppose also $n = 10$ and the range of each mapping u_i is $[0, 1]$. Then the range of $\sum_{i=1}^n u_i(\cdot)$ is $[0, 10]$ and it seems plausible to use $\delta = 1$. Let us now consider objects differing only on one attribute. We have $a_i \succ_i b_i$ iff $(a_i, a_{-i}) \succ (b_i, a_{-i})$ iff $\sum_{j=1}^n u_j(a_j) > u_i(b_i) + \sum_{j \neq i} u_j(a_j) + 1$ iff $u_i(a_i) > u_i(b_i) + 1$. Since, the range of u_i is $[0, 1]$, it will never be the case that $u_i(a_i) > u_i(b_i) + 1$ and, hence $a_i \sim_i b_i$ for all $a_i, b_i \in X_i$. In other words, the marginal preference $\succsim_i$ is completely uninformative: it does not discriminate any level of X_i. This case is obviously extreme but it is not uncommon that $\succsim_i$ discriminates only few levels.

Is there a relation on X_i that has stronger links with the global preference $\succsim$ than the marginal preference $\succsim_i$? The answer is the *marginal trace* $\succsim_i^{\pm}$ that is defined below.

Definition 3.7 (Marginal Trace)
The marginal trace $\succsim_i^{\pm}$ of relation $\succsim$ on the product set $X = \prod X_i$ is the relation on X_i defined by:

$$a_i \succsim_i^{\pm} b_i \text{ iff } \begin{cases} \text{for all } c, d \in X, \\ [(b_i, c_{-i}) \succsim d] \Rightarrow [(a_i, c_{-i}) \succsim d] \text{ and} \\ [c \succsim (a_i, d_{-i})] \Rightarrow [c \succsim (b_i, d_{-i})] \end{cases} \tag{3.20}$$

In other words, $a_i \succsim_i^{\pm} b_i$ iff substituting b_i by a_i in an alternative does not change the way this alternative compares to others.

In the case of Example 3.5, one has $a_i \succsim_i^{\pm} b_i$ iff $u_i(a_i) \geq u_i(b_i)$, which is easily verified. Suppose indeed that $(b_i, c_{-i}) \succsim d$ for some $c_{-i} \in X_{-i}$ and $d \in X$; this means that

$$u_i(b_i) + \sum_{j \neq i} u_j(c_j)) \geq \sum_{j=1}^{n} u_j(d_j) + 1. \tag{3.21}$$

Substituting b_i by a_i : $u_i(a_i) \geq u_i(b_i)$ preserves the inequality.

In models in which $\succsim$ is not supposed to be a weak order, the information conveyed in the marginal preferences may be insufficient to reconstruct the preference. As we shall see, the marginal traces, when they are weak orders, always convey enough information. The reason why the insufficiency of marginal preferences did not show up in the decomposable model is a consequence of the following result.

Proposition 3.1 (Marginal Preferences and Marginal Traces) *If a preference relation $\succsim$ on X is reflexive and transitive, its marginal preferences $\succsim_i$ and its marginal traces $\succsim_i^{\pm}$ are confounded for all i.*

The proposition almost immediately results from the definitions of marginal preferences and traces. It makes clear that there is no need worrying about marginal traces unless $\succsim$ is not transitive. More exactly, as we shall see below, the notion that conveys all the information needed to reconstruct the global preference from relations on each scale X_i is always the marginal traces; but when $\succsim$ is reflexive and transitive, you may equivalently use marginal preferences instead. The converse of the proposition is not true however: there are cases where $\succsim$ is not transitive (e.g. when $\succsim$ is a semiorder) and $\succsim_i = \succsim_i^{\pm}$ (see Bouyssou and Pirlot, 2004, Example 4).Instead of generalising again the decomposable model in order to encompass preferences that are for instance semiorders, we propose and study a much more general model. It is so general that it encompasses all relations on X. Considering this model as a framework, we introduce successive specialisations that will bring us back to the decomposable model, but "from above", i.e. in a movement from the general to the particular. In this specialisation process, it is the marginal trace—not the marginal preference—that is the central tool.

3.3.3 Generalising Decomposable Models Using Marginal Traces

Consider the very general representation of a relation $\succsim$ described by:

$$x \succsim y \Leftrightarrow F(u_1(x_1), u_2(x_2), \ldots, u_n(x_n), u_1(y_1), u_2(y_2), \ldots, u_n(y_n)) \geq 0 \qquad (L0)$$

The main difference w.r.t. the decomposable model is that the evaluations of the two alternatives are not dealt with separately.

If no property is imposed on function F, the model is trivial since any relation can be represented within it. It obviously generalises the decomposable model and encompasses as a special case the representation involving a threshold described in Example 3.5 (in which the preference is a semiorder).

It is easy to obtain representations that guarantee simple properties of $\succsim$. For instance, $\succsim$ is reflexive iff it has a representation in model $(L0)$ with $F([u_i(x_i)];[u_i(x_i)]) \geq 0$; $\succsim$ is complete iff it has a representation in model $(L0)$ with $F([u_i(x_i)];[u_i(y_i)]) = -F([u_i(y_i)];[u_i(x_i)])$. What if we impose monotonicity conditions on F? The natural ones in view of the decomposable model are (1) F increasing in its first n arguments and decreasing in its last n arguments and (2) F non-decreasing in its first n arguments and non-increasing in its last n arguments. The following axioms are closely linked with imposing monotonicity properties to F and, as we shall see, with properties of the marginal traces.

Definition 3.8 (Axioms $AC1, AC2, AC3, AC4$) We say that $\succsim$ satisfies:

$$AC1_i \quad \text{if} \quad \left.\begin{array}{r}(x_i, a_{-i}) \succsim y \\ \text{and} \\ (z_i, b_{-i}) \succsim w\end{array}\right\} \rightarrow \left\{\begin{array}{l}(z_i, a_{-i}) \succsim y \\ \text{or} \\ (x_i, b_{-i}) \succsim w,\end{array}\right.$$

$$AC2_i \quad \text{if} \quad \left.\begin{array}{r}y \succsim (x_i, a_{-i}) \\ \text{and} \\ w \succsim (z_i, b_{-i})\end{array}\right\} \Rightarrow \left\{\begin{array}{l}y \succsim (z_i, a_{-i}) \\ \text{or} \\ w \succsim (x_i, b_{-i}),\end{array}\right.$$

$$AC3_i \quad \text{if} \quad \left.\begin{array}{r}(x_i, a_{-i}) \succsim y \\ \text{and} \\ w \succsim (x_i, b_{-i})\end{array}\right\} \Rightarrow \left\{\begin{array}{l}(z_i, a_{-i}) \succsim y \\ \text{or} \\ w \succsim (z_i, b_{-i}),\end{array}\right.$$

for all $x_i, z_i \in X_i$, all $a_{-i}, b_{-i} \in X_{-i}$ and all $y, w \in X$.

It satisfies $AC4_i$ if $\succsim$ satisfies $AC3_i$ and, whenever one of the conclusions of $AC3_i$ is false, then the other one holds with $\succ$ instead of $\succsim$.

We say that $\succsim$ satisfies $AC1$ (resp. $AC2$, $AC3$, $AC4$) if it satisfies $AC1_i$ (resp. $AC2_i, AC3_i, AC4_i$) for all $i \in N$. We also use $AC123_i$ (resp. $AC123$) as shorthand for $AC1_i$, $AC2_i$ and $AC3_i$ (resp. $AC1$, $AC2$ and $AC3$).

The intuition behind these axioms is the following. Take axiom $AC1_i$. It suggests that x_i and z_i can be compared: either x_i corresponds to a "level" on a "scale" on X_i that is "above" z_i or the other way around. Suppose indeed that x_i is involved in an alternative that is preferred to another one ($(x_i, x_{-i}) \succsim y$); suppose further that substituting z_i to x_i would not allow to preserve the preference ($Not[(z_i, x_{-i}) \succsim y]$). Then $AC1_i$ says that substituting z_i by x_i when z_i is involved in an alternative that is preferred to another ($(z_i, z_{-i}) \succsim w$) will always preserve the preference (i.e. we have: $(x_i, z_{-i}) \succsim w$). One can interpret such a situation by saying that x_i is "above" z_i. The "being above" relation on X_i is what we call the *left marginal trace* of $\succsim$ and we denote it by $\succsim_i^+$; it is defined as follows:

$$x_i \succsim_i^+ z_i \Leftrightarrow [(z_i, z_{-i}) \succsim w \Rightarrow (x_i, z_{-i}) \succsim w]. \tag{3.22}$$

We explained above that $AC1_i$ meant that x_i and z_i can always be compared, which, in terms of the left trace, interprets as: "We may not have at the same time $Not[x_i \succsim_i^+ z_i]$ and $Not[z_i \succsim_i^+ x_i]$". It is easy to see that supposing the latter would amount to have some z_{-i} and some w such that:

$$(z_i, z_{-i}) \succsim w \text{ and } Not[(x_i, z_{-i}) \succsim w]$$

and at the same time, for some x_{-i} and some y,

$$(x_i, x_{-i}) \succsim y \text{ and } Not[(z_i, x_{-i}) \succsim y],$$

which is exactly the negation of $AC1_i$. Axiom $AC1_i$ thus says that the left marginal trace $\succsim_i^+$ is complete; since it is transitive by definition, $\succsim_i^+$ is a weak order.

$AC1_i$ deals with levels involved in alternatives that are preferred to other ones, thus in the strong (lefthand side) position in the comparison of two alternatives; in contrast, $AC2_i$ rules the behaviour of $\succsim$ when changing levels in alternatives in the weak position (another alternative is preferred to them). Clearly, $AC2_i$ is concerned with a *right marginal trace* $\succsim_i^-$ that is defined as follows:

$$y_i \succsim_i^- w_i \Leftrightarrow [x \succsim (y_i, y_{-i}) \Rightarrow x \succsim (w_i, y_{-i})]. \tag{3.23}$$

Through reasoning as above, one sees that $AC2_i$ is equivalent to requiring that $\succsim_i^-$ is a complete relation and thus a weak order (since it is transitive by definition).

At this stage, it is natural to wonder whether the left marginal trace is related to the right one. The role of $AC3_i$ is to ensure that $\succsim_i^+$ and $\succsim_i^-$ are not incompatible, i.e. that one cannot have at the same time $Not[x_i \succsim_i^+ y_i]$ and $Not[y_i \succsim_i^- x_i]$. If $\succsim_i^+$ and $\succsim_i^-$ are complete, this means that one cannot have $[y_i \succ_i^+ x_i]$ and $[x_i \succ_i^- y_i]$ (where $\succ_i^+$ and $\succ_i^-$ denote the asymmetric part of $\succsim_i^+$ and $\succsim_i^-$, respectively) or, in other words, that $[x_i \succ_i^+ y_i]$ implies $[x_i \succsim_i^- y_i]$ and $[x_i \succ_i^- y_i]$ implies $[x_i \succsim_i^+ y_i]$. As a consequence of $AC123_i$, the intersection of the (complete) relations $\succsim_i^+$ and $\succsim_i^-$ is a complete relation, that is nothing else than the marginal trace $\succsim_i^\pm$ since Definition (3.20) is equivalent to

$$a_i \succsim_i^\pm b_i \Leftrightarrow a_i \succsim_i^+ b_i \text{ and } a_i \succsim_i^- b_i.$$

The links between the above axioms and the marginal traces can be directly exploited in the construction of a monotone numerical representation of $\succsim$ in model $(L0)$. We have the following result (Bouyssou and Pirlot, 2004, Theorem 2).

Proposition 3.2 (Representation in Models L**)** *A preference relation* $\succsim$ *on* X *admits a representation in model* $(L0)$ *with* F *non-decreasing in its first* n *arguments and non-increasing in the last* n *arguments if and only if it is reflexive and satisfies* $AC1$, $AC2$ *and* $AC3$.

In order to make it clear to the reader, how the marginal traces intervene in the construction of the representation, we describe how a representation can be obtained with F monotone as indicated. Due to the fact that $\succsim$ satisfies $AC123$, we know that the marginal traces $\succsim_i^\pm$ are weak orders. Take for u_i, any numerical representation of the weak order $\succsim_i^\pm$, i.e., u_i is any real-valued function defined on X_i, such that

$$x_i \succsim_i^\pm z_i \text{ iff } u_i(x_i) \geq u_i(z_i).$$

Define then F as follows:

$$F([u_i(x_i)];[u_i(y_i)]) = \begin{cases} +\exp(\sum_{i=1}^n (u_i(x_i) - u_i(y_i))) & \text{if } x \succsim y, \\ -\exp(\sum_{i=1}^n (u_i(y_i) - u_i(x_i))) & \text{otherwise.} \end{cases} \quad (3.24)$$

It can easily be shown that this representation satisfies the requirements. Clearly, the choice of the exponential function in the definition of F is arbitrary; any other positive and non-decreasing function could have been chosen instead. Again the choice of a representation u_i of the weak orders $\succsim_i^\pm$ is highly arbitrary. We are thus far from the uniqueness results that can be obtained for the representation of preferences in the additive utility model (3.1). All these representations are however equivalent from the point of view of the description of a preference.

Table 3.3 Main models using traces on levels and their characterisation

Models	Definition	Conditions
$(L0)$	$x \succsim y \Leftrightarrow F([u_i(x_i)], [u_i(y_i)]) \geq 0$	$\varnothing$
$(L1)$	$(L0)$ with $F([u_i(x_i)], [u_i(x_i)]) = 0$	refl.
$(L2)$	$(L1)$ with $F([u_i(x_i)]; [u_i(y_i)]) = -F([u_i(y_i)]; [u_i(x_i)])$	cpl.
$(L3)$	$(L0)$ with $F(\nearrow, \searrow)$	
$\Updownarrow$		$AC123$
$(L4)$	$(L0)$ with $F(\nearrow\!\!\nearrow, \searrow\!\!\searrow)$	
$(L5)$	$(L1)$ with $F(\nearrow, \searrow)$	
$\Updownarrow$		refl., $AC123$
$(L6)$	$(L1)$ with $F(\nearrow\!\!\nearrow, \searrow\!\!\searrow)$	
$(L7)$	$(L2)$ with $F(\nearrow, \searrow)$	cpl., $AC123$
$(L8)$	$(L2)$ with $F(\nearrow\!\!\nearrow, \searrow\!\!\searrow)$	cpl., $AC4$

$\nearrow$ means nondecreasing, $\searrow$ means nonincreasing
$\nearrow\!\!\nearrow$ means increasing, $\searrow\!\!\searrow$ means decreasing
refl. means reflexive, *cpl.* means complete

3.3.4 Models Using Marginal Traces

At this point, it might be useful to give a full picture of the models based on marginal traces. We have identified above three variants of model $(L0)$: those corresponding respectively to reflexive or complete preference $\succsim$ or to a preference with complete marginal traces. To each variant, one can associate particular features of the numerical representation in model $(L0)$. Systematising the analysis, we may define the variants of model $(L0)$ listed in Table 3.3. This table also shows a characterisation of the models using the axioms introduced in the previous section.

3.3.5 Properties of Marginal Preferences in $(L0)$ and Variants

We briefly come back to the analysis of marginal preferences in connection with the variants of $(L0)$ characterised above. As stated before (Proposition 3.1), we know that for reflexive and transitive preferences, $\succsim_i = \succsim_i^{\pm}$. For reflexive preferences, $x_i \succsim_i^{\pm} z_i$ implies $x_i \succsim_i z_i$.

The incidence of axioms $AC1$, $AC2$, $AC3$ and $AC4$ on marginal preferences is summarised in the next proposition (Bouyssou and Pirlot, 2004, Proposition 3 and Lemma 4.3).

Proposition 3.3 (Properties of Marginal Preferences)

1. *If $\succsim$ is reflexive and either $AC1_i$ or $AC2_i$ holds then $\succsim_i$ is an interval order.*
2. *If, in addition, $\succsim$ satisfies $AC3_i$ then $\succsim_i$ is a semiorder.*
3. *If $\succsim$ is reflexive and $AC4_i$ holds then $\succsim_i$ is a weak-order and $\succsim_i = \succsim_i^{\pm}$.*

The preference $\succsim$ in Example 3.5, page 57 has marginal preferences $\succsim_i$ that are semiorders, while marginal traces are the natural weak orders on $\mathbb{R}$. From the latter, applying Proposition 3.2 (in its version for sets X of arbitrary cardinality), we deduce that $\succsim$ satisfies $AC123$. Applying the third part of Proposition 3.3, we deduce further that $\succsim$ does not satisfy $AC4$.

3.3.5.1 Separability and Independence

$AC1$, $AC2$, $AC3$ and $AC4$ also have an impact on the separability and independence properties of $\succsim$ (Bouyssou and Pirlot, 2004, Proposition 3.1 and Lemma 4.3).

Proposition 3.4 (Separability and Independence) *Let $\succsim$ be a reflexive relation on X. We have:*

1. *If $\succsim$ satisfies $AC1_i$ or $AC2_i$ then $\succsim$ is weakly separable for $i \in N$.*
2. *If $\succsim$ satisfies $AC4_i$ then $\succsim$ is independent for $\{i\}$,*

The preference $\succsim$ in Example 3.5 (p. 57) is weakly separable for all i (since $\succsim$ satisfies $AC123$ and in view of part 1 of proposition 3.4); although $\succsim$ does not satisfy $AC4$, it is easy to see, applying the definition, that $\succsim$ is also independent for all i.

3.3.5.2 The Case of Weak Orders

The case in which $\succsim$ is a weak order is quite special. We have the following result (Bouyssou and Pirlot, 2004, Lemma 5 and Lemma 4.3).

Proposition 3.5 (Case of Weakly Ordered Preferences) *Let $\succsim$ be a weak order on a set X. Then:*

1. *[$\succsim$ is weakly separable] $\Leftrightarrow$ [$\succsim$ satisfies $AC1$] $\Leftrightarrow$ [$\succsim$ satisfies $AC2$] $\Leftrightarrow$ [$\succsim$ satisfies $AC3$],*
2. *[$\succsim$ is weakly independent] $\Leftrightarrow$ [$\succsim$ satisfies $AC4$],*
3. *If $\succsim$ is weakly separable, the marginal preference $\succsim_i$ equals the marginal trace $\succsim_i^{\pm}$, for all i, and these relations are weak orders.*

This result recalls that for analysing weakly separable weak orders, marginal traces can be substituted by marginal preferences (as is classically done); it also shows that weak separability masks $AC123$.

Example 3.6 (Min and LexiMin) In Example 3.2, we have shown that comparing vectors of satisfaction degrees associated with a set of constraints could be done by comparing the lowest satisfaction degree in each vector, i.e.

$$x \succsim y \Leftrightarrow \min(x_1, \ldots, x_n) \geq \min(y_1, \ldots, y_n),$$

where x and y are n-tuples of numbers in the $[0, 1]$ interval. This method for comparing vectors is known as the "Min" or "MaxMin" method. Clearly, the preference $\succsim$ that this method yields is a weak order; it is not weakly independent as was shown in Example 3.2, but it is weakly separable since $\succsim_i^{\pm}$ is just the natural weak order on the interval $[0, 1]$; the relation $\succsim$ thus satisfies $AC123$ but not $AC4$. By Proposition 3.5.3, $\succsim_i^{\pm} = \succsim_i$, for all i.

A refinement of the "Min" or "MaxMin" method is the "LexiMin" method; the latter discriminates between alternatives that the former leaves tied. When comparing alternatives x and y, LexiMin ranks x before y if $\min x_i > \min y_i$; in case the minimal value of both profiles are equal, LexiMin looks at the second minimum and decides in favour of the alternative with the highest second minimum; if again the second minima are equal, it goes to the third and so on. Only alternatives that cannot be distinguished when their coordinates are rearranged in non-decreasing order will be indifferent for LexiMin.

The preference yielded by LexiMin is again an independent weak order and $\succsim_i^{\pm} = \succsim_i$, for all i.

3.3.6 *Eliciting the Variants of Model (L0)*

This family of models suggests an elicitation strategy similar to that for the decomposable model but based on the marginal traces instead of the marginal preferences. It is not likely however that such a general model could serve as a basis for a direct practical elicitation process; we think instead that it is a framework for conceiving more specific models associated to a method; the additive value function model could be considered in this framework. Although it may seem unrealistic to work in such a general framework, Greco et al. (1999) have proposed to do so and elicit preferences using an adapted rough sets approach (indirect approach).

3.4 Following Another Path: Models Using Marginal Traces on Differences

The generalisation of the additive value model has been pursued to its most extreme limits since, with model $(L0)$, we encompass all possible binary relations on a product set. This process has relied on the marginal traces on the sets X_i. Those

Definition 3.9 (Marginal Trace on Differences $\succsim_i^*$) The marginal trace on differences $\succsim_i^*$ is the relation on the pairs of levels X_i^2 defined by:

$$(x_i, y_i) \succsim_i^* (z_i, w_i) \text{ iff } \begin{cases} \text{for all } a_{-i}, b_{-i} \in X_{-i}, \\ (z_i, a_{-i}) \succsim (w_i, b_{-i}) \Rightarrow (x_i, a_{-i}) \succsim (y_i, b_{-i}). \end{cases} \tag{3.27}$$

Intuitively, if $(x_i, y_i) \succsim_i^* (z_i, w_i)$, it seems reasonable to conclude that the preference difference between x_i and y_i is not smaller that the preference difference between z_i and w_i. Notice that, by construction, $\succsim_i^*$ is reflexive and transitive.

Contrary to our intuition concerning preference differences, the definition of $\succsim_i^*$ does not imply that there is any link between two "opposite" differences (x_i, y_i) and (y_i, x_i). Henceforth we introduce the binary relation $\succsim_i^{**}$ on X_i^2.

Definition 3.10 (Marginal Trace on Differences $\succsim_i^{**}$) The marginal trace on differences $\succsim_i^{**}$ is the relation on the pairs of levels X_i^2 defined by:

$$(x_i, y_i) \succsim_i^{**} (z_i, w_i) \text{ iff } [(x_i, y_i) \succsim_i^* (z_i, w_i) \text{ and } (w_i, z_i) \succsim_i^* (y_i, x_i)]. \tag{3.28}$$

It is easy to see that $\succsim_i^{**}$ is transitive and *reversible*, i.e.

$$(x_i, y_i) \succsim_i^{**} (z_i, w_i) \Leftrightarrow (w_i, z_i) \succsim_i^{**} (y_i, x_i). \tag{3.29}$$

The relations $\succsim_i^*$ and $\succsim_i^{**}$ both appear to capture the idea of comparison of preference differences between elements of X_i induced by the relation $\succsim$. Hence, they are good candidates to serve as the basis of the definition of the functions p_i. They will not serve well this purpose however unless they are complete as we shall see.

3.4.3 A General Family of Models Using Traces on Differences

In the same spirit as we generalised the decomposable model to the models based on marginal traces, we envisage here a very general model based on preference differences. It formalises the idea of measuring "preference differences" separately on each dimension and then combining these (positive or negative) differences in order to know whether the aggregation of these differences leads to an advantage for x over y. More formally, this suggests a model in which:

$$x \succsim y \Leftrightarrow G(p_1(x_1, y_1), p_2(x_2, y_2), \ldots, p_n(x_n, y_n)) \geq 0 \tag{D0}$$

where p_i are real-valued functions on X_i^2 and G is a real-valued function on $\prod_{i=1}^n p_i(X_i^2)$.

As already noted by Goldstein (1991), all binary relations satisfy model $(D0)$ when X is finite or countably infinite. Necessary and sufficient conditions for the non-denumerable case are well-known (Bouyssou and Pirlot, 2002b).

As for the variants of model $(L0)$, it is easy to impose conditions on G that will result in simple properties of $\succsim$. Assume $\succsim$ has a representation in model $(D0)$; then

- $\succsim$ is reflexive iff $G([p_i(x_i, x_i)]) \geq 0$, for all x_i;
- $\succsim$ is independent iff $p_i(x_i, x_i) = 0$ for all x_i; in addition, $\succsim$ is reflexive iff $G(\mathbf{0}) \geq 0$ and $\succsim$ is irreflexive iff $G(\mathbf{0}) < 0$.
- $\succsim$ is complete iff p_i is skew-symmetric and G is odd, i.e. $p_i(x_i, y_i) = -p_i(y_i, x_i)$ for all x_i, y_i and $G(-\mathbf{p}) = -G(\mathbf{p})$ for all $\mathbf{p} = (p_1, \ldots, p_n)$.

Again, as for the models based on marginal traces, the monotonicity of G is related to the properties of traces on differences (3.27) and (3.28). The axioms needed to guarantee the monotonicity of G are very much looking like $AC1$, $AC2$ or $AC3$ because traces are involved.

Definition 3.11 We say that relation $\succsim$ on X satisfies:
$RC1_i$ if

$$\left.\begin{array}{r}(x_i, a_{-i}) \succsim (y_i, b_{-i})\\ \text{and}\\ (z_i, c_{-i}) \succsim (w_i, d_{-i})\end{array}\right\} \Rightarrow \left\{\begin{array}{l}(x_i, c_{-i}) \succsim (y_i, d_{-i})\\ \text{or}\\ (z_i, a_{-i}) \succsim (w_i, b_{-i}),\end{array}\right.$$

$RC2_i$ if

$$\left.\begin{array}{r}(x_i, a_{-i}) \succsim (y_i, b_{-i})\\ \text{and}\\ (y_i, c_{-i}) \succsim (x_i, d_{-i})\end{array}\right\} \Rightarrow \left\{\begin{array}{l}(z_i, a_{-i}) \succsim (w_i, b_{-i})\\ \text{or}\\ (w_i, c_{-i}) \succsim (z_i, d_{-i}),\end{array}\right.$$

for all $x_i, y_i, z_i, w_i \in X_i$ and all $a_{-i}, b_{-i}, c_{-i}, d_{-i} \in X_{-i}$.

$RC3_i$ if $\succsim$ satisfies $RC2_i$ and when one of the conclusions of $RC2_i$ is false then the other holds with $\succ$ instead of $\succsim$.

We say that $\succsim$ satisfies $RC1$ (resp. $RC2$) if it satisfies $RC1_i$ (resp. $RC2_i$) for all $i \in N$. We also use $RC12$ as shorthand for $RC1$ and $RC2$.

Condition $RC1_i$ implies that any two ordered pairs (x_i, y_i) and (z_i, w_i) of elements of X_i are comparable in terms of the relation $\succsim_i^*$. Indeed, it is easy to see that supposing $Not[(x_i, y_i) \succsim_i^* (z_i, w_i)]$ and $Not[(z_i, w_i) \succsim_i^* (x_i, y_i)]$ is the negation of $RC1_i$. Similarly, $RC2_i$ implies that the two opposite differences (x_i, y_i) and (y_i, x_i) are linked. In terms of the relation $\succsim_i^*$, it says that if the preference difference between x_i and y_i is not at least as large as the preference difference between z_i and w_i then the preference difference between y_i and x_i should be at least as large as the preference difference between w_i and z_i (Bouyssou and Pirlot, 2002b, Lemma 1).

Proposition 3.6 (Completeness of the Traces on Differences) *We have:*

1. *[$\succsim_i^*$ is a weak order] $\Leftrightarrow$ $RC1_i$,*
2. *[$\succsim_i^{**}$ is a weak order] $\Leftrightarrow$ [$RC1_i$ and $RC2_i$].*

Here again (like for the models based on marginal traces, see Sect. 3.3.3) the links between $RC1$, $RC2$ and properties of $\succsim_i^*$ and $\succsim_i^{**}$ play a fundamental role in the construction of a representation of a preference in model $(D0)$ with a monotone G function. Axiom $RC2$ introduces a *mirror effect* on preference differences: under $RC2_i$, the difference of preference (y_i, x_i) is the mirror image of (x_i, y_i) (Bouyssou and Pirlot, 2002b, Theorem 1).

Proposition 3.7 (Representation in Model D) *A preference relation $\succsim$ on X admits a representation in model $(D0)$ with G nondecreasing in all its n arguments iff $\succsim$ satisfies $RC1$. It admits such a representation with, in addition, $p_i(x_i, y_i) = -p_i(y_i, x_i)$ iff $\succsim$ satisfies $RC1$ and $RC2$.*

The construction of a representation under the hypotheses of the theorem helps to make the theorem more intuitive. We outline this construction below.

Suppose that $\succsim$ satisfies $RC1$. We know, by Proposition 3.6.1 that $\succsim_i^*$ is a weak order on the set of pairs of levels X_i^2 for all i. Select, for all i, a real-valued function p_i that represents the weak order $\succsim_i^*$, i.e. that satisfies:

$$p_i(x_i, y_i) \geq p_i(z_i, w_i) \text{ iff } (x_i, y_i) \succsim_i^* (z_i, w_i),$$

for all $x_i, y_i, z_i, w_i \in X_i$. Then define G as follows:

$$G([p_i(x_i, y_i)]) = \begin{cases} \exp \sum_{i=1}^n p_i(x_i, y_i) & \text{if } x \succsim y \\ -\exp[-\sum_{i=1}^n p_i(x_i, y_i)] & \text{otherwise.} \end{cases} \tag{3.30}$$

It can easily be shown that G is well-defined. The choice of the exponential function and the sum operator is purely arbitrary; any other increasing function defined on the real numbers and taking positive values would do as well. The role of such a function is to ensure that in each of the two sub-domains $x \succsim y$ and "otherwise", the function G is increasing in the p_i's; since the relation $\succsim$ is itself non-decreasing with respect to the relations $\succsim_i^*$ for all i, raising the value of a p_i (which represents $\succsim_i^*$) may only result in remaining in the same sub-domain or passing from the domain "otherwise" to the domain "$x \succsim y$"; the value of G is negative in the former sub-domain and positive in the latter and in each sub-domain, G is increasing. This proves that G is increasing in all its arguments p_i.

The second case, in which $\succsim$ satisfies $RC1$ and $RC2$ is dealt with similarly. Since in this case $\succsim_i^{**}$ is a weak order, we use functions p_i that represent $\succsim_i^{**}$ instead of $\succsim_i^{*}$. We may moreover exploit the reversibility property (3.29) of $\succsim_i^{**}$ to ensure that we may choose a skew-symmetric function p_i to represent $\succsim_i^{**}$. Then we define G as in (3.30). In the same case, we may also get a representation in which G is increasing (instead of non-decreasing) by defining G as follows:

$$G([p_i(x_i, y_i)]) = \begin{cases} \exp \sum_{i=1}^{n} p_i(x_i, y_i) & \text{if } x \succ y \\ 0 & \text{if } x \sim y \\ -\exp\left[-\sum_{i=1}^{n} p_i(x_i, y_i)\right] & \text{otherwise.} \end{cases} \tag{3.31}$$

Combining the various additional properties that can be imposed on $\succsim$, we are lead to consider a number of variants of the basic $(D0)$ model. These models can be fully characterised using the axioms $RC1$, $RC2$ and $RC3$. The definition of the models as well as their characterisation are displayed in Table 3.4.

Table 3.4 Main models using traces on differences and their characterisation

Models	Definition	Conditions
$(D0)$	$x \succsim y \Leftrightarrow G([p_i(x_i, y_i)]) \geq 0$	$\varnothing$
$(D1)$	$(D0)$ with $p_i(x_i, x_i) = 0$	
$\Updownarrow$		ind.
$(D2)$	$(D0)$ with p_i skew symmetric	
$(D3)$	$(D0)$ with p_i skew symmetric and G odd	cpl., ind.
$(D4)$	$(D0)$ with $G(\nearrow)$	
$\Updownarrow$		$RC1$
$(D8)$	$(D0)$ with $G(\nearrow\!\nearrow)$	
$(D5)$	$(D1)$ with $G(\nearrow)$	
$\Updownarrow$		$RC1$, ind.
$(D9)$	$(D1)$ with $G(\nearrow\!\nearrow)$	
$(D6)$	$(D2)$ with $G(\nearrow)$	
$\Updownarrow$		$RC12$
$(D10)$	$(D2)$ with $G(\nearrow\!\nearrow)$	
$(D7)$	$(D3)$ with $G(\nearrow)$	cpl., $RC12$
$(D11)$	$(D3)$ with $G(\nearrow\!\nearrow)$	cpl., $RC3$

$\nearrow$ means nondecreasing, $\nearrow\!\nearrow$ means increasing
cpl. means completeness, *ind.* means independence

3.4.4 Eliciting Models Using Traces on Differences

We suppose that $\succsim$ is reflexive and satisfies $RC1$, i.e., we place ourselves in model $(D5)$ [equivalent to $(D9)$]. In that model $\succsim_i^*$ is a weak order on the "differences of preference" $(x_i, y_i) \in X_i^2$, for all i, and the functions p_i may be chosen to be numerical representations of $\succsim_i^*$. To each pair of alternatives $x, y \in X$ is henceforth associated a profile $\overline{p} = (p_1, \ldots, p_n)$ of differences of preferences ($p_i = p_i(x_i, y_i)$, for $i = 1, \ldots, n$). The function G may be conceived of as a rule that assigns a value to each profile; in model $(D5)$, G is just supposed to be nonincreasing [not necessarily increasing if we choose to represent $\succsim$ into model $(D5)$ instead of the equivalent model $(D9)$] and therefore we may choose a very simple form of G that codes profiles in the following way:

$$G(\overline{p}) = \begin{cases} +1 & \text{if } \overline{p} \text{ corresponds to } x \succ y; \\ 0 & \text{if } \overline{p} \text{ corresponds to } x \sim y; \\ -1 & \text{if } \overline{p} \text{ corresponds to } Not[\, x \succsim y \,]. \end{cases} \tag{3.32}$$

The strategy for eliciting such a model (in a direct manner) may thus be as follows:

1. for all i, elicit the weak order $\succsim_i^*$ that ranks the differences of preference; choose a representation p_i of $\succsim_i^*$
2. elicit the rule (function) G that assigns a category (coded $+1$, 0 or -1) to each profile $\overline{p}$.

The initial step however is more complex than with the decomposable model, because we have to rank-order the set X_i^2 instead of X_i. In case it may be assumed that the difference of preference is reversible [see (3.29)] almost half of the work can be saved since only the "positive" (or only the "negative") differences must be rank-ordered.[4] The difficulty, that remains even in the reversible case, may motivate the consideration of another family of models that rely both on marginal traces and on traces on differences (see Bouyssou et al., 2006, Sect. 6.4). In some of these models, $\succsim_i^*$ is reacting positively (or non-negatively) to marginal traces and therefore, the elicitation of p_i may benefit of its monotonicity w.r.t. marginal traces.

Models $(D4)$, $(D5)$, $(D6)$ and $(D7)$, in which G is a nondecreasing function, can be elicited in a similar fashion. The situation is different when a representation with G increasing is sought, in particular for model $(D11)$. For such representations, the definition of G by (3.32) is no longer appropriate and defining G requires more care and effort. We do not enter into this point.

[4] In case of a tie, i.e. whenever $(x_i, y_i) \sim_i^* (z_i, w_i)$, one has however to look explicitly at the relation between the reverse differences (y_i, x_i) and (w_i, z_i) since all cases ($\succsim_i^*$, $\sim_i^*$ or $\precsim_i^*$) can possibly show up.

3.4.5 Examples of Models that Distinguish No More Than Three Classes of Differences

We show in this section that simple majority (or Condorcet method), weighted majority, qualified majority and lexicographic method can be represented in some of the models $(D1)$ to $(D11)$. We consider in addition, a variant of the ELECTRE I procedure in which the profile of preferences on each dimension are not weak orders but semiorders. In each of these cases, the relation that orders the differences of preference on each criterion is revealed by the global preference relation.

We say that a relation $\succsim$ defined on a product set $X = \prod_{i=1}^{n} X_i$ is the result of the application of a majority or a lexicographic rule if there is a relation S_i on each X_i such that $\succsim$ can be obtained by aggregating the n relations S_i using that rule. Those S_i's will usually be *weak orders* but we shall also consider more general structures like semiorders. In the sequel, we refer to S_i as to the *a priori preference relation* on X_i.

Take the example of the simple majority rule. We say that $\succsim$ is a simple majority preference relation if there are relations S_i that are weak orders on the corresponding X_i such that:

$$x \succsim y \text{ iff } \begin{cases} \text{the number of criteria on which } x_i \, S_i \, y_i \\ \text{is at least as large as} \\ \text{the number of criteria such that } y_i \, S_i \, x_i. \end{cases} \tag{3.33}$$

In the rest of this section, P_i will denote the asymmetric part of a relation S_i defined on X_i and its symmetric part will be denoted by I_i. In the first five examples, the S_i's are supposed to be weak orders.

3.4.5.1 Simple Majority or Condorcet Method

A relation $\succsim$ on X is a *simple majority relation* if there is a weak order S_i on each X_i such that

$$x \succsim y \text{ iff } |\{i \in N : x_i S_i y_i\}| \geq |\{i \in N : y_i S_i x_i\}|. \tag{3.34}$$

In other terms, $x \succsim y$ if the "coalition" of criteria on which x is at least as good as y is at least as large as the "opposite coalition", i.e. the set of criteria on which y is at least as good as x. The term "coalition" is used here for "set", in reference with social choice. We do not, apparently, distinguish between the case in which x_i is better than y_i $(x_i P_i y_i)$ and that in which they are indifferent $(x_i I_i y_i)$. Note that the criteria for which x_i is indifferent with y_i appear in both coalitions and hence cancel. We could thus define a simple majority relation in an equivalent fashion by $x \succsim y$ iff $|\{i \in N : x_i P_i y_i\}| \geq |\{i \in N : y_i P_i x_i\}|$.

Such a relation can be represented in model $(D11)$ by defining

$$p_i(x_i, y_i) = \begin{cases} 1 \text{ if } x_i P_i y_i \\ 0 \text{ if } x_i I_i y_i \\ -1 \text{ if } y_i P_i x_i \end{cases} \quad (3.35)$$

and

$$G([p_i]) = \sum_{i \in N} p_i. \quad (3.36)$$

We have indeed that $x \succsim y$ iff $G([p_i(x_i, y_i)]) = |\{i \in N : x_i P_i y_i\}| - |\{i \in N : y_i P_i x_i\}| \geq 0$, which is clearly equivalent to Definition (3.34).

This representation of a simple majority relation can furthermore be called *regular* in the sense that the functions p_i are numerical representations of the weak orders $\succsim_i^{**}$; the latter has exactly three equivalence classes, namely, the set of pairs (x_i, y_i) such that $x_i P_i y_i$, the set of pairs for which $x_i I_i y_i$ and the set of those such that $y_i P_i x_i$. Observe that the relation $\succsim_i^*$ distinguishes the same three classes; hence $\succsim_i^* = \succsim_i^{**}$.

3.4.5.2 Weighted Simple Majority or Weighted Condorcet Method

A relation $\succsim$ on X is a *weighted simple majority relation* if there is a vector of normalised weights $[w_i]$ (with $w_i \geq 0$ and $\sum_{i \in N} w_i = 1$) and a weak order S_i on each X_i such that

$$x \succsim y \text{ iff } \sum_{i \in N : x_i S_i y_i} w_i \geq \sum_{j \in N : y_j S_j x_j} w_j. \quad (3.37)$$

In this model, the coalitions of criteria are weighted: they are assigned a value that is the sum of those assigned to the criteria belonging to the coalition. The preference of x over y results from the comparison of the coalitions like in the simple majority rule: $x \succsim y$ if the coalition of criteria on which x is at least as good as y *does not weigh less* than the opposite coalition. Like for simple majority, we could have defined the relation using strict *a priori* preference, saying that $x \succsim y$ iff $\sum_{i \in N : x_i P_i y_i} w_i \geq \sum_{j \in N : y_j P_j x_j} w_j$.

A representation of a weighted majority relation in model $(D11)$ is readily obtained letting:

$$p_i(x_i, y_i) = \begin{cases} w_i \text{ if } x_i P_i y_i \\ 0 \text{ if } x_i I_i y_i \\ -w_i \text{ if } y_i P_i x_i \end{cases} \quad (3.38)$$

and

$$G([p_i]) = \sum_{i \in N} p_i. \tag{3.39}$$

We have that $x \succsim y$ iff $G([p_i(x_i, y_i)]) = \sum_{i \in N: x_i P_i y_i} w_i - \sum_{j \in N: y_j P_j x_j} w_j \geq 0$.

This representation is *regular* since p_i is a numerical representation of $\succsim_i^{**}$ and $\succsim_i^{**}$ has only three equivalence classes as in the case of simple majority.

3.4.5.3 Weighted Qualified Majority

A relation $\succsim$ on X is a *weighted qualified majority relation* if there is a vector of normalised weights $[w_i]$ (i.e. with w_i non-negative and summing up to 1), a weak order S_i on each X_i and a threshold δ between $\frac{1}{2}$ and 1 such that

$$x \succsim y \text{ iff } \sum_{i \in N: x_i S_i y_i} w_i \geq \delta. \tag{3.40}$$

In contrast with the previous models, the preference does not result here from a comparison of coalitions but from stating that the coalition in favour of an alternative is *strong enough*, i.e. that the measure of its strength reaches a certain threshold δ (typically above one half). Even when δ is set to 0.5, this method is not equivalent to weighted simple majority, with the same weighting vector $[w_i]$, due to the inclusion of the criteria on which x and y are indifferent in both the coalition in favour of x against y and that in favour of y against x. Take for example two alternatives x, y compared on five points of view; suppose that the criteria all have the same weight, i.e. $w_i = 1/5$, for $i = 1, \ldots, 5$. Assume that x is preferred to y on the first criterion ($x_1 P_1 y_1$), x is indifferent to y on the second and third criteria ($x_2 I_2 y_2$; $x_3 I_3 y_3$) and y is preferred to x on the last two criteria ($y_4 P_4 x_4$; $y_5 P_5 x_5$). Using the weighted majority rule [Eq. (3.37)], we get $y \succ x$ since the coalition in favour of x against y is composed of criteria 1, 2, 3 (weighting 0.6) and the opposite coalition contains criteria 2, 3, 4, 5 (weighting 0.8). Using the weighted qualified majority with threshold δ up to 0.6, we get that $x \sim y$ since both coalitions weigh at least 0.6.

Note that when the criteria have equal weights ($w_i = 1/n$), weighted qualified majority could be simply called *qualified majority*; the latter has the same relationship with weighted qualified majority as weighted simple majority with simple majority.

Qualified weighted majority relations constitute a basic component of the ELECTRE I and ELECTRE II methods (Roy, 1971) as long as there are no vetoes.

Any weighted qualified majority relation admits a representation in model ($D8$). Let:

$$p_i(x_i, y_i) = \begin{cases} w_i - \frac{\delta}{n} \text{ if } x_i S_i y_i \\ \\ -\frac{\delta}{n} \text{ if } Not[x_i S_i y_i] \end{cases} \tag{3.41}$$

and

$$G([p_i]) = \sum_{i \in N} p_i. \tag{3.42}$$

We have that

$$\begin{aligned} x \succsim y \text{ iff } G([p_i(x_i, y_i)]) &= \sum_{i \in N: x_i S_i y_i} (w_i - \frac{\delta}{n}) - \sum_{j \in N: Not[x_j S_j y_j]} \frac{\delta}{n} \\ &= \sum_{i \in N: x_i S_i y_i} w_i - \delta \\ &\geq 0. \end{aligned} \tag{3.43}$$

In this representation, p_i is a numerical representation of $\succsim_i^*$ but not of $\succsim_i^{**}$. The former has two equivalence classes: the pairs (x_i, y_i) that are in S_i form the upper class of the weak order; those that are not in S_i form the lower class. Note that there are no further distinctions between pairs; all pairs in the upper class contribute the same amount $w_i - \frac{\delta}{n}$ to the value of the coalition while the pairs of the lower class all contribute the same amount $-\frac{\delta}{n}$. The comparison of preference differences in this model is thus rather poor (as is the case of course with the two previous models).

The relation $\succsim_i^{**}$ is also a weak order; it has three equivalence classes. It makes a distinction between $x_i P_i y_i$ and $x_i I_i y_i$ (a distinction that is not made by $\succsim_i^*$): both cases play the same role when comparing (x_i, y_i) to other pairs (since what counts in formula (3.40) is whether or not (x_i, y_i) belongs to S_i); it is no longer the case when comparing (y_i, x_i) to other pairs since, then, $x_i I_i y_i$ counts in the coalition in favour of y against x while $x_i P_i y_i$ does not.

3.4.5.4 Lexicographic Preference Relations

A preference relation is lexicographic if the criteria are linearly ordered and if they are considered in that order when comparing alternatives: the first criterion, in that order, that favours one alternative with respect to another determines the global preference. Denoting by $>_l$ a linear order on the set of criteria, we rank-order the criteria according to it: $1^l >_l 2^l >_l \ldots >_l n^l$. We thus have the following definition. A relation $\succsim$ on X is a *lexicographic* preference relation if there is a linear order $>_l$ on the set of criteria and a weak order (or a semiorder) S_i on each X_i such that:

$$x \succ y \text{ if } \begin{cases} x_{1^l} P_{1^l} y_{1^l} \text{ or} \\ x_{1^l} I_{1^l} y_{1^l} \text{ and } x_{2^l} P_{2^l} y_{2^l} \text{ or} \\ x_{i^l} I_{1^l} y_{i^l} \forall i = 1, \ldots, k-1 \text{ and } x_{k^l} P_{k^l} y_{k^l}, \\ \text{for some } k \text{ such that } 2 \leq k \leq n. \end{cases} \tag{3.44}$$

and $x \sim y$ if $x_{i^l} I_{i^l} y_{i^l}$, for all $i \in N$. In words, $x \sim y$ if x_i is a priori indifferent to y_i, for all i; $x \succ y$ if, for the first index k^l for which x_{i^l} is not a priori indifferent to y_{i^l}, one has x_{k^l} a priori preferred to y_{i^l}.

Such a relation can be viewed (as long as there are only finitely many criteria) as a special case of a weighted majority relation. Choose a vector of weights w_i in the following manner: for all $i \in N$, let w_{i^l} be larger than the sum of all remaining weights (in the order $>_l$), i.e.:

$$\begin{aligned} w_{1^l} &> w_{2^l} + w_{3^l} + \ldots + w_{n^l} \\ w_{2^l} &> w_{3^l} + \ldots + w_{n^l} \\ &\ldots \\ w_{(n-1)^l} &> w_{n^l} \end{aligned} \tag{3.45}$$

Using these weights in (3.38) and (3.39) which define a representation for weighted majority relations, one gets a representation for lexicographic relations in model $(D11)$.

3.4.5.5 Other Forms of Weighted Qualified Majority

Instead of imposing—in an absolute manner—a threshold above 0.5 for defining a weighted qualified majority, as is done in Sect. 3.4.5.3, we may alternatively impose a relative majority threshold, in an additive or a multiplicative form. A preference relation $\succsim$ on X is a *weighted majority relation with additive threshold* if there is vector of normalised weights $[w_i]$ (with $w_i \geq 0$ and $\sum_{i \in N} w_i = 1$), a weak order or semiorder S_i on each X_i and a non-negative threshold γ such that

$$x \succsim y \text{ iff } \sum_{i \in N: x_i S_i y_i} w_i \geq \sum_{j \in N: y_j S_j x_j} w_j - \gamma. \tag{3.46}$$

Table 3.5 Models distinguishing no more than three classes of differences of preferences

Aggregation rule	General model	Special models
Weighted simple majority (see Sect. 3.4.5.2)	$(D11)$	$(D11)$ + additive
Weighted qualified majority (see Sect. 3.4.5.3)	$(D10)$	$(D8)$ + additive
Lexicographic (see Sect. 3.4.5.4)	$(D11)$	$(D11)$ + additive
Weighted majority with add. threshold (see Sect. 3.4.5.5)	$(D7)$	$(D10)$ + additive (with constant: Eq. (3.46))
Weighted majority with mult. threshold (see Sect. 3.4.5.5)	$(D7)$	$(D6)$ + linear

A relation $\succsim$ is a *weighted majority relation with multiplicative threshold* $\rho \geq 1$ if

$$x \succsim y \text{ iff } \sum_{i \in N: x_i S_i y_i} w_i \geq \frac{1}{\rho} \sum_{j \in N: y_j S_j x_j} w_j, \tag{3.47}$$

with $[w_i]$ and S_i as in the case of an additive threshold.

Constructing preference relations using these rules resembles what is known as the TACTIC method; it was proposed and studied in Vansnick (1986) with the possible adjunction of vetoes. In the original version of TACTIC, the preference is defined as an asymmetric relation $\succ$; the symmetric version that we consider here obtains from the original one just by saying that $x \succsim y$ if and only if we have not $y \succ x$.

It is easy to provide a representation of a weighted majority relation with additive threshold in model $(D10)$ or $(D7)$, but a representation in model $(D11)$ is in general not possible (Bouyssou et al., 2006). Turning to weighted majority relations with multiplicative threshold, one observes that $\succsim$ is complete and can be represented in model $(D6)$ or $(D7)$ but $\succsim$ does not fit in model $(D11)$ since, in general, indifference is not "narrow" (Bouyssou et al., 2006).

Table 3.5 provides a summary of the main models applicable to preferences that distinguish no more than three classes of differences of preference on each dimension.

3.4.6 Examples of Models Using Vetoes

Vetoes could be introduced in all the examples dealt with in the previous section (Sect. 3.4.5). We shall only consider the cases of qualified weighted majority relations (see Sect. 3.4.5.3) with vetoes (the relations that are the basic ingredients in the ELECTRE I and II methods).

The intuition one can have about a *veto* is the following. Consider an alternative x and a criterion i on which the level of the performance x_i of x is much worse than the level y_i of another alternative y. A veto of y on x on criterion i consists in rejecting the possibility that x be globally preferred to y irrespective of the performances of x and y on the criteria other than i. In other words, a veto on criterion i forbids to declare that $x \succsim y$ if (x_i, y_i) is a "negative" difference that is "large enough in absolute value", with respect to relation $\succsim_i^*$ or $\succsim_i^{**}$ (in the latter case, this is equivalent to saying that (y_i, x_i) is a large enough "positive" difference). Of course, in case the difference (x_i, y_i) leads to a veto on declaring x preferred to y, it is certainly because we do not have $x_i S_i y_i$, but, instead, $y_i P_i x_i$, and "even more". We thus define the veto relation V_i as a subset of relation P_i consisting of all pairs $(y_i; x_i)$ such that the presence of the reverse pair (x_i, y_i) in two alternatives x and y prohibits $x \succsim y$; V_i is an asymmetric relation.

Suppose that, for all i, X_i is a subset of the real numbers (X can be seen, in a sense, as a performance table) and that S_i is a semiorder determined by the following condition:

$$x_i S_i y_i \Leftrightarrow x_i \geq y_i - \tau_{i,1} \tag{3.48}$$

where $\tau_{i,1}$ is a non-negative threshold. This is similar to the situation described in Sect. 3.4.5.3 with the example of the cost (except that the cost is to be minimised; here we prefer the larger values): the values x_i and y_i are indifferent ($x_i I_i y_i$) if they differ by less than the threshold $\tau_{i,1}$; x_i is strictly preferred to y_i ($x_i P_i y_i$) if it passes y_i by at least the value of the threshold. In such a case, a convenient way of defining the veto relation V_i, a subset of P_i, is by means of another threshold $\tau_{i,2}$ that is larger than $\tau_{i,1}$. We say that the pair (y_i, x_i) belongs to the veto relation V_i if the following condition is satisfied:

$$y_i V_i x_i \Leftrightarrow y_i > x_i + \tau_{i,2}. \tag{3.49}$$

Clearly, the veto relation defined above is included in P_i. Assume indeed that $y_i V_i x_i$; since $\tau_{i,2}$ is larger than $\tau_{i,1}$, we have $y_i > x_i + \tau_{i,2} > x_i + \tau_{i,1}$, yielding $y_i P_i x_i$. We call $\tau_{i,2}$, a *veto threshold*; the relation V_i defined by (3.49) is a strict semiorder, i.e. the asymmetric part of a semiorder; it is contained in P_i that is also a strict semiorder, namely, the asymmetric part of the semiorder S_i. In such a situation, when comparing an arbitrary level x_i to a fixed level y_i, we can distinguish four relative positions of x_i with respect to y_i that are of interest. These four zones are shown on Fig. 3.9; they correspond to relations described above, namely:

If x_i belongs to:	Then:
Zone I	$x_i P_i y_i$
Zone II	$x_i I_i y_i$
Zone III	$y_i P_i x_i$ and *Not*[$y_i V_i x_i$]
Zone IV	$y_i P_i x_i$ and $y_i V_i x_i$

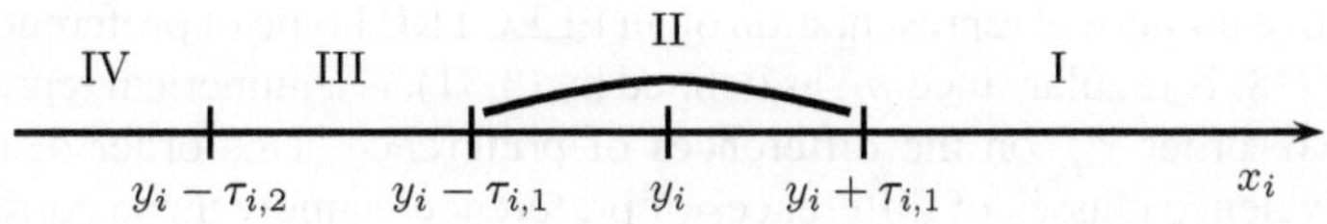

Fig. 3.9 Relative positions of an arbitrary level x_i with respect to a fixed level y_i

3.4.6.1 Weighted Qualified Majority with Veto

Starting with both an a priori preference relation S_i (a semiorder) and an a priori veto relation V_i (a strict semiorder included in P_i) on each set X_i, we can define a global preference relation of the ELECTRE I type as follows:

$$x \succsim y \text{ iff } \begin{cases} \sum_{i \in N: x_i S_i y_i} w_i \geq \delta \\ \text{and} \\ \text{there is no dimension } i \text{ on which } y_i V_i x_i, \end{cases} \tag{3.50}$$

where $(w_1, \ldots, w_n)$ denotes a vector of normalised weights and δ, a threshold between $1/2$ and 1. The global preference of the ELECTRE I type is thus a weighted qualified majority relation (in which the a priori preferences may be semiorders instead of weak orders) that is "broken" as soon as there is a veto on any single criterion, i.e. as soon as the performance of an alternative on some dimension is sufficiently low as compared to the other. It is not difficult to provide a representation of such a preference relation $\succsim$ in model $(D8)$ letting:

$$p_i(x_i, y_i) = \begin{cases} w_i \text{ if } x_i S_i y_i \\ 0 \text{ if } y_i P_i x_i \text{ but } Not[\, y_i V_i x_i \,] \\ -M \text{ if } y_i V_i x_i, \end{cases} \tag{3.51}$$

where M is a large positive constant and

$$G([p_i]) = \sum_{i \in N} p_i - \delta. \tag{3.52}$$

If no veto occurs in comparing x and y, then $G([p_i(x_i, y_i)]) = \sum_{i: x_i S_i y_i} w_i - \delta$, which is the same representation as for the weighted qualified majority without veto (Sect. 3.4.5.3). Otherwise, if, on at least one criterion j, one has $y_j V_j x_j$, then $G([p_i(x_i, y_i)]) < 0$, regardless of x_{-j} and y_{-j}. The effect of the constant M in the definition of p_i is to make it impossible for G to pass or reach 0 whenever any of the terms p_i is equal to $-M$.

The above numerical representation of an ELECTRE I type of preference relation in model $(D8)$ is regular since p_i, as defined by (3.51), is a numerical representation of the weak order $\succsim_i^*$ on the differences of preference. This order distinguishes three equivalence classes of differences of preference, namely those corresponding respectively to the cases where $x_i\, S_i\, y_i$, $y_i\, P_i\, x_i$ but $Not[\, y_i\, V_i\, x_i\,]$ and $y_i\, V_i\, x_i$.

The representation above is probably the most natural and intuitive one. Since the set of relations that can be described by (3.50) contains the weighted qualified majority relations, it is clear from Sect. 3.4.5.3 that one cannot expect that weighted qualified majority relations with veto admit a representation in model $(D7)$ or $(D11)$. They however admit a representation in model $(D6)$ and in its strictly increasing yet equivalent version $(D10)$. For a representation in model $(D6)$, we may choose for p_i a numerical representation of the weak order $\succsim_i^{**}$ that determines five equivalence classes of differences of preference, namely:

$$p_i(x_i, y_i) = \begin{cases} M & \text{if } x_i\, V_i\, y_i \\ w_i & \text{if } x_i\, P_i\, y_i \text{ and } Not[\, x_i\, V_i\, y_i\,] \\ 0 & \text{if } x_i\, I_i\, y_i \\ -w_i & \text{if } y_i\, P_i\, x_i \text{ and } Not[\, y_i\, V_i\, x_i\,] \\ -M & \text{if } y_i\, V_i\, x_i, \end{cases} \tag{3.53}$$

where M is a positive constant larger than w_i. The function G can be defined by

$$G([p_i(x_i, y_i)]) = \begin{cases} \sum_{i:x_i\, S_i\, y_i} \min(p_i(x_i, y_i), w_i) - \delta & \text{if, for all } j \in N,\ Not[\, y_j\, V_j\, x_j\,] \\ -1 & \text{if, for some } j \in N,\ y_j\, V_j\, x_j. \end{cases} \tag{3.54}$$

A strictly increasing representation [in model $(D10)$] obtains by the usual construction (with an exponential function).

Remark 3.1 The relations defined by means of vetoes that are described in this section constitute a very particular subclass of relations for which five classes of differences of preference can be distinguished. There are of course many other ways of defining models of preference that distinguish five classes of differences.

3.4.7 *Examples of Preferences that Distinguish a Large Variety of Differences*

Contrary to the examples discussed so far in which the relations $\succsim_i^*$ or $\succsim_i^{**}$ distinguish a small number of classes of preference differences (typically three or five classes for $\succsim_i^{**}$ in the above examples), there are very common cases where there is a large number of distinct classes, possibly an infinite number of them.

The most common model, the additive value model, usually belongs to the class of models in which $\succsim_i^{**}$ makes subtle distinctions between differences of preferences; indeed its definition, Eq. (3.1), p. 37, can be rewritten in the following manner:

$$x \succsim y \text{ iff } \sum_{i=1}^{n} (u_i(x_i) - u_i(y_i)) \geq 0. \tag{3.55}$$

The difference $u_i(x_i) - u_i(y_i)$ can often be interpreted as a representation $p_i(x_i, y_i)$ of $\succsim_i^{**}$; the preference then satisfies model $(D11)$. Let us take a simple example; assume that $X_i = \mathbb{R}$, that the number of dimensions n is equal to 2 and that $u_i(x_i) = x_i$ for $i = 1, 2$. The preference is defined by:

$$\begin{aligned} x \succsim y \text{ iff } & x_1 + x_2 \geq y_1 + y_2 \\ \text{iff } & (x_1 - y_1) + (x_2 - y_2) \geq 0. \end{aligned} \tag{3.56}$$

In such a case, $p_1(x_1, y_1) = x_1 - y_1$ is a numerical representation of the relation $\succsim_1^{**}$ on the differences of preference on the first dimension X_1 (and similarly for $x_2 - y_2$ on X_2). The pair (x_1, y_1) corresponds to an at least as large difference of preference as (z_1, w_1) iff $x_1 - y_1 \geq z_1 - w_1$; indeed, if $(z_1, a_2) \succsim (w_1, b_2)$ for some "levels" a_2, b_2 in X_2, then substituting (z_1, w_1) by (x_1, y_1) results in $(x_1, a_2) \succsim (y_1, b_2)$ and, conversely, if $(y_1, c_2) \succsim (x_1, d_2)$ for some c_2, d_2 in X_2, then $(w_1, c_2) \succsim (z_1, d_2)$ [by definition of $\succsim_1^{**}$, see (3.28) and (3.27)]. We have furthermore that both preferences obtained after these substitutions are strict as soon as $(x_1, y_1) \succ_1^{**} (z_1, w_1)$, i.e. as soon as $x_1 - y_1 > z_1 - w_1$. This strict responsiveness property of $\succsim$ is characteristic of model $(D11)$, in which indifference is "narrow" as was already mentioned at the end of Sect. 3.4.5.3. Indeed if $(z_1, a_2) \succsim (w_1, b_2)$, we must have:

$$(z_1 - w_1) + (a_2 - b_2) = 0$$

and substituting (z_1, w_1) by (x_1, y_1) results in $(x_1 - y_1) + (a_2 - b_2) > 0$ as soon as $x_1 - y_1 > z_1 - w_1$.

Thus, any increase or decrease of $p_i(x_i, y_i)$ breaks indifference. This is also the case with the additive difference model (3.25) (with $p_i(x_i, y_i) = \Phi_i(u_i(x_i) - u_i(y_i))$) and the nontransitive additive model (3.26).

Remark 3.2 (From Ordinal to Cardinal) The framework based on marginal traces on differences that we studied in the present Sect. 3.4 is general enough to encompass both "non-compensatory" and "compensatory" preferences, for instance, preferences based on a majority or a lexicographic rule (three classes of differences of preference) and those represented in an additive manner (that can potentially distinguish an unbounded number of differences). A weighted qualified majority rule, for instance, can be said to be *ordinal* or *purely non-compensatory*; from the representation of the procedure [Eqs. (3.41), (3.42)], one can see that the full weight w_i associated to a dimension is credited to an alternative x, as compared to an alternative y, as soon as the preference difference $p_i(x_i, y_i)$ is in favour of x on that dimension. In this model, the preference difference $p_i(x_i, y_i)$ is positive as soon as x_i is preferred to y_i, w.r.t. some a priori preference relation S_i on X_i, hence the denomination of "ordinal".

On the opposite, in the additive value model [Eq. (3.55)], a large difference of preference on one dimension can be compensated by small differences of opposite sign on other dimensions: the procedure is compensatory and it uses the full power of the numbers p_i in arithmetic operations like sums and differences; we call it "cardinal".

Between those two extremes, the other procedures can be sorted in increasing order of the number of classes of differences of preference they permit to distinguish. This can be seen as a picture of a transition from "ordinal" to "cardinal" or, alternatively, from non-compensatory to compensatory procedures. Of course, the type of model is determined by the richness of the preferential information available.

3.5 Models with Weakly Differentiated Preference Differences

In Sect. 3.4.5, we have investigated a variety of models in which the number of classes of differences of preference is reduced to at most three. Can one provide a unified framework for discussing and understanding all those variants of a majority rule? It is our aim in this section to briefly describe such a framework. All the preferences described in the above-mentioned sections have some right to be called *concordance* relations. The term "concordance" was introduced by Roy (1968, 1971) in the framework of the ELECTRE methods [see also Roy (1996), Roy and Bouyssou (1993, sections 5.2 and 5.3) and Roy (1991); Roy and Vanderpooten (1996)]. It specifies an index (the so-called *concordance index*) that measures the strength of the coalition of criteria saying that an alternative x is at least as good as an alternative y. Here we use this term in the same spirit for qualifying a preference relation that results from the comparison of the strengths of coalitions of criteria: we have in mind all preference relations studied in Sect. 3.4.5.[5]

An earlier investigation of preference relations of this type in a conjoint measurement framework is due to Fishburn (1976) through its definition of *non-compensatory* preferences [see also Bouyssou and Vansnick (1986)]. Recently, Bouyssou and Pirlot (2002a), Bouyssou and Pirlot (2005) proposed a precise definition of concordance relations and showed that they can be described within the family of models that rely on traces on differences (Sect. 3.4.3). It is the goal of this section to outline those results. Similar ideas have been developed by Greco et al. (2001).

[5] The lexicographic preference described in Sect. 3.4.5.4 enters into this framework but can be seen as a limit case.

3.5.1 Concordance Relations

In a conjoint measurement context, a concordance relation is characterised by the following features.

Definition 3.12 A reflexive relation $\succsim$ on X is a concordance relation if there are:

- a complete binary relation S_i on each X_i,
- a binary relation $\trianglerighteq$ between subsets of N having N for union that is monotonic with respect to inclusion, i.e. such that for all $A, B, C, D \subseteq N$,

$$[A \trianglerighteq B, C \supseteq A, B \supseteq D, C \cup D = N] \Rightarrow C \trianglerighteq D, \tag{3.57}$$

such that, for all $x, y \in X$,

$$x \succsim y \Leftrightarrow S(x, y) \trianglerighteq S(y, x), \tag{3.58}$$

where $S(x, y) = \{i \in N : x_i S_i y_i\}$.

In this definition, we interpret S_i as the *a priori* preferences on the scale co-domain X_i of each dimension; in cases of practical interest, S_i will usually be a weak order or a semiorder (but we do not assume this for the start) and the global preference of x over y results from the comparison of the coalitions of criteria $S(x, y)$ and $S(y, x)$. The former can be seen as the list of reasons for saying that x is at least as good as y, while the latter is a list of reasons supporting that y is at least as good as x. In order to compare coalitions of criteria, we assume that there is a relation $\trianglerighteq$ on the power set of the set N that allows us to decide whether a subset of criteria constitutes a stronger argument than another subset of criteria; the interpretation of such a relation is straightforward when the compared subsets are the lists of dimensions $S(x, y)$ and $S(y, x)$ involved in the comparison of two alternatives x and y. Note that $\trianglerighteq$ enables us only to compare "complete" coalitions of criteria, i.e. those having N for their union.

The weighted majority relation (Sect. 3.4.5.2), typically, fulfills the requirements for a concordance relation as defined above. In this example, the strength of a subset of criteria can be represented by the sum of their weights and comparing $S(x, y)$ to $S(y, x)$ amounts to comparing two numbers, namely the sums of the weights of the dimensions that belong respectively to $S(x, y)$ and $S(y, x)$. In such a case, $\trianglerighteq$ can be extended to a weak order on the power set of N and this weak order admits a numerical representation that is additive with respect to individual dimensions:

$$S(x, y) \trianglerighteq S(y, x) \text{ iff } \sum_{i \in S(x,y)} w_i \geq \sum_{i \in S(y,x)} w_i. \tag{3.59}$$

In our general definition however, we neither postulate that $\trianglerighteq$ is a weak order nor that it can be additively represented on the basis of "weights" of individual criteria.

On the relation $\trianglerighteq$, we only impose a quite natural property (3.57), namely that it is monotonic with respect to the inclusion of subsets of criteria.

The interesting feature of concordance relations is that they can easily be characterised within the family of models (Dk) that rely on preference differences. The main result, obtained in Bouyssou and Pirlot (2005, Theorem 1), establishes that concordance relations are exactly those preferences for which the traces on differences $\succsim_i^{**}$ are weak orders with no more than three equivalence classes. This result will be part 1 of Theorem 3.4 stated below on p. 85. Concordance relations consequently form a subclass of the relations belonging to model $(D6)$.

3.5.1.1 The Relation $\trianglerighteq$

As a consequence of this result, *all* preferences described in Sect. 3.4.5 admit a representation as a concordance relation and can be described by (3.58), i.e.:

$$x \succsim y \Leftrightarrow S(x, y) \trianglerighteq S(y, x),$$

for some $\trianglerighteq$ and some S_i satisfying the requirements of Definition 3.12. We emphasise that this is true not only for simple weighted majorities (Sect. 3.4.5.2) but also for *qualified* majorities (Sect. 3.4.5.3) or lexicographic preferences (Sect. 3.4.5.4) that are not primarily defined through comparing coalitions (qualified majority is defined through comparing the "pros" in favour of x against y to a threshold; lexicographic relations arise from considering the most important criterion and only looking at the others when alternatives are tied on the most important one). Part 1 of Theorem 3.4 says that all these relation can *also* be represented according with Eq. (3.58) using an appropriate definition of $\trianglerighteq$ and S_i. Of course, we cannot ensure that $\trianglerighteq$ can be represented in general according with Eq. (3.59), i.e. in an additive manner.

3.5.1.2 The Relations S_i

The link between S_i and $\succsim$ is given by:

$$x_i S_i y_i \Leftrightarrow (x_i, y_i) \succsim_i^* (x_i, x_i). \tag{3.60}$$

The interpretation of this definition is clear (at least for reflexive and independent preferences $\succsim$ with which all "null differences" (x_i, x_i), for $x_i \in X_i$, are indifferent with respect to relation $\succsim_i^*$): $x_i S_i y_i$ means that the difference of preference (x_i, y_i) is "non negative", in the sense that it is at least as large as the "null difference" (x_i, x_i) or any other null difference (z_i, z_i).

For a general concordance relation $\succsim$, it can be shown that S_i is complete but not necessarily transitive; the marginal traces $\succsim_i^+$ and $\succsim_i^-$ are included in S_i, which in turn is contained in the marginal preference $\succsim_i$.

We summarise the above results in the following theorem that is based on Bouyssou and Pirlot (2005, theorems 2 and 4). Note that the latter paper provides conditions, expressed in terms of the relation $\succsim$, that are equivalent to requiring that the traces on differences $\succsim_i^{**}$ have at most three equivalence classes.

Theorem 3.4 (Concordance Relation)

1. *A relation $\succsim$ on X is a concordance relation iff it is reflexive, satisfies $RC12$ and its traces on differences $\succsim_i^{**}$ have at most three equivalence classes.*
2. *The relations S_i that intervene in the definition of concordance relations are semiorders iff $\succsim$ satisfies, in addition, $AC123$.*
3. *These relations are weak orders as soon as $\succsim$ satisfies $AC4$.*

3.5.1.3 Concordance-Discordance Relations

Concordance-discordance relations are similar to concordance relations but, in addition, their representation also involves a veto. They can be studied and characterized in the same spirit as concordance relations (Bouyssou and Pirlot, 2009).

References

Arrow, K. J. (1951). *Social choice and individual values*. New York: Cowles Foundations and Wiley.

Bouyssou, D. (1986). Some remarks on the notion of compensation in MCDM. *European Journal of Operational Research, 26*, 150–160.

Bouyssou, D., & Pirlot, M. (2002a). A characterization of strict concordance relations. In D. Bouyssou, É. Jacquet-Lagrèze, P. Perny, R. Słowinski, D. Vanderpooten, & Ph. Vincke (Eds.), *Aiding decisions with multiple criteria: Essays in honour of Bernard Roy* (pp. 121–145). Dordrecht: Kluwer.

Bouyssou, D., & Pirlot, M. (2002b) Nontransitive decomposable conjoint measurement. *Journal of Mathematical Psychology, 46*, 677–703.

Bouyssou, D., & Pirlot, M. (2004). Preferences for multi-attributed alternatives: Traces, dominance and numerical representations. *Journal of Mathematical Psychology, 48*(3), 167–185.

Bouyssou, D., & Pirlot, M. (2005). A characterization of concordance relations. *European Journal of Operational Research, 167*, 427–443.

Bouyssou, D., & Pirlot, M. (2009). An axiomatic analysis of concordance-discordance relations. *European Journal of Operational Research, 199*, 468–477.

Bouyssou, D., & Vansnick, J.-Cl. (1986). Noncompensatory and generalized noncompensatory preference structures. *Theory and Decision, 21*, 251–266.

Bouyssou, D., Marchant, Th., Pirlot, M., Perny, P., Tsoukiàs, A., & Vincke, Ph. (2000). *Evaluation and decision models: A critical perspective*. Dordrecht: Kluwer.

Bouyssou, D., Marchant, Th., Pirlot, M., Tsoukiàs, A., & Vincke, Ph. (2006) *Evaluation and decision models with multiple criteria: Stepping stones for the analyst*. New York: Springer.

Brans, J.P., & Vincke, Ph. (1985) A preference ranking organisation method. (The PROMETHEE method for multiple criteria decision-making). *Management Science, 31*(6), 647–656.

Debreu, G. (1960) Topological methods in cardinal utility theory. In K. J. Arrow, S. Karlin, & P. Suppes (Eds.), *Mathematical methods in the social sciences* (pp. 16–26). Stanford: Stanford University Press.

Dubois, D., & Fortemps, Ph. (1999). Computing improved optimal solutions to max-min flexible constriant satisfaction problems. *European Journal of Operational Research, 118*, 95–126.

Dubois, D., Fargier, H., & Prade, H. (1995). Fuzzy constraints in job-shop scheduling. *Journal of Intelligent Manufacturing, 6*, 215–234.

Dubois, D., Fargier, H., Perny, I., & Prade, H. (2003). A characterization of generalized concordance rules in multicriteria decision-making. *International Journal of Intelligent Systems, 18*(7), 751–774.

Edwards, W. (1971). Social utilities. *Engineering Economist, 6*, 119–129.

Fishburn, P. C. (1967). Methods of estimating additive utilities. *Management Science, 13*(7), 435–453.

Fishburn, P. C. (1970). *Utility theory for decision making*. New York: Wiley.

Fishburn, P. C. (1976). Noncompensatory preferences. *Synthese, 33*, 393–403.

Fishburn, P. C. (1990a). Continuous nontransitive additive conjoint measurement. *Mathematical Social Sciences, 20*, 165–193.

Fishburn, P. C. (1990b). Additive non-transitive preferences. *Economic Letters, 34*, 317–321.

Fishburn, P. C. (1991a). Nontransitive preferences in decision theory. *Journal of Risk and Uncertainty, 4*, 113–134.

Fishburn, P. C. (1991b). Nontransitive additive conjoint measurement. *Journal of Mathematical Psychology, 35*, 1–40.

Goldstein, W. M. (1991). Decomposable threshold models. *Journal of Mathematical Psychology, 35*, 64–79.

Greco, S., Matarazzo, B., & Słowiński, R. (1991). Rough approximation of a preference relation by dominance relations. *European Journal of Operational Research, 117*, 63–83.

Greco, S., Matarazzo, B., & Słowiński, R. (2001, 30 May–2 June). Axiomatic basis of noncompensatory preferences. In Communication to *FUR X*, Torino.

Keeney, R. L. (1992). *Value-focused thinking. A path to creative decision making*. Cambridge: Harvard University Press.

Keeney, R. L., & Raiffa, H. (1976). *Decisions with multiple objectives: Preferences and value tradeoffs*. New York: Wiley.

Krantz, D. H. (1964). Conjoint measurement: The Luce-Tukey axiomatization and some extensions. *Journal of Mathematical Psychology, 1*, 248–277.

Krantz, D. H., Luce, R. D., Suppes, P., & Tversky, A. (1971). *Foundations of measurement*, vol. 1: *Additive and polynomial representations*. New York: Academic Press.

Luce, R. D. (1956). Semiorders and a theory of utility discrimination. *Econometrica, 24*, 178–191.

Luce, R. D. (2000). *Utility of gains and losses: Measurement-theoretic and experimental approaches*. Mahwah, NJ: Lawrence Erlbaum Association.

Luce, R. D., Tukey, J. W. (1964). Simultaneous conjoint measurement: A new type of fundamental measurement. *Journal of Mathematical Psychology, 1*, 1–27.

Perny, P. (1992). *Modélisation, agrégation et exploitation de préférences floues dans une problématique de rangement*. Thèse de doctorat, Université Paris Dauphine.

Raiffa, H. (1969, December). Preference for multi-attributed alternatives. RAND Memorandum, RM-5868-DOT/RC.

Roy, B. (1968). Classement et choix en présence de points de vue multiples (la méthode ELECTRE). *RIRO, 2*, 57–75.

Roy, B. (1971). Problems and methods with multiple objective functions. *Mathematical Programming, 1*, 239–266.

Roy, B. (1991). The outranking approach and the foundations of ELECTRE methods. *Theory and Decision, 31*, 49–73.

Roy, B. (1996). *Multicriteria methodology for decision aiding*. Dordrecht: Kluwer. Original version in French (1985). *Méthodologie multicritère d'aide à la décision*. Paris: Economica.

Roy, B., & Bouyssou, D. (1993). *Aide multicritère à la décision : méthodes et cas*. Paris: Economica.

Roy, B., & Vanderpooten, D. (1996). The european school of mcda: Emergence, basic features and current works. *Journal of Multi-Criteria Decision Analysis, 5*(1), 22–37.

Tversky, A. (1969). Intransitivity of preferences. *Psychological Review, 76*, 31–48.

Vansnick, J. Cl. (1986). De Borda et Condorcet à l'agrégation multicritère. *Ricerca Operativa, 40*, 7–44.

Vincke, Ph. (1992). *Multicriteria decision-aid*. New York: Wiley.

Vind, K. (1991). Independent preferences. *Journal of Mathematical Economics, 20*, 119–135.

von Winterfeldt, D., & Edwards, W. (1986). *Decision analysis and behavorial research*. Cambridge: Cambridge University Press.

Wakker, P. P. (1989). *Additive representations of preferences: A new foundation of decision analysis*. Dordrecht: Kluwer.

Wakker, P. P. (1991). Additive representations of preferences, a new foundation of decision analysis; the algebraic approach. In J.-P. Doignon & J.-Cl. Falmagne (Eds.), *Mathematical psychology: Current developments* (pp. 71–87). Berlin: Springer.

Chapter 4
Building Recommendations

Denis Bouyssou, Thierry Marchant, Marc Pirlot, Alexis Tsoukiàs, and Philippe Vincke

Abstract This chapter briefly presents a number of techniques that can be used to build recommendations in each of three classical problem statements (choosing, ranking, and sorting) on the basis of a preference model. We start with the simple case of a preference model based on a value function. We then turn to more complex cases.

4.1 Introduction

In Chap. 3, various preference models for alternatives evaluated on several attributes/criteria were presented. Two main types of preference models were analyzed:

- preference models based on *value functions* leading to a weak order on the set of alternatives,
- preference models in which incomparability and/or intransitivity may occur.

This chapter is based on Bouyssou et al. (2006, , Chap. 7).

D. Bouyssou (✉) • A. Tsoukiàs
CNRS–LAMSADE & Université Paris Dauphine, Place du Maréchal de Lattre de Tassigny, F-75775 Paris Cedex 16, France
e-mail: bouyssou@lamsade.dauphine.fr; tsoukias@lamsade.dauphine.fr

T. Marchant
Department of Data analysis, Ghent University, H. Dunantlaan 1, B-9000 Gent, Belgium
e-mail: Thierry.Marchant@UGent.be

M. Pirlot
Université de Mons, Faculté Polytechnique, 9, Rue de Houdain, 7000 Mons, Belgium
e-mail: marc.pirlot@umons.ac.be

P. Vincke
Ecole Polytechnique, Université libre de Bruxelles, Campus de la Plaine, CP210/01, boulevard du Triomphe, 1050 Bruxelles, Belgium
e-mail: Philippe.Vincke@ulb.ac.be

R. Bisdorff et al. (eds.), *Evaluation and Decision Models with Multiple Criteria*, International Handbooks on Information Systems,
DOI 10.1007/978-3-662-46816-6_4

Preference models are tools built by the analyst in the course of a decision aiding study, the main phases of which were described in Chap. 2. Having built one or several preference models does not mean that the work of the analyst is over. Going from a preference model to *recommendations* requires many different tasks. Some of them are rather informal, involving, e.g., a good communication strategy with the actors in the decision process, the need for transparency in this process, a sound management of multiple stakeholders, etc. We discuss here the formal tasks that are involved in the elaboration of a recommendation.

The nature of this recommendation that is looked for will be of crucial importance in this phase of the decision aiding study. The central element here is the *problem statement* that has been agreed upon at the problem formulation stage of the decision aiding process (see Chap. 2). We will restrict our attention here to the three main problem statements introduced in Roy (1996).

4.1.1 Choosing

The first problem statement, *choosing*, is quite familiar in Operational Research and in Economics. The task of the analyst is formulated in such a way that he either tries to isolate, in the set A of potential alternatives, a subset A' that is likely to contain the most desirable alternatives in A given the information available or to propose a procedure that will operate such a selection.

Examples in which such a problem statement seems appropriate are not difficult to find: a recruiter wants to select a unique applicant, an engineer wants to select the best possible technical device, a patient wants to choose the best possible treatment among those offered in a hospital, a manager wants to optimise the supply policy of a factory (for other examples, see Chaps. 7 and 14 in this volume). In all these examples, the selection is to be made on the sole basis of the comparison of potential alternatives. In other words, the "best" alternatives are not defined with respect to norms but with respect to the set of alternatives A; the evaluation is only *relative*. Therefore, it may occur that the subset A', while containing the most desirable alternatives within A, only contains poor ones.

4.1.2 Ranking

The second problem statement, *ranking*, is also familiar in Operational Research and Economics. The problem is formulated in such a way that the analyst tries to rank order the set of potential alternatives A according to their desirability or to propose a procedure that will operate such a ranking. The evaluation is performed, as in the preceding problem statement, on a *relative* basis: the top ranked alternatives are judged better than the others while nothing guarantees that they are "satisfactory".

It is not difficult to find examples in which this problem statement seems appropriate. A sports league wants to rank order the teams at the end of the season. An academic programme has to select a number of applicants: a competitive exam is organized which leads to rank ordering the applicants according to an "average grade" and applicants are then selected in the decreasing order of their average grades until the size of the programme is reached. An R&D department has to finance a number of research projects subject to a budget constraint: research projects are then rank ordered and financed till the budget constraint is binding. In practice, some authors tend to use a ranking problem statement whereas a choice problem statement would seem more natural (see Chap. 12 in this volume). This is often motivated by the fact that the ranking problem statement leads to richer information than the choice problem statement.

4.1.3 Sorting

The third problem statement, *sorting*, is designed to deal with absolute evaluation. The problem is here formulated in such a way that the analyst tries to partition the set of alternatives into several categories, the definition of these categories being intrinsic, or to propose a procedure that will generate such a partition. The essential distinctive characteristics of this problem statement therefore lie in the definition of the categories. Two main cases arise.

The definition of the categories may not refer to the desirability of the alternatives. Many problems that arise in pattern recognition, speech recognition or diagnosis are easily formulated in this way. We will only discuss here the case in which the definition of the categories refers to the *desirability* of the alternatives, e.g., a credit manager may want to isolate "good" risks and "bad" risks, an academic programme may wish to only enroll "good" students, etc. A crucial problem here will lie in the definition of the categories, i.e., of the *norms* defining what is a "good" risk, what is a "good" student. Several chapters in this volume (see Chaps. 15 and 19) adopt this problem statement.

4.1.4 Outline

In Sect. 4.2, we tackle the simple case in which the preference model takes the form of a value function. Section 4.3 is devoted to the case of making a recommendation on the basis of *several* value functions. Such a situation frequently arises when using Linear Programming-based assessment techniques of an additive value function. In Sect. 4.4 we deal with the more delicate case of deriving a recommendation on the basis of less well-structured preference models like the ones that are obtained with the so-called outranking methods, which includes the ELECTRE methods.

4.2 A Single Value Function

Many of the preference models envisaged in Chap. 3 are based on value functions. This means that the analyst has built a real-valued function V on the set of alternatives A that induces binary relation $\succsim$ on A, interpreted as an "at least as good" relation letting, for all $a, b \in A$:

$$a \succsim b \Leftrightarrow V(a) \geq V(b). \tag{4.1}$$

Such a relation $\succsim$ is a weak order (it is complete and transitive). It is therefore simple to use it to build a recommendation involving only a relative evaluation of the alternatives, the hard work involved in the assessment of a value function being rewarded at this stage of the decision aiding process.

In this section, we suppose that the value function V is only constrained by (4.1). This means that any increasing transformation of V would carry the same information as V.

4.2.1 Choosing

In a choosing problem statement, it is natural to look for alternatives that would be "at least as good" as all other alternatives, i.e., to identify the set $G(A, \succsim)$ of *greatest alternatives* in A given the binary relation $\succsim$ defined by:

$$G(A, \succsim) = \{a \in A : a \succsim b, \forall b \in A\}.$$

Since $\succsim$ is complete and transitive, $G(A, \succsim)$ will, in general,[1] be nonempty. Finding the alternatives in $G(A, \succsim)$ is equivalent to finding the solutions to the following optimisation problem:

$$\max_{a \in A} V(a).$$

Note that the set of solutions to this optimisation problem is unchanged if V is replaced by any value function satisfying (4.1), i.e., by any value function obtained from V applying to it an increasing transformation.

The set $G(A, \succsim)$ may contain more than one element. In this case, all alternatives in $G(A, \succsim)$ are indifferent and compare in the same way to all other alternatives. Therefore, the preference model defined by V offers no means of distinguishing

[1]This is true when A is finite. The general case may be more tricky: while the relation $\geq$ on $\mathbb{R}$ is complete and transitive, $G(\geq, \mathbb{R})$ is clearly empty. The same is true with $\geq$ on the open $]0, 1[$ interval.

between them. All alternatives in $G(A, \succsim)$ are strictly preferred to all alternatives outside $G(A, \succsim)$. The rejection of the latter therefore seems fully justified: all recommended alternatives are judged strictly better than all rejected alternatives.

The set of maximal alternatives $M(A, \succsim)$ in A, given the binary relation $\succsim$, is defined by:

$$M(A, \succsim) = \{a \in A : Not[b \succ a], \forall b \in A\},$$

where $\succ$ is the asymmetric part of $\succsim$. It is often presented as the central notion in a choosing problem statement. When $\succsim$ is complete, we always have $G(A, \succsim) = M(A, \succsim)$. When A is finite, it is easy to show that $M(A, \succsim)$ is nonempty when $\succsim$ has no circuit in its asymmetric part $\succ$. For finite sets, the absence of any circuit in $\succ$ is, in fact, a necessary and sufficient condition for $M(B, \succsim)$ to be nonempty for all nonempty sets $B \subseteq A$.

4.2.2 Ranking

Let us now envisage the case of a ranking problem statement. The hard work of building a value function also pays off here since the binary relation $\succsim$ induced on A by the value function V (or by any increasing transformation of V) rank orders the alternatives from the best to the worst, which is precisely what is wanted. Apart from the necessity of conducting a robustness analysis, no additional work is required (on the notion of robustness analysis, see Roy, 1998, 2010).

4.2.3 Sorting

In both problem statements involving only a *relative evaluation* of alternatives, we have seen that the value function model provided an almost immediate way of deriving a recommendation. The situation is slightly more complex in a sorting problem statement, which calls for an *absolute evaluation*. It is indeed necessary to define the "norms" that will give sense to such an evaluation.

We will only envisage the case in which the absolute evaluation that is sought takes the form of a sorting of the alternatives between r ordered categories $C^1, C^2, \ldots, C^r$, with C^1 containing the least desirable alternatives. The definition of each category involves the definition of norms. These norms usually take two distinct forms. They may be modelled as *prototypes* of alternatives belonging to a category or as *limiting profiles* indicating the limit of each category. A "good" student may be defined using examples of past students in the programme: this would define the prototypes of the category of "good students". Alternatively, we could define, as is done in the French *baccalauréat*, an average grade above which, students are considered to be "good". This average grade implicitly defines a limiting profile for the category of "good students".

4.2.3.1 Limiting Profiles

When each category C^k is delimited by a limiting profile π^k, an alternative a should belong at least to the category C^k when it is preferred to π^k. It then becomes easy to use a value function to sort the alternatives: alternative $a \in A$ will belong to C^k if and only if $V(\pi^k) < V(a) < V(\pi^{k+1})$, where the unlikely cases of equality are dealt with conventionally, depending on the definition of the limiting profiles π^k. Note that the definition of a limiting profile implies that there is only one such profile per category. The main problem here lies in the definition of the limiting profiles π^k. We shall come back to this point in Sect. 4.3.3.

4.2.3.2 Prototypes

The situation is more delicate when categories are defined via prototypes. Suppose that category C^k has been defined by a set $P^{k,1}, P^{k,2}, \ldots$ of prototypes. A first step in the analysis consists in checking whether this information is consistent with the value function V, i.e., if the prototypes defining a category C^k are all preferred to the prototypes defining the category C^ℓ when $k > \ell$.

When this consistency test fails, the analyst may wish to reconsider the definition of V or of the various prototypes. When the prototypes are consistent, we may easily associate to each category C^k, its lowest prototype L^k and its highest prototype H^k in terms of the value function V. If $V(a) \in [V(L^k); V(H^k)]$, alternative a should be assigned to the category C^k. If this simple rule allows to assign each alternative to a well-defined category, no further analysis is required. When this is not the case, i.e., when there are alternatives $a \in A$ such that $V(a)$ falls between two intervals, we may either try to refine the information defining the categories, e.g., try to ask for new prototypes, or apply a simple rule e.g., replacing the intervals $[V(L^k); V(H^k)]$ by the interval $[(V(H^{k-1}) + V(L^k))/2; (V(H^k) + V(L^{k+1}))/2]$. Ideally we would need a similarity measure between alternatives and prototypes that would allow to classify a as a member of C^k if a is close to one or several of the prototypes defining C^k. The simple rule envisaged above amounts to using V as a very rough similarity measure since this amounts to saying that a is more similar to b than it is to c if $|V(a) - V(b)| < |V(a) - V(c)|$. It should however be noted that the assessment procedures of V do not necessarily guarantee that such a measure is appropriate. In general, this would call for the modelling of "preference differences" between alternatives, e.g., using a model in which:

$$a \succsim b \Leftrightarrow V(a) \geq V(b) \text{ and} \tag{4.2}$$

$$(a,b) \succsim^* (c,d) \Leftrightarrow V(a) - V(b) \geq V(c) - V(d), \tag{4.3}$$

where $\succsim^*$ is a binary relation on A^2 such that $(a, b) \succsim^* (c, d)$ is interpreted as "the preference difference between a and b is at least as large as the preference difference between c and d". A common mistake here is to use any V satisfying (4.2) as if it would automatically satisfy (4.3).

4.3 A Set of Value Functions

Motivated by the assessment of an additive value function via Linear Programming, this section studies techniques to build a recommendation on the basis of *several* value functions that cannot be deduced from one another using an increasing transformation. This is the case with techniques such as UTA (Jacquet-Lagrèze and Siskos, 1982). This method uses LP techniques to assess an additive value function, which, in general, leads to several possible value functions.

4.3.1 Choosing with a Set of Additive Value Functions

Suppose for example that, e.g., because we have assessed an additive value function with UTA, we have an entire set $\mathscr{V}$ of value functions compatible with the available information. Two main ways of exploiting this set $\mathscr{V}$ may be envisaged within a choosing problem statement.

The simplest way of using the set $\mathscr{V}$ is to consider that an alternative $a \in A$ should be included in the set $A' \subseteq A$ of recommended alternatives as soon as there is one additive value function in $\mathscr{V}$ such that using this function, a is at least as good as any other alternative in A.

When the set $\mathscr{V}$ comes from Linear Programming-based assessment techniques, such a test is easily performed using LP, since the elements in $\mathscr{V}$ correspond to the solution of a set of linear constraints. In fact, we only have to test whether the system of inequalities $V(a) \geq V(b)$, for all $b \in A$, is consistent for some $V \in \mathscr{V}$. This requires solving a linear programme for each alternative $a \in A$. This idea has been systematized in Greco et al. (2008, 2009).

The above technique is very cautious and is likely to lead to quite large choice sets. A more refined analysis is based on the "proportion" of value functions $V \in \mathscr{V}$ for which an alternative is optimal. The "more functions" V in $\mathscr{V}$ give a as the optimal solution, the more confident we are in the fact that a can be recommended. In general, such an analysis unfortunately requires solving difficult computational problem (see Bana e Costa, 1986, 1988), even when $\mathscr{V}$ is defined by the solutions of a set of linear constraints. A possible solution would be to sample a few value functions within $\mathscr{V}$. Indeed, when $\mathscr{V}$ is defined by linear constraints, Jacquet-Lagrèze and Siskos (1982) suggested a simple way to build a finite subset $\mathscr{V}'$ of $\mathscr{V}$ that is "representative" of the whole set $\mathscr{V}$. An alternative approach is to use Monte-Carlo simulation (Charnetski and Soland, 1978; Lahdelma et al., 1998)

4.3.2 Ranking with a Set of Additive Value Functions

The crudest way of using the information contained in $\mathcal{V}$ is to build a partial preorder (i.e., a reflexive and transitive relation) T such that:

$$aTb \Leftrightarrow V(a) \geq V(b) \text{ for all } V \in \mathcal{V}, \tag{4.4}$$

i.e., letting a be ranked before b if it is so for every admissible function V in $\mathcal{V}$.

Testing if aTb can easily be done using LP when $\mathcal{V}$ is defined via linear constraints (this idea has been systematized in Greco et al. (2008) and Greco et al. (2009)). The use of such a technique is however limited since it implies solving $n(n-1)$ linear programmes when $|A| = n$. Furthermore, such a unanimity argument is likely to lead to a very poor recommendation: many alternatives will be incomparable when $\mathcal{V}$ is large.

When $|A|$ is too large to allow the use of the technique described above or when a richer result is sought, one may either try to restrict the domain $\mathcal{V}$ through emphasizing interaction with the decision maker during the assessment phase, or work with a representative set of value functions $\mathcal{V}'$, as mentioned above. Quite interesting examples of such techniques can be found in Siskos (1982).

4.3.3 Sorting with a Set of Additive Value Functions

In the techniques envisaged so far we did not consider the definition of the "norms" that are necessary to sort alternatives. A useful technique, in the spirit of UTA, consists in assessing the additive value function using examples of alternatives belonging to each of the ordered categories, that we called prototypes in Sect. 4.2.3.2. Such examples may come from past decisions or may be obtained from the decision maker as prototypical examples of each category. We may then try to infer limiting profiles and an additive value function on the basis of such information.

This amounts to assessing an additive value function V and thresholds s_k such that, for all prototypes $P^{k,j}$ of category C^k we have $V(P^{k,j}) \in [s^k, s^{k+1}[$. This is the basis of the UTADIS technique (see Jacquet-Lagrèze, 1995; Zopounidis and Doumpos, 2000b, 2001, 2002) and its variants (Zopounidis and Doumpos, 2000a).

Basically UTADIS uses a number of prototype alternatives for each ordered category whereas UTA uses a weak order on a subset of reference alternatives. Such a technique extends the traditional methods of discrimination used in Statistics considering the possibility of nonlinear value functions. As in Statistics, the assessment may use "cost of misclassification" which simply amounts to weighting the deviation variables in the LP used to assess the value function V appropriately. As in UTA, this leads to a whole set of possible additive value functions with associated limiting thresholds.

The way to make use of such information to build a recommendation has not been thoroughly studied in the literature. When the set $\mathscr{V}$ is defined via linear constraints, it is easy to use LP to compute for each alternative the subset of categories to which they may belong. This is computationally intensive. Another way to proceed is to consider a subset $\mathscr{V}'$ of representative additive value functions. For each alternative $a \in A$, it is easy to compute a set of possible assignments using $\mathscr{V}'$. One may then, for example, use the frequency with which each alternative is assigned to a category to devise a recommendation. For developments along this line, see Greco et al. (2010).

4.4 Other Preference Models

As argued in Chap. 3, the assessment of a value function is a demanding task. The analyst may then wish to use aggregation technique that have a more "ordinal" character. The price to pay for using such models is that the preference models to which they lead may be intransitive and/or incomplete. Using them to derive a recommendation is a difficult task. For space reasons, we restrict our attention to the case of crisp binary relations (the case of valued relations is dealt with in Bouyssou et al., 2006, , Chap. 7).

Suppose that you have built a preference relation on a set of alternatives using one of the techniques presented in Chap. 3 that does not guarantee the transitivity or the completeness of the result. This does not necessarily mean that *any* preference structure can be obtained with such a method. Let us first show, that for a number of well known techniques, this is unfortunately true.

Consider simple majority, i.e., the simplest "ordinal" technique for comparing alternatives. On each criterion, we suppose that alternatives can be compared using a weak order. Simple majority amounts to declaring that:

$$x \succsim y \Leftrightarrow |P(x, y)| \geq |P(y, x)|$$

where $P(x, y)$ denotes the set of criteria on which x is preferred to y. Clearly, a relation $\succsim$ obtained in such a way is always complete. Let T be any complete binary relation on a finite set of alternatives A. Besides completeness, no hypothesis is made on T; it may be the most intransitive relation you can think of, with circuits of any length in its asymmetric part. The surprising and disturbing fact, proved by McGarvey (1953), is that it is always possible to see T as the result of a simple majority aggregation. Extending this result, Bouyssou (1996) has shown that *any* reflexive relation on a finite set of alternatives may be obtained with ELECTRE I (Roy, 1968). Therefore, we have to tackle here quite a large class of preference models.

4.4.1 Motivating Examples

Many techniques for building recommendations on the basis of a non-necessarily transitive or complete binary relation have been proposed in the literature on Multiple Criteria Decision Making (MCDM). Most of them were justified on an ad hoc basis. But the intuition supporting these techniques might not work well in all cases. Let us illustrate this point with two examples.

Example 4.1 (Choice Procedures and Dominated Alternatives) Consider a set of alternatives $A = \{a, b, c, d\}$ evaluated on three criteria. Suppose that, on each criterion, alternatives are weakly ordered by a binary relation S_i. Suppose that the preference on each criterion are such that, using an obvious notation for weak orders:

$$a P_1 b P_1 c P_1 d,$$
$$c P_2 d P_2 a P_2 b,$$
$$d P_3 a P_3 b P_3 c,$$

where P_i denotes the asymmetric part of S_i.

Alternative b is *strongly dominated* by alternative a (a is strictly preferred to b on all criteria). Intuitively, this gives a decisive argument not to include b in the set of recommended alternatives.

Suppose then that the above information is aggregated into a binary relation S using simple majority. It is not difficult to see that S is such that: $aPb, aPc, bPc, cPd, dPa, dPb$, where P denotes the asymmetric part of S. It is obvious that S is not well suited to select a subset of alternatives since its asymmetric part P contains a circuit involving all alternatives (aPb, bPc, cPd, dPa). The simplest way to get rid of such a circuit is to consider that all alternatives included in a circuit should be considered "equivalent". This can be done by considering the *transitive closure* of the relation, i.e., the smallest transitive relation containing it. But using the transitive closure of S would then lead to consider that all alternatives are equivalent and, hence, to propose the whole set A as the set of recommended alternatives. This is not sound since we have shown that b should *not* be recommended.

Example 4.2 (Ranking Procedures and Monotonicity) Let $A = \{a, b, c, d, e, f, g\}$. Using the result of Bouyssou (1996), we know that if we use simple majority or ELECTRE I, we might end up with a complete binary relation S such that: $aPb, aPf, bPc, bPd, bPe, bPf, cPa, cPe, cPf, cPg, dPa, dPc, dPe, dPf, dPg, ePa, ePf, ePg, fPg, gPa, gPb$, where P denotes the asymmetric part of S.

In order to obtain a ranking on the basis of such information, one may use a measure of the "desirability" of each alternative. A simple measure of the desirability of an alternative x consists in counting the number of alternatives y

such that xSy minus the number of alternatives z such that zSx. This measure is called the *Copeland score* of an alternative (Laslier, 1997).

A simple way of building a ranking on A goes as follows. Define the first equivalence class of the ranking as the alternatives that have obtained a maximal Copeland score. Remove these alternatives from the set of alternatives. Define the second equivalence class of the ranking as the alternatives with maximal Copeland scores in the reduced set. Repeat this procedure as long as there are unranked alternatives. Such a ranking procedure is intuitively appealing and leads to the following ranking, using obvious notations:

$$d \succ c \succ e \succ [a, g] \succ b \succ f,$$

which does not seem unreasonable.

Consider now a relation identical to the one above except that we now have aPd instead of dPa. Intuition suggests that the position of a has improved and we reasonably expect that this is reflected in the new ranking. But applying the same ranking method as before now leads to:

$$[b, c, d] \succ e \succ [a, f, g].$$

Such a result is quite disappointing since, before a was improved, a was ranked before b while, after the improvement of a, b is ranked before a.

These two examples show that the definition of sound procedures for deriving a recommendation on the basis of a non-necessarily transitive or complete binary relation is a difficult task. Intuitively appealing procedures sometimes produce disappointing results.

4.4.2 Choice Procedures

Let A be a set of alternatives. Suppose that you have built a preference relation S on A using an aggregation technique. Let us call $\mathcal{S}$ the set of all conceivable preference relations that can be obtained using such a technique. As shown above, $\mathcal{S}$ consists of all reflexive binary relations with ELECTRE I and all complete binary relations with simple majority. A choice procedure C is a function associating a nonempty subset $C(S)$ of A with each element S of $\mathcal{S}$. The choice procedure C should:

- be such that $C(S)$ is as small as possible given the available information,
- be such that there are clear arguments to justify the elimination of the alternatives in $A \setminus C(S)$, i.e., the alternatives that are not selected,
- be such that there is no built-in bias in favour of some alternatives, i.e., that the only arguments that can be taken into account in the determination of $C(S)$ are how these alternatives are related in terms of the relation S. Technically, this leads to requiring that C is *neutral*, i.e., that $C(S) = \sigma[C(S^\sigma)]$, where σ is any

one-to-one function on A and S^σ is the binary relation in $\mathscr{S}$ such that, for all $a, b \in A$, $S(a,b) = S^\sigma(\sigma(a), \sigma(b))$.

- react to the improvement of an alternative in the expected direction. Technically, the procedure should be *monotonic*, i.e., if $a \in C(S)$ and S' is identical to S except that $[aS'b$ and $Not[aSb]]$ or $[Not[bS'a]$ and $bSa]$, for some $b \in A$, then we should have $a \in C(S')$.

Let $S \in \mathscr{S}$. We shall always denote by P (resp. I) the asymmetric (resp. symmetric) part of S and J the associated incomparability relation, i.e., for all $a, b \in A$, aJb iff $[Not[aSb]$ and $Not[bSa]]$.

4.4.2.1 Procedures Based on Covering Relations

Suppose that there exists $a \in A$ such that aPb, for all $b \in A \setminus \{a\}$. Such an alternative is usually called a *Condorcet winner*. In this case, letting $C(S) = \{a\}$ seems to be the only reasonable choice. In fact, by construction:

- when there is a Condorcet winner, it is necessarily unique,
- there is *direct evidence* that a is better than all other alternatives.

Unfortunately, the existence of a Condorcet winner is an unlikely situation and we must agree on what to do in the absence of a Condorcet winner.

A simple extension of the notion of a Condorcet winner is that of *greatest* alternatives already introduced. Remember that an alternative $a \in A$ belongs to the set $G(A, S)$ of greatest alternatives in A given S if aSb, for all $b \in A$. If a belongs to $G(A, S)$, we have direct evidence that a is at least as good as any other alternative in A. Contrary to the case of Condorcet winners, there may be more than one greatest alternative. When the set of greatest alternatives is nonempty, it is tempting to put all alternatives on $G(A, S)$ in $C(S)$.

This seems a natural choice. Indeed, all greatest alternatives are indifferent, so there is no direct evidence that would allow to further refine the choice set $C(S)$. Contrary to the case in which S is a weak order, it should however be noted that there might be *indirect* evidence that allows to distinguish between greatest alternatives. As shown in the following example, indirect evidence may be usefully employed to narrow down the set of selected alternatives.

Example 4.3 Suppose that $A = \{a, b, c\}$ and S be such that aIb, bIc and aPc. Although both a and b belong to $G(A, S)$, we can use the way a and b compare to a third alternative, c, to distinguish between them. Here, since aPc while bIc, it is very tempting to use this indirect evidence to narrow $C(S)$ down to $\{a\}$.

Unfortunately, there is no clear-cut way of defining what should count as an *indirect evidence* that an alternative is better than another and to balance it with the direct evidence.

Suppose first that aPb so there is direct evidence that a is superior to b. If, for all $c \in A$, we have $cPa \Rightarrow cPb$, $cIa \Rightarrow cSb$, $bPc \Rightarrow aPc$ and $bIc \Rightarrow aSc$, there is no indirect evidence that b could be superior to a. In such a case, we say that a strongly covers b ($aSCb$) and it seems that the selection of b would be quite unwarranted. A cautious selection would then seem to be to select all alternatives that are not strongly covered by any other, i.e., the set $M(A, SC)$ of maximal alternatives in A for SC. When A is finite, $M(A, SC)$ is always nonempty since the strong covering relation is asymmetric and transitive and, thus, has no circuit. Therefore letting $C(S) = M(A, SC)$ defines a selection procedure. Note that the use of this selection procedure would allow to avoid selecting a strongly dominated alternative as was the case with the procedure envisaged in Example 4.1 since, in this example, a strongly covers b. With such a procedure, the rejection of the elements in $A \setminus C(S)$ would seem fully justified since for each $b \in A \setminus C(S)$, there would be an $a \in C(S)$ such that aPb. We leave to the reader the, easy, task of showing that this selection procedure is neutral and monotonic.

The relation SC is likely to be rather poor, so that the above procedure may result in large choice sets. In order to reject an alternative, it is necessary to have direct evidence against it and no indirect evidence in its favour. In Example 4.3, it would not allow to distinguish between the two greatest alternatives a and b since there is no direct evidence for a against b.

A less stringent procedure would consist in saying that the selection of b is unwarranted as soon as there is an alternative a such that there is direct evidence that a is at least as good as b while there is no indirect evidence that b is better than a. This would lead to the definition of a covering relation in which a weakly covers b ($aWCb$) as soon as aSb and for all $c \in A$, we have $cPa \Rightarrow cPb$, $cIa \Rightarrow cSb$, $bPc \Rightarrow aPc$ and $bIc \Rightarrow aSc$. Therefore, the weak covering relation WC is identical to the strict covering relation SC except that aIb is compatible with $aWCb$. Contrary to SC, the relation WC is not asymmetric. It is reflexive and transitive so its asymmetric part has no circuit. When A is finite, letting $C(S) = M(A, WC)$ therefore defines a selection procedure. For each non selected alternative b, there is a selected alternative a such that either aPb or aIb, while there is no indirect evidence that b might be superior to a. The theoretical properties of this choice procedure are quite distinct from the one relying on the strong covering relation (Dutta and Laslier, 1999; Peris and Subiza, 1999), while remaining neutral and monotonic.

A weakness of the procedure given above is that when a and b are incomparable, it is impossible to distinguish between them even when there is strong indirect evidence that one is better to the other. It is possible to modify the definition of the weak covering relation requiring only that there is no direct evidence against a, i.e., that aSb or aJb, while still requiring that there is no indirect evidence that b is superior to a. This very weak covering relation is still reflexive and transitive. Taking the maximal alternatives in A for the very weak covering relation therefore defines a selection procedure. It refines the above selection procedure based on the weak covering relation. This is however a price to pay. Using such a choice set does not prevent the existence of a non selected alternative b such that there is no alternative in the choice set for which there is direct evidence that it is at least as good as b. Therefore, the narrowing of the choice set, considering the very weak covering relation, may be judged unsatisfactory.

We refer to Dutta and Laslier (1999), Laslier (1997) and Peris and Subiza (1999) for a thorough study of the properties of choice sets that are based on some idea of "covering" i.e., mixing direct and indirect evidence to justify the selection of $C(S)$.

4.4.2.2 Procedures Based on Kernels

Quite a different path was taken by Roy (1968) and Roy and Skalka (1984) in the ELECTRE I and ELECTRE IS methods (a similar idea is already detailed in von Neumann and Morgenstern, 1947, , in the context of Game Theory). Note that the selection procedure is clear as soon as S is transitive. In fact, in such a case, the set of maximal elements in A, i.e., $M(A, S) = \{a \in A : Not[bPa] \text{ for all } b \in A\}$ is always nonempty and such that, for all $b \notin M(A, S)$, there is an alternative $a \in M(A, S)$ such that aSb. In fact, when S is transitive, the set $M(A, S)$ coincides with the set of maximal alternatives for the weak covering relation since, in this case, $S = WC$.

For $B \subseteq A$, we say that B is *dominating* if for all $c \notin B$ there is an alternative $b \in B$ such that bSc. Therefore the selection of the alternatives in a dominating subset always justifies the non selection of the other alternatives. By construction, the set A itself is dominating. When A is finite, there are therefore dominating subsets of minimal cardinality. If there is only one such dominating subset, it is a good candidate for the choice set $C(S)$. When S has circuits, there may be more than one dominating subset of minimal cardinality. Taking their union will generally result in quite an undiscriminating procedure. This is illustrated in the following example.

Example 4.4 Let $A = \{a, b, c, d, e\}$. Suppose that S is such that aPb, bPc, cPd, dPe and ePa. This relation has 5 dominating subsets of minimal cardinality, i.e., $\{a, c, e\}$, $\{a, b, d\}$, $\{a, c, d\}$, $\{b, c, e\}$ and $\{b, d, e\}$. The union of the minimal dominating subsets is A.

B. Roy therefore suggested to consider the relation S' obtained by reducing the circuits in S, i.e., to consider all alternatives that are involved in a circuit as a single alternative. Working with S' instead of S amounts to considering that all alternatives involved in a circuit compare similarly with alternatives outside the circuit. This is frequently a strong hypothesis implying the loss of a lot of information (this would be the case in Example 4.4). The following example illustrates the process of reducing the circuits of S.

Example 4.5 Let $A = \{a, b, c, d, e, f\}$ and consider the binary relation S such that: $aSb, aSc, aSd, aSe, aSf, bSc, bSf, cSa, cSe, dSe, eSf$. In order to build the relation S' obtained by reducing the circuits in S we need to find the maximal circuits in S (i.e., circuits that are not included in other circuits). There is only one circuit in S: aSb, bSc and cSa. Therefore the three alternatives a, b and c are replaced by a single one, say x, and there is an arc from x to another alternative if there is an arc in S going from either a, b or c to this alternative. Similarly there is an arc going from an alternative to x if there was an arc going from this alternative to either a, b or c in S. Therefore the binary relation S' is such that: $xS'd, xS'e, xS'f, dS'e, eS'f$.

A famous result of Graph Theory (Berge, 1970; Roy, 1969–70) says that when a graph has no circuit, it has a unique *kernel*, defined as a dominating subset that is internally stable, i.e., such that there is no arc between any of its elements (this implies that the kernel is a minimal dominating subset). Reducing the circuits and taking the kernel of the relation is the selection procedure proposed in ELECTRE I. It is easy to verify that it is neutral and monotonic.

The procedure in ELECTRE IS (see Roy and Bouyssou, 1993; Roy and Skalka, 1984) amounts to a more sophisticated reduction of the circuits that takes the way the relation S has been defined into account. For recent developments along this line, including the extension of the notion of kernel to valued binary relation, see Bisdorff et al. (2008) (see also Chap. 5).

4.4.2.3 Other Procedures

The use of covering relations and of the notion of kernel are far from being the only possible choices to devise a selection procedure (Laslier, 1997; Peris and Subiza, 1999; Schwartz, 1986). Some of the possibilities that we do not investigate here are:

- selection procedures based on the consideration of relations close to S for which the choice is simple, e.g, orders or weak orders (see Barthélémy et al., 1989; Laslier, 1997; Charon and Hudry, 2007),
- selection procedures based on scores, e.g., Copeland scores (see van den Brink and Gilles, 2003; Henriet, 1985; Rubinstein, 1980),
- selection procedures that directly operate on the evaluations of the alternatives without building a relation S as an intermediate step (see Fishburn, 1977).

4.4.3 Ranking Procedures

Let A be a set of alternatives. Suppose that you have built a crisp relation S on A using some kind of aggregation technique. Let $\mathscr{S}$ be the set of all conceivable preference relations that can be obtained using such a technique. A ranking procedure $\succsim$ is a function associating a reflexive and transitive binary relation $\succsim(S)$ on A with each element S of $\mathscr{S}$. The task of building a transitive result on the basis of a binary relation, that might not be transitive or complete is not easy: we are in fact looking for a much richer result than that obtained using choice procedures. We expect such a ranking procedure to be:

- *neutral*, i.e., insensitive to the labelling of the alternatives,
- *faithful*, i.e., if S is a reflexive and transitive relation, we should have $\succsim(S) = S$,
- *monotonic*, i.e., the position of a in the ranking $\succsim(S)$ should not decrease if S is substituted by a relation S' in which the position of a has improved (see Example 4.2).

Clearly, this list is only partial, e.g., we would also expect the ranking $\succsim(S)$ to be linked to the covering relations defined above (see Vincke, 1992).

Several types of ranking procedures have been suggested in the literature:

1. Ranking procedures based on the transitive closure of S,
2. Ranking procedures based on scores, e.g., the Copeland score,
3. Ranking procedures based on the repeated use of a choice mechanism (as in Example 4.2),

We briefly illustrate each type of procedure below.

4.4.3.1 Procedures Based on the Transitive Closure

Let S be a reflexive binary relation on A. A simple way to obtain a reflexive and transitive relation $\succsim(S)$ on the basis of S is to take its transitive closure $\hat{S}$, i.e., the smallest transitive relation containing S. This defines a ranking procedure; it is easy to see that it is neutral, faithful and monotonic. In view of our discussion of choice procedures, the main defect of this ranking procedure should be apparent. All alternatives that are involved in a circuit of S will be equally ranked if we let $\succsim(S) = \hat{S}$. This often results in a huge loss of information.

A closely related ranking procedure is the one used in ELECTRE II (Roy and Bertier, 1973). It was originally designed to produce a reflexive and transitive relation on the basis of two nested reflexive relations. We present it below in the special case in which there is only one relation (the role of the second one being only to possibly refine the equivalence classes that are obtained).

Consider any reflexive relation S on A. The ranking procedure of ELECTRE II first consists, as with ELECTRE I, in reducing the circuits that may exist in S, replacing all alternatives involved in a circuit by a single vertex in the associated graph. Once this is done, we obtain, by construction, a relation with no circuit. We use this relation to build two weak orders. In the first one, T_1, the first equivalence class consists of the maximal elements (there is no element that is strictly preferred to them) of the relation with no circuit. These elements are then removed from the set of alternatives. The second equivalence class of T_1 consists of the maximal elements of the relation among those remaining and so forth.

The second weak order T_2 is obtained in a dual way, building the last equivalence class consisting of the minimal elements first (they are preferred to no other element) in the relation with no circuit, removing these elements from the set of alternatives and building the penultimate equivalence class of T_2 as the minimal elements among those remaining and so forth. In general, T_1 and T_2 are not identical. The reflexive and transitive relation $\succsim(S)$ is then taken to be the intersection of these two weak orders. Let us illustrate this process using a simple example.

Example 4.6 Let $A = \{a_1, a_2, \ldots, a_9\}$ and let S be such that: $a_1 S a_2, a_1 S a_4, a_1 S a_5$, $a_2 S a_3$, $a_3 S a_1, a_4 S a_6$, $a_6 S a_7, a_7 S a_9, a_8 S a_9$. The relation S has a circuit: $a_1 S a_2$, $a_2 S a_3$, $a_3 S a_1$. We therefore replace S on A with the relation S' on A' defined by: $bS'a_4, bS'a_5, a_4 S' a_6, a_6 S' a_7, a_7 S' a_9, a_8 S' a_9$, where a_1, a_2 and a_3 have been replaced by b. The relation S' has no circuit. Its set of maximal elements consists of $\{b, a_8\}$. Once these elements have been removed, the set of maximal elements is $\{a_4, a_5\}$. At the next iteration, we obtain $\{a_6\}$, then $\{a_7\}$ and $\{a_9\}$. Therefore the weak order T_1 is, using obvious notation:

$$[a_1, a_2, a_3, a_8] T_1 [a_4, a_5] T_1 a_6 T_1 a_7 T_1 a_9.$$

In a dual way, we obtain the weak order T_2:

$$[a_1, a_2, a_3] T_2 a_4 T_2 a_6 T_2 [a_7, a_8] T_2 [a_5, a_9].$$

The relations T_1 and T_2 are not identical. Taking their intersection leads to, abusing notation:

$$\begin{aligned}
[a_1, a_2, a_3] \succ a_4 \succ a_6 \succ a_7 \succ a_9&,\\
[a_1, a_2, a_3] \succ a_8&,\\
a_4 \succ a_5&,\\
a_8 \succ a_7, a_8 \succ a_5&,\\
a_5 \succ a_9&.
\end{aligned}$$

What can be said of this result? First observe that the rationale for building two weak orders and for defining $\succsim(S)$ as their intersection is to introduce incomparability between alternatives that are difficult to compare using S. This is, for instance, the case between a_5 and all alternatives except a_1 or between a_8 and all alternatives except a_9. In this respect the success of the procedure is only limited since we finally conclude that $[a_1, a_2, a_3] \succ (S) a_8$, $a_8 \succ (S) a_7$, $a_4 \succ (S) a_5$ and $a_5 \succ (S) a_9$.

Let us also note that we would have obtained a similar result starting with the transitive closure $\hat{S}$ of S instead of S. Observe that, simply taking $\succsim(S) = \hat{S}$, would have probably been a better choice in this example.

The final result of the ranking procedure is obtained by taking the intersection of two weak orders. Since it is well-known that there are reflexive and transitive relations that cannot be obtained in such a way (Dushnik and Miller, 1941), this procedure is not faithful. We leave the proof that this procedure is indeed neutral and monotonic to the reader (this is detailed in Vincke, 1992).

4.4.3.2 Copeland Scores

We have seen that the procedure suggested in ELECTRE II does not satisfy all the requirements we intuitively would like to see satisfied. A simpler ranking procedure consists in rank ordering the elements in A according to their Copeland scores, i.e., the number of alternatives that they beat minus the number of alternatives that beat them. With Example 4.6, this would, abusing notation, give the weak order:

$$a_1 \succ a_8 \succ [a_2, a_3, a_4, a_6, a_7] \succ a_5 \succ a_9.$$

We cannot expect faithfulness with such a procedure, since the result of the procedure is obviously complete (note that the procedure treats indifference and incomparability similarly). On the other hand, such a procedure is neutral and monotonic.

The ranking procedure based on Copeland scores was characterized by Rubinstein (1980) (for the case of tournaments, i.e., complete and antisymmetric relations) and Henriet (1985) (for the case of complete relations). It is not difficult to extend Henriet's result to cover the case of an arbitrary reflexive relation (see Bouyssou, 1992). The main distinctive characteristic of this ranking procedure is that it is insensitive to the presence of circuits in S since the contribution of any circuit to the Copeland scores of the alternatives in the circuit is always zero.

Ranking procedures based on scores are quite common as soon as one deals with valued binary relations (a topic that is outside the scope of the present text). Let us simply mention here that the "net flow" score used in the PROMETHEE method (Brans and Vincke, 1985) can be seen as an extension of the Copeland score to the valued case (Bouyssou, 1992) (see Chap. 19). Other scores, e.g., scores that do not make use of the cardinal properties of the valuations can be envisaged (Bouyssou and Pirlot, 1997). Other ways of using scores are considered in Dias and Lamboray (2010).

4.4.3.3 Ranking by Repeated Choice

A possible way of combining the simplicity of such a ranking procedure with a move towards faithfulness consists in using the Copeland scores iteratively to build two weak orders T_1 and T_2. This would consist here in building the first equivalence class of a weak order T_1 with the alternatives having the highest Copeland scores, and iterating the procedures after having removed the already-ranked alternatives. For the relation in Example 4.6, we would obtain:

$$a_1 T_1 [a_2, a_4, a_8] T_1 a_6 T_1 a_7 T_1 [a_3, a_5, a_9].$$

Using a dual principle, we could also build a weak order T_2 the last equivalence class of which consists of alternatives having minimal Copeland scores and reiterate the process on the set of unranked alternatives. This would yield:

$$[a_1, a_2, a_3, a_8] T_2 a_4 T_2 a_6 T_2 [a_5, a_7] T_2 a_9.$$

Taking the intersection of these two weak orders is a much simplified version of the ranking procedure implemented in ELECTRE III (Roy, 1978). This leads to:

$$a_1 \succ [a_2, a_8] \succ a_4 \succ a_6 \succ a_7 \succ a_5 \succ a_9,$$
$$[a_2, a_8] \succ a_3 \succ a_5.$$

Such a result does not seem to lead us closer to an adequate restitution of the uncertain positions of a_8 and a_5 within S. Furthermore, as observed in Example 4.2, such a ranking procedure is not monotonic, which seems to be a serious shortcoming.

4.4.4 Sorting Procedures

We have seen that the lack of transitivity and/or completeness raised serious difficulties when it comes to devising choosing and ranking procedures. These difficulties are somewhat less serious here. This is because, with sorting procedures, the assignment of an alternative only depends on its comparison to carefully selected reference actions defining the categories. The use of such reference points implies that, contrary to the case of choice and ranking procedures, the distinction between the phase of building a relation S and then using this relation in order to reach conclusions is blurred with the sorting problem statement. Reference points are used from the beginning and the relation S is mainly used to compare the alternatives in A to these reference points.

Early attempts to propose sorting procedures are Massaglia and Ostanello (1991), Moscarola and Roy (1977) and Roy (1981). A more general approach to the problem was suggested in Roy and Bouyssou (1993) and Yu (1992) with the so-called ELECTRE TRI approach that we present below.

4.4.4.1 An Overview of ELECTRE TRI

We consider the case of r ordered categories $C^1, C^2, \ldots, C^r$, with C^r containing the most desirable alternatives. We suppose, for the moment, that each category C^k is delimited by a limiting profile π^k. It is not restrictive to suppose that π^{k+1} strictly dominates[2] π^k, for all k. Furthermore, we can always find an alternative π^{r+1} that

[2]That is, π^{k+1} is at least as good as π^k on all criteria and strictly better on some criterion.

strongly dominates[3] all other alternatives in A and, conversely, an alternative π^1 that is strongly dominated by all other alternatives.

How can we use a preference relation between the alternatives in A and the set of limiting profiles to define a sorting procedure? Intuitively, since π^k is the lower limit of category C^k, we can apply the following two rules:

- if an alternative a is preferred to π^k, it should at least belong to category C^k,
- if π^k is preferred to a, a should at most belong to category C^{k-1},

the case in which a is indifferent to π^k is dealt with conventionally depending on the definition of the limiting profiles π^k.

When the relation S is complete and transitive, these two rules lead to unambiguously assign each alternative to a single category.

The situation is somewhat more complex when S is intransitive or incomplete. When S is compatible with the dominance relation (which is not a very restrictive hypothesis), as we have supposed that π^k strictly dominates π^{k-1}, it is possible to show (see Roy and Bouyssou, 1993, , Chap. 5) that when an alternative a is compared to the set of limiting profiles $\pi^1, \pi^2 \dots, \pi^{r+1}$, three distinct situations can arise:

1. $\pi^{r+1} P a, \pi^r P a, \dots, \pi^{k+1} P a, a P \pi^k, a P \pi^{k-1}, \dots, a P \pi^1$. In such a case, there is little doubt on how to assign a to one of $C^1, C^2, \dots, C^r$. Since $a P \pi^k$, a should be assigned at least to category C^k. But since $\pi^{k+1} P a$, a should be assigned at most to C^k. Hence, a should belong to C^k.
2. $\pi^{r+1} P a$, $\pi^{r+2} P a, \dots,$ $\pi^{\ell+1} P a$, $a I \pi^\ell$, $a I \pi^{\ell-1}, \dots,$ $a I \pi^{k+1}$, $a P \pi^k, \dots,$ $a P \pi^1$. The situation is here more complex. Since $\pi^{\ell+1} P a$, alternative a must be assigned at most to category C^ℓ. Similarly since $a P \pi^k$, a must be assigned at least to category C^k.

   The fact that a is indifferent to several consecutive limiting profiles is probably a sign that the definition of the categories is too precise with respect to the binary relation that is used by the sorting procedure: the profiles are too close to one another. This would probably call for a redefinition of the categories and/or for a different choice for S. In such a situation, an optimistic attitude consists in assigning a to the highest possible category, i.e., C^ℓ. A pessimistic attitude would assign a to C^k.
3. $\pi^{r+1} P a, \pi^r P a, \dots, \pi^{\ell+1} P a, a J \pi^\ell, a J \pi^{\ell-1}, \dots, a J \pi^{k+1}, a P \pi^k, \dots, a P \pi^1$. In this situation, a is incomparable to several consecutive profiles. This is a sign that, although we are sure that a must be assigned at most to category C^ℓ and at least to category C^k, the relation S does not provide enough information to opt for a category within this interval. Again, an optimistic attitude in such a situation consists in assigning a to the highest possible category, i.e., C^ℓ. A pessimistic attitude would be to assign a to C^k.

[3]That is, it is strictly better on all criteria.

The assignment procedure described above is the one introduced in ELECTRE TRI (Roy and Bouyssou, 1993; Yu, 1992) in which a is assigned to one of $C^1, C^2, \ldots, C^r$ using an optimistic procedure and a pessimistic procedure. Alternative a is always assigned to a higher category when using the optimistic procedure than when using the pessimistic procedure.

When S is identical to a dominance relation, the optimistic procedure suggested above coincides with a disjunctive sorting procedure. In fact a will be assigned to C^ℓ as soon as $\pi^{\ell+1} P a$ and $Not[\pi^\ell P a]$, which means that ℓ is the highest category such that, on some criterion $i \in N$, a is better than π^ℓ. Conversely, the pessimistic procedure coincides with a conjunctive assignment strategy: a will be assigned to C^k as soon as $Not[a P \pi^{k+1}]$ and $a P \pi^k$, which amounts to saying that k is the lowest category such that a dominates π^k.

It is worth noting that although the authors of this method have coupled this procedure with a particular definition of S (a crisp relation based on a concordance discordance principle), it can be applied to any relation that is compatible with a dominance relation.

An axiomatic analysis of ELECTRE TRI was recently proposed in Bouyssou and Marchant (2007a,b). For applications of ELECTRE TRI, see for instance Chaps. 9 and 7

4.4.4.2 Implementation of ELECTRE TRI

The ELECTRE TRI procedure described above supposes that the analyst has defined:

- the limiting profile π^k for each category C^k,
- the parameters involved in the definition of S: weights, indifference and preference thresholds, veto thresholds.

This is overly demanding in most applications involving the use of a sorting procedure. In many cases however, it is possible to obtain examples of alternatives that should be assigned to a given category. Like in the UTADIS method described earlier (see Sect. 4.3.3), one may use a "learning by examples" strategy to assign a value to these parameters. Several strategies for doing this were investigated in Dias and Mousseau (2006), Dias et al. (2002), Mousseau et al. (2001), Mousseau and Słowiński (1998), and Ngo The and Mousseau (2002). In Dias et al. (2002) and Dias and Mousseau (2003) a way to derive robust conclusions with ELECTRE TRI on the basis of several relations S is suggested. This shows that the analysis in Sect. 4.3 can be applied to preference models that are not based on a value function. An approach to the derivation of robust conclusions with ELECTRE TRI based on Monte-Carlo simulation is presented in Tervonen et al. (2009).

4.5 Conclusion

The difficulties presented in Sect. 4.4 raise the question of how to analyse and compare procedures designed to build recommendations. We would like to conclude with some thoughts on this point. Two main routes can be followed. The first one (see, e.g., Bouyssou and Vincke, 1997; Vincke, 1992) consists in defining a list of properties that seem "desirable" for such a technique (for example, never select a dominated alternative or respond to the improvement of an alternative in the expected way). Given such a list of properties one may then try:

- to analyse whether or not they are satisfied by a number of techniques,
- to establish "impossibility theorems", i.e., subsets of properties that cannot be simultaneously fulfilled,
- to determine, given the above-mentioned impossibility theorems, the techniques that satisfy most properties.

The second one (see, e.g., Bouyssou, 1992; Bouyssou and Perny, 1992; Bouyssou and Pirlot, 1997; Pirlot, 1995) consists in trying to find a list of properties that would "characterize" a given technique, i.e., a list of properties that this technique would be the only one to satisfy. This allows to emphasize the specific features of an exploitation technique and, thus, to compare it more easily with others.

These two types of analysis are not unrelated: ideally they should merge at the end, the characterizing properties exhibited by the second type of analysis being parts of the list of "desirable" properties used in the first type of analysis. Both types of analysis have their own problems. In the first, the main problem consists in defining the list of "desirable" properties. These properties should indeed cover every aspect of what seems to be constitutive of an "appropriate" technique. In the second, the characterizing properties will only be useful if they have a clear and simple interpretation, which may not always be the case when analysing a complex technique. We do hope that such analyses will continue to develop.

Let us finally mention that we have restricted our attention to procedures that only operate on the basis of the relation S. In particular, this excludes the use of some "reference points", i.e., of alternatives playing a particular role, as advocated by Dubois et al. (2003). When such reference points are taken into account, the separation between the phases of building a relation S and exploiting it in order to build a choice set is blurred. Indeed, it is then tempting to compare alternatives only to the reference points and not amongst themselves. Such approaches may offer an interesting alternative to the procedures presented above. They have not been worked out in much detail to date. In particular, the selection in practice of appropriate reference points does not seem to be an obvious task.

References

Bana e Costa, C. A. (1986). A multicriteria decision aid methodology to deal with conflictuous situation on weights. *European Journal of Operational Research, 26*, 22–34.

Bana e Costa, C. A. (1988). A methodology for sensitivity analysis in three-criteria problems: a case study in municipal management. *European Journal of Operational Research, 33*, 159–173.

Barthélemy, J. -P., Guénoche, A., & Hudry, O. (1989). Median linear orders: heuristics and a branch and bound algorithm. *European Journal of Operational Research, 42*, 313–325.

Berge, C. (1970). *Graphes et hypergraphes*. Paris: Dunod.

Bisdorff, R., Meyer, P., & Roubens, M. (2008). RUBIS: a bipolar-valued outranking method for the choice problem. *4OR. A Quarterly Journal of Operations Rsearch, 6*(2), 143–165.

Bouyssou, D. (1992). Ranking methods based on valued preference relations: a characterization of the net flow network. *European Journal of Operational Research, 60*, 61–67.

Bouyssou, D. (1996). Outranking relations: do they have special properties? *Journal of Multi-Criteria Decision Analysis, 5*, 99–111.

Bouyssou, D., & Marchant, T. (2007a). An axiomatic approach to noncompensatory sorting methods in MCDM, I: the case of two categories. *European Journal of Operational Research, 178*(1), 217–245.

Bouyssou, D., & Marchant, T. (2007b). An axiomatic approach to noncompensatory sorting methods in MCDM, II: more than two categories. *European Journal of Operational Research, 178*(1), 246–276.

Bouyssou, D., Marchant, T., Pirlot, M., Tsoukiàs, A., & Vincke, P. (2006). *Evaluation and decision models: Stepping stones for the analyst*. Boston: Springer.

Bouyssou, D., & Perny, P. (1992). Ranking methods for valued preference relations: a characterization of a method based on entering and leaving flows. *European Journal of Operational Research, 61*, 186–194.

Bouyssou, D., & Pirlot, M. (1997). Choosing and ranking on the basis of fuzzy preference relations with the "min in favor". In G. Fandel, & T. Gal (Eds.), *Multiple criteria decision making*. Proceedings of the Twelfth International Conference, Hagen (Germany) (pp. 115–127). Heidelberg: Springer.

Bouyssou, D., & Vincke, P. (1997). Ranking alternatives on the basis of preference relations: a progress report with special emphasis on outranking relations. *Journal of Multi-Criteria Decision Analysis, 6*, 77–85.

Brans, J. -P., & Vincke, P. (1985). A preference ranking organisation method (The PROMETHEE method for multiple criteria decision-making). *Management Science, 31*(6), 647–656.

Charnetski, J., & Soland, R. (1978). Multiple-attribute decision making with partial information: the comparative hypervolume criterion. *Naval Research Logistics Quarterly, 25*, 279–288.

Charon, I., & Hudry, O. (2007). A survey on the linear ordering problem for weighted or unweighted tournaments. *4OR, 5*(1), 5–60.

Dias, L., & Mousseau, V. (2003). IRIS: a DSS for multiple criteria sorting problems. *Journal of Multi-Criteria Decision Analysis, 12*, 285–298.

Dias, L. C., & Lamboray, C. (2010). Extensions of the prudence principle to exploit a valued outranking relation. *European Journal of Operational Research, 201*(3), 828–837.

Dias, L. C., & Mousseau, V. (2006). Inferring ELECTRE's veto-related parameters from outranking examples. *European Journal of Operational Research, 170*(1), 172–191.

Dias, L. C., Mousseau, V., Figueira, J., & Clímaco, J. N. (2002). An aggregation/disaggregation approach to obtain robust conclusions with ELECTRE TRI. *European Journal of Operational Research, 138*, 332–348.

Dubois, D., Fargier, H., Perny, P., & Prade, H. (2003). A characterization of generalized concordance rules in multicriteria decision-making. *International Journal of Intelligent Systems, 18*(7), 751–774.

Dushnik, B., & Miller, E. (1941). Partially ordered sets. *American Journal of Mathematics, 63*, 600–610.

Dutta, B., & Laslier, J. -F. (1999). Comparison functions and choice correspondences. *Social Choice and Welfare, 16*, 513–532.
Fishburn, P. C. (1977). Condorcet social choice functions. *SIAM Journal on Applied Mathematics, 33*, 469–489.
Greco, S., Figueira, J., & Słowiński, R. (2009). Building a set of additive value functions representing a reference preorder and intensities of preference: GRIP method. *European Journal of Operational Research, 195*(2), 460–486.
Greco, S., Mousseau, V., & Słowiński, R. (2008). Ordinal regression revisited: multiple criteria ranking using a set of additive value functions. *European Journal of Operational Research, 191*(2), 415–435.
Greco, S., Mousseau, V., & Słowiński, R. (2010). Multiple criteria sorting with a set of additive value functions. *European Journal of Operational Research, 207*(3), 1455–1470.
Henriet, D. (1985). The Copeland choice function: an axiomatic characterization. *Social Choice and Welfare, 2*, 49–64.
Jacquet-Lagrèze, É. (1995). An application of the UTA discriminant model for the evaluation of R&D projects. In P. Pardalos, Y. Siskos, & C. Zopounidis (Eds.), *Advances in multicriteria analysis* (pp. 203–211). Dordrecht: Kluwer.
Jacquet-Lagrèze, É., & Siskos, J. (1982). Assessing a set of additive utility functions for multicriteria decision making: the UTA method. *European Journal of Operational Research, 10*, 151–164.
Lahdelma, R., Hokkanen, J., & Salminen, P. (1998). SMAA - stochastic multiobjective acceptability analysis. *European Journal of Operational Research, 106*(1), 137–143.
Laslier, J. -F. (1997). *Tournament solutions and majority voting*. Berlin: Springer.
Massaglia, R., & Ostanello, A. (1991). N-Tomic: a support system for multicriteria segmentation problems. In P. Korhonen, A. Lewandowski, & J. Wallenius (Eds.), *Multiple criteria decision support*. LNEMS (Vol. 356, pp. 167–174). IIASA. Heidelberg: Springer.
McGarvey, D. C. (1953). A theorem on the construction of voting paradoxes. *Econometrica, 21*, 608–610.
Moscarola, J., & Roy, B. (1977). Procédure automatique d'examen de dossiers fondée sur une segmentation trichotomique en présence de critères multiple. *RAIRO / Operations Research, 11*(2), 145–173.
Mousseau, V., Figueira, J., & Naux, J. P. (2001). Using assignment examples to infer weights for ELECTRE TRI method: some experimental results. *European Journal of Operational Research, 130*, 263–275.
Mousseau, V., & Słowiński, R. (1998). Inferring an ELECTRE TRI model from assignment examples. *Journal of Global Optimization, 12*, 157–174.
Ngo The, A., & Mousseau, V. (2002). Using assignment examples to infer category limits for the ELECTRE TRI method. *Journal of Multi-Criteria Decision Analysis, 11*(1), 29–43.
Peris, J. E., & Subiza, B. (1999). Condorcet choice correspondences for weak tournaments. *Social Choice and Welfare, 16*, 217–231.
Pirlot, M. (1995). A characterisation of 'min' as a procedure for exploiting valued preference relations and related results. *Journal of Multi-Criteria Decision Analysis, 4*, 37–56.
Roy, B. (1968). Classement et choix en présence de points de vue multiples (la méthode ELECTRE). *RIRO, 2*, 57–75.
Roy, B. (1969/1970). *Algèbre moderne et théorie des graphes orientées vers les sciences économiques et sociales* (Vols. I and II). Paris: Dunod.
Roy, B. (1978). ELECTRE III: un algorithme de classement fondé sur une représentation floue des préférences en présence de critères multiples. *Cahiers du CERO, 20*, 3–24.
Roy, B. (1981). A multicriteria analysis for trichotomic segmentation problems. In P. Nijkamp, & J. Spronk (Eds.), *Multiple criteria analysis: Operational methods* (pp. 245–257). Aldershot: Gower Publishing Company.
Roy, B. (1996). *Multicriteria methodology for decision aiding*. Dordrecht: Kluwer. Original version in French (1985). "*Méthodologie multicritère d'aide à la décision*. Paris: Economica

Roy, B. (1998). A missing link in OR-DA: robustness analysis. *Foundations of Computing and Decision Sciences, 23*(3), 141–160.
Roy, B. (2010). Robustness in operational research and decision aiding: a multi-faceted issue. *European Journal of Operational Research, 200*(3), 629–638.
Roy, B., & Bertier, P. (1973). La méthode ELECTRE II: une application au media-planning. In M. Ross (Ed.), *OR'72* (pp. 291–302). Amsterdam: North-Holland.
Roy, B., & Bouyssou, D. (1993). *Aide multicritère à la décision: méthodes et cas*. Paris: Economica.
Roy, B., & Skalka, J. -M. (1984). ELECTRE IS: aspects méthodologiques et guide d'utilisation. Technical Report. Paris: Université Paris Dauphine (Document du LAMSADE, 30).
Rubinstein, A. (1980). Ranking the participants in a tournament. *SIAM Journal of Applied Mathematics, 38*, 108–111.
Schwartz, T. (1986). *The logic of collective choice*. New York: Columbia University Press.
Siskos, J. (1982). A way to deal with fuzzy preferences in multi-criteria decision problems. *European Journal of Operational Research, 10*, 314–324.
Tervonen, T., Figueira, J. R., Lahdelma, R., Almeida-Dias, J., & Salminen, P. (2009). A stochastic method for robustness analysis in sorting problems. *European Journal of Operational Research, 192*, 236–242.
van den Brink, R., & Gilles, R. P. (2003). Ranking by outdegress for directed graphs. *Discrete Mathematics, 271*(1–3), 261–270.
Vincke, P. (1992). Exploitation of a crisp relation in a ranking problem. *Theory and Decision, 32*, 221–240.
von Neumann, J., & Morgenstern, O. (1947). *Theory of games and economic behavior* (2nd ed.). Princeton: Princeton University Press.
Yu, W. (1992). *Aide multicritère à la décision dans le cadre de la problématique du tri: concepts, méthodes et applications*. Thèse de doctorat, Université Paris Dauphine, Paris.
Zopounidis, C., & Doumpos, M. (2000a). Building additive utilities for multi-group hierarchical discrimination: the MHDIS method. *Optimization Methods & Software, 14*(3), 219–240.
Zopounidis, C., & Doumpos, M. (2000b). PREFDIS: a multicriteria decision support system for sorting decision problems. *Computers & Operations Research, 27*(7–8), 779–797.
Zopounidis, C., & Doumpos, M. (2001). A preference disaggregation decision support system for financial classification problems. *European Journal of Operational Research, 130*(2), 402–413.
Zopounidis, C., & Doumpos, M. (2002). Multicriteria classification and sorting methods: a literature review. *European Journal of Operational Research, 138*(2), 229–246.

Part II
Case Studies of MCDA Applications

Chapter 5
The EURO 2004 Best Poster Award: Choosing the Best Poster in a Scientific Conference

Raymond Bisdorff

Abstract The chapter concerns the attribution of the EURO Best Poster Award at the 20th EURO Conference, held in Rhodes, July 2004. We present the historical decision making process leading to the selection of the winner, followed by a thorough discussion of the constructed outranking models and of the best choice recommendation.

Introduction

In this chapter, we report the elaboration of a recommendation for selecting the winner in a competition for the *EURO Best Poster Award* (EBPA[1]) at the EURO 2004 Conference in Rhodes (Greece). From an MCDA point of view, the application discussed here concerns a *unique best choice* decision problem based on multiple ordinal performance assessments given by the EBPA jury members, i.e. a multiple criteria group best choice decision problem.

The initiator of the EBPA, i.e. the Programme and Organisation Committees of the EURO 2004 Conference nominated five members in the award jury and fixed in advance four performance criteria: *Scientific Quality*, *Contribution to Theory and Practice of OR*, *Originality*, and *Presentation Quality*, to be taken into account in decreasing order of significance for selecting the EBPA winner. The call for participation in the EBPA resulted eventually in a pool of 13 poster submissions. Unfortunately, being quite busy at the conference, not all jury members had the possibility to inspect and evaluate all the competing posters. As a result the EBPA jury was left with an incomplete performance tableau showing some irreducibly

[1] A glossary with abbreviations and symbols is provided at the end of the chapter.

R. Bisdorff (✉)
Faculty of Science, Technology and Communication, Computer Science and Communication Research Unit, University of Luxembourg, 6, rue Richard Coudenhove-Kalergi, 1359 Luxembourg, Luxembourg
e-mail: raymond.bisdorff@uni.lu

R. Bisdorff et al. (eds.), *Evaluation and Decision Models with Multiple Criteria*, International Handbooks on Information Systems,
DOI 10.1007/978-3-662-46816-6_5

missing values. With the help of an outranking based decision aiding process, the EBPA jury could nevertheless agree on a unanimous final decision which was presented and scientifically argumented at the closing session of the EURO 2004 Conference.

The goal of this chapter is to present, comment and redo this decision aiding process from an a posteriori—2010—perspective.[2] We therefore, first, report the historical case with its decision making process,—the involved actors, and—in particular, the actual decision aiding process with the historical unique best choice recommendation. We continue in a second section with discussing and analyzing more specifically the modelling of the EBPA jury's preferences. Finally, we propose a (re)building of the best choice recommendation with a particular focus on its robustness.

5.1 The Historical Case

In this first section we are going to present in detail the historical decision making process, followed by a thorough review of all the objects appearing in this decision making process. We close this section with a view on the decision aiding process actually put into practice by the chair of the EBPA jury.

5.1.1 *The Decision Making Process*

The decision making process we are going to describe here covers a period of approximately 3 months: from May to July 2004. We may grosso modo distinguish six steps.

Step 1: Defining and Configuring the Decision Problem

Apart from the traditional contributed and invited presentations, the Programme Committee (PC) of the 20th European Conference on Operational Research (EURO 2004) invited for special *discussion presentations*—a new kind of EURO K[3] conference participation consisting in a 30 min presentation in front of a poster in the style of natural sciences conferences. In order to promote this new type of poster presentations, the EURO 2004 conference organizers decided to attribute a special

[2]The seminal articles (Bisdorff et al., 2006, 2008) of the RUBIS decision aiding methodology date from 2006 and 2008.

[3]EURO K conferences, organised every 3 years, are the main dissemination instrument of EURO—the Federation of European Operational Research Societies, see http://www.euro-online.org.

EURO Best Poster Award consisting of a diploma and a prize of 1,000€ to the best poster. The actual selection procedure was dedicated to a special EBPA jury composed of three members of the Conference Programme Committee including the PC chair[4] and two members from the Organizing Committee. Furthermore, four selection criteria, in decreasing order of significance, were recommended: scientific quality, contribution to OR theory and practice, originality, and presentation quality.

Step 2: Collecting the Competing Posters

Besides invited and contributed paper submissions, the EURO 2004 Programme Committee had called for discussion presentations based on posters to be held in parallel in an exhibition space in the main lobby of the conference. Each presentation scheduled in such a session lasted 30 min, whereas the poster was informally exhibited during a whole day (see Fig. 5.1). At the end of the day all the posters were changed. Among the contributions suitable for a discussion presentation session we may distinguish contributions by authors willing to present a poster or to present more than one paper, contributions selected by the Programme Committee, and European Working Group promotional presentations. Only the first three types of contributions were eligible for the best poster award.

Eventually 99 discussion presentations were scheduled at the EURO XX Conference in eight sessions: MA (Monday 9:00–10:30), MC (Monday 14:00–15:30), MD (Monday 16:00–17:30), TA (Tuesday 9:00–10:30), TC (Tuesday 14:00–15:30), TD

Fig. 5.1 The poster exhibition during the conference

[4]The author of this chapter.

(Tuesday 16:00–17:30), WA (Wednesday 9:00–10:30) and WC (Wednesday 14:00–15:30) in separated time slots of 30 min parallel to the 15 or 16 regular organized and contributed session streams. They gave the authors the possibility to present and discuss their ongoing work with their poster illustration in the background. As illustrated in Fig. 5.1, the posters attracted a large and interested audience.

Step 3: Gathering the Performance Assessments

The actual evaluation of the competing posters by the five jury members was done at the occasion of the discussion presentations in front of the poster. The grading on the four selection criteria, recommended by the EBPA organizer, was guided by an evaluation sheet template provided by the jury chair (see Fig. 5.2).[5]

template

EURO Best Poster Award 2004

Evaluation sheet

Evaluator:

Evaluation marks should be given from 0 (very weak) – 10 (excellent)

authID	Scientific quality	Contribution to theory or practice of OR	Originality	Presentation quality
P_01				
P_02				
P_03				
P_04				
P_05				
P_06				
P_07				
P_08				
P_09				
P_10				
P_11				
P_12				
P_13				

Fig. 5.2 The evaluation sheet used by the jury members

[5]Here the evaluation sheet template has been made anonymous. The real instance showed the actual coordinates of the poster authors instead of the abstract identifier shown here.

Step 4: Aggregating all the Preferential Information

Considering the ordinal nature of the recommended grading scale, the chair of the EBPA jury decided to follow an ordinal aggregation method and to aggregate the jury members' evaluations into a global valued outranking relation, representing the bipolar valued characterisation of pairwise "at least as good" preference situations on the set of competing posters. All jury members were considered equi-significant whereas decreasing integer significance weights (from 4 to 1) were allocated, in accordance with the EBPA organizers regulations, to the four recommended selection criteria.

Step 5: Selecting the Best Poster

The EBPA jury was asked to select the best—in the sense of the selection criteria retained by the Programme Committee—out of the 13 competing posters on the basis of their grades as gathered in the individual evaluation sheets. In July 2004, the jury unanimously accepted the best choice recommendation elaborated by their chair on the basis of the proposed global pairwise outranking relation and consequently attributed the EURO Best Poster Award 2004 to poster p_{10}, a poster with title: *Political Districting via Weighted Voronoï Regions* and authored by Federica RICCA, Bruno SIMEONE and Isabella LARI from the University of Rome "La Sapienza".

Step 6: Auditing the Result

The report on the selection procedure of the EBPA 2004 was eventually presented by the Programme Committee Chair at the closing session of the EURO 2004 conference. The audience positively acknowledged the winner and the arguments which led the jury to particularly select this poster.

Before looking more precisely at the actual decision aiding process which guided the EBPA jury in the selection procedure, we review, first, the formal MCDA data appearing in this application.

5.1.2 The Formal Data of the Decision Problem

We may distinguish a list of general MCDA data that can be identified in the decision making process above.

The Actors and Stakeholders

1. The EBPA responsible organizer: in fact the joint EURO 2004 Programme and Organising Committees;
2. The EBPA jury: The Programme Committee nominated a jury of five members, three members of the Programme Committee (J. Blazewicz, R. Bisdorff (chair), G. Wäscher) and two members of the Organising Committee (N. Matsatsinis, C. Zopounidis), to evaluate the submitted posters on the basis of the proposed selection criteria and eventually attribute the award to the best submission. The chair of the award jury acted as decision analyst.
3. The authors having submitted their poster to the EBPA;
4. The conference participants: witness of the eventual winner and potentially the actual auditor of the overall decision making process.

The Potential Decision Alternatives

The Conference organizers offered the EURO Best Poster Award EBPA 2004 with the goal to encourage discussion presentations based on posters. This award, granted during the Closing session, consisted in a diploma and a prize of 1,000€. All accepted discussion presentations authors were invited to compete for the EBPA. In order to participate the authors had to submit a reduced electronic PDF version of their poster before June 15th 2004. Thirteen candidates actually submitted an abstract and an image of their poster in due time. These were the potential decision alternatives for the best choice decision problem under review, denoted A in the sequel.

The subjects of the competing posters concern:—a variety of traditional OR topics like inventory planning and project management tools;—discrete mathematics problems with set covering and dice games;—applications in software development, in data and information systems, in the wood industry, in higher education, in the banking industry, and in political districting.

The Selection Criteria

To evaluate the submitted poster images, the Programme Committee retained the officially recommended selection criteria: *Scientific Quality* (sq), *Contribution to OR Theory and/or Practice* (tp), *Originality* (or) and *Presentation Quality* (pq) in decreasing order of importance.

The Performance Tableau

The EBPA jury members were invited to listen to the discussion presentations and evaluate the corresponding poster. In Table 5.1 are shown, for instance, the evaluation marks given by three jury members.

Table 5.1 Evaluation marks given by three jury members j_1, j_2 and j_3

	Scientific quality			Theory or practice of OR			Originality			Presentation quality		
Poster ID	j_1	j_2	j_3	j_1	j_2	j_3	j_1	j_2	j_3	j_1	j_2	j_3
p_1	4	7	5	4	7	6	4	7	6	4	7	5
p_2	/	1	6	/	1	7	/	1	8	/	3	9
p_3	6	6	7	8	9	7	6	7	7	6	6	9
p_4	8	9	9	7	8	6	8	8	7	8	6	7
p_5	8	6	8	8	7	9	8	5	7	8	8	8
p_6	5	5	5	5	7	5	5	5	5	5	7	6
p_7	6	5	6	7	8	7	6	5	5	8	8	5
p_8	4	/	5	4	/	5	4	/	7	7	/	10
p_9	/	/	5	/	/	5	/	/	7	/	/	10
p_{10}	9	9	8	9	9	9	9	9	9	9	10	10
p_{11}	6	9	8	6	8	6	6	9	7	8	9	8
p_{12}	4	5	7	4	5	7	4	3	7	4	5	3
p_{13}	4	8	8	4	8	8	4	6	7	4	9	9

We may notice that j_1 expressed himself moderately by using only a reduced set of ordinal values: from 4 (lowest) to 9 (highest). Jury member j_2 used nearly the whole range of the given ordinal performance scale, from 1 (lowest) to 10 (highest), whereas j_3 used almost only the upper part (from 5 to 10) of the performance scale. Beside this apparent incommensurability of the jury members' ordinal performance evaluations, a further serious problem represents the fact that not all five jury members did provide marks for all the competing posters. Jury member j_1, for instance, did not mark posters p_2 and p_9, whereas j_2 did not mark posters p_8 and again p_9 (see the slash (/) denotation in Table 5.1). This lack of information results from the fact that some jury members, due to availability constraints during the conference days, could not attend the public presentation of one or the other poster. All the posters in competition were, however, evaluated by at least two members of the award jury (see Appendix "The Complete Performance Tableau").

Finally, we may have a detailed look at the actual decision aiding process that was guiding the selection procedure of the EBPA jury.

5.1.3 The Decision Aiding Process

In order to assist the EBPA jury in selecting the winner among the competing posters, the chair of the EBPA jury, a professional decision aid specialist, deployed a standard multiple criteria base decision aiding procedure. Four steps of this historical procedure are worthwhile to be reported here:—guiding the individual evaluation process of the jury members;—aggregating the collected individual preferences into a global pairwise outranking relation;—building a unique best poster recommendation (BCR) for the EBPA jury;—and, evaluating the robustness of the proposed BCR.[6]

Guiding the Evaluations of the Jury Members

To harmonize as far as possible the evaluation process, a common evaluation sheet template (see Fig. 5.2) was distributed to all the EBPA jury members. The main purpose of this template was to guide the jury members in their individual grading of the competing posters.

The filled in evaluation sheet for jury member 2 is shown in Fig. 5.3. It is worthwhile noticing the missing data; some posters were not evaluated by all the jury members. Jury member 2, for instance, did not provide evaluations for posters 8 and 9 (see Fig. 5.3).

jury member 2

EURO Best Poster Award 2004

Evaluation sheet

Evaluator: jury member 2

Evaluation marks should be given from 0 (very weak) – 10 (excellent)

authID	Scientific quality	Contribution to theory or practice of OR	Originality	Presentation quality
P_01	7	7	6	7
P_02	1	1	1	3
P_03	6	9	7	6
P_04	9	8	8	6
P_05	6	7	5	8
P_06	5	7	5	7
P_07	5	8	5	8
P_08	NA	NA	NA	NA
P_09	NA	NA	NA	NA
P_10	9	9	9	10
P_11	9	8	9	9
P_12	5	5	3	5
P_13	8	8	6	9

Fig. 5.3 Evaluation sheet filled in by the jury member 2

[6]A glossary with abbreviations and symbols is provided at the end of the chapter.

	p01	p02	p03	p04	p05	p06	p07	p08	p09	p10	p11	p12	p13
p01	0.00	16.00	-52.00	-76.00	-8.00	36.00	-32.00	52.00	30.00	-92.00	26.00	-84.00	-44.00
p02	-16.00	0.00	-32.00	-32.00	-32.00	-16.00	-16.00	-20.00	22.00	-52.00	-10.00	-32.00	-48.00
p03	64.00	48.00	0.00	8.00	32.00	96.00	72.00	92.00	38.00	-68.00	62.00	16.00	-8.00
p04	96.00	36.00	24.00	0.00	52.00	96.00	64.00	96.00	38.00	-44.00	50.00	40.00	8.00
p05	28.00	36.00	44.00	-4.00	0.00	100.00	56.00	96.00	38.00	-48.00	50.00	4.00	0.00
p06	8.00	16.00	-80.00	-80.00	-32.00	0.00	-16.00	72.00	30.00	-100.00	26.00	-92.00	-60.00
p07	36.00	44.00	-36.00	-8.00	-40.00	72.00	0.00	64.00	30.00	-80.00	38.00	0.00	-28.00
p08	0.00	20.00	-68.00	-60.00	-40.00	32.00	-20.00	0.00	42.00	-96.00	34.00	-68.00	-48.00
p09	-14.00	-2.00	-30.00	-30.00	-18.00	-2.00	-26.00	-2.00	0.00	-38.00	-22.00	-26.00	-30.00
p10	100.00	60.00	100.00	68.00	100.00	100.00	80.00	100.00	42.00	0.00	62.00	76.00	60.00
p11	42.00	22.00	-26.00	-42.00	-42.00	-14.00	-22.00	18.00	38.00	-62.00	0.00	-38.00	-14.00
p12	96.00	32.00	40.00	24.00	28.00	92.00	56.00	88.00	38.00	-36.00	50.00	0.00	12.00
p13	100.00	52.00	40.00	20.00	60.00	60.00	40.00	92.00	38.00	-4.00	62.00	28.00	0.00

Fig. 5.4 Valued pairwise outranking characteristics (weighted majority margins in the range $-100\,\%$ to $+100\,\%$)

Constructing an Overall Pairwise Outranking Relation

From the five eventually gathered evaluations sheets (see Appendix "The Complete Performance Tableau"), it becomes readily apparent that the collected gradings were all expressed on, in principle, non commensurable ordinal grading scales with eleven grades from 0 (very weak) to 10 (excellent). The chair of the EBPA, being a specialist in the aggregation of non compensating, ordinal and possibly partial preference statements (Bisdorff, 2002), the construction into a global preference on the level of the jury as a whole was done with a specially adapted outranking approach, a forerunner of the RUBIS method (Bisdorff et al., 2008). In accordance with the recommended ranking of the selection criteria, a significance of 4 points was given to the *Scientific Quality*, 3 points to the *Contribution to OR Theory and/or Practice*, 2 point to the *Originality*, and, 1 point to the *Presentation Quality*. All jury members were considered equi-significant. The resulting historical global valued outranking relation is shown in Fig. 5.4. The positive figures denote pairwise "*at least as good as*" situations that are validated by a weighted majority of jury members, whereas the negative figures denote non validated situations.

Building the Best Poster Recommendation

To find now the best poster to recommend for the EBPA, the EBPA jury chair was looking for the smallest subset of posters such that:—every non selected one was positively outranked by at least one of the selected poster (external stability);—and, the selected posters do not outrank each other (internal stability). Such a best choice set corresponds to a dominating kernel of the outranking digraph (see Bisdorff et al., 2006).

The historical global outranking relation luckily delivered a unique outranking kernel: singleton $\{p_{10}\}$, in fact a CONDORCET winner (see Fig. 5.4). Poster p_{10} hence represents in view of the global outranking relation the evident recommendation for the EBPA winner.

Evaluating the Robustness of the Recommendation

It remained however to verify that the result obtained was not, in fact, an artifact of the chosen numerical significance weight vector. Luckily again, the jury chair could prove that his apparent best choice recommendation was only depending on the officially recommended ordered significance of the selection criteria, but not on the effective numerical values used for the construction of the global valued outranking relation (see Bisdorff, 2004).

In the next section, we present and discuss now in detail, the construction of the global preferences of the EBPA jury with the help of an outranking approach.

5.2 Models of Apparent Preferences

Due to both the ordinal character of the performance scales and the presence of missing values, it was not possible, in the limited time span available at the EURO 2004 Conference, to construct the overall preferences of the jury members with a value oriented decision aiding approach. To transform the ordinal marks into commensurable values would have needed a sophisticated preference elicitation procedure involving time consuming interviews of each jury member. Instead, the chair of the jury adopted a more descriptive, order statistics approach, inspired from social choice theory and generally promoted under the name "outranking approach" (see Roy and Bouyssou, 1993). In this section we are presenting in detail how this approach may allow us to model the apparent preferences of the EBPA jury members.

5.2.1 *Pairwise* "at least as good as" *Situations*

Defining Marginal "*at least as good as*" Statements

Let F denote the set of four selection criteria to be taken into account and let J denote the set of five jury members. If we consider, for instance, the evaluation of the posters for jury member j in J with respect to their scientific quality (sq), that is the main criterion for selecting the best poster, we may qualify the validation of pairwise "poster x is at least as good as poster y" situations, denoted $x \succsim_{sq}^{j} y$, with

Table 5.2 Pairwise performance comparisons by jury member j_1 on criterion sq

$r(\succcurlyeq^1_{sq})$	p_1	p_2	p_3	p_4	p_5	p_6	p_7	p_8	p_9	p_{10}	p_{11}	p_{12}	p_{13}
p_1	–	0	−1	−1	−1	−1	−1	+1	0	−1	+1	−1	+1
p_2	0	–	0	0	0	0	0	0	0	0	0	0	0
p_3	+1	0	–	−1	−1	+1	+1	+1	0	−1	+1	+1	+1
p_4	+1	0	+1	–	+1	+1	+1	+1	0	−1	+1	+1	+1
p_5	+1	0	+1	+1	–	+1	+1	+1	0	−1	+1	+1	+1
p_6	+1	0	−1	−1	−1	–	−1	+1	0	−1	+1	−1	+1
p_7	+1	0	+1	−1	−1	+1	–	+1	0	−1	+1	+1	+1
p_8	+1	0	−1	−1	−1	−1	−1	–	0	−1	+1	−1	+1
p_9	0	0	0	0	0	0	0	0	–	0	0	0	0
p_{10}	+1	0	+1	+1	+1	+1	+1	+1	0	–	+1	+1	+1
p_{11}	+1	0	−1	−1	−1	−1	−1	+1	0	−1	–	−1	+1
p_{12}	+1	0	+1	−1	−1	+1	+1	+1	0	−1	+1	–	+1
p_{13}	+1	0	−1	−1	−1	−1	−1	+1	0	−1	+1	−1	–

the help of a bipolar[7] characteristic function $r(x \succcurlyeq^j_{sq} y)$ defined for all couple of posters (x, y) as follows:

$$r(x \succcurlyeq^j_{sq} y) := \begin{cases} +1 & \text{if} \quad g^j_{sq}(x) \geqslant g^j_{sq}(y), \\ -1 & \text{if} \quad g^j_{sq}(x) < g^j_{sq}(y), \\ 0 & \text{otherwise, i.e. when} \\ & g^j_{sq}(x) = \text{'}/\text{'} \text{ or } g^j_{sq}(y) = \text{'}/\text{'}. \end{cases} \tag{5.1}$$

In Formula (5.1), $g^j_{sq}(x)$ and $g^j_{sq}(y)$ represent jury member j's performance evaluation of posters x, respectively y, with respect to preference viewpoint sq. In Table 5.2, we may read for instance that for jury member j_1, posters p_1 and p_8 are each one judged at least as good as the other $\big(r(p_1 \succcurlyeq^{j_1}_{sq} p_8) = r(p_8 \succcurlyeq^{j_1}_{sq} p_1) = +1\big)$. In Table 5.1, we see indeed that j_1 evaluated them equally with value $g^{j_1}_{sq}(p_1) = g^{j_1}_{sq}(p_8) = 4$. We also may note that poster p_1 is in fact not judged at least as good as poster p_3 ($r(p_3 \succcurlyeq^{j_1}_{sq} p_1) = +1$ and $r(p_1 \succcurlyeq^{j_1}_{sq} p_3) = -1$). This time, $g^{j_1}_{sq}(p_3) = 6$ against $g^{j_1}_{sq}(p_1) = 4$. It is also noteworthy that posters p_2 and p_9, as they were not evaluated by this jury member, may not be compared to any of the other posters ($r(x \succcurlyeq^{j_1}_{sq} y) = 0$ for $x \in \{p_2, p_9\}$ and $y \in A - \{p_2, p_p\}$). The trivial reflexive comparison is globally ignored in this analysis.

In general, three different preferential situations may thus be characterised:

- Poster x is *better than* poster y (strict preference): $r(x \succcurlyeq^j_{sq} y) = +1$ and $r(y \succcurlyeq^j_{sq} x) = -1$.

[7] See (Bisdorff, 2002; Bisdorff et al., 2008).

- Poster x is *as good as* poster y (indifference): $r(x \geqslant_{sq}^{j} y) = +1$ and $r(y \geqslant_{sq}^{j} x) = +1$.
- Posters x and y are *mutually incomparable*: $r(x \geqslant_{sq}^{j} y) = 0$ and $r(y \geqslant_{sq}^{j} x) = 0$. Neither a preference, nor an indifference can be validated (indeterminacy).

It is important to notice that the bipolar characterisation $r(\geqslant)$ from A^2 to $\{-1, 0, +1\}$ forgets the actual performance values. The very magnitude of the performance differences is thereby ignored. Only the sign of the difference or a null difference are discriminated. We completely respect hence the purely ordinal character of the given performance measure scales. One may however consider that it is not always sure that a one point difference on a 0 to 10 points scale is really signifying a preference situation for sure. In many real decision aid cases, it is therefore opportune to analyze the actual preference discriminating power of the underlying performance measure scales.

Discriminating Non Equivalent Performances

In Eq. (5.1) we have implicitly assumed that, for all the award jury members $j \in J$, a positive difference of one point on all the performance scales, indicates a clearly better performing situation. Indeed, with $g_{sq}^{j_2}(p_6) = 5$ and $g_{sq}^{j_2}(p_7) = 7$ jury member j_2 may validate that p_7 is at least as good as poster p_6 ($r(p_7 \geqslant_{sq}^{j_2} p_6) = +1$), but, may be, not the converse situation ($r(p_6 \geqslant_{sq}^{j_2} p_7) = -1$). Indeed, in the context of solely ordinal performance evaluations, the actual confirmed preference discrimination threshold is commonly set equal to one ordinal level difference. For the decision aiding practice, it may be opportune, the case given, to assume that a clearly warranted preference situation is only given when a positive difference of at least two ordinal levels is observed. Depending on the actual discrimination of the ordinal performance evaluations, a one level difference may some time be seen as a still more or less equivalent performance, either, supporting, an indifference statement, or, indicating the hesitation between an indifference or a preference statement (see Bisdorff, 2002; Bisdorff et al., 2008).

For each jury member $j \in J$ and each preference point of view $f \in F$, we denote h_f^j, respectively p_f^j (with $0 \leqslant h_f^j < p_f^j \leqslant 10$), the indifference, respectively preference, threshold we may observe on the performance scale of preference point of view f for jury member j. For all couple (x, y) of decision alternatives where we dispose of valid performance evaluations $g_f^j(x)$ and $g_f^j(y)$, we may thus extend the definition of the bipolar-valued characteristic function r of the pairwise "at least as good as" $(x \geqslant_f^j y)$ comparison as follows:

$$r(x \geqslant_f^j y) := \begin{cases} -1 & \text{if} \quad g_f^j(x) - g_f^j(y) \leqslant -p_f^j \\ +1 & \text{if} \quad g_f^j(x) - g_f^j(y) \geqslant -h_f^j \\ 0 & \text{otherwise} \end{cases} \tag{5.2}$$

Table 5.3 Comparing the posters from the *Scientific Quality* (*sq*) point of view

$r(\succcurlyeq_{sq})$	p_1	p_2	p_3	p_4	p_5	p_6	p_7	p_8	p_9	p_{10}	p_{11}	p_{12}	p_{13}
p_1	–	+0.2	−0.2	−0.2.	−0.2	+0.2	−0.4	+0.6	+0.4	−0.2.	+0.2	−0.2.	−0.6
p_2	**−0.2**	–	**−0.6**	**−0.6**	**−0.6**	**−0.2**	**−0.2**	**−0.2**	**0**	**−0.6**	**−0.4**	**−0.6**	**−0.6**
p_3	+0.2	+0.6	–	−0.6	−0.2	+0.2	+0.8	+0.2	+0.4	−0.2.	+0.6	−0.2	+0.6
p_4	**+0.2**	**+0.6**	**+0.6**	–	**+0.6**	**+0.2**	**+0.8**	**+0.2**	**+0.4**	**+0.2**	**+0.6**	**+0.6**	**+0.2**
p_5	+0.2	+0.6	+0.2	−0.2	–	+0.2	+0.8	+0.2	+0.4	−0.2	+0.6	+0.2	+0.2
p_6	+0.2	+0.2	−0.6	−0.6	−0.6	–	+0.8	+0.2	+0.4	−0.2	+0.2	−0.2	−0.6
p_7	+0.4	+0.6	−0.4	−0.4	−0.8	+0.8	–	+0.8	+0.4	−0.8	+0.2	−0.4	−0.4
p_8	+0.2	+0.2	−0.6	−0.6	−0.6	+0.6	0	–	+0.4	−0.2	+0.2	−0.2	−0.6
p_9	0	0	−0.4	−0.4	−0.4	0	−0.4	0	–	−0.4	−0.4	−0.4	−0.4
p_{10}	**+0.2**	**+0.6**	**+0.2**	**+0.2**	**+0.2**	**+0.2**	**+0.8**	**+0.2**	**+0.4**	–	**+0.6**	**+0.6**	**+0.6**
p_{11}	+0.6	+0.4	−0.2	−0.6	−0.6	−0.2	−0.2	+0.2	+0.4	−0.6	–	−0.6	−0.2
p_{12}	+0.2	+0.6	+0.2	−0.2	+0.2	+0.2	+0.8	+0.2	+0.4	+0.2	+0.6	–	+.2
p_{13}	+0.2	+0.6	+0.6	−0.2	+0.6	+0.6	+0.4	+0.2	+0.4	+0.2	+0.6	+0.2	–

Bolded table entries are referred to in the chapter text

If $g^j_f(x)$ or $g^j_f(y)$ are not available, we put $r(x \succcurlyeq^j_f y)$ to the neutral value 0.

In Table 5.1 one may notice for instance that jury member j_2 has evaluated posters p_3, p_4 and p_5 on the criterion *Originality* with 7, 8, respectively 5 points. Suppose now that jury member j_2 admitted on his performance scale a preference threshold of 2 points and an indifference threshold of 0 points. In this case, $r(p_3 \succcurlyeq^{j_2}_{or} p_4)$ becomes 0 as $g^{j_2}_{or}(p_3) - g^{j_2}_{or}(p_4) = 7 - 8 = -1$ which is higher than the negative preference threshold, but lower than the indifference threshold. Whereas, $r(p_5 \succcurlyeq^{j_2}_{or} p_3)$ becomes -1 as $g^{j_2}_{or}(p_5) - g^{j_2}_{or}(p_3) = 5 - 7 = -2$ which is equal to the negative preference threshold. Similarly, $r(p_4 \succcurlyeq^{j_2}_{or} p_3)$ or $r(p_4 \succcurlyeq^{j_2}_{or} p_5)$ would both become $+1$. In case we encounter missing evaluations, as noticed before in Table 5.1, the bipolar characteristic function r will qualify any involved pairwise comparison as indeterminate, i.e. r will always take the neutral value 0.

Considering that we have to take into account the preferences of the five jury members on each one of the four selection criteria, we are in fact confronted in this decision aiding problem with $5 \times 4 = 20$ individual "*at least as good as*" characterisations similar to the one shown in Table 5.3. How to aggregate this information into an overall global preference model will be described step by step hereafter.

5.2.2 Aggregating per Viewpoint or per Jury Member

We will start by marginally aggregating the opinions of all the jury members concerning one specific preference point of view, namely the apparent *Scientific Quality* (*sq*) of the competing posters.

Appreciating the Posters from the *Scientific Quality* Viewpoint

Inspired by social choice theory (Fishburn, 1977; Sen, 1986; Arrow and Raynaud, 1986), we shall take the individual $r(\succcurlyeq_{sq}^{j})$ characterisations of the five members of the award jury as a kind of pairwise voting result and balance the pro votes $(+1)$ against the con votes (-1) of a given "*at least as good*" statement. 0-valued characterisations are counted as abstentions. We thus obtain for the *Scientific Quality* criterion a bipolar characteristic function r of the overall "*poster x is at least as good as poster y*" statement with respect to the *Scientific Quality* viewpoint, denoted $(x \succcurlyeq_{sq} y)$ and defined as follows on each couple $(x, y) \in A^2$:

$$r(x \succcurlyeq_{sq} y) := \sum_{j \in J} \left(\frac{r(x \succcurlyeq_{sq}^{j} y)}{|J|} \right) \tag{5.3}$$

The result of this aggregation operator r is shown in Table 5.3 and which admits the following semantics:

- A value of $+1.0$, respectively -1.0, means that, from the *sq* point of view, all five jury members *unanimously* judge poster x at least as good as poster y, respectively *not* at least as good as poster y.
- A positive value means that, from the *sq* point of view, *more* jury members judge poster x *at least as good as* poster y *than not*.
- A negative value signifies that, from the *sq* point of view, *more* jury members judge poster x *not at least as good as* poster y *than not*.
- The *null* value indicates an *indeterminate* situation, where the positive and the negative votes concerning the pairwise comparison of their scientific quality are balanced, and where no overall pro or con judgment hence can be made apparent.

This bipolarly valued characterisation $r(\succcurlyeq_{sq})$ has a nice order statistical property (see Barbut, 1980). $r(\succsim)$ represents in fact a *median characterisation* between a disjunctive $(\max_{j \in J}[r(\succcurlyeq_{sq}^{j})])$ and a conjunctive $(\min_{j \in J}[r(\succcurlyeq_{sq}^{j})])$ aggregation of the individual characterisations $r(\succcurlyeq_{sq}^{j})$. From an exploratory and descriptive data analysis point of view, the so characterised $\succcurlyeq_{sq}$ relation represents a compromise relation which is at minimal ordinal disagreement with all the individual "*at least as good as*" statements expressed. It gives us a convincing and reliable *central* model of the preferences of the EBPA jury from the *Scientific Quality* point of view. In Table 5.3 we show the result for all pairwise comparisons of the posters. Take for instance the comparison of posters p_4 and p_1, where we notice that $r(p_4 \succcurlyeq_{sq} p_1) = +0.2$ and $r(p_1 \succcurlyeq_{sq} p_4) = -0.2$. Poster p_4 is judged having a better scientific quality than poster p_1 by a majority of jury members. Conversely, poster p_1 is judged having a better scientific quality than poster p_1 only by a minority of jury members. Moreover, as $r(p_4 \succcurlyeq_{sq} p_i) > 0$ for $p_{i \neq 4} \in A$, poster p_4 shows a positive majority margin with all the other posters. A majority of jury members expresses thereby that poster p_4 is at least as good as any of the other posters. A same situation may be verified for poster p_{10}.

Poster p_2 compares, on the contrary, negatively with all the other posters, except poster p_9, with which it appears mutually incomparable. So a majority of jury members express that poster p_2 is *not* at least as good as all the other posters, except for poster p_9.

It is worthwhile noticing here that we obtain this clear result even when jury members j_1 and j_2, did not provide performance evaluations for posters p_2 and p_9. Three jury members out of five have actually not conjointly evaluated this pair of posters and the remaining two jury members are divided in their opinions. Hence we obtain an indeterminate situation: $r(p_2 \succcurlyeq_{sq} p_9) = 0$ and $r(p_9 \succcurlyeq_{sq} p_2) = 0$. Both posters appear incomparable under the available information.

We may in fact compute such a bipolar-valued characterisation of the overall result on each of the four selection criteria and analyze the partial results from each preference point of view. However, we are now more interested in making apparent the overall preferences of each individual jury member by aggregating the comparisons over all the four imposed preference points of view.

Aggregating Individual Opinions

Instead of aggregating the opinions of all jury members with respect to one preference dimension, as we did before, we may also aggregate the opinions of each jury member on all the selection criteria. To do so, we must take into account the hierarchy of significance that the decision problem organizer, i.e. the EURO 2004 Programme and Organising Committees, wished to give the four imposed selection criteria, i.e. $sq \succ tp \succ or \succ pq$. With no precise indications from the jury, the decision analyst fixed somehow arbitrarily the corresponding normalized numerical significance weights to: $w_{sq} = 0.4$, $w_{tp} = 0.3$, $w_{or} = 0.2$, and $w_{pq} = 0.1$. Hence, the total significance is, as required for a normalized significance weight vector, equal to 1.0.

We may now characterise a global "*at least as good as*" relation for each jury member, denoted $\succcurlyeq^j$ for $j = 1$ to 5 and defined in the following way:

$$r(x \succcurlyeq^j y) := \sum_{f \in F} \left(r(x \succcurlyeq^j_f y) \cdot w_f \right) \tag{5.4}$$

Similar to the previous marginal aggregation concerning only the scientific quality of the competing posters, Eq. (5.4) delivers again a median characterisation in between the disjunction or the conjunction of the individual $r(x \succcurlyeq^j_f y)$ characterisations along all selection criteria $f \in F$, but weighted by their significance w_f. Again, the so characterised relation $\succcurlyeq^j$ represents a significant compromise of the individual preference statements of a jury member j taking into account the specific significance of each preference dimension f in $F = \{sq, tp, or, pq\}$.

In Table 5.4 is shown the result for jury member j_3 for instance. One may notice in the upper left corner that $r(p_1 \succcurlyeq^{j_3} p_2) = -1$ and $r(p_2 \succcurlyeq^{j_3} p_1) = +1$. Which

Table 5.4 Overall pairwise comparisons for jury member j_3

$r(\succcurlyeq^j)$	p_1	p_2	p_3	p_4	p_5	p_6	p_7	p_8	p_9	p_{10}	p_{11}	p_{12}	p_{13}
p_1		**−1.0**	−1.0	−0.4	−0.4	+0.8	−0.4	+0.4	+0.4	**−1.0**	−0.8	−0.4	−1.0
p_2	**+1.0**		+0.2	**+0.2**	+0.2	+1.0	+1.0	+0.8	+0.8	**−0.6**	+0.2	+0.2	−0.4
p_3	**+1.0**	**+0.6**		+0.2	+0.2	+1.0	+1.0	+0.8	+0.8	**−1.0**	+1.0	+0.2	−0.4
p_4	**+1.0**	+0.2	+0.2		+0.8	+1.0	+1.0	+0.8	+0.8	**−0.2**	+0.4	+0.8	+0.2
p_5	**+0.4**	−0.2	+0.2	+0.4		+1.0	+0.4	+0.8	+0.8	**−0.2**	+0.4	+0.4	+0.2
p_6	0	−1.0	−1.0	−1.0	−0.4		+0.4	+0.4	+0.4	**−1.0**	−0.8	−1.0	−1.0
p_7	**+0.6**	+0.4	−0.4	−0.4	−0.4	+0.8		+0.4	+0.4	**−1.0**	−0.2	−0.4	−1.0
p_8	**+0.4**	−0.8	−0.4	−0.4	+0.2	+1.0	−0.4		+1.0	**−0.8**	+0.4	−0.4	−0.4
p_9	**+0.4**	−0.8	−0.4	−0.4	+0.2	+1.0	−0.4	+1.0		**−0.8**	−0.4	−0.4	−0.4
p_{10}	**+1.0**	**+1.0**	**+1.0**	**+0.2**	**+1.0**	**+1.0**	**+1.0**	**+1.0**	**+1.0**		**+1.0**	**+1.0**	**+1.0**
p_{11}	**+0.8**	+0.4	+0.8	0	0	+0.8	+0.8	+0.8	+0.8	**−1.0**		0	−0.6
p_{12}	**+1.0**	−0.2	+0.2	+0.2	+1.0	+1.0	+0.4	+0.8	+0.8	**−0.2**	+0.4		+0.2
p_{13}	**+1.0**	+0.6	+1.0	+0.2	+1.0	+1.0	+1.0	+0.8	+0.8	**−0.2**	+0.2	+1.0	

signifies that poster p_2 is *performing better than* poster p_1 on all four selection criteria. For posters p_3 and p_2, however,

$$\begin{aligned} r(p_3 \succcurlyeq^{j_3} p_2) &= 0.4 \cdot r(p_3 \succcurlyeq^{j_3}_{sq} p_2) \;+\; 0.3 \cdot r(p_3 \succcurlyeq^{j_3}_{tp} p_2) \\ &\quad + 0.2 \cdot r(p_3 \succcurlyeq^{j_3}_{or} p_2) \;+\; 0.1 \cdot r(p_3 \succcurlyeq^{j_3}_{pq} p_2) \\ &= 0.4 \cdot (+1) \;+\; 0.3 \cdot (+1) \;+\; 0.2 \cdot (-1) \;+\; 0.1 \cdot (+1) \\ &= +0.6 \end{aligned}$$

Positive validation of the "*poster p_3 is at least as good as poster p_2*" statement from the *Scientific Quality* (0.4), *Contribution to OR Theory and/or Practice* (0.3) and *Presentation Quality* (0.1) points of view is counter-balanced by the negative validation from the *Originality* (0.2) point of view. Conversely, positive validation of the "*poster p_2 is at least as good as poster p_3*" statement from the *Contribution to OR Theory and/or Practice* (0.3), the *Originality* (0.2), and the *Presentation Quality* (0.1) points of view is counter-balanced by the negative validation from the *Scientific Quality* (0.4) point of view. Globally they are therefore appreciated to be more or less equally good.

As $r(p_i \succcurlyeq^{j_3} p_1) \geq 0$ for all $p_{i \neq 1} \in A$ (see Table 5.4: Column p_1), all posters are considered by j_3 to be *at least as good as* p_1. On the contrary, as $r(p_i \succcurlyeq^{j_3} p_{10}) < 0)$ (see Table 5.4: Column p_{10}), all posters $p_{i \neq 10}$ are *not* considered to be *at least as good as* poster p_{10}. Furthermore, as $r(p_{10} \succcurlyeq^{j_3} p_i) > 0$ for all $p_{i \neq 10} \in A$, poster p_{10} is considered by j_3 to be *globally better than* any other poster. In social choice theory terms, p_{10} gives a CONDORCET *winner* for jury member j_3.

We may compute such a global "*at least as good as*" characterisation $r(\succcurlyeq^j)$ for all five jury members. In order to analyze now the potential disagreements between the individual jury members' global preferences, we may use a Kendall like distance

Table 5.5 Average disagreement between jury members and between preference viewpoints (in %)

$K(\succcurlyeq^{j_r}, \succcurlyeq^{j_s})$	j_2	j_3	j_4	j_5	$K(\succcurlyeq_{f_r}, \succcurlyeq_{f_s})$	tp	or	pq
j_1	31.3	32.2	33.1	31.3	sq	12.9	12.9	18.6
j_2		27.9	28.5	20.2	tp		11.8	19.5
j_3			29.2	25.7	or			19.1
j_4				37.1				

(see Bisdorff, 2008), denoted K, between the bipolar-valued characteristics of their apparent "*at least as good as*" statements. Let r and s be two jury member.

$$K(\succcurlyeq^r, \succcurlyeq^s) = \sum_{x \neq y \in A} \left(\frac{|r(x \succcurlyeq^r y) - r(x \succcurlyeq^s y)|}{2 \cdot |A|(|A| - 1)} \right) \tag{5.5}$$

As the bipolar characterisations may take values from -1.0 to $+1.0$, the disagreement distance K varies between 0.0 (no disagreement at all) and 1.0 (total disagreement). In case one relation is completely indeterminate and the other completely determined (with solely $+1.0$ or -1.0 values), one would obtain a K value of 0.5.

In the left part of Table 5.5 are shown the disagreement distances we obtain between the jury members. One may notice here that jury member j_1 is more or less equally distant to all the other jury members ($K(\succcurlyeq^1, \succcurlyeq^j) \approx 32\,\%$ for $j \neq 1 \in J$). Whereas, jury member j_5 shows a more differentiated situation with most disagreements with j_4 ($K(\succcurlyeq^5, \succcurlyeq^4) = 37.1\,\%$) and less with j_2 ($K(\succcurlyeq^5, \succcurlyeq^2) = 20.2\,\%$). In fact, we may verify with the help of this K measure, that the views of the jury members on the competing posters significantly disagree one from the other. This observation guarantees somehow that the jury members have indeed expressed each one independently their own personal view on the competing posters.[8]

Similarly, the right part of Table 5.5 shows the disagreement distances between the four preference viewpoints[9] Most disagreement (19.5 %) is here observed between the *Scientific Quality* (sq) and the *Presentation Quality* (pq). The least disagreement (11.8 %) is observed between the *Contribution to OR Theory and/or Practice* (tp) and *Originality* (or). It is worthwhile noticing that the disagreements between the preference viewpoints appear less important than those between the jury members. It seams as if, for *Scientific Quality*, *Contribution to OR Theory*

[8]The very short time period available between the posters' evaluation and the final selection of the best posters is another procedural circumstance of the decision making process which made it rather difficult for the jury members to coordinate before the final selection procedure.

[9]See global outranking per preference viewpoint in the Appendix "Overall Outranking per Preference Viewpoint".

and/or Practice and *Originality*, high and low appreciations have been somehow more correlated[10] in the performance evaluations.

Finally, we still have to aggregate these individual global preference statements of the jury members on all the weighted selection criteria into an overall global characterisation of the pairwise outranking situations which become apparent between the competing posters.

5.2.3 *Aggregating into a Global* "outranking" *Statement*

Three strategies are available for the overall aggregation of the preferences:

1. First, aggregate the jury members' opinions on each preference point of view and then only, aggregate over the selection criteria.
2. Aggregate first over the selection criteria for each jury member and then only, aggregate to a global consensus among the jury members.
3. Or, we may directly aggregate all individual opinions over all the preference points of view.

We propose here to follow the third strategy.

Aggregating All Opinions from Every Point of View

All five award jury members, renowned experts in the field of Operations Research, are by nomination to be considered equal in significance for aggregating the preferential information.[11] Mixing this equi-significance of the five jury members with the imposed differentiated significance of the four selection criteria, we consider now to be in the presence of $5 \times 4 = 20$ criteria that we may gather into four equi-significance classes listed hereafter in decreasing order of importance: $\{sq^j \mid j \in J\}$, $\{tp^j \mid j \in J\}$, $\{or^j \mid j \in J\}$, and $\{pq^j \mid j \in J\}$.

Following a similar numerical weighting strategy as in the preceding section, we associate the following normalized significance weight vector $\mathbf{w}$ with these four equivalence classes: $w^j_{sq} = 0.4/5$, $w^j_{tp} = 0.3/5$, $w^j_{or} = 0.2/5$ and $w^j_{pq} = 0.1/5$, for $j = 1$ to 5. Note that we recover hence the same relative weights $w_{sq} = 0.4$, $w_{tp} = 0.3$, $w_{or} = 0.2$ and $w_{pq} = 0.1$ for each preference dimension as before. We

[10]A common misunderstanding holds this apparent statistical correlation as the sufficient sign of a violation of the required preferential independence hypothesis. However, significant statistical correlations may well appear with preferentially independent criteria.

[11]Except perhaps, the chair of the award jury, who may influence the final balance if an indeterminate situation arises. This was not the case here. On the contrary a clear and convincing solution appeared, as we will see later on.

will use this property when discussing alternative overall aggregation strategies in the next Paragraph.

All the 20 criteria in our case here are by design non-redundant, exhaustive and consistent. We are, hence, in the presence of a coherent family of criteria (see Roy and Bouyssou, 1993) and a weighted additive aggregation of the individual criterion based characterisations may be used. As done before already, and considering the given significance vector $\mathbf{w}$, we may therefore compute the characterisation r of a global "poster x is at least as good as poster y" statement, denoted $(x \succsim_w y)$, as follows:

$$r(x \succsim_{\mathbf{w}} y) := \sum_{f \in F \wedge j \in J} \left(r(x \geqslant_f^j y) \cdot w_f^j \right) \tag{5.6}$$

This $r(\succsim_{\mathbf{w}})$ function, defined on all the couples of posters, characterises what is commonly called a *pairwise outranking* situation (see Roy, 1991). As all the bipolar characteristic function before, It takes value in a rational[12] interval $[-1.0, +1.0]$ with the following semantics:

1. $r(x \succsim_{\mathbf{w}} y) = +1.0$: all jury members *unanimously validate* on all the selection criteria the statement that poster x is at least as good as poster y on all selection criteria.
2. $+1.0 > r(x \succsim_{\mathbf{w}} y) > 0.0$: a *significant weighted majority* of jury members *validates* the statement that poster x is at least as good as poster y. For short we say that poster x outranks poster y.
3. $r(x \succsim_{\mathbf{w}} y) = -1.0$: No jury member validates on any preference dimension the statement that poster x is at least as good as poster y. In negative terms, all jury members *unanimously invalidate* such a statement.
4. $-1.0 < r(x \succsim_{\mathbf{w}} y) < 0.0$: Under the given significance vector $\mathbf{w}$, a*significant weighted minority* of jury members only *validates* the statement that poster x is at least as good as poster y. In negative terms, a *significant weighted majority* of jury members in fact *invalidates* this statement. Symmetrically to the positive case, we say here for short that poster x does not outrank poster y.
5. $r(x \succsim_{\mathbf{w}} y) = 0.0$: Under the given significance vector $\mathbf{w}$, the statement that poster x is at least as good as poster y may *neither be validated, nor, invalidated*. The overall weighted preferential judgment is, so to say, *suspended*.

In Table 5.6 is shown the bipolar characterisation of the "*global outranking*" statement on all the pairs of posters in the EBPA competition.

The bipolar-valued characteristic function $r(\succsim)$ still preserves the nice order statistical property we have mentioned in the previous section when appreciating

[12]As the r characteristic is supposed to admit only rational values, one may admit without loss of generality, that it is always possible to express the significance weights with a set of integer numbers. Here the corresponding integer numbers would be 4 for the *Scientific Quality*, 3 for the *Contribution to OR Theory and/or Practice*, 2 to the *Originality*, and 1 to the *Presentation Quality* point of view.

Table 5.6 Global outranking of the posters considering significance vector **w**

$r(\succsim_{\mathbf{w}})$	p_1	p_2	p_3	p_4	p_5	p_6	p_7	p_8	p_9	p_{10}	p_{11}	p_{12}	p_{13}
p_1	–	+0.16	−0.52	−0.76	+0.08	+0.36	−0.32	+0.52	+0.30	**−0.92**	+0.26	−0.84	−0.44
p_2	−0.16	–	−0.32	−0.32	−0.32	−0.16	−0.16	−0.16	+0.22	**−0.52**	−0.10	−0.32	−0.48
p_3	+0.64	+0.48	–	+0.08	+0.32	+0.96	+0.72	+0.92	+0.38	**−0.68**	+0.62	+0.16	−0.08
p_4	+0.96	+0.36	+0.24	–	+0.52	+0.96	+0.64	+0.96	+0.38	**−0.44**	+0.50	+0.40	+0.08
p_5	+0.28	+0.36	+0.44	−0.04	–	**+1.0**	+0.56	+0.96	+0.38	**−0.48**	+0.50	+0.04	**±0.0**
p_6	+0.08	+0.16	−0.80	−0.80	−0.32	–	−0.16	+0.72	+0.30	**−1.0**	+0.26	−0.92	−0.60
p_7	+0.36	+0.44	−0.36	−0.08	−0.40	+0.72	–	+0.64	+0.30	**−0.80**	+0.38	±0.0	−0.28
p_8	**±0.0**	+0.20	−0.68	−0.60	−0.40	+0.32	−0.20	–	+0.42	**−0.96**	+0.34	−0.68	**−0.48**
p_9	−0.14	−0.02	−0.30	−0.30	−0.18	−0.02	−0.26	−0.02	–	**−0.38**	−0.22	−0.26	−0.30
p_{10}	**+1.0**	**+0.60**	**+1.0**	**+0.68**	**+1.0**	**+1.0**	**+0.80**	**+1.0**	**+0.42**	–	**+0.62**	**+0.76**	**+0.60**
p_{11}	+0.42	+0.22	−0.26	−0.42	−0.42	−0.14	−0.22	+0.18	+0.38	**−0.62**	–	−0.38	−0.14
p_{12}	+0.96	+0.32	+0.40	+0.24	+0.28	+0.92	+0.56	+0.88	+0.38	**−0.36**	+0.50	–	+0.12
p_{13}	**+1.0**	+0.52	+0.40	+0.20	+0.60	+0.60	+0.40	+0.92	+0.38	**−0.04**	+0.62	+0.28	–

the posters from a single point of view, and when aggregating the opinions of a jury member. In the disagreement K-distance sense [see Eq. (5.5)], $r(\succsim)$ represents indeed again a weighted *median* characterisation between the all *disjunctive* ($\max_{f \in F, j \in J}[r(\geqslant^j_f) \cdot w^j_f]$) and the all *conjunctive* ($\min_{f \in F, j \in J}[r(\geqslant^j_f) \cdot w^j_f]$) aggregation of the individual "*at least as good as*" characterisations (see Barbut, 1980).

From an exploratory and descriptive data analysis point of view, the global outranking relation represents therefore a convincing compromise which is at minimal ordinal disagreement distance with all the individual "*at least as good as*" relations. It gives us hence a convincing and reliable *central* model of the global preferences of the EBPA jury.

Stability with Respect to Marginal Aggregation Strategies

As mentioned before, we could have followed two alternate strategies for aggregating the individual preferences:

1. First aggregate the opinions of the jury members on each preferential point of view, and then, propose a global compromise viewpoint;
2. Or, first, aggregate all preference points of view for each individual jury member, and then, propose the consensus opinion of the whole jury.

However, it is easy to verify that our linear formulation [see Eq. (5.6)] of the bipolar characterisation of the global "$x \succsim_{\mathbf{w}} y$" statement, coupled with the consistent choice of the individual weights w^j_f, induces in fact the equivalence of all three potential aggregation strategies.

Proposition 1

$$r(x \succsim_{\mathbf{w}} y) = \sum_{j \in J} \big(r(x \succsim^j y)/|J|\big) = \sum_{f \in F} \big(r(x \succsim_f y) \cdot w_f\big). \qquad (5.7)$$

Proof Note that $r(x \succsim^j y) = \sum_{f \in F} \left[r(x \succsim^j_f y) \cdot w_f\right]$ and that $w_f = \sum_{j \in J} w^j_f = \sum_{j \in J} w_j/|J|$. Similarly, $r(x \succsim_f y) = \sum_{j \in J} \left[r(x \succsim^j_f y) \cdot w^j\right]$ and that $w_j = \sum_{f \in F} w^j_f$.

All three strategies lead hence naturally to the same weighted bipolar characterisation of the global pairwise "*outranking*" statement. It is evident that this result is mainly dependent on the effective verification of the preferential independence and significance of points of view, as well as, of the individual jury members.

Having herewith modelled the overall preferences of the award jury on all the competing posters, we are now prepared for rebuilding the historical best poster recommendation submitted to the decision of the EBPA jury members.

5.3 Rebuilding the Best Poster Recommendation

As mentioned in the methodological part (see Chap. 4, Sect. 4.4), a global outranking relation as constructed in the preceding section, apart from being trivially reflexive, a fact that we ignore deliberately in this case study, has commonly no further structural properties that would allow to implement a simple choice function for determining the globally best decision alternative. In this case here, however, we are lucky. A clear winner is appearing as we will discover soon.

5.3.1 Exploiting the CONDORCET *Graph*

The semantics of the bipolar-valued characterisation of the global outranking relation give access to a crisp graph called CONDORCET[13] graph and denoted $C(A, \mathrm{S})$, where A represents the set of competing posters and S[14] represents a crisp outranking relation defined on A as follows:

$$(x\,\mathrm{S}\,y) \quad \text{is} \quad \begin{cases} \textit{true}\ (+) & \text{when} \quad r(x \succsim_{\mathrm{w}} y) > 0, \\ \textit{false}\ (-) & \text{when} \quad r(x \succsim_{\mathrm{w}} y) < 0, \\ \textit{indeterminate}\ (0) & \text{when} \quad r(x \succsim_{\mathrm{w}} y) = 0. \end{cases} \tag{5.8}$$

The S relation may thus only render a partially defined crisp outranking on A. In Table 5.6, we see, for instance, that $r(p_8 \succsim_{\mathrm{w}} p_1) = 0$. Consequently, $p_8\,\mathrm{S}\,p_1$ is indeterminate, i.e. the global outranking situation between p_8 and p_1 appears neither validated, nor invalidated. The cumulative significance of weighted positive (validating) arguments is here exactly counterbalanced by the cumulative significance of the weighted negative (invalidating) arguments and no global conclusion concerning the validation or not of the outranking situation in question can be drawn. This is not a symmetrical situation, however. The converse global outranking situation, where we see that $r(p_1 \succsim_{\mathrm{w}} p_8) = +0.52$), is, however, strongly validated with more than 75 % significance.[15] Several other similar indeterminate cases do appear in the CONDORCET graph under review (see Table 5.6).

[13]We follow here a suggestion made by Barbut (1980) who calls a median cut graph after Marie Jean Antoine Nicolas de Caritat, marquis de CONDORCET (1743–1794). A French mathematician and political scientist who is the inventor of the pairwise voting procedure named after him.

[14]The S notation comes from the French term "*surclasser*" (to *outrank*).

[15]Passing from the r characteristic function to classic election style majority percentages is readily achieved by shifting the r value up by 1.0 and dividing the result by 2.0. For instance, $r(p_{10} \succsim_{\mathrm{w}} p_9) = 0.42$, which gives in percentages: $(0.42 + 1.0)/2.0 = 0.71 = 71\,\%$.

Table 5.7 The CONDORCET outranking relation

x S y	p_1	p_2	p_3	p_4	p_5	p_6	p_7	p_8	p_9	p_{10}	p_{11}	p_{12}	p_{13}
p_1		+	−	−	+	+	−	+	+	−	+	−	−
p_2	−		−	−	−	−	−	−	+	−	−	−	−
p_3	+	+		+	+	+	+	+	+	−	+	+	−
p_4	+	+	+		+	+	+	+	+	−	+	+	+
p_5	+	+	+	−		+	+	+	+	−	+	+	0
p_6	+	+	−	−	−		−	+	+	−	+	−	−
p_7	+	+	−	−	−	+		+	+	−	+	0	−
p_8	0	+	−	−	−	+	−		+	−	+	−	−
p_9	−	−	−	−	−	−	−	−		−	−	−	−
$\mathbf{p_{10}}$	**+**	**+**	**+**	**+**	**+**	**+**	**+**	**+**	**+**		**+**	**+**	**+**
p_{11}	+	+	−	−	−	−	−	+	+	−		−	−
p_{12}	+	+	+	+	+	+	+	+	+	−	+		+
p_{13}	+	+	+	+	+	+	+	+	+	−	+	+	

Based on this CONDORCET graph (see the + and − denotation in Table 5.7), three progressively extended exploitation approaches become available:

1. Determine the CONDORCET *winner(s)*, if there is one or more, or
2. Determine its *top equivalence class* if the CONDORCET graph shows a transitive global outranking, or
3. Determine its *outranking kernel(s)*, if there is one (or more).

The CONDORCET Winner

In CONDORCET's method, the winner of an election is a decision alternative that, if it exists, outranks all the other competing alternatives. Note that, as CONDORCET was essentially considering a strict preference model, the CONDORCET winner, if it existed, was necessarily unique. As the outranking relation here is not an asymmetric relation, we may find, the case given, several such CONDORCET winners in a global outranking graph $C(A, \succsim)$.

Careful inspection, now, of the Table 5.6—line by line—makes it apparent that poster p_{10} represents obviously such a CONDORCET winner. It outranks positively (see Table 5.7) all other posters with a comfortable minimal weighted significance of 71 % (see line p_{10} in Table 5.6).

We are lucky in the case here. No other competing poster is in a similar good situation, and p_{10} may thus be recommended, on the basis of the given outranking graph as the winner of the EURO 2004 BPA competition.

The Top Strongly Connected Component

Already CONDORCET himself noticed that his pairwise voting approach could end up with cyclic strict global preferences, an apparent *social choice paradox*, named after him. In the multiple criteria based aggregation of "*at least as good as*" statements, such potentially cyclic outrankings are, however, *not* considered to be *paradoxical* or even problematic at all. They simply show, the case given, that each preference dimension may well express cyclically opposed preferential opinions, so that no global consensus on a unique linearly ordered common point of view is possible. Roy and Bouyssou (1993) propose therefore, in the ELECTRE method (see Sect. 4.4.2), to collapse the strongly connected components (maximal cycles in fact) of the CONDORCET graph into potential equivalence classes of decision alternatives, and to exploit the so-reduced CONDORCET graph for building the best choice recommendation.

From our crisp $C(A, S)$ graph, we obtain the following, linearly ordered, strong components (see Fig. 5.5a): $\{\mathbf{p_{10}}\} \succ \{p_3, p_4, p_5, p_{12}, p_{13}\} \succ \{p_7\} \succ \{p_1, p_6, p_8, p_{11}\} \succ \{p_2\} \succ \{p_9\}$. A CONDORCET winner, the case given, necessarily appears as best singleton strongly connected component. We find here again confirmed that poster p_{10} clearly dominates indeed all the other competing posters. Considering furthermore the depth of the linear ordering of the strong components, we may notice that the five jury members do share apparently loads of

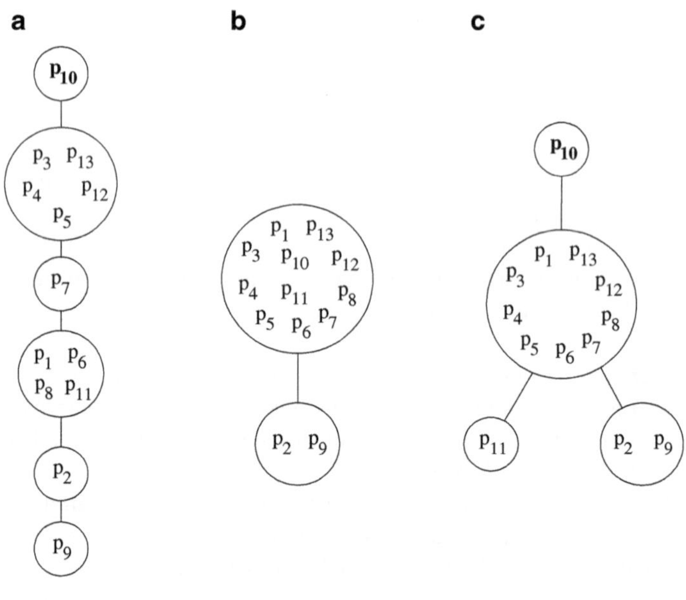

Fig. 5.5 Hasse diagrams of strongly connected components reduced outranking graph with 1 level preference discrimination (**a**), with 2 levels preference discrimination (**b**), and with additional veto effects (**c**)

preferential opinions. A significant majority, for instance, shares the opinion that p_9 is the worst candidate (see Table 5.7 line p_9). The global outranking gives therefore this weak ordering of the competing posters. This opportune situation is, however, not generally given. There might appear for instance several CONDORCET winners due, for instance, to a less precise discrimination of the individual performances.

Let's consider for the moment that a real better performing situation is only warranted when we observe a positive difference of at least two ordinal levels, a not unreasonable working hypothesis. We consequently obtain a much less clear cut global outranking picture. Two strong components only remain (see Fig. 5.5b), where $\{p_2, p_9\}$ is the less preferred of both. All the other competing posters are now considered to be equally preferred. The top strong component gathers under this working hypothesis, 11 of the 13 best choice candidates. It obviously does not represent anymore a satisfactory potential best choice recommendation.

However, two CONDORCET winners do appear now: poster p_{10}, as well as poster p_{13}, outrank all the other candidates in this revised CONDORCET graph (See lines p_{10} and p_{13} in Table 5.8). By recognizing these CONDORCET winners directly from the values of the weighted bipolar characterisation $r(\succsim_{\mathbf{w}})$, one would readily notice that poster p_{10} gives a CONDORCET winner with at least 71 % significance support in both cases (see line p_{10} both in Table 5.6 and in Table 5.8). Whereas poster p_{13}, actually a CONDORCET winner only in the reduced preference discrimination case (see Table 5.8) and with at least 62 % of significance only, gives a somehow less convincing best poster candidate.

The Outranking Kernel

It becomes apparent from the preceding considerations, that, in order to be suitable in a decision aiding problem, a best choice recommendation should correspond to a *maximal* or, if not available, to a somehow *initial* node of the global outranking relation. A CONDORCET winner, if it exists, fulfills ideally this condition. If the CONDORCET graph is a, perhaps partial, weak order, the maximal equivalence class, or classes the case given, give a potential set of somehow equivalent best poster candidates. The overall aggregation may, however, yield a CONDORCET graph which generally shows neither a transitive nor a complete crisp outranking. An extension of the maximality condition (see Roy, 1985), leads therefore to the following three conditions, a suitable best choice recommendation should fulfill:

1. All decision alternatives, not retained as candidate for the best choice, should be rejected with objective reasons. The best choice recommendation should outrank the rejected alternatives, a fact called "*externally stable*".
2. The recommended set of potential best alternatives should be as limited in cardinality as possible, ideally a singleton.
3. The best choice candidates retained in a choice recommendation should be perceived either equivalent or incomparable, a fact called "*internally stable*".

Table 5.8 Global outranking of the posters with a preference discrimination threshold of two points

$r(\succsim_w)$	p_1	p_2	p_3	p_4	p_5	p_6	p_7	p_8	p_9	p_{10}	p_{11}	p_{12}	p_{13}
p_1	–	+0.32	−0.32	−0.40	±0.0	+0.66	+0.04	+0.70	+0.34	**−0.84**	+0.36	−0.62	−0.26
p_2	−0.16	–	−0.24	−0.32	−0.32	−0.16	−0.16	−0.18	+0.32	**−0.48**	−0.02	−0.32	−0.40
p_3	+0.82	+0.54	–	+0.16	+0.50	+0.98	+0.72	+0.96	+0.40	**−0.40**	+0.62	+0.34	+0.14
p_4	+0.98	+0.46	+0.60	–	+0.66	+0.98	+0.70	+0.96	+0.38	**−0.06**	+0.56	+0.68	+0.16
p_5	+0.58	+0.42	+0.46	+0.18	–	+1.0	+0.62	+0.96	+0.38	**−0.22**	+0.50	+0.22	+0.16
p_6	+0.40	+0.24	−0.42	−0.56	−0.16	–	−0.18	+0.78	+0.30	**−0.96**	+0.26	−0.48	−0.46
p_7	+0.48	+0.44	+0.10	−0.04	−0.16	+0.74	–	+0.64	+0.30	**−0.62**	+0.46	+0.10	−0.06
p_8	+0.20	+0.32	−0.40	−0.50	−0.22	+0.54	−0.06	–	+0.42	**−0.86**	+0.34	−0.52	−0.42
p_9	−0.08	+0.10	−0.30	−0.24	−0.18	−0.02	−0.18	−0.02	–	**−0.34**	−0.22	−0.20	−0.30
p_{10}	**+1.0**	**+0.60**	**+1.0**	**+0.76**	**+1.0**	**+1.0**	**+0.80**	**+1.0**	**+0.42**	–	**+0.62**	**+0.88**	**+0.64**
p_{11}	+0.42	+0.26	−0.25	−0.28	−0.34	+0.18	−0.04	+0.32	+0.38	**−0.50**	–	−0.24	±0.0
p_{12}	+0.96	+0.44	+0.60	+0.46	+0.42	+0.94	+0.68	+0.90	+0.38	**−0.02**	+0.56	–	+0.28
p_{13}	**+1.0**	**+0.56**	**+0.50**	**+0.36**	**+0.60**	**+0.80**	**+0.40**	**+0.94**	**+0.40**	**+0.24**	**+0.62**	**+0.40**	–

A choice recommendation fulfilling these three conditions is actually called an *outranking kernel.*[16] And, both CONDORCET winners, mentioned in the previous section, represent two such outranking kernels observed in the corresponding CONDORCET graphs. However, as we have already mentioned, they are not one as well determined as the other. This insight gives us the hint that the CONDORCET graph, due to its crisp polarization effect, is not well suited for discriminating between several best poster candidates. And we might, instead, have advantage in formulating a best poster recommendation directly from the bipolar-valued outranking characterisation.

5.3.2 The RUBIS *Best Choice Method*

This approach has been promoted under the name RUBIS by Bisdorff et al. (2008). It results from general mathematical and algorithmic results obtained for computing best choice recommendations in bipolar-valued directed graphs (see Bisdorff et al., 2006). We shall briefly outline the main theoretical concepts and formulas.

Similar to the bipolar characterisation of a pairwise outranking situation between competing posters, one may also thus characterise the more or less validation of the fact that a given subset of decision alternatives represents a suitable best choice recommendation. We need only to adequately characterise the statement that the corresponding choice is internally and externally stable.

Let $Y \subseteq A$ be a non empty subset of potential best choice candidates. We denote $\Delta^{\mathrm{ind}}(Y)$, respectively $\Delta^{\mathrm{dom}}(Y)$ or $\Delta^{\mathrm{abs}}(Y)$, the bipolar characteristic value we may attribute to the statement that "Y is internally stable", respectively "Y is *dominantly stable*" or "Y is *absorbingly* stable". Formally, we define these values for all couples $(x, y) \in A^2$ $(x \neq y)$ of posters as follows:

$$\Delta^{\mathrm{ind}}(Y) := \begin{cases} 1.0 & \text{if } \; |Y| = 1, \\ \min_{(x \neq y) \in Y^2} \left[r(x \succsim_{\mathrm{w}} y) \right] & \text{otherwise.} \end{cases} \tag{5.9}$$

$$\Delta^{\mathrm{dom}}(Y) := \begin{cases} 1.0 & \text{if } \; Y = A, \\ \min_{x \notin Y} \left[\max_{y \in Y} r(y \succsim_{\mathrm{w}} x) \right] \end{cases} \tag{5.10}$$

$$\Delta^{\mathrm{abs}}(Y) := \begin{cases} 1.0 & \text{if } \; Y = A, \\ \min_{x \notin Y} \left[\max_{y \in Y} r(x \succsim_{\mathrm{w}} y) \right] \end{cases} \tag{5.11}$$

We get the same semantics as with the bipolar characterisation of the preferential statements. With stab $\in$ {ind, dom, abs},

1. $\Delta^{\mathrm{stab}}(Y) = 1.0$ signifies that it is *certainly validated* that Y yields a choice recommendation which verifies the respective stability condition.

[16] See glossary entry "Kernel" at the end of the chapter.

2. $\Delta^{\text{stab}}(Y) > 0.0$ signifies that it is *more validated than invalidated* that Y yields a choice recommendation which verifies the respective stability condition.
3. $\Delta^{\text{stab}}(Y) = -1.0$ signifies that it is *certainly invalidated* that Y yields a choice recommendation which verifies the respective stability conditions.
4. $\Delta^{\text{stab}}(Y) < 0.0$ signifies that it is *more invalidated than validated* that Y yields a choice recommendation which verifies the respective stability conditions.
5. $\Delta^{\text{stab}}(Y) = 0.0$ signifies as usual an indeterminate situation where neither the validation, nor the invalidation may be assumed.

We have shown in Bisdorff et al. (2006), that the kernels of the CONDORCET graph correspond bijectively to the choice sets that are internally and dominantly stable.

In Table 5.9 we show the evaluation of the stability conditions for all potential singletons and some pairs of posters. It appears, that poster p_{10}, with $\Delta^{\text{ind}}(p_{10}) = 1.0$, $\Delta^{\text{dom}}(p_{10}) = +.42$ and $\Delta^{\text{abs}}(p_{10}) = -1.0$, yields the unique internal and dominantly stable choice recommendation available in the bipolar valued global outranking relation $\succsim_{\mathbf{w}}$ defined on A. In Fig. 5.6a, we may see indeed that p_{10}

Table 5.9 Internal and external stability of potential best choice recommendations

choice (Y)	Δ^{ind}	Δ^{dom}	Δ^{abs}	choice (Y)	Δ^{ind}	Δ^{dom}	Δ^{abs}
$\{\mathbf{p_{10}}\}$	**+1.0**	**+0.42** (71 %)	**−1.0**	$\{p_{05}\}$	+1.0	−0.48	−0.42
$\{\mathbf{p_{13}}\}$	+1.0	**−0.04** (48 %)	−0.60	$\{p_{02}\}$	+1.0	−0.52	−0.02
$\{\mathbf{p_9}\}$	**+1.0**	**−0.38**	**+0.22**	$\{p_{11}\}$	+1.0	−0.62	−0.22
$\{\mathbf{p_9}, \mathbf{p_{10}}\}$	**−0.42**	**+0.60** (80 %)	**+0.22**	$\{p_{03}\}$	+1.0	−0.68	−0.80
$\{p_{10}, p_{13}\}$	−0.60	+0.42	−0.60	$\{p_{07}\}$	+1.0	−0.80	−0.32
$\{p_{12}\}$	+1.0	−0.36	−0.92	$\{p_{01}\}$	+1.0	−0.92	−0.16
$\{p_{10}, p_{12}\}$	−0.76	+0.42	−0.92	$\{p_{08}\}$	+1.0	−0.96	−0.20
$\{p_{04}\}$	+1.0	−0.44	−0.80	$\{p_{06}\}$	+1.0	−1.0	−0.16

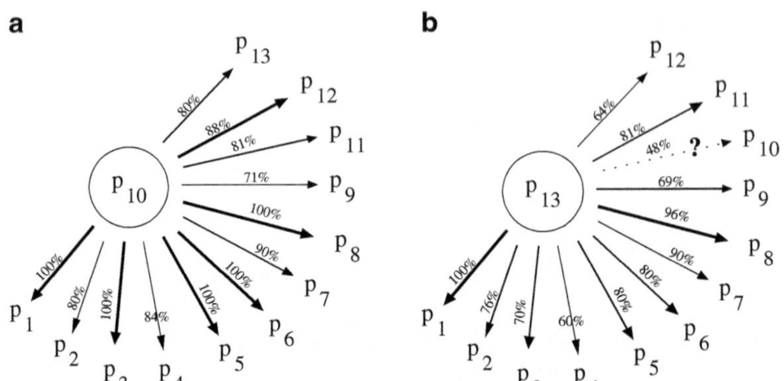

Fig. 5.6 Dominance stability of singletons $\{p_{10}\}$ and $\{p_{13}\}$ in the global weighted outranking graph

outranks all other competing posters with a minimum significance of 71 %[17] and is not outranked for certain by any other candidate. It is worthwhile mentioning that poster p_{13} appears as second potential choice recommendation as it also outranks all other competing posters, except poster p_{10}, with a minimal significance of 64 % (see Fig. 5.6b). It also gets apparent in Table 5.9, that poster p_9 yields the unique absorbingly stable choice with 61 % of significance. This candidate is outranked by all the other competing posters with a minimum significance of 61 %. Finally, it is worthwhile noticing that, the pair $\{p_9, p_{10}\}$ would potentially yield a significantly outranking (80 % of significance), but, at the same time, significantly outranked (61 % of significance) choice recommendation. This recommendation would, however, not be stable. Poster p_9 is indeed outranked by poster p_{10} with a significance of 76 % (see Table 5.6). Similarly, all other pairs are not internally stable.

Besides these singletons and pairs mentioned so far, no other small subset of competing posters is convincingly outranking all the others. At the sight of the results shown in Table 5.9, we may hence conclude that poster p_{10} represents definitely the best candidate that we may recommended the EBPA jury to attribute the EBPA.

But is this result not an artifact of our preference modelling strategy? Isn't this result an anecdotal consequence of the numerical significance weights we are using in the computation of the bipolar valued characterisation of the global outranking situations? Answering these questions is the subject of the following, last, section.

5.3.3 Robustness Analysis

Three strategies for testing the stability of the previous result with respect to some variants of the preference model construction are proposed hereafter:

1. Taking into account large positive and negative performance differences. This is the specialty of the ELECTRE outranking concept.
2. Requiring a qualified—high—significance level for the validation of an outranking statement.
3. Testing the stability of the CONDORCET graph with respect to the numerical significance weights.

Taking into Account Considerable Large Performance Differences

In the Electre methods, Roy (1991), Roy and Słowiński (2008) suggest polarizing the global outranking situation by, on the one hand, cutting those arcs in the

[17]The conversion formula for percentages is $(\Delta^{\text{stab}}(Y) + 1.0)/2.0$.

CONDORCET graph where a worst performance (a veto) is challenging an otherwise significant "*at least as good as*" situation and, on the other hand, reinforcing those significant "*at least as good as*" situations where a best performance (a counter-veto) may be observed. Let us set somehow arbitrarily such veto or counter-veto threshold, denoted v_j for $j \in J$, to the maximum spread of the performances given by each jury member minus one point on all the criteria.[18] From Table 5.14 in Appendix "The Complete Performance Tableau", we see that for j_1 it is 4 points, for j_2 it is 7 points, for j_3 it is 6 points, for j_4 it is 5 points, and for j_5 it is 7 points.

In order to detect these veto situations, denoted $\lll^j_f$, we are using again a bipolar characteristic function $r(\lll^j_f)$, defined as follows on all couples (x, y) in A^2:

$$r(x \lll^j_f y) = \begin{cases} +1 & \text{if} \quad g^j_f(x) - g^j_f(y) \leqslant -v_j, \\ -1 & \text{if} \quad g^j_f(x) - g^j_f(y) \geqslant +v_j, \\ 0 & \text{otherwise.} \end{cases} \tag{5.12}$$

Note that the bipolar symmetric negation of a serious worst performance (veto) situation $\lll^j_f$, namely changing the sign of its $r(\lll^j_f)$ value, gives the characteristic value of the corresponding very best performance (counter-veto) situations, denoted $\ggg^j_f$.

Extending the ideas of Roy (1991), we may now describe a pairwise global outranking situation,[19] denoted $x\, \tilde{\mathrm{S}}\, y$, with the help of the following bipolar characteristic function r:

$$r(x\, \tilde{\mathrm{S}}\, y) = \begin{cases} r(x \succsim_{\mathrm{w}} y) \quad \text{if} \quad \forall f \in F, \forall j \in J : \big(r(x \lll^j_f y) = -1\big) \\ \qquad\qquad \wedge \big(r(x \ggg^j_f y) = -1\big), \\ +1 \quad \text{if} \quad r(x \succsim_{\mathrm{w}} y) > 0.0 \text{ and } \exists f \in F, j \in J : \big(r(x \ggg^j_f y) = +1\big) \\ \qquad\qquad \text{and } \nexists f \in F : \big(r(x \lll^j_f y) = +1\big), \\ -1 \quad \text{if} \quad r(x \succsim_{\mathrm{w}} y) < 0.0 \text{ and } \exists f \in F : \big(r(x \lll^j_f y) = +1\big) \\ \qquad\qquad \text{and } \nexists f \in F, j \in J : \big(r(x \ggg^j_f y) = +1\big), \\ 0 \quad \text{otherwise.} \end{cases} \tag{5.13}$$

[18]The EBPA 2004 jury members did not feel any need to consider such veto effects when deliberating on the final best poster choice. This is certainly related to the easy dominating situation of poster p_{10}.

[19]The classical outranking relation, as used in the various ELECTRE methods, differs slightly from our bipolar definition here in the sense that the large performance difference polarization is solely operated for a veto situation, but not for a counter-veto situation. This unipolar handling may induce, however, abusive strict invalidation of otherwise more or less validated outranking situations (Bisdorff, 2013).

The resulting semantics (see Bisdorff, 2013) are the following:

- $r(\tilde{\mathrm{S}})$ remains unchanged with $r(\succsim_{\mathrm{w}})$ in case we do not observe any veto or counter-veto situation.
- We get a positively polarized validation, i.e. $r(x \succsim_{\mathrm{w}} y) \rightarrow +1.0$, in case we observe a significant positive outranking coupled with a very best performance (a counter-veto) on at least one criterion and we observe no serious counter-performance raising a veto on some other criterion.
- We get a negatively polarized invalidation, i.e. $r(x \succsim_{\mathrm{w}} y) \rightarrow -1.0$, in case we have a significant negative outranking coupled with a serious worst performance on at least one criterion and we observe no counter-veto on some other criterion.
- In all the other cases, i.e. when we observe conjointly best and worst performances, or a positive validation coupled with a serious worst performance, or a negative validation coupled with a very best performance, we admit the neutral zero value. Neither a validation, nor an invalidation of the global outranking situation may then be assumed and we suspend the validation of the corresponding outranking statement.

In Table 5.10 we may see the effect of this veto and counter-veto polarization. Many pairwise outrankings, like $p_3 \,\tilde{\mathrm{S}}\, p_1$ or $p_1 \,\tilde{\mathrm{S}}\, p_3$ appear now, either certainly validated, or, certainly invalidated. Take poster p_{10} for instance. It outranks now the other posters with certitude, except poster p_4, where, nevertheless, the polarized validation is highly significant (76 %). In this large-performance-differences (LPD) polarized outranking graph, poster p_{10} becomes on the one hand, an even more convincing CONDORCET winner. Whereas, poster p_{13} on the other hand, does no more positively outrank poster p_{10} ($r(p_{13} \,\tilde{\mathrm{S}}\, p_{10}) = 0.0$), and so does no more qualify as second CONDORCET winner.

The LPD[20] polarization induces four strong components:

$$\{p_{10}\} \succ \{p_1, p_3, p_4, p_5, p_6, p_7, p_8, p_{12}, p_{13}\} \succ \begin{cases} \{p_2, p_9\} \\ \{p_{11}\} \end{cases}$$

where poster p_{10} remains, as CONDORCET winner, the singleton top strong component. However, the so collapsed CONDORCET graph shows a partial weak order instead of the previous linear ordering (see Fig. 5.5c). The two worst strong components $\{p_2, p_9\}$ and $\{p_{11}\}$ appear now mutually incomparable.

The kernel extraction delivers now three solutions: $\{p_{10}\}$ as *outranking* kernel with a dominance significance of 76 %, and two overlapping *outranked* kernels: $\{p_9, p_{11}\}$ and $\{p_2, p_{11}\}$ with absorbency significance of 61 %, respectively 55 %.

Poster p_{10} is, under these working hypotheses, even more convincingly to be recommended for getting the EBPA. But are we not fooled by weakly significant validations and invalidations of global weighted outranking situations?

[20] See the glossary at the end of chapter.

Table 5.10 Global outranking with veto and counter-veto effects

$r(\widetilde{S})$	p_1	p_2	p_3	p_4	p_5	p_6	p_7	p_8	p_9	p_{10}	p_{11}	p_{12}	p_{13}
p_1	–	+0.32	**−1.0**	−1.0	−1.0	+0.66	±0.0	+0.70	+1.0	**−1.0**	+1.0	−1.0	−1.0
p_2	−0.16	–	−1.0	−1.0	−1.0	−0.16	−1.0	−0.18	+0.32	**−1.0**	±0.0	−1.0	−1.0
p_3	**+1.0**	+1.0	–	+0.16	+0.50	+0.98	+0.72	+1.0	+0.40	**−0.40**	+1.0	+0.34	+1.0
p_4	+1.0	+1.0	+0.60	–	+0.66	+0.98	+0.70	+1.0	+0.38	**−0.06**	+1.0	+0.68	+1.0
p_5	+1.0	+1.0	+0.46	+0.18	–	+1.0	+0.62	+1.0	+1.0	**−0.22**	+1.0	+0.22	±0.0
p_6	+0.40	+0.24	−0.42	−0.56	−0.16	–	+0.18	+0.78	+1.0	**−1.0**	+1.0	−0.48	−1.0
p_7	+1.0	+1.0	+0.10	−0.04	−0.16	+0.74	–	+0.64	+1.0	**−1.0**	+1.0	+0.10	±0.0
p_8	+0.20	+0.32	−1.00	−1.00	−1.0	+0.54	−0.06	–	+0.42	**−1.0**	+1.0	−0.52	−1.0
p_9	−1.0	+0.10	−0.30	−0.24	−1.0	−1.0	−1.0	−0.02	–	**−1.0**	±0.0	−1.0	−1.0
p_{10}	**+1.0**	**+1.0**	**+1.0**	**+0.76**	**+1.0**	**+1.0**	**+1.0**	**+1.0**	**+1.0**	–	**+1.0**	**+1.0**	**+1.0**
p_{11}	±0.0	±0.0	−1.0	−1.0	−1.0	±0.0	−1.0	±0.0	±0.0	**−1.0**	–	−1.0	−1.0
p_{12}	+1.0	+1.0	+0.60	+0.46	+0.42	+0.94	+0.68	+0.90	+1.0	**−1.0**	+1.0	–	±0.0
p_{13}	+1.0	+1.0	±0.0	±0.0	±0.0	+1.0	±0.0	+1.0	+1.0	**±0.0**	+1.0	±0.0	–

Requiring a Qualified Significance Level

Until now, we have indeed considered that a simple majority of weighted significance is sufficient for validating, respectively invalidating, a given global outranking situation. Let us for one moment be more suspicious and require instead a qualified majority of at least 75 % significance. Translated into bipolar characteristic terms, we will require a bipolar characteristic value of at least 0.5, respectively at most −0.5, for validating, respectively invalidating, the global weighted outranking relation, a situation we will denote $S_{75\%}$. We have consequently to adapt the definition of the associated crisp outranking relation from Eq. (5.8) on all the couples (x, y) of posters as follows:

$$x \, S_{75\%} \, y \text{ is } \begin{cases} \textit{true } (+) & \text{if} \quad r(x \succsim_{\mathrm{w}} y) \geqslant 0.5, \\ \textit{false } (-) & \text{if} \quad r(x \succsim_{\mathrm{w}} y) \leqslant -0.5, \\ \textit{indeterminate } (0) & \text{if} \quad -0.5 < r(x \succsim_{\mathrm{w}} y) < 0.5\,. \end{cases} \tag{5.14}$$

In Table 5.11, we show the corresponding 75 % qualified significance denotation we obtain on the global weighted outranking relation $\tilde{S}$ under the working hypothesis of widened preference thresholds (2 points) and by taking into account the polarizing effects of large performance differences. Compared to Table 5.7, much more outranking situations get indeterminate now, like $p_1 \, S \, p_2$ and $p_2 \, S \, p_1$ for instance. Only poster p_{10} outranks all the other posters with a sufficiently high significance. Notice that poster p_{13} does not anymore yield an alternative CONDORCET winner besides p_{10}. Indeed, $p_{13} \, S \, p_{10}$ can now no more be validated. We thus obtain one outranking singleton kernel: $\{p_{10}\}$, and one outranked kernel $\{p_2, p_9, p_{11}\}$. Posters p_2, p_9 and p_{11} appear clearly outranked at this qualified significance level.

Table 5.11 The 75 % significance qualified outranking relation

$x \, S_{75\%} \, y$	p_1	p_2	p_3	p_4	p_5	p_6	p_7	p_8	p_9	p_{10}	p_{11}	p_{12}	p_{13}
p_1		0	−	−	−	+	0	+	+	−	+	−	−
p_2	0		−	−	−	0	−	0	0	−	0	−	−
p_3	+	+		0	0	+	+	+	0	0	+	0	+
p_4	+	+	+		+	+	+	+	0	0	+	+	+
p_5	+	+	0	0		+	+	+	+	0	+	0	0
p_6	0	0	0	−	0		0	+	+	−	+	0	−
p_7	+	+	0	0	0	+		+	+	−	+	0	0
p_8	0	0	−	−	−	+	0		0	−	+	−	−
p_9	−	0	0	0	−	−	−	0		−	0	−	−
$\mathbf{p_{10}}$	**+**	**+**	**+**	**+**	**+**	**+**	**+**	**+**	**+**		**+**	**+**	**+**
p_{11}	0	0	−	−	−	0	−	0	0	−		−	−
p_{12}	+	+	+	0	0	+	+	+	+	−	+		0
p_{13}	+	+	0	0	0	+	0	+	+	0	+	0	

All the preceding analysis evidently depends on the numeric significance weight vector $\mathbf{w}$ we have chosen for computing the overall global outranking relation $\succsim_{\mathbf{w}}$. The organizers of the EBPA did not fix these weights, instead they only imposed a significance hierarchy of the selection criteria. Let us finally study the very impact of the choice of the significance weight vector $\mathbf{w}$ on our best choice recommendation.

Stability of the CONDORCET Graph

The question we must ask at this point is whether the bipolar characterisation of the global outranking may not appear as an artifact induced by our more or less arbitrarily chosen cardinal significance weights: $w_{sq} = 0.4$, $w_{tp} = 0.3$, $w_{or} = 0.2$, and $w_{pq} = 0.1$?

Let $\mathscr{W}$ denote the set of all possible weight vectors we may define on a family F of criteria. Let $\geqslant_{\mathbf{w}}$ be a significance preorder[21] associated with F via the natural $\geqslant$ relation on the significance values in the given weight vector $\mathbf{w}$. The symmetric part $=_{\mathbf{w}}$ of the relation $\geqslant_{\mathbf{w}}$ induces s ordered equi-significance classes, denoted $\Pi^{\mathbf{w}}_{(1)} <_{\mathbf{w}} \ldots <_{\mathbf{w}} \Pi^{\mathbf{w}}_{(s)}$, with $1 \leq s \leq |F|$. The criteria gathered in each equi-significance class have the same weight in $\mathbf{w}$ and, for $1 \leqslant i < j \leqslant s$, those of equi-significance class $\Pi^{\mathbf{w}}_{(i)}$ have a higher weight than those of class $\Pi^{\mathbf{w}}_{(j)}$. In our case here, we observe in fact $s = 4$ such equi-significance classes: one for each preference viewpoint f in F gathering the equi-significant opinions of all the five jury members.[22]

Let $\mathscr{W}_{=_{\mathbf{w}}} \subset \mathscr{W}$ denote the set of all significance weight vectors that are compatible with the equivalence part $=_{\mathbf{w}}$. Let $\mathscr{W}_{\geqslant_{\mathbf{w}}} \subset \mathscr{W}$ denote the set of all significance weight vectors that are compatible with $\geqslant_{\mathbf{w}}$,and let $\mathbf{w} \in \mathscr{W}$. The CONDORCET *robustness denotation* (Bisdorff, 2004) of $\succsim_{\mathbf{w}}$, denoted $[\![\succsim_{\mathbf{w}}]\!]$, is defined, for all $(x, y) \in A \times A$, as follows:

$$[\![x \succsim_{\mathbf{w}} y]\!] := \begin{cases} 4 & \text{if } r(x \succsim_{\mathbf{v}} y) = +1.0 \ \ \forall \mathbf{v} \in \mathscr{W}; \\ 3 & \text{if } r(x \succsim_{\mathbf{v}} y) > 0.0 \ \ \forall \mathbf{v} \in \mathscr{W}_{=_{\mathbf{w}}}; \\ 2 & \text{if } \left[r(x \succsim_{\mathbf{v}} y) > 0.0 \ \ \forall \mathbf{v} \in \mathscr{W}_{\geqslant_{\mathbf{w}}}\right] \\ & \quad \wedge \left[\exists \mathbf{v}' \in \mathscr{W} : r(x \succsim_{\mathbf{v}'} y) < +1.0\right]; \\ 1 & \text{if } \left[r(x \succsim_{\mathbf{w}} y) > 0.0\right] \wedge \left[\exists \mathbf{v}' \in \mathscr{W}_{\geqslant_{\mathbf{w}}} : r(x \succsim_{\mathbf{v}'} y) \leqslant 0.0\right]; \\ 0 & \text{if } r(x \succsim_{\mathbf{w}} y) = 0.0; \\ -1 & \text{if } \left[r(x \succsim_{\mathbf{w}} y) < 0.0\right] \wedge \left[\exists \mathbf{v}' \in \mathscr{W}_{\geqslant_{\mathbf{w}}} : r(x \succsim_{\mathbf{v}'} y) \geqslant 0.0\right]; \\ -2 & \text{if } \left[r(x \succsim_{\mathbf{v}} y) < 0.0 \ \ \forall \mathbf{v} \in \mathscr{W}_{\geqslant_{\mathbf{w}}}\right] \\ & \quad \wedge \left[\exists \mathbf{v}' \in \mathscr{W} : r(x \succsim_{\mathbf{v}'} y) > -1.0\right]; \\ -3 & \text{if } r(x \succsim_{\mathbf{v}} y) < 0.0 \ \ \forall \mathbf{v} \in \mathscr{W}_{=_{\mathbf{w}}}; \\ -4 & \text{if } r(x \succsim_{\mathbf{v}} (x, y)) = -1.0 \ \ \forall \mathbf{v} \in \mathscr{W}; \end{cases} \quad (5.15)$$

[21] As classically done, $>_{\mathbf{w}}$ denotes the asymmetric part of $\geqslant_{\mathbf{w}}$, whereas $=_{\mathbf{w}}$ denotes its symmetric part.

[22] See the complete set of global outrankings from each preference point of view in Appendix "Overall Outranking per Preference Viewpoint".

with the following semantics:

- $[\![x \succsim_{\mathbf{w}} y]\!] = \pm 4$ if, either, the jury *unanimously validates* (resp. *invalidates*) the outranking situation between x and y on all the selection criteria, or, we observe an effective counter-veto or a veto situation;
- $[\![x \succsim_{\mathbf{w}} y]\!] = \pm 3$ if a significant majority of the jury *validates* (resp. *invalidates*) the outranking situation between x and y for any significance weights of the selection criteria;
- $[\![x \succsim_{\mathbf{w}} y]\!] = \pm 2$ if a *significant majority* of the jury *validates* (resp. *invalidates*) the outranking situation between x and y for all $\geqslant_{\mathbf{w}}$-compatible significance weights;
- $[\![x \succsim_{\mathbf{w}} y]\!] = \pm 1$ if a significant weighted majority of criteria *validates* (respectively *invalidates*) this outranking situation for $\mathbf{w}$ but not for all $\geqslant_{W}$-compatible weights;
- $[\![x \succsim_{\mathbf{w}} y]\!] = 0$ if the total significance of the warranting criteria is *exactly balanced* by the total significance of the not warranting criteria for $\mathbf{w}$.

Let us start by presenting the notation which allows us to detail the construction of the CONDORCET robustness denotation associated with a valued outranking relation $\succsim_{\mathbf{w}}$ and a significance weight vector $\mathbf{w}$.

We recall that $r(\succsim_f)$ represents the sum of the jury's members opinions on preference point of view f. When changing the sign of $r(\succsim_f)$, we may as well represent the sum of the jury's members *negated* opinions on this preference point of view f. From this fact it follows that $r(x \succsim_{\mathbf{w}} y) > 0.0$ is verified for all $\mathbf{w} \in \mathscr{W}_{\mathbf{w}}$ if and only if $r(x \succsim_{\mathbf{w}} y) - r(x \not\succsim_{\mathbf{w}} y) > r(x \not\succsim_{\mathbf{w}} y) - r(x \succsim_{\mathbf{w}} y)$ is also verified (Bisdorff, 2004). The latter inequality gives us the operational key for implementing a test for the presence of a CONDORCET robustness of degree ± 2. The same weights w_f and $-w_f$, denoting the "*affirmative*", respectively the "*refutative*", significance of each preference point of view, appear on each side of these inequalities. Furthermore, the sum of the coefficients $r(x \succsim_f x)$ and $r(x \not\succsim_f x)$—that constitute the terms $r(x \succsim_{\mathbf{w}} y)$ and $r(x \not\succsim_{\mathbf{w}} y)$—are equal for all couples (x, y) of posters. These coefficients may appear therefore as some kind of "*credibility*" distribution on the set of positive and negative significance weights.

To illustrate this insight, let us order the sequence $F_{\pm}$ of negative and positive preference points of view from the most significant negative one to the most significant positive one: $F_{\pm} := [-sq, -td, -or, -pq, pq, or, td, sq]$. Let us furthermore denote $r(x \succsim_{f(k)} y)$, respectively $r(x \not\succsim_{f(k)} y)$, for $(k) = (1), \ldots, (2s)$ indexing the ordered entries in the sequence $F_{\pm}$, the bipolar characteristics of the individual outranking situations gathered in the same equi-significance class $\Pi^{\mathbf{w}}_{f(k)}$.

In the first line of Table 5.12, we may for instance, observe the distribution of $r(p_{10} \succsim_f p_1)$ over the ordered sequence $F_{\pm}$. The jury unanimously validates the outranking on all the selection criteria. Hence, $[\![p_{10} \succsim_{\mathbf{w}} p_1]\!] = +4$. The positive outranking results remains indeed valid with any significance weight vector, even one where the jury members would be attributed different significance weights. Consider now, in the second part of Table 5.12, the distribution of $r(p_{10} \succsim_f p_4)$

Table 5.12 Repartition of the bipolar characterisation $r(\succsim)$ into negative and positive arguments

$F_{\pm}$	$-sq$	$-tp$	$-or$	$-pq$	$+pq$	$+or$	$+tp$	$+sq$
$p_{10} \succsim_{(f)} p_1$	0	0	0	0	**1.0**	**1.0**	**1.0**	**1.0**
$p_{10} \succsim_{(f)} p_4$	0	0	0	0	1.0	1.0	1.0	**0.2**
$p_{10} \not\succsim_{(f)} p_4$	**0.2**	1.0	1.0	1.0	0	0	0	0
$p_1 \succsim_{(f)} p_2$	0	0	0	0.2	0	0.2	0.2	0.2
$p_1 \not\succsim_{(f)} p_2$	0.2	0.2	0.2	0	0.2	0	0	0
$C^{\mathbf{w}}_{(k)}(p_1, p_2)$	0	0	0	**0.2**	**0.2**	**0.4**	**0.6**	**0.8**
$\overline{C^{\mathbf{w}}_{(k)}}(p_1, p_2)$	**0.2**	**0.4**	**0.6**	**0.6**	**0.8**	**0.8**	**0.8**	**0.8**
$p_4 \succsim_{(f)} p_{10}$	0	1.0	0.6	1.0	0	0	0	0.2
$p_4 \not\succsim_{(f)} p_{10}$	0.2	0	0	0	1.0	0.6	1.0	0
$C^{\mathbf{w}}_{(k)}(p_4, p_{10})$	**0**	**1.0**	1.6	2.6	2.6	2.6	2.6	2.8
$\overline{C^{\mathbf{w}}_{(k)}}(p_4, p_{10})$	**0.2**	**0.2**	0.2	0.2	1.2	1.8	2.8	2.8

and $r(p_{10} \not\succsim_f p_4)$ over the ordered sequence $F_{\pm}$. The jury unanimously validates again this outranking situation, but only on three of the four selection criteria. From the *Scientific Quality* point of view, however, only a majority of 60 % validates it. Hence, $[\![p_{10} \succsim_{\mathbf{w}} p_4]\!] = +3$. The positive outranking result remains indeed valid with any significance weight vector where the jury members are consider equi-significant.

Furthermore, let $C^{\mathbf{w}}_{f(k)}(x, y) := \sum_{i=1}^{k} \big[r(x \succsim_{f(i)} y)\big]$ be the cumulative sum of "*outranking*" characteristics for all preference points of view having significance at least equal to the one associated to $f_{(k)}$, and let $\overline{C^{\mathbf{w}}_{f(k)}}(x, y) := \sum_{i=1}^{k} \big[-r(x \succsim_{f(i)} y)\big]$ be the same cumulative sum of the negation of these characteristics.

In the third part of Table 5.12, we may see these cumulative repartition for the comparison of posters p_1 and p_2. As $C^{\mathbf{w}}_{(k)}(p_1, p_2)$ for $f_{(k)}$ in $F_{\pm}$ is strictly lower than the cumulative repartition of $\overline{C^{\mathbf{w}}_{(k)}}(p_{10}, p_4)$, we are thus sure that $r(p_{10} \succsim_{\mathbf{w}} p_4)$ will stay strictly positive for all $\mathbf{w} \in \mathscr{W}_{\mathbf{w}}$. Hence, $[\![p_1 \succsim_{\mathbf{w}} p_2]\!] = +2$. This ± 2 denotation test of Proposition 2 corresponds in fact to the verification of *stochastic dominance-like* conditions (see Bisdorff, 2004). And, in the absence of a ± 4 or ± 3 denotation, the following proposition gives us the corresponding test for the presence of a ± 2 denotation:

Proposition 2 (Bisdorff, 2004) *Let $\succsim_{\mathbf{w}}$ represent the global weighted outranking relation obtained with significance weight vector* **w**.

$$[\![x \succsim_{\mathbf{w}} y]\!] = +2 \;\Leftrightarrow\; \begin{cases} \forall k \in 1, \ldots, s : \; C^{\mathbf{w}}_{f(k)}(x, y) \leqslant \overline{C^{\mathbf{w}}_{f(k)}}(x, y)\,; \\ \exists k \in 1, \ldots, s : \; C^{\mathbf{w}}_{f(k)}(x, y) < \overline{C^{\mathbf{w}}_{f(k)}}(x, y). \end{cases} \tag{5.16}$$

The respective negative degree $[\![x \succsim_{\mathbf{w}} y]\!] = -2$ may be checked with similar conditions using reversed inequalities.

A ± 1 CONDORCET robustness denotation, corresponding to the observation of a weighted majority (resp. minority) in the absence of the ± 2 case, is simply verified as follows:

$$[\![x \succsim_{\mathbf{w}} y]\!] = \pm 1 \iff \big((x \succsim_{\mathbf{w}} y) \gtrless 0.0 \big) \wedge [\![x \succsim_{\mathbf{w}} y]\!] \neq \pm 2 \big). \tag{5.17}$$

This situation is illustrated in the fourth part of Table 5.12, where we may notice that the cumulative repartition of the bipolar characterisation of $p_4 \succsim p_{10}$ is neither strictly lower nor strictly greater than its negation. Hence, $[\![p_4 \succsim_{\mathbf{w}} p_{10}]\!] \neq \pm 2$. The apparent result that p_4 does not outrank poster p_{10} ($r(p_4 \succsim_{\mathbf{w}} p_{10}) = -0.44$; see Table 5.6 in Sect. 5.2.3) is thus not stable for all **w**-order compatible significance vectors and $[\![p_4 \succsim_{\mathbf{w}} p_{10}]\!]$ is equal to -1.

The CONDORCET robustness degrees of the global outranking statements $\succsim_{\mathbf{w}}$ for all couples of competing posters are shown in Table 5.13. We notice now that the previous best choice recommendation, namely poster p_{10} becomes positively confirmed. Indeed, with a robustness degree of at least $+3$, i.e. *positively outranking with any $=_{\mathbf{w}}$-compatible weight vector*, i.e. even totally independent of any significant differentiation of the preference points of view, poster p_{10} is definitely confirmed as the unique *robust* CONDORCET winner. There is even evidence that p_{10} *unanimously outranks* posters p_1, p_3, p_5, p_6 and p_8. Inspecting Column p_{10} of the same Table 5.13, we may furthermore notice that no other poster positively outranks p_{10}. The jury members even unanimously invalidate the statement that p_6 and p_{11} might outrank p_{10}. The CONDORCET robustness analysis shows, by the way, that poster p_4 is, apart from p_{10}, positively outranking all other competing poster with any $\geqslant_{\mathbf{w}}$-compatible weight vector. Finally, poster p_9 is definitely confirmed to be outranked with any $\geqslant_{\mathbf{w}}$-order compatible weight vector, and so can be rejected with good reasons, even if it has not been evaluated by some jury members.

Table 5.13 CONDORCET robustness degrees of the weighted outranking relation

$[\![x \succsim_{\mathbf{w}} y]\!]$	p_1	p_2	p_3	p_4	p_5	p_6	p_7	p_8	p_9	$\mathbf{p_{10}}$	p_{11}	p_{12}	p_{13}
p_1		+2	−3	−3	−1	+2	−2	+2	+3	**−3**	+3	−3	−2
p_2	−2		−2	−2	−2	−2	−2	−3	+3	**−3**	−1	−2	−3
p_3	+3	+3		+1	+1	+3	+3	+3	+3	**−3**	+3	+1	−1
p_4	+3	+3	+2		+3	+3	+3	+3	+3	**−1**	+3	+2	+2
p_5	+3	+3	+2	−1		+4	+3	+3	+3	**−3**	+3	+1	+0
p_6	+1	+2	−3	−3	−2		−2	+3	+3	**−4**	+3	−3	−3
p_7	+2	+2	−3	−1	−3	+3		+3	+3	**−3**	+3	+0	−3
p_8	+0	+3	−3	−3	−3	+2	−3		+3	**−3**	+3	−2	−3
p_9	−3	−3	−3	−3	−3	−3	−2	−3		**−3**	−2	−2	−3
$\mathbf{p_{10}}$	**+4**	**+3**	**+4**	**+3**	**+4**	**+4**	**+3**	**+4**	**+3**		**+3**	**+3**	**+3**
p_{11}	+2	+2	−3	−3	−3	−2	−3	+2	+3	**−3**		−3	−2
p_{12}	+3	+2	+2	+1	+3	+3	+3	+2	+3	**−1**	+3		+2
p_{13}	+4	+3	+3	+1	+3	+3	+3	+3	+3	**−1**	+3	+2	

5.4 Conclusions

To conclude this long methodological study of the EBPA case, let us enumerate some remarks, first, on the case itself, and later more generally concerning our approach to MCDA decision aiding practice.

1. **Auditing**: Regarding the output of the historical decision making process, the actual decision to attribute the EBPA to poster p_{10} can be transparently legitimated, both from the preference modelling—, as well as, from the best unique choice recommendation viewpoint. Computing the underlying global outranking relation and the corresponding best choice recommendation requires, apart from the official set of selection criteria with its significance preorder pre-settled institutionally by the EBPA organizer, no further model parameters. The only clearly needed information here are in fact the individual ordinal performance assessments delivered by the jury members with respect to the officially recommended selection criteria. This cognitive task corresponds well, however, with their scientific and professional qualification. Indeed, the official nomination into the jury is precisely based on this reputation and guarantees therefore the official expert status of the jury members.
2. **MAVT Approach**: Would a value theory based approach, in this case, do the same job? This is doubtful for two reasons:

    a. The actual decision making process shows that the EBPA jury has to come to its conclusion after all the poster sessions have happened and before the actual closing session begins where the winner has to be announced. This leaves very little time—a single physical meeting of the jury members—to elicit all the cognitively complex model parameters like swing weights or value trade offs between the selection criteria which would, the case given, be needed for a conjoint measurement of the overall performances.
    b. The presence of some missing evaluations represents furthermore an irreducible problem for all value theory approach. By nature, the value theory approach can indeed not positively take into account non existing evaluations. Either, partially evaluated posters would have to be dropped from the contest (a solution difficult to legitimate by the EBPA jury), or, a fictive neutral value would have to be artificially fixed to fill in the missing values.

    The social choice theory approach, that underlies the outranking methodology, fits, on the contrary, quite well here with the actual group decision problem the EBPA jury has to tackle. Achieving or validating decisions by implicit or explicit voting procedures is quite acceptable in our culture and the five jury members are by nature to be considered equi-significant for the selection of the best poster. A jury member, considered as a voter, may, by the way, abstain himself from delivering his opinion. This feature, present in every practical voting system, is effectively available in the RUBIS outranking approach and naturally allows for coherently tackling missing performance assessments.

3. **Ranking Versus Selecting**: Finally, it is interesting to compare our approach with the case study concerning the choice of a cooling system for a power plant (see Chap. 8). There, the best choice decision problem is treated as a ranking problem with the argument that the output of ranking methods is *richer*. Clearly, a value theory approach will not make the difference between selection and ranking procedures as a total ranking will anyway be available beforehand to the selection procedure via the global value assessments of the decision alternatives. In the outranking approach, however, things are more subtle in the sense that constructing a complete ranking may in practice need much more preferential information (in order to be richer as claimed before) than a direct best choice selection procedure like the RUBIS method. But this additional preferential information, needed for a complete ranking of the decision alternatives, generally represents the most doubtful part of the preference modelling assumptions, especially when the multiple criteria don't reveal a trivial concordance for easily rendering a global ranking. Here we painfully recover Arrow's impossibility theorem in the sense that making globally concordant a family of, otherwise discordant, criteria definitely needs a strong arbiter, i.e. a dictator principle generally hidden behind non trivial model parameters, who induces insidiously the requested, complete and transitive, global preference. As put to the point by Roy,[23] it is precisely the parsimony and the simplicity of the preference modelling parameters that represent the practical advantage of an outranking approach, and in particular of the RUBIS best choice method when applied to solve this decision aiding problem.

Appendix 1: The Complete Performance Tableau

The evaluation of the 13 competing posters on all four selection criteria by all the jury members are expressed in Table 5.14 on a common ordinal performance scale from 0 (lowest) to 10 (highest). The *slash* symbol (/) represents not available evaluations (see the corresponding paragraph in Sect. 5.1.3) at the moment where the award jury had to select the award winner.

[23]"... The goal of our research was to design a resolution method ... that is easy to put into practice, that requires as few and reliable hypotheses as possible, and that meets the needs [of the decision maker] ... " (Roy et al., 1966).

Table 5.14 Evaluation marks given by all the jury members on all the competing posters

	Scientific quality					Theory or practice of OR					Originality					Presentation quality				
Poster ID	j_1	j_2	j_3	j_4	j_5	j_1	j_2	j_3	j_4	j_5	j_1	j_2	j_3	j_4	j_5	j_1	j_2	j_3	j_4	j_5
p_1	4	7	5	5	3	4	7	6	5	3	4	6	6	7	3	4	7	5	6	2
p_2	/	1	6	2	/	/	1	7	3	/	/	1	8	3	/	/	3	9	7	/
p_3	6	6	7	6	2	8	9	7	6	4	6	7	7	7	5	6	6	9	7	5
p_4	8	9	9	8	6	7	8	6	7	4	8	8	7	7	4	8	6	7	7	6
p_5	8	6	8	7	2	8	7	9	7	0	8	5	7	7	2	8	8	8	6	5
p_6	5	5	5	6	2	5	7	5	5	0	5	5	5	6	2	5	7	6	5	5
p_7	6	5	6	6	/	7	8	7	6	/	6	5	5	6	/	8	8	5	3	/
p_8	4	/	5	6	2	4	/	5	6	0	4	/	7	5	2	7	/	10	5	4
p_9	/	/	5	3	/	/	/	5	3	/	/	/	7	3	/	/	/	10	3	/
p_{10}	9	9	8	8	4	9	9	9	7	6	9	9	9	7	7	9	10	10	8	7
p_{11}	6	9	8	7	5	6	8	6	6	5	6	9	7	8	5	8	9	8	7	3
p_{12}	4	5	7	5	/	4	5	7	5	/	4	3	7	5	/	4	5	3	3	/
p_{13}	4	8	8	8	8	4	8	8	7	10	4	6	7	7	8	4	9	9	8	10

The complete performance table, encoded in XMCDA-2.0 format under the name `bpaeuro20.xml`, may be downloaded from the webpage http://leopold-loewenheim.uni.lu/Digraph3/handbook/chapter-5. An extract of the XMCDA-2.0 encoding is shown hereafter:


```xml
<?xml version="1.0" encoding="UTF-8"?>
<xmcda:XMCDA
  xmlns:xmcda=
  "http://www.decision-deck.org/2009/XMCDA-2.0.0"
  instanceID="void">

 <projectReference id="bpaeouro20" name="bpaeouro20.xml">
    <title>The EURO 20 Best Poster Award</title>
    <author>Raymond Bisdorff</author>
    <version>D2 MCDA Applications Book</version>
 </projectReference>

 <alternatives mcdaConcept="alternatives">
    <description>
      <subTitle>List of competing posters.</subTitle>
    </description>
    <alternative id="p01" name=""
                mcdaConcept="potentialDecisionAction">
      <description>
        <comment>submitted poster</comment>
      </description>
      <type>real</type>
      <active>true</active>
    </alternative>
    ...
    ...
  </alternatives>
```


(continued)

```
   <criteria  mcdaConcept="criteria">
      <description>
         <subTitle>Family of criteria</subTitle>
      </description>

      <criterion  id="or2"
                  name="or2"
                  mcdaConcept="criterion">
         <description>
            <comment>
               Originality evaluated by jury member j−2
            </comment>
            <version>performance</version>
         </description>
         <active>true</active>
         <criterionValue>
            <value><real>0.04</real></value>
         </criterionValue>
         <scale>
            <quantitative>
               <preferenceDirection>max</preferenceDirection>
               <minimum><real>0.0</real></minimum>
               <maximum><real>10.0</real></maximum>
            </quantitative>
         </scale>
         <thresholds>
            <threshold  id="pref"
                  name="preference"
                  mcdaConcept=
               "performanceDiscriminationThreshold">
               <linear>
                  <slope><real>0.0</real></slope>
                  <intercept><real>1.0</real></intercept>
               </linear>
            </threshold>
         </thresholds>
      </criterion>
      ...
      ...
   </criteria>
   <performanceTable  mcdaConcept="performanceTable">
     <description>
        <subTitle>Rubis Performance Table.</subTitle>
     </description>
     <alternativePerformances>
        <alternativeID>p01</alternativeID>
        <performance>
          <criterionID>or2</criterionID>
          <value><real>6.00</real></value>
        </performance>
        ...
        ...
     </alternativePerformances>
   </performanceTable>
</xmcda:XMCDA>
```

Appendix 2: Overall Outranking per Preference Viewpoint

The following tables (Tables 5.15, 5.16, 5.17, and 5.18) may be computed with the `Digraph3` collection of Python3 modules (Bisdorff, 2014), as shown in Listing 5.1

Listing 5.1 Computing with the Python3 `outrankingDigraphs` module (Bisdorff, 2014)

```
#!/usr/bin/env python3
# MCDA Applications Handbook
# Chapter on BPA Euro 2004: Appendix 2
#---------------------------------------

from outrankingDigraphs import *

# load the complete performance tableau from file bpaeuro20.xml
T = XMCDA2PerformanceTableau('bpaeuro20')

# gather the individual preference viewpoints from all 5 jury members
Sq = ['sq1', 'sq2', 'sq3', 'sq4', 'sq5']
Tp = ['tp1', 'tp2', 'tp3', 'tp4', 'tp5']
Or = ['or1', 'or2', 'or3', 'or4', 'or5']
Pq = ['pq1', 'pq2', 'pq3', 'pq4', 'pq5']

# gather the family F of preference viewpoints
F = [Sq, Tp, Or, Pq]

# generate and show the outranking relation Sf per viewpoint f in F
for f in F:
    print 'Global outranking relation from viewpoint %s' %f
    Sf = BipolarOutrankingDigraph(T,coalition=F,Normalized=True)
    Sf.showRelationTable()
```

Table 5.15 Compairing the posters from the *Scientific Quality* (*sq*) point of view

$r(\succcurlyeq_{sq})$	p_1	p_2	p_3	p_4	p_5	p_6	p_7	p_8	p_9	p_{10}	p_{11}	p_{12}	p_{13}
p_1	–	+0.2	−0.2	−1.0	−0.2	+0.2	−0.4	+0.6	+0.4	−1.0	+0.2	−1.0	−0.6
p_2	−0.2	–	−0.6	−0.6	−0.6	−0.2	−0.2	−0.2	0	−0.6	−0.4	−0.6	−0.6
p_3	+0.2	+0.6	–	−0.6	−0.2	+1.0	+0.8	+1.0	+0.4	−1.0	+0.6	−0.2	−0.6
p_4	+1.0	+0.6	+0.6	–	+0.6	+1.0	+0.8	+1.0	+0.4	+0.2	+0.6	+0.6	+0.2
p_5	+0.2	+0.6	+1.0	−0.2	–	+1.0	+0.8	+1.0	+0.4	−0.2	+0.6	+0.2	+0.2
p_6	+0.2	+0.2	−0.6	−0.6	−0.6	–	0	+1.0	+0.4	−1.0	+0.2	−1.0	−0.6
p_7	+0.4	+0.6	−0.4	−0.4	−0.8	+0.8	–	+0.8	+0.4	−0.8	+0.2	−0.4	−0.4
p_8	+0.2	+0.2	−0.6	−0.6	−0.6	+0.6	0	–	+0.4	−1.0	+0.2	−1.0	−0.6
p_9	0	0	−0.4	−0.4	−0.4	0	−0.4	0	–	−0.4	−0.4	−0.4	−0.4
p_{10}	+1.0	+0.6	+1.0	+0.2	+1.0	+1.0	+0.8	+1.0	+0.4	–	+0.6	+0.6	+0.6
p_{11}	+0.6	+0.4	−0.2	−0.6	−0.6	−0.2	−0.2	+0.2	+0.4	−0.6	–	−0.6	−0.2
p_{12}	+1.0	+0.6	+1.0	−0.2	+0.2	+1.0	+0.8	+1.0	+0.4	+0.2	+0.6	–	+0.2
p_{13}	+1.0	+0.6	+0.6	−0.2	+0.6	+0.6	+0.4	+1.0	+0.4	+0.2	+0.6	+0.2	–

Table 5.16 Compairing the posters from the *Contribution to OR Theory and/or Practice* (tp) point of view

$r(\succcurlyeq_{sq})$	p_1	p_2	p_3	p_4	p_5	p_6	p_7	p_8	p_9	p_{10}	p_{11}	p_{12}	p_{13}
p_1	–	+0.2	−1.0	−0.6	+0.2	+0.6	−0.8	+0.6	+0.4	−1.0	+0.2	−0.6	−0.6
p_2	−0.2	–	−0.2	−0.2	−0.2	−0.2	−0.2	−0.2	+0.4	−0.6	0	−0.2	−0.6
p_3	+1.0	+0.6	–	+1.0	+1.0	+1.0	+0.8	+1.0	+0.4	−0.2	+0.6	+0.6	+0.2
p_4	+1.0	+0.2	−0.6	–	+0.2	+1.0	+0.4	+1.0	+0.4	−1.0	+0.2	+0.6	−0.2
p_5	+0.2	+0.2	−0.2	−0.2	–	+1.0	0	+1.0	+0.4	−0.6	+0.2	−0.2	−0.2
p_6	+0.2	+0.2	−1.0	−1.0	+0.2	–	−0.8	+0.6	+0.4	−1.0	+0.2	−1.0	−0.6
p_7	+0.8	+0.6	−0.4	+0.8	0	+0.8	–	+0.8	+0.4	−0.8	+0.6	+0.8	0
p_8	−0.2	+0.2	−1.0	−0.6	−0.2	+0.2	−0.4	–	+0.4	−1.0	+0.2	−0.6	−0.6
p_9	−0.4	0	−0.4	−0.4	0	0	−0.4	0	–	−0.4	−0.4	−0.4	−0.4
p_{10}	+1.0	+0.6	+1.0	+1.0	+1.0	+1.0	+0.8	+1.0	+0.4	–	+0.6	+1.0	+0.6
p_{11}	+0.6	+0.4	−0.2	−0.2	−0.2	+0.2	−0.2	+0.2	+0.4	−0.6	–	−0.2	−0.2
p_{12}	+1.0	+0.2	−0.6	+0.6	+0.2	+1.0	0	+1.0	+0.4	−1.0	+0.2	–	−0.2
p_{13}	+1.0	+0.6	+0.2	+0.6	+0.6	+0.6	+0.4	+1.0	+0.4	−0.2	+0.6	+0.6	–

Table 5.17 Compairing the posters from the *Originality* (or) point of view

$r(\succcurlyeq_{sq})$	p_1	p_2	p_3	p_4	p_5	p_6	p_7	p_8	p_9	p_{10}	p_{11}	p_{12}	p_{13}
p_1	–	+0.2	−0.6	−0.6	+0.2	+0.6	+0.4	+0.6	0	−0.6	+0.2	−1.0	+0.2
p_2	−0.2	–	−0.2	−0.2	−0.2	−0.2	−0.2	−0.2	+0.4	−0.2	0	−0.2	−0.2
p_3	+1.0	+0.2	–	+0.2	+0.6	+1.0	+0.8	+1.0	+0.4	−0.6	+0.6	+0.2	+0.6
p_4	+1.0	+0.2	+0.6	–	+1.0	+1.0	+0.8	+1.0	+0.4	−0.6	+0.6	−0.2	+0.6
p_5	+0.2	+0.2	+0.2	+0.2	–	+1.0	+0.8	+1.0	+0.4	−0.6	+0.6	−0.2	+0.2
p_6	−0.6	+0.2	−1.0	−1.0	−0.2	–	+0.4	+0.6	0	−1.0	+0.2	−1.0	−0.6
p_7	−0.4	+0.2	−0.4	−0.8	−0.4	+0.8	–	+0.4	0	−0.8	+0.2	−0.4	−0.4
p_8	−0.2	+0.2	−0.6	−0.6	−0.2	−0.2	−0.4	–	+0.4	−1.0	+0.6	−0.6	−0.2
p_9	0	0	0	0	0	0	0	0	–	−0.4	0	0	0
p_{10}	+1.0	+0.6	+1.0	+1.0	+1.0	+1.0	+0.8	+1.0	+0.4	–	+0.6	+0.6	+0.6
p_{11}	+0.2	0	−0.2	−0.2	−0.2	−0.2	−0.2	+0.6	+0.4	−0.6	–	−0.2	+0.2
p_{12}	+1.0	+0.2	+1.0	+0.6	+0.6	+1.0	+0.8	+1.0	+0.4	−0.2	+0.6	–	+0.6
p_{13}	+1.0	+0.2	+0.2	+0.2	+0.6	+0.6	+0.4	+1.0	+0.4	−0.2	+0.6	−0.2	–

Table 5.18 Compairing the posters from the *Presentation Quality* (pq) point of view

$r(\succcurlyeq_{sq})$	p_1	p_2	p_3	p_4	p_5	p_6	p_7	p_8	p_9	p_{10}	p_{11}	p_{12}	p_{13}
p_1	–	−0.2	−0.2	−0.6	−1.0	−0.2	0	−0.2	+0.2	−1.0	+0.8	−0.6	−0.6
p_2	+0.2	–	+0.2	+0.2	+0.2	+0.2	+0.2	−0.2	+0.2	−0.6	+0.6	+0.2	−0.2
p_3	+0.6	+0.2	–	−0.2	−0.2	+0.6	0	+0.2	+0.2	−1.0	+0.8	+0.2	−0.2
p_4	+0.6	+0.2	+0.6	–	+0.2	+0.6	+0.4	+0.6	+0.2	−1.0	+0.8	+0.2	−0.6
p_5	+1.0	+0.2	+0.6	+0.6	–	+1.0	+0.8	+0.6	+0.2	−1.0	+0.8	+0.6	−0.6

(continued)

Table 5.18 (continued)

$r(\succcurlyeq_{sq})$	p_1	p_2	p_3	p_4	p_5	p_6	p_7	p_8	p_9	p_{10}	p_{11}	p_{12}	p_{13}
p_6	+0.6	−0.2	−0.6	−0.6	−1.0	–	0	+0.2	+0.2	−1.0	+0.8	−0.2	−0.6
p_7	+0.4	−0.2	0	0	0	0	–	0	+0.2	−0.8	+0.8	0	−0.4
p_8	+0.2	+0.2	−0.2	−0.6	−0.6	+0.6	0	–	+0.6	−0.6	+0.8	+0.2	−0.2
p_9	−0.2	−0.2	−0.2	−0.2	−0.2	−0.2	+0.2	−0.2	–	−0.2	+0.6	+0.2	−0.2
p_{10}	+1.0	+0.6	+1.0	+1.0	+1.0	+1.0	+0.8	+1.0	+0.6	–	+0.8	+1.0	+0.6
p_{11}	−0.4	−0.6	−0.8	−0.8	−0.8	−0.8	−0.4	−0.8	+0.2	−0.8	–	−0.4	−0.4
p_{12}	+0.6	−0.2	−0.2	+0.2	+0.2	+0.2	+0.8	−0.2	+0.2	−1.0	+0.8	–	−0.2
p_{13}	+1.0	+0.6	+0.6	+0.6	+0.6	+0.6	+0.4	+0.2	+0.2	−0.2	+0.8	+0.6	–

Glossary

Abbreviations and Terms

BCR: Best choice recommendation promoted by the RUBIS decision aiding methodology (see Bisdorff et al., 2008). It consists in a minimal, strict outranking, stable and maximal determined bipolar-valued choice set, computed directly on the given bipolar-valued outranking graph.

DECISION DECK: The DECISION DECK project aims at collaboratively developing Open Source software tools implementing Multiple Criteria Decision Aiding (MCDA) methods. Its purpose is to provide effective tools for three types of users:

- practitioners who use MCDA tools to support actual decision makers involved in real world decision problems;
- teachers who present MCDA methods in courses, for didactic purposes;
- researchers who want to test and compare methods or to develop new ones.

More information may be found on the official web site of the DECISION DECK Project: http://www.decision-deck.org.

EBPA: Euro 2004 Best Poster Award (see Bisdorff, 2004).

ELECTRE: Multiple criteria decision aiding methods, originating from seminal work of B. Roy (early seventies) with contributions from numerous PhD students and senior researchers that collaborated with him during the eighties and nineties when visiting his Laboratoire d'Analyse et de Modélisation des Systèmes d'aide à la Décision (Lamsade) (see http://www.lamsade.dauphine.fr) at Université Paris-Dauphine.

EURO: The Association of European OR Societies (see http://www.euro-online.org).

Kernel: An *outranking* (respectively *outranked*) *kernel* in a directed outranking graph corresponds to a *dominant* (respectively an *absorbent*) and *independent* subset of decision alternatives. The dominant version, also called *game solution*, is due to Von Neumann and Morgenstern (1944), whereas the absorbent version is due to Berge. The name "noyau" (kernel) proposed by Berge (1956), probably stems from the zero values (algebraic kernels) of the GRUNDY function which deliver internally and externally stable solutions for NIM like game (see Berge, 2001).

LPD: Large Performance Differences. The LPD polarized characterisation of an outranking situation allows to take into account large performance differences when assessing its validation (see Bisdorff (2013)).

RUBIS: Multiple criteria decision aiding method for selecting the unique best decision alternative from a bipolar-valued outranking digraph (see Bisdorff et al., 2008).

XMCDA: Standard XML encoding norm for MCDA Applications data (see Chap. 20 in this handbook).

Symbols

A: Set of conference posters competing for the best poster award.

J: Index set for the award jury members j_k, $k = 1, \ldots, 5$, nominated for selecting the best poster.

F: Official set of EBPA selection criteria: *Scientific Quality* (*sq*), *Contribution to OR Theory and/or Practice* (*tp*), *Originality* (*or*), and *Presentation Quality* (*pq*). Each $f \in F = \{sq, tp, or, pq\}$ is also called a *preference viewpoint*.

$\mathbf{x} \geqslant^{\mathbf{j}}_{\mathbf{f}} \mathbf{y}$: Individual statement of jury member j that poster x is at least as good as poster y with respect to preference viewpoint f (see Eq. (5.2)).

$\mathbf{x} \succcurlyeq^{\mathbf{j}} \mathbf{y}$: Overall statement of jury member j that poster x is at least as good as poster y with respect to all the given selection criteria (see Eq. (5.4)).

$\mathbf{x} \succcurlyeq_{\mathbf{f}} \mathbf{y}$: Global statement of all jury members that poster x is at least as good as poster y with respect to preference point of view f (see Eq. (5.3)).

$\mathbf{x} \succsim \mathbf{y}$: Global outranking statement of all jury members that poster x is at least as good as poster y with respect to all the given selection criteria. This situation is commonly referred as poster x globally *outranks* poster y (see Eq. (5.6)).

$\mathbf{C(A, S)}$: The CONDORCET graph, i.e. the median cut crisp directed graph, associated with the bipolar-valued characterisation of the global outranking statements. $x \,\mathrm{S}\, y$, for $(x, y) \in A^2$, is true (respectively false) if the bipolar characteristic function $r(x \succsim_{\mathbf{w}} y)$ of the global outranking situation $x \succsim_{\mathbf{w}} y$ shows a significant weighted majority (respectively minority) of epistemic support considering the significance weight vector $\mathbf{w}$.

$\mathbf{x \tilde{S} y}$: ELECTRE like outranking statement, polarizing the global outranking statement with *veto* and *counter-veto* effects (see Eqs. (5.12) and (5.13) (Bisdorff, 2013)).

$\mathbf{r(x\,R\,y)}$: bipolar characteristic function of pairwise relational statement $x \,\mathrm{R}\, y$ with $\mathrm{R} \in \{\geqslant^{j}_{f}, \succcurlyeq_{f}, \succcurlyeq^{j}, \succsim, \tilde{\mathrm{S}}\}$ defined on A and taking values in the rational interval $[-1.0, +1, 0]$. Positive values validate, whereas negative values invalidate, the relational $x \,\mathrm{R}\, y$ statement. The zero value signifies an indeterminate situation, i.e. where the relational $x \, \mathrm{R} \, y$ statement appears neither validated nor invalidated (Bisdorff, 2002).

$[\![\mathbf{x} \succsim_w \mathbf{y}]\!]$: CONDORCET robustness denotation associated with global weighted outranking relation $\succsim_{\mathbf{w}}$. See Definition 5.15 (Bisdorff, 2004).

References

Arrow, K. J., & Raynaud, H. (1986, March) *Social choice and multicriterion decision-making*. MIT Press books (vol. 1). Cambridge: MIT Press.

Barbut, M. (1980). Médianes, Condorcet et Kendall. *Mathématiques et Sciences Humaines, 69*, 9–13.

Berge, C. (1956). *La fonction de Grundy d'un graphe infini. Comptes Rendus. Académie des Sciences, Paris, 242*, 1404–1405.

Berge, C. (2001). *The theory of graphs* (original title: *The theory of graphs and its applications*). Mineola, NY: Dover. (Originally published by Wiley 1962).

Bisdorff, R. (2002). Logical foundation of multicriteria preference aggregation. In D. Bouyssou, E. Jacquet-Lagrèze, P. Perny, R. Słowiński, D. Vanderpooten, & P. Vincke (Eds.), *Aiding decisions with multiple criteria* (pp. 379–403). Boston: Kluwer Academic Publishers.

Bisdorff, R. (2004). Concordant outranking with multiple criteria of ordinal significance. *4OR, 2* (4), 293–308.

Bisdorff, R. (2008). On clustering the criteria in an outranking based decision aid approach. In H. A. L. Thi, P. Bouvry, & D. Pham (Eds.), *Computation and optimization in information systems and management sciences*. CCIS (pp. 409–418). Springer, Heidelberg.

Bisdorff, R. (2013). On polarizing outranking relations with large performance differences. *Journal of Multi-Criteria Decision Analysis, 20*, 3–12.

Bisdorff, R. (2014). Digraph3: a collection of python3 modules for computing with outranking digraphs. http://leopold-loewenheim.uni.lu/Digraph3/docSphinx/html.

Bisdorff, R., Meyer, P., & Roubens, M. (2008 June). Rubis: a bipolar-valued outranking method for the best choice decision problem. *4OR: A Quarterly Journal of Operations Research, 6*(2), 143–165.

Bisdorff, R., Pirlot, M., & Roubens, M. (2006). Choices and kernels from bipolar valued digraphs. *European Journal of Operational Research, 175*, 155–170.

Fishburn, P. C. (1977). Condorcet social choice functions. *SIAM Journal on Applied Mathematics, 33*(3), 469–489.

Roy, B. (1985). *Méthodologie multicritère d'aide à la décision*. Paris: Economica.

Roy, B. (1991). The outranking approach and the foundations of ELECTRE methods. *Theory and Decision, 31*(1), 49–73.

Roy, B., & Bouyssou, D. (1993). *Aide Multicritère à la Décision : Méthodes et Cas*. Paris: Economica.

Roy, B., Benayoun, R., & Sussmann, B. (1966). ELECTRE: une méthode pour guider le choix en présence de points de vue multiples. Technical Report 49, Société d'Economie et de Mathématique Appliqué, Direction Scientifique.

Roy, B., Słowiński, R. (2008). Handling effects of reinforced preference and counter-veto in credibility of outranking. *European Journal of Operational Research, 188*(1), 185–190.

Sen, A. K. (1986) Social choice theory. In K. J. Arrow, & M. D. Intriligator (Eds.), *Handbook of mathematical economics* (vol. 3, pp. 1073–1181). New York: North-Holland.

Von Neumann, J., & Morgenstern, O. (1944). *Theory of games and economic behaviour*. Princeton: Princeton University Press.

Editors' Comments on "The EURO 2004 Best Poster Award"

This chapter describes a decision making process, in which a committee has to award a prize to the best in a series of posters presented at a conference. Besides the context of **group decision making**, the main singularity of this study is the fact that not all experts have evaluated all posters so that the evaluation matrix involves missing values. The chapter is also an illustration of the use of a specific outranking method, designed by the author and selecting the best item or a subset of top items from the set of all alternatives.

The author of this study was appointed chair of the jury of the Best Poster Award at the EURO 2004 Operational Research Conference in Rhodos. One may thus consider that the **client** was EURO, the Federation of European OR Societies. More precisely, the Programme and the Organizing Committees of the conference appointed five of their members to constitute the **jury**. The benefit for the client here is mostly symbolic, as EURO is a non-profit organization whose aim is to promote OR and help to disseminate its most promising scientific achievements. In the particular case of the award, the **client's goal** was to stimulate the submission of (good) posters at its conferences, presumably in view of limiting the number of parallel regular communications sessions.

The **client's priorities** were communicated to the jury through the specification of four criteria (scientific quality, contribution to theory and practice of OR, originality and quality of presentation). As a further indication, it was specified that these criteria should "be taken into account in decreasing order of significance". The jury was thus to act firstly as a **group of experts** evaluating the posters on the four specified criteria. And secondly, they were supposed to play the role of **decision makers** having to choose the best poster. This group, which was making the decision on behalf of the EURO federation, felt the need to justify its decision. Indeed, the winner was not only announced at the closing session of the conference, but also, the evaluation procedure and the arguments which led the jury to make its decision were presented to the audience in the closing session.

This application illustrates the case of a decision delegated to a committee (i.e. the jury). It shows how the committee worked to reach a decision. Since the president of the jury is an expert in decision aiding, he acted both as member of the jury and as an **analyst**. The present study briefly describes the process by which the jury came up with a decision (in Sect. 5.1). The remaining—and largest—part of the chapter can be described as an *a posteriori* consolidation of the jury decision. The real **decision process** was conducted under time pressure since the decision had to be made before the end of the conference. Therefore, the author felt the need to come back to the model, analyze it more in depth and "re-build" the recommendation, taking pains to make sure that it was robust, i.e. insensitive to the options taken during the preference modeling phase.

The problem, the jury was in charge of, was definitely a **choice problem**. The definition of the alternatives and the specification of the relevant points of view was straightforward. The alternatives were simply the 13 posters competing for the award. The points of view to be taken into consideration in the evaluation were specified by the Programme and Organization Committees of the conference. Furthermore, the latter even gave indications regarding the relative importance of the specified viewpoints.[24]

The choice of a multicriteria **evaluation method** was made by the president of the jury who opted for an outranking method. Each member of the jury was asked to assess each competing poster on each point of view by a mark from 0 to 10 (from "very weak" to "excellent"). These marks were considered as ordinal evaluations. Due to some constraints not all the jury members could assess all the posters so that some entries were missing in the evaluation matrix. The **preference modelling** and **aggregation method** that were used are similar to the ELECTRE I method (Roy, 1968; Roy and Bouyssou, 1993) (see also Chap. 3, Sect. 3.5, and Chap. 4, Sect. 4.2.2). They differ from it mainly by the following features:

- the outranking relation that is built is valued and bipolar, with the special value 0 coding indeterminateness, i.e. meaning that no judgment can be made about the concerned comparison of items;
- the best alternative or the set of top alternatives ("best choice" set) are determined directly from the valued outranking relation by a specially designed algorithm (the RUBIS method).

An interesting feature of this method is that it rather naturally allows to deal with **missing data** (using the special value 0). The advantages of the **best choice** set yielded by the RUBIS method as compared to the usual kernel obtained on the basis of a crisp relation are discussed in detail.

Two manners of aggregating the jury members judgments are considered. In the first approach, the pairwise comparisons of all posters are performed for each jury member and the resulting valued relations are summed up (i.e., the values on homologous arcs in the outranking relations of all jury members are summed up) resulting in an overall **outranking relation**, which is exploited by means of the RUBIS method. The second approach counts the number of jury members who give a better mark to a poster than to another on each point of view; a weighted sum of these numbers then yields the value on the corresponding arc of the overall outranking relation. Both approaches obviously yield the same outranking relation due to the fact that the aggregation both over the criteria and over the jury members is performed by using a sum (or a weighted sum); these sums can be permuted.

The construction of the valued outranking relation is rather transparent since it is obtained, for each pair of items, as a weighted sum of the number of jury members who prefer an item over the other on each point of view. Such a simple formulation allows to **analyse the robustness** of the best choice set when varying some preference modeling options, e.g. when introducing vetoes and counter-vetoes, or imposing a qualified majority instead of a simple one, or liberating oneself

[24] An XMCDA 2-0 encoding of the performance tableau may be downloaded from the webpage http://leopold-loewenheim.uni.lu/Digraph3/handbook/chapter-5/.

from hypotheses on the criteria weight values. In the present case study, the unique best poster is particularly stable, which is not surprising in view of the evaluation matrix. But the method does not reveal only evidences. The robustness analysis also points rather clearly to the posters that would be natural candidates for the second best.

The study confirms very neatly the **decision made** by the jury. It is also a good illustration of the author's methodology.

In the framework of outranking methods, the proposed model shows interesting features among which I would pinpoint the transparency of the bipolar valued outranking relation and its ability to accommodate missing evaluations in a straightforward way. The method however requires more systematic testing since finding the best choice in the present case study seems rather easy. It would be of great interest to see how the "best choice set" yielded by the RUBIS algorithm behaves in more delicate decision cases.

References

Roy, B. (1968). Classement et choix en présence de points de vue multiples: La méthode ELECTRE. *Revue Francaise d'Informatique et de Recherche Opérationnelle, 8*, 57–75.

Roy, B., & Bouyssou, D. (1993). *Aide Multicritère à la Décision : Méthodes et Cas*. Paris: Economica.

Chapter 6
Multicriteria Evaluation-Based Framework for Composite Web Service Selection

Salem Chakhar, Serge Haddad, Lynda Mokdad, Vincent Mousseau, and Samir Youcef

Abstract The present paper seeks to propose a general framework to composite Web services selection. The proposed framework extends the conventional Web services architecture by adding a new component in the registry devoted to multicriteria classification of compositions into different ordered Quality of Service (QoS) classes. This additional component takes as input the specification of the desired service, a set of functional and non-functional evaluation criteria, a set of QoS-ordered classes, and a set of preference parameters, and generates as output a classification of composite Web services into different QoS-ordered classes. In addition to the description of the proposed framework, the paper proposes solutions to construct, evaluate and classify composite Web services. The paper also briefly presents the developed prototype and then illustrates and discusses some computational aspects of the proposed framework using numerical data.

S. Chakhar
Portsmouth Business School, University of Portsmouth, Portland Building, Portland Street, Portsmouth, PO1 3AH, UK
e-mail: salem.chakhar@port.ac.uk

S. Haddad
Laboratoire Spécification et Vérification, École Normale Supérieure de Cachan, 61, Avenue du Président Wilson, 94235 Cachan Cedex, France
e-mail: haddad@lsv.enscachan.fr

L. Mokdad
LACL, Faculté des Sciences et Technologies, Université Paris XII, 61 Avenue du Général de Gaulle, 94010 Créteil Cedex, France
e-mail: lynda.mokdad@univ-paris12.fr

V. Mousseau (✉)
Laboratoire Génie Industriel, Ecole Centrale Paris, Grande Voie des Vignes, 92295 Châtenay-Malabry Cedex, France
e-mail: vincent.mousseau@ecp.fr

S. Youcef
LAMSADE, Université Paris-Dauphine, Place du Maréchal de Lattre de Tassigny, 75775 Paris Cedex 16, France
e-mail: samir.youcef@lamsade.dauphine.fr

R. Bisdorff et al. (eds.), *Evaluation and Decision Models with Multiple Criteria*, International Handbooks on Information Systems,
DOI 10.1007/978-3-662-46816-6_6

6.1 Introduction

Individual Web services are conceptually limited to relatively simple functionalities modelled through a collection of simple operations. However, for certain types of applications, it is necessary to combine a set of individual Web services to obtain more complex ones, called *composite* or *aggregated* Web services (Dustdar and Schreiner, 2005). One important issue within Web services composition is related to the selection of the most appropriate one among the different possible compositions. A possible solution is to use the Quality of Service (QoS) aspects to evaluate, compare and select the most appropriate composition(s). The QoS is defined as a combination of the different attributes of the Web service such as availability, response time, throughput, etc. The QoS is an important element of Web services and software quality evaluation (Blin and Tsoukiàs, 2001; Briand et al., 2002; Fenton and Pfleeger, 1997; Morisio et al., 2002, 2003). Currently, most of works use successive evaluation of different, non-functional, aspects of Web services in order to attribute a general "level of quality" to different composite Web services and to select the "best" one from these services. In these works, the evaluation of composite Web services is based either on a single criterion or, at best, on a weighted sum of several quantitative evaluation criteria. Both evaluation techniques are not appropriate in practice since: (1) a single criterion cannot encompass all the facets of the problem, (2) weighted sum-like aggregation rules may lead to the compensation problem since worst evaluations can be counterbalanced by higher evaluations, and (3) several QoS evaluation criteria are naturally qualitative ones but weighted sum-like aggregation rules cannot deal with this type of evaluation criteria.

The goal of this research is to propose a general framework to composite Web services selection based on *multicriteria evaluation* (Figueira et al., 2005a). The proposed framework extends the conventional Web services architecture by adding a new *Multicriteria Evaluation Component* (MEC) in the registry devoted to multicriteria classification of compositions into different QoS-ordered classes. The MEC takes as input the specification of the desired service, a set of functional and non-functional evaluation criteria, a set of QoS-ordered classes, and a set of preference parameters, and generates as output a classification of composite Web services into different QoS-ordered classes. In addition to the description of the proposed framework, the paper proposes solutions to construct, evaluate and classify composite Web services. The paper also briefly presents the developed prototype and then illustrates and discusses some computational aspects of the proposed framework using numerical data.

The classification of compositions is grounded on several criteria and takes the form of a qualitative scale with a finite set of evaluation levels corresponding to ordered QoS classes. The assignment of composite Web services into different QoS classes is based on the use of a multicriteria classification method. In this paper, the multicriteria classification method ELECTRE TRI (Figueira et al., 2005b) will be used. The application of this method requires the specification of a set of preference information such as criteria weights. The definition of these parameters requires an important cognitive effort from the consumer. To reduce this effort, MEC uses a specific Web service permitting to deduce the preference parameter values from a set of holistic information provided by the consumer. In this paper, the holistic information takes the form of the assignment of some typical composite Web services into different QoS classes.

The chapter is organized as follows. Section 6.2 discusses some related work. Section 6.3 presents the architecture of the proposed framework. Section 6.4 details the architecture of the multicriteria evaluation component while Sects. 6.5, 6.6 and 6.7 present proposed solutions to respectively construct, evaluate and classify composite Web services. The following section briefly describes the developed prototype while Sect. 6.9 illustrates the framework using numerical data. Some computational aspects related to the proposed framework are discussed in Sect. 6.10. Section 6.11 concludes the chapter.

6.2 Related Work

We discuss here a selection of proposals to composite Web services multicriteria evaluation and selection. Menascé (2004) considers two evaluation criteria (time and cost) and assigns to each one a weight between 0 and 1. The single combined score is computed as a weighted average of the scores of all criteria. The best composition of Web services can then be decided on the basis of the optimum combined score. One important limitation of this proposal is the compensation problem mentioned earlier.

In Georgakopoulos et al. (1999), the service definition models the concept of "placeholder activity" to cater for dynamic composition of Web services. A placeholder activity is an abstract activity replaced on the fly with an effective activity. Casati et al. (2000) deal with dynamic service selection based on user requirements expressed in terms of a query language. Klingemann (2000) considers the problem of dynamically selecting several alternative tasks within workflow using QoS evaluation. In Benatallah et al. (2002), the service selection is performed locally on the basis of a selection policy involving the parameters of the request, the characteristic of the services, the history of past executions and the status of the ongoing executions. One important shortcoming of Benatallah et al. (2002), Casati et al. (2000), Georgakopoulos et al. (1999) and Klingemann (2000) is the use of local selection strategy. In other words, services are considered as independent. Within this strategy, there is no guarantee that the selected Web service is the best one.

Zeng et al. (2003) propose the use of linear programming techniques to compute the "optimal" execution plans for composite Web service. However, the multi-attribute decision making approach used by the authors has the same limitation as weighted-sum aggregation rules, i.e., the compensation problem. Maximilien and Singh (2004) propose an ontology-based framework for dynamic Web service selection. However, they consider only a single criterion, which is not enough to take into account all the facets of the problem.

Menascé and Dubey (2007) extend the work of Menascé et al. (2007) on QoS brokering for *Service-Oriented Architectures* (SOA) by designing, implementing, and experimentally evaluating a service selection QoS broker that maximizes a utility function for service consumers. These functions allow stakeholders to ascribe a value to the usefulness of a system as a function of several QoS criteria such as response time, throughput, and availability. This framework is very demanding in terms of preference information from the consumers. Indeed, consumer should provide the QoS broker with their utility functions and their cost constraints on the requested services. Once again, the limitation of this work is the use of a weighted-sum optimization criterion, leading to the compensation problem as already mentioned. One important finding of this paper is the fact that the QoS broker uses the analytic queuing models to predict the QoS values of the various services that could be selected under varying workload conditions.

Ma and Zhang (2008) use genetic algorithms for Web service selection with global QoS constraints. The authors integrate two policies (an enhanced initial policy and an evolution policy), which matter permits to overcome several shortcomings of genetic algorithms.

6.3 Extended Web Services Architecture

6.3.1 Conventional Web Services Architecture

The Web service architecture is defined by the World Wide Web Consortium (W3C) (see http://www.w3.org/) in order to determine a common set of concepts and relationships that allow different implementations to work together (Champion et al., 2000). Figure 6.1 shows a graphical representation of the traditional Web service architecture. The conventional Web service architecture consists of three entities: the service provider, the service registry and the service consumer. The service provider creates or simply offers the Web service. The service provider needs to describe the Web service in a standard format, which is often XML (eXtensible Markup Language), and to publish it in a central service registry. The service registry contains additional information about the service provider, such as address and contact of the providing company, and technical details about the service. The service consumer retrieves the information from the registry and uses the service description obtained to bind and then invoke the Web service. The appropriate methods associated with these different operations are depicted in Fig. 6.1 by the keywords "publish", "bind" and "find".

The Web services architecture is loosely coupled and service oriented. The Web Service Description Language (WSDL) uses the XML format to describe the methods provided by a Web service. This includes input and output parameters,

Fig. 6.1 Conventional architecture of Web services

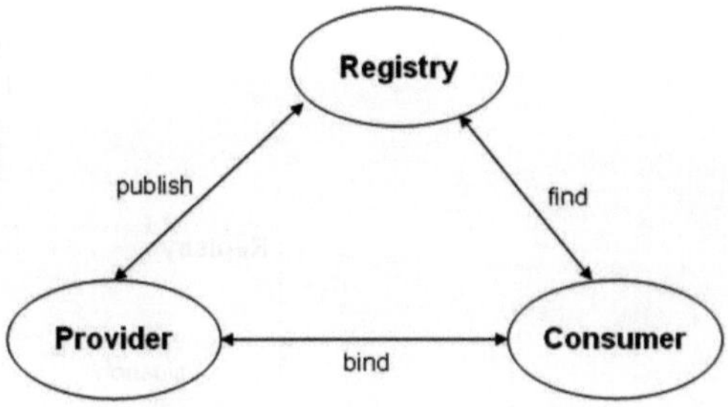

data types and the transport protocol, which is typically HTTP (HyperText Transfer Protocol). The Universal Description Discovery and Integration standard (UDDI) suggests means to publish details about a service provider, the services that are stored and the opportunity for service consumers to find service providers and Web service details. The Simple Object Access Protocol (SOAP) is generally used for XML formatted information exchange among the entities involved in the Web service model.

6.3.2 Proposed Web Services Architecture

As underlined earlier, the proposed framework extends the conventional Web services architecture by adding a new Multicriteria Evaluation Component (MEC) in the registry devoted to multicriteria evaluation. The general schema of the extended architecture is given in Fig. 6.2. According to the requirement of the consumer, the registry opts either for conventional evaluation or for multicriteria evaluation. By default, the registry uses conventional evaluation; multicriteria evaluation is used only if the consumer explicitly specifies this in the SOAP message addressed to the registry. This ensures the flexibility of the proposed architecture.

As stated earlier, the application of a multicriteria method needs the definition of a set of preference parameters, which needs an important cognitive effort from the consumer. To reduce this effort, MEC uses a specific Web service called WS-IRIS, which is a Web version of IRIS[1] system (Dias and Mousseau, 2003), permitting to infer the different preference parameter values. The input for WS-IRIS is a set of learning examples obtained by assigning some typical composite Web services into different QoS classes. These assignment examples will be used by WS-IRIS to infer the preference parameters necessary to apply the multicriteria classification method, which is ELECTRE TRI (Figueira et al., 2005b) in this paper.

As shown in Fig. 6.2, the three basic operations denoted by "publish", "bind" and "find" still exist. In addition, two new operations, denoted by keywords "infer" and

[1]Interactive Robustness analysis and Inference for Sorting problems.

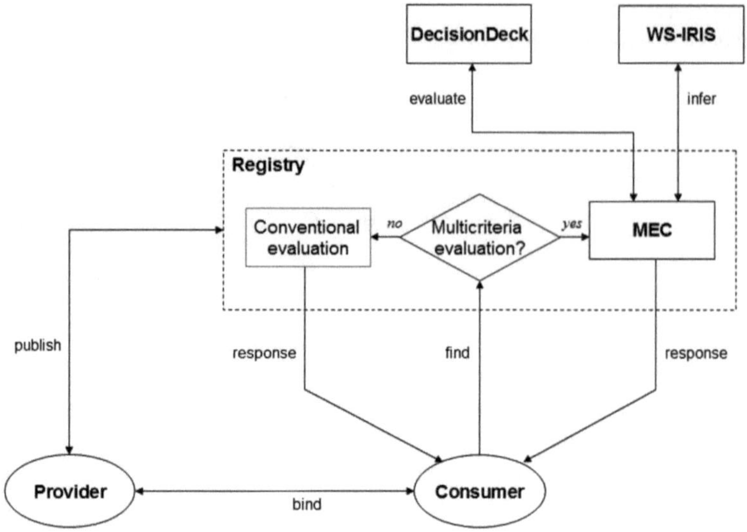

Fig. 6.2 Extended architecture of Web services

"evaluate", are included in the extended architecture. The first permits to handle data exchange between MEC and WS-IRIS. The latter permits to handle data exchange between MEC and Decision Deck platform. This platform is issued from the D2-Decision Deck project.[2] It consists of a Web-based framework to assist decision makers in evaluating alternatives in a multicriteria and multi-experts context.

To achieve the interaction among the entities of the extended Web service model, we need to enrich some SOAP protocols and add new ones. More specifically, we need to extend protocols of consumer request to registry and registry response to consumer; and add the ones relative to MEC request to WS-IRIS and WS-IRIS response to MEC.

6.4 Functional Architecture of MEC

The functional architecture of MEC component is depicted in Fig. 6.3. Basically, it takes as input the specification of the desired composite Web service, a set of functional and non-functional evaluation criteria, a set of QoS-ordered classes, and a set of assignment examples. All these pieces of information are extracted from the SOAP message sent by the consumer to the registry. MEC applies then the multicriteria method ELECTRE TRI to classify the composite Web services

[2]More information on this project is available at: www.decision-deck.org/.

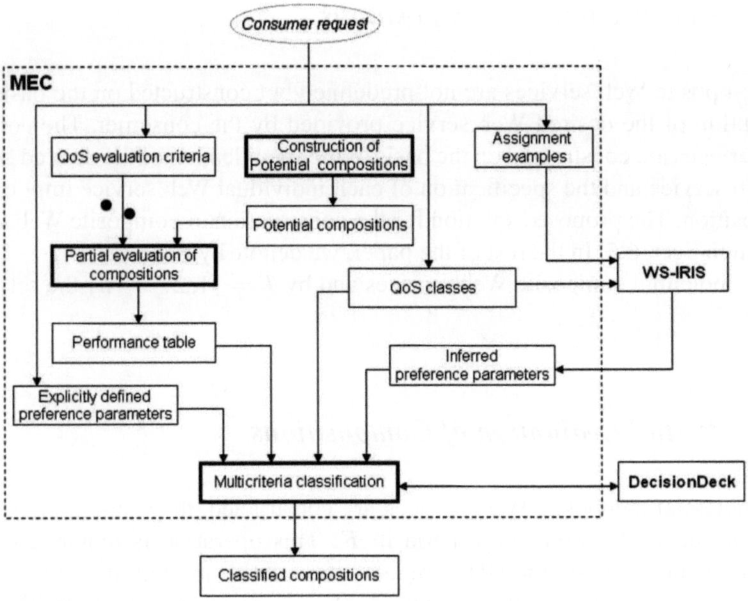

Fig. 6.3 Architecture of MEC

into different QoS-ordered classes. The final choice should be performed by the consumer, based on the recommendation of MEC.

Operationally, MEC stars by constructing the set of potential compositions which are then evaluated with respect to each QoS evaluation criterion. This operation leads to the creation of a performance table that summarizes the evaluation of all compositions with respect to all criteria. The performance table along with the preference parameters are then used as input to multicriteria classification in order to assign each of the obtained potential compositions into a single QoS class.

6.4.1 Identification of QoS Evaluation Criteria

The set of QoS evaluation criteria considered in a given application is extracted from the "find" SOAP message sent by the consumer to the registry. There are several QoS evaluation criteria. For convenience, a comprehensive list of commonly used criteria is given in the appendix. In the rest of the paper, we denote by $F = \{g_1, g_2, \cdots, g_m\}$ the set of m evaluation criteria and by $J = \{1, 2, \cdots, m\}$ the set of their indices. Theoretically, there is no limit to the number of criteria but at least two criteria should be provided. We observe also that a large set increases the cognitive effort required from the consumer and a few ones do not permit to encompass all the facets of the selection problem.

6.4.2 Construction of Compositions

The composite Web services are not predefined but constructed on the basis of the description of the desired Web service provided by the consumer. The composite Web services are constructed on the basis of the specification of the desired composite Web service and the specification of each individual Web service implied in the composition. The proposed solution for the construction of composite Web services is given in Sect. 6.5. In the rest of the paper, we denote by $K = \{k_1, k_2, \cdots, k_n\}$ the set of n potential composite Web services and by $I = \{1, 2, \cdots, n\}$ the set of their indices.

6.4.3 Partial Evaluation of Compositions

Once potential composite Web services are constructed, they should be evaluated with respect to all evaluation criteria in F. This operation is required since the evaluations provided by the UDDI registry are relative to individual Web services participating in the composition and not to the composition as a whole. The partial evaluation of a composite Web service $k_i \in K$ with respect to criterion $g_j \in F$ is denoted by $g_j(k_i)$. The matrix $[g_j(k_i)]$, $\forall i \in I, \forall j \in J$ is called the *performance table*. The computing of $g_j(k_i)$, $\forall i \in I, \forall j \in J$, will be dealt with in Sect. 6.6.

6.4.4 Definition of Preference Parameters

Most of multicriteria methods require the definition of a set of preference parameters such as criteria weights. This is also the case with the multicriteria classification method included in MEC. The value for the preference parameters can either be provided explicitly by the consumer or deduced from the assignment examples provided by the consumer and extracted from the "find" SOAP message sent by the consumer to the registry. These approaches to specify the preference parameter values can be used jointly. In the second approach, MEC uses the WS-IRIS Web service to infer the desired preference parameter values from the assignment examples.

6.4.5 Multicriteria Classification

The objective of multicriteria classification is to use the ELECTRE TRI method (Figueira et al., 2005b) to assign each of the composite Web services into a single QoS class. The QoS classes $Cl_1, Cl_2, \cdots, Cl_l$ are defined in terms of a set of multidimensional profiles as will be explained in Sect. 6.7. At this level, we simply mention that QoS classes are ordered from best to worst. This means that compositions assigned to the highest QoS class Cl_l are preferred to those assigned to Cl_{l-1}, which are themselves preferred to those assigned to Cl_{l-2}, and so on. More details on multicriteria classification are given in Sect. 6.7.

6.5 Constructing Potential Composite Web Services

Following Menascé (2004), a Web service is defined as follows.

Definition 6.1 A **Web service** S_i is a tuple (F_i, Q_i, H_i), where:

- F_i is a description of the service's functionality,
- Q_i is a specification of its QoS evaluation criteria, and
- H_i is its cost specification.

Menascé (2004) uses the term "attribute" instead of "criteria". The latter is more general and hence it is adopted here. A Web service's QoS evaluation criterion may be any one of the list provided in the appendix. A Web service's cost is often related to its quality. Faster, reliable, secure services will be more expensive, for example, but there could also be penalties associated with the fact of not meeting certain QoS goals or service-level agreements (SLAs) (Menascé, 2004).

A composition operation implies several individual Web services. The relationships among the individual Web services may be represented by a connected and directed graph $G = (X, V)$ where $X = \{S_i, S_j, \cdots, S_m\}$ is the set of individual Web services and $V = \{(S_i, S_j) : S_i, S_j \in X \wedge S_i \text{ can invoke } S_j\}$. The graph $G = (X, V)$ is called the **composition graph**. Figure 6.4, which is reproduced from Menascé (2004), presents a composition graph example implying six individual Web services S_1, S_2, S_3, S_4, S_5 and S_6. The edges in this figure represent different types of invocation. The latter ones correspond to different BPEL (Business Process Execution Language) constructors. The basic BPEL constructors are:

- *Sequential Invocation*. A Web service is activated as a result of the completion of one of a set of mutually exclusive predecessor activities. These activities may be listed with the XML `<sequence>` tag, that is, in lexical order. *Example*: S_2 and S_6 in Fig. 6.4.
- *Parallel Invocation* (*Fork*). It represents a point in the process where a single thread of control splits into multiple threads of control which can be executed in parallel. This pattern is supported by BPEL using XML `<flow>` tag. *Example*: S_1 in Fig. 6.4 which can invoke S_2 and S_3 in parallel.
- *Probabilistic Invocation*. A probability value p on an outgoing arrow from S_i to S_j indicates that S_i invokes S_j with probability p. If no value is indicated, the probability is assumed to be 1. *Example*: S_3 in Fig. 6.4 which can invoke S_4 with probability p_1 or S_5 with probability p_2.

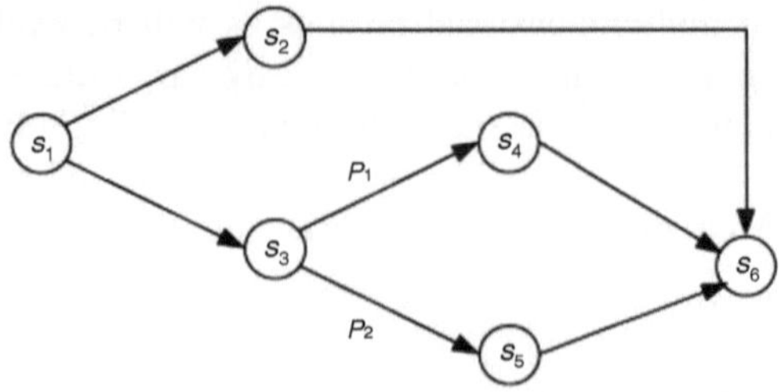

Fig. 6.4 An example of composition graph

- *Conditional Invocation*. Represents a situation where one or several branches are chosen. The first situation can directly be implemented using <switch> constructor and the second through control links inherited from XLANG. There is no example of conditional invocation in Fig. 6.4.
- *Synchronized Invocation (Join)*. A Web service is activated only when all of its predecessor Web services have completed. It can be implemented using control links inherited from XLANG. *Example*: S_6 in Fig. 6.4 which requires the completion of Web services S_4 and S_5.

We assume that each Web service S_i has a unique functionality F_i. However, the same functionality may be provided by different providers. Let P_i be the collection of providers supporting functionality F_i of Web service S_i: $P_i = \{s_i^1, s_i^2, \cdots, s_i^{n_i}\}$ where n_i is the number of providers in P_i. A composite Web service is defined as follows.

Definition 6.2 Let $S_1, S_2, \cdots, S_n$ be a set of n individual Web services such that $S_i = (F_i, Q_i, H_i)$ with $i = 1, \cdots, n$. Let P_i be the collection of Web services supporting functionality F_i. Let $G = (X, V)$ be the composition graph associated with $S_1, S_2, \cdots, S_n$. A **composite Web service** k is an instance $\{s_1, s_2, \cdots, s_n\}$ of G defined such that $s_1 \in P_1, s_2 \in P_2, \cdots, s_n \in P_n$.

It is clear that this definition may lead to a large number of compositions. Some solutions to avoid this problem will be introduced in Sect. 6.9.

To take into account the invocation probabilities associated with some Web services, we define a new function, called π, as follows:

$$\begin{aligned} \pi: \quad & X \times X && \rightarrow [0, 1] \\ & S_i \times S_j && \rightarrow \pi(S_i, S_j) \end{aligned}$$

The number $\pi(S_i, S_j)$ represents the probability that S_i invokes S_j.

Example 6.1 Consider the graph of Fig. 6.4 and suppose that:

- $P_1 = \{s_1^1, s_1^2, s_1^3, s_1^4\}$
- $P_2 = \{s_2^1, s_2^2, s_2^3\}$
- $P_3 = \{s_3^1, s_3^2\}$
- $P_4 = \{s_4^1\}$

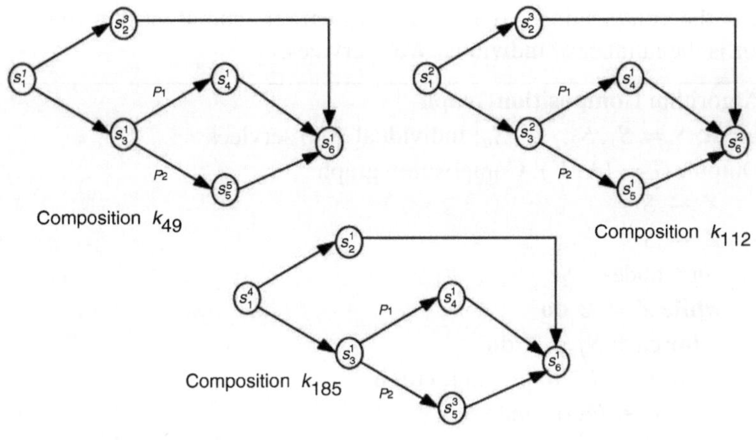

Fig. 6.5 Composed Web services k_{49}, k_{112} and k_{185}

- $P_5 = \{s_5^1, s_5^2, s_5^3, s_5^4, s_5^5\}$
- $P_6 = \{s_6^1, s_6^2\}$

where s_i^j is the jth provider of Web service S_i. Then, the following are some composite Web services:

- k_{49} associated with $G_{49} = (X_{49}, V_{49})$ where:
  - $X_{49} = \{s_1^1, s_2^3, s_3^1, s_4^1, s_5^5, s_6^1\}$
  - $V_{49} = \{(s_1^1, s_2^3); (s_1^1, s_3^1); (s_2^3, s_6^1); (s_3^1, s_4^1); (s_3^1, s_5^5); (s_4^1, s_6^1); (s_5^5, s_6^1)\}$
  - $\pi(s_3^1, s_4^1) = p_1; \pi(s_3^1, s_5^5) = p_2$
- k_{112} associated with $G_{112} = (X_{112}, V_{112})$ where:
  - $X_{112} = \{s_1^2, s_2^3, s_3^2, s_4^1, s_5^1, s_6^2\}$
  - $V_{112} = \{(s_1^2, s_2^3), (s_1^2, s_3^2), (s_3^2, s_4^1), (s_3^2, s_5^1); (s_4^1, s_6^2); (s_5^1, s_6^2)\}$
  - $\pi(s_3^2, s_4^1) = p_1; \pi(s_3^2, s_5^1) = p_2$
- k_{185} associated with $G_{185} = (X_{185}, V_{185})$ where:
  - $X_{185} = \{s_1^4, s_2^1, s_3^1, s_4^1, s_5^3, s_6^1\}$
  - $V_{185} = \{(s_1^4, s_2^1); (s_1^4, s_3^1); (s_3^1, s_4^1); (s_3^1, s_5^3); (s_4^1, s_6^1); (s_5^3, s_6^1)\}$
  - $\pi(s_3^1, s_4^1) = p_1; \pi(s_3^1, s_5^3) = p_2$

Figure 6.5 shows graphically the composite Web services k_{49}, k_{112} and k_{185}.

To construct the set of potential compositions, we have incorporated two algorithms in the MEC. The first one, called **CompositionGraph** which is given below, permits to construct the composition graph. In this algorithm, $\Gamma^+(x)$ returns the set of successors of node x: $\Gamma^+(x) = \{y \in X : (x, y) \in V\}$. The input of **CompositionGraph** algorithm is the description of the different individual Web services stored in the UDDI registry and the invocation probability function π. The output is the composition graph G defined earlier. The algorithm runs in $O(n^2)$ where n is the number of individual Web services.

```
Algorithm CompositionGraph
Input: S = S_1, S_2, ··· , S_n: Individual Web services
Output: G = (X, V): Composition graph
X ← S
Z ← S
curr_node← S_1
while Z ≠ ∅ do
  for each S_j ∈ X do
    if S_j ∈ Γ+(curr_node) then
      V ←(curr_node,S_j)
    end if
  end for
  Z ← Z\ curr_node
  curr_node← pick a node in Z
end while
return G
```

The second algorithm, given hereafter, is **CompositionsConstruction** that generates the potential compositions. The algorithm **CompositionsConstruction** proceeds as follows. First a tree T is constructed using **ConstructTree** procedure. The construction of this tree is explained in the next paragraph. Then, **CompositionsConstruction** uses the composition graph G to construct the different compositions as instances of the graph G. More concretely, compositions are then defined, using **ElementaryPath** function, as elementary paths in T. The complexity of algorithm **CompositionsConstruction** is $O(r_1 \times (r_2 + r_3))$ where $r_1 = |V|$ is the cardinality of V, $r_2 = \prod_{i=1}^{n} |P_i|$ is the number of compositions and r_3 is the complexity of **ElementaryPath**.

Now we come to the explanation of how the tree T is constructed by **ConstructTree** function. First, we mention that the tree T should have $n + 1$ levels (recall that n is the number of provides in P). Then, the nodes of the ith level are the providers in P_i. For each node in level i, we associate the providers in set P_{i+1} as sons. The same reasoning is used for $i = 1$ to $n - 1$. The nodes of level $n - 1$ are associated with the providers in P_n. Finally, a root r is added to T as the parent of nodes in the first level (representing the providers in P_1). Then, the set of nodes for each composition is obtained as an elementary path in T, as explained earlier. Figure 6.6 shows a schematic representation of the tree associated with composition graph given in Fig. 6.4. The first elementary path is composed of $s_1^1, s_2^1, s_3^1, s_4^1, s_5^1$ and s_6^1. The last elementary path is $s_1^4, s_2^3, s_3^2, s_4^1, s_5^5$ and s_6^2. Thus, the node set of k_1 is $X_1 = \{s_1^1, s_2^1, s_3^1, s_4^1, s_5^1, s_6^1\}$ and the node set of k_{240} is $X_{240} = \{s_1^4, s_2^3, s_3^2, s_4^1, s_5^5, s_6^2\}$.

Algorithm **CompositionsConstruction**

Input: $G = (X, V)$: Composition graph, $P = \{P_1, P_2, \cdots, P_n\}$: Providers

Output: K: Potential compositions

```
T ← ConstructTree(X,P)
t ← 1
K ← ∅
while t <= ∏_{i=1}^{n} |P_i| do
  X_t ← ElementaryPath(T)
  for each (S_h, S_k) ∈ V do
    V_t ← (s'_h, s'_k)
  end for
  k_t ← G_t = (X_t, V_t)
  K ← K ∪ k_t
  t ← t + 1
end while
return K
```

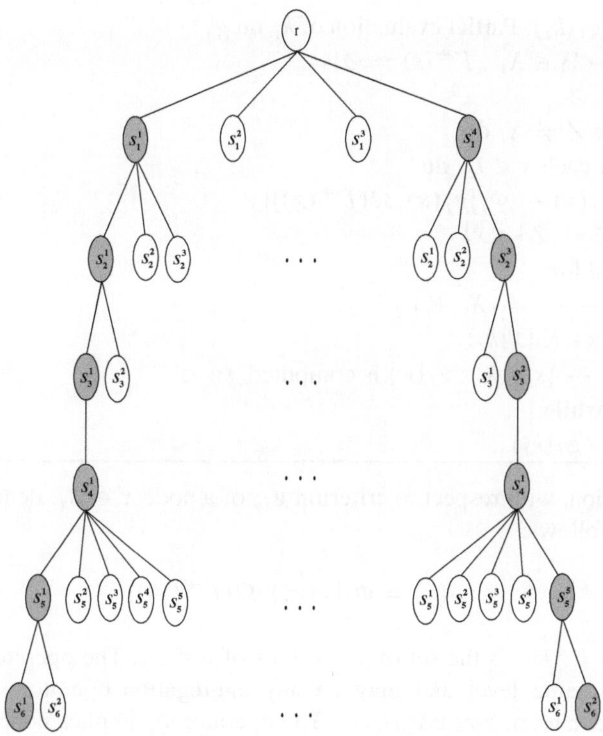

Fig. 6.6 Schematic representation of tree T

6.6 Evaluation of Compositions

As defined earlier, a potential composition is an instance of the composition graph $G = (X, V)$. Each composition can be seen as collection of individual Web services. The evaluations provided by the UDDI registry are relative to these individual Web services. However, to evaluate and compare the different potential compositions, it is required to define a set of rules to combine the partial evaluations (i.e. with respect to individual Web services) to obtain partial evaluations that apply to the whole composition.

To compute the partial evaluations $g_j(k_i)$ $(j = 1, \cdots, m)$ of different compositions k_i $(i = 1, \cdots, n)$, we need to define a set of m aggregation operators $\Phi_1, \Phi_2, \cdots, \Phi_m$, one for each evaluation criterion. The partial evaluation of a composition k_i on criterion g_j, $g_j(k_i)$, is computed as follows. It consists in applying a bottom-top scan on graph $G_i = (X_i, V_i)$ and to apply the aggregation operator Φ_j on each node. Algorithm **PartialEvaluation** below implements this idea. It runs on $O(r^2)$ where $r = |X|$ is the number of nodes in the composition graph.

Algorithm **PartialEvaluation**
Input: $k_i = G_i(X_i, V_i)$: Composition, Φ_j: Aggregation operators
Output: $g_j(k_i)$: Partial evaluation of k_i on g_j
$L_r \leftarrow \{s \in X_i : \Gamma^+(s) = \varnothing\}$
$Z \leftarrow \varnothing$
while $Z \neq X_i$ **do**
  for each $x \in L_r$ **do**
    $v_j(x) \leftarrow \Phi_j[g_j(x), \Omega(\Gamma^+(x))]$
    $Z \leftarrow Z \bigcup \{x\}$
  end for
  $k_t \leftarrow G_t = (X_t, V_t)$
  $K \leftarrow K \cup \{k_t\}$
  $L_r \leftarrow \{s \in X_i : v_j(w)$ is computed $\forall w \in \Gamma^+(s)\}$
end while
return $g_j(k_i)$

The valuation, with respect to criterion g_j, of a node $x \in X_i$, denoted $v_j(x)$, is computed as follows:

$$v_j(x) = \Phi_j[g_j(x), \Omega(\Gamma^+(x))]$$

Recall that $\Gamma^+(x)$ is the set of successors of node x. The operator Ω involves nodes on the same level and may be any aggregation operator such as `sum`, `product`, `max`, `min`, `average`, etc. The operator Φ_j implies nodes on different levels and vary according to the BPEL constructors (see Sect. 6.5) associated with node x. It may be the `sum`, `product`, `max`, `min`, or `average`.

It is important to note that when the criterion is ordinal, it is not possible to use the probability associated with the branches of a `<switch>` constructor. To avoid this problem, we may use one of the following rules (other rules may also be applied):

- ignore the probabilities and proceed as with the `< flow>` BPEL constructor,
- use the partial evaluation associated with the most probable branch,
- use the majority rule (when there are at least three branches),
- use the intermediate level between the partial evaluations associated with the most probable branch and the least probable branch,
- use the intermediate level between the highest partial evaluation and the lowest partial evaluation.

In what follows, we provide the proposed formulas for computing $v_j(x)$ $(j = 1, \cdots, 4)$ for response time, availability, cost and security evaluation criteria, denoted g_1, g_2, g_3 and g_4, respectively. Evaluation criteria g_1 and g_3 are to be minimized while criteria g_2 and g_4 are to be maximized. The three first criteria are quantitative. The latter is an ordinal one.

First, we mention that the following formulas apply for non-leaf nodes, i.e., $x \in X_i$ such that $\Gamma^+(x) \neq \varnothing$. For leaf nodes, i.e. $x \in X_i$ such that $\Gamma^+(x) = \varnothing$, the partial evaluation on a criterion g_j is simply $v_j(x) = g_j(x)$.

6.6.1 Response Time (g_1)

The response time of a non-leaf node x is computed as follows:

$$v_1(x) = g_1(x) + \max\{v_1(y) : y \in \Gamma^+(x)\} \tag{6.1}$$

or

$$v_1(x) = g_1(x) \quad + \sum_{y \in \Gamma^+(x)} \pi(x, y) \cdot v_1(y) \tag{6.2}$$

Equation (6.1) applies for the `<flow>` or the sequential BPEL constructors. Equation (6.2) applies when the constructor `<switch>` is used. Here: Φ_1 is the `sum` and Ω is the `max` [for Eq. (6.1)] or the `sum` [for Eq. (6.2)].

6.6.2 Availability (g_2)

For the availability, two formulas may be applied:

$$v_2(x) = g_2(x) \quad \cdot \prod_{y \in \Gamma^+(x)} v_2(y) \tag{6.3}$$

or

$$v_2(x) = g_2(x) \quad \cdot \sum_{y \in \Gamma^+(x)} \pi(x, y) \cdot v_2(y) \tag{6.4}$$

Equation (6.3) applies for the `<flow>` BPEL or the sequential constructors. Equation (6.4) applies when the constructor `<switch>` is used. Here: Φ_2 is the `product` and Ω is the `product` [for Eq. (6.3)] or the `sum` [for Eq. (6.4)].

6.6.3 Cost (g_3)

For cost criterion, two formulas may be used:

$$v_3(x) = g_3(x) \quad + \sum_{y \in \Gamma^+(x)} v_3(y) \tag{6.5}$$

or

$$v_3(x) = g_3(x) \quad + \sum_{y \in \Gamma^+(x)} \pi(x, y) \cdot v_3(y) \tag{6.6}$$

Equation (6.5) applies for the `<flow>` or the sequential BPEL constructors. Equation (6.6) applies when the constructor `<switch>` is used. Here, the `sum` operator is used for both Φ_3 and Ω.

6.6.4 Security (g_4)

Finally, for security criterion, we have:

$$v_4(x) = \min\{g_4(x), \min_{y \in \Gamma^+(x)} \{v_4(y)\}\} \tag{6.7}$$

Here, both Φ_4 and Ω are the `min` operator. Recall that security criterion is an ordinal one. Equation (6.7) applies when the `<flow>` BPEL constructor is used.

Table 6.1 Evaluations of providers of Web service S_1

	Response time (g_1)	Availability (g_2)	Cost (g_3)	Security (g_4)
s_1^1	2.0	0.99	0.4	1
s_1^2	1.7	0.95	0.5	2
s_1^3	1.6	0.80	0.7	3
s_1^4	3.4	0.94	0.1	5

Table 6.2 Evaluations of providers of Web service S_2

	Response time (g_1)	Availability (g_2)	Cost (g_3)	Security (g_4)
s_2^1	2.0	0.99	0.7	5
s_2^2	3.0	0.89	0.6	2
s_2^3	2.5	0.82	0.4	1

Table 6.3 Evaluations of providers of Web service S_3

	Response time (g_1)	Availability (g_2)	Cost (g_3)	Security (g_4)
s_3^1	2.0	0.85	0.4	4
s_3^2	1.7	0.84	0.5	2

Table 6.4 Evaluations of providers of Web service S_4

	Response time (g_1)	Availability (g_2)	Cost (g_3)	Security (g_4)
s_4^1	1.8	0.89	0.3	5

When the constructor <switch> is used, one of the rules mentioned above should be used.

These different equations are illustrated through the example that follows.

Example 6.2 For better illustration of the previous formulas, consider again the composition graph of Fig. 6.4 and the three compositions k_{49}, k_{112} and k_{185} given in Fig. 6.5. Suppose that $p_1 = 0.4$ and $p_2 = 0.6$. The objective is to show the computing of partial evaluations of k_{49}, k_{112} and k_{185} with respect to four evaluation criteria: Response time (g_1), Availability (g_2), Cost (g_3) and Security (g_4). The evaluation of the providers of Web services S_1 to S_6 with respect to g_1, g_2, g_3 and g_4 are given in Tables 6.1, 6.2, 6.3, 6.4, 6.5, and 6.6, respectively. Recall that evaluation criteria g_1 and g_3 are to be minimized while criteria g_2 and g_4 are to be maximized. Recall also that the three first criteria are quantitative. The latter is ordinal for which the following five-level scale is used: 1:"very low", 2: "low", 3: "average", 4: "high", and 5: "very high".

Illustrating now the computing for partial evaluation of composition k_{49} with respect to response time criterion (g_1). To compute $g_1(k_{49})$, Algorithm **PartialEvaluation** is used on $G_{49} = (X_{49}, V_{49})$. Details of computing are given below. Recall that aggregation mechanism Φ_1 associated with g_1 is the `sum` operator.

Table 6.5 Evaluations of providers of Web service S_5

	Response time (g_1)	Availability (g_2)	Cost (g_3)	Security (g_4)
s_5^1	3	0.86	0.5	1
s_5^2	1.5	0.60	0.6	2
s_5^3	2	0.99	0.8	5
s_5^4	2.5	0.82	1.2	4
s_5^5	3	0.90	0.6	3

Table 6.6 Evaluations of providers of Web service S_6

	Response time (g_1)	Availability (g_2)	Cost (g_3)	Security (g_4)
s_6^1	3	0.8	0.23	5
s_6^2	2.5	0.92	0.5	3

First, for leaf-node s_6^1, we have $v_1(s_6^1) = g_1(s_6^1) = 3.0$. Then, for nodes s_4^1 and s_5^5, we apply Eq. (6.1):

$$\begin{aligned} v_1(s_4^1) &= g_1(s_4^1) + \max\{v_1(s_6^1)\} \\ &= 1.8 + 3.0 \\ &= 4.8. \end{aligned}$$

$$\begin{aligned} v_1(s_5^5) &= g_1(s_5^5) + \max\{v_1(s_6^1)\} \\ &= 3.0 + 3.0 \\ &= 6.0. \end{aligned}$$

For node s_3^1, we apply Eq. (6.2):

$$\begin{aligned} v_1(s_3^1) &= g_1(s_3^1) + (p_1 \cdot v_1(s_4^1) + p_2 \cdot v_1(s_5^5)) \\ &= 2.0 + (0.4 \times 4.8 + 0.6 \times 6) \\ &= 7.52. \end{aligned}$$

For node s_2^3, we apply Eq. (6.1):

$$\begin{aligned} v_1(s_2^3) &= g_1(s_2^3) + \max\{v_1(s_6^1)\} \\ &= 2.5 + 3.0 \\ &= 5.5. \end{aligned}$$

For node s_1^1, we apply Eq. (6.1):

$$\begin{aligned} v_1(s_1^1) &= g_1(s_1^1) + \max\{v_1(s_2^3), v_1(s_3^1)\} \\ &= 2.0 + \max\{5.5, 7.52\} \\ &= 2.0 + 7.52 \\ &= 9.52. \end{aligned}$$

The partial evaluation of composition k_{49} on criterion response time is then $g_1(k_{49}) = 9.52$.

Consider now the evaluation of composition k_{49} on security criterion (g_4). For leaf-node s_6^1, we have $v_4(s_6^1) = g_4(s_6^1) = 5$. For nodes s_4^1 and s_5^5, we apply Eq. (6.7):

$$\begin{aligned} v_4(s_4^1) &= \min\{g_4(s_4^1), \min\{v_4(s_6^1)\}\} \\ &= \min\{5, \min\{5\}\} \\ &= 5. \end{aligned}$$

$$\begin{aligned} v_4(s_5^5) &= \min\{g_4(s_5^5), \min\{v_4(s_6^1)\}\} \\ &= \min\{3, \min\{5\}\} \\ &= 3. \end{aligned}$$

For node s_3^1, we apply Eq. (6.7). Remark that the security criterion is an ordinal one. Thus, we have used the first rule in the list given earlier, that is, we have ignored the probabilities p_1 and p_2 and proceed as with the < `flow`> BPEL constructor by using the `min` operator.

$$\begin{aligned} v_4(s_3^1) &= \min\{g_4(s_3^1), \min\{v_4(s_4^1), v_4(s_5^5)\}\} \\ &= \min\{4, \min\{5, 3\}\} \\ &= 3. \end{aligned}$$

For node s_2^3, we apply Eq. (6.7):

$$\begin{aligned} v_4(s_2^3) &= \min\{g_4(s_2^3), \min\{v_4(s_6^5)\}\} \\ &= \min\{1, 5\} \\ &= 1. \end{aligned}$$

Table 6.7 Partial evaluations of compositions k_{49}, k_{112} and k_{185}

Composition	Response time (g_1)	Availability (g_2)	Cost (g_3)	Security (g_4)
k_{49}	9.52	0.39567	2.14	1
k_{112}	8.42	0.48296	2.82	1
k_{185}	10.32	0.48093	2.16	4

For node s_1^1, we apply Eq. (6.7):

$$\begin{aligned} v_4(s_1^1) &= \min\{g_4(s_1^1), \min\{v_4(s_2^3), v_4(s_3^1)\}\} \\ &= \min\{1, \min\{1, 3\}\} \\ &= 1. \end{aligned}$$

Finally, the partial evaluation of composition k_{49} on g_4 is: $g_4(k_{49}) = 1$

The partial evaluation of compositions k_{49}, k_{112} and k_{185} with respect to the four criteria g_1, g_2, g_3 and g_4 is summed-up in Table 6.7.

Algorithm **PartialEvaluation** presented earlier permits to evaluate a given composition on a single criterion. Algorithm **PerformanceTable** below permits to obtain the complete performance table containing the evaluations of all potential compositions $k_i \in K$ with respect to all evaluation criteria $g_j \in F$. **PerformanceTable** is straightforward. It simply loops on the set of compositions K and on the set of criteria F and calls Algorithm **PartialEvaluation** to compute the partial evaluation of each composition in K with respect to each criterion in F. Algorithm **PerformanceTable** runs on $O(n \times m \times r)$ where n is the number of compositions, m is the number of evaluation criteria and r is the complexity of **PartialEvaluation**.

Algorithm **PerformanceTable**

Input: $K = \{k_1, k_2, \cdots, k_n\}$: Compositions, $\Phi_1, \cdots, \Phi_m$: Aggregation operators

Output: PerforTable: performance table

01. PerforTable $\leftarrow$ matrix of n rows and m columns
02. **for** $i = 1$ to n **do**
03.   **for** each $j = 1$ to m **do**
04.   PerforTable(i, m) $\leftarrow$ **PartialEvaluation**$(G_i(X_i, V_i), \Phi_j)$
05.   **end for**
06. **end for**
07. return PerforTable

One important remark to conclude this section is related to the evaluation of individual Web services. In the formulas given above, we have supposed that the partial evaluations of individual Web services $g_j(.)$ are available on the UDDI registry. However, this is not always true because these pieces of information may not be specified by the providers.

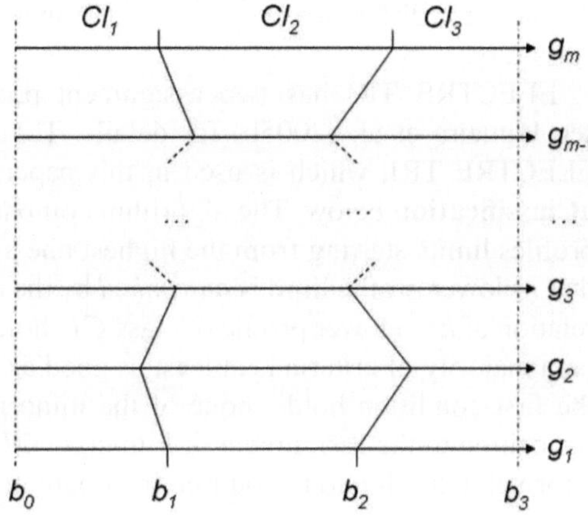

Fig. 6.7 Definition of three classes in terms of the profile limits

6.7 Multicriteria Classification of Compositions

The objective of this section is to evaluate the QoS of each composition. The formal model used to specify the evaluation of compositions is grounded on the multicriteria classification method. Let $\mathscr{E}$ be an ordinal scale composed of a finite set of l evaluation levels: $\varepsilon_1 \prec \varepsilon_2 \prec \cdots \prec \varepsilon_l$. Each level can be seen as a QoS class. Let Γ denote a multicriteria classification method. Then, to evaluate the overall QoS level of compositions, we need to apply the multicriteria classification method Γ to assign to each composition $k \in K$ a level on $\mathscr{E}$:

$$\Gamma \ : \ \begin{array}{ccc} K & \longrightarrow & \mathscr{E} \\ k & \longrightarrow & \Gamma(k) \end{array} \tag{6.8}$$

Different multicriteria classification methods can be applied. In this paper, the multicriteria classification method ELECTRE TRI (Figueira et al., 2005b) has been selected and used. ELECTRE TRI assigns objects described by several criteria to ordered classes. It uses multidimensional profiles $b_1, b_2, \cdots, b_{l-1}$ to define the limits of l QoS-ordered classes. Figure 6.7 shows the definition of three classes Cl_1, Cl_2, and Cl_3 in terms of two profile limits b_1 and b_2. Each profile is defined as a vector of m elements where m is the number of considered QoS evaluation criteria, denoted $g_1, g_2, \cdots, g_m$ in Fig. 6.7. Profiles b_0 and b_3 are defined as a vector of lower and higher boundaries of evaluation criteria scales.

In order to represent decision maker's preferences, ELECTRE TRI uses weights $w_1, w_2, \cdots, w_m$, indifference thresholds $q_1, q_2, \cdots, q_m$ preference thresholds $p_1, p_2, \cdots, p_m$ and veto thresholds $v_1, v_2, \cdots, v_m$, all of them are associated to criteria. Threshold $q_j(b_h)$ represents the largest difference $g_j(k) - g_j(b_h)$ preserving an indifference between k and b_h with respect to criterion g_j. Threshold $p_j(b_h)$ represents the smallest difference $g_j(k) - g_j(b_h)$ compatible with a preference in favor of k with respect to criterion g_j. Threshold $v_j(b_h)$ represents the smallest difference $g_j(b_h) - g_j(u)$ incompatible with the assignment of k to class Cl_h.

ELECTRE TRI has two assignment procedures: optimistic and pessimistic; see Figueira et al. (2005b) for details. The pessimistic assignment procedure of ELECTRE TRI, which is used in this paper, is given in Algorithm **MulticriteriaClassification** below. The algorithm compares each composition k to each of the profiles limits starting from the highest one and assign k to the first class Cl_h such that its lower profile limit is *outranked* by the evaluation vector of k. The outranking relation of k on lower profile of class Cl_h holds if and only if (1) the evaluation of k on a majority of criteria is at least as good as the lower profile of Cl_h and (2) when the first condition holds, none of the minority of criterion shows an "important" opposition to the assignment of k to class Cl_h; see, e.g., Figueira et al. (2005b) for a formal definition to the outranking relation.

```
Algorithm MulticriteriaClassification
Input: K: List of compositions
Output: Assignment of compositions to different QoS classes
l ← number of classes
result ← ∅
for each k in K do
    h ← l
    assigned ← False
    while h ≥ 0    and    not(assigned) do
        if AssignmentTest(k, b_h) then
            result ←result ∪{(k, Cl_k)}
            assigned ← True
        end if
        h ← h − 1
    end while
    Assign k to class Cl_{l+}
end for
return result
```

The algorithm runs in $\theta(r \times l)$, where r is the number of compositions in K and l is the number of classes. The function **AssignmentTest** in Algorithm **MulticriteriaClassification** permits to check if the outranking relation holds or not. This requires the computing of the *credibility indexes* $\sigma(k, b_h) \in [0, 1]$ measuring the level to which a given composition k *outranks* (i.e. at least as good as) the profile b_h. As far as this present paper is concerned, it is sufficient to know that a composition k is assigned to class Cl_h only and only if $\sigma(k, b_h)$ is greater or equal to $\lambda \in [0.5, 1]$, where λ is a *cutting level* representing the lowest value for the credibility indexes $\sigma(k, b_h)$ to validate the outranking situation of k upon b_h. Mathematically, the assignment rule of ELECTRE TRI is defined as

$$\sigma(k, b_h) \geq \lambda \Leftrightarrow k \in Cl_{h+1}, \tag{6.9}$$

where Cl_{h+1} is the class delimited by profiles b_h and b_{h+1}. This assignment rule is implemented by Algorithm **AssignmentTest** below. This algorithm runs in $O(m)$, where m is the number of evaluation criteria.

Algorithm **AssignmentTest**
Input: k: Composition, b_h: Profile, λ: Cutting level, F: List of criteria
Output: Boolean: *True* if sentence (6.9) holds; *False* otherwise

for each $j \in J$ **do**
    if $g_j(b_h) - g_j(u) \geq p_j(b_h)$ **then** $c_j \leftarrow 0$
    else if $g_j(b_h) - g_j(k) \leq q_j(b_h)$ then $c_j \leftarrow 1$
        else $c_j \leftarrow (p_j(b_h) - g_j(b_h) + g_j(k))/(p_j(b_h) - q_j(b_h))$
        end if
    end if
end for
$c \leftarrow \sum_{j \in J} w_j \cdot c_j$
for each $j \in J$ **do**
    if $g_j(k) \leq g_j(b_h) + p_j(b_h)$ **then** $d_j \leftarrow 0$
    else if $g_j(k) > g_j(b_h) + v_j(b_h)$ then $d_j \leftarrow 1$
        else $d_j \leftarrow (v_j(b_h) - g_j(k) + g_j(b_h))/(v_j(b_h) - p_j(b_h))$
        end if
    end if
end for
$J' \leftarrow \{j \in J : d_j > c\}$
$d \leftarrow \prod_{j \in J'} (1 - d_j)/(1 - c)$
if $c \cdot d \geq \lambda$ **then** return true **else** return false **end if**

6.8 Implementation Issues

A prototype supporting the proposed architecture has been developed. This section briefly presents this prototype.

6.8.1 Prototype Architecture

The prototype has been developed on the basis of the architecture given in Fig. 6.2. It is implemented using Apache jUDDI Version 0.4rc4 which is an open source

UDDI implementation compliant with Version 2.0 specification. MySQL Version 5.0.16 is used to implement the jUDDI database. The UDDI4J (version 2.0.4) is an open source Java class library that provides an APIs (Application Programming Interfaces) to interact with a jUDDI. They are grouped in three API categories: (1) Iniquity APIs set, (2) Publication APIs set and (3) Security APIs set.

We have used Java as the programming language. The Java language has been selected since (1) it is portable and can be interpreted by any operating system implementing the Java Virtual Machine; and (2) the API of the jUDDI registry is coded in Java.

The prototype contains three parts:

- The jUDDI registry which is the heart of the prototype and which is enriched by adding the MEC;
- The WS-IRIS Web service that will be used by MEC to infer the values of the preference parameters required to apply the multicriteria classification method;
- The DecisionDeck, which is a Web-based framework devoted to multicriteria evaluation.

In the current version of the prototype, the WS-IRIS Web service is not directly accessible to the consumer. Further, the Decision Deck platform is not used in the current version of the prototype. However, the system is parameterized for a future use of other multicriteria evaluation methods available on this platform.

6.8.2 Presentation of the jUDDI Registry

We provide here a very brief presentation of the jUDDI registry. More information is available at http://juddi.apache.org/. The jUDDI is an open source Java implementation of the UDDI specification for Web Services. The jUDDI information model is composed of data structure instances expressed in XML schema. They are stored in the jUDDI registries. A service is discovered by sending requests based on service information. The four core data elements within the jUDDI data model are: (1) the *businessEntity* that contains information business, such as name and contact (each entity may provide various *businessEntity* elements); (2) the *businessService* contains information about published services; (3) the *bindingTemplate* represents a service implementation and provides the information needed to bind with the service; and (4) the *tModel* which is used to check the presence of a variety of concepts and to point to their technical definitions.

6.8.3 Extension of the jUDDI Registry

Currently, the jUDDI registry does not permit to compare different Web services having the same functionality. In other words, Web services supporting a requested functionality are returned to the consumer in the order of their subscription in the jUDDI registry. To avoid this problem, we have extended the jUDDI by adding different methods that implement the different algorithms presented previously. More precisely and in addition to the existing entities, we defined the following elements:

- *QoSInscription*: contains customers who wish to take into account the QoS in their search of services in the extended registry;
- *QoSDescription*: contains the QoS values for each service provider. The provider requests service publication and providers the QoS values. The latter are checked and validated by the registry manager. Note that QoS values can be updated by the registry manager, and if a value is not provided, thus it is valued at worst. The *QoSDescription* table refers to the *bindingTemplate* table that stores Web services instances. It also refers to the *tModel*.
- *QoSParameters*: contains the different parameters required to use the multicriteria classification method ELECTRE TRI.
- *inferParameters* that permits to infer the preference parameters by calling the W-IRIS Web service.
- *classifywithQoS* that implements the pessimistic multicriteria assignment algorithm of ELECTRE TRI.

The extended registry includes extensions to the UDDI4J Inquiry and Publication API sets in order to manipulate the QoS related data. The extended registry is managed by registry manager, who implements the QoS management operations. Several simulations conduced by the authors show the compatibility of the extended registry with the basic UDDI and both types of UDDI registries and can coexist in the same environment.

6.9 Illustrative Application

As an illustration, we consider the same composition graph example introduced in Sect. 6.6 and shown in Fig. 6.5. The objective is to classify the different potential compositions into different QoS classes. Four classes Cl_1, Cl_3, Cl_3 and Cl_4 have been defined for this example. The profile limits associated with these classes are given in Table 6.8. Next, we suppose that the consumer is not able to provide all the required preference parameters. Instead, s/he provides the assignment examples given in Table 6.9, which can be used to infer the different preference parameter values. The columns "Lower Class" and "'Upper Class" are, respectively, the lowest and highest classes to which composition k_i should be assigned. Compositions for which the lowest and highest classes are equal correspond to exact assignments, i.e., only one class is possible. The other assignment examples correspond to the case where a range of classes is possible. For instance, composition k_{181} in Table 6.9 must be assigned to Cl_1 while composition k_{11} may be assigned to Cl_1, Cl_2 or Cl_3.

Table 6.8 Parameters of profile limits

g_j	$g(b_3)$	q_3	p_3	$g(b_2)$	q_2	p_2	$g(b_1)$	q_1	p_1
g_1	8.295	0	0.25	9.17	0	0.25	10.045	0	0.25
g_2	0.56553	0	0.03	0.46119	0	0.03	0.35685	0	0.03
g_3	2.27	0	0.02	2.76	0	0.02	3.25	0	0.02
g_4	4	0	1	3	0	1	2	0	1

Table 6.9 Assignment examples

k_i	Description	$g_1(k_i)$	$g_2(k_i)$	$g_3(k_i)$	$g_4(k_i)$	Lower Class	Upper Class
k_{11}	$\{s_1, s_1, s_2, s_1, s_1, s_1\}$	9.22	0.45946	2.48	1	Cl_1	Cl_3
k_{44}	$\{s_1, s_3, s_1, s_1, s_2, s_2\}$	8.12	0.41817	2.68	1	Cl_1	Cl_2
k_{110}	$\{s_2, s_3, s_1, s_1, s_5, s_2\}$	8.72	0.50216	2.78	2	Cl_3	Cl_4
k_{118}	$\{s_2, s_3, s_2, s_1, s_4, s_2\}$	8.12	0.46967	3.24	2	Cl_3	Cl_4
k_{129}	$\{s_3, s_1, s_1, s_1, s_5, s_1\}$	9.12	0.38604	2.74	3	Cl_2	Cl_3
k_{134}	$\{s_3, s_1, s_2, s_1, s_2, s_2\}$	7.42	0.40317	3.38	2	Cl_2	Cl_3
k_{144}	$\{s_3, s_2, s_1, s_1, s_2, s_2\}$	7.72	0.36676	3.18	2	Cl_2	Cl_4
k_{159}	$\{s_3, s_2, s_2, s_1, s_5, s_1\}$	8.82	0.34296	2.74	2	Cl_2	Cl_3
k_{181}	$\{s_4, s_1, s_1, s_1, s_1, s_1\}$	10.92	0.44145	2.08	1	Cl_1	Cl_1
k_{216}	$\{s_4, s_2, s_2, s_1, s_3, s_2\}$	9.52	0.56506	2.8	2	Cl_1	Cl_2
k_{220}	$\{s_4, s_2, s_2, s_1, s_5, s_2\}$	10.12	0.53294	2.68	2	Cl_1	Cl_2
k_{222}	$\{s_4, s_3, s_1, s_1, s_1, s_2\}$	10.42	0.48356	2.32	1	Cl_1	Cl_1

The inference of the missing preference parameter values requires the resolution of a mathematical program (see Dias et al. 2002). The computational complexity for solving the mathematical program varies in the sense that the program to solve may be linear or nonlinear. Specifically, with an outranking relation, obtaining a global optimum is not obvious and requires the resolution of a nonlinear mathematical program. One possible solution to overcome this difficulty is to use "partial" inference procedures. Indeed, if the value of some preference parameters can be considered as known, "partial" inference procedures can be applied to infer the other parameters. The partial inference is useful in situations in which the value of some parameters can reasonably be set. If not, it is possible to partition the parameters in sets, and proceed through a sequence of partial inference procedures in which the value of some parameters is fixed. In this paper, the inference procedure is used to infer the cutting level and the weights of the different evaluation criteria. The other (fixed) parameters are provided in Table 6.10. The values for these parameters are defined by the authors after several simulations.

The output of the inference procedure is given in Table 6.11. According to Table 6.11, "Response time" (g_1) and "Availability" (g_2) evaluation criteria have the same relative importance with weights $w_1 = w_2 = 0.32502$. Equally, "Cost" (g_3) and "Security" (g_4) evaluation criteria are of equal importance with $w_3 = w_4 = 0.17498$. The value of the cutting level is 0.57507.

Table 6.10 Fixed preference parameters

Preference parameter	Response time (g_1)	Availability (g_2)	Cost (g_3)	Security (g_4)
Indifference threshold (q_j)	0	0	0	0
Preference threshold (p_j)	0.25	0.03	0.02	1
Veto threshold (v_j)	0	0	0	0

Table 6.11 Inferred preference parameters

Parameter	λ	w_1	w_2	w_3	w_4
Inferred value	0.57507	0.32502	0.32502	0.17498	0.17498

Table 6.12 Result of classification for the assignment examples

k_i	Description	Worst class	Inferred class	Best class
k_{11}	$\{s_1, s_1, s_2, s_1, s_1, s_1\}$	Cl_2	Cl_3	Cl_3
k_{44}	$\{s_1, s_3, s_1, s_1, s_2, s_2\}$	Cl_2	Cl_2	Cl_2
k_{110}	$\{s_2, s_3, s_1, s_1, s_5, s_2\}$	Cl_3	Cl_3	Cl_3
k_{118}	$\{s_2, s_3, s_2, s_1, s_4, s_2\}$	Cl_3	Cl_3	Cl_3
k_{129}	$\{s_3, s_1, s_1, s_1, s_5, s_1\}$	Cl_2	Cl_3	Cl_3
k_{134}	$\{s_3, s_1, s_2, s_1, s_2, s_2\}$	Cl_2	Cl_2	Cl_2
k_{144}	$\{s_3, s_2, s_1, s_1, s_2, s_2\}$	Cl_2	Cl_2	Cl_2
k_{159}	$\{s_3, s_2, s_2, s_1, s_5, s_1\}$	Cl_2	Cl_2	Cl_2
k_{180}	$\{s_4, s_1, s_1, s_1, s_1, s_1\}$	Cl_1	Cl_1	Cl_1
k_{216}	$\{s_4, s_2, s_2, s_1, s_3, s_2\}$	Cl_2	Cl_2	Cl_2
k_{220}	$\{s_4, s_2, s_2, s_1, s_5, s_2\}$	Cl_2	Cl_2	Cl_2
k_{222}	$\{s_4, s_3, s_1, s_1, s_1, s_2\}$	Cl_1	Cl_1	Cl_1

Table 6.13 Best compositions

k_i	Description	Response time (g_1)	Availability (g_2)	Cost (g_3)	Security (g_4)
k_{16}	$\{s_1, s_1, s_2, s_1, s_3, s_2\}$	8.12	0.66199	3.2	1
k_{36}	$\{s_1, s_2, s_2, s_1, s_3, s_2\}$	8.12	0.59512	3.1	1
k_{66}	$\{s_2, s_1, s_1, s_1, s_3, s_2\}$	8.12	0.64281	3.2	2
k_{76}	$\{s_2, s_1, s_2, s_1, s_3, s_2\}$	7.82	0.63524	3.3	2
k_{78}	$\{s_2, s_1, s_2, s_1, s_4, s_2\}$	8.12	0.56703	3.54	2
k_{86}	$\{s_2, s_2, s_1, s_1, s_3, s_2\}$	8.12	0.57787	3.1	2
k_{96}	$\{s_2, s_2, s_2, s_1, s_3, s_2\}$	7.82	0.57107	3.2	2

The obtained preference parameters are then used in order to apply ELECTRE TRI. The result of classification for the assignment examples is summed up in Table 6.12. The list of best compositions (those belonging to Cl_4) is shown in Table 6.13. For convenience, Table 6.13 contains also the partial evaluations of best compositions.

6.10 Discussion

In this section, we discuss the computational behavior of compositions construction and evaluation solutions. Indeed, the solution proposed to define the composite Web services may lead to a large set of potential compositions. To guarantee a minimum level of efficiency, it is required that the time to construct, evaluate and compare the different potential compositions does not exceed the response time of the worst composition. Naturally, the worst composition k_w may be a fictive one. It can be defined as the one such that $\forall j \in J$:

- $g_j(k_w) \leq \min_{k \in K} g_j(k)$ if preference increases on g_j.
- $g_j(k_w) \geq \max_{k \in K} g_j(k)$ if preference decreases on g_j.

Another possible solution follows. Let $\mathscr{T}(k)$ be the response time of composition k and τ the time required to construct, evaluate and compare potential compositions. The number τ may be estimated on the basis of the complexity of the different algorithms and on the average execution time of basic operations. Then, the following proposition should be verified:

Proposition 6.1 *If* $\mathscr{T}(k_w) > \tau$, *then use* MEC. *Otherwise, use conventional evaluation.*

This rule may be included in the registry and applied to orient the system towards conventional evaluation or towards multicriteria evaluation.

In addition to this proposition, the framework may be further enhanced through some basic notions in multicriteria analysis. First, the number of potential compositions may be largely reduced using dominance relation. This allows to eliminate all the compositions which are dominated by at least another one. Let k_i and k_l be two composite Web services from K. Suppose that preference is increasing on all criteria (this is not restrictive). Then, service k_i *dominates* service k_l, denoted $k_i \Delta k_l$, if and only if $g_j(k_i) \geq g_j(k_l); \forall j \in J$, with at least one strict inequality. Only non dominated composite Web services are considered in the multicriteria evaluation step.

Another solution consists in using some elementary multicriteria methods. Two typical elementary multicriteria methods are the conjunctive and disjunctive decision rules. In the conjunctive method, we define, for each criterion g_j, a minimal satisfaction level $\hat{g_j}$. A composition k_i is acceptable if and only if:

$$g_j(k_i) \geq \hat{g_j}, \forall j \in J$$

A more drastic choice consists in eliminating any composition having performance vector $(g_1(k_i), g_2(k_i), \cdots, g_m(k_i))$ dominated by the vector $(\hat{g_1}, \hat{g_2}, \cdots, \hat{g_m})$. The disjunctive method is similar to the previous one but a composition is acceptable if it exceed at least one satisfaction level:

$$\exists j \in J : g_j(k_i) > \hat{g_j}$$

More complex elementary methods as the *elimination by aspect* (EBA) and *lexicographic elimination* ones may also be used. With EBA method, a set of satisfaction levels are defined and applied progressively. In each step, the composition that fails to verify these satisfaction levels is eliminated. The procedure is repeated for all the remaining compositions using the next criterion. The lexicographic elimination method supposes that an order on the evaluation criteria is established and that the $(k - 1)$ next criteria may be ignored if the first k criteria are sufficient to make a decision.

6.11 Conclusion

We have proposed a framework for composite Web services selection based on multicriteria evaluation. The framework extends the conventional Web services architecture by adding a multicriteria evaluation component in the registry devoted to multicriteria evaluation. This additional component takes as input a set of composite Web services and a set of evaluation criteria. The output is a set of recommended composite Web services. We also proposed solutions to construct and evaluate the different potential compositions. Equally, we discussed the computational behavior of the framework and proposed some solutions to reduce the complexity of the solution. To show the feasibility of our proposal, an illustrative example is included in the paper. A prototype implementing the proposed framework is under development.

Currently, we are concerned with the finalization of the prototype. Aside from this, there are several directions for future research. One point to investigate is related to the extension of the framework to support dynamic composition. The basic change concerns the construction of the potential compositions and their evaluations.

Appendix: Description of Some QoS Criteria

This appendix presents a comprehensive list of commonly used criteria in Web services evaluation. For each criterion, we provide a brief description, the type (quantitative or qualitative), and the preference direction where "max" means "the higher, the better" and "min" means "the lower, the better" (Table 6.14).

Table 6.14 Description of some QoS criteria

Name	Description	Type	Preference
Availability	The degree to which a system, subsystem, or equipment is operable and in a committable state at the start of a mission, when the mission is called for at an unknown, i.e., a random, time. In others terms, availability is the proportion of time a system is functional	Quantitative	max
Response time	The lapse of time from request sending to response reception	Quantitative	min
Throughput	The rate at which a service can process requests	Quantitative	max
Reliability	The likelihood of success using a service	Quantitative	max
Security	It captures the level and kind of security a service provides	Qualitative	max
Robustness	The degree to which a system or component can function correctly in the presence of invalid inputs or stressful environment conditions	Qualitative	max
Scalability	It defines whether the service capacities can be increased as needed	Qualitative	max
Integrity	The quality aspect of how the Web service maintains the correctness of the interaction with respect to the source. Proper execution of Web service transactions will provide the correctness of interaction. A transaction refers to a sequence of activities to be treated as a single unit of work. All the activities have to be completed to make the transaction successful. When a transaction does not complete, all the changes made are rolled back	Qualitative	max
Reputation	It is a measure of trustworthiness. It mainly depends on end user's experiences of using a service	Qualitative	max
Latency	The amount of time it takes a packet to travel from Web service to another Web service	Quantitative	min
Accuracy	Represents the error rate generated by the Web service. It can be measured by the numbers of errors generated in a certain time interval	Quantitative	max
Regulatory	The quality aspect of the Web service according to rules, law, compliance with standards, and the established service level agreement. Strict adherence to correct versions of standards by service providers is necessary for proper invocation of Web services by service requestors	Qualitative	max
Authentication	The capacity of a service to authenticate other entities—users or other Web services—in order to access them	Qualitative	max

(continued)

Table 6.14 (continued)

Name	Description	Type	Preference
Confidentiality	The capacity that a Web service respect that a given data should be treated properly, so that only authorized entities (or Web services) can access or modify the data	Qualitative	max
Traceability	The capacity that a Web service traces itself history when a request was serviced	Qualitative	max
Auditability	The capacity that a Web service encrypts data	Qualitative	max
Non-repudiation	The fact that an entity (service) cannot deny requesting a service after the fact	Qualitative	max
Accessibility	The degree that a Web service is capable of serving a Web service request. It may be expressed as a probability measure denoting the success rate or chance of a successful service instantiation at a point in time. There could be situations when a Web service is available but not accessible	Qualitative	max
Cost	Web service cost specification	Quantitative	min

References

Benatallah, B., Dumas, M., Sheng, Q. Z., & Ngu, A. (2002). Declarative composition and peer-to-peer provisioning of dynamic Web services. In *Proc. of ICDE'02* (pp. 297–308). San Jose: IEEE Computer Society.

Blin, M. J., & Tsoukiàs, A. (2001). Multicriteria methodology contribution to software quality evaluations. *Software Quality Journal, 9*, 113–132.

Briand, L., Morasca, S., & Basili, V. (2002). An operational process for goal-driven definition of measures. *IEEE Transactions on Software Engineering, 28*, 1106–1125 (2002)

Casati, F., Ilnicki, S., Jin, L.-J., Krishnamoorthy, V., & Shan, M.-C. (2000). eFlow: a platform for developing and managing composite e-services. In *Technical Report HPL-2000-36*, Palo Alto: HP Laboratoris.

Champion, M., Newcomer, E., & Orchard, D. (2000). Web service architecture. In *W3C draft*.

Dias, L. C., Mousseau, V., Figueira, J., & Clímaco, J. (2002). An aggregation/disaggregation approach to obtain robust conclusions with ELECTRE TRI. *European Journal of Operational Research, 138*, 332–348.

Dias, L., & Mousseau, V. (2003). IRIS: A DSS for multiple criteria sorting. *Journal of Multi-Criteria Decision Analysis, 12*, 285–298.

Dustdar, S., & Schreiner, W. (2005). A survey on Web services composition. *International Journal of Web and Grid Services, 1*, 1–30.

Fenton, N. A., & Pfleeger, S. L. (1997). *Software metrics*. Boston: PWS Publishing Co.

Figueira, J., Greco, S., & Ehrgott, M. (Eds.) (2005). *Multiple criteria decision analysis: State of the art surveys*. New York: Springer.

Figueira, J., Mousseau, V., & Roy, B. (2005). ELECTRE methods. In J. Figueira, S. Greco, & M. Ehrgott (Eds.), *Multiple criteria decision analysis: State of the art surveys* (pp. 133–162). New York: Springer.

Georgakopoulos, D., Schuster, H., Cichocki, A., & Baker, D. (1999). Managing process and service fusion in virtual enterprises. *Information System, 24*, 429–456.

Klingemann, J. (2000). Controlled flexibility in workflow management. In *Proc. of the 12th international conference on advanced information systems (CAiSE)* (pp. 126–141). Sweden: Stockholm.

Ma, Y., & Zhang, C. (2008). Quick convergence of genetic algorithm for QoS-driven Web service selection. *Computer Networks, 52*, 1093–1104.

Maximilien, E. M., & Singh, M. P. (2004). A Framework and ontology for dynamic Web services selection. *IEEE Internet Computing, 8*, 84–93.

Menascé, D. A. (2004). Composing Web servies: A QoS view. In *IEEE internet computing*.

Menascé, D. A., & Dubey, V. (2007). In *Utility-based QoS brokering in service oriented architectures*.

Menascé, D. A., Ruan, H., & Gomma, H. (2007). QoS management in service oriented architectures. *Performance Evaluation Journal, 64*, 646–663.

Morisio, M., Seaman, C., Basili, V., Parra, A., Kraft, S., & Condon, S. (2002). COTS-based software development: Processes and open issues. *Journal of Systems and Software, 61*, 189–199.

Morisio, M., Stamelos, T., & Tsoukiàs, A. (2003). Software product and process assessment through profile-based evaluation. *International Journal of Software Engineering and Knowledge Engineering, 13*, 495–512.

Zeng, L., Bentallah, B., Dumas, L., Kalagnanam, J., & Sheng, Q. Z. (2003). Quality driven web service composition. In *Proc. of the 12th international conference on World Wide Web* (pp. 411–421), Budapest. New York: ACM Press.

Editors' Comments on "Multi-Criteria Evaluation-Based Framework for Composite Web Services"

The chapter by Chakhar, Haddad, Mokdad, Mousseau and Youcef presents a framework and a software prototype for composite web selection. It addresses the problem of a user (the consumer), who wishes to use services available on the Internet to perform some task, needing possibly to perform a composition of services offered by different providers located anywhere in the world. This is a very timely topic in today's "cloud computing" world, motivating much research on how can web services be described, evaluated, and composed (e.g., the reader may see the special issue Ranjan et al. 2012). This framework acknowledges three types of **actors**: the service provider who offers an elementary service, the registry manager who informs about elementary service objective performances, and the consumer (decision maker) who performs a subjective overall evaluation.

The chapter relates to the problem formulation stage (see Chap. 2) mainly in addressing the problem of constructing the set of alternatives. The chapter also relates to other chapters (see for example Chaps. 16, 12 or 10) in the use of the ELECTRE TRI aggregation method, although other aggregation approaches are discussed.

The authors suggest that the **decision process objective** of the consumer is to obtain a set of recommended solutions (composite web services), which would already be very helpful because the problem has typically a combinatorial nature: the components of the web service can be combined in different ways using distinct providers. They suggest therefore the use of a sorting **problem**

statement, according to which each potential composite web service is assigned to a performance class. Presumably, the consumer would then examine in more detail the choices available in the best class. Other authors, however, have tackled the problem of selecting the best service according to a (more demanding) ranking problematic, typically using weighted sums (Ranjan et al., 2012; Toma et al., 2007) or the AHP approach (Garg et al., 2013).

Each element of the **alternatives set** is a composite web service, i.e., a "portfolio" of individual services structured according to precedence relations. The authors explain how several algorithms are used to construct each possible combination. Each elementary service can be evaluated on a number of **criteria**, and other algorithms are run to determine the composite service's evaluation on each criterion. A list of criteria is suggested, which is quite comprehensive although it does not include a recent concern Garg et al. (2013), which is environmental sustainability. Indeed, as described in another chapter in this book (see Chap. 10), different service providers may have different performances concerning data center environmental impacts.

In terms of evaluating composite web services, the first of the **stages** is to evaluate each element on a number of criteria, and then to evaluate possible compositions. The evaluation of compositions is first made on a intra-criterion basis, one criterion at a time. This entails some sort of **aggregation** of elementary performances using operators such as sum, product, max, etc., depending on the performance metric. It is assumed that a registry manager updates the provider's performances.[3] At a second stage, the evaluations of each composite web service are aggregated using the ELECTRE TRI method to yield a classification. However, the authors discuss that other less sophisticated methods could be used instead.

Although the framework and prototypes developed have a clear practical applicability, there was not a specific **client** organization for this chapter and therefore the authors assume a hypothetical decision maker. No **analyst** is explicitly mentioned, thereby assuming the consumer would be able to use the proposed tools on his or her own. To help this hypothetical decision maker, an indirect **elicitation process** is proposed. This consists in inferring the parameters of the ELECTRE TRI aggregation method from classification examples provided by the decision maker. This process is illustrated through a small example yielding as a **tangible result** the classification of composite each composite web service in one of four possible classes.

[3]Nowadays web pages such as http://cloudharmony.com/benchmarks already divulge performance metrics of cloud services providers.

References

Garg, S., Versteeg, S., & Buyya, R. (2013). A framework for ranking of cloud computing services. *Future Generation Computer Systems, 29*(4), 1012–1023. Special Section: Utility and Cloud Computing.

Ranjan, R., Buyya, R., & Benatallah, B. (2012). Special section: software architectures and application development environments for cloud computing. *Software: Practice and Experience, 42*(4), 391–394.

Toma, I., Roman, D., Fensel, D., Sapkota, B., & Gomez, J. (2007). A multi-criteria service ranking approach based on non-functional properties rules evaluation. In B. Krämer, K.-J. Lin, & P. Narasimhan (Eds.), *Service-oriented computing – ICSOC 2007*. Lecture notes in computer science (vol. 4749, pp. 435–441). Heidelberg: Springer.

Chapter 7
Site Selection for a University Kindergarten in Madrid

Tommi Tervonen, Gabriela Fernández Barberis, José Rui Figueira, and María Carmen Escribano

Abstract In this paper we present a case study of a real-life multicriteria decision making problem of choosing the site for a university kindergarten in Madrid. The largest private university of Madrid, San Pablo CEU, needs to build a kindergarten for staff children. This study consists of two phases. In the first phase, an approximate model was presented to the decision makers in order to motivate re-activating the process. In the second phase, a more detailed model with new alternatives was introduced. The criteria measurements as well as the preferences contain large uncertainties. Therefore, the problem is solved by using the SMAA-III method that allows to model uncertainties through joint probability distributions.

7.1 Introduction

Choosing a site for a new facility is among the traditional multiple criteria decision making problems. This type of problems typically consists of a finite set of alternative sites that are evaluated in terms of several criteria. The criteria often take into account socio-economical, logistical, and environmental aspects of the problem setting. Although the ultimate goal is to choose the site to build in, it is common to use a ranking method to obtain also some backup alternatives, in the case that the most preferred one cannot be implemented. Many modern multiple criteria ranking methods have been applied in similar settings, see e.g. Barda et al. (1990), Erkut and Moran (1991), Erkut et al. (2008), Hokkanen et al. (1997, 1999), Karkazis (1998),

T. Tervonen (✉)
Erasmus University Rotterdam, P.O. Box 1738, 3000 DR Rotterdam, The Netherlands
e-mail: tommi@smaa.fi

G. Fernandes Barberis • M.C. Escribano
Department of Quantitative Methods, San Pablo - CEU University, 28003 Madrid, Spain

J.R. Figueira
CEG-IST Instituto Superior Técnico, Universidade de Lisboa, A. Rovisco Pais 1, 1049-001 Lisbon, Portugal
e-mail: jose.figueira@mines.inpl-nancy.fr

R. Bisdorff et al. (eds.), *Evaluation and Decision Models with Multiple Criteria*, International Handbooks on Information Systems,
DOI 10.1007/978-3-662-46816-6_7

Keeney (1980), Lahdelma and Salminen (2002), Karagiannidis and Moussiopoulos (1997), Norese (2006), Partovi and Burton (1992), Queiruga et al. (2008), and Wu et al. (2007).

In this paper we present a real-life case study of siting a university kindergarten. The Fundación Universitaria San Pablo—Centro de Estudios Universitarios (abbreviated as CEU from now on) is among the largest universities in Madrid, Spain. It has received a petition from the teachers and other staff of the university to arrange a kindergarten for the staff children. This petition was received already in 1996, but the project was frozen because no agreement for the location could be reached. In early 2007, a two-phase decision making process for choosing the site was initiated by the university professors. In the first phase, an initial analysis was made in order to motivate re-activation of the project without requiring interaction from the Decision Makers (DMs). In the second phase, the model was revised and the DMs gave more precise preference information so that the most preferred alternatives could be recognized.

The case study considered in this paper had a preliminary phase in which PROMETHEE method (Brans and Vincke, 1985) and generalized criteria were used (Barberis et al., 2006). Equal weights were considered in the preliminary phase without justification. In the face of ignorance about preferences, it is advisable not to use geometrical or other means to model ignorance, because even small alterations of the weights might give different results. This is especially the case with outranking methods (see e.g. Figueira et al. 2005b) due to their sensitive preference model (Lahdelma and Salminen, 2002). For an example of alteration of results because of small changes in weights, see Tervonen et al. (2007).

The problem consists of ordinal and imprecise cardinal criteria measurements and partially missing preference information. Stochastic Multicriteria Acceptability Analysis (SMAA) methods have been used successfully in such site selection problems, see e.g. Hokkanen et al. (1999), Lahdelma et al. (2002), or Tervonen and Figueira (2008) for a full survey on SMAA methods. These problems have included environmental and/or socio-economical criteria that are also present in this study. ELECTRE methods are used widely in discrete decision making problems (e.g. Figueira et al., 2005b; Hokkanen et al., 1997; Karagiannidis and Moussiopoulos, 1997; Norese, 2006). They have the advantage that a utility or a value function does not need to be defined, therefore requiring less interaction with the DMs. Our problem has these characteristics: the criteria measurements are uncertain and preferences cannot be elicited in the first phase because we need results to motivate the DMs. Therefore, we have chosen to analyze the problem with SMAA-III (Tervonen and Lahdelma, 2007). It allows to apply ELECTRE III with imprecise values for the model parameters. We also cross-validate the results by applying SMAA-3 (Hokkanen et al., 1998) that uses a less discriminative maximin exploitation rule.

SMAA-III applies probability distributions to model imprecision. Although we believe that the approach taken in SMAA-III is the most appropriate one for this study, we note that there are also other approaches. These include entropy methods (Abbas, 2006), interval methods (Mustajoki et al., 2005), Dempster-Shafer theory (Beynon et al., 2000), rough sets and fuzzy sets (Figueria et al., 2005a). An important reason for choosing the method is also that the analysts (us) are more familiar with SMAA-III than with the other pre-mentioned methods, therefore lowering the risk of incorrect analysis due to misunderstanding the method prerequisites.

This paper starts by presenting the applied method, SMAA-III, in Sect. 7.2. The case study is presented in Sect. 7.3, followed by a discussion of the results in Sect. 7.4. Conclusions end the paper in Sect. 7.5.

7.2 SMAA-III

SMAA-III (Tervonen and Lahdelma, 2007) is designed to solve a discrete ranking problem that consists of a set of alternatives evaluated in terms of multiple criteria. It is based on ELECTRE III (see e.g. Belton and Stewart, 2002; Figueira et al., 2005b; Roy, 1978) for constructing a ranking of alternatives, extending it by allowing imprecise parameter values. ELECTRE III has two phases. In the first phase, an outranking relation between pairs of alternatives is formed. When an alternative outranks another, it is considered "*as good as or better than*" the other. The second phase consists of exploiting this relation, producing a final partial pre-order and a median pre-order.

ELECTRE III applies pseudo-criteria in constructing the outranking relation. A pseudo-criterion is defined with two thresholds: an indifference threshold for defining the difference in a criterion that the DM finds insignificant, and a preference threshold for the smallest difference that is considered absolutely preferred. Between these two lies a zone of "*hesitation*" between indifference and strict preference. ELECTRE III also defines a third threshold, the veto threshold. It is the smallest (negative) difference that cancels (raises "*veto*" against) the outranking relation. In addition to the thresholds, preferences are quantified through a weight vector $w = (w_1, \ldots, w_j, \ldots, w_n)$. Without loss of generality, we assume that $\sum_j w_j = 1$.

For more details on how ELECTRE III constructs the ranking, see e.g. Belton and Stewart (2002) or Roy (1978). In the original ELECTRE III, a median pre-order is computed based on the two complete pre-orders and the final partial pre-order. The median pre-order removes incomparabilities in the final partial pre-order. SMAA-III applies simulation and studies the effect of changing parameter values and criteria evaluations on the results. The imprecision of the parameters is quantified in theory through joint density functions, but in practice independent uniform distributions on intervals or Gaussian distributions are used. Monte Carlo simulation is used in SMAA-III to compute three types of descriptive measures: rank acceptability indices, pair-wise winning indices, and incomparability indices.

The rank acceptability index measures the share of feasible weights that grant an alternative a certain rank in the median pre-order by simultaneously taking into account imprecision in all parameters and criteria evaluations. It represents the share of feasible parameter combinations that make the alternative acceptable for a particular rank, and it is most conveniently expressed as percentage. The most acceptable ("*best*") alternatives are those with high acceptability for the best ranks. Evidently, the rank acceptability indices are within the range [0,1], where 0 indicates that the alternative will never obtain a given rank and 1 indicates that it will always obtain the given rank with any feasible choice of parameters. Thus, the rank acceptability indices are a measure of robustness of the ranking.

The pair-wise winning index describes the share of weights that place an alternative on a better rank than another one. An alternative that has a pair-wise winning index of 1 with respect to another one always obtains a better rank, and can thus be said to dominate it in a wide sense. The pair-wise winning indices are especially useful when trying to distinguish between the ranking differences of two alternatives. Because the number of ranks in the median pre-order of different simulation runs varies, two alternatives might obtain similar rank acceptability indices although one is in fact inferior. In these cases looking at the pair-wise winning indices between this pair of alternatives can help to determine whether one of the alternatives is superior to the other or if they are equal in "*goodness*".

Because median pre-orders are used in computing the rank acceptability indices, it is not anymore possible to model incomparability. For this reason, SMAA-III includes an incomparability index that measures the share of feasible parameter values that cause two alternatives to be incomparable. When the criteria measurements and other parameters are imprecise, the three different indices can be used to measure robustness of the analysis. For example, pair-wise winning indices show how the mutual goodness of a pair of alternatives changes with different feasible parameter values. If an alternative is deemed the preferred one and still has a relatively low (less than 60 %) pair-wise winning index with another alternative, the parameters should be defined more precisely. Sometimes this is not possible, and less crucial decisions can be made based on such imprecise conclusions. With decisions having larger impact, the process should be iterated until sufficient pair-wise winning indices are obtained.

7.3 Case Study

The CEU has received a petition from the teachers and other personnel of the university to arrange a kindergarten for the staff children within the university premises. CEU has various installations dispersed widely in Madrid. The future location for the kindergarten can be chosen within these installations, or in the residential zones west of Madrid. The choice of location has clearly multi-dimensional effects; not only the accessibility and the price of construction and maintenance have to be taken into account, but also the possible size of the kindergarten and the effects to the surrounding city view.

The original petition was received already in 1996, and a committee was formed with experts in various disciplines (architects, builders, environmental technicians, municipal technicians, biologists, etc) was created to make an ordinal evaluation of possible locations. They met twice, first for a brainstorming session and second time for expressing preferences for possible locations. No agreement was reached over the location, and the project was frozen for more than 10 years. Lately the University Board of Directors has received a large amount of requests from the teachers and employees concerning building the kindergarten. Detailed geographical, demographical, and economical studies were conducted to probe possible locations in the Madrid Community area. In order to re-activate the project, we first did an initial, imprecise analysis for motivational purposes. We used for it criteria measurements and possible locations from 10 years ago.

There was no preference information available as the DMs were not consulted. To probe for good compromise alternatives and to raise discussion, we used weight lower bounds of 0.1 to avoid extreme weight combinations. There were in total five criteria used, therefore the weights were modeled with a joint uniform distribution bounded within 0.1–0.6 for each weight (for more details on this technique, see Tervonen and Lahdelma 2007).

The initial phase resulted in a decision to re-activate the project and to do a more thorough analysis. We then re-evaluated the alternatives, and found that one of them did not belong to CEU anymore. A residential zone alternative was split into three different locations. All the criteria measurements were updated to correspond with the current situation. In this manner we formed a multiple criteria decision making problem in which seven alternatives were to be ranked with respect to five criteria. The criteria were the same that were used in the first phase of the study, chosen after discussions with different educational bodies of the CEU. In their opinion, these five criteria take into account all relevant aspects of the problem:

- ACC: accessibility to the center of city. The metropolitan area of Madrid covers a wide area, causing transportation accessibility to be of importance when choosing a site for a new facility. In a city with heavy traffic congestion, the actual distance might not correlate with accessibility, and therefore we have chosen to measure it in minutes by public transportation from a central transport hub.
- SIZ: size (in children) of the kindergarten to be built as measured with a number of day-care places. The Spanish government regulates (BOE, 2007a,b) the maximum number of children for m^2 and the required common services. The number of day-care places can be derived from the estimated building specifications.
- COP: land and construction price in euros. The sites have differing costs of location and construction depending on the building location (e.g. residential zone, city center or outskirts).
- EFF: effects to the city landscape. Government regulations define that effects to urban landscape, green spaces, and cultural heritage must be estimated. We measure them with this ordinal criterion.
- MAC: maintenance cost of the facility in euros/month, measured by estimating total fixed and variable costs (supplies, personnel, taxes, etc).

The seven alternative locations for the kindergarten are all located in the west side of the centre of Madrid. Figure 7.1 shows a map of the locations. Notice that two alternatives are so close to each other that they are shown in the map as a single location: Campus Moncloa and San Dominique. These reside within 50 m in the same street.

The criteria measurements revised for the second phase of the study are presented in Table 7.1. The accessibility criterion (ACC) is measured in minutes by public transportation from the Avenida América metro station. This metro station is a major

Fig. 7.1 Alternative locations in the map of central-western Madrid

Table 7.1 Criteria measurements

Alternative	ACC	SIZ	COP	EFF	MAC
Campus Montepríncipe	52.5 ± 5.24	234	3,937,880	3	39,000–48,000
Campus Moncloa	39.17 ± 5.85	159	4,729,000	7	26,000–32,000
Campus Argüelles	36.67 ± 6.06	167	5,238,520	5	28,500–35,000
San Dominique	38.33 ± 6.06	134	4,068,450	6	23,500–29,000
Majadahonda	46.33 ± 3.83	159	3,146,000	4	27,500–33,500
Pozuelo	42.83 ± 3.19	167	3,317,270	1	28,500–35,000
Las Rozas	49 ± 3.52	201	3,904,800	2	34,000–42,000

transport hub for central Madrid. It incorporates train, bus, and metro stations, and is used by a large amount of commuting workers to arrive to the central Madrid area. For defining measurements for the accessibility criterion, faculty staff accustomed to travel in Madrid approximated the mean times to travel from the Avenida América metro station to the desired location during a weekday. Separate approximations were done for six different time slices: 6:30–10, 10–13, 13–16, 16–19, 19–21, and 21–24. After this, we calculated the mean and standard deviations for each alternative based on these approximations, and modeled the criteria measurements as Gaussian distributed values. It should be noted, that although the uncertainties of the measurements are correlated in the approximations, probably the real values underlying these means are not correlated. Therefore we do not model the criterion

Table 7.2 The number of different classrooms for each alternative

Alternative	0–1 years	1–2 years	2–3 years	3–6 years
Campus Montepríncipe	4	4	3	3
Campus Moncloa	2	2	3	3
Campus Argüelles	3	2	2	3
San Dominique	2	2	2	2
Majadahonda	2	2	2	3
Pozuelo	3	2	2	3
Las Rozas	3	3	3	3

through a multivariate Gaussian distribution as it has been done by, for example, in Tervonen et al. (2008).

For measuring the size of the kindergarten (SIZ), we calculated the number of kindergarten places that would be available in the final installation. In Spain there are two government rules that regulate the amount of children allowed in kindergartens (BOE, 2007a,b). These divide the kindergarten education into two cycles and take into account the age of children. For the first cycle, we have three age classes: 0–1 years, 1–2 years, and 2–3 years. The regulated number of children in the classroom for these are 8, 12–14, and 16–20, respectively. The second cycle comprises of children of ages 3–6. For children of these ages there can be between 20 and 25 in a classroom.

The size of the kindergarten as well as the construction costs depend on the number of classrooms. Our estimates for these numbers are presented in Table 7.2. We model the number of children with exact value that is the maximum number of children allowed with this amount of classrooms. For example, for Campus Montepríncipe, the SIZ is $4 \times 8 + 4 \times 14 + 3 \times 20 + 3 \times 25 = 223$ children. The minimum infrastructure for each building is a W.C., a multiple purpose room, a playground, and a classroom for every group of children. The sizes of classrooms are regulated by two government orders. These obligate two square meters for each child, and a minimum size of $30\,m^2$ for a classroom (BOCM, 2004; BOE, 2007a). Therefore the sizes are $30\,m^2$ for classrooms of children of 0–1 and 1–2 years, $40\,m^2$ for 2–3 years and $50\,m^2$ for 3–6 years. The infrastructure requirements are used to estimate the total land area required by the alternatives. We use Gaussian distribution for the land and construction price (COP). Standard deviation is set to 5 % of the mean value, so that the 95 % confidence intervals are mean $\pm 10\,\%$. The land prices were obtained from the El País newspaper for second hand housing mean prices in the corresponding areas (El País, 2007). The estimated construction prices were obtained from Madrid (2007).

Effects to the city landscape (EFF) measure both the effect during construction as well as the possible negative effect after completion. We chose to measure the effect as an ordinal criterion: the alternatives were ranked based on expert views. It would have been quite hard to come up with a cardinal values to measure the effects, similarly that has been reported in the literature when measuring effects on the landscape or environment (Hokkanen et al., 1997; Lahdelma et al., 2000; Martin et al., 2007).

The DMs provided us with imprecise weight information: the ACC and COP criteria were considered to be the most important ones with approximated weights of 0.3. After them, the next important one was considered to be SIZ with a weight of 0.2. EFF and MAC were considered the least important ones with estimated weights of 0.1. Although the DMs provided these exact weight values, they showed uncertainty about the values. To model this behavior, we considered the weights to be uncertain within intervals of the elicited value ± 0.05.

This enforces weight bounds as shown in Table 7.3. It should be noted, that these weight bounds preserve the ordinal information present in the original weights; for example, ACC and COP can never have lower weights than the rest of the criteria. We have estimated preferences also in terms of imprecise indifference- and preference thresholds. For all cardinal criteria except the maintenance cost we use direct imprecise thresholds. For maintenance cost the threshold is defined as imprecise percentage of the value. The thresholds are presented in Table 7.3. It should be noted, that we do not apply veto thresholds in our study.

We executed the analysis with SMAA-III and cross-validated the results with a modified SMAA-3 method. It takes into account all ranks and produces rank acceptability indices with a meaning similar to those of SMAA-III, but uses a less discriminative maximin exploitation rule. This was done because up to our best knowledge SMAA-III has not been used before in real-life decision making contexts as is the case with SMAA-3. The cross-validation gave additional security in the results. Both of these analyses were done with the open source CSMAA software v1.0 (see www.smaa.fi). The rank acceptability indices and pair-wise winning indices of the SMAA-III analysis are shown in Tables 7.4 and 7.5, respectively. The incomparability indices are not presented as they are not relevant in this study. Neither are presented the rank acceptability indices of the modified SMAA-3 analysis, because the results are similar to those of the SMAA-III analysis.

Table 7.3 Imprecise weights and thresholds

Criterion	ACC	SIZ	COP	EFF	MAC
Weight	$0.25 - 0.35$	$0.15 - 0.25$	$0.25 - 0.35$	$0.05 - 0.15$	$0.05 - 0.15$
Indif TH	6.5 ± 1.5	1.5 ± 1.5	$10{,}000 \pm 5{,}000$	–	$3 \pm 2\,\%$
Pref TH	12.5 ± 2.5	3 ± 1	$100{,}000 \pm 50{,}000$	–	$8 \pm 2\,\%$

Table 7.4 Rank acceptability indices of the SMAA-III analysis

Rank	1	2	3	4	5	6	7
Montepríncipe	13	19	19	19	17	10	2
Moncloa	9	15	17	16	17	17	10
Argüelles	36	16	14	12	12	7	2
San Dominique	3	10	16	22	22	19	8
Majadahonda	4	9	14	19	22	20	12
Pozuelo	37	23	16	11	7	4	1
Las Rozas	18	25	20	17	12	7	1

Table 7.5 Pair-wise winning indices of the SMAA-III analysis

	Monte- príncipe	Mon- cloa	Argü- elles	S. Domi- nique	Majada- honda	Pozuelo	Las Rozas
Monteprincipe	0	57	36	64	66	28	39
Moncloa	38	0	28	52	55	22	31
Argüelles	60	67	0	74	74	45	53
S. Dominique	32	44	23	0	50	15	24
Majadahonda	29	40	21	45	0	15	22
Pozuelo	67	72	50	82	81	0	58
Las Rozas	53	65	41	73	73	36	0

7.4 Discussion

The resulting indices of the analysis give quite high first rank acceptability to Campus Argüelles and Pozuelo. However, as we are using quite uncertain criteria measurements as well as thresholds and weights, all alternatives that obtain significant first rank acceptability should be taken into account. This means, that Monteprincípe, Moncloa, and Las Rozas are viable choices as well. As it can be seen from the pair-wise winning indices, all of them obtain higher ranks than Argüelles and Pozuelo with a reasonable share of parameter combinations. Therefore the "*true*" parameters might as well lie in these, relatively small sets of values.

Although the results contain high uncertainties, recommendations have to be given. Pozuelo and Campus Argüelles seem to be the "best" alternatives with no further information. There is a clear "*trade-off*" between the two alternatives: Pozuelo is a residential zone alternative away from the city center, while Campus Argüelles resides in the center of Madrid. An interesting fact is that they are equal in size, both being good compromise alternatives in that aspect. Campus Argüelles is more accessible alternative, but also expensive and causing possibly high effects to the city landscape. For deciding between these two, we presented the results to the University Board of Directors.

The University Board of Directors examined carefully the results. During several meetings of the Board, discussions took place with respect to measuring their preferences. They reckoned that the problem of weighting decision criteria is hard. Furthermore, they acknowledged the fact that in the case of collective decisions it is very difficult to achieve consensus. As they acknowledged the hardness of making group decisions with highly imprecise data, the results of the analysis were accepted and discussion continued about the results. Between the two "*best*" alternatives, Pozuelo and Campus de Argüelles, the Board considered that Pozuelo is more preferred one in the current situation. The most important reason for this was that at present it is hard to have access to the land in the central area of Madrid where Campus Argüelles is situated. The question of buying property is currently complicated in Spain because of the state of markets. Buying centrally situated property would imply extra financial uncertainties not taken into consideration during the model building phase.

Even though the Board agreed on choosing Pozuelo for the location of building the kindergarten, the project was postponed due to ongoing change of members in the University Board. The decision making process ended with these conclusions. The initial enthusiasm and the decision to re-activate the project because of structured decision analysis not requiring too much interaction from the DMs was in the end overtaken by the current administrative situation. We believe that taking into account the importance of the problem presented in this paper, the forthcoming new members of the University Board will show sensibility in relation with the crucial social problem and re-activate the project again in the near future.

7.5 Conclusions

In this paper we presented a real-world case study of choosing a location for a kindergarten of the largest private university of Madrid. The study contained some important particularities: the initial phase of the process was to re-activate the project without requiring interaction from the Decision Makers (DMs). The SMAA-III ranking method was chosen because it allows the analysis to be done with imprecise criteria measurements and missing preference information. Initial phase of the project was considered a success: the University Board of Directors decided to re-activate the process and the model was revised with up-to-date data. New alternatives were also discovered and old ones not viable anymore removed from the model. In the second phase, more preference information was included in the model as well. In the end of the process, the DMs could identify the most preferred alternative. However, the implementation is delayed because of changes in the university administration.

The initial phase of re-activation of the process without requiring interaction from the DMs could be applied similarly in other decision making contexts as well. Whenever older, more imprecise data is available, a possible initial phase with an uncertain model can allow savings to be obtained. Future research should evaluate applicability of this type of two phase decision analysis in other real-life problems.

References

Abbas, A. (2006). Maximum entropy utility. *Operations Research, 54*(2), 277–290.

Barberis, G. F., & Rodenas, M. E. (2006). Nuevos criterios generalizados para modelar las preferencias del decisor en los métodos de relaciones de superación. *Rect, 7*(1), 95–117.

Barda, O., Dupuis, J., & Lencioni, P. (1990). Multicriteria location of thermal power plants. *European Journal of Operational Research, 45*, 332–346.

Belton, V., & Stewart, T. J. (2002). *Multiple criteria decision analysis - An integrated approach*. Dordrecht: Kluwer Academic Publishers.

Beynon, M., Curry, B., & Morgan, P. (2000). The Dempster-Shafer theory of evidence: an alternative approach to multicriteria decision modelling. *Omega, 28*, 37–50.

BOCM, Order 2879/2004. (2004). Boletín Oficial de la Comunidad de Madrid 26.7.2004, Spain, 2004.

BOE, Order 1848/2005. (2007a). Boletín Oficial del Estado 28.2.2007, Spain.

BOE, Order 609/2007. (2007b). Boletín Oficial del Estado 28.2.2007, Spain.

Brans, J. P., & Vincke, P. (1985). The PROMETHEE method for multiple criteria decision making. *Management Science, 31*(6), 647–656.

El País. (2007). Section properties, second hand housing. *El País* 27.4.2007, Spain, 2007.

Erkut, E., Karagiannidis, A., Perkoulidis, G., & Tjandra, S. (2008). A multicriteria facility location model for municipal solid waste management in North Greece. *European Journal of Operational Research, 187*(16), 1402–1421.

Erkut, E., & Moran, S. (1991). Locating obnoxious facilities in the public sector: an application of the analytic hierarchy process to multiple landfill siting decisions. *Socio-Economic Planning Sciences, 25*(2), 89–102.

Figueira, J., Greco, S., & Ehrgott, M. (Eds.). (2005a). *Multiple criteria decision analysis: State of the art surveys*. New York: Springer Science+Business Media Inc.
Figueira, J., Mousseau, V., & Roy, B. (2005b). ELECTRE methods, Chap. 4. In: Figueira, J., Greco, S., Ehrgott, M. (Eds.), *Multiple criteria decsion analysis: State of the art surveys*. New York: Springer Science+Business Media Inc.
Hokkanen, J., Lahdelma, R., Miettinen, K., & Salminen, P. (1998). Determining the implementation order of a general plan by using a multicriteria method. *Journal of Multi-Criteria Decision Analysis, 7*(5), 273–284.
Hokkanen, J., Lahdelma, R., & Salminen, P. (1999). A multiple criteria decision model for analyzing and choosing among different development patterns for the Helsinki cargo harbor. *Socio-Economic Planning Sciences, 33*, 1–23.
Hokkanen, J., & Salminen, P. (1997). Choosing a solid waste management system using multicriteria decision analysis. *European Journal of Operational Research, 98*, 19–36.
Karagiannidis, A., & Moussiopoulos, N. (1997). Application of ELECTRE III for the integrated management of municipal solid wastes in the Greater Athens area. *European Journal of Operational Research, 97*, 439–449.
Karkazis, J. (1998). Facilities location in a competitive environment – a PROMETHEE based multiple criteria analysis. *European Journal of Operational Research, 42*(3), 294–304.
Keeney, R. (1980). *Siting energy facilities*. New York: Academic.
Lahdelma, R., & Salminen, P. (2002). Pseudo-criteria versus linear utility function in stochastic multi-criteria acceptability analysis. *European Journal of Operational Research, 141*, 454–469.
Lahdelma, R., Salminen, P., & Hokkanen, J. (2000). Using multicriteria methods in environmental planning and management. *Environmental Management, 26*(6), 595–605.
Lahdelma, R., Salminen, P., & Hokkanen, J. (2002) Locating a waste treatment facility by using stochastic multicriteria acceptability analysis with ordinal criteria. *European Journal of Operational Research, 142*, 345–356.
Madrid. (2007). *Sistema de ayuda al contribuyente para la determinación de bases imponibles en los impuestos sobre transmisiones patrimoniales y actos jurídicos documentados, y sucesiones y donaciones*. Consejaría de Hacienda, Dirección General Tributos, de la Comunidad de Madrid, Spain, 2007.
Martin, C., Ruperd, Y., & Legret, M. (2007). Urban stormwater drainage management: the development of a multicriteria decision aid approach for best management practices. *European Journal of Operational Research, 181*(1), 338–349.
Mustajoki, J., Hämäläinen, R. P., Salo, A. (2005). Decision support by interval SMART/SWING - incorporating imprecision in the SMART and SWING methods. *Decision Sciences, 36*(2), 317–339.
Norese, M. (2006). ELECTRE III as a support for participatory decision-making on the localisation of waste-treatment plants. *Land Use Policy, 23*, 76–85.
Partovi, F., & Burton, J. (1992). An analytical hierarchy approach to facility layout. *Computers & Industrial Engineering, 22*(4), 447–457.
Queiruga, D., Walther, G., González-Benito, J., & Spengler, T. Evaluation of sites for the location of WEEE recycling plants in Spain. *Waste Management, 28*(1), 181–190.
Roy, B. (1978). Un algorithme de classement fondé sur une representation floue des preferences en présence de critères multiples. *Cahiers du CERO, 20*(1), 3–24.
Tervonen, T., & Figueira, J. R. (2008). A survey on stochastic multicriteria acceptability analysis methods. *Journal of Multi-Criteria Decision Analysis, 15*(1–2), 1–14.
Tervonen, T., Figueira, J. R., Lahdelma, R., & Salminen, P. (2007). *Towards robust ELECTRE III with simulation: theory and software of SMAA-III*. Research report 1/2007 of the Centre for Management Studies of Instituto Superior Técnico, Technical University of Lisbon, Portugal, 2007.
Tervonen, T., Hakonen, H., & Lahdelma, R. (2008). Elevator planning with stochastic multicriteria acceptability analysis. *Omega, 36*(3), 352–362.

Tervonen, T., & Lahdelma, R. (2007). Implementing stochastic multicriteria acceptability analysis. *European Journal of Operational Research, 178*(2), 500–513.

Wu, C., Lin, C., & Chen, H. (2007). Optimal selection of location for Taiwanese hospitals to ensure a competitive advantage by using the analytic hierarchy process and sensitivity analysis. *Building and Environment, 42*(3), 1431–1444.

Editors' Comments on "Site Selection for a University Kindergarten in Madrid"

The chapter by T. Tervonen, G. Fernandez Barberis, J. Figueira and M. Escribano describes a real-world application which aims at supporting a decision problem concerning the location of a Kindergarten for a university (Fundaciòn Universitaria San Pablo—Centro de Estudios Universitarios) in Madrid. Hence, this case study can be viewed, at least partly, as a decision problem involving geographical aspects and geo-referenced data (see also Chaps. 9 and 12).

The decision process started with a petition of the University staff asking for a kindergarten. A first study was conducted in 1996, but led to no agreement concerning the location and the project was then frozen. This Chapter describes how this location problem has been re-activated and reconsidered in 2007.

The **set of alternatives**, seven (7) possible locations for the kindergarten, was clearly defined and corresponds to the locations initially considered in 1996. These seven alternative locations were evaluated on five (5) **criteria**: Accessibility to the city center, Size, Investment costs, Effect on the city landscape, and Maintenance costs.[1] Although the decision to be made concerned the choice of a single location, formulating the **problem statement** as ranking the seven alternatives from the best to the worst was considered as a relevant way of studying the decision problem.

The application is based on the use of the SMAA-III **aggregation method** (see Tervonen et al. 2007). This SMAA-III method considers the Electre III outranking ranking method (see Chap. 4, Sect. 4.4.3, and Figueira et al. 2005) as way to rank alternatives. However, the specificity of the SMAA-III method comes from the fact that uncertainty is attached to the preference parameters (and possibly alternatives evaluations). This uncertainty is modeled by probability distributions. Rank acceptability indices and pairwise comparison indices are computed using a Monte Carlo simulation approach.

A peculiarity of this application comes from the fact that there was little preference information available for a thorough **elicitation process** and seemingly no way to collect more specific preference information. More specifically, the DMs were only able to provide a rough interval in which the weights of criteria could vary; similar intervals for the preference and indifference thresholds were also

[1]An XMCDA 2.0 encoded performance tableau with average model parameters may be downloaded from the webpage http://leopold-loewenheim.uni.lu/Digraph3/handbook/chapter-7.

elicited. In this context, the use of a Monte Carlo simulation based approach as used in the SMAA methods seems relevant. In this application, it could have been interesting to refine/reduce with the DMs the uncertainty concerning the preference parameters on the basis of the results obtained in the first stage of the analysis. It seems that the involvement of the DMs did not make it possible to conduct such iterated analysis.

The study has lead to a recommendation: two of the alternatives came out as the best possible locations for the kindergarten. Such recommendation stemming from the preference model is indeed a **tangible result**, as in many standard decision aiding processes. In this study, such tangible result does not exist as it is an ex-post study. Discussions among the member the University board led to the choice of one single alternative, but the decision process did not led to an actual decision.

References

Figueira, J., Mousseau, V., & Roy B. (2005). ELECTRE methods. In: J. Figueira, S. Greco, & M. Ehrgott (Eds.), *Multiple criteria decision analysis: State of the art surveys* (pp. 133–162). Boston/Dordrecht/London: Springer.

Tervonen , T., & Lahdelma, R. (2007). Implementing stochastic multicriteria acceptability analysis. *European Journal of Operational Research, 178*(2), 500–513.

Chapter 8
Choosing a Cooling System for a Power Plant in Belgium

Marc Pirlot, Jacques Teghem, Berthold Ulungu, Léon Duvivier, Pierre Bulens, and Coralie Goffin

Abstract This chapter reports on a simulated decision aiding process aiming at choosing a cooling system for a new power plant. The study took place in a research contract between MathRO, the Mathematics and Operations Research unit at UMONS, and Laborelec, a technical competence centre of the Belgian power industry. The goal of the contract was to show whether and how multiple criteria decision methods could help taking the environmental and societal aspects of technical choices into account in a relevant way. In this perspective, the case of the choice of a cooling system for the Saint-Ghislain power plant was conceived as a validation exercise.

8.1 Introduction

In the fall of 2001, the team of L. Duvivier at Laborelec asked the laboratory of Mathematics and Operational Research (MathRO) of the Faculté Polytechnique de Mons, Belgium, to enter into a 2 years project under a research contract. Laborelec is a technical competence centre in charge of energy processes and energy use in Belgium. The team headed at that time by L. Duvivier was especially involved in

M. Pirlot (✉) • J. Teghem • B. Ulungu
Université de Mons, Faculté Polytechnique, Mons, Belgium
e-mail: marc.pirlot@umons.ac.be; jacques.teghem@umons.ac.be; berthold.ulungu@umons.ac.be

P. Bulens
Laborelec, Rodestraat 125, 1630 Linkebeek, Belgium
e-mail: pierre.bulens@ laborelec.com

L. Duvivier
Business Development, Laborelec, Rodestraat 125, 1630 Linkebeek, Belgium
e-mail: leon.duvivier@laborelec.com

C. Goffin
Sustainable Process Technologies, Laborelec, Rodestraat 125, 1630 Linkebeek, Belgium
e-mail: coralie.goffin@laborelec.com

R. Bisdorff et al. (eds.), *Evaluation and Decision Models with Multiple Criteria*,
International Handbooks on Information Systems,
DOI 10.1007/978-3-662-46816-6_8

the environmental aspects of these activities. The general mission underlying this contract was to show Laborelec how it is possible to take environmental and societal aspects into account, on top of costs as was traditionally done, in technical decisions related to the building of power plants and the management of power generation. The project started with a one day seminar in which MathRO explained what MCDA was all about to an audience composed of members of Laborelec and other persons responsible for the engineering and management of power generation. Then it was decided that the appropriateness and usefulness of MCDA methods would best be illustrated by working out a few case studies. The first case that was submitted was an *ex post* evaluation of the selection of a cooling system for a newly constructed power plant in Saint-Ghislain, close to the city of Mons in Belgium. This power plant is equipped with a combined cycle gas turbine cooled by an air condenser composed of 24 large fans.

In view of studying the case, a working group was settled, composed of members of MathRO, Laborelec and Tractebel (an engineering consultancy company, now in the GDF Suez group). The working group included the authors of this paper. We emphasize that the process starting at that time was an *ex post* evaluation exercise; it was not a real decision process. It aimed at validating the use of a multicriteria methodology for taking into account environmental and societal aspects in technical choices. In this process, the members of Laborelec and Tractebel played the role of the decision makers. The members of MathRO acted as analysts. External experts were asked to assess the alternatives on selected criteria or indicators. Note that the members of Laborelec did not act as decision makers in the usual sense since the decision had already been made. They could be called *observers*: they witnessed the simulated decision aiding process with the aim to make up their mind about the reliability and appropriateness of such a process for ulterior decisions of a similar type that could be done using MCDA methods. In this case study Laborelec figures as client of MathRO.

8.2 Formulation of the Problem by the Working Group

Three half-a-day meetings of the working group were dedicated to the presentation and the analysis of the problem in view of gradually elaborating the various objects of a multicriteria decision process:

- the specification of the alternatives,
- a clear view of the goal of the analysis (often called the "problématique" in French, see Roy 1985),
- the various viewpoints that matter in this case,
- and a way of assessing the alternatives on these viewpoints.

Table 8.1 List of the alternatives

Label	Description
A_1	Once through
A_2	After cooling tower with natural air flow
A_3	Half-closed cycle with fixed concentration factor and forced air flow
A_4	Half-closed cycle with fixed concentration factor and hybrid air flow
A_5	Half-closed cycle with fixed concentration factor and natural air flow
A_6	Half-closed cycle with variable concentration factor and natural air flow
A_7	Air condenser with forced air flow

8.2.1 The Alternatives

The determination of the alternatives was intensively discussed during the first meeting. The main issue was to determine to which degree of detail the alternatives should be described and whether variants of each alternative should be considered. For instance, should we consider a certain cooling system and the same cooling system with a noise barrier wall as distinct alternatives. For this example, the answer was negative. Several variants of similar systems were nevertheless considered. Note also that the definition of the alternatives was not fully independent from considerations about their assessment. L. Duvivier eventually came to the second meeting with the set of seven alternatives described in Table 8.1

We do not enter into a more precise, technical, description of these alternatives. Let us simply say that systems A_1 to A_6 all require water as a cooling fluid that must be taken from a river or a canal. System A_1 is the simplest one can think of. Water is taken from the environment, used for cooling the turbine and then rejected in the environment without treatment. In A_2 to A_6, water taken from the environment is used for cooling a fluid in a primary circuit and is cooled in some way before being returned to the environment. These alternatives differ by the fact that the air flow used to cool the water is natural or forced and by the concentration factor. The reader should focus attention on alternatives A_1, A_3 and A_7 since these will emerge from the analysis.

8.2.2 The Decision **Problématique**

Although the problem was initially formulated as a choice problem, the analyst is asked to establish a ranking of all the retained alternatives. This is because there are relatively few of them; choosing one alternative in the set is considered too easy. In order to put more pressure on MCDA methods, the client asks for a ranking of all alternatives. The validation of the methodology will rely on whether experts of the domain are eventually convinced that the produced ranking makes sense.

8.2.3 Points of View and Indicators

It has been clear from the start that Laborelec wanted to integrate three points of view in the preference model: cost, societal aspects and environmental aspects. As far as costs are concerned, Tractebel has an expert practice of cost evaluation that is not to be questioned. Their experts are able to assess the costs of all sorts of equipments composing various sorts of power plants. They include all kinds of costs such as investment, running, maintenance and dismantling costs in their assessments. Even the impact of the type of cooling system on the thermodynamic working conditions of the turbine and hence on the quantity of power produced is taken into account. Strong uncertainty factors however threaten the reliability of the estimations, such as for instance, the actual lifetime of the plant, the price of energy during the lifetime of the equipment, the discount rate of the investment. In spite of these uncertainties, the costs are considered as well mastered, at least in relative terms, i.e. the cost ratios of the various solutions. Table 8.2 shows the relative costs of the alternatives on a scale ranging from 0 to 10. The more expensive alternative (A_7) receives the maximal mark, while the cheaper one (A_1) is valued approximately to 6.5.

The discussion in the working group thus focussed on the identification of indicators likely to describe all aspects of the viewpoints that are relevant for the choice of a cooling system. The initial option aiming at defining objective, measurable, indicators had to be abandoned. In this logic, a way of measuring the environmental impact included an index such as the losses of fish at the water intake of the power plant (such a study had been performed for another power plant on the Meuse river near Liège). Unfortunately, such studies were too specialized and the few available indices were not sufficient to give an appropriate picture even of the biological impact of the various equipments. It was eventually decided to retain seven aspects representing the societal point of view and four aspects representing the environmental viewpoint; these 11 aspects are described in Tables 8.3 and 8.4. Some of these aspects are self-explanatory. Others require precise delimitation to prevent taking account of characteristics of some systems redundantly, under the heading of more than one aspect. For instance, a large cooling tower emitting its plume of water vapor may impact both the "view" and the "image" aspects. Its impact may be negative on "view" since the tower is perceived by some as a ugly object in the landscape. The plume may be perceived as threatening (e.g. because

Table 8.2 Relative costs of the alternatives on a 0–10 scale. The more expensive one receives the mark "10"

$A1$	6.551
A_2	9.531
A_3	6.779
A_4	8.482
A_5	7.989
A_6	8.002
A_7	10

Table 8.3 List of societal aspects

Identifier	Description
no	*no*ise: noise generated by the functioning of the cooling system
vi	*vi*ew: harmonious visual integration in the landscape
im	*im*age: image of the site as perceived by the public
hp	*h*ealth of *p*ersonnel: health risks faced by the workers on site
hr	*h*ealth of *r*esidents: health risks faced by the residents living in the neighborhood of the site
sp	*s*afety of *p*ersonnel: risk of accidents at work faced by the personnel
sr	*s*afety of *r*esidents: risk of accidents faced by the residents and other persons in the neighborhood of the site

Table 8.4 List of environmental aspects

Identifier	Description
tm	in*t*ake of *m*atter from the environment, which is not entirely restored to the environment in its initial state
cs	*c*hemical *s*pill: release of traces of chemicals used for cleaning the system in the environment
hi	*h*eat *i*nput: impact of the heat released locally
bi	*b*iological *i*mpacts: impacts on the local ecosystem

some people interpret it as pollution or even suspect it could be radioactive), which negatively affects the "image" aspect.

Not all the retained aspects can be assessed by means of objective measurements in the present state of knowledge. In particular, evaluating these aspects in quantitative terms, e.g. social or environmental costs, and aggregating them with monetary costs using tradeoffs appears to be out of reach. It has been decided that they would be submitted to subjective evaluation by experts. Twelve persons working in different departments of Laborelec, Electrabel and Tractebel were chosen to act as experts; they were selected for their knowledge of the problem and because they represent various points of view on the problem: technical, financial, environmental.

8.2.4 Assessment Procedure

The working group designed a questionnaire to be submitted to the experts. The experts were asked to assess all seven alternatives on the 11 aspects described above. For all aspects (but the cost) the assessment scale was the [0, 10] interval. In order to ease the task of the experts and also the further bipolar interpretation of the obtained assessments, three reference points were specified on the 0–10 scale:

- level "2" (resp. "8") represents a very unsatisfactory (resp. satisfactory) level
- level "5" represents the boundary between unsatisfactory and satisfactory.

Fig. 8.1 Expert 1's graphical assessment of the "harmonious visual integration" aspect

The scales were described to the experts as "at least" qualitative or ordinal. This means that the most important point they have to pay attention to is correctly ordering the alternatives on each scale, with respect to the corresponding aspect. However, while assigning alternatives to levels on the scale, the experts are asked to try to reflect as much as possible the differences between alternatives on each aspect as they perceive them. The definition of the reference points suggests that the difference between the unsatisfactory level "2" and the boundary level "5" could be similar in terms of preference to that between "5" and the satisfactory level "8". It may sound very optimistic, or even unrealistic, to hope that the assessments provided by the experts could be treated as marginal value functions, which would in particular imply that equal intervals on a scale represent equal preference differences. We were nevertheless planning to use a weighted sum of these evaluations since it was out of question to spend the time and effort needed to build an additive value function, using one of the numerous methods developed to do this in a reliable way (see e.g. von Winterfeldt and Edwards 1986). Since it is far from granted that equal intervals on the scale represent equal value differences, we will also use a fully ordinal aggregation model (an outranking method of the ELECTRE type, see Roy and Bouyssou 1993).

The questionnaire submitted to the experts asks for assessments on the [0, 10] scale in graphical mode. As a matter of illustration, Fig. 8.1 shows the qualitative assessment of the alternatives from the "harmonious visual integration" viewpoint by Expert 1.

8.2.5 Relative Importance of the Criteria

Obtaining reliable information about the relative importance of the criteria is both crucial and quite delicate especially when no aggregation model has been chosen beforehand. Indeed the meaning of importance coefficients attached to the criteria strongly depends on the type of aggregation model (see Roy and Bouyssou 1993; Belton and Stewart 2001 or Vansnick 1986); correlatively the way of questioning about the importance of the criteria depends on the model. In additive value function models, the weights associated with the criteria are tradeoffs and depend on the choice of a "measurement unit" on each scale. In outranking methods, weights of criteria are added to measure the strength of coalitions of criteria. Assuming that equal length intervals on any scale represent equal differences of preference, one might question the experts in view of determining tradeoffs. This would amount to ask for instance how many units on the scale of the "harmonious visual integration" aspect would the expert agree to abandon in order to pass from 2 to 5 on the "noise" criterion. In the present context, it was not possible to envisage using such a time consuming and cognitively demanding methodology. A similar conclusion prevails when concerned with a sound elicitation of weights to be used in an outranking method. Finally, the working group decided that the information on the weights would be collected in a similar form as the assessment of the alternatives on the various aspects. Each expert will be asked to assess the relative importance of the criteria on the [0, 10] interval. Again, reference points have been determined: "2" (resp. "8") represents a criterion of very little importance (resp. a very important criterion); level "5" is associated with a criterion of medium importance.

Considering that it would be hard to compare directly the importance of a societal aspect such as "health of personnel" to an environmental one such as "biological impacts", it has been taken advantage of the hierarchical structure of the criteria. The working group determined that the experts would be asked to give a mark from 0 to 10 to each aspect in order to reflect its relative importance within the viewpoint it belongs to (societal or environmental); then they would mark in a similar way the three major viewpoints (cost, societal, environmental) for their contribution in the global objective. In order to assign a weight to each of the 12 criteria (including cost), based on each expert assessment, a fraction of the sum of the weights (100 %) was first assigned to each of the three groups of criteria proportionally to the marks given by the expert; second, a weight was assigned to each aspect in a group of criteria proportionally to the marks given by the expert. For instance, Expert 1 provided assessments of the various aspects as described in Table 8.6. From this table, straightforward computations yield $\frac{8}{21}$ (resp. $\frac{6}{21}, \frac{7}{21}$ as a weight for "cost" (resp. "societal", "environmental" groups of criteria). Then, in the group of societal criteria, "noise" receives a fraction equal to $\frac{9}{50}$ of the total weight of the group, i.e. $\frac{9}{50} \times \frac{6}{21} \approx 5.1\,\%$. The procedure is similar for all criteria of any of the groups.

8.2.6 Assessments Obtained from the Experts

The questionnaire was submitted to 12 experts as said above. It starts with a short description of the decision problem, of the alternatives and the hierarchy of criteria, of the scale and the interpretation of the reference points. The experts are then asked to fill in a form in with their assessments. For testing purposes, a first version of the assessment form was administered to six out of the twelve experts. After

Table 8.5 Assessment of the alternatives by Expert 1

	no	vi	im	hp	hr	sp	sr	tm	cs	hi	bi
A_1	9	9	9	8	9	8	8	4	1	3	1
A_2	7	2	1	6	7	6	8	2	2	3	3
A_3	2	5	4	6	7	6	8	6	6	5	6
A_4	3	4	4	6	7	6	8	6	6	5	6
A_5	5	2	2	6	7	6	8	6	4	3	4
A_6	2	5	4	6	7	6	8	6	6	5	6
A_7	2	6	7	6	9	6	8	9	9	7	8

Table 8.6 Importance of the major viewpoints and of their various aspects as assessed by Expert 1

cost	soc							env			
8	6							7			
	no	vi	im	hp	hr	sp	sr	tm	cs	hi	bi
	9	2	5	8	9	8	9	5	8	8	6

reformulation of some of the questions, a second version of the questionnaire was submitted to the remaining six experts.

Of the responses received from the experts, one answer form could not be exploited (the fourth expert in the first wave misunderstood the instructions; only one alternative was assessed on each criterion). An example of responses, those made by Expert 1, are reproduced in Tables 8.5 and 8.6. Note that the experts have not been asked to assess the alternatives on the cost criterion since a quantitative evaluation of this viewpoint was already available.

8.3 Weighted Sum Approach

Let us assume that the values given by the experts on all aspects but the "cost" dimension are good estimates of marginal value functions and, in addition, that the weights provided by the same experts can be considered as tradeoffs between the eleven last aspects. Under this hypothesis, there is a straightforward way, namely, a weighted sum, that yields an additive value function allowing to rank the alternatives taking into account the eleven aspects of the societal and environmental points of view. A serious problem remains for incorporating the "cost" dimension into the overall value. Indeed, if we may argue that the scales on which the eleven latter aspects have been assessed are of the same nature, this is not the case with the "cost" aspect, which has been assessed using an economic evaluation procedure. Since there was no possibility of questioning a decision maker on tradeoffs between "cost" and some other aspect (for instance, constructing a *standard sequence* on the cost criterion by means of indifference judgments as explained in Sect. 3.2.4; see also von Winterfeldt and Edwards, 1986, p. 266), we made several hypotheses on the possible tradeoff between cost and the other aspects. More precisely, we assumed that the marginal value function on "cost" is linear, which is reasonable since there was no indication that some amount would constitute a breakpoint[1] on the "cost" scale. Hence, what we had to do was just to properly scale the cost assessments.

8.3.1 Hypotheses on the Cost Criterion

The following three hypotheses have been formulated:

1. **Hypothesis** α assumes that considering *relative costs*, i.e. dividing all costs by the larger one, as shown in Table 8.2, makes the cost scale comparable to the 11 other ones. Of course, one has to take into account that cost has to be minimized, hence we have to subtract all values in Table 8.2 from 10, yielding finally scaling α_i of the costs. The value associated with alternative A_i, for $i = 1$ to 7, on the cost aspect is computed as follows:

$$\alpha_i = 10 \times \left(1 - \frac{\text{cost}(A_i)}{\text{cost}(A_7)}\right).$$

   With this scaling, the worst alternative (A_7) receives value 0 and the better one (A_1) receives value 3.45 (approximately)[2].
2. **Hypothesis** β is the most extreme interpretation of the cost scale: it assigns value 0 to the more expensive alternative A_7 and value 10 to the cheaper A_1. Hence scaled value β_i of alternative A_i for $i = 1$ to 7 is defined as:

$$\beta_i = 10 \times \left(1 - \frac{\text{cost}(A_i) - \text{cost}(A_1)}{\text{cost}(A_7) - \text{cost}(A_1)}\right).$$

3. **Hypothesis** γ constitutes an intermediate interpretation in which, the worst alternative (A_7) receives the value 2 ("very unsatisfactory" level) and the better one (A_1) receives the value 8 ("very satisfactory" level). Scaled value γ_i of alternative A_i for $i = 1$ to 7 is defined as:

$$\gamma_i = 2 + 6 \times \left(1 - \frac{\text{cost}(A_i) - \text{cost}(A_1)}{\text{cost}(A_7) - \text{cost}(A_1)}\right).$$

[1]That is, a cost level above which a unit cost difference has not the same value as a unit cost difference below this level.

[2]Note that the scale origin can be translated without any impact **on the ranking** obtained via a weighted sum or an additive value function. Here we could equivalently say that A_7 receives mark 2 ("very unsatisfactory" level) and A_1 receives 5.45. Or else that A_1 receives 8 ("very satisfactory" level) and A_7 receives $8-3.45 = 4.55$. Or even that A_1 receives 10 ("ideal" value) and A_7 receives $10 - 3.45 = 6.55$. Only differences matter to the ranking in such models.

Table 8.7 Impact of the three hypotheses on the importance of the criteria

Hypotheses	α	γ	β
A_7	0	2	0
A_1	3.449	8	10
Range	3.449	6	10
Ratio	1	1.74	2.9

8.3.1.1 Comments

- Using the three scalings described above, we cover a range of different interpretations of the cost criterion with respect to the scale proposed for the experts'assessment on the other aspects. Table 8.7 shows the values of the best and the worse alternatives on the cost criterion according with the three hypotheses we considered. We see that the range of the scaled cost criterion varies from 1 to almost 3 depending on the hypothesis made. Accordingly, without changing the weight of the cost criterion, we make it three times as influent by adopting hypothesis β instead of α and 1.74 times more influent by adopting γ instead of α. Therefore the choice of an hypothesis on the cost that would faithfully reflect the way the decision maker considers the role of the cost is likely to be crucial. We shall work under the three above hypotheses and formulate conclusions in all three cases.
- Hypothesis α should not be considered as an extreme one. One could think of other hypotheses that would give lesser influence to cost. For instance, one might consider that cost(A_1) is quite satisfactory, assigning mark 8 to it while A_7 is more expensive but still affordable, assigning mark 6 to it. In fact, reasoning in relative terms on the cost criterion is quite common and in this view, scaling α is the natural one.

8.3.2 Scores of the Alternatives Under the Various Hypotheses on Cost

We can now compute the scores of the alternatives for each expert under each hypothesis. Table 8.8 shows these scores under hypothesis α, for example. Experts are labeled R1 to R12, "R" standing for "respondent". Expert R4 is lacking since his/her answer could not be exploited, as mentioned previously. A better way of visualizing the distribution of the scores among the various experts is through using boxplots. In each box of a boxplot, the lower (resp. central, upper) horizontal segment represents the first (resp. second, third) quartile of the distribution of the scores. Looking at Figs. 8.2, 8.3 and 8.4 clearly shows a number of facts. Under hypothesis α, almost all experts agree that A_7 has the highest score followed by A_1.

Table 8.8 Scores for the 11 experts under hypothesis α

	R1	R2	R3	R5	R6	R7	R8	R9	R10	R11	R12
A_1	4.46	5.36	5.43	5.29	4.43	5.02	4.22	3.93	4.13	4.10	5.47
A_2	2.75	6.58	3.95	3.23	2.49	3.64	3.59	2.18	2.79	2.72	3.95
A_3	4.72	6.56	3.21	4.72	3.85	4.57	3.44	4.03	4.57	3.45	3.98
A_4	4.11	6.94	3.41	4.07	3.54	4.14	2.91	3.82	3.91	3.23	3.65
A_5	3.78	6.84	4.08	4.00	3.68	4.20	3.65	3.34	4.11	3.01	4.38
A_6	4.26	7.03	3.08	4.22	3.51	4.16	3.19	3.86	4.10	3.08	3.65
A_7	4.52	8.60	6.60	5.48	5.80	5.48	6.18	4.51	5.33	3.49	6.19

Under hypothesis γ (the intermediate one w.r.t. the importance of cost), alternative A_7 goes down, having scores similar to A_1, while A_3 slowly emerges. Under β, the hypothesis that gives cost three times as much importance as α, the distribution of scores of A_1 is in the lead, followed by A_3 and then A_7, which still stands before the rest of the alternatives. Our first impression, which will be confirmed in the sequel, is that A_1, A_3 and A_7 lead the race and their final rank will eventually depend on the importance of the cost criterion.

Note also that there seems to be an "outlier" among the experts. Expert 2 (labeled "R2" in Table 8.8 and in the boxplot figures) tends to systematically assign higher marks to all alternatives. His/her scores consistently appear above the boxes in almost all boxplots. Since the order in which Expert 2 ranks the alternatives remains consistent with that of the other experts, there is no indication that this expert has made atypical judgments. It just shows that he/she considers differently the reference levels provided on the scales, the relative positions of the alternatives being similar for this expert and the other ones.

Another way of visualizing the rankings of the alternatives by the experts, which result from the computed scores under the various hypotheses, is by looking at Fig. 8.5. In this figure, each alternative is attached a rank number according to its position in the ranking of the alternatives derived from the scores computed for each expert under hypothesis α. The alternative ranked in the first position receives rank number 7; the alternative in the last position receives rank number 1. From this figure, we can see that the alternative which is most often in the first position is A_7; a sensible synthetic ranking is A_7 followed by A_1 followed by A_3 and then the others. This ranking of the first three alternatives is also the one we obtain the average rank number. If we compare the alternatives as represented by their ranks frequency distribution, using stochastic dominance (i.e. by comparing coordinatewise the cumulative distributions of their rank frequencies), we obtain that $A7$ dominates all other alternatives, $A3$ and $A1$ are not comparable, $A3$ dominates all others, while $A1$ dominates all others except $A5$.

Similar representations for the rankings of the alternatives under hypotheses γ and β show that the position of A_7 declines. Under γ the ordering given by both

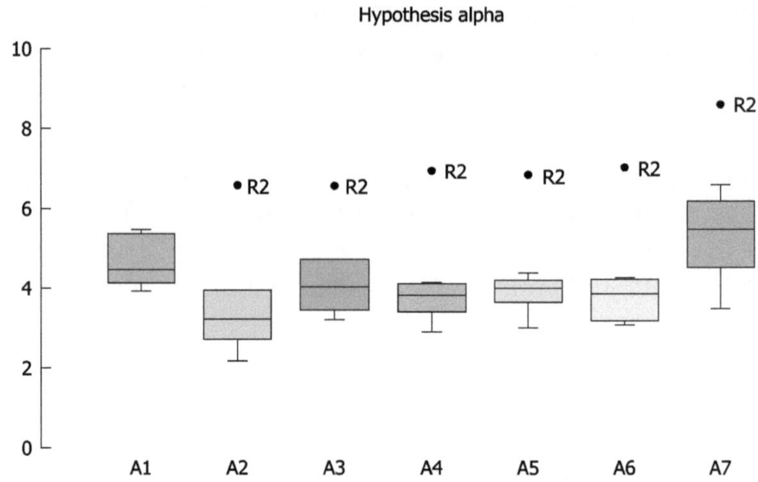

Fig. 8.2 Boxplots under hypothesis α

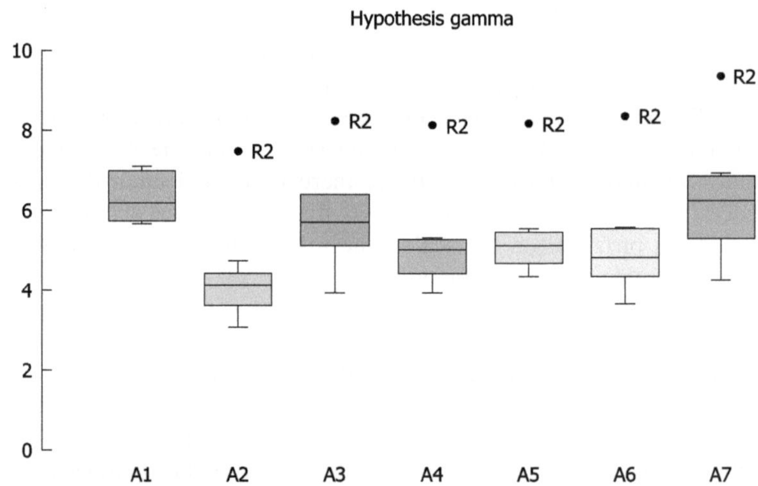

Fig. 8.3 Boxplots under hypothesis γ

stochastic dominance and average rank is $A_1 \succ A_7 \succ A_3$ (where $\succ$ stands for "is preferred to"). Under β, stochastic dominance and average rank again agree on the following ordering $A_1 \succ A_3 \succ A_7$; even in this case A_7 continues to stand before the remaining alternatives.

The latter analysis confirms that the focus is on alternatives A_1, A_3, A_7 and that discriminating between them will force the decision maker to take a position w.r.t. the importance of the cost criterion.

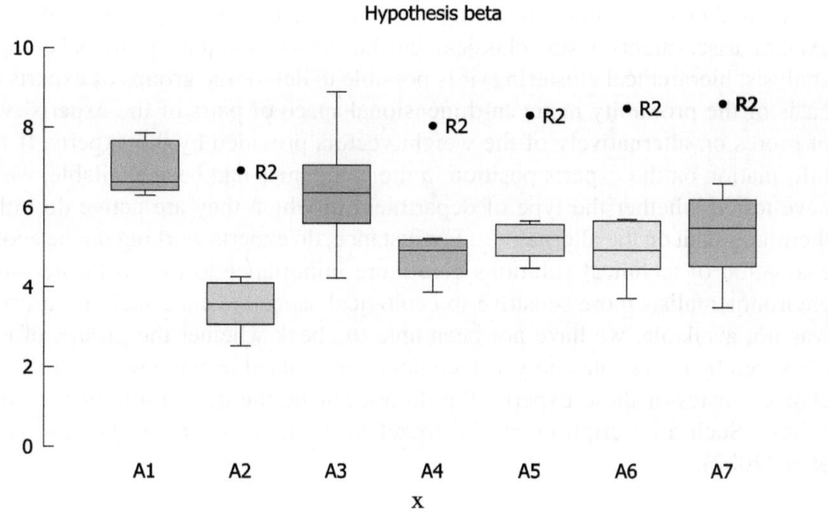

Fig. 8.4 Boxplots under hypothesis β

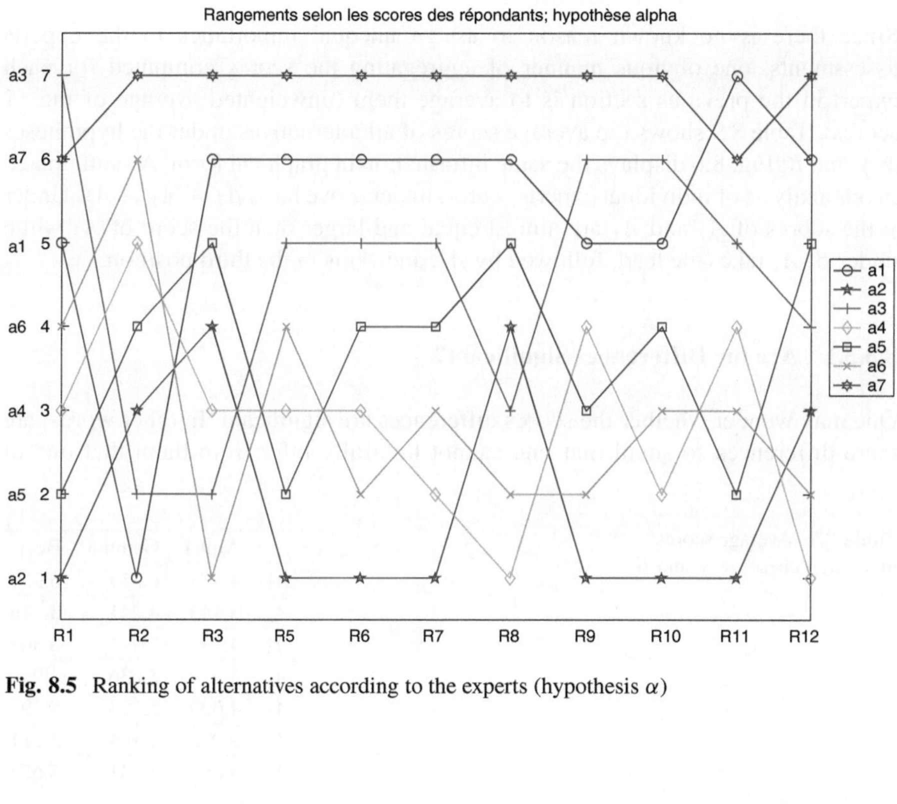

Fig. 8.5 Ranking of alternatives according to the experts (hypothesis α)

A number of further interesting observations can be made by analyzing the experts' assessments. Using classical data analysis techniques (principal component analysis, hierarchical clustering) it is possible to determine groups of experts on the basis of the proximity in seven-dimensional space of pairs of the experts' vectors of scores or, alternatively of the weight vectors provided by the experts. If further information on the experts position in the companies had been available, we could have tested whether the type of department in which they are active do influence their judgment on the alternatives. For instance, do experts working on the economic evaluation of technical solutions give more importance to the cost criterion? Are environmentalists more sensitive to ecological aspects? Since such an information was not available, we have not been able to check whether the groups of experts identified by using data analysis techniques are related in some way to professional characteristics of these experts. We do not pursue the description of the obtained results. Such a description can be found in the final report on the case (Ulungu et al., 2002).

8.3.3 *Aggregating the Experts Scores*

Since there is no known reason to assign unequal importance to the experts assessments, one obvious manner of aggregating the scores computed for each expert in the previous section is to average them (unweighted average of the 11 scores). Table 8.9 shows the average scores of all alternatives under the hypotheses α, γ and β; Fig. 8.6 displays the same information in graphical form. As anticipated in our analysis of individual experts scores, under α, we have $A_7 \succ A_1 \succ A_3$. Under γ the scores of A_7 and A_1 are almost equal and larger than the score of A_3 while under β, A_1 takes the lead, followed by A_3, and A_7 is in the third position.

8.3.3.1 Are the Differences Significant?

One may wonder whether the scores differences are significant. In other words, are there differences so small that one cannot faithfully infer from them that one of

Table 8.9 Average scores under hypotheses α, γ and β

	Alpha	Gamma	Beta
A_1	4.713	6.259	6.939
A_2	3.443	4.241	3.746
A_3	4.282	5.771	6.362
A_4	3.974	5.036	4.954
A_5	4.099	5.284	5.397
A_6	3.922	5.104	5.211
A_7	5.652	6.331	5.652

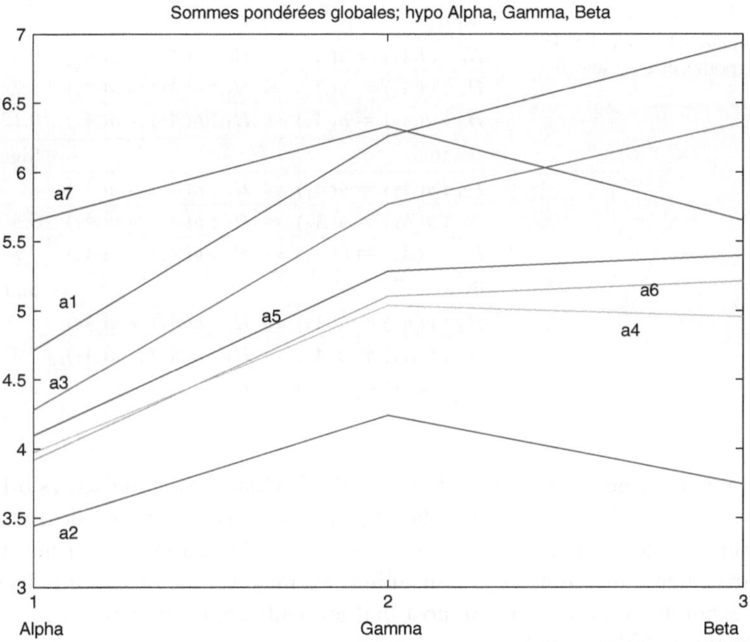

Fig. 8.6 Average scores under hypotheses α, γ and β

the alternatives involved has a strictly better position than the other in the ranking? There are mainly two approaches that can be thought of to deal with this question in the present context.

1. Monetary equivalent of a given score difference. Knowing the cost of the alternatives (which we are not allowed to reveal here) it is possible to determine the monetary value of one unit difference on the average score (which by the way depends on the hypotheses α, γ or β). To fix the ideas, let us assume that the cost of A_7 is 1 million €. In this case, A_1 would cost approximately 655 k€. Under hypothesis α, this cost difference is represented by the interval [0, 3.55] on the cost scale. Therefore, a difference of 1 unit on the cost criterion scale would represent 100 k€. The average weight of the cost criterion is 0.3398, as can be computed from the experts assessments (see also Table 8.12). Hence, under hypothesis α, a difference of 0.1 on the overall score can be obtained through a cost difference of Δ k€, where Δ is the solution of the following equation:

$$0.1 = 0.3398 \times \frac{\Delta}{100}$$

Table 8.10 t-tests of mean scores equality for A_1, A_3, A_7 under hypotheses α, γ and β

Alpha	Signif. (%)
$H_0 : u(A_7) = u(A_1)$ vs $H_1 : u(A_7) > u(A_1)$	0.65 %
$H_0 : u(A_1) = u(A_3)$ vs $H_1 : u(A_1) > u(A_3)$	8 %
$H_0 : u(A_7) = u(A_3)$ vs $H_1 : u(A_7) > u(A_3)$	0.15 %
Gamma	Signif. (%)
$H_0 : u(A_7) = u(A_1)$ vs $H_1 : u(A_7) > u(A_1)$	41 %
$H_0 : u(A_1) = u(A_3)$ vs $H_1 : u(A_1) > u(A_3)$	5.5 %
$H_0 : u(A_7) = u(A_3)$ vs $H_1 : u(A_7) > u(A_3)$	9 %
Beta	Signif. (%)
$H_0 : u(A_1) = u(A_3)$ vs $H_1 : u(A_1) > u(A_3)$	3 %
$H_0 : u(A_3) = u(A_7)$ vs $H_1 : u(A_3) > u(A_7)$	7 %
$H_0 : u(A_1) = u(A_7)$ vs $H_1 : u(A_1) > u(A_7)$	2.5 %

From this, we get that $\Delta \approx 29.4$ k€ ≈ 30 k€. Considering the scores difference between A_7 and A_1 under hypothesis γ, for instance, we may ask the decision maker whether a difference of $6.331 - 6.259 = 0.0720$ matters or not; in order to give such a difference some meaning, we may tell the decision maker that it corresponds to a difference in cost that amounts approximately to 21.2 k€, all other things being equal.

2. Since the average scores result from the aggregation of 11 individual judgements, it may be argued that they are averages in a statistical sense. Hence we may envisage to perform pairwise comparisons of means tests in order to decide whether an average score can be considered larger than another, taking into account the variability of experts judgements (considered as independent realizations of random variables). Table 8.10 displays the significance levels (p-value) of one-sided t-tests for means equality (u denotes the random variable "score of the alternatives"); we have tested the hypotheses that we formulated above while analyzing individual experts scores, namely

   - $A_7 \succ A_1 \succ A_3$ under hypothesis α
   - $A_7 \succ A_1 \succ A_3$ under hypothesis γ
   - $A_1 \succ A_3 \succ A_7$ under hypothesis β

   In the first case, the hypothesis is validated except that the equality of the scores of A_1 and A_3 is not rejected at the 5 % significance level (p-value = 8 %). Under γ, one cannot reject any of the three equalities at the 5 % significance level; however, we are not far from rejecting $u(A_1) = u(A_3)$ in favor of $u(A_1) > u(A_3)$ (p-value = 5.5 %) and $u(A_7) = u(A_3)$ in favor of $u(A_7) > u(A_3)$ (p-value = 9 %). Under hypothesis β, the first and the third inequalities are validated while the second one $u(A_3) > u(A_7)$ is borderline (p-value = 7 %).

Note that the just described usage of formal statistical tests is not above criticism. Here are three reasons that may question the validity of the conclusions drawn from these tests:

- it is not clear that the experts assessments can be considered as independent realizations of random variables, *a fortiori* normal variables. This is a key hypothesis which is at the basis of the construction of t-tests; we have little possibility of testing such an hypothesis due to the small number of respondents.
- our hypotheses related to the ordering of the alternatives have been formulated on the basis of the experts assessments, while it is assumed in statistical theory that the hypotheses must pre-exist data collection; this biases the results.
- in each case, three *non-independent* pairwise tests have been performed, which implies that significance levels are not reliably estimated.

In spite of these weaknesses, we consider that statistical tests are useful in this context, not so much for establishing a specific ordering of the alternatives on firm scientific grounds, but instead for identifying significant differences taking into account the variability of the experts judgments. For instance, the difference between $u(A_1)$ and $u(A_3)$ under hypothesis γ, which is approximately 0.49, corresponds to a 5 % significant difference, which is usually considered, in statistics, as sufficient for excluding that $u(A_1) = u(A_3)$.

8.3.4 Conclusion for the Weighted Sum Approach

At this stage we have reached some firm conclusions even though we cannot formally make a recommendation to the decision maker. Indeed our conclusions are conditional on further but well-defined information on the importance of the cost criterion. Independently from that, we have seen that we may focus on alternatives A_1, A_3 and A_7. In the three hypotheses we made on the importance of the cost criterion, A_3 never comes in the first position; either A_1 or A_7 has the lead. Hence the crucial point is to determine the importance of the cost. The eventual implementation of A_7 in the Saint-Ghislain plant gives us an a posteriori clear answer to this question. It was indeed hypothesis α that correctly reflected the importance of the "cost" dimension in the mind of the decision makers.

In order to more firmly establish this conclusion, we still have to examine one important issue. In using the weighted sum approach as we did, we assumed that the experts' assessments are strongly related to marginal value functions and, in our case, that equal differences on the assessment scales reflect equal differences of preference. In Sect. 8.2.4, we claimed that the scales could also be interpreted as purely qualitative, which means that only the ordering of the values matters. In order to confirm the conclusions of the weighted sum approach, we still need to verify whether similar conclusions are obtained using a qualitative interpretation of the experts assessments. This is the subject of the next section.

8.4 Outranking Approach

For aggregating qualitative criteria, we have used the ELECTRE II method (Roy and Bouyssou, 1993). Basically, in this method, we compare alternatives in pairwise manner deciding that alternative A is preferred to B (A *outranks* B) if A is at least as good as B on a majority of criteria and there is no strong opposition to this assertion.

The notion of majority of criteria is determined by means of weights attached to criteria and one (or several) majority threshold(s). Note that the weights here have not the same meaning as in a weighted sum: they are no tradeoffs but rather they measure the importance of each criterion in such a way that the strength of a coalition is measured by the sum of the weights of the criteria belonging to it. The entire weight of a criterion enters in the coalition of criteria in favor of A as compared to B as soon as the performance of A is at least as good as that of B on this criterion, no matter by what amount it is better. Such a feature makes the procedure well-suited for qualitative scales on which comparing differences of performance hardly make any sense. Needless to say, the weight values used in ELECTRE II may differ from tradeoffs used in a weighted sum.

The impossibility of comparing differences of performance is not absolute however. In some cases, certain negative performance differences may seem unacceptable as such. A "strong opposition" or *veto* occurs when alternative A is unacceptably worse than B on some criterion, so bad indeed that it would be nonsense to claim that A is preferred to B.

Since alternatives are compared in pairs, and the result only relies on the comparison of their performances, independently of third party alternatives, the obtained preference relation can be guaranteed neither to be transitive (Condorcet paradox) nor complete. Deriving a complete ranking of the alternatives from a relation which is not a complete weak order requires additional processing, which is often called exploitation procedure or ranking procedure (see Sect. 4.4.3). The exploitation procedure usually used in the ELECTRE II method is called *distillation* and possibly yields two different rankings: one is obtained by first considering the alternatives that are not outranked by others (possibly after reducing the circuits of the outranking relation), extracting them and then iterating the process on the remaining ones; we call this ranking "descending". The other is obtained in the opposite way, by first considering and extracting the alternatives which do not outrank any other, then iterating; we call this ranking "ascending". The two rankings may differ; a third "median ranking" can be constructed by ranking the alternatives according with their average positions in the descending and ascending rankings (see also Sect. 4.4.3.3). Another–simpler–exploitation procedure consists in ordering the alternatives in decreasing order of the number of alternatives that they outrank (descending ranking) or in increasing order of the number of alternatives which outrank them (ascending ranking). In this work, we used the latter exploitation procedure, obtaining also a median ranking by averaging the ranks of the alternatives in the descending and ascending rankings.

Finally, a distinctive character of ELECTRE II w.r.t. ELECTRE I is the fact that the distillation procedure usually involves two outranking relations; the latter, respectively called *strong* and *weak* outranking are obtained by using two or three different majority thresholds and usually two veto thresholds. While comparing A to B, strong outranking occurs when the more demanding conditions of majority and/or non-veto are fulfilled, while weak outranking obtains whenever weaker majority and/or non-veto conditions apply. The distillation process is primarily based on strong outranking; weak outranking intervenes for breaking ties. For a more precise description of the rules of ELECTRE II, see Roy and Bouyssou (1993); Vincke (1992) or Belton and Stewart (2001).

8.4.1 Applying ELECTRE II *to Individual Experts Judgments*

In our report (Ulungu et al., 2002), we describe how we applied ELECTRE II to the individual experts judgments in order to obtain a descending (resp. ascending, median) ranking of the alternatives for each expert. To do this, we attached the same weights to the criteria as we did in the weighted sum. There are two main reasons that justify this unorthodox—yet not uncommon—option. First, the only information available on the relative importance of the criteria are the experts' assessments. Second, the experts were asked to assess the relative importance of the criteria, which is not specially oriented towards obtaining tradeoff values. Since the evaluation scales of the criteria were the normalized [0, 10] interval, one may hope that the experts' weights are both tradeoffs and measure the importance of the criteria. From a practical point of view, it is important for the success of the ELECTRE II method that the weights are not too contrasted. Indeed, if the weight of a particular criterion is close to 50 % it is very hard to reach a majority in the comparison of A and B if this criterion is not in favor of A, so that such a criterion tends to play a dictatorial role. In our case the three groups of criteria are well-balanced, each one receiving about one third of the total on average. The fact that the cost criterion has no sub-criteria will however play a central role in our analysis. Indeed, when comparing A to B, all the weight of the cost criterion goes with the cheaper alternative. On the contrary, when comparing two alternatives on the societal or the environmental block of criteria, some sub-criteria may turn in favor of one alternative and other sub-criteria in favor of the other. Hence, not all the weight of these blocks necessarily go with one or the other alternative. We will come back on this point later.

In our analysis of individual experts assessments, we used three sets of three majority thresholds together with fixed veto thresholds. We shall not expose in detail the results of this exploration (the results of the procedure using one of the sets of thresholds will be described below in Sect. 8.4.5). The same alternatives A_1, A_3 and A_7 tend to emerge. The main observation is the following. As soon as we use majority thresholds larger than $1 - w_1$, where w_1 stands for the weight of the cost criterion for the concerned expert, alternative A_7 does not outrank any other alternative. Indeed, since A_7 is the most expensive alternative, the weight of the coalition in favor of A_7, when compared to any other alternative, never passes $1 - w_1$. As a mechanical consequence, for such majority thresholds, A_7 is in a very bad position in the descending ranking. It may however be in good position in the ascending ranking since, being good in many sub-criteria of the societal and environmental groups, it is seldom outranked.

8.4.2 *Obtaining Global Rankings in the Outranking Approach*

Various approaches can be envisaged in the framework of the outranking methods to obtain global rankings synthesizing the experts judgments. We describe two of them below that we call Path 1 and Path 2 respectively. In essence, Path 1 consists in building rankings for each expert then aggregate them in a global ranking. Path 2 takes the other way around: the experts assessments are first aggregated then an outranking method is applied to the aggregated assessments.[3] Here are more detailed descriptions of the procedures:

- **Path 1** Use the ascending (resp. descending) rankings obtained in the analysis of individual expert judgments and aggregate these rankings into a *social*[4] preference relation by means of a majority rule (Condorcet) for instance. In other words, an alternative is ranked before another if it is ranked in a better position by a majority of individuals. Since the resulting relation is not an order, in general (due to possible *Condorcet effects*), an exploitation procedure is then needed to derive a "social" ordering.
- **Path 2** Compute average assessments of the alternatives on the criteria and average weights (averaging over experts); apply ELECTRE II to these averaged assessments and weights.

Path 1 is more consistent with a qualitative interpretation of the experts assessments. This approach presents however a number of difficulties. One is the need for selecting parameters such as majority thresholds adapted to each expert (these parameters should indeed be determined taking the experts weights into consideration and the latter vary with the experts). Another difficulty arises from the fact that the aggregation of the individual rankings by using a majority rule is likely to yield

---

[3]This reminds us of the two paradigms "Compare then Aggregate" vs. "Aggregate then Compare" described by Grabisch and Perny (2003). The context is different however since, for Grabisch and Perny, "aggregate" concerns criteria, while in our case, it applies to experts.

[4]Here we use the terminology of Social Choice theory, that aims at aggregating orders representing the preference of individuals into a socially acceptable preference relation (see e.g. Sen (1986) for more detail).

a preference relation that is not an ordering; applying an exploitation procedure to it will hence be required. There are also positive arguments in favor of Path 2. Due to the relative consistency of the experts judgments, which can be observed in several figures or tables including Figs. 8.2 and 8.5 and Table 8.8, one may think that the averaged assessments of each alternative on each criterion and the averaged weights are representative of "social" assessments and can be interpreted at least as qualitative evaluations. We shall thus start our analysis along Path 2, which is simpler to put into practice, and return to Path 1, in a less detailed analysis, for confirmation purposes in the end.

8.4.3 *Applying* ELECTRE II *to Aggregated Judgements*

Tables 8.11 and 8.12 below contain the assessments and weights averaged over the 11 experts. We observe that A_1 is assigned a very poor evaluation (1.82) on criterion *heath input* ("hi") as well as on *biological impact* ("bi"). Both A_1 and A_2 also perform very poorly on criterion *intake of matter* ("tm"). As already observed, in Table 8.12, the *cost* criterion constitutes an indivisible block weighing 0.3398 on its own. Note also that we don't need hypotheses α, β or γ like in the additive value function approach. Indeed, the criteria scales are considered ordinal: the size of the evaluation differences does not matter, only their sign does. From the above data, we can directly compute the *concordance* matrix, which provides the strength of the coalition of criteria (i.e. sum of the weights) in favor of any alternative when compared to any other. Looking at the concordance matrix in Table 8.13, the main observation is that the maximal coalition in favor of A_7 weighs 0.6602, which

Table 8.11 Averaged assessments of the 11 experts

	cost	no	vi	im	hp	hr	sp	sr	tm	cs	hi	bi
A_1	3.45	8.91	8.18	6.55	7.36	7.64	7.82	8.00	2.27	4.64	1.82	2.82
A_2	0.47	5.73	3.36	3.09	5.09	6.45	5.64	6.45	2.64	4.64	4.09	4.00
A_3	3.22	3.18	3.91	4.27	4.18	5.27	5.27	6.55	4.55	4.64	5.27	4.82
A_4	1.52	3.45	4.27	4.91	4.55	5.73	5.36	6.45	5.09	4.64	5.18	5.00
A_5	2.01	5.36	3.36	4.09	4.82	6.18	5.55	6.45	4.55	4.09	4.91	4.73
A_6	2.00	3.27	3.82	4.27	3.91	5.45	5.18	6.55	4.64	5.36	4.64	4.45
A_7	0.00	3.45	6.09	8.18	7.91	8.82	6.55	8.00	9.18	9.36	8.55	9.00

Table 8.12 Average weights

cost	0.3398						
soc	no	vi	im	hp	hr	sp	sr
	0.0482	0.0409	0.0430	0.0514	0.0503	0.0448	0.0444
env	tm	cs	hi	bi			
	0.0679	0.0872	0.0905	0.0915			

Table 8.13 Concordance matrix based on averaged assessments

	A_1	A_2	A_3	A_4	A_5	A_6	A_7
A_1	0	0.7501	0.7501	0.7501	0.7501	0.6629	0.5182
A_2	0.3371	0	0.2819	0.3263	0.3672	0.1947	0.388
A_3	0.3371	0.8053	0	0.562	0.8053	0.7464	0.3398
A_4	0.3371	0.8053	0.5252	0	0.4654	0.5286	0.388
A_5	0.2499	0.7181	0.2626	0.579	0	0.7166	0.388
A_6	0.3371	0.8053	0.341	0.4714	0.2834	0	0.3398
A_7	0.5263	0.612	0.6602	0.6602	0.612	0.6602	0

is exactly $1 - w_1$, where w_1 is the weight of the cost criterion, i.e. 0.3398. This means that 0.6602 is a critical value for the majority threshold. For all value larger than 0.6602 of such a threshold, alternative A_7 will not outrank any of the other alternatives.

8.4.3.1 Selection of a Set of Parameters

In order to keep things as simple as possible, we decided to use only two majority thresholds $c_1 > c_2$. In a first approach we do not consider any veto; in a second time, we will examine what happens if we set the value of a veto threshold to 6. This value is the difference between the reference levels 2 and 8 on all subjective assessment scales, i.e. the difference between a very satisfactory and a very unsatisfactory level. Alternative A thus strongly (resp. weakly) outranks alternative B if the set of criteria on which A is at least as good as B weighs at least c_1 (resp. c_2) and there is no veto, on any criterion, of B against A (i.e. on no criterion, the evaluation of A is below the evaluation of B minus the veto threshold).

Since we know that A_7 is a potential choice, and even has actually been chosen, it seems reasonable to admit that the value of the majority threshold c_1 should not exceed 0.6602, otherwise A_7 would not outrank any other alternative. We thus chose the following values for c_1 and c_2:

$$c_1 = 0.6 \qquad c_2 = 0.501$$

The value of c_2 is set to the smallest possible value for strict majority. With these values and without using any veto threshold, we obtain the three rankings represented in Fig. 8.7. As in Fig. 8.5, "7" encodes the first position and "1" the last one. We see that A_1 and A_7 share the first position and are followed by A_3 in all three rankings. Since our choice for c_1 was rather arbitrary, we now perform sensitivity analysis mainly on the values of this threshold.

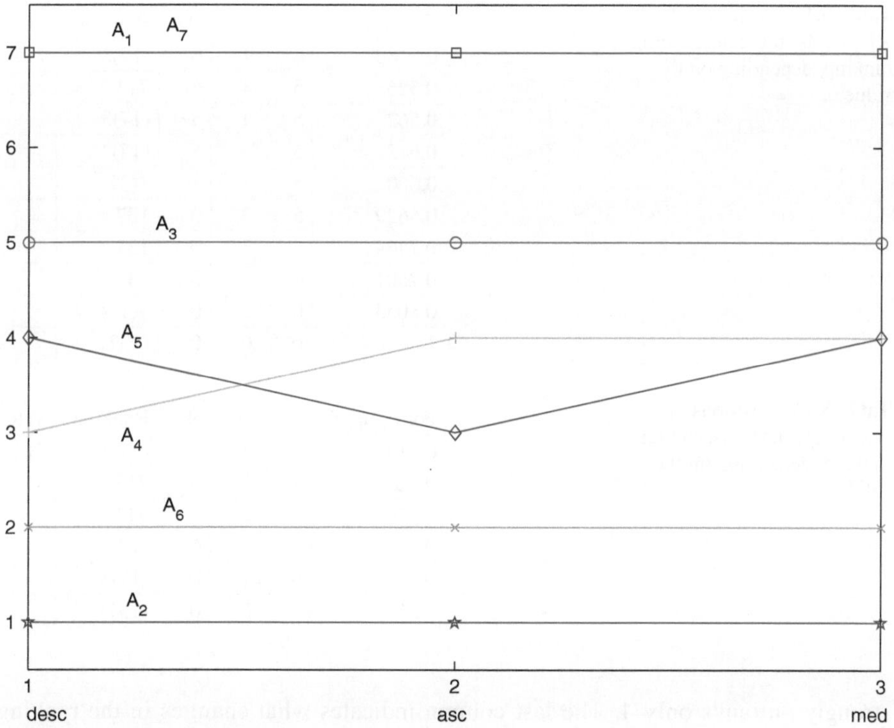

Fig. 8.7 Descending, ascending and median rankings obtained using ELECTRE II. The median ranking is a form of average of descending and ascending rankings

8.4.4 Sensitivity Analysis

Using our simplified ELECTRE II method, it is easy to establish the complete evolution of the relative positions of A_1, A_3 and A_7 in the rankings while c_1 is moved from 0.5 to 1. This can be done directly by considering the concordance matrix in Table 8.13. Table 8.14 shows the relative positions of these alternatives in the descending ordering, i.e. when alternatives are ranked in decreasing order of the number of alternatives that they outrank. Column 1 lists the values of c_1 for which there is a change in the number of alternatives that are outranked by A_1, A_3 or A_7 in the strong outranking relation (without veto). Columns 2 to 4 display the number of alternatives outranked by A_1, A_3 and A_7, respectively, when majority threshold c_1 ranges in the interval starting from the value in the previous row until the value in the current row. The fifth column shows the relative positions of A_1, A_3, A_7 in the descending order before ties have been broken by using threshold c_2. The ranking on A_1, A_3, A_7 is coded as an ordered list of their indices; parentheses indicate ties. For instance, on the first row, "(17)3" stands for $A_1 \sim A_7 \succ A_3$; the ordering is so because A_1 and A_7 both strongly outrank six alternatives while A_3

Table 8.14 Positions of A_1, A_3, A_7 in the descending ranking, depending on the value of c_1

For c_1 up to	A_1	A_3	A_7	Ranking	Veto
0.5182	6	4	6	(17)3	713
0.5263	5	4	6	713	
0.562	5	4	5	(17)3	
0.612	5	3	5	(17)3	
0.6602	5	3	3	1(37)	
0.6629	5	3	0	137	
0.7464	4	3	0	137	
0.7501	4	2	0	137	
0.8053	0	2	0	3(17)	
1	0	0	0	(137)	

Table 8.15 Positions of A_1, A_3, A_7 in the ascending ranking, depending on the value of c_1

For c_1 up to	A_1	A_3	A_7	Ranking	Veto
0.5182	1	3	1	(17)3	713
0.5252	1	3	0	713	
0.5263	1	2	0	713	
0.6602	0	2	0	(17)3	
0.7501	0	1	0	(17)3	
1	0	0	0	(137)	

strongly outranks only 4. The last column indicates what changes in the ranking when a veto is introduced. Using a veto threshold equal to 6, only a few vetoes occur (see Table 8.11): A_7 against A_1 on all four environmental sub-criteria and A_7 against A_2 on *tm*. The effect of introducing these vetoes is very limited: A_1 no longer strongly outranks A_7 for $c_1 \leq 0.5182$ resulting in a number of alternatives outranked by A_1 reduced by one unit (5 instead of 6) and A_7 having the lead (713). Table 8.15 contains similar information for the ascending ranking. Here alternatives are ranked in increasing order of the number of alternatives by which they are strongly outranked, which information is displayed in columns 2 to 4 for A_1, A_3 and A_7. The fifth column shows the resulting ascending rankings. For instance, for values of c_1 ranging from 0.5182 to 0.5263 the order is $A_7 \succ A_1 \succ A_3$. Column 6 shows the influence of the veto, which only intervenes for breaking a tie in case $0.5 \leq c_1 < 0.5182$.

To complete the analysis, note the following facts:

1. The only possible influence of the weak outranking relation, defined through assigning a value to threshold c_2, consists in breaking ties of the descending or ascending rankings. It is easy to infer, from Tables 8.14 and 8.15, which values of c_2, with $0.5 \leq c_2 < c_1$, will result in breaking ties. For example, considering the descending ranking with $0.562 < c_2 \leq 0.6602$, we see that the relative positions of A_1, A_3, A_7 is (17)3, A_1 and A_7 being tied. If we set c_1 to a value between 0.5 and 0.5263 (the latter excluded), A_1 and A_7 remain tied (because they are tied in the weak outranking relation without veto) while setting c_1 to a value comprised between 0.5263 and 0.562 (the latter excluded) brakes the tie in favor of A_7.

2. For some values of c_1, some alternatives can gain better positions than A_1, A_3 or A_7. For example, this is the case with A_4 and A_6, which reach a better position than A_7 in the descending ranking for values of c_1 ranging from 0.6602 to 0.8053 and a better position than A_1 for c_1 ranging from 0.7501 to 0.8053. Such a phenomenon does not occur for $c_1 < 0.6602$, in which case A_1, A_3 and A_7 always occupy the first three positions, in various orders and possibly with ties.

8.4.4.1 Conclusion

From the above extensive study of the rankings, obtained by varying c_1 and c_2, we have got further insight in our problem. We are able to confirm that the following question is a crucial one: can an alternative be preferred to another while it is more expensive? If the answer is "yes" then c_1 has to be set to a value smaller than 0.6602 and A_1, A_7 are the two alternatives that emerge. A_1 is never ranked before A_7 but it may happen that they are tied. If we consider that the striking advantage of A_7 over A_1 on all four criteria of the environmental block does more than balancing the disadvantage of A_7 on the cost point of view, then A_7 is the alternative that should be chosen. Since we know that A_7 has been chosen in the Saint-Ghislain plant, we may conclude that the answer is indeed "yes". We may however make the exercise of determining what would have been the conclusion if the answer to the question had been "no". Then c_1 should be set to at least 0.6602. If $0.6602 \leq c_1 < 0.7501$, A_1 is the first choice, followed by A_3. Finally, for $0.7501 \leq c_1 < 0.8053$, A_3 is in the first position followed by A_4 and A_6. For $c_1 > 0.8053$ all alternatives are tied in the strong outranking relation and any discrimination originates from the weak outranking relation.

8.4.5 *Other Path to Outranking*

We turn finally to the other approach described in Sect. 8.4.2, that was referred to as "Path 1". It consists of applying ELECTRE II to the assessments provided by each expert, using a majority rule to aggregate the eleven descending (resp. ascending, median) rankings obtained into a "collective" or "social" preference relation and eventually derive rankings from these relations.

8.4.5.1 Applying ELECTRE II to Individual Experts Assessments

As weights associated with the criteria we use those deduced from each expert assessment of the importance of the criteria. The delicate question of assigning values to the majority thresholds and veto thresholds is still more delicate here since it would require to examine in detail the concordance matrix of each expert. Instead we shall use standard values of these thresholds, inspired by our experience with

"Path 2". We adopt the more traditional version of ELECTRE II a version with three majority thresholds c_1, c_2, c_3 (where $0.5 \leq c_3 < c_2 < c_1$) and two veto thresholds v_1, v_2 (where $v_2 < v_1$).[5] The values of these thresholds are set as follows (they are one of the three sets of three values used in the exploration alluded to in Sect. 8.4.1):

$$c_1 = 0.7 \quad c_2 = 0.6 \quad c_3 = 0.501$$
$$v_1 = 6 \quad v_2 = 4$$

The strong outranking relation is determined by applying either of the following two rules: alternative A *strongly outranks* B if the strength of the coalition of criteria on which A is at least as good as B passes threshold c_1 (resp. c_2) and there is no criterion on which B is at an advantage over A by a difference at least equal to the veto threshold v_1 (resp. v_2). The weak outranking relation is determined by similar rules: alternative A *weakly outranks* B if it does not strongly outrank B and the strength of the coalition of criteria on which A is at least as good as B passes threshold c_2 (resp. c_3) while there is no criterion on which B is at an advantage over A by a difference at least equal to the veto threshold v_1 (resp. v_2).

Using these rules and then exploiting the resulting strong and weak outranking relations by means of the simplified exploitation procedure described in the preamble of Sect. 8.4, we obtain three rankings for each expert. The descending and ascending rankings of all individual experts are respectively represented in Figs. 8.8 and 8.9 using our usual convention, i.e. 7 for the first ranked alternative, 6 for the second, etc. We observe more variability than in the ranking obtained with weighted sum scores for individual experts (Fig. 8.5) but similar trends nevertheless appear: A_1 and A_7 ahead in ascending and even descending rankings; A_3 emerging in the first positions only in descending rankings.

8.4.5.2 Aggregation of Individual Rankings Using a Majority Rule

For each type of rankings (descending, ascending, median), we apply the majority rule to each pair of alternatives: A is preferred or indifferent to B if it occupies better or identical position in the rankings of at least six experts. If the *majority relation* obtained in this way is not a ranking, we apply to it the "simple" exploitation procedure that we used in ELECTRE II. We obtain the following rankings: A_1 and A_7 are tied in the first position in all rankings; A_3 follows in second position, alone for the descending ranking, tied with A_5 in the ascending ranking. This confirms our

[5]Note that using uniform veto threshold implies strong assumptions on the scales of the criteria. In view of the construction of the scales for all criteria but the cost, these assumptions seem fulfilled here. For the cost criterion, we consider the scale related to hypothesis α (see Sect. 8.3.1) in which the maximal cost difference is smaller than 4. This means that we exclude all veto effect due to cost. The reason for that is that cost has already a considerable influence due to its weight (around 0.33) and the fact that it is not split into sub-criteria contrary to the societal and environmental blocks of criteria.

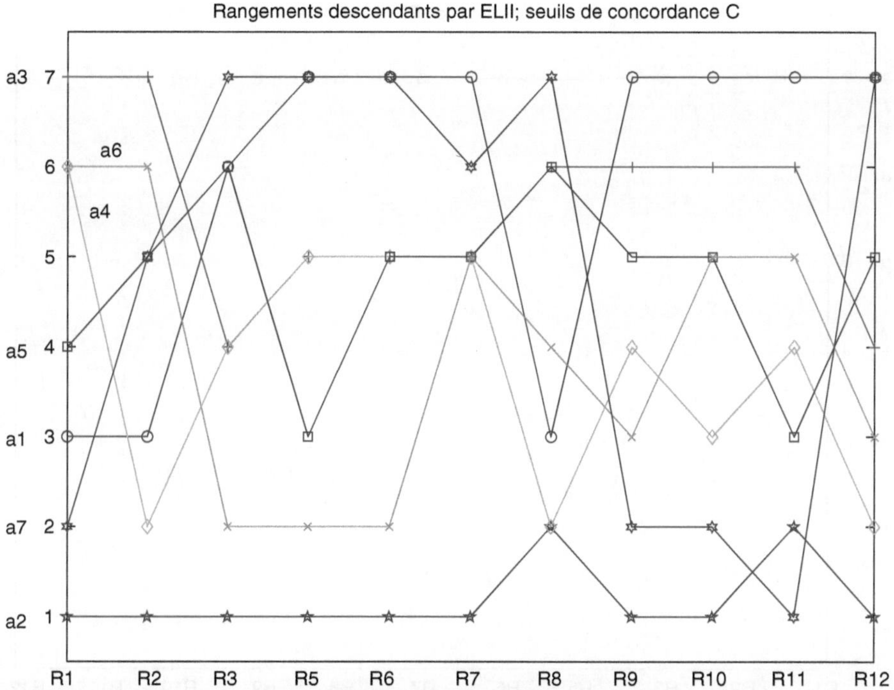

Fig. 8.8 Descending rankings of individual experts

Descending	Ascending	Median
(17)35(46)2	(17)(35)(46)2	(17)35462

previous conclusions, even though the setting of the parameters in the ELECTRE II method has been done in a rough manner.

8.5 Conclusions

At the end of such a detailed study of this rich application, a number of conclusions can be drawn, both on the case itself but also, more generally, in a methodological perspective. We list the main issues below, starting with considerations directly in relation to the case.

1. In both the approaches we have used, the same triplet of alternatives emerges: A_1, A_3, A_7. The assessments that have been collected do not point unambiguously to one of them. Clearly some additional information is needed to further discriminate between these three alternatives. The main merit of both the weighted sum and the outranking approaches has been to focus the attention

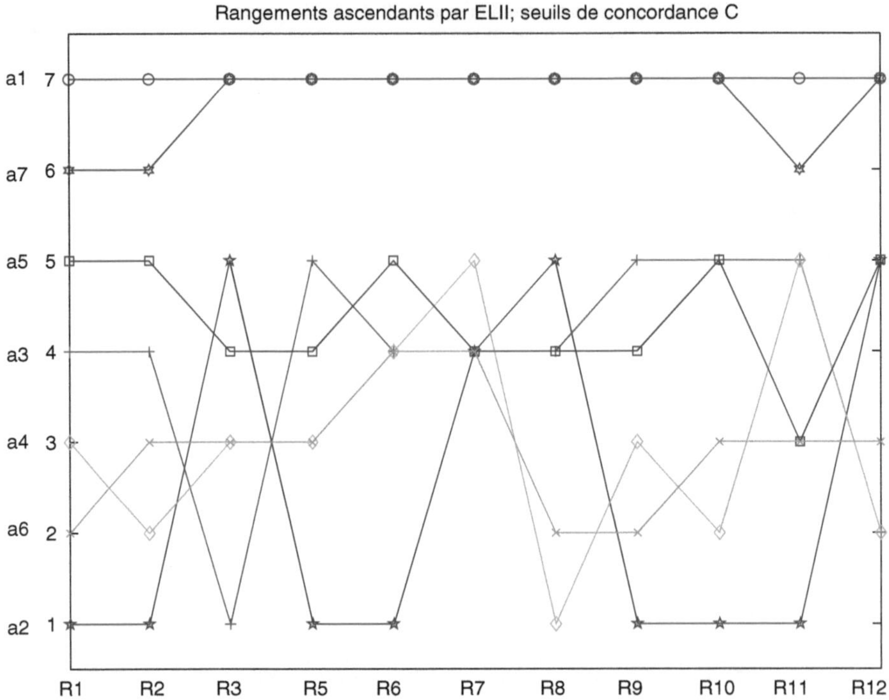

Fig. 8.9 Ascending rankings of individual experts

on a crucial question related to the importance of the cost criterion. Not only did both approaches help identifying this crucial question, but they helped in giving a precise formulation of this question:

- in the weighted sum model, the question of the importance of the cost is formulated as that of an appropriate scaling of the cost criterion; three hypotheses have been formulated (α, γ, β); these formulations are concrete enough to enable opening a dialog with the decision maker in order to determine which hypothesis should be considered most adequate. In our case, the answer was given by facts, namely that an alternative had already been chosen and this choice was unambiguously supporting hypothesis α.
- in the outranking model, the same question is formulated in a language that is appropriate for this model. The question is simply: Is it conceivable to declare that an alternative is better than another if it is more expensive? Here again the answer comes from facts.

Once it has been agreed that cost is not of prominent importance (more precisely, if we discard hypothesis β in the weighted sum model or we determine that appropriate majority thresholds should be less than 1 minus the weight of the cost, in the outranking methods), we can mainly eliminate A_3 and we are left with A_1 and A_7. From the interactions we had with the experts, we could understand that A_1 was not a very attractive alternative due to the current concern with environmental issues and the quite bad performances of A_1 on all 4 environmental criteria. This information was an indication that tended to validate hypothesis α in the weighted sum model. In the same way, it gives credit to the sets of parameters of ELECTRE II for which A_7 is placed alone in the first position of the rankings and not tied with A_1.

2. Regarding the goal of the study, an ex post study aiming at validating the use of multiple criteria decision aiding methods for technical choices in the power generation industry, we can certainly emphasize the following points:

    - the case study has clearly shown that the methods used have the potential to help a decision maker getting deeper insight into his/her problem and focussing on the main questions. Hence they favor a decision making process that is truly a *learning process*.
    - such a process has also the virtue of providing the decision maker with *arguments* that could help him/her *justifying* the final choice to third parties. This is especially important in the context of power generation since the producers are increasingly forced to justify their choices in the media.
    - confronting several methods as we did, establishes the final recommendation more solidly. In our case, very different interpretations of the expert assessments (quantitative or qualitative) lead essentially towards similar conclusions, which consolidates these conclusions.

3. There are several methodological points in this application that would deserve in depth discussion. We present four of them, in the form of *assertions* followed by a brief argumentation:

    - *Treating choice problem by ranking methods is at an advantage.* While the initial question was *choosing* a cooling system, we treated the case as a *ranking* problem. There is an advantage in doing so. The output of ranking methods being richer (a ranking of the alternatives instead of one (or several) distinguished alternative(s)), there are many more opportunities for invalidating the underlying model than with choice methods. In the latter, the decision maker might have nothing to object against the alternative recommended as the best choice while the position of some alternatives in a recommended ranking could appear as inconsistent with the decision maker's intuition or knowledge. In other words, ranking methods favor deeper investigation during the validation phase than choice models; once the model has been validated, the decision maker can be more confident in the recommendation.
    - *Simplifying* ELECTRE II *allows to issue more convincing recommendations.* We plead here for more transparent outranking methods, closer to simple majority rules that are their essence. The simple version of ELECTRE II (with two majority thresholds and one veto threshold together with a simplified exploitation procedure) that we used in Sect. 8.4.4 allowed us to view the full landscape of possible rankings (obtained by varying the value of the main thresholds). It makes the link between parameters settings and the corresponding rankings as transparent as possible.

- *In most applications, it is fruitful to use both a value function approach and an outranking method.* In most applications, the information needed to properly apply either a value function method or an outranking method is not fully available. Therefore the analyst is led to make many assumptions on the interpretation of the available information and fill the blanks by reasonable working hypotheses. This reduces the confidence one can have in the outputs of the decision aiding process. Using two fundamentally different approaches (such as value function and outranking) and seeing that they can agree on similar recommendations substantially strengthens the conclusions of the decision aiding process.
- *Cases in which several experts assess the alternatives offer good perspectives of progress related to the treatment of uncertainty and imprecision.* In the end of Sect. 8.3.3 we addressed the question of significant differences in the constructed value function. We feel that interesting theoretical considerations could be developed by observing and taking advantage of the variability in the experts' assessments. We used straightforward—statistical and non statistical—approaches in the end of the above-mentioned section, drawing also the attention of the reader to the difficulties of a statistical approach. Nevertheless we think that it should be possible to adapt the classical statistical model to deal with uncertainty in this context, as we suggest in the last lines of Sect. 8.3.3.

Appendix: Assessments Made by the Experts

This appendix contains all the responses made by the experts that have been questioned both on the importance of the criteria and the evaluation of the alternatives on the various criteria but cost. The evaluation of the cost of the alternatives by a specialist is also provided but in relative terms only. These data should permit the reader to reconstruct all our computations as well as experimenting other approaches on the same data and comparing the results with those we have obtained (Tables 8.16, 8.17, 8.18, 8.19, 8.20, 8.21, 8.22, 8.23, 8.24, 8.25, 8.26, 8.27, and 8.28).

Table 8.16 Relative costs of the alternatives on a 0–10 scale

$A1$	6.551
A_2	9.531
A_3	6.779
A_4	8.482
A_5	7.989
A_6	8.002
A_7	10

Table 8.17 Importance of criteria and alternatives performance assessment by Expert 1

cost	soc							env			
8	6							7			
	no	vi	im	hp	hr	sp	sr	tm	cs	hi	bi
	9	2	5	8	9	8	9	5	8	8	6

	no	vi	im	hp	hr	sp	sr	tm	cs	hi	bi
A_1	9	9	9	8	9	8	8	4	1	3	1
A_2	7	2	1	6	7	6	8	2	2	3	3
A_3	2	5	4	6	7	6	8	6	6	5	6
A_4	3	4	4	6	7	6	8	6	6	5	6
A_5	5	2	2	6	7	6	8	6	4	3	4
A_6	2	5	4	6	7	6	8	6	6	5	6
A_7	2	6	7	6	9	6	8	9	9	7	8

Table 8.18 Importance of criteria and alternatives performance assessment by Expert 2

cost	soc							env			
8	7							6			
	no	vi	im	hp	hr	sp	sr	tm	cs	hi	bi
	8	3	4	6	6	4	3	3	5	7	5

	no	vi	im	hp	hr	sp	sr	tm	cs	hi	bi
A_1	9	9	2	6	7	6	7	3	2	2	2
A_2	7	2	2	6	7	6	7	3	2	5	4
A_3	2	5	5	6	7	6	7	7	8	9	7
A_4	2	5	5	6	7	6	7	7	7	7	7
A_5	7	2	5	6	7	6	7	7	4	7	7
A_6	2	5	5	6	7	6	7	7	8	9	7
A_7	2	5	8	7	9	6	7	10	10	10	9

Table 8.19 Importance of criteria and alternatives performance assessment by Expert 3

cost	soc							env			
1	3							2			
	no	vi	im	hp	hr	sp	sr	tm	cs	hi	bi
	7	8	9	10	10	10	10	6	10	8	9

	no	vi	im	hp	hr	sp	sr	tm	cs	hi	bi
A_1	9	1	9	8	8	5	5	0	9	0	8
A_2	3	8	2	5	6	5	5	0	8	2	5
A_3	1	6	5	1	1	5	5	3	1	6	2
A_4	1	4	7	3	3	5	5	4	2	6	2
A_5	3	8	7	5	6	5	5	3	1	6	2
A_6	1	6	7	1	1	5	5	1	5	4	0
A_7	1	5	9	9	10	5	5	10	10	10	10

Table 8.20 Importance of criteria and alternatives performance assessment by Expert 5

cost	soc							env			
8	6							7			
	no	vi	im	hp	hr	sp	sr	tm	cs	hi	bi
	5	9	6	4	4	2	2	5	6	8	8

	no	vi	im	hp	hr	sp	sr	tm	cs	hi	bi
A_1	8	10	6	8	8	8	9	9	9	2	2
A_2	3	1	1	8	8	6	5	7	8	5	5
A_3	3	2	3	5	5	5	9	7	7	7	8
A_4	3	2	3	5	5	5	9	7	7	7	8
A_5	3	1	1	5	5	5	5	7	7	7	8
A_6	3	2	3	4	5	5	9	7	7	7	8
A_7	4	8	8	8	8	8	10	10	10	10	10

Table 8.21 Importance of criteria and alternatives performance assessment by Expert 6

cost	soc							env			
6	8							7			
	no	vi	im	hp	hr	sp	sr	tm	cs	hi	bi
	7	6	5	10	10	9	9	6	8	7	10

	no	vi	im	hp	hr	sp	sr	tm	cs	hi	bi
A_1	9	9	5	8	6	9	9	1	2	1	1
A_2	4	2	2	3	6	5	7	2	2	2	2
A_3	4	2	2	3	6	5	7	3	5	4	3
A_4	4	2	2	3	6	5	7	4	5	4	4
A_5	4	2	2	3	6	5	7	4	5	4	4
A_6	4	2	2	3	6	5	7	3	5	4	3
A_7	7	6	8	6	9	7	8	9	10	8	9

Table 8.22 Importance of criteria and alternatives performance assessment by Expert 7

cost	soc							env			
8	8							8			
	no	vi	im	hp	hr	sp	sr	tm	cs	hi	bi
	8	8	9	10	10	10	10	7	8	8	9

	no	vi	im	hp	hr	sp	sr	tm	cs	hi	bi
A_1	9	10	9	4	8	8	9	2	4	4	4
A_2	8	3	8	4	8	5	9	4	4	4	4
A_3	7	3	8	4	8	6	9	4	4	4	4
A_4	8	4	8	4	8	7	9	4	4	4	4
A_5	9	3	8	4	8	5	9	4	4	4	4
A_6	7	3	8	4	8	6	9	4	4	4	4
A_7	8	3	9	9	9	6	9	9	8	9	9

Table 8.23 Importance of criteria and alternatives performance assessment by Expert 8

cost	soc							env			
8	7							9			
	no	vi	im	hp	hr	sp	sr	tm	cs	hi	bi
	7	5	8	9	9	9	9	4	7	9	9

	no	vi	im	hp	hr	sp	sr	tm	cs	hi	bi
A_1	10	10	3	8	8	10	10	0	7	0	0
A_2	7	5	5	7	7	3	3	2	7	7	3
A_3	3	4	6	4	4	1	1	3	0	6	5
A_4	2	6	4	5	5	0	0	5	0	6	5
A_5	5	5	7	7	7	3	3	3	0	6	5
A_6	3	6	5	4	4	1	1	6	5	3	4
A_7	4	7	10	10	10	8	8	10	10	10	10

Table 8.24 Importance of criteria and alternatives performance assessment by Expert 9

cost	soc							env			
8	5							8			
	no	vi	im	hp	hr	sp	sr	tm	cs	hi	bi
	8	8	8	8	5	2	2	8	8	8	8

	no	vi	im	hp	hr	sp	sr	tm	cs	hi	bi
A_1	10	9	8	8	8	8	8	0	2	2	2
A_2	5	2	2	4	7	5	8	0	2	5	4
A_3	4	5	3	6	6	7	8	2	5	5	5
A_4	4	6	7	5	8	7	8	4	5	5	5
A_5	5	2	2	4	7	5	8	2	5	5	5
A_6	5	2	2	4	7	5	8	2	3	3	4
A_7	3	7	9	8	8	6	8	8	8	7	7

Table 8.25 Importance of criteria and alternatives performance assessment by Expert 10

cost	soc							env			
8	5							8			
	no	vi	im	hp	hr	sp	sr	tm	cs	hi	bi
	7	6	8	10	10	10	10	5	5	5	5

	no	vi	im	hp	hr	sp	sr	tm	cs	hi	bi
A_1	8	8	6	10	10	10	10	0	5	0	2
A_2	5	5	4	5	5	9	9	2	5	2	3
A_3	2	4	5	4	7	9	9	5	5	5	5
A_4	3	4	5	4	6	9	9	5	5	5	5
A_5	4	5	4	5	5	9	9	5	5	5	5
A_6	2	4	5	4	7	9	9	5	5	5	5
A_7	1	4	6	10	10	6	10	8	10	10	10

Table 8.26 Importance of criteria and alternatives performance assessment by Expert 11

cost	soc							env			
8	7							6			
	no	vi	im	hp	hr	sp	sr	tm	cs	hi	bi
	8	6	5	7	7	8	8	5	7	6	7

	no	vi	im	hp	hr	sp	sr	tm	cs	hi	bi
A_1	7	5	7	5	3	6	5	4	2	4	4
A_2	6	2	2	3	3	6	3	4	4	5	5
A_3	3	5	4	2	4	3	4	5	4	3	3
A_4	4	6	5	4	4	4	4	5	4	4	4
A_5	6	2	2	3	3	6	3	4	4	3	3
A_6	3	5	4	2	5	4	4	5	4	3	3
A_7	2	8	8	4	5	4	5	8	8	3	7

Table 8.27 Importance of criteria and alternatives performance assessment by Expert 12

cost	soc							env			
10	10							10			
	no	vi	im	hp	hr	sp	sr	tm	cs	hi	bi
	10	10	10	10	10	10	10	10	10	10	10

	no	vi	im	hp	hr	sp	sr	tm	cs	hi	bi
A_1	10	10	8	8	9	8	8	2	8	2	5
A_2	8	5	5	5	7	6	7	3	7	5	6
A_3	4	2	2	5	3	5	5	5	6	4	5
A_4	4	4	4	5	4	5	5	5	6	4	5
A_5	8	5	5	5	7	6	7	5	6	4	5
A_6	4	2	2	5	3	5	5	5	7	4	5
A_7	4	8	8	10	10	10	10	10	10	10	10

Table 8.28 Normalised weights computed from importance assessment by the experts

	cost	no	vi	im	hp	hr	sp	sr	tm	cs	hi	bi
R1	0.3810	0.0514	0.0114	0.0286	0.0457	0.0514	0.0457	0.0514	0.0617	0.0988	0.0988	0.0741
R2	0.3810	0.0784	0.0294	0.0392	0.0588	0.0588	0.0392	0.0294	0.0429	0.0714	0.1000	0.0714
R3	0.1667	0.0547	0.0625	0.0703	0.0781	0.0781	0.0781	0.0781	0.0606	0.1010	0.0808	0.0909
R5	0.3810	0.0446	0.0804	0.0536	0.0357	0.0357	0.0179	0.0179	0.0617	0.0741	0.0988	0.0988
R6	0.2857	0.0476	0.0408	0.0340	0.0680	0.0680	0.0612	0.0612	0.0645	0.0860	0.0753	0.1075
R7	0.3333	0.0410	0.0410	0.0462	0.0513	0.0513	0.0513	0.0513	0.0729	0.0833	0.0833	0.0938
R8	0.3333	0.0365	0.0260	0.0417	0.0469	0.0469	0.0469	0.0469	0.0517	0.0905	0.1164	0.1164
R9	0.3810	0.0465	0.0465	0.0465	0.0465	0.0290	0.0116	0.0116	0.0952	0.0952	0.0952	0.0952
R10	0.3810	0.0273	0.0234	0.0312	0.0090	0.0390	0.0390	0.0390	0.0952	0.0952	0.0952	0.0952
R11	0.3810	0.0544	0.0408	0.0340	0.0476	0.0476	0.0544	0.0544	0.0571	0.0800	0.0686	0.0800
R12	0.3333	0.0476	0.0476	0.0476	0.0476	0.0476	0.0476	0.0476	0.0833	0.0833	0.0833	0.0833

References

Belton, V., & Stewart, T. (2001). *Multiple criteria decision analysis: An integrated approach.* Dordrecht: Kluwer.
Grabisch, M., & Perny, P. (2003). Agrégation multicritère. In B. Bouchon, & C. Marsala (Eds.), *Utilisations de la logique floue* (pp. 81–120). Paris: Hermès.
Roy, B. (1985). *Méthodologie multicritère d'aide à la décision.* Paris: Economica.
Roy, B., & Bouyssou, D. (1993). *Aide Multicritère à la Décision: Méthodes et Cas.* Paris: Economica.
Sen, A. K. (1986). Social choice theory. In K. J. Arrow, & M. D. Intriligator (Eds.), *Handbook of mathematical economics* (vol. 3, pp. 1073–1181). Amsterdam: North-Holland.
Ulungu, B., Pirlot, M., & Teghem, J. (2002, May). Choix d'un système de refroidissement pour la centrale TGV de Saint Ghislain. Technical report, Faculté Polytechnique de Mons, 88 p.
Vansnick, J. -C. (1986). On the problems of weights in MCDM (the noncompensatory approach). *European Journal of Operational Research, 24*, 288–294.
Vincke, Ph. (1992). *Multi-criteria decision aid.* New York: Wiley. Original version in French (1989). *L'aide multicritère à la décision.* Éditions de l'Université de Bruxelles — Éditions Ellipses, Brussels.
von Winterfeldt, D., & Edwards, W. (1986). *Decision analysis and behavorial research.* Cambridge: Cambridge University Press.

Editors' Comments on "Choosing a Cooling System for a Power Plant in Belgium"

The application described by M. Pirlot, J. Teghem, B. Ulungu, P. Bulens and C. Goffin aims at supporting the choice of a cooling system for a power plant. More precisely, this application studies the benefit of using multiple criteria decision aiding methods in order to account for environmental and societal issues in addition to a standard cost analysis in such a technico-economic decision.

Decisions related to the energy sector provide a wide scope of potential application of the MCDA methods. Beyond the application described in this chapter, the three following in this book also consider MCDA application involving energy issues: Chap. 9 (localization of windfarms in Corsica), Chap. 10 (assessment of environmental sustainability of data centers) and Chap. 11 (Cost analysis of a nuclear fuel repository). It should be emphasized that the issue of considering simultaneously qualitative (societal and environmental) criteria with cost related criteria (quantitative) is of a high importance.

The client of the study was Laborelec, a technical competence center in charge of energy processes and energy use in Belgium. Laborelec worked for 2 years on a contract with a team of **analysts** composed of researchers from the MATHRO department at the University of Mons. The aims of this joint work was to extend the "traditional" cost based approach, and also to integrate issues dealing with societal and environmental concerns in investment decisions.

The **set of alternatives**, seven (7) possible cooling systems for the power plant, was clearly defined at the beginning of the decision process. Although the decision to be made concerned the choice of a single cooling system, formulating the **problem statement** as ranking the seven alternatives from the best to the worst was considered as a relevant way of studying the decision problem.

In this study the **criteria** considered in the decision problem were firstly cost related (investment, running, maintenance and dismantling cost), but also societal (safety, health, noise, ...) and environmental (chemical spill, impact on local ecosystem...). Costs were previously assessed by experts, and the other 11 criteria were evaluated qualitatively by a group of 12 experts.[6]

A specificity of this study comes from the fact that the team of analysts did not choose a single method to elaborate a recommendation, but rather adopted a "preference investigation" perspective. As it was an ex-post study, they tried several aggregation methods, in a *what if* analysis. Such analysis made it possible to highlight under which hypothesis, alternatives can be reasonably ranked on top of the ranking. The **aggregation methods** considered are the weighted sum (see Chap. 4, Sect. 4.2, and Bouyssou et al. 2006) and Electre II (see Chap. 4, Sect. 4.4.3, and Figueira et al. 2005).

In this application's **elicitation process**, the team of analysts collected the evaluation from 12 experts on 11 criteria related to environmental and societal points of view. Each expert was asked to answer on a qualitative [0–10] scale; in order to support experts in the expression of their judgments, semantic anchors were defined (2: very unsatisfactory level, 5: boundary between satisfactory/unsatisfactory, 8: very satisfactory level). Extensive analysis of the experts judgment variability is one of the particular interests of this chapter.

An interesting aspect of this application deals with the perspective by which the team of analysts did conduct the study; as opposed to many standard multicriteria decision aiding applications, the **goal of the application** is not to provide recommendations concerning the best decision (in terms of choosing a cooling systems among the possible alternatives). Indeed this study was conducted ex-post, after the actual decision was made. In contrast, the team of analysts worked in order to come out with an increased understanding of what precisely means to make such a choice (integrating societal and environmental issues into a cost analysis for an investment decision in the energy sector). This means particularly, which multicriteria methods (several ones) could be used, how to actually use them in this context, what are the underlying hypotheses concerning the context, what benefit could be expected.

A tangible result of a standard decision aiding process usually is the recommendations stemming from the decision aiding model. In this study, such a tangible result does not exist as it is an ex-post study. However the main **tangible result** is the study itself, which shows in detail how the decision process could have

---

[6]An XMCDA 2-00 encoded performance tableau with average evaluations of the seven cooling alternatives on all the criteria may be downloaded from the webpage http://leopold-loewenheim.uni.lu/Digraph3/handbook/chapter-8/.

benefited from the use different methods. As an **intangible result**, another important benefit that comes out of this study is the increased knowledge that the Laborelec participants gained in conducting this study with the analyst. It is highly probable that the experts involved will be more inclined to use MCDA methods in future applications and better understand which are the benefits they can expect from such decision aid modeling.

References

Bouyssou, D., Marchant, T., Pirlot, M., Tsoukias, A., & Vincke, P. (2006). *Evaluation and decision models with multiple criteria stepping stones for the analyst*. International series in operations research and management science (vol. 86). New York: Springer.

Figueira, J., Mousseau, V., & Roy, B. (2005). ELECTRE methods. In J. Figueira, S. Greco, & M. Ehrgott (Eds.), *Multiple criteria decision analysis: State of the art surveys* (pp. 133–162). Boston: Springer.

Chapter 9
Participative and Multicriteria Localization of Wind Farm Projects in Corsica Island: Decision Aid Process and Result

Pascal Oberti and Christophe Paoli

Abstract The purpose of this chapter is to present the main results of a decision aid process which we have applied to help policymakers for the localization of a wind farm in Corsica (Western Mediterranean Island, French region). This process has been applied in a participatory context of multiple stakeholders open to the public. The first section presents a brief introduction about this real case study ordered by the Economic Development Agency of the Territorial Collectivity of Corsica. The second section is devoted to the study context and the decision aid process. The third section describes the simulated projects of wind farms and the family of evaluation criteria. The fourth section deals with the performance table and the recommendations of localization. A discussion about the case study is delivered in the fifth section. Finally, the last section is devoted to the conclusion and proposals for enlargements.

9.1 Introduction

The promotion of electricity produced from renewable energy is a high priority of the European Union. While France is overdue in this domain, the Corsica Island appears as a French pioneer region. This region managed by the Territorial

---

P. Oberti (✉)
University of Corsica - CNRS UMR 6240 LISA, Corte, France
e-mail: pascal.oberti@univ-corse.fr

C. Paoli
Department of Computer Engineering, Galatasaray University, No: 36, 34357 Ortakoy, Istanbul, Turkey

University of Corsica - CNRS UMR 6134 SPE, Corte, France
e-mail: cpaoli@gsu.edu.tr; christophe.paoli@univ-corse.fr

R. Bisdorff et al. (eds.), *Evaluation and Decision Models with Multiple Criteria*, International Handbooks on Information Systems,
DOI 10.1007/978-3-662-46816-6_9

Collectivity of Corsica (CTC[1]) has formalized this ambition in the second energy planning (Conseil exécutif de la Corse, 2005). The objective is to produce 25–30 % of electricity from renewable energies by the year 2015. Underdeveloped in the island (Notton et al., 2005), the wind industry is one of the privileged sectors. In order to integrate wind farm projects into human territories, the CTC and its Agency for Economic Development (ADEC[2]) needed a methodology to facilitate an early participation of local citizens in wind farm projects. In this context, the ADEC has ordered a pilot study to the University of Corsica. Before detailing the decision aid process and the main results, we give some brief preliminary considerations on the type and number of studied projects, the motives that have led to the evaluation criteria and the contribution of Geographic Information Systems (GIS).

Five potential sites were considered to study the localization of wind turbines on the **Municipality of Bonifacio** (Southern Corsica). Various factors have guided the determination of these territories: the municipal cadastre, the existence of previous industrial projects, the specific wind zoning of the Municipality, the existence of ecological zones, the sites at lower altitudes with good wind potential. Thus, two new siting territories, not considered by investors in the past, have been introduced. For each of the five territories, variants of wind farms have been simulated and the optimal configuration, that maximizes under constraints the potential production (producible) of electricity, has been retained. Among the five projects achieved two were eliminated for their non-integration (visual and/or acoustic) on the municipalities (Bonifacio and the surrounding). Finally, three wind farms were projected. This number was considered sufficient by the actors for several reasons: the necessary limitation of wind power into the electrical grid of the island of Corsica (small and not interconnected with the French territory) in order to not introduce a strong random part on the supply-demand balance of electricity—the preference for dispersion of wind farms in Corsica rather than concentration, to operate several wind regimes—the possibility to include two other sites in the wind zoning of the municipality, offering expansion areas. Of course, methodology can be applied to a larger number of projects. The three wind farm projects were compared on a family of six evaluation criteria. These were selected to take into account the concerns of the actors who participated in the study process, but also from information available. Thus, the stakes associated with criteria are energy, visual, ecological and spatial.

GIS tools were important complements to the multiple criteria outranking modeling, and have helped to identify: constraints definition of projects in each area of implementation, such as exclusion zones for wind turbines (Fig. 9.1)—integration constraints of projects, on considerations of sound and visual impacts—criteria for evaluation, such as producible (Fig. 9.2 in Appendix 4) and visibility of projects (Figs. 9.2 and 9.3 in Appendix 4)—a spatial projection of sites and recommendations of a wind farm, for inclusion in the Local Urban Plan (PLU[3]) of Bonifacio.

[1]For “Collectivité Territoriale de Corse” in French.

[2]For “Agence de Développement Economique de la Corse” in French.

[3]For “Plan Local d’Urbanisme” in French.

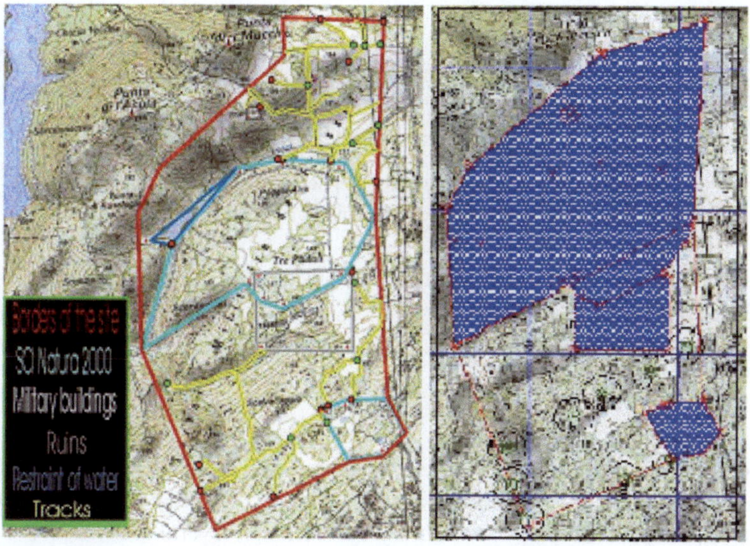

Fig. 9.1 Frasselli project—zoning and optimal positioning of wind turbines

More broadly, GIS have been efficient communication tools between institutional, scientific, technical actors, and local citizens.

The remainder of this chapter is organized as follows: Sect. 9.2 presents the context of the study and the decision aid process. Section 9.3 describes the actions set and how the criteria have been constructed. The performance table and the wind farm projects recommendations are detailed in the Sect. 9.4. Comments on the case study are proposed in the Sect. 9.5 and the last section concludes and suggests perspectives.

9.2 Context of the Study and Decision Aid Process

9.2.1 Decision Problem and Actors

The acceptability and the localization of future wind farm projects are decision problems encountered by the CTC and the ADEC. Although producing clean electricity is central, it is important to avoid localizations only guided by industrial interests, not accepted by local citizens which ultimately could involve a non integration of wind power into the Corsican electricity system.

The ADEC wanted to have a decision aid methodology to deal with wind farms localization. This methodology should be independent of the project holders, scientifically rigorous, and reproducible in other places. The question to be answered was: how and where to localize a wind farm into the territory?

Table 9.1 Actors of the study

Groups of actors		Acronyms	Individuals
Corsica's agency for economic development (*economic operations*)		ADEC	2
City council of Bonifacio	Majority	MAIRM	5
	Opposition	MAIRO	2
	Town planning and other services	MAIRS	3
Regional direction of environment ("natures and landscapes" service)		DIREN	3
Electricity of France		EDF	2
University of Corsica (physics, economics and data-processing departments)		UCPP	7
Local citizens		CITOYL	30
Tourists		TOUR	6

Through its experience in multiple criteria decision aid, the University of Corsica has been selected to make this original study. The methodology has been applied on the Municipality of Bonifacio, which was selected for several reasons:

- a high wind potential, with wind speed averages between 7.76 and 8.2 m/s, the presence of old windmills, an ancient wine business using a private wind turbine,
- the absence of wind farm, despite several preindustrial projects,
- the favorable opinion of the city council of Bonifacio concerning wind farm installation, wishing to register a specific zoning in its PLU.

Besides the municipality of Bonifacio, the surrounding municipalities that could be impacted by the building of wind farms have been considered.

Sixty actors have participated in the study, according to different levels: information, consultation, and dialogue. Groups of actors are gathered in the following Table 9.1.

Participants have been selected according to their official responsibilities of **decision makers** (CTC-ADEC, City council, DIREN, EDF), issuing opinions and permissions on the permit to construct a wind farm, their recognized expertise, technical or scientific, necessary for the evaluation exercise, and to constitute an **evaluator's** group. Other participants have freely integrated the study process, following its opening to the public announced by the press. This includes local citizens, who may be affected by the consequences of wind farm projects, and even tourists coming to inquire about the ongoing study. Let us note that the final decision to grant (or not) the building permit belongs to the Prefect of the region.

Corsica is one of the 26 regions of France and is designated as a "territorial collectivity" by law. Thus, the island enjoys greater powers, such as energy policy. ADEC, which is an agency of CTC, aims to stimulate economic development i.e. industry, trade, craft, energy equipments, renewable energies, information and communication technology. The Economic Engineering Department of the ADEC was the **client**, term that means the actor "...requesting the study and responsible for allocating the means to conduct it" (Roy, 1996).

The Regional direction of environment (DIREN), attached to the French Ministry of Ecology, is responsible for preserving the environment and sustainable development. The service "nature and landscapes" of the DIREN has contributed to the study on the choice of observation points of the landscape, concerning the visibility of wind farms, the question of noise impact, the provision of GIS ecological zones of Southern Corsica, and the potential environmental degradation of wind farm projects.

Electricity of France (EDF[4]), one of whose activities is the management of electricity network, has brought its skills on the connection of wind farms, electrical losses involved and the limited power to install.

The University of Corsica (UCPP[5]), provided expertise in renewable energy, economics of sustainable development and computer science; and also the **analyst** to apply the multiple criteria approach and ensure an independent study of wind projects investors.

At local level, the city council of Bonifacio was broken down into three groups of actors: the majority, the opposition, the planning service. Were provided the preliminary wind projects studied by industrialists in the past, the draft of the PLU. Meeting workspaces were made available, and visits sites have been facilitated. Local citizens, members of an association of environmental protection or residents, were present at a public conference and public meeting. They questioned the independence of the ongoing evaluation, and were seeking additional visual simulations (in 2D and 3D) to assess the landscape impact. They also expressed their priorities on the criteria, which resulted in a specific set of importance coefficients.

Tourists were **third party** in the process: "those … who do not actively participate in shaping the decision, but who are affected by its consequences and whose preferences must be considered when arriving at the decision" (Roy, 1996). They have been present during a summer school, to get information about the study.

Actor's participation took the form of plenary working meetings, restricted technical meetings, study on sites, public meetings and public conference during a summer school. Timing and agendas of the meetings are presented in Appendix 1.

9.2.2 General Structure of the Decision Aid Process

Given the complexity of the problem, this pilot study was obviously multidisciplinary with the following theoretical and methodological foundations:

- economics of environment and natural resources (Faucheux and Noël, 1995), sustainable development and governance (Froger, 2001);
- physics of renewable energies (Landberg, 1999; Mortensen and Petersen, 1997);
- multicriteria decision aiding (Roy, 1996) in participative context (Froger and Oberti, 2002), applied to environment (Maystre et al., 1994).

[4]For "Electricité de France" in French.

[5]For "Université de Corse Pasquale Paoli" in French.

A combination of tools has been used to complete this study:

- tools to analyze spatial and temporal data of various units of measurement including qualitative terms,
- tools to facilitate communication between actors, to share results and have a coherent approach.

The general structure of the process which consists of three key steps is given in Appendix 2. Three main stages are distinguished. During the first implementation of the stages I and II, the participation involving public actors remains institutional, technical and scientific. Then the stage III opens the decision aid process to civil society who is concerned with the possible wind farm localizations.

The stage I of the process was to determine **relevant territories for wind farm installation**. Several data had to be collected:

- time series of wind speed and direction over 20 years, measured at the meteorological station of Météo France,
- GIS maps (from DIREN) in LAMBERT IV earth projection, on obstacles and rough terrain, topography, locations of homes, wind potential, PLU zoning and ecological zones.

These data have been analyzed by physicists of renewable energies using **WASP**[6] software in order to estimate the wind potential. At the end of stage I, we have identified and delimited five possible territories (Frasselli, Arapa, Monte Corbu, Francolo, Valle Torta) whose altitudes vary between 65 and 334 m.

Stage II of the process has proposed to adapt the **simulation of wind farms to each territory**. This rational integration has been based on the optimization of an electrical production function under physical and geographical constraints.

Various wind farm parameters have been studied, and also maps of potential sound and visual impacts have been obtained in order to facilitate communication between actors. Thus, several configurations of wind farms were simulated using the **WindFarmer** software[7] (Hassan and Ltd, 2002). Because of their acoustic impacts (exceeding the limits imposed by law, maximum + 5 dB(A) the day and maximum + 3 dB(A) the night) or/and visual impacts (at least 75 % of visibility), two wind farm projects (Corbu, Arapa) were eliminated. Into the enlarged municipal territory, their integrations have been considered impossible or weak. The three other projects (Frasselli, Francolo, Valle Torta) were insufficient, satisfactory or high.

Stage III of the process was related to the **participative recommendations for wind farm projects**. The goal was firstly to evaluate the three retained actions, through criteria about concerns (energetic, visual, ecological, and spatial) of the involved actors; secondly to try to determine a preferential ranking of these actions. The stage III includes ten phases organizing the participation. Reader can refer to Froger and Oberti (2002). The search of compromise solutions and a partial or total

[6]http://www.wasp.dk.

[7]http://www.garradhassan.com/products/ghwindfarmer.

order of wind farms project led us to use the **ELECTRE III** (Figueira et al., 2005) outranking approach. In this framework, **revised Simos' procedure** (Figueira and Roy, 2002) implemented by **SRF** software, were applied to determine numerical values for the weights of criteria.

9.3 Actions Set and Criteria Family

9.3.1 Simulated Projects of Wind Farms

The projects of wind farms studied are not industrial projects but simulations using the WindFarmer software. This stems from the nature of the study, commissioned to public purpose and methodology, but also because the municipality of Bonifacio had only old projects.

Therefore, for each of the five possible territories of installation, **variants** of wind farm project have been generated, by changing parameters (wind turbine type, power, height, positioning with wake effect[8] and turbulence, visibility, noise impact). Among all simulated configurations, has been selected the one that maximized the potential of electricity generation under constraints of a total power of 10–20 MW, a number of wind turbines from 5 to 10 and to be outside the exclusion zones.

Thus at the end of stage II, we have retained three potential actions that are three simulated wind farm projects. Each one is related (1) to a specific localization (borders and obstacles) (2) and to a specific set of optimal wind farm parameters.

The wind farm project of **Frasselli** is located at the northwest of Bonifacio, on an army ground which is part of a plateau rising to 214 m. Because of previous industrial projects and the favorable opinion of the city council of Bonifacio concerning wind farm installation, Frasselli has been added to the PLU draft. The different zonings of the site and the optimal positioning of wind turbines are presented on Fig. 9.1.

Two exclusion areas (blue polygons on the Fig. 9.1) were identified on the ground, making impossible the installation of wind turbines. These principal sub-zones are community interest sites which have been included in Natura 2000 network.[9] Occupying 116 ha, these remarkable Mediterranean temporary ponds make the site of Frasselli significant for this natural habitat. The maintenance of ecological function of this land excludes the installation of wind turbines making the soil impermeable because of the need of concrete foundations (150 m^3).

On Fig. 9.1, the optimal localizations of the wind turbine are symbolized by circles outside the exclusion areas. Thus the Frasselli project contains **nine Vestas**

[8]Losses in the electric energy production due to a disturbance between wind generators.

[9]Europe-wide network of sites tasked with the preservation of natural heritage: http://www.natura.org.

Table 9.2 Frasselli project—Lambert IV earth projections

Borders of the site		Wind turbines		Exclusion zones			
				X(E)	Y(N)	X(E)	Y(N)
X(E)	**Y(N)**	X(E)	Y(N)	Zone 1		Zone 2	
571,176	4,131,340	571,056	4,129,046	570,766	4,128,579	569,503	4,129,052
571,093	4,129,926	570,948	4,128,264	570,911	4,128,641	569,445	4,129,994
571,166	4,128,655	569,886	4,128,066	571,166	4,128,655	569,605	4,130,316
571,286	4,128,447	569,858	4,128,320	571,286	4,128,447	570,483	4,131,109
571,169	4,128,305	569,977	4,127,831	571,169	4,128,305	570,219	4,129,503
570,950	4,128,265	570,301	4,128,545	570,950	4,128,265	570,343	4,129,397
569,995	4,127,779	570,817	4,128,864	–	–	570,304	4,129,028
569,503	4,129,052	570,637	4,128,106	–	–	570,928	4,129,028
569,445	4,129,994	570,486	4,128,716	–	–	570,928	4,129,547
569,605	4,130,316	–	–	–	–	–	–
570,483	4,131,109	–	–	–	–	–	–

V63 of 1.5 MW for which the Lambert IV earth projections are presented on the Table 9.2.

By minimizing the wake effects, the ground surface necessary to the installation would reach **70,63 ha**. Without taking into account electrical losses and production stoppages, this wind farm could produce 37,908 MWh/year.

The two other projects were defined according to the same method. We have distinguished:

- The **Francolo** project, a former motocross track at an altitude of 65 m, located at the northeast of the Municipality, near a trunk road. After optimization, **five turbines Bonus of 2 MW** have been positioned, which would produce 21,909 MWh/year, except electrical losses and production stoppages
- The **Valle Torta** project, very close to the previous project, located on a small valley at the northeast of the Municipality, culminating with 82 m of altitude. After optimization, **seven turbines Bonus of 2 MW** have been localized, which would produce 30,227 MWh/year.

In addition let us note that assuming that no more than two projects should be realizable in the future. Indeed actors consider that three potential actions is a sufficient number.

9.3.2 Criteria of Evaluation

In order to evaluate and compare wind farm projects, **six criteria** have been retained (Table 9.3) and associated with four concerns of actors.

Table 9.3 Concerns of actors and evaluation criteria

Concerns of actors, evaluators	Associated criteria, (unities/items), optimizations	Principles of criteria construction
Energy, EDF, UCPP	PROD: annual net producible, (MWh/year), maximization	Probabilistic analysis of wind (Wasp). Estimating a production function of electricity (WindFarmer). Calculation of the electric losses (network connection, intentional or accidental production stoppages). Estimating the amount of electrical energy delivered to the community of users
Visual, DIREN, UCPP	VBON: visibility from the town of Bonifacio, (%), minimization	Surface of wind turbines, visible to the naked eye from an observation point, divided by the total surface of wind turbines (WindFarmer). From a given observation area, minimum and maximum values of visible parts, aggregated by a rule of type "maximum otherwise arithmetic mean"
	VHAB: visibility from the closest habitation, (%), minimization	
	VAIL: visibility from elsewhere, (%), minimization	
Ecological, MAIRS, DIREN, UCPP	DECO: potential environmental degradation, (points on 36), minimization	Potential negative impacts of the wind farm (building site, delivery, activity) with the environmental functions (ecological areas, hunting reserves, supply of the migratory birds, ground)
Spatial, MAIRM, UCPP	CONF: potential conflicts of uses or/and potential functional conflicts, (non-existent, limited, moderated, considerable, high), minimization	Pace of site frequentation. Incompatibility, or not, of the wind farm with existing private/public uses of the site. Deprivation, or not, of a common interest alternative project/purpose, considering the short or medium term

It should be noted that for all actors in the decision aid process, the visual impact from the city and from elsewhere (neither city nor the habitations close to a wind farm project, municipalities bordering of Bonifacio) were first concerns. The criteria construction is specified in the four following subsections.

9.3.2.1 Annual Net Producible

The producible is an estimation of the electrical energy amount delivered to the final consumers. During the construction of criterion PROD, we have considered that:

1. according EDF, the losses of power related to the network connection are 40 kW for 10 km of cable,
2. according the energy model of RETScreen International,[10] the losses due to intentional or accidental production stoppages vary from 2 % until respectively 7 % and 6 %.

[10]http://www.retscreen.net.

Table 9.4 Calculation of the annual net producible for Frasselli project

Power of the park (MW)	15
Annual producible with wake effect (MWh/year)	37,908
Distance to the 90 kV transformer (km)	9.953
Annual electric losses of connecting (MWh/year)	111
Losses by stops, volunteer or fortuitous (%)	5
Net annual producible (MWh/year)	35,902

These data have been specified by the physicists of University of Corsica (UCPP) for each wind project. The application of the criterion PROD for the Frasselli project gives, without decimal, $37{,}908 - 111 - (37908 \times 5\,\%) = 35{,}902$ (MWh/year) (Table 9.4).

9.3.2.2 Criteria of Visibility

Visual impacts have been geographically differentiated, and the minimal and maximal values have been computed using the GIS embedded in WindFarmer. The synthesis of the results has been realized according to the following **aggregation rule**:

1. for each observation place, if the maximal visibility of the wind farm is at least equal to 50 %, the synthesis corresponds to the maximal visibility, otherwise the synthesis corresponds the arithmetic mean of the minimal and maximal visibilities;
2. for a criterion, if several observation places are distinguished, we compute the arithmetic mean of the synthesized visibilities.

Suggested by the analyst, this principle has been adopted by all the actors. The physicists of the UCPP have had the responsibility to implement these three criteria of visibility. Their application to the Frasselli project is described on the Table 9.5. For example, from nearby homes the park would be visible at $56.25\,\% = ((0 + 0.25)/2 + 100)/2$.

Let us note that VAIL, the visibility from elsewhere, considers points of observation located on:

1. the Municipality of Bonifacio, except the city and the habitations close to a wind farm project. For example the sites such as beaches, places of worship, places to hike have been retained;
2. the four Municipalities bordering of Bonifacio, namely Pianotolli-Caldarello, Figari, Sotta and Porto-Vecchio.

Table 9.5 Visibilities of the wind project of Frasselli, in %

VBON		VHAB				VAIL									
		Observation places				Observation places									
		Poggio d'Olmo		Suartone		Gurgazu		Caldarello		Pianotoli Caldarello		Pertusato		La Trinité	
Min	Max	Min	Max	Min	Max	Min	Max	Min	Max	Min	Max	Min	Max	Min	Max
0	50	0	25	0	100	10	75	50	100	1	75	0	75	20	75
50		12.5		100		75		100		75		75		75	
		56.25				80									

9.3.2.3 Potential Environmental Degradation

The principle of construction of the criterion DECO does not result from a true impact study. This is a summary and preliminary assessment. Formally, it is a total score to minimize, ranging from 0 to 36 points, aggregating the elementary scores by simple addition. **Numerical encoding** of information meets the following logic:

- **increasing linear difference** between successive levels, from bottom to the top of the scales, allowing to appreciate the possible impact of a wind farm on a site Natura 2000, on the grounds because of the deforestation, the access and the electric connection;
- **equivalence or numerical prioritization** among the other elements of information.

The construction of the criterion (Table 9.6) has been supervised by the analyst and the DIREN, and has been accepted by all the others actors. The scores were obtained according to the importance and equivalence of listed information elements. The value 0 was assigned when the damage was considered negligible. The maximum value depends on the type of numerical encoding and number of items to be encoded. Elements of the ground impact assessment were all considered equivalent, which leads to the same scores (0, 1, 3). In contrast, the European Community importance of a site (Natura 2000) was considered as a priority on the national interest (French inventory of ZNIEFF[11] areas); ZNIEFF of type I, small areas, were considered more vulnerable than ZNIEFF II, large natural areas. This hierarchy explains the maximum scores of 10, 2 and 1. The reasoning was similar to the Important Bird Areas[12] (IBA) , exceeding the national level.

An application of this criterion DECO with the Frasselli project (Appendix 3, Table 9.14) has given an evaluation of ten points out of 36, by the sum of resulting scores.

9.3.2.4 Potential Conflicts of Uses or Functional Conflicts

Finally, the criterion CONF has been associated with a **verbal scale of five risks levels encoded by increasing linear difference**. The construction principles of scale were semantic. Actors have connected the potential conflicts with the attendance rate of sites, its compatibility with the presence of wind farms, the opportunity cost related to another type of project or future of the site, the term of achievement (Table 9.7).

The wind project of Frasselli should have limited risks. According to the city council (MAIRM, MAIRS), the possible presence of a farmer on the site should not be problematic, and the access tracks to the park could serve a future technical

[11]For “Zone Naturelle d’Intérêt Ecologique, Faunistique et Floristique” in French.

[12]For “Zones Importantes pour la Conservation des Oiseaux” in French.

Table 9.6 Construction of the potential ecological degradation criterion

Background information	Scores
Site of Community Importance (SCI) - Natura 2000	–
Territory of installation close (less than 150 m) to a Natura 2000 site:	–
Relative surface (SR):	–
15–100 % : remarkable site for this habitat, noted A	6
2–15 % : very important site for this habitat, noted B	3
Inferior to 2 % : important site for this habitat, noted C	1
Relative population (PR):	–
15–100 % : remarkable site for this species, noted A	10
2–15 % : very important site for this species, noted B	6
Inferior to 2 % : Lower than 2 %: important site for this species, noted C	3
Presence of the species, but non significant, noted D	1
Territory of establishment distant (minimum 150 m) from a Natura 2000 site	0
Natural zones of ecological, faunal and floral interest - ZNIEFF type I	–
Presence of the installation territory in the area	2
Installation territory out of area	0
Natural zones of ecological, faunal and floral interest - ZNIEFF type II	–
Presence of the installation territory in the area	1
Installation territory out of area	0
Avifauna	–
Important Bird Areas (IBA):	–
Presence of the installation territory close (less than 150 m) to the area	6
Installation territory distant (minimum 150 m) from the area	0
Hunting preserve:	–
Presence of the installation territory in a reserve	1
Installation territory out of reserve	0
Migrations of birds:	–
No behavior of massive passage, but possible sourcing in situ	1
No behavior of massive passage on the installation territory	0
Impacts on the grounds	–
Deforestation:	–
Considerable: wooded area with small access	3
Possible but limited: existing access, and spaces to possibly release	1
Non necessary: land already and sufficiently deforested	0
Access track:	–
Creation or reinforcement of the existing surface from at least 20 %	3
Reinforcement of the existing surface of less than 20 %	1
No necessary creation or reinforcement	0
Connection with the public network of electricity:	–
Indirect: at least one close ground to cross on more than 1 km	3
Quasi-direct: at least one close ground to cross on maximum 1 km	1
Direct: no need to cross one or more close grounds	0
Total of the scores	36

Table 9.7 Preference scale for criterion CONF

Levels of risk	Meanings
Non-existent (0)	Low human frequentation of the site, compatible with wind project, or/and absence of alternative project/ purpose of common interest in the short-term
Limited (1)	Occasional human frequentation of the site, compatible with wind project, or/and non-realizable alternative project/purpose of common interest in the short-term
Moderated (3)	Seasonal human frequentation, or weekly, of the site, compatible with wind project or requiring a limited redevelopment; or/and probable alternative project/purpose of common interest in the medium term
Considerable (6)	Seasonal human frequentation, or weekly, of the site, requiring a real refitting of wind project; or/and realizable alternative project/purpose of common interest in the medium term
High (10)	High human frequentation, even daily, of the site, incompatible with wind project; or/and realizable alternative project/purpose of common interest in the short-term

hiding center of waste. Thus constructed, the six criteria were used to evaluate the three wind farm projects.

9.4 Multiple Criteria Evaluation and Wind Farm Project Recommendations

In the framework of outranking ELECTRE approach (Figueira et al., 2005), different types of values are distinguished on each criterion: evaluations of all the actions, in a performance table; importance coefficients or normalized weights; discrimination thresholds, taking into account the imperfect nature of evaluations, and veto thresholds, setting a limit on compensation of poor evaluations by good evaluations of an action compared to another. In a participatory process, theses values are generally not consensual. Therefore several sets of information may be retained and introduced individually in multiple criteria computations. The values obtained in the study are delivered in three subsections that follow.

9.4.1 Performance Table

The evaluation of all projects through the family criteria has led us to a single performance table. Indeed, each intersection of row and column includes only one value, because actors agreed results delivered by the evaluators. Detailed presentations, about construction of criteria and preference scales, have facilitated the consensus achievement (Table 9.8).

Table 9.8 Performance table

		Criteria					
		PROD	VBON	VHAB	VAIL	DECO	CONF
Terms of scale		MWh/year	%	%	%	Points	Numerical
Optimization		Maximization	Minimization				
Wind farm projects	Frasselli	35,902	50	56.25	80	10	1
	Francolo	20,975	5	52.5	25	1	3
	Valle Torta	28,950	0	40	3.7	2	1

The imperfection of these evaluations and the search for a good compromise project, have required the determination thresholds on criteria.

9.4.2 Thresholds on Criteria

There are no true values for thresholds, but assigned values being the most convenient and accepted by actors for expressing imperfect knowledge and preference limits.

The indifference threshold, when it is strictly positive, take into account:

1. margins of **imprecision** (due to imperfect geographical coordinates, wind speed extrapolations), of **ill-determination** (due to the technology type selected in future by industrialists) and of **uncertainty** (due to the connecting paths to electrical network, dependant on agreements with the landowners), limiting the relevance of the evaluations resulting from criteria PROD, VBON, VHAB, and VAIL;
2. **non-significant difference of values** (criteria DECO).

The thresholds of preference and veto results more from a subjective appreciation of actors. The first expresses a significant difference of values, the other sets a limit to the compensation between performances.

The decision aid process has delivered the following thresholds values (Table 9.9).

Let us note two particularities concerning thresholds of the criterion PROD. Firstly, they have been expressed as percentages instead of MWh/year. Physicists of the UCPP (actors UCPP1 and UCPP2) encountered difficulties in expressing the differences of producible reflecting situations of indifference, preference or veto between two wind farm projects. However, evaluate thresholds as dimensionless numbers constituted an intelligible exercise. Technically, this is to define **variable thresholds** on the preference scale of the criterion. Using scientific and technical literature, evaluators knew relative error margins on the producible, facilitating the evaluation of indifference threshold, and establish a relation with the others. The veto threshold value, which is 100 %, expresses that a project producing less than

Table 9.9 Thresholds on criteria

		Criteria						
		PROD		VBON	VHAB	VAIL	DECO	CONF
Terms of scale		MWh/year		%	%	%	Points	Numerical
Optimization		Maximization		Minimization				
Criteria thresholds by actors	Indifference	UCPP1	UCPP2	5			1	0
		5 %	10 %					
	Preference	20 %	30 %	20			3	1
	Veto	100 %		50			6	9

Table 9.10 SRF parameters

Actors	MAIRM	MAIRO	ADEC	DIREN	CITOYL
Z	3.58	3.57	3.54	3.53	3.57
Number of white card between PROD and other criteria of best ranks	1				

twice the amount of another project, may not catch his disadvantage on another criterion at least. Secondly, **two sets of threshold values** have been distinguished for PROD, because the physicists had different opinions on the indifference (5 % or 10 %) and the preference (20 % or 30 %). They were inserted individually in multiple criteria calculations.

Furthermore, to give a **veto power** to the criterion CONF, qualitative in the beginning, a numerical encoding by increasing linear difference was performed.

9.4.3 Relative Importance of Criteria

In the ELECTRE framework, the importance coefficients of criteria are intrinsic weights: they can not be interpreted as substitution rates, but as voting power accorded to each criterion.

Normalized weights of criteria were obtained with the **revised Simos' procedure** (Figueira and Roy, 2002) implemented in SRF software. The actors have retained (1) only one white card, between criterion PROD and the other of best ranks (2) an importance factor (Z), between the first package of criterion and the last, that varies in the range [3.53; 3.58] (Table 9.10).

Computed weights are the following (Table 9.11). Notably, this phase reveals that the actors were generally agreed on the most important criteria (VBON, VAIL, DECO) and the least important criteria (PROD).

Each set of weights were inserted individually in multiple criteria calculations.

Table 9.11 Sets of normalized criteria weights

		Criteria					
		PROD	VBON	VHAB	VAIL	DECO	CONF
Weights of the criteria by actors	MAIRM	0.0613	0.2193	0.1667	0.2193	0.1667	0.1667
	MAIRO	0.0649	0.2315	0.1757	0.2315	0.2315	0.0649
	ADEC	0.0535	0.1893	0.1893	0.1893	0.1893	0.1893
	DIREN	0.0561	0.1982	0.1511	0.1982	0.1982	0.1982
	CITOYL	0.1007	0.2193	0.18	0.2193	0.2193	0.0614

Table 9.12 Enlarged table of performances

		Criteria						
		PROD		VBON	VHAB	VAIL	DECO	CONF
Terms of scale		MWh/year		%	%	%	points	numerical
Optimization		Maximization		Minimization				
Wind farm projects	Frasselli	35,902		50	56.25	80	10	1
	Francolo	20,975		5	52.5	25	1	3
	Valle Torta	28,950		0	40	3.7	2	1
Weights of the criteria by actors	MAIRM	0.0613		0.2193	0.1667	0.2193	0.1667	0.1667
	MAIRO	0.0649		0.2315	0.1757	0.2315	0.2315	0.0649
	ADEC	0.0535		0.1893	0.1893	0.1893	0.1893	0.1893
	DIREN	0.0561		0.1982	0.1511	0.1982	0.1982	0.1982
	CITOYL	0.1007		0.2193	0.18	0.2193	0.2193	0.0614
Criteria thresholds by actors	Indifference	UCPP1	UCPP2	5			1	0
		5 %	10 %					
	Preference	20 %	30 %	20			3	1
	Veto	100 %		50			6	9

9.4.4 Outranking Aggregation and Recommendations

The participative process gives an enlarged table of performances. The enlargement corresponds to the possible presence of several values within the traditional table structure (evaluations, relative weights of criteria, and thresholds on the latter), because of differentiated judgments according to the actors (Table 9.12).

In fact, this synthetic presentation counts, here, ten cases (one consensual evaluation table, five sets of weights, two sets of thresholds). Thus, the method ELECTRE III was implemented ten times. The recommendations on wind farm projects results of:

1. the application of ELECTRE III method, on each ten cases, in order to check out coincidence, or not, of the preferential ranking;

Table 9.13 Results of ELECTRE III method

Final outranking graph	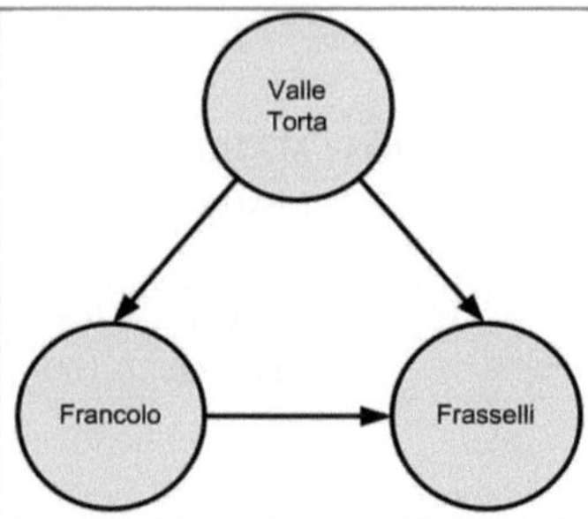		
Final preorder	Rank 1	Rank 2	Rank 3
	Valle Torta	Francolo	Frasselli

2. a new optimization of the better compromise wind farm project, using the WindFarmer software, defining the number of wind turbines, the unit power, height, positioning on site, form of installation, ground surface, borders of the installation site;
3. translation of the recommended territory in compatible files with the numerized PLU of the Municipality, using the MapInfo software.

Concerning the application of ELECTRE III method, all the results converge (Table 9.13), for ascending and descending distillations, even after a sensitivity robustness analysis.

These scientific recommendations, which indicate Valle Torta as the better compromise wind farm project, have been adopted unanimously by the actors of the decision aid process. Occupying the second rank, Francolo project offers a site geographically close, which in future would extend the project of Valle Torta. Last of the ranking the Frasselli project can be eliminated, because of **four veto situations** expressed by the very important criteria DECO and VAIL.

A last optimization of Valle Torta project (Appendix 4) allowed to obtain a better variant: (1) a greater visual integration (2) an increased power (3) a limited surface on the ground. Thus, the **final collective recommendations** were the following ones:

install a farm of 10 unaligned wind turbines on the site of Valle Torta. Each one is of maximum 100 meters high, blades included, and with unit power near to 2 MW.

In terms of decision, these recommendations were registered in the PLU of Bonifacio. Also, at the regional level, a final study report was realized for ADEC.

9.5 Comments on the Case Study

This study constitutes a first case in Corsica. All in all, it was well accepted, at regional and local levels. Various lessons were delivered by this real world application.

Concerning the construction of criteria, like producible and visibilities, the roles of the analyst and evaluators were crucial, to attach these first to a **collective interest**. Indeed, the WindFarmer software, like other reference, is used by industrialists of wind to evaluate variants of project-bases on the aforementioned criteria. However, without taking account the electrical loss of connection with the electrical network, the producible would have been estimate not for the community of users, but at the wind park level, for the needs of the project holder. Also, the visibility can be apprehended starting from observations points interesting only certain strong actors, with the detriment of the others (small residential communities, environment users, neighbor Municipalities, ...).

Furthermore, the coexistence of **several scientific disciplines**, required to find a manner of combining the analytical tools of each one, which in particular supposes (1) to determine the complementarities (2) to have a common language. Outranking approach constituted an adaptable but rigorous methodology. For example, variable thresholds (%) for criterion PROD were helpful. A clear and illustrated documentation was also important to maintain the knowledge of concepts among actors.

Concerning the study process, the major stake was the opening to local civil society, not only to inform it or consult it, but so:

1. set up a dialogue around the visual impacts of wind farm projects, implying new simulations 2D and 3D, upon request, during the assemblies;
2. to attest that scientists and analyst, were not alibis of town councilors;
3. to convince that there was no hidden truth, revealed by dominant models and software, that the citizens were to follow, but that on the contrary, their opinions were taken into account through these tools, as well as those of the other actors.

Also let us note that, at the end of last public assembly, **an industrialist has appeared in the process**, to expose a poster on a preliminary wind farm project. This one (a) related to the site of Frasselli, ranked last in our study (b) constituted higher machine (approximately 130 m) (c) was partially established in the temporary pond Natura 2000 (d) delivered a visual simulation 3D in a single point of the town of Bonifacio.

Another **intervention of external actors** occurred after delivering the final report. An energy advisor, unavailable during application, but then again depending, commissioned a review from an office. The goal was to publish it, in appendix of a regional planning document being prepared, to put forward without scientific argument the site of Frasselli. The same critic deplored the fact that analyst has not made contact with a farm operator, an approach that was inconsistent with the purpose study, methodological and public. This brief episode, finally without any consequence, was instructive on the logic of external actors in the process of decision support, and links that can be established between them in the actual process of decision.

9.6 Conclusion and Enlargements

This pilot study, founded on a multiple criteria aid to participative decision (Froger and Oberti, 2002) was appreciated by the actors for (1) its increased **transparency** (2) the **opening** to the disciplines and local civil society (3) the **rigor** of the approach.

In addition, exogenous decisions of the study had incidences on the wind sector development, as well in Bonifacio as in Corsica. Indeed, during the elaboration of wind regional plan, the CTC did not deliver an opinion any more on real wind farm projects, as long as the public document was not finalized and was not adopted. Also, at the national level, the ministerial decision to decrease the tariff of obligatory buying, by EDF of the wind electricity produced in Corsica, reduced the attractiveness of the region and the profitability of the industrial projects. To date, no new wind farm was delivered in the island since December 2003, and only 18 MW have been installed. Let us stress that the second energy plan of Corsica fixed the objective of 100 MW in 2015.

Vested powers imply that CTC has rigorous and operating evaluation tools, producing recommendations of projects more quickly than currently. A larger partnership than an ad hoc pilot study is to be considered.

In the future two proposals for enlargement are considered. A **software project**, called Ev@l, will try to (1) increase the productivity of the analyst, to produce multiple criteria calculations in multi-actors context (2) to **facilitate the structuring of an evaluation process** (3) to communicate with a GIS. A favorable opinion was given by the competitiveness cluster CAPENERGIES (Corsica committee), for the MECADEPPE project which includes functionalities dedicated to energy. A request for certification is actually in process. Finally we wish to explore new areas by proposing to formalize a generic decision aid process at the territorial level. We think that knowledge representation languages and recent works developed for the semantic web will be useful.

Acknowledgements This work was supported by the Territorial Collectivity of Corsica and its Agency for Economic Development. We thank Vallée J.-C., Ferracci M. (ADEC), the City council of Bonifacio, Muselli M., Poggi P., Darras C. and Tinti B. (University of Corsica).

Appendix 1: Timing and Agendas of the Meetings

Tasks/Months	1	2	3	4	5	6	7	8	9	10	11	12	13	14	15	16	17
Plenary working meetings:	■				■	■		■			■		■		■		■
Objectives of the study	■				■	■		■									
Methodology and documentation	■				■	■		■			■		■		■		■
Steering committee	■				■	■		■									
Working group								■			■		■		■		■
Sites and wind farm projects	■					■		■			■		■		■		■
Stakeholders concerns	■				■	■		■			■		■		■		■
Evaluation criteria						■		■			■		■				
Evaluation of projects, thresholds						■		■			■		■		■		■
Actors' priorities on criteria family															■		
Weights of criteria															■		
Recommendations of projects															■		■
Registration in PLU draft															■		■
Restricted technical meetings:	■	■	■	■	■	■	■	■	■		■	■	■	■	■	■	■
Time series of wind			■	■	■	■											
GIS of wind potential					■	■	■	■	■								
GIS of topography and housing					■	■											
GIS of environmental zones													■	■	■		
Orthophoto													■	■	■		
Grid connection	■			■	■		■	■				■		■			
PLU draft														■	■		■
Previous wind farm projects	■	■	■	■	■												
Locations to investigate	■	■	■	■	■	■	■	■	■		■	■	■	■	■	■	■
Simulations of wind farm projects				■	■	■	■	■	■		■	■	■	■	■	■	■
Visual and acoustic impacts				■	■	■	■	■	■		■	■	■	■	■	■	■
Territorial integration						■		■				■					

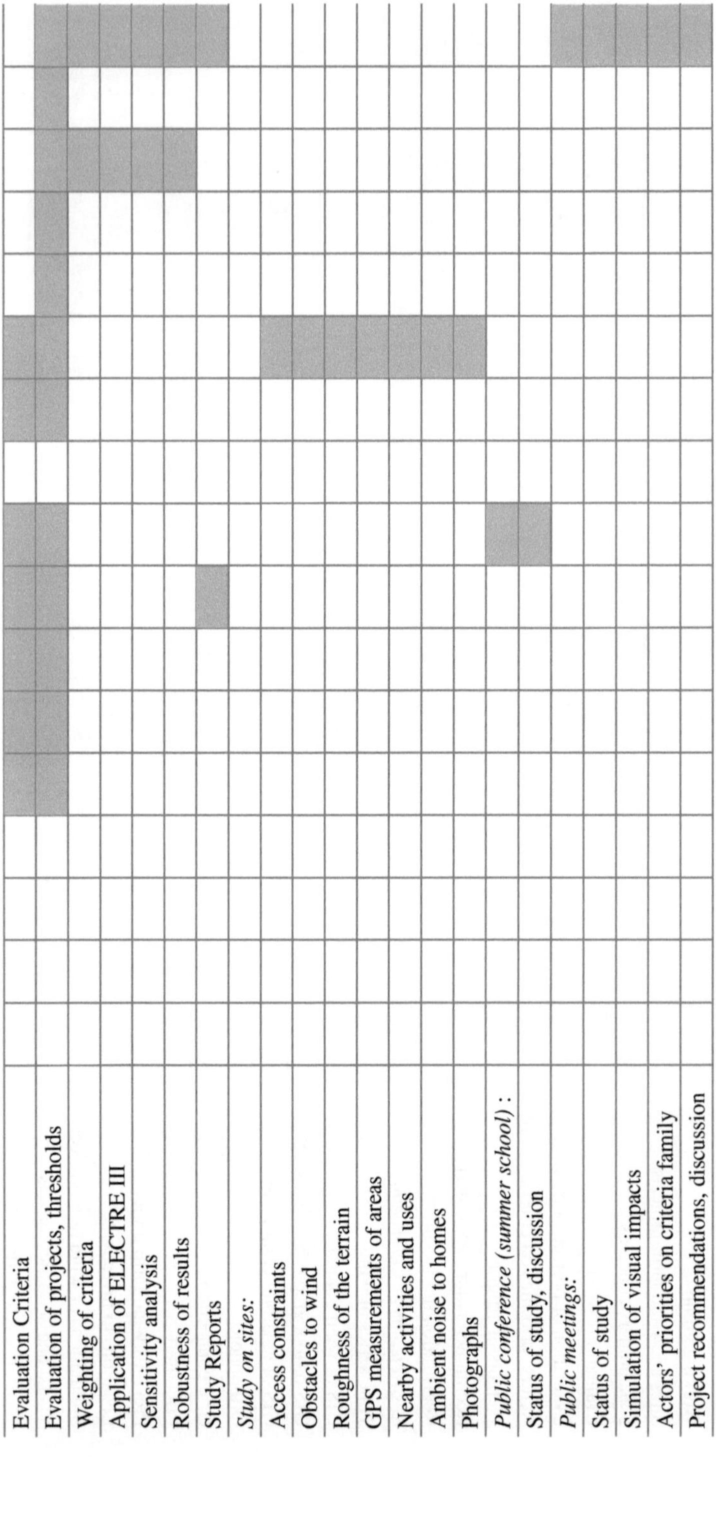
Evaluation Criteria
Evaluation of projects, thresholds
Weighting of criteria
Application of ELECTRE III
Sensitivity analysis
Robustness of results
Study Reports
Study on sites:
Access constraints
Obstacles to wind
Roughness of the terrain
GPS measurements of areas
Nearby activities and uses
Ambient noise to homes
Photographs
Public conference (summer school) :
Status of study, discussion
Public meetings:
Status of study
Simulation of visual impacts
Actors' priorities on criteria family
Project recommendations, discussion

Appendix 2: General Structure of the Process

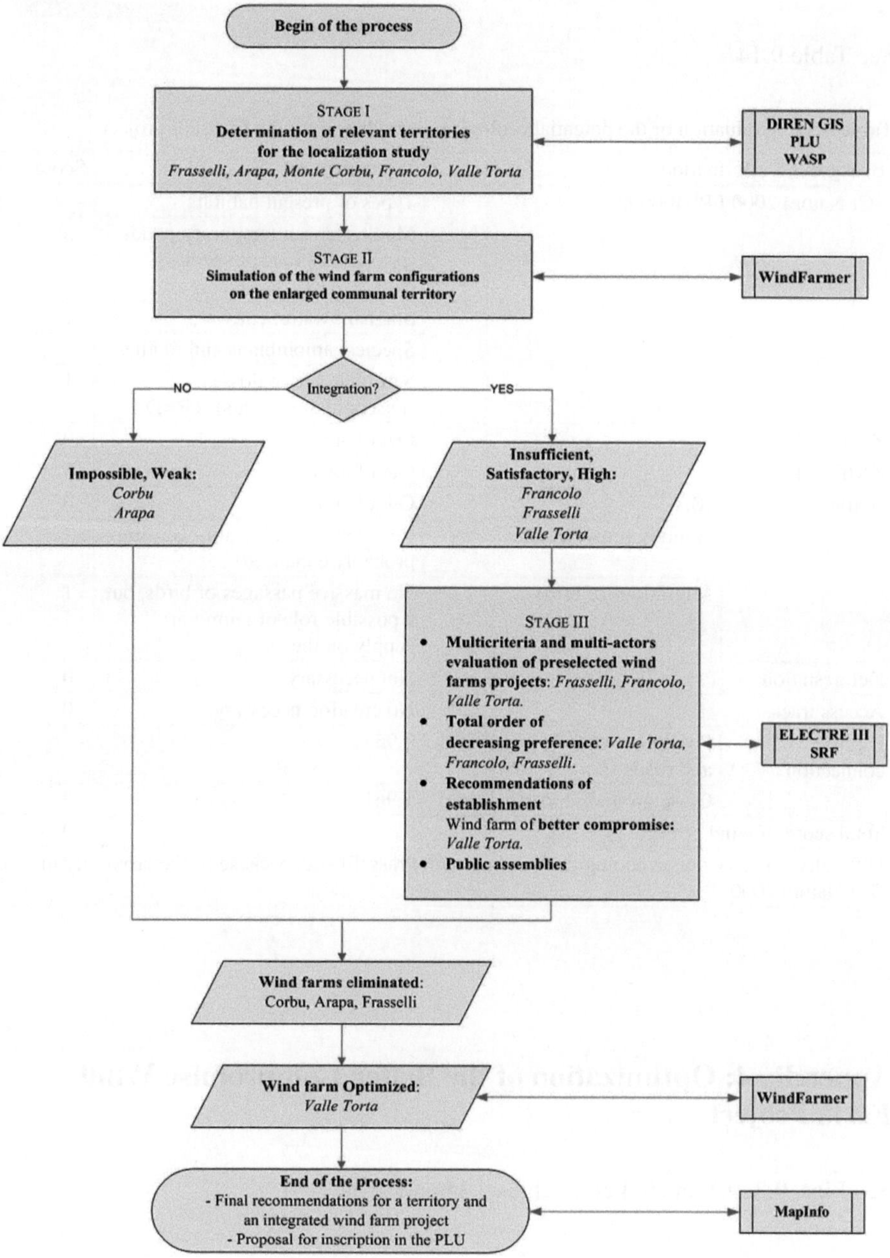

Appendix 3: Example of Application for the Potential Ecological Degradation Criterion

See Table 9.14.

Table 9.14 Evaluation of the potential ecological degradation for the Frasselli project

Background information		Wind project of Frasselli	Scores
SCI Natura 2000 FR9400608		Types of present habitats	–
		Mediterranean temporary ponds (priority habitats or species): couv = 10 %, SR=B	3
		Stagnant water: couv = 5 %	1
		Species: amphibians and reptiles	–
		Sardinian Discoglosse (Discoglossus sardus), PR=D	1
ZNIEFF I		Out of area	0
ZNIEFF II		Out of area	0
Avifauna	IBA	Out of area	0
	Hunting preserve	Yes (density and quality Birdlife probably enhanced)	1
	Migrations of birds	No massive passages of birds, but a possible role of temporary supply on the site	1
Deforestation		Not necessary	0
Access track		No creation necessary	0
Electric connection	Possibility of following tracks and roads (km)	9.953	–
	Close ground(s) to cross (km)	1.961	3
Total score of wind project			10
Difficulty: to carry out an ecological building with Frasselli site, because of the proximity in SCI Natura 2000			

Appendix 4: Optimization of the Better Compromise Wind Farm Project

See Figs. 9.2, 9.3 and 9.4 and Tables 9.15 and 9.16.

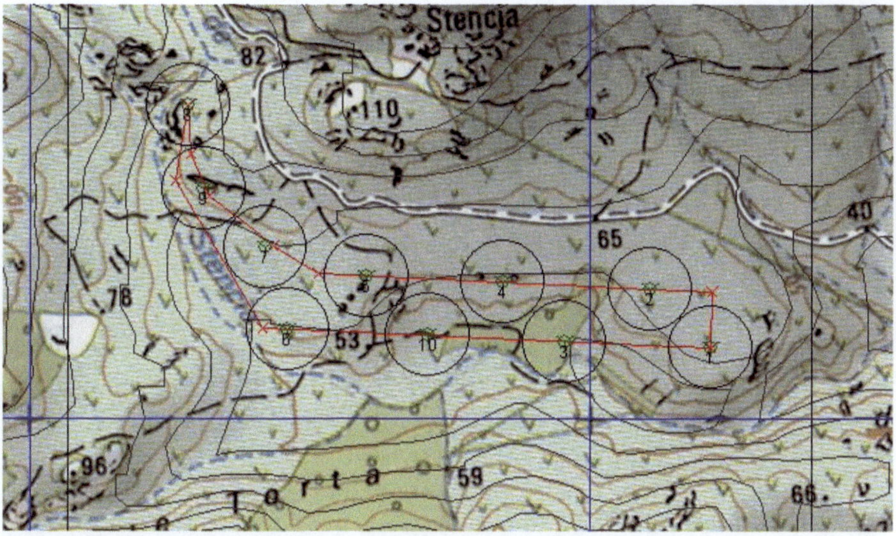

Fig. 9.2 Zoning of the Valle Torta site and optimal positioning of wind turbines

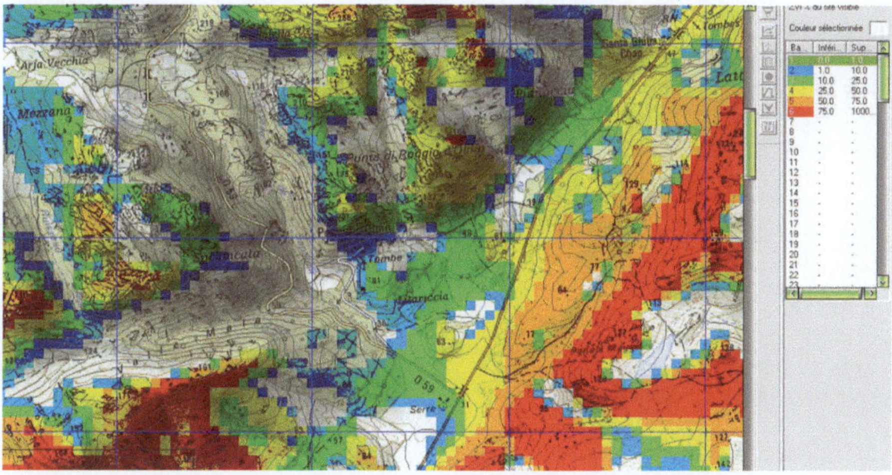

Fig. 9.3 2D visibility with the close habitations of the hamlet Poggio d'Olmo

Fig. 9.4 3D visibility with the close habitations of the hamlet Poggio d'Olmo

Table 9.15 Calculation of the net annual producible for Valle Torta project

Power of the park (MW)	20
Annual producible with wake effect (MWh/year)	37,479
Distance to the 90 kV transformer (km)	7.197
Annual electric losses of connecting (MWh/year)	59
Losses by stops, volunteer or fortuitous (%)	4 %
Net annual producible (MWh/year)	35,920

Table 9.16 Visibilities of the wind project of Valle Torta, in %

		VHAB				VAIL									
		Observation places				Observation places									
VBON		Poggio d'Olmo		Suartone		Gurgazu		Caldarello		Pianotoli Caldarello		Pertusato		La Trinité	
Min	Max	Min	Max	Min	Max	Min	Max	Min	Max	Min	Max	Min	Max	Min	Max
0	0	0	3	0	75	1	17	0	0	0	0	1	4	0	0
0		1.5		75		9		0		0		2.5		0	
		38.25				2.3									

References

Conseil exécutif de la Corse. (2005) *Plan énergétique de la corse*. Technical report, Collectivité Territoriale de Corse (CTC), Nov 2005.

Faucheux, S., & Noël, J. -F. (1995). *Economie des ressources naturelles et de la environnement*. Série Economie. Collection U, 1995. ISBN:978-2200214425.

Figueira, J., Mousseau, V., & Roy, B. (2005). *Multiple criteria decision analysis: State of the art surveys*, chapter ELECTRE methods (pp. 133–162). International Series in Operations Research and Management Science. New York: Springer.

Figueira, J., & Roy, B. (2002). Determining the weights of criteria in the electre type methods with a revised simos' procedure. *European Journal of Operational Research, 139*(2), 317–326.

Froger, G. (2001). *Gouvernance 1: Gouvernance et développement durable*. Bâle: Helbing & Lichtenhahn.

Froger, G., & Oberti, P. (2002). Gouvernance et développement durable. l'aide multicritere deă la décision participative. *Sciences de la société, 57*, 57–74.

Hassan, G., & P. Ltd, (2002). *WindFarmer - Theory Manual*. Number no 093/BR/ 01 Issue 07, Oct 2002.

Landberg, L. (1999). Short-term prediction of the power production from wind farms. *Journal of Wind Engineering and Industrial Aerodynamics, 80*(1–2), 207–220.

Maystre, L. Y., Pictet, J., & Simos, J. (1994). *Méthodes multicriteres ELECTRE*. Paris: Geodif.

Mortensen, N.G., & Petersen, E.L. (1997). *Influence of topographical input data on the accuracy of wind flow modelling in complex terrain*, Proceedings of the European Wind Energy Conference, Dublin, October 6-9, 317–320.

Notton, G., Cristofari, C., Poggi, P., & Oberti, P. (2005). Contexte insulaire de la production d'énergie électrique: Corse, île des énergies renouvelables? *Revue de l'energie, 72*(564), 78–91.

Roy, B. (1996). *Multicriteria methodology for decision aiding*. Dordrecht: Kluwer Academic.

Editors' Comments on "Participative and Multicriteria Localization of Wind Farm Projects in Corsica Island"

Oberti and Paoli consider in their chapter an application in the field of production of renewable energy. Policymakers face a situation in which the objective is to promote renewable energies and to increase the proportion of electricity produced by renewable energy. Within this context, Oberti and Paoli supported a participative decision process to support stakeholders in the choice of location of wind farm projects in Corsica Island. Such public decision process arise frequently and common characteristic are: strategic decisions which have long term consequences, multiple stakeholders having possibly divergent objectives, multiple perspectives/criteria by which the problem can be approached, difficulties in assessing alternatives. Another public decision application can be found in this book (see Chap. 15).

The client of the study was Agency for Economic Development of Corsica, but the authors describe how the 60 **stakeholders** were involved in the participative process (Economic development agency, city council representatives, regional direction for environmental, local citizens, tourists, university of Corsica. . .). Considering the large number of participants to the project, the problem definition and formulation stages (see Chap. 2) have been an important part of the study.

The **objective of the intervention** was to gather all relevant stakeholders and lead them to a common understanding of the issues involved in the choice of the best location of wind farms. In this perspective, the selection of potential sites, the definition of evaluation criteria, the use of a Geographical Information System to put these criteria into practice with the actual data constitute a considerable achievement in this application. Therefore, the application of the ELECTRE III method (see Chap. 4, Sect. 4.4.4) to rank the potential sites should not be seen as the main output of the application.

One of the interesting features of this chapter concerns the fact that the application deals with geo-referenced entities, and explicitly considers the link between two related fields: Multiple criteria decision Aid (MCDA) on one hand, and Geographical Information Systems (GIS) and spatial decision problems, on the other hand. The link between these two fields has been studied in several Ph.D. theses (e.g. Laaribi 1994; Chakhar 2006; Lidouh 2014) and books Malczewski (1999), Malczewski and Rinner (2014) (see also Malczewski 2006 for a literature review).

Another positive and interesting aspect of this application concerns the participative aspect of the decision aid process. Such perspective focuses on the organizational aspects of the decision aid process, the active participation and involvement of the stakeholders, which fosters the acceptance the decision aid model appropriation of the related recommendations.

Among the interesting links between GIS and MCDA, the construction of criteria explicitly involving geo-referenced data is of particular interest. In this application, the "visual impact" of the wind farms is evaluated by a criterion which accounts for the surface of the territory from which these wind farms are visible. Considering the hilly landscape of Corsica, it is easy to understand that an advanced use of GIS was necessary to build the evaluation criteria.

Concerning the choice of the **aggregation method** (ELECTRE III method), it can be justified by the diversity in the way the criteria were elaborated: some criteria are evaluated on a qualitative linguistically defined scale (e.g. potential conflict of use of the site), the annual electricity production is evaluated MWh/year, and the visual impact criterion is the result of relatively sophisticated computations.

As far as the use, in this application, of the ELECTRE III ranking method is concerned, alternative ways to analyze the relative advantages and drawback of the sites could have been considered. The case study considered a very limited number (3) of potential sites; therefore, instead of applying the ELECTRE III ranking method, it could have been relevant to limit the analysis to the construction of the outranking relation, and, to propose a synthetic representation of the arguments (pros and cons) at stake in the pairwise comparisons of the three potential sites.

The first **tangible outcome** of this application is the comparison of the potential sites involved in this pilot study. Further (more interesting) outcomes are the criteria that have been elaborated during this pilot study. More **intangible results** of this work are related to the fact that the stakeholders with various objectives have elaborated a common analysis of this difficult and strategic decision concerning the selection of sites for wind farms.

References

Chakhar, S. (2006). *Cartographie décisionnelle multicritère: formalisation et implémentation informatique*. Ph.D., Université Paris-Dauphine, 2006.
Laaribi, A. (1994). *Systèmes d'information géographique et analyse multicritère: Intégration pour l'aide à la décision à référence spatiale*. Ph.D. thesis, Université Laval, Québec, 1994.
Lidouh, K. (2014). *Integration of Multi-Criteria Tools in Geographical Information Systems*. Ph.D., Université Libre de Bruxelles, 2014.
Malczewski, J. (1999). *GIS and multicriteria decision analysis* (392 pp.). New York: Wiley. ISBN:978-0471329442.
Malczewski, J. (2006). GIS-based multicriteria decision analysis: a survey of the literature. *International Journal of Geographical Information Science, 20*(7), 703–726.
Malczewski, J., & Rinner, C. (2014). *Multicriteria decision analysis in geographic information science*. New York: Wiley.

Chapter 10
Multi-Criteria Assessment of Data Centers Environmental Sustainability

Miguel Trigueiros Covas, Carlos A. Silva, and Luis C. Dias

Abstract The size and capacity of Data Centers (DCs) is growing at a rapid pace to meet the increased demand of data processing and storage capacity requested by a digital information society. Since DCs are infrastructures that have large energy consumption, there is a need to change their design approach to make them more efficient and more environment friendly. This research was motivated by the planning of a new DC in Portugal. It proposes a multi-criteria framework to assess the sustainability of a DC, which includes a new metric to evaluate the DC efficiency taking into account the environmental conditions of the DC location. ELECTRE TRI was chosen for aggregating different metrics concerning the environmental sustainability of a DC into sustainability categories. The evaluation methodology allows some freedom for each DC to place more weight on the aspects in which it is stronger, an analysis facilitated by the IRIS decision support system.

10.1 Introduction

As our society shifts from paper-based to digital information management, the demand for data processing and storage has increased significantly across all activity sectors. Data Centers (DCs), by their data processing and storage capacity, are essential for the development of the new paradigm of collaborative networked

M.T. Covas
Portugal Telecom, Portugal
e-mail: miguel.a.covas@telecom.pt

C.A. Silva
IN+ Center for Innovation Technology and Policy Research (IST), Technical University of Lisbon, Lisbon, Portugal

MIT Portugal Program, Sustainable Energy Systems, Lisbon, Portugal
e-mail: carlos.santos.silva@ist.utl.pt

L.C. Dias
INESC Coimbra and Faculty of Economics, University of Coimbra, Coimbra, Portugal

MIT Portugal Program, Sustainable Energy Systems, Lisbon, Portugal
e-mail: lmcdias@fe.uc.pt

R. Bisdorff et al. (eds.), *Evaluation and Decision Models with Multiple Criteria*, International Handbooks on Information Systems,
DOI 10.1007/978-3-662-46816-6_10

society. With the increasing use of the Internet, telecommunications services, and IT networks internal to organizations, the number of servers and their power consumption has risen rapidly over the last years. Due to this, the implications to the capacity of power grids to supply larger amounts of electricity and the carbon emissions associated with electricity generation are getting the attention and concern from both industry and public policy makers (EPA, 2007; European Commission, 2008). In addition, the increasing costs of electricity are making IT companies aware of the importance of implementing an optimized infrastructure necessary to support the new IT equipment. Therefore, social, environmental and economic interests are leveraging the development of more sustainable DCs.

This work was motivated by a new DC that is going to be built in Portugal by a telecommunications company. Its purpose was to help this telecommunications company assess the sustainability of its planned new DC in a simple way that could be used as a standard by this industry. There were already concrete plans for the new DC (namely its location has already been made public) but a few design options were still under consideration and not yet definitely decided. Nevertheless, rather than focusing solely on this particular problem, we intend to propose a general framework to assess DC sustainability taking into account several environmental criteria.

The study involved the authors and three DC experts from the telecommunications company, spanning around 3 months in time. The authors were the analysts, who suggested a Multi-Criteria Decision Analysis (MCDA) methodology and provided guidance in its use. The set of criteria was based on a literature review on DC metrics and incorporating other sustainability concerns of the problem owner. The discussions among analysts and experts led to the suggestion of replacing the most used criterion in the industry by a variant that takes meteorological data into account. This discussion led the team to propose a benchmarking tool that would encourage DC designers to take as much advantage as possible of the opportunities they have to increase the energy efficiency of the DC.

This chapter proceeds as follows: Sect. 10.2 briefly introduces the problem of assessing sustainability. Section 10.3 presents a review of the main metrics to evaluate the DCs performance. Section 10.4 presents a new metric to evaluate the DC efficiency taking into account the environmental conditions of the DC location. In Sect. 10.5, a framework to assess the DC environmental sustainability performance is proposed. Section 10.6 describes the application of the proposed framework that motivated this work. Finally, Sect. 10.7 draws the main conclusions of this study.

10.2 Sustainability Assessment

Sustainable development is a compromise between environmental, social and economic goals of a community enabling the well-being for the present and future generations. In the words of the World Commission on Environment and

Development (1987) sustainable development is a "development that meets the needs of the present without compromising the ability of future generations to meet their own needs". Several definitions have been proposed since then (Pezzoli, 1997) but there seems to be a consensus that sustainable development is a multi-dimensional issue that can involve a large amount of complex information (Ghosh et al., 2006). According to Ciegis et al. (2009), addressing sustainability implies the problem of its measurement. This can be addressed by indicators, which are quantitative or qualitative measures, that should be simple (with a transparent method of calculation), and should have wide coverage and that allows setting trends (Böhringer and Jochem, 2007; Ciegis et al., 2009; Valentin and Spangenberg, 2000). Thus, the development of sustainable strategies without indicators or qualitative reasoning would be lacking a solid foundation, as indicators are an instrument to evaluate environmental, social and economic goals. Though there is no single measure that could encompass all aspects of the concept sustainability (Ciegis et al., 2009), a collection of indicators chosen and analyzed under multiple criteria could better describe such complex concept (Gasparatos et al., 2008).

These criteria must be credible, relevant, attainable and measurable/verifiable (Global Ecolabelling Network (GEN), 2004). Elghali et al. (2007) established three sets of criteria to assess the sustainability of a bioenergy system: economic viability; environmental performance, including, but not limited to, low carbon dioxide emissions; and social acceptability. For an urban sustainability assessment, Munda (2005) established the city product per person for the economic dimension, the use of private car and the solid waste generated per capita criteria for the environmental dimension and the crime rate, houses owned, and the mean travel time to work among others criteria for the social. Other criteria examples used to assess sustainability, as gross domestic product, pollution emissions (CO_2, SO_2; NO_x) and water consumption, can be found in the literature (Gasparatos et al., 2008; Munda and Saisana, 2011). But how can this set of multi-dimensional indicators be aggregated?

Often, some indicators improve while others deteriorate. For example, when incomes grow, SO_2 might go down while CO_2 increases (Munda, 2005). The aggregation of several criteria implies taking a position on the fundamental issue of compensability. Compensability refers to the existence of trade-offs, i.e. the possibility that a good score on one indicator can compensate a very bad score on another indicator, which is often considered to be unwarranted or at least undesirable for sustainability assessment (Munda and Nardo, 2005). But at the end, the different stakeholders want to have a clear and simple message regarding the aggregated analysis of the different sustainability criteria. This can be addressed by a label.

According to Boer (2003) it is difficult to fully specify what sustainability ideally means at a level of a product, production process or producer. In the absence of a fully specified ideal model, two strategies based on sustainability labeling can be developed. One strategy, based on identifying relevant "ideals" to pursue (e.g. recycling), or a strategy based on identifying "ills" to escape from (e.g. dependence on pesticide use). For Lindblom (1990) it is easier for a heterogeneous society to agree on the "ills" (e.g. poverty) to be avoided than on the "ideals" to be achieved (e.g.

distribution of income). To Boer (2003), sustainability labeling is similar to quality assurance in the marketplace, as it reveals differences between more sustainable and less sustainable practices. It is not just a message about a product or service, but a claim stating that it has particular properties, and this is the goal of a label.

There are multiple stakeholders with interest in sustainability labeling. For industry, labeling products or services is a way to improve its competitive position in the market. For consumers, a label is a distinctive symbol revealing differences between more or less sustainable practices. For policymakers, it is a tool to address the economic interest of consumers (correction of asymmetric information), or to achieve broader sustainability objectives. For non-governmental organizations, creating a sustainability label could be a way to pressure the industry or consumers to make progress towards sustainability.

We can establish two main types of labels (Wiel and McMahon, 2005): endorsement labels and comparative labels. Endorsement labels are essentially "seals of approval" given according to specified criteria. An endorsement label could be specifically conceived for energy efficiency (e.g. US Energy Star) to provide accurate information to end users to make an informed choice and to select more energy efficient products (Saidi et al., 2011) or for environmental friendliness (e.g. the European Union Eco-Label) (Harrington and Damnics, 2004) to provide critical quality assurance information on environmental impacts of the products (Bratt et al., 2011), endorsing products that have low impact on a wide range of environment factors. Comparative labels, as the European Union Energy Label, allow consumers to compare performance among similar products using either discrete categories of performance or a continuous scale. Both endorsement and comparative labels can coexist, and can be mandatory or voluntary. Several labeling programs examples (e.g. air conditioners; fans; heat pumps) can be found around the world (Harrington and Damnics, 2004).

Labels can help organizations to better understand and improve the sustainability of their products or services. However, the authors could not find in the literature a label or tool addressing the Data Center environmental sustainability in more than one dimension.

10.3 Data Center Metrics

The objective of building a framework to assess the environmental performance of DCs led the authors to perform a literature review to compile the most used metrics in this context. These are presented in Table 10.1.

The Green Grid defines several metrics to evaluate DCs. The Power Usage Effectiveness (PUE) and the Data Center Infrastructure Efficiency (DCiE) metrics address the energy efficiency of the DC infrastructure (Green Grid, 2007); the Carbon Usage Effectiveness (CUE) (Green Grid, 2010a) addresses the carbon emissions associated with the DC operation (in terms of CO_2-equivalent emissions); the Water Usage Effectiveness (WUE) (Green Grid, 2011) addresses the water usage in DCs, including the water used for humidification and water evaporated

Table 10.1 Data center metrics

Metric	Definition
Power Usage Effectiveness (PUE)	$PUE = \frac{\text{Total facility power}}{\text{IT equipment power}}$
Data Center Infrastructure Efficiency (DCiE)	$DCiE = \frac{1}{PUE} \times 100$
Carbon Usage Effectiveness (CUE)	$CUE = \frac{CO_2 \text{ emitted } (kgCO_2eq)}{\text{Unit of energy (kWh)}} \times PUE$
Water Usage Effectiveness (WUE)	$WUE = \frac{\text{Annual site water usage}}{\text{IT equipment energy}}$
Energy Reuse Effectiveness (ERE)	$ERE = (1 - \frac{\text{Reuse energy}}{\text{Total energy}}) \times PUE$
Compute Power Efficiency (CPE)	$CPE = \frac{\text{IT equipment utilization}}{PUE}$
Power Overhead Multiplier (SI-POM)	$SI\text{-}POM = \frac{\text{DC power consumption at the utility meter}}{\text{Total hardware power consumption at the plug for all IT}}$
Hardware Power Overhead Multiplier (H-POM)	$H\text{-}POM = \frac{\text{AC hardware load at the plug}}{\text{DC hardware compute load}}$
Deployed Hardware Utilization Ratio (DH-UR)	$DH\text{-}UR = \frac{\text{No. of servers running live applications}}{\text{Total no. of servers actually deployed}}$
Corporate Average Data Center Efficiency (CADE)	Facility efficiency × IT asset efficiency

Where:

Facility energy efficiency (%) = IT load/total power consumed by the DC
Facility utilization (%) = Actual IT load (servers, storage, network equipment) used/facility Capacity
IT utilization (%) = Average CPU utilization
IT energy efficiency (%) = CPU loading/Total CPU power
Facility efficiency = Facility energy efficiency (%) × Facility utilization (%)
IT asset efficiency = IT utilization (%) × IT energy efficiency (%)

on-site for energy production or cooling of the DC and its support systems. The Green Grid developed also the Energy Reuse Effectiveness (ERE) (Green Grid, 2010b) metric, to measure the benefit of reusing the energy produced in the DC on other external infrastructures, and the Compute Power Efficiency (CPE) metric (Green Grid, 2008a), which seeks to quantify the overall efficiency of a DC taking into account the fact that not all electrical power delivered to the IT equipment is transformed by that equipment into a useful work product.

The Uptime Institute (Stanley et al., 2007) defined other metrics. The Site Infrastructure Power Overhead Multiplier (SI-POM), similar to the PUE metric, indicates how much of the DCs site power is consumed in overhead instead of being used by the IT equipment. The IT Hardware Power Overhead Multiplier (H-POM) addresses the IT equipment efficiency, by evaluating how much of the power input in the hardware is wasted in power supply conversion losses or diverted to internal fans,

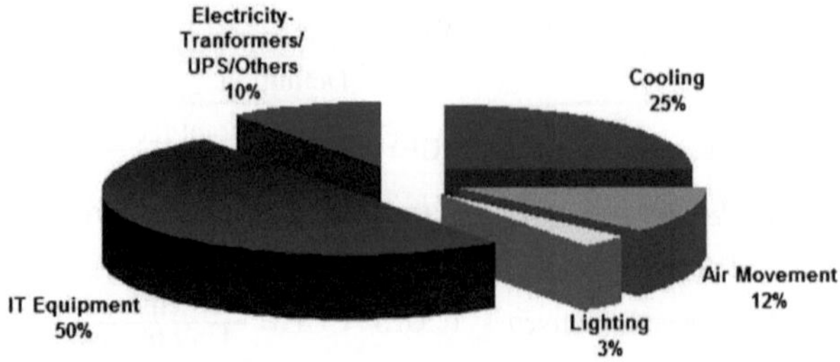

Fig. 10.1 Energy usage in a data center (Emerson, 2007)

rather than in useful computing components. The Deployed Hardware Utilization Ratio (DH-UR) indicates the fraction of the deployed IT equipment in the DC that is not running any application or handling data. Finally, the Corporate Average Data Center Efficiency (CADE) metric, defined together by the Uptime Institute and McKinsey (Kapan et al., 2008), addresses both the physical infrastructure and the IT systems.

Other examples of DC metrics can be found on the Uptime Institute (2012) or in the Green Grid (2012) organizations. All these metrics are ratios that can be used to assess the efficiency of a DC. However it seems that no attempt has been done to develop an integrated indicator or a label. And despite the diversity of the existing metrics, the PUE has been used worldwide by the industry as a tool for measuring and benchmarking DCs energy efficiency. In fact, the European Union, the United States of America and Japan established in February 2010 an agreement to use the PUE as the metric guide for DCs energy efficiency (Energy Star, 2011).

The use of PUE only for benchmarking purposes must be, however, carefully analyzed, since we need to understand the conditions of the DC infrastructure. First, the operation constraints such as the redundancy level of a DC can influence the PUE, as the use of more levels of standby electrical infrastructure to reduce downtime may introduce additional power losses. Furthermore, PUE does not account for the environmental conditions of the DC site, which can influence the energy efficiency of the facility due to the needs of the cooling systems, which are responsible for the consumption of a considerable amount of energy (around 37 %, according to Emerson 2007 in Fig. 10.1). In particular, depending on the geographic location of the DCs, the potential to use free cooling solutions (air-side economizer system) can vary and influence directly the amount of energy that can be saved by using cold outside air to directly or indirectly cool the computer room, avoiding the use of the chillers as cooling systems. We propose therefore a new metric that copes with this issue.

10.4 A New Metric: TRUE

As mentioned in the previous section, PUE has been adopted as the metric guide to evaluate DCs efficiency. However, the use of the PUE metric in this study raised some concerns among the analysts and participating DC specialists as they concluded that it does not necessarily foster energy efficiency practices. The following example demonstrates this.

Consider two DCs at two different locations with the same systems (IT; power distribution, generators, UPS, etc.) but with different cooling systems. Let us suppose that one of the DCs is located in a warmer climate, but they have the same PUE. This means that their cooling infrastructures (all else being equal) are using the same amounts of energy, which means that under the PUE metric, they could be considered equally efficient. However, it is easier for a DC located in a very cold climate (e.g., in the Arctic region) to profit from free cooling than for a DC located in a warmer climate such as Portugal. Thus, the DC located in the colder region is not taking advantage of the local conditions and it is not being as energy efficient as it could be.

The problem owners were not considering the possibility of building a DC in the Arctic. The problem owners do need that some of their employees live near the DC and that other personnel, including clients of the DC, can easily visit the DC for maintenance or other operations. The public image of the telecommunications company might also be at stake if it opted to build its flagship DC in another country. The problem owners main concern is that the DC is as energy efficient as it could be. Thus, benchmarking based on the PUE metric may not be totally fair.

The PUE metric does to some extent penalize DCs in countries with warmer climates. If the climate is taken into account, we could consider that the DC located in the colder climate is less efficient, since it is not able to profit from a better free cooling potential in order to use less energy for the cooling infrastructure. It is therefore necessary to develop another metric that will encourage a DC to profit as much as possible from the free cooling potential of the region it is located at.

We developed a metric called Temperature of the Region Usage Effectiveness (TRUE), to take into account the efficient use of the air free cooling potential—and corresponding impact on energy use in a DC location. As discussed, the cooling system represents more than one third of the energy consumption but the type of system and its efficiency depends on the location temperature conditions. The TRUE metric is thus a correction factor to the PUE metric that tries to incorporate the temperature conditions impact on efficiency, using a correction factor which describes the number of hours per year at which the temperature of the region where the DC is located has an average value that allows to use free cooling systems.

Free cooling can be used only in climate zones where the outside air temperature and humidity conditions are appropriate. For the ASHRAE (American Society of Heating, Refrigerating and Air Conditioning Engineers) (2008) and the European Commission (2010), DCs should be designed to operate at "inlet" (supply air) temperatures between 18 °C and 27 °C, to maximize energy efficiency. Following these recommendations and considering that for "inlet" temperatures up to 25 °C the server fans will already run at high speed and consume more energy (ASHRAE, 2008; Sartor and Greenberg, 2008; Bean, 2011), and that the usual temperature gains when using free cooling technology are 4 °C (Dunnavant, 2011), we established 21 °C as the top limit for the outside air temperature to allow the use of free cooling.

We did not set any limit for humidity levels because depending of the free cooling technology (direct or indirect) this constraint can be easily managed.

The TRUE metric is defined as follows. Let us first note that PUE (Table 10.1) can be rewritten as:

$$PUE = \frac{\text{Cooling System Power+IT Eq.Power+Lighting Power+Other(e.g. UPS)}}{\text{IT Equipment Power}}. \quad (10.1)$$

Thus, we define TRUE as:

$$TRUE = \frac{\text{IT Eq.Power+Lighting Power+Other(e.g.UPS)}}{\text{IT Equipment Power}} + C_f \times \frac{\text{Cooling System Power}}{\text{IT Equipment Power}}, \quad (10.2)$$

where:

$$C_f = \frac{1}{8{,}760} \sum_{t=-\infty}^{21} n_t. \quad (10.3)$$

Here, C_f is the Correction Factor, n_t is the annual number of hours per year with average temperature t and 8,760 is the total number of hours per year.

The success of PUE is mainly due to two reasons: it is easy to understand and it does not require complex mathematical formulas to be applied. With the aim to maintain a straightforward and easy way to calculate the metric, we defined the simplified TRUE metric as follows:

$$TRUE' = 1 + C_f \times (PUE - 1) \quad (10.4)$$

In this case, the correction factor is also affecting the entire electric infrastructure system of the DC (e.g. lighting, that could represent 3 % of the energy consumption in the DC), even though its performance is not influenced by the outdoor temperature conditions. All the calculations reported in this article are based on this simplified version of TRUE.

In Fig. 10.2 we can see the impact of the climate region around the world on the TRUE metric. For instance, a DC in Lisbon with a PUE of 1.25 has better TRUE (1.193) than one DC with a PUE of 1.25 in London (TRUE = 1.24). This means that a DC in London that has the same IT infrastructure than one in Lisbon and has the same PUE is not really taking full advantage of its location in terms of free cooling potential.

This metric could be a stimulus for the organizations to pursue the effective use of the natural resources to maximize the operational efficiency and reduce the impact on the environment and resources, i.e., an enabler for the development of more sustainable DCs. However, it still does not take into account other issues, such as carbon emissions associated with the electricity consumption or the use of water. Thus, the analysis of DCs sustainability and efficiency should take into consideration other metrics.

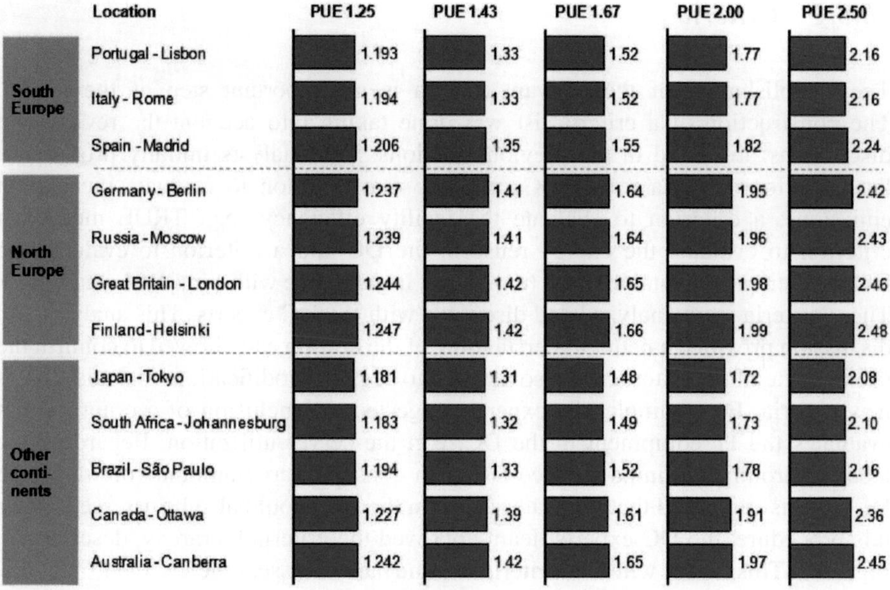

Fig. 10.2 TRUE metric for temperatures below 21 °C—cities around the world

10.5 A Framework to Assess the Data Center Environmental Performance

In the previous sections we reviewed the most common metrics to assess DC efficiency and introduced a new metric that considers the temperature of the region where the DC is located. The discussion about this new metric led us to conclude that the assessment methodology should be designed in a way that fosters DC planners to be as efficient as possible given the conditions of the DC's environment. Metrics can help organizations to better understand and improve the sustainability of their DCs, as well as, to help the decision makers in the deployment of new DC. It is important for the organizations to continue improving the effective use of resources to maximize operational efficiency and reduce the impact on resources and environment.

This section presents a tool to help DC managers to assess the environmental sustainability performance of their DC, using MCDA. This tool was developed by taking into account the DCs experts point of view. These experts (a team of three) possess a large experience in running DC facilities and were also able to represent the points of view of the telecommunications company.

10.5.1 Criteria

The establishment of the relevant criteria is an important step of the model. The construction of a criteria list was done taking into account the review and discussions presented in the previous sections. The analysts initially proposed a list with four criteria to the DCs experts: one criterion to evaluate the carbon emissions, a criterion to evaluate the facility efficiency (e.g. TRUE metric), a criterion to evaluate the energy reuse in the DC and a criterion to evaluate the DC local environmental impacts (e.g. noise, interference with protected areas, etc.). These criteria were analyzed and discussed with the DC experts. This analysis and discussion provided a better understanding of the criteria and allowed to confirm the use of some of the criteria and also allowed to suggest modifications and addition of new criteria. For example, the experts suggested the inclusion of a criterion that evaluates the IT equipment in the DC, e.g. the server utilization. Regarding the local environmental impact, since DCs can consume large amounts of water, the DC experts suggested that the water usage in the DC should also be assessed. After this procedure, the DC experts' team approved the criteria hierarchy, described in Fig. 10.3. This model with five criteria was the basis to assess the DC environmental sustainability.

10.5.2 Criteria Evaluation

The criteria to assess (and encourage) the DC environmental sustainability performance are from different nature and both qualitative and quantitative data are used. This diversity led to the use of different types of scales for the different criteria. The criteria assessment was done by the analysts in collaboration with the DCs experts.

1. *CEF (Carbon Emission Factor)*: DCs can be large consumers of electricity, and depending on the electricity energy resource they can be responsible for large amounts of carbon emissions. CEF represents the carbon emissions per kWh consumed by the DC, evaluated in $kgCO_2eq/kWh$. Its evaluation can range

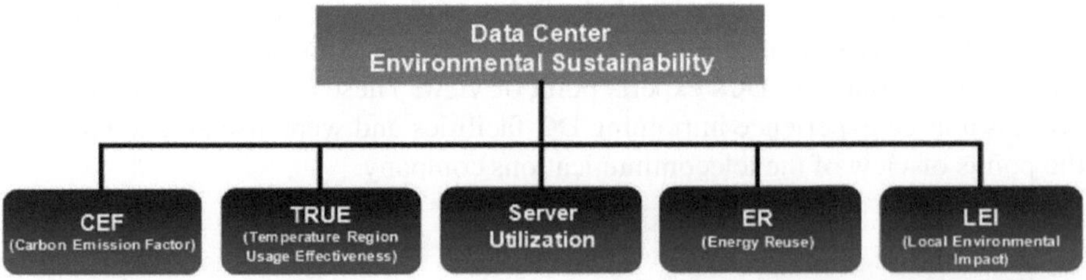

Fig. 10.3 Main criteria to assess the data center environmental sustainability class performance

from 0 (e.g. use of only renewable energy resources) to infinity, where 0 is the best score.

2. *TRUE (Temperature of the Region Usage Effectiveness)*: The TRUE metric described in Sect. 10.4, measures the DC support infrastructure energy efficiency taking into account the temperature in the area of its location. Its evaluation results from applying the metric, and can range from 1 to infinity (1 is the best score).
3. *Server Utilization*: This criterion addresses the efficiency of the IT systems. Server Utilization can include multiple systems (Central processing unit (CPU), memory, disk, network). According with the DCs experts, this depends on the intended use of the utilization data and the sophistication of the management infrastructure and applications. The experts evaluate this criterion by considering the CPU average utilization in percentage that can range from 0 % to 100 % (the best score).
4. *ER (Energy Reuse)*: This criterion measures the percentage of the thermal energy generated by the DC (e.g. heat released by the IT equipment) that is being reused in other parts of the facility (e.g. dehumidification) or in other nearby external facilities (e.g. greenhouses). Its evaluation can range from 0 % to 100 % (the best score).
5. *LEI (Local Environmental Impact)*: The aim of this criterion is to assess the local environmental impact of the DC on a qualitative scale. This criterion considers three different sub-criteria: Water Usage (WU), Interference with Protect Areas (IPA) and Local Impact Pollution (LIP), described as follows:

   (a) *Water Usage (WU)*: the DCs can be very large consumers of water. For example, a 1 MW DC operating with water-cooled chillers and cooling towers can consume up to 68,000 L/day to dissipate the heat generated by the IT equipment (Sharma et al., 2009). However, in general it is very difficult to establish water consumption values, so the WU evaluation was done by the perception of the DCs experts regarding the impact of the use of water. They attributed levels between 1 and 5 (the best score), as described in Table 10.2. In the evaluation, the use of water is related to the site location also, as in some areas the use of water, even if large, may not be an important constraint (e.g. if the DC is located on the shore of a large river).

   (b) *Local Impact Pollution (LIP)*: to evaluate this criterion we initially proposed a list of three criteria to the DCs experts: noise (no noise impact or no impact on neighbors) and water pollution (no pollution of surface/underground natural watercourse and no water temperature increase) and ozone depletion (no degradation of the ozone layer caused by the use of cooling refrigerants or fire extinguishing gases). DCs experts suggested the inclusion of a new criterion that evaluates recycling programs, namely plans for IT equipment and packaging material recycling. Therefore, there was agreement on four sub-criteria for LIP evaluation: noise, water pollution, ozone depletion and recycling programs. Five LIP levels

Table 10.2 WU, LIP and IPA qualitative scale description

Water usage (WU)		Local impact pollution (LIP)		Interference with protect areas (IPA)	
Description	Level	Description	Level	Description	Level
No water consumption or use	5	Local impacts are negligible	5	Outside reserves and natural parks	5
Consumption of alternative water sources, i.e. non potable water (e.g. rainwater harvesting)	4	Non-negligible but small impact in one of the aspects	4		
Use of water (from a lake, river, ocean) but without/negligible water consumption	3	Non-negligible but small impact in two of the aspects	3		
Consumption from large potential water sources (lakes, rivers, reservoirs, aquifers), i.e. ample water availability, without putting in risk the water resource over time	2	An obvious impact in one or more aspects or a small impact in three or more aspects	2		
Consumption of potable water, public water supply, water-scarce region	1	An excessive impact (given existing norms) in one or more aspects	1	Inside reserves and natural parks	1

were defined (see Table 10.2) according to fulfillment of the described criteria.

(c) *Interference with Protect Areas (IPA)*: reserves and natural parks should be avoided to locate the DC. Therefore DCs located in protected regions, e.g. natural parks, should be classified as having a poor environmental concern. If located outside protected areas, they should be classified as having an excellent environmental concern, as depicted in Table 10.2.

As mentioned the aim of LEI is to assess the local environmental impact of the DC. The authors and the DCs experts agreed that a good performance in one criterion should not be allowed to compensate a poor performance in another criterion. After discussing this issue, it was defined that the LEI performance is set by the minimum value performance of the WU, IPA and LIP criteria. For example, if a DC has a 4 in the WU, a 5 in the IPA and a 2 in the LIP criterion, the LEI performance will be 2.

10.5.3 The ELECTRE TRI Method as the Evaluation Tool

The ELECTRE TRI method (Yu, 1992) belongs to the ELECTRE family of multi-criteria methods developed by Bernard Roy and his co-workers (Roy, 1991, 1996). This method was specifically designed for multi-criteria sorting problems, i.e., to assign each alternative to one of a set of predefined ordered categories according to a set of evaluation criteria. ELECTRE TRI allows an evaluation in absolute terms, i.e., alternatives are not compared against each other but to predefined norms. The result of such analysis is a partition of the set of alternatives into several categories defined with respect to these norms (called by Roy 1996 the sorting problem formulation). Another feature is that ELECTRE models allow incomparability. Incomparability occurs when some alternatives are so different that a direct comparison is hard to justify. ELECTRE TRI does not require converting the performance criteria into a uniform scale range, as it allows the inclusion of criteria measured in different units and even measured in qualitative terms.

To establish the environmental sustainability framework to assess the DC performance several categories are pre-established to represent different environmental sustainability levels. Considering the nature of the criteria (different value scales and different value domains, qualitative data), the preference for a non-compensatory method and the possibility of using a method where the assignments of alternatives are independent from each other, are the main reasons for choosing ELECTRE TRI.

The pessimistic variant of ELECTRE TRI method was applied using the decision support software called IRIS (Dias and Mousseau, 2003a,b), which was designed to address the problem of assigning a set of alternatives to predefined ordered categories, according to their evaluations (performances) at multiple criteria. For details about the ELECTRE TRI variant used see Dias and Mousseau (2003a,b) and Dias et al. (2002).

10.5.4 Model Parameters

The use of ELECTRE TRI requires to set the parameters that represent the preferences of the decision makers. In this case, this was done by the authors in collaboration with the DCs experts. The group agreed that for the study's purposes it would suffice to sort the possible alternatives (Data Centers) into five categories (levels) of environmental sustainability performance, in accordance to what it is used in energy efficiency comparative labels, according to the Table 10.3 (columns 1 and 2).

In addition to the categories definition, it is also necessary to define the category boundaries or limit profiles that represent the limit between two consecutive categories. The definition of the limit profiles was performed taking into account some support information.

Table 10.3 Environmental sustainability categories: levels and boundaries

Environmental sustainability categories	Description	CEF (kgCO_2eq/kWh) (Carbon Emission Factor)	TRUE (Temperature Region Usage Effectiveness)	Server utilization (%)	ER (%) (Energy Reuse)	LEI (Local Environmental Impact)
A+	DC with an excellent performance	≤ 0.18	≤ 1.25	≥ 50	≥ 45	5
A	DC with a very good performance	]0.18, 0.36]	]1.25, 1.43]	[35, 50[	[30, 45[	4
B	DC with a good performance	]0.36, 0.57]	]1.43, 1.67]	[20, 35[	[15, 30[	3
C	DC with a reasonable performance	]0.57, 0.79]	]1.67, 2]	[5, 20[	[0.1, 15[	2
D	DC with a poor performance	> 0.79	> 2	< 5	< 0.1	1

For the CEF criterion profiles, it was considered the carbon emissions produced by the different power generation technologies (EDP, 2012). The values have the following rationale: according to EDP (2012) the CEF is 0.36 $kgCO_2eq/kWh$ if electricity is generated by natural gas power plants, 0.78 $kgCO_2eq/kWh$ in case electricity is generated by fuel power plants, and 0.9 $kgCO_2eq/kWh$ in case electricity is generated by coal power plants. Illustrative scenarios were used to assess the category limits presented in Column 3 of Table 10.3: category A could represent a DC powered with a mix of 50 % of natural gas power plants and 50 % of nuclear and renewable plants; category B could represent a mix of natural gas (50 %) and fuel power plants (50 %); and category C could represent a mix of natural gas power plants (25 %), fuel power plants (50 %) and coal plants (25 %).

The TRUE criterion considers the classification proposed by the Green Grid (2008b) for the PUE metric, see column 4 of Table 10.3. For the Server Utilization criterion, the DC experts established the limits presented in column 5 of Table 10.3. For the ER criterion, the experts defined values described in column 6 of Table 10.3. For the LEI it was straightforward to establish the values presented in column 7 of Table 10.3.

Based on the criteria description presented, the categories range values for each criterion were established. Five categories were considered, where D (category C1) is the worst, described as Poor performance, and A+ (category C5) is the best category described as Excellent performance, see Fig. 10.4. Table 10.4 indicates the values considered for the reference profiles, e.g. for indicator ER we have boundaries $b_1 = 0.1$, $b_2 = 15$, $b_3 = 30$, $b_4 = 45$.

The next step consisted in defining the indifference ($q_j(b_h)$) and preference ($p_j(b_h)$) threshold values for each category, as well as, the veto ($v_j(b_h)$) thresholds. The thresholds $q_j(b_h)$ and $p_j(b_h)$ intervene when checking if a criterion agrees with an outranking. A criterion agrees fully with the outranking if the alternative is not worse than the profile by a difference larger than $q_j(b_h)$; it agrees partially if this difference lies between $q_j(b_h)$ and $p_j(b_h)$; it does not agree if the difference is $p_j(b_h)$ or higher. In the latter case, it will oppose a partial veto if the difference lies between $p_j(b_h)$ and $v_j(b_h)$, or it will oppose a complete veto if the difference is $v_j(b_h)$ or higher. A veto means that the outranking is not accepted even if all other criteria support it. Table 10.4 displays the IRIS thresholds that must be entered; these thresholds can be set independently for each category.

It was established that an alternative (a DC) should be at least C (Reasonable performance) in all criteria in order to be classified as A (Very good performance), by setting a veto threshold for all criteria to reach category C4 ($g_j(b_3) - v_j(b_3) =$

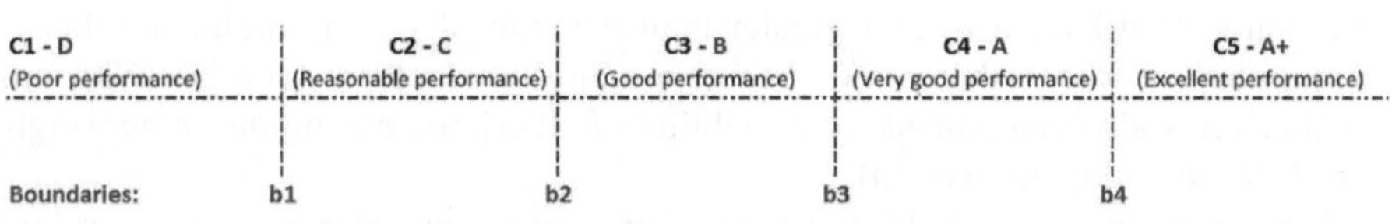

Fig. 10.4 Relation between the environmental sustainability categories and the category profiles

Table 10.4 Category boundaries and preference discrimination thresholds

	CEF	TRUE	Server utilization	ER	LEI
Parameter	k_1	k_2	k_3	k_4	k_5
$g(b_1)$	0.79	2	5	0.1	2
q_1	0.0395	0.100	0.25	0	0
p_1	0.11	0.165	2.5	0	0
v_1	–	–	–	–	–
$g(b_2)$	0.57	1.67	20	15	3
q_2	0.0285	0.084	1	0.75	0
p_2	0.11	0.165	7.5	7.45	0
v_2	–	–	–	–	–
$g(b_3)$	0.36	1.43	35	30	4
q_3	0.018	0.072	1.75	1.5	0
p_3	0.105	0.12	7.5	7.5	0
v_3	0.43	0.57	30	29.9	2
$g(b_4)$	0.18	1.25	50	45	5
q_4	0.009	0.063	2.5	2.25	0
p_4	0.09	0.09	7.5	7.5	0
v_4	0.39	0.42	30	30	2
Preference direction	Min	Min	Max	Max	Max

$g_j(b_1)$). Similarly, it was also established that an alternative should be at least B (Good performance) in all criteria in order to be classified as A+ (Excellent performance), by setting a veto threshold for all criteria to reach category C4 ($g_j(b_4) - v_j(b_4) = g_j(b_2)$).

Regarding the indifference and preference thresholds, it was defined for all criteria (except the LEI) an indifference threshold of 5 % of the boundary value, and a preference threshold equal to half of the difference between adjacent categories.

Concerning the criteria weights, there was a consensus that the evaluation methodology should allow some freedom for each DC to place more weight on the aspects in which it is stronger, in the spirit of Data Envelopment Analysis (see Madlener et al. 2009 for another example in which this type of approach was used). This avoids the controversial question of defining a precise weight for each criterion and allows DCs with different profiles to attain the best categories. Let us note however that the veto thresholds prevent a DC with a major weakness from reaching the top categories. It was defined that each criterion weight can vary from 10 % to 30 %. As we have five criteria, with this range of values it is guaranteed that each criterion cannot have a weight greater than the sum of the minimum weights of the number of criteria that can constitute a majority (i.e. three criteria). With this approach it is also guaranteed the possibility of all criteria having the same weight (i.e. 20 %, the midpoint weight).

For the majority threshold, the value 0.66 was set in order to ensure a robust majority. This means that in order to say that an alternative is at least as good as a category limit profile, at least 66 % of the criteria must be in concordance with this affirmation (after the weighting).

10.6 Application of the Model

In this section the proposed framework has been applied to a case study, the new DC that is going to be built in Portugal by Portugal Telecom (PT). The application of the model aimed at evaluating some different variants for the DC, as well as to assess the impact of the TRUE metric by considering (hypothetical) scenarios in which the same DC would be built in other locations.

PT announced on February 4th 2011 the construction of a new DC in Covilhã region (a region in the center of Portugal). According to the company this new DC will be the largest ever built in Portugal, with an initial investment cost between 30 and 50 million Euro, and its main focus is to provide cloud computing services. It will have an area over 45,000 m^2 and a power capacity of 40 MW. This critical facility will be a worldwide energy efficiency reference, with an expected PUE of 1.15, and it will use free cooling solutions and renewable energies (the DC will be powered by its own wind farm of 28 turbines in a total of 56 MW installed capacity Camara Municipal da Covilhã 2011; Portugal Telecom 2011).

The hypothetic scenarios refer to Data Centers located in areas with different environmental conditions, such as free cooling potential or electricity carbon emission factor, represented by the countries UK, Poland and France.

10.6.1 Criteria Evaluation

1. *CEF (Carbon Emission Factor)*: We used the CEF published by the International Energy Agency (2010). For Portugal, the CEF was 0.395 $kgCO_2eq/kWh$. For the other countries considered in the comparative analysis we considered for United Kingdom that the CEF was 0.497 $kgCO_2eq/kWh$, for Poland it was 0.660 $kgCO_2eq/kWh$ and for France it was 0.086 $kgCO_2eq/kWh$. Taking into account that the DC in Covilhã will have a wind farm that will be able to produce 23 %[1] of the annual electricity needs, the CEF can be reduced to 0.305 $kgCO_2eq/kWh$.

[1] Considering the following assumption: 56 MW of installed capacity; 2,000 h/year equivalent production at maximum capacity; 40 MW average consumption power directly consumed by the DC; the excess energy from the wind park is considered to be injected into the national grid and thus is not considered.

2. *TRUE (Temperature of the Region Usage Effectiveness)*: this value was obtained taking into account a PUE of 1.15 and the temperature data of the different regions.
3. *Server Utilization*: according to PT, the main focus of this DC is to provide cloud computing services. Since the average CPU utilization in typical DCs is around 20 % according to Meisner et al. (2009), VanGeet (2011), and considering the PT orientation, we established an average CPU utilization of 40 %.
4. *ER (Energy Reuse)*: according to PT's plans, we assumed that the DC will reuse at least 5 % of the waste heat from the IT equipment in heating the offices spaces.
5. *LEI (Local Environmental Impact)*: it was established the WU of 3, since the water consumption will be negligible and will be pumped from river Zezere (a large river in the neighborhood). The DC is located outside of reserves and natural parks and it was considered that local impact pollution of the DC will be negligible.

10.6.2 Data Center Environmental Sustainability Performance Results

This section presents the IRIS results for the DC sustainability. We considered seven different scenarios described as follows:

1. DC_PT_Covilha: the base scenario, taking into account the criteria values described in the previous section.
2. DC_PT_Covilha S1: similar to the first scenario, but without the existence of the wind farm, i.e., with an increase of the CEF.
3. DC_PT_Covilha S2: similar to the first scenario, but without the existence of the wind farm and without reuse of the energy from the IT equipment.
4. DC_PT_Covilha S3: similar to the first scenario, but without the existence of the wind farm, without reuse of the energy from the IT equipment and a decrease of the WU to 1 (i.e. LEI criterion performance equal to 1).
5. DC_PT_London: similar to the second scenario (no wind farm), but in this case the location of the DC is in London, with different temperature conditions, as well as, with different CEF.
6. DC_PT_Krakow: similar approach to the DC_PT_London scenario.
7. DC_PT_Paris: similar approach to the DC_PT_London scenario.

The criteria values used in this section for the several scenarios are summarized in Table 10.5. Although the scenarios have the same Server Utilization, this indicator contributes to define the category assignment.

The results from IRIS are depicted in Fig. 10.5a. Since the weights are allowed to vary, there are cases in which IRIS yields more than one category: in these cases the category would depend on more precise choices for the weight values. In a "benefit of doubt" (Cherchye et al., 2007) or benevolent perspective in the spirit of Data

Table 10.5 Criteria values for Portugal telecom data

Data center	Location	Free cooling (h/year)	PUE	CEF ($kgCO_2eq/kWh$)	TRUE	Server utiliz. (%)	Energy reuse (%)	LEI
				$g_1(.)$	$g_2(.)$	$g_3(.)$	$g_4(.)$	$g_5(.)$
DC_PT_Covilha	Covilhã, Portugal	7,400	1.15	0.305	1.127	40	5	3
DC_PT_CovilhaS1	Covilhã, Portugal	7,400	1.15	0.395	1.127	40	5	3
DC_PT_CovilhaS2	Covilhã, Portugal	7,400	1.15	0.395	1.127	40	0	3
DC_PT_CovilhaS3	Covilhã, Portugal	7,400	1.15	0.395	1.127	40	0	1
DC_PT_London	London, UK	8,551	1.15	0.497	1.146	40	5	3
DC_PT_Krakow	Krakow, Poland	8,308	1.15	0.66	1.142	40	5	3
DC_PT_Paris	Paris, France	8,178	1.15	0.086	1.140	40	5	3

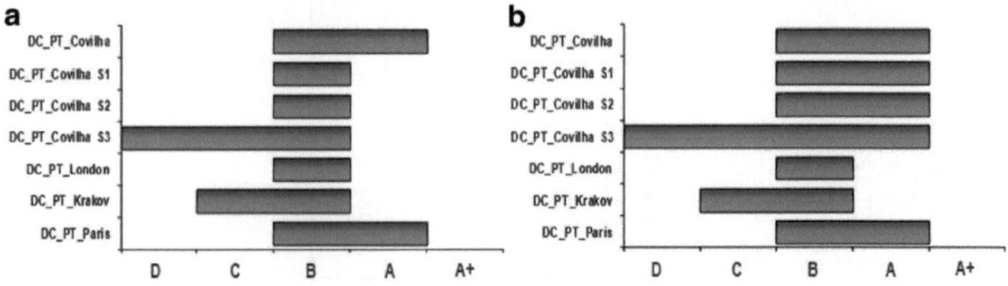

Fig. 10.5 IRIS results for the PT DC. (**a**) IRIS parameters set with the established Veto conditions. (**b**) IRIS parameters set without veto conditions for category A, only the defined veto conditions for A+

Envelopment Analysis (Madlener et al., 2009), each DC would be attributed the highest category allowed by the results.

In this case, the PT DC can reach an A level or label, but not an A+. If the wind farm is not considered or if the DC does not reuse the heat from the IT equipment, the maximum performance is reduced to B. A decrease in the WU criterion may bring the classification down to D, but only if the water criterion is considered to be more important than the others.

If a similar DC was installed in London, the potential performance (B level) would be similar to the DC installed in Covilha (without the wind farm), but if it was installed in Krakow the potential performance would vary between B and C. This is due to the high level of carbon emissions of Poland (0.660 $kgCO_2eq/kWh$). However, and due to the low carbon emissions of France, if a similar DC was installed for example in Paris, then CEF would decrease considerably and the DC could reach an A label (even without a wind farm).

In Fig. 10.5b we change the veto conditions previously established by eliminating veto condition for category A and maintaining the condition of veto for the category A+. In this scenario the range of the results can be improved, in particular the alternatives in Portugal could all reach category A. Is also interesting to highlight that London and Krakow alternatives did not change their potential.

It is also interesting to notice that no DC can ever achieve an A+ label, even if we reduce requirements of the veto conditions for this level [e.g. from all alternatives must be at least B (Good performance) to C (Reasonable performance)]. In this particular case, there are no differences in the results when compared to the ones obtained in Fig. 10.5b.

Comparing the two sets of results, it was felt that it would be important to take into account the veto thresholds under this type of evaluation, so that the best categories will not be achieved by DCs that are weak in one of the criteria. Another aspect that was considered noteworthy is that this tool encourages PT to build a wind farm in order to improve the CEF. Alternatively, if this were a possibility, PT could buy cleaner energy in terms of CO_2 from a different grid, since this allows the Paris scenario to attain category A.

Given this set of results, the DC experts and the authors felt the tool was able to produce results that were aligned with the preferences they constructed during the discussions they had for this study.

10.7 Conclusions

We present a tool to assess the DC environmental sustainability performance using MCDA, pursuing the idea that the environmental categorization of DCs should encompass multiple dimensions. The tool is based on the outranking method ELECTRE TRI due to the nature of the data (quantitative, qualitative, different scales), the desire to avoid compensation among criteria, as well as the recognition that it would be misleading to provide results other than a separation of the alternatives among categories. With the involvement of a team of DC experts, five categories (levels) of environmental sustainability performance were defined, where D is the least preferred (worst category) and A+ is the most preferred (best category), as well as, the several criteria to evaluate the sustainability.

In total, 5 criteria were established, one of which was a new metric reflecting the concerns of the problem owners about the PUE metric. The DC should be encouraged to profit as much as possible from free cooling but taking into account what the location of the DC allows, bearing in mind that there are practical barriers to choosing an ideally cold place. DCs in warmer climates have less opportunity to improve energy efficiency by drawing upon external air than DCs in cooler climates. The TRUE does not contradict that the regions with a higher free cooling potential are potentially better areas to install a DC; it indicates that certain installations, even if they have a higher PUE, can in fact be more efficient if they take more advantage of the climate. A smaller differential between PUE and TRUE leads to a lower potential investment needed to achieve the same levels of efficiency. The TRUE provides a way to improve DCs benchmarking but mostly to determine opportunities to consider the use of alternative cooling strategies. It can help DC decision making processes related to site planning.

The tool was applied to several scenarios for the new PT data center, some of which were only hypothetical. Due to the lack of information some assumptions were taken. Considering identical DCs, more effort is required from a DC located in Portugal to reach A+ level than from one in France, due to the low carbon emission factor in this country. The results show that the tool helps to visualize the state of the DC quickly, and the flexibility in assigning weights according to the type/use of the DC provides additional value to this tool, because the decisions makers (e.g. DC managers) have the ability to control the importance of each variable in the problem resolution in a transparent way, giving them the sense of ownership of the evaluation model.

Using these results, further analysis with more accurate data can be conducted to identify possibly improvements in the DCs. Indeed, one of the intangible results of this study was the knowledge transfer from the analysts to the company about the use of MCDA. The company wishes to use this approach for helping making architecture choices, in the planning phase for a new data center or a major renovation of an existing infrastructure. It can also help DC decision making processes related to Data Center site selection, e.g. looking for sites where the use of the heat recovered from the DC can be increased (e.g. swimming pools; greenhouses, etc.). In general terms, we can also conclude that this study helped the company to better define the vision or goals of what should be a sustainable DC, identifying what must be assessed to evaluate a DC's environmental sustainability performance.

Although this study did not aim at selecting the best design for the new DC, it had an indirect impact through the learning process that occurred. The classification of the alternatives, although imprecise, helped the telecommunications company to understand which options would be important to obtain a good classification if this type of labeling was adopted by the industry. Initially the company was mostly concerned about PUE, but this study contributed to the emergence of other concerns leading it to pursue good performances in other criteria. For instance, the company is now considering architecture choices in order to improve the heat recovering from the DC. These efforts will be pursued even though this would not be sufficient to achieve the best category (despite the company's effort to have a strategy focused on energy efficiency and an IT resources optimization via increasing the virtualization and server utilization levels).

With more sustainable DCs, organizations can better manage the increased computing needs, i.e. they can meet the future business needs and at the same time lower their energy costs. The future poses serious challenges for DC managers, such as energy cost, water cost, carbon taxation, and general environmental concerns. Organizations that proactively focus on these issues will manage better the DC total cost of ownership and consequently reduce their business risks.

Our contribution with this tool is not to provide an absolute measure of the DC environmental sustainability, but instead to provide a way according to the specificities of each DC to assess their potential sustainability by addressing several issues and help organizations to determine strategies to improve DCs operational efficiency and reduce the impact on resources and environment. If new indicators appear that the DCs managers would like to analyze and incorporate, with this flexible tool we can easily adopt them if necessary.

The authors hope that this framework may help the industry to have a common understanding of Data Center Sustainability measurement, and can generate dialogue to improve it. An industry consensus about a sustainability assessment tool for DCs such as the one proposed here can yield several benefits: it can foster the promotion of sustainable DCs industry internationally, it can facilitate transparency and accountability by organizations and provides to stakeholders a universally applicable and comparable framework, from which one can understand disclosed information. Finally, such a framework could be a tool to communicate with customers, to help them to buy services from more eco-friendly Data Centers.

Acknowledgements This work has partially been supported by MIT Portugal Program, Sustainable Energy Systems and the Programa de Financiamento Plurianual de Unidades de I&D from the Portuguese Science and Technology Foundation (FCT) to the research activities of the associated laboratory LARSYS and INESC Coimbra (UID/MULTI/00308/2013).

References

ASHRAE. (2008). *ASHRAE environmental guidelines for datacom equipment*. Technical Report.

Bean, D. M. J. H. (2011). *Energy impact of increased server inlet temperature*. Technical Report. DELL and APC.

Boer, J. (2003). Sustainability labelling schemes: The logic of their claims and their functions for stakeholders. *Business Strategy and the Environment, 12*, 254–264.

Böhringer, C., & Jochem, P. (2007). Measuring the immeasurable - a survey of sustainability indices. *Ecological Economics, 63*, 1–8.

Bratt, C., Hallstedt, S., Robèrt, K. -H., Broman, G., & Oldmark, J. (2011). Assessment of eco-labelling criteria development from a strategic sustainability perspective. *Journal of Cleaner Production, 19*(14), 1631–1638.

Camara Municipal da Covilhã. (2011). http://www.cm-covilha.pt/simples/?f=5443. 11.12.11.

Cherchye, L., Moesen, W., Rogge, N., & Puyenbroeck, T. (2007). An introduction to benefit of the doubt composite indicators. *Social Indicators Research, 82*, 111–145.

Ciegis, R., Ramanauskiene, J., & Startiene, G. (2009). Theoretical reasoning of the use of indicators and indices for sustainable development assessment. *Inzinerine Ekonomika-Engineering Economics Journal, 3*, 33–40.

Dias, L., & Mousseau, V. (2003a). IRIS: A DSS for multiple criteria sorting problems. *Journal of Multi-Criteria Decision Analysis, 12*, 285–298.

Dias, L., & Mousseau, V. (2003b). *IRIS - interactive robustness analysis and paramenters inference for multi criteria sorting problems (version 2.0)*. Technical Report. User Manual, INESC Coimbra - Institute of Systems Engineering and Computers.

Dias, L., Mousseau, V., Figueira, J., & Clímaco, J. (2002). An aggregation/disaggregation approach to obtain robust conclusions with ELECTRE TRI. *European Journal of Operational Research, 138*(2), 332–348.

Dunnavant, K. (2011). Indirect air-side economizer cycle data center heat rejection. *ASHRAE Journal, 53*, 44–54.

EDP. (2012). http://www.edp.pt/pt/aedp/unidadesdenegocio/producaodeelectricidade/Pages/CompromissoAmbiental.aspx.

Elghali, L., Clift, R., Sinclair, P., Panoutsou, C., & Bauen, A. (2007). Developing a sustainability framework for the assessment of bioenergy systems. *Energy Policy, 35*, 6075–6083.

Emerson. (2007). *Five strategies for cutting data center energy costs through enhanced cooling efficiency*. Technical Report. Columbus, OH: Emerson Network Power.

Energy Star. (2011). Harmonizing global metrics for data center energy efficiency. http://www.energystar.gov/index.cfm?c=prod_development.server_efficiency. 04.01.11.

EPA. (2007). *Report to Congress on server and data center energy efficiency*. Technical Report. US Environmental Protection Agency Public Law 109-431.

European Commission. (2008). *Code of conduct on data centres energy efficiency version 1.0*. Technical Report.

European Commission. (2010). *2010 best practices for the EU code of conduct on data centers*. Technical Report. Version 2.0.

Gasparatos, A., El-Haram, M., & Horner, M. (2008). A critical review of reductionist approaches for assessing the progress towards sustainability. *Environmental Impact Assessment Review, 28*, 286–311.

Ghosh, S., Vale, R., & Vale, B. (2006). Indications from sustainability indicator. *Journal of Urban Design, 11*(2), 263–275.
Global Ecolabelling Network (GEN). (2004). *Introduction to ecolabelling*. Technical Report.
Green Grid, T. (2007). *The Green Grid data center power efficiency metrics: PUE and DCiE*. Technical Report. Beaverton, OR: The Green Grid.
Green Grid, T. (2008a). *A framework for data center energy productivity*. Technical Report.
Green Grid, T. (2008b). *Rating data centers for energy efficiency*. Technical Report.
Green Grid, T. (2010a). *Carbon usage effectiveness (CUE): A Green Grid data center sustainability metric*. Technical Report. Beaverton, OR: The Green Grid.
Green Grid, T. (2010b). *ERE: A metric for measuring the benefit of reuse energy form a data center*. Technical Report. Beaverton, OR: The Green Grid.
Green Grid, T. (2011). *Water usage effectiveness (WUE): A Green Grid data center sustainability metric*. Technical Report. Beaverton, OR: The Green Grid.
Green Grid, T. (2012). http://www.thegreengrid.org/. 17.01.12.
Harrington, L., & Damnics, M. (2004). *Energy labelling and standards programs throughout the world*, 2nd ed. Technical Report. The National Appliance and Equipment Energy Efficiency Committee - Australia.
International Energy Agency. (2010). *CO2 emissions from fuel combustion - highlights*. Technical Report. I E A Statistics.
Kapan, J., Forrest, W., & Kindler, N. (2008). *Revolutionizing data center energy efficiency*. Technical Report. McKinsey&Company.
Lindblom, C. (1990). *Inquiry and change. The troubled attempt to understand and shape society*. New Haven, CT: Yale University Press.
Madlener, R., Antunes, C. H., & Dias, L. C. (2009). Assessing the performance of biogas plants with multi-criteria and data envelopment analysis. *European Journal of Operational Research, 197*(3), 1084 – 1094.
Meisner, D., Gold, B., & Wenisch, T. (2009). Powernap: Eliminating server idle power. In *Architectural Support for Programming Languages and Operating Systems - ASPLOS'09*. New York: ACM.
Munda, G. (2005). Measuring sustainability: A multi-criterion framework. *Environment, Development and Sustainability, 7*, 117–134.
Munda, G., & Nardo, M. (2005). Constructing consistent composite indicators: The issue of weights. Technical Report. European Commission – Joint Research Center, Office for Official Publications of the European Communities, Luxembourg [EUR 21834 EN].
Munda, G., & Saisana, M. (2011). Methodological considerations on regional sustainability assessment based on multicriteria and sensitivity analysis. *Regional Studies, 45*(2), 261–276.
Pezzoli, K. (1997). Sustainable development: A transdisciplinary overview of literature. *Journal of Environmental Planning and Management, 40*, 549–574.
Portugal Telecom. (2011). http://www.telecom.pt/InternetResource/PTSite/PT/Canais/Media/press_releases/Portugal+Telecom+implementa+um+dos+maiores+Data+Center+da+Europa+na+Covilha.htm.
Roy, B. (1991). The outranking approach and the foundations of ELECTRE methods. *Theory and Decision, 31*, 49–73.
Roy, B. (1996). *Multicriteria methodology for decision aiding*. Dordrecht: Kluwer Academic.
Saidi, M., Sajadi, B., & Sayyadi, P. (2011). Energy consumption criteria and labeling program of wet cooling towers in Iran. *Energy and Buildings, 43*, 2712–2717.
Sartor, D., & Greenberg, S. (2008). *Save energy now in federal data centers*. Technical Report. Lawrence Berkeley National Laboratory.
Sharma, R., Shah, A., Bash, C., Christian, T., & Patel, C. (2009). Water efficiency management in datacenters: Metrics and methodology. In *Sustainable Systems and Technology, ISSST '09*. Phoenix, AZ: IEEE International. Print ISBN: 978-1-4244-4324-6. DOI: 10.1109/ISSST.2009.5156773.
Stanley, J., Brill, K., & Koomey, J. (2007). *Four metrics define data center "greenness"*. Technical Report. Uptime Institute.

Uptime Institute. (2012). http://uptimeinstitute.org/. 17.01.12.

Valentin, A., & Spangenberg, J. (2000). A guide to community sustainability indicators. *Environmental Impact Assessment Review, 20*, 381–392.

VanGeet, O. (2011). *Best practices guide for energy-efficient data center design*. Technical Report. U.S Department of Energy.

Wiel, S., & McMahon, J. (2005). *Energy efficiency labels and standards: A guidance for appliance, equipment and lighting*, 2nd ed. Technical Report. Washington: Collaborative Labeling and Appliance Standards Program (CLASP).

World Commission on Environment and Development (WCED). (1987). *Our common future*. Oxford: Oxford University Press.

Yu, W. (1992). ELECTRE TRI: Aspects méthodologiques et manuel d'utilisation. Technical Report. Document du LAMSADE. Paris:Université de Paris–Dauphine, Working Paper No. 74.

Editors' Comments on "Multi-Criteria Assessment of Data Centers' Environmental Sustainability"

The **main contribution** of Chapter "Multi-Criteria Assessment of Data Centers' Environmental Sustainability", by M.T. Covas, C.A. Silva and L.C. Dias is the assessment of the environmental sustainability performance of Data Centers (DC) that underlie most common Internet and telecommunications services available today, proposing a framework for that purpose. This case study is hence related to the energy/environment field, a most popular application area for MCDA and a topic that is well covered in this book (see Chaps. 8–14).

The **main objective** of this application is to help a telecommunications company assess the sustainability of its planned new data center (different variants) in a simple way that could be used as a standard by this industry. **Other objectives** are to propose: (1) a general framework for assessing the environmental sustainability of data centers, and (2) a new metric for measuring the efficiency of such data centers.

The **client** of the decision aid application was a telecommunications operator in Portugal. Three experts from the client organization participated in model building (definition of criteria, judging the adequacy of the method, setting preference-related parameters). The three authors of the chapter acted as analysts. Their role was, in particular, to suggest the MCDA methodology and to provide guidance in its use. Experts and analysts collaborated for elaborating a DC assessment framework. One of the authors is a member of the client organization and therefore also acted as a Data Center expert.

Identified **phases** in the process concern: (1) building a set of criteria, (2) elaborating the scales of the criteria and determining how to asses the DC's on these scales, and (3) selecting a model for aggregating the evaluations of the DC's on the criteria and determining the model's parameters. The **duration** of the process was about 3 months, from after the new Data Center location was announced. Hence the main goal was not to assess this particular DC. The planned DC was more used as a reference alternative; the **set of alternatives** used to elaborate or validate the evaluation model were either variants pertaining to choices the client has to make (building a wind farm, reuse of heat) or fictitious (assessing the results if the Data Center was built elsewhere).

The decision **problem statement** in this case study was ordinal sorting, interpreted as an evaluation method. Based on a literature review on Data Center metrics and incorporating other sustainability concerns of the client the analysts propose five **performance criteria**, four quantitative and one qualitative. No uncertainties were considered for the alternatives' performances and the model parameters, except the criteria weights. Each weight is allowed to vary in an interval. The **handling of uncertainties** shares characteristics with Data Envelopment Analysis: the evaluation methodology allows, for each DC, to put more weight on the criteria on which it is stronger.

Due to, first, the type of result sought (a level on an ordered scale), secondly, the wish to avoid making explicit trade-offs between the criteria, and, thirdly, the wish to deny that a very good performance on one criterion can compensate a poor performance on another criterion (by using veto) a valued outranking **model of preference aggregation** is chosen. And, considering chosen the decision problem statement (ordinal sorting) the ELECTRE TRI method with five sorting categories is applied in this case study. The **parameter setting**, i.e., the category limiting profiles, the discrimination thresholds for indifference, preference and veto situations, as well as criteria weights constraints were directly given by the client. Divergence among actors is addressed by agreement between the experts, and a **sensitivity analysis** of the effect of considering veto situations or not is performed.

Among the **tangible results** and artifacts achieved in this case study are:

1. The criticism of the PUE metric, generally agreed upon as the measure of DC's energy efficiency, and the proposal of an alternative metric (TRUE) taking into account the temperature of the region, which has an impact on the efficiency of the cooling system,
2. The proposal of a set of criteria and the implementation of an evaluation model, including category definitions, for assessing the sustainability of data centers,
3. An agreement about the parameter values and weight constraints to be used,
4. A tool for disclosing Data Centers' sustainability performance, suitable for organizations of any size or type, and from any geographic region, and allowing comparability between Data Centers that tackle sustainability with different strategies,
5. A (imprecise) classification of the alternatives in ordered categories (more precisely, the alternatives are assigned to an interval of possible categories).

As **intangible results** we may list in this study, first, a knowledge transfer about MCDA from the analysts to the client organization. The decision aid also helped the company to better define the vision or goals what should be a sustainable DC. Establishing the framework helped to identify what must be assessed to evaluate a DC sustainability performance. The Client wishes to use this approach for helping making architecture choices, in the planning phase for a new data center or a major renovation of an existing building. It can also help Data Center decision making processes related to site selection, e.g. looking for sites where can be increased the use of the heat recovered from the Data Center (e.g. swimming pools; greenhouses, etc.). This framework may furthermore help the industry to have a common understanding of Data Center Sustainability measurement, and can generate dialogue to improve it. It can also foster the promotion of sustainable Data Centers industry internationally. It facilitates transparency and accountability by organizations and provides to stakeholders a universally applicable and comparable framework, from which they can understand disclosed information. Finally, this environmental sustainability assessment framework could be a tool to communicate with customers, to help them to buy services from more eco-friendly Data Centers.

The **impact of the decision aiding** is to help the client to understand which options would be important to obtain a good classification if this type of categorization is adopted by the industry. It helped the client to extend its concerns beyond the PUE metric, in order to be as good as possible in terms of the other criteria. The tool helped to make architecture choices, in the planning phase for a new data center in order to improve the heat recovering from the DC. Despite the company's effort to have a strategy focused on energy efficiency (an excellent PUE performance) and an IT resources optimization (e.g. increasing the virtualization and server utilization levels), this would not be sufficient to achieve the best category.

Chapter 11
The Cost of a Nuclear-Fuel Repository: A Criterion Valuation by Means of Fuzzy Logic

Pierre Louis Kunsch and Mathieu Vander Straeten

Abstract In this chapter a fuzzy methodology is presented for the valuation of criteria for which the level of available knowledge is limited or inexistent. Due to this lack of knowledge, statistical techniques and data mining are only useable in a limited way. The criteria valuations rely on the elicitation of experts' knowledge. For coping with criteria valuations in a similar uncertainty context a three-tiered fuzzy inference system has been developed. Details on the fuzzy rules and implications in this fuzzy inference system are provided. This approach has been used in practice for the cost and financial analysis of radioactive-waste-management projects. The case study on a nuclear-fuel repository is a fictive simulation of an actual project assessment. It is presented along with the Fuzzy Inference System software, called FIS Tool, which has been developed for the analysis. It is thought that the approach can be extended to different criteria valuations, particularly in the field of environmental management.

11.1 Introduction

In many decision problems giving a numerical value to a criterion (criterion valuation) is a difficult task. Many examples may be found in environmental management: frequently the valuations do not rest on firm statistical grounds; no, or limited data are available from measurements or past experience. For example, little is known on the exact lifetime of off-shore wind turbines, or their possible impact on the bird—or fish—populations; the precise impact of bio-fuels on the environment and the food crisis; the precise marginal costs of CO_2 abatement, etc. Because available data are scarce, at least at the onset of a technology, or a new practice, it may be difficult, or impossible to elaborate probability distributions of values on the basis of the sole Bayesian techniques. By the same token, because of accumulating experience and learning feedbacks, uncertain criteria valuations get

P.L. Kunsch (✉) • M. Vander Straeten
CoDE Department, Université libre de Bruxelles (ULB), CP 165/15, 50 Avenue F.D. Roosevelt, 1050 Brussels, Belgium
e-mail: pikunsch@ulb.ac.be

R. Bisdorff et al. (eds.), *Evaluation and Decision Models with Multiple Criteria*, International Handbooks on Information Systems,
DOI 10.1007/978-3-662-46816-6_11

more refined in the course of time: in principle uncertainties are decreasing as time goes by, providing more knowledge and experience to decision-makers. In many cases expert opinions may be the sole, or at least the most important, source of data. It is where fuzzy logic may assist for criterion valuations: this technique is well adapted because experts' opinions are not only quantitative assessments, but also largely semantic statements.

In the present chapter this situation of diverging opinions and limited information about true values of a criterion will be assumed. A methodology to be discussed below has been developed by the first author in several papers (Kunsch et al., 1999; Kunsch and Fortemps, 2002; Kunsch, 2003; Fiordaliso and Kunsch, 2005) to cope with the criteria valuation problem in such uncertainty contexts, often characterized by long-term horizons.

To illustrate the proposed approach, uncertainties on costs issues will be in the foreground. Criteria of a different nature may possibly be considered in further developments of the methodology, however. A simplified case study addresses the future-cost valuation of a geological repository for disposing of spent-nuclear fuel. This is a good case for illustrating the approach: today no or limited real-scale experience is available for such repositories, but this situation is expected to be dynamically changing during the foreseen extended time horizon. A convenient instrument is needed allowing periodic re-assessments of the project costs, as more and more knowledge on the design and realisation aspects becomes available. In this repository planning the impact of cost uncertainties have important intergenerational financial impacts. It is why financial provisions have to be set aside today in order to approach a fair share of the financial burden between present and future consumers.

Section 11.2 introduces the case of the nuclear-fuel repository, and presents the requirements of the cost-valuation approach. Two types of uncertainties are distinguished in order to elaborate technology and project contingency factors. In Sect. 11.3 the fuzzy methodology is presented to address the two types of uncertainty by means of fuzzy logic. The software tool developed to collect and aggregate expert opinions is described from Fiordaliso and Kunsch (2005). The elicitation procedure and the results of the case study are presented in Sect. 11.4. Section 11.5 contains a discussion on the gathered practical experience using the software developed for the analysis. Section 11.6 provides conclusions and prospects for future work on more general tools for criteria valuations.

11.2 Case Study: Budgeting a Nuclear-Fuel Repository

11.2.1 Technical Background

The methodology to be described here has been used by the first author in the framework of his activities as economist and financial expert with the Belgian agency for radioactive waste management ONDRAF/NIRAS. The elaboration of the approach is the result of a scientific collaboration with Faculté Polytechnique de Mons, Mons, Belgium. It started from the first author's own ideas for translating into fuzzy logic the recommendations of the nuclear industry about addressing budget uncertainties in nuclear projects (Biewald and Bernow, 1991). This work was originally rather exploratory, and no guidelines or specifications were issued from waste-management authorities for initiating it. Later on the methodology has been used in practice for economic and financial valuations of radioactive-waste management projects (Kunsch et al., 1999; Kunsch, 2003, 2008), though for a limited number of projects in Belgium and abroad. Dedicated software has been developed for an easier data acquisition. It is of course hoped for that in the long term the proposed approach for preparing budgets for waste-management projects can still develop, and be more widely used by responsible agencies, the potential '*clients*'.

A simplified case on the budgeting of a spent-nuclear-fuel repository is presented here. Due to the lack of space only basic information on spent-fuel management is provided. Details about the nuclear-fuel repository concepts in different countries can be found in the sites of national agencies responsible for radioactive-waste management, like www.nirond.be (Belgium), www.andra.fr (France), www.skb.se (Sweden), www.nda.gov.uk (UK), etc. General economic and financial information on radioactive-waste management is provided in European Commission (1996) and Kunsch (2008).

The spent-fuel repository is excavated into a geological host rock, e.g., clay, granite, salt dome, or others, several hundreds meters below the surface. Extensive R&D programmes have to be performed by the responsible national waste-management agency, prior to building and operating the repository. The objective of the R&D programmes is to validate the repository design, and to verify the ability of the host rock in containing the radioactivity during very long-time periods. Today such studies are underway in most countries with a nuclear-power-plant programme. No such facility is yet operational, so that the availability of design data is limited, or nonexistent. Roughly speaking, the repository is built and operated in several phases, according to the following general scenario:

- After a suitable area has been selected: access roads and other surface infrastructures are made available, facilities and offices are built on the surface;
- An on-site conditioning facility for spent fuel is built. In this facility spent fuel elements are placed into special sheaths (canisters) after a sufficiently long cooling-off period in dry storage;
- Access wells and ramps are built down to an underground service area to which the conditioned spent fuel elements are brought prior to disposal;
- A underground network of access and specially designed disposal galleries is built for disposing of the conditioned spent-fuel elements;
- Fuel elements are disposed of in the disposal galleries. The galleries are progressively backfilled with bentonite as the disposal operations proceeds;
- After all spent-fuel elements have been disposed of the underground structures, wells and ramps are all closed-down and backfilled;

- Finally all surface infrastructures are decommissioned and demolished.

The spent-fuel repository constitutes a very large and complex project for which many tasks have to be investigated, and carefully designed. The status of knowledge of such projects and their technology is still at a relatively early stage in most countries. In the complete estimation of a realisation budget for the repository 30–50 tasks are identified (see ONDRAF/NIRAS 2001). Table 11.1 presents a simplified list of 19 main tasks, only provided for illustrative purposes in normalised cost units, but with no direct reference to any existing or planned repository.

11.2.2 Principles of the Valuation

Regarding the preparation of a budget for the repository it is assumed that engineers establish a basic '*nominal*' value of the different task costs at the time of the valuation. Remember here that the resulting budget and schedule should be periodically revisited, as time proceeds, and more experience and knowledge are gained.

Project managers agree to regard the cost values as lower, '*optimistic*' assessments from the engineers, and not accounting for contingencies. The purpose of experts' interrogation is to provide information on the amount of uncertainty. The deliverable from the experts will thus be contingency factors to be applied to the basic cost estimates for all tasks, in order to obtain a good confidence of a realistic global cost estimate, given the present level of knowledge.

All data listed in Table 11.1 are only indicative, because of the required confidentiality on real waste-management projects in Belgium and abroad. The basic costs without contingencies per task are normalised to a total of 1,000. The mean (expected) durations of tasks are given in the last but one column on the right; the last column on the right indicates the correlation groups between some task costs, as explained in Sect. 11.2.4.

Additional schedule data may be added for PERT-network evaluations, including a precedence table for tasks, and optimistic and pessimistic duration values attached to each task. The PERT network will be briefly discussed in Sect. 11.2.5.

The Electric Power Research Institute (EPRI) has elaborated recommendations on how to valuate contingency factors for nuclear projects (Biewald and Bernow, 1991). These recommendations appear in the form of rules, which can be easily interpreted as fuzzy rules, as will be later explained in Sect. 11.3. These recommendations are assumed to be applicable to the repository project. EPRI considers that the basic costs estimates must take into account two types of contingencies factors:

1. Technology factors related to the knowledge level of the technology;
2. Project factors related to the knowledge level of the project.

Table 11.1 Basic data for the repository realisation stages and tasks

Stages	Task ID	Tasks	C	D	G
Preliminary	1	Siting	50	6	1
Preliminary	2	Qualification of site	99	7	2
Surface operations	3	Construction of surface infrastructure	68	7	3
Surface operations	4	Local infrastructure of the disposal site	2	2	4
Mining	5	Construction of wells and ramps	37	4	5
Mining	6	Construction of the disposal zone	106	6	5
Mining	7	Construction of the underground service zone	65	3	5
Surface operations	8	Preparation time before underground operations	0	2	
Fuel conditioning on site	9	Construction of the fuel conditioning facility	148	3	6
Fuel conditioning on site	10	Procurement of conditioning canisters	215	18	7
Fuel conditioning on site	11	Conditioning fuel in the canisters	17	18	8
Disposal operations	12	Disposing of spent fuel elements	109	15	9
Disposal operations	13	Preparation time before backfilling operations	0	2	
Closure and backfilling of disposal zone	14	Backfilling of the disposal galleries with bentonite	68	15	10
Closure and backfilling	15	C&B of the underground service zone	3	2	11
Closure and backfilling	16	C&B of wells and ramps	9	2	11
Closure and backfilling	17	C&B of the conditioning facility	3	3	12
Closure and backfilling	18	Preparation time before decommissioning surface facilities	0	2	
Closure and backfilling	19	Decommissioning of the surface facilities	1	3	13

Details are set out in the text
(C) Normalized costs
(D) Mean durations (Years)
(G) Correlation groups

11.2.3 Technology Factors

The technology contingency factor, called T-factor, used in the EPRI recommendations is a multiplicative factor larger than one, but with no defined upper limit, to be applied to the nominal task cost, i.e., the basic task cost provided in the first place by engineers without contingency. For this particular design item of the repository, at the time of the assessment, the T-factor relates to the limited technological '*Level of Knowledge*'. The latter is represented by the T-*level*, for realising any task with a technological content. The T-level is measured on a [0, 1] scale:

T-level = 0 corresponds to a fully new technological task for which no prior knowledge is available;
T-level = 1 corresponds to a fully known task from the technological point of view, for which many prior data are available.

The definition of a T-factor (noted T_f in the following text) in function of the T-level, i.e., in this case the availability of data, is given by EPRI in the form of recommendations for picking up a value in a range of values representing $(T_f - 1)$ (%). Five '*fuzzy*'-like T-levels T_1, T_2, T_3, T_4, T_5 are defined by EPRI:

$$\begin{array}{ll} T_1 \text{ no or limited data} & T_f - 1 : 40\,\% \text{ to unlimited} \\ T_2 \text{ bench scale data} & T_f - 1 : 30\,\% \text{ to } 70\,\% \\ T_3 \text{ small pilot data plant} & T_f - 1 : 20\,\% \text{ to } 35\,\% \\ T_4 \text{ full scale module data} & T_f - 1 : 5\,\% \text{ to } 20\,\% \\ T_5 \text{ operational data} & T_f - 1 : 1\,\% \text{ to } 10\,\% \end{array} \tag{11.1}$$

Note that overlaps do exist for different T-levels, and that no upper bound for $(T_f - 1)$ is prescribed for level $T1$.

Assume for example that the level of technology is T-level = T_2 (bench scale data) for some cost item with nominal cost C_0, and that experts agree to choose $T_f - 1 = 40\,\%$ for this level of technology maturity, so that, if C_T is the cost including technological contingencies:

$$T_f = 140\,\% \; ; \; C_T = C_0 \times 1.4 \tag{11.2}$$

The definition of T_f requires two decisions for each task valuation, i.e., first to select a T-level in a first step, and then to choose on this basis in a second step a $(T_f - 1)$ value in the corresponding range (11.1). These decisions are made by experts on the technological design of the considered task, e.g., the construction of disposal galleries for the spent-fuel repository. The T_f on a particular task cost is a multiplicative contingency factor increasing the nominal task costs:

$$C_T(task) = C_0(task) \cdot T_f(task) \tag{11.3}$$

Technological uncertainties are genuine; it means that their nature is not probabilistic like in the case of risk assessments for which probability distributions can be provided. The global cost C_T for the whole project is thus simply the addition of the partial task costs in (11.3):

$$C_T(project) = \sum_{\text{all tasks}} C_T(task) \tag{11.4}$$

The resulting global-cost assessment of the project is conservative, because no uncertainty compensation will appear in (11.4), like it would in the combination of partially uncorrelated random variables. Implicitly full correlation is thus assumed between all tasks costs affected by technological uncertainties, though correlation has only a meaning in risk theory (see below in Sect. 11.2.4 on project factors for a discussion on cost correlations). The global T-factor for the repository project is then given by:

$$T_f(project) = \frac{C_T(project)}{\sum_{\text{all tasks}} C_0(task)} \tag{11.5}$$

11.2.4 Project Factors

Some unforeseen events may occur during the construction work, or the operations of the repository, like delays in procurement, excavating difficulties, bad weather or working conditions, etc., causing delays and cost increases. The task contingency factors—also called '*P-factors*'—called in the following text P_f's—take these unforeseen events into account for all tasks, even those with no marked technological content. A procedure comparable to the one exposed in Sect. 11.2.3 for T_f's will be followed for P_f's, but with some differences. This occurs in the way project contingencies—sometimes called project uncertainties by abuse of language—are to be combined, up to the global project level. P_f's are risk factors, by contrast with T_f's representing genuine uncertainties, see Sect. 11.2.3. Some further probabilistic treatment is thus needed.

The procedure for determining P_f's begins, as for T_f's, with the EPRI recommendations (Biewald and Bernow, 1991). The P_f of some specific task has to do with the more or less advanced project '*Level of Knowledge*', as seen from the perspective of drafting detailed plans, defining time schedules, etc. The degree of project advancement of some task representing the project is called accordingly P-level, and it is measured on a $[0, 1]$ scale:

P-level $= 0$ corresponds to a completely preliminary task or project estimate, something like an exploratory artist view, i.e., a non-existent project '*Level of Knowledge*' from the perspective of the drafting office;

P-level = 1 corresponds to a completely finalised task or project planning, i.e., a finalised project '*Level of Knowledge*' available to the drafting office.

The definition of some P_f in function of the P-level is given by EPRI in the form of recommendations for picking up a value in a range of values representing $(P_f - 1)$ (%). Four echelons of the P-level P_1, P_2, P_3, P_4 are defined by EPRI:

$$\begin{array}{ll} P_1 \text{ Simplified estimates} & P_f - 1 : 30\,\% \text{ to } 50\,\% \\ P_2 \text{ Preliminary estimates} & P_f - 1 : 15\,\% \text{ to } 30\,\% \\ P_3 \text{ Detailed estimates} & P_f - 1 : 10\,\% \text{ to } 20\,\% \\ P_4 \text{ Finalised estimates} & P_f - 1 : 5\,\% \text{ to } 10\,\% \end{array} \quad (11.6)$$

Assume for example that the P-level of a specific task is estimated to be P_2 ('*Preliminary estimates*') with a cost including the corresponding technological T-factor to be $C_T(task)$ according to (11.3). Further assume that experts agree to choose from (11.6) for the P_2 echelon the value 27 %, so that $C_{PT}(task)$ is the cost of the task including both project and technological contingency factors:

$$C_{PT}(task) = C_T(task) \times 1.27 \quad (11.7)$$

In general the task cost, including both technology and project contingency factors, is calculated to be:

$$C_{PT}(task) = C_T(task) \cdot P_f(task) \quad (11.8)$$

Finally, all partial task costs including the individual T_f's and P_f's are combined to produce a global cost including the global technological and project contingency margins. But task costs including P_f's cannot be simply added in order to obtain the global maximum costs, like it is done in the case of T_f's in (11.4), because of the stochastic nature of unforeseen events assessed by the P_f's. Some task costs are correlated with respect to the P-factors, while some others are not. A simple addition of task P_f's would therefore be too conservative. Because of this situation, '*correlation groups*' are defined. As an example from the last column on the right in Table 11.1, a distinct correlation group (Group 5) comprises all underground mining tasks in the repository project; comparable difficulties and delays, causing cost increases, may indeed occur when digging shafts or tunnels in the host rock.

In general it will not be possible to give an accurate value to the correlation coefficient in a pair of cost items in some correlation group. To make things simpler and in the sense of conservatism, it has been assumed that all tasks within the same correlation group are fully correlated, i.e. the correlation matrix of tasks in the corresponding correlation group has coefficients all equal to one.

In practice, each task cost including technology and project contingency factors is handled as a stochastic variable within the interval:

$$\tilde{C}(task) \in \left[C_T(task); C_{PT}(task)\right] \quad (11.9)$$

where $C_T(task)$ includes the technological contingency factor T_f as given in Eq. (11.3); $C_{PT}(task)$ is given in (11.8). The range of uncertainty on the task cost $P_u(task)$ is thus given by:

$$P_u(task) = C_{PT}(task) - C_T(task) = C_T(task) \cdot \big(P_f(task) - 1\big) \tag{11.10}$$

It is reasonable to use a uniform probability distribution in this range. Given the correlation groups, and the uniform probability distribution of all task costs in (11.10), Monte-Carlo simulations are then performed for obtaining the global-cost probability distribution—with and without discounting. Simulation is quite time-consuming, however, and specialised software may be used. It is why using a global P-factor for the whole project makes the valuations handier, also for establishing a cost schedule for all tasks and globally (see Sect. 11.2.5).

In summary, a global P-factor is evaluated for the whole project, taking into account the existence of correlation groups; it is applied to all partial task costs. The average value $\mu(task)$ and the standard deviation $\sigma(task)$ of each uniformly distributed task cost including both T_f and P_f are immediately calculated from (11.10) as being:

$$\mu(task) = C_T(task) + \frac{P_u(task)}{2} \tag{11.11}$$

$$\sigma(task) = \frac{P_u(task)}{\sqrt{12}} = \frac{P_u(task)}{2\sqrt{3}} \tag{11.12}$$

The average value $\mu(g_i)$ and the standard deviation $\sigma(g_i)$ of the correlated tasks in group g_i are adding up, as full correlation within each group has been assumed:

$$\mu(g_i) = \sum_{tasks \in g_i} \mu(task) \tag{11.13}$$

$$\sigma(g_i) = \sum_{tasks \in g_i} \sigma(task) \tag{11.14}$$

The average global maximum cost M of the repository project is given by:

$$M(project) = \sum_{all g_i} \mu(gi) \tag{11.15}$$

Because by definition correlation groups are stochastically independent the standard deviations of the total costs of all tasks in the joined groups are adding according to the '*Square Root of the Sum of the Squares*' (SRSS) rule to give the global standard deviation of the repository project:

$$\Sigma(project) = \sigma\Big(\bigcup_{all g_i} g_i\Big) = \sqrt{\sum_{all g_i} \sigma^2(g_i)} \tag{11.16}$$

Considering the total uncertainty of the repository as being the upper limit of an equivalent rectangular distribution, one obtains for the maximum global cost of the repository project, including both technological and project contingencies:

$$C_{Max}(project) = M(project) + \sqrt{3}\Sigma(project) \tag{11.17}$$

This maximum cost value corresponds to a confidence level of about 96 % with respect to the global average value and the standard deviation in (11.15) and (11.16), in the approximation of a Gaussian shape for the probability distribution of the global cost. The global project P-factor $P_f(project)$ is then given by:

$$P_f(project) = \frac{M(project) + \sqrt{3}\Sigma(project)}{C_T(project)} \tag{11.18}$$

In this global approach for the repository-funding calculations, the task costs with both technology and contingency factors are given by the following expression:

$$C_{T,P}(task) = C_T(task) \cdot P_f(task) \tag{11.19}$$

The task costs are evenly distributed over the duration period for obtaining a cost schedule used for discounting. It has been verified that the resulting global, undiscounted or discounted, costs are close to the results obtained with Monte-Carlo simulations performed on the basis of (11.11), (11.12), and the correlation groups of tasks from Table 11.1. Those calculations have also shown that the assumption of a Gaussian probability distribution of the global costs of the repository project is generally acceptable.

11.2.5 Dynamic Aspects in PERT Network

Discounted costs are the basis for funding, i.e., financial means that must be set aside to cover as exactly as possible, and in due time, all the future repository costs. The choice of a discount rate is an important issue in the financial calculations, which will not be further discussed here (see Kunsch 2007; Kunsch et al. 2008). Uncertainties in the realisation schedule of the repository are another very important issue in calculating discounted costs. To account for such uncertainties resulting from schedule changes, a PERT network is used (Moder et al. 1983; Buckley et al. 2002, , Chap. 6), showing the successive tasks in the project, and the order in which they have to be completed. Within such networks the tasks durations are treated either as stochastic variables in stochastic PERT, or as fuzzy variables in fuzzy PERT (Lootsma 1989; Buckley et al. 2002, , Chap. 6). For each task three values represent respectively: the Optimistic (O), the Expected (likeliest) (E), and the pessimistic (P) assumptions, corresponding to respectively minimum, median and maximum task durations. The sensitivity of funding with changes in the realisation schedule is analysed as follows:

- In stochastic (classical) PERT task durations represented by Beta-PERT distributions match the three (O; E; P) durations; correlations between some task durations are used, when appropriate. By means of Monte Carlo simulations probability distributions of discounted costs are obtained, in order to determine the required repository funding at any given confidence level;
- In fuzzy PERT, used in the software to be introduced in Sect. 11.3.4, task durations are represented by triangular fuzzy *MF*'s from the three (O; E; P) durations, so that, for any given α-cut (Buckley et al., 2002), three cost schedules and the corresponding discounted costs are calculated.

Comparisons of both PERT versions show that fuzzy PERT gives rather conservative results regarding the project durations (Lootsma, 1989). For actual project management managers will generally prefer classical PERT, as being less conservative, and more familiar to them.

11.3 Aggregation of Expert Opinions with Fuzzy Logic

11.3.1 The Principles of Fuzzy Inference Systems (FIS) for the Analysis

Fuzzy logic, or fuzzy reasoning, sometimes called '*computing with words*' is close to the natural language. It is why it is well adapted for collecting and aggregating opinions. Also fuzzy logic operator and rules are able to approximate any real function, whatever its properties (non-linearity, discontinuity, etc.). This property of '*universal approximator*' is very useful in many problems, including engineering control (Passino and Yurkovich, 1997), and decision-making. As an example of the latter applications, Kunsch and Springael (2005, 2008), discuss the evolution of marginal CO_2 abatement cost and interest rates obtained from experts' panels for the purpose of elaborating carbon tax policies. The theoretical aspects of aggregating complex functions resulting from experts' elicitations will not be further discussed here. The important literature on fuzzy logic, and the way to use it in aggregating experts' opinions by means of statistical or fuzzy approaches (Meyer and Booker, 2001; Meyer et al., 2002; McCarthy, 2007), will not be reviewed either.

Basic knowledge of fuzzy techniques is assumed for applications in economics, engineering (Buckley et al., 2002), and decision-making (Bouyssou et al., 2006). Only main findings regarding the implementation of a Fuzzy Inference System (*FIS*) for the cost assessments of radioactive-waste management are summarised from previous publications (Kunsch et al., 1999; Kunsch and Fortemps, 2002; Kunsch, 2003; Fiordaliso and Kunsch, 2005).

With an eye on the repository case study in Sect. 11.2 the following criterion-valuation assumptions are made in the present section:

- Some criterion with a lot of uncertainties is to be evaluated today: the criterion valuation is assumed to change over time with gathering new information and knowledge;
- A long-term horizon has to be considered for the criterion evolution;
- At time of valuation limited information or data are available: experts' opinions are considered to compensate for lacking knowledge;
- The value of the criterion is directly linked to today's '*Level of Knowledge*', as measured by some '*Proxy*' variable. The word '*Proxy*' is commonly used in decision theory to name a factor standing as a measurable representative (proxy) for another not directly observable, and therefore not directly measurable variable. Here the '*Level of Knowledge*' is meant (Kunsch et al., 1999).

Consider next to the repository case study introduced in Sect. 11.2 a choice problem between several advanced energy systems. The criterion '*Investment cost*' of each technology is considered to be a very important, but uncertain one in the development stage. Moreover, its value over a long time horizon will be changing with learning effects, economies of scale, etc. Sparse or no statistical data from past full-scale implementation are available, so that decision-makers are still depending on experts' cost assessments. Each expert considers that uncertainties on the cost estimate are strongly linked to the present level of knowledge about each specific technology. A '*preliminary design*' will indeed induce a larger grade of cost uncertainty than a '*finalised design*'. To evaluate the level of knowledge experts consider that a useful '*Proxy*' would be the Research and Development (R&D) budget still needed to bring the present incomplete design to a finalised design. Therefore the valuation fits a three-tiered valuation scheme for each technology cost valuation with technological uncertainties:

$$\text{Proxy R\&D budget} \rightarrow \text{Level of technology knowledge} \rightarrow \text{Valuation of uncertain costs,} \tag{11.20}$$

and more generally:

$$\text{Proxy} \rightarrow \text{Level of knowledge} \rightarrow \text{Valuation with contingencies,} \tag{11.21}$$

This scheme may be used for any criterion in which contingencies are dynamically lifting thanks to gathered experience and knowledge. In particular it is applicable to the EPRI-recommendations (11.1) and (11.6) for nuclear projects.

The *FIS* over three steps for implementing this scheme is as follows:

1. In the first step, *FIS*(1), each expert (i) makes an unconditional fuzzy guess on the '*Proxy*', e.g. in the form of a fuzzy membership function $MF(i)$, like:

$$FIS(1): \text{IF '}Expert\text{' is } Expert(i) \text{ THEN '}Proxy\text{' is } MF(i) \tag{11.22}$$

The experts' guesses are aggregated by fuzzy inference in order to obtain an aggregated (crisp) proxy value, e.g., the R&D budget. This aggregation process takes into account a credibility factor attached to the opinion of each expert (see Sect. 11.3.2).

2. In the second step, *FIS*(2), the links between the '*Proxy*' and '*Level of Knowledge*' are given by conditional fuzzy rules, like:

$$FIS(2): \text{IF '}\mathit{Proxy}\text{' is '}\mathit{High}\text{' THEN '}\mathit{Level\ of\ Knowledge}\text{'is'}\mathit{Low}\text{'} \tag{11.23}$$

where '*High*' would represent an important R&D budget, and '*Low*' a simplified design in the energy-system example. Although the rules are the same for all experts, they must take into account the credibility factors attached to the experts' opinions (see Sect. 11.3.3).

3. In the final third step, *FIS*(3), the link between '*Level of Knowledge*' and '*Criterion Value*' is in turn given by a set of conditional fuzzy rules, like:

$$FIS(3): \text{IF '}\mathit{Level}\text{' is '}\mathit{Low}\text{' THEN '}\mathit{Criterion\ contingency\ factor}\text{'is'}\mathit{High}\text{'} \tag{11.24}$$

where the attribute '*Criterion contingency factor*' in the conclusion refers to the cost valuation in the practical cases discussed here.

In the most general case (11.21) the chain includes three $FIS(i)$, $i = 1, 2, 3$ for aggregating the experts' opinions to a final criterion assessment. Of course in some problems *FIS*(1) alone may be used, e.g., if the assessment of a '*Proxy*', like '*R&D budget*', is required as a stand-alone criterion; or the combined $\{FIS(1), FIS(2)\}$ may be sufficient to derive some criterion valuation from the '*Proxy*'. The $FIS(i)$ are the cornerstones of a general methodology for evaluating criteria on the basis of experts' opinions.

The repository case study in Sect. 11.2 includes all three $FIS(i)$, $i = 1, 2, 3$. This is shown in Fig. 11.1. The EPRI recommendations (11.1) and (11.6) are translating into fuzzy rules for deriving two contingency factors per task.

Table 11.2 summarises the characteristics of the three *FIS* in the software implementation that has been developed for assessing the cost of projects in radioactive-waste management. The methodological details are presented in the following sub-sections indicated in the first column. The choices mentioned in this table for particular rules, implications, and defuzzification techniques will be elaborated as we will proceed through the three *FIS* steps.

In the following of this section, the three *FIS* are illustrated by using the Fuzzy Toolbox of MATLAB® for evaluating the technological contingency factor in (11.1) for some task of the repository project presented in Sect. 11.2. Dedicated *FIS* software is presented in Sect. 11.3.5.

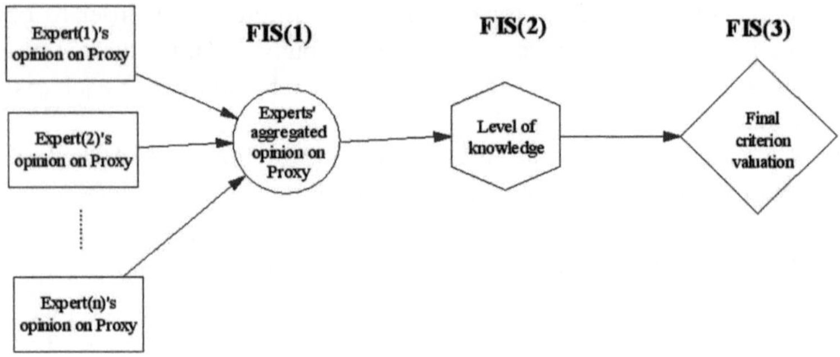

Fig. 11.1 The three-tiered *FIS* for the criteria valuation on the basis of a '*Proxy*' and the corresponding '*Level of Knowledge*'

Table 11.2 The characteristics of the three fuzzy inference systems to be discussed in Sects. 11.3.2–11.3.4

Fuzzy inference system	Links	Rules	Implication	Defuzzification technique
FIS(1) (11.22)	Expert-proxy	Unconditional for each expert	Kleene-Dienes (KD)	Max (min) of modes: whatever is most conservative
FIS(2) (11.23)	Proxy-status	Conditional	Mamdani	Center of Gravity (COG)
FIS(3) (11.24)	Status-final	Conditional	Progressive (Goguen)	Max (min) of modes: whatever is most conservative

11.3.2 Unconditional Proxy Valuation *FIS*(1)

Typical unconditional rules for *FIS*(1) are given in (11.22). These rules are unconditional by expert because there is no other input than the expert's identity. It will be assumed in the following that the R&D budget is chosen as a '*Proxy*' for the technology knowledge level in (11.1) for some task in the repository project. A credibility factor is given to each expert's opinion, as further explained in Sect. 11.4.1. Three experts' opinions are elicited. The first ranked opinion is rather reliable, so that it gets a credibility factor $u = 0.8$; the second ranked opinion gets the somewhat lower value $u = 0.75$; the third less credible opinion gets $u = 0.65$. Assume further that all experts agree on the same universe of discourse represented in relative units by the [0, 100] interval, and the use of five triangular membership functions (*MF*'s) [Very Low (*VL*), Low (*L*), Medium (*M*), High(*H*), Very High(*VH*)] evenly-distributed over this interval. The five *MF*'s represent the five echelons for the R&D budget proxy according to (11.1). Assume further that

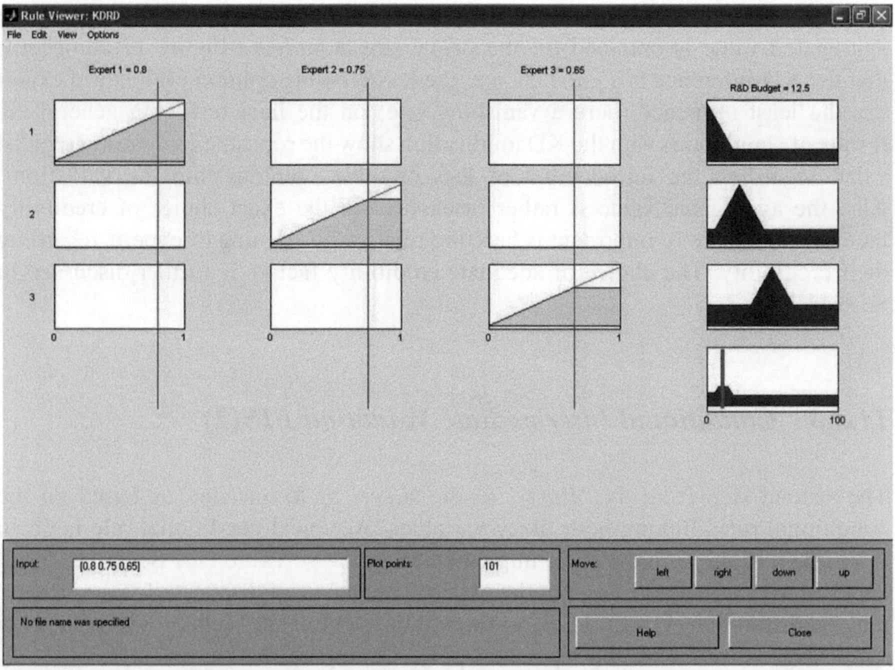

Fig. 11.2 The valuation of the R&D budget (12.5 in arbitrary units) as a '*Proxy*' for the T-level in (11.1) using the Kleene-Dienes implication with three experts with credibility factors [0.8, 0.75, 0.65], and five evenly distributed triangular *MF*'s over the common universe of discourse in [0, 100]. The *MF*'s choice of the experts is given in (11.25)

the input *MF*'s to the unconditional rules in (11.22) for the three experts are as follows (see Fig. 11.2):

$$\text{Expert}(1): \ MF(1) = VL; \quad \text{Expert}(2): \ MF(2) = L; \quad \text{Expert}(3): \ MF(3) = M \tag{11.25}$$

The valuation of the unconditional rule of each expert is made with the Kleene-Dienes (KD) implication defined as follows (Kunsch et al., 1999; Kunsch and Fortemps, 2002):

$$R(u, v) = \max(1 - u, v) \tag{11.26}$$

where u represents the credibility factor of the expert, and v the *MF* he(she) selects for the '*Proxy*'. The aggregation of preferences is made by conjunction, using the 'min' operator. The KD implication has been chosen as explained in detail in Kunsch and Fortemps (2002) because it filters the '*noise*' induced by the less assured opinions. Figure 11.2 illustrates the rules in action for finding the aggregated R&D budget.

The conservative Maxmode is used here for defuzzification. In this way an aggregated value is obtained for the proxy '*R&D budget*'. Figure 11.2 confirms that the KD-inference is a good choice: the less credible opinion of the third expert has the least influence (here a vanishing one) on the final result. In general the results of simulations with the KD implication show the robustness of the aggregated value regarding the introduction of less credible opinions into the valuations. Also the aggregated value is rather insensitive to the exact choice of credibility factors; what is more important is here the relative positioning of experts regarding their credibility. The choice of adequate credibility factors is further discussed in Sect. 11.5.

11.3.3 Conditional Intermediate Valuation $FIS(2)$

The second step from the '*Proxy*' to the '*Level of Knowledge*' is based on the conditional rules linking both fuzzy variables. A typical conditional rule is given in (11.23). In the actual *FIS*(2) implemented in the software (see Sect. 11.3.5) all experts share the same rules, but the experts' universes of discourse for the '*Proxy*' may be different (see Sect. 11.3.2). According to (11.1) the technological '*Level of Knowledge*' (T-level) in the repository project is represented by five *MF*'s (*VL, L*, M, H, *VH*), from '*Very Low*' to '*Very High*', evenly distributed over the common universe of discourse [0, 1] on the output side of the rule (see Fig. 11.3). The *MF*'s are linked in reverse order to the corresponding five *MF*'s representing the '*Proxy*' R&D budget. In the same way four levels are considered for the '*Proxy*' representing the Project '*Level of Knowledge*', according to (11.6).

FIS(2) has thus two inputs to each rule: the credibility factor of the corresponding expert, and the aggregated value obtained by *FIS*(1) on the '*Proxy*'. This is shown in Fig. 11.3.

Firstly, the 'min' operator selects in each partial rule the smaller value u between on one hand the expert's credibility factor, and, on the other hand, the membership grade of the '*Proxy*' input. Secondly, the Mamdani inference, commonly used in engineered control systems (Passino and Yurkovich, 1997) gives the partial conclusion to each expert's rule by means of the 'min' operator:

$$R(u, v) = \min(u, v) \tag{11.27}$$

where v is the *MF* on the conclusion side of the considered expert's rule.

The aggregation to a global result is then made by means of the 'max' operator. For the Mamdani inference it is usual to use the Center-of-Gravity (COG) defuzzication.

In Fig. 11.3 only the two more credible experts have been kept; the value for '*R&D Budget*' comes as the output from *FIS*(1). The quite low R&D budget of 12.5 (relative arbitrary unit) provided from *FIS*(1) gives a crisp quite high value of 81.5 % for the technology knowledge level.

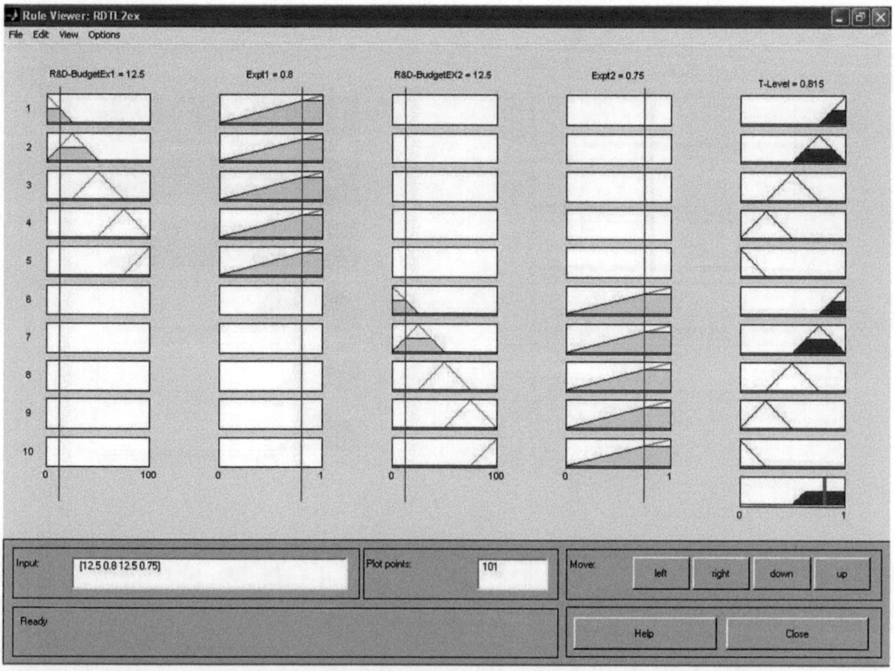

Fig. 11.3 The valuation of the technology '*Level of Knowledge*' (T-level) from the '*Proxy*' in *FIS*(2) using the Mamdani inference system. The less credible expert may be ignored

11.3.4 Conditional Final Valuation FIS(3)

A typical conditional rule for *FIS*(3) is given in (11.24) for evaluating '*Criterion contingency factor*' from '*Level of Knowledge*'. The merits of different implications to be used in this last inference system have been discussed from the point of view of dynamic uncertainties in Kunsch et al. (1999) and Kunsch and Fortemps (2002). Because uncertainties are due to decrease over time with the level of knowledge towards the actual project realisation, it is more appropriate to use gradual rules, rather than certainty or possibility rules, as used in *FIS*(2). It is why the choice has been made of using the Goguen implication for the fuzzy rules. The latter reads as follows:

$$R(u, v) = 1 \quad \text{if } u = 0; \quad R(u, v) = \min(1, v/u) \quad \text{otherwise.} \tag{11.28}$$

As for the KD implication, rules with less credibility on the input side produce less decisive information on the conclusion side. It is why the 'min' aggregation operator is used. The Goguen implication interpolates between the two most possible *MF*'s on the output side, manifesting the property of 'universal approximators' shared by all *FIS* (see Sect. 11.2.1).

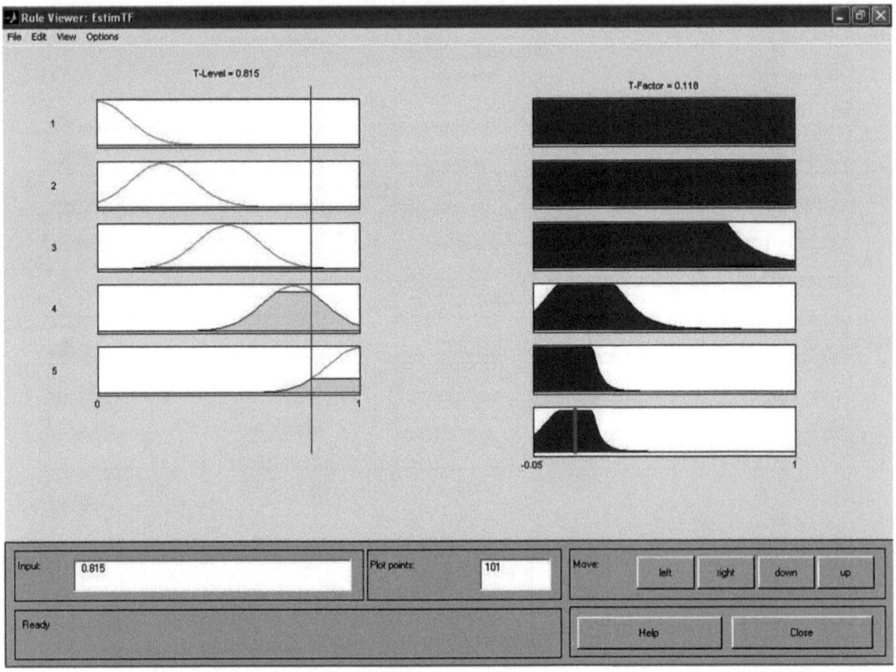

Fig. 11.4 The final valuation of the contingency factor $(T_f - 1)$ of the technology cost from the technology knowledge level by means of Goguen implication. The global output interpolates between the most possible *MF*'s on the output side

The use of the Goguen implication is illustrated in Fig. 11.4 for linking according to (11.1) in reverse order the T-level in [0, 1] to the T-factor in an interval to be defined, depending on the problem. In this example [0, 1] has been chosen, meaning that $T_f \leq 2$.

Five evenly distributed gaussian-shaped *MF*'s represent the T-level; five trapezoidal-like *MF*'s represent the T-factor. The output of the implication is thus the value of the multiplicative contingency factor $(T_f - 1)$ for the cost value including technological uncertainties. MaxMode is here again the most conservative defuzzifying technique, providing a final value of 1.118 for the cost contingency factor, thus increasing the cost without uncertainties by about 12 %.

11.3.5 The FIS Tool software

In Sects. 11.3.1–11.3.4 a mock-up using the Fuzzy Toolbox of MATLAB® has been used for the preliminary methodological development of the fuzzy procedure. This compiled piece of software was not found to be practical for the operational use by real experts. There was a need for developing specialised software including the three-tiered *FIS*, and an interface for inputting experts' data. In a first stage the FIS Tool software was developed on behalf of the Belgian waste-management agency ONDRAF/NIRAS for its own repository project (Kunsch, 2003; Fiordaliso and Kunsch, 2005). It has been later developed to make it more flexible for simulating any other project. Though the present version of FIS Tool is still fully dedicated to cost estimates in radioactive waste management, other applications with other types of problems and criteria may fit into similar software, as said earlier. As visible on the screen in Fig. 11.5, the data of experts are entered by means of the interface in the '*Design Proxy*' panel, corresponding to *FIS*(1). All calculations corresponding to *FIS*(2) are performed in the background, while the panel '*Margins Fuzzy Systems*' displays the evaluations with the Goguen implications in *FIS*(3). The global results are displayed in the panel '*Calendar*' which lets appear the distributions of undiscounted and discounted costs in time for all tasks and globally for different durations scenarios. The cost schedules are calculated by fuzzy PERT for the different duration scenarios (minimum, median, maximum) described in Sect. 11.2.5. All detailed and global cost results can be easily exported to spreadsheets for further treatment, in particular graphical displays, or stochastic PERT, more familiar to project engineers than fuzzy PERT (see Sect. 11.2.5).

The data introduced by means of the '*Design Proxy*' interface in Fig. 11.5 are now shortly presented. The particular task '*Backfilling of the disposal galleries with*

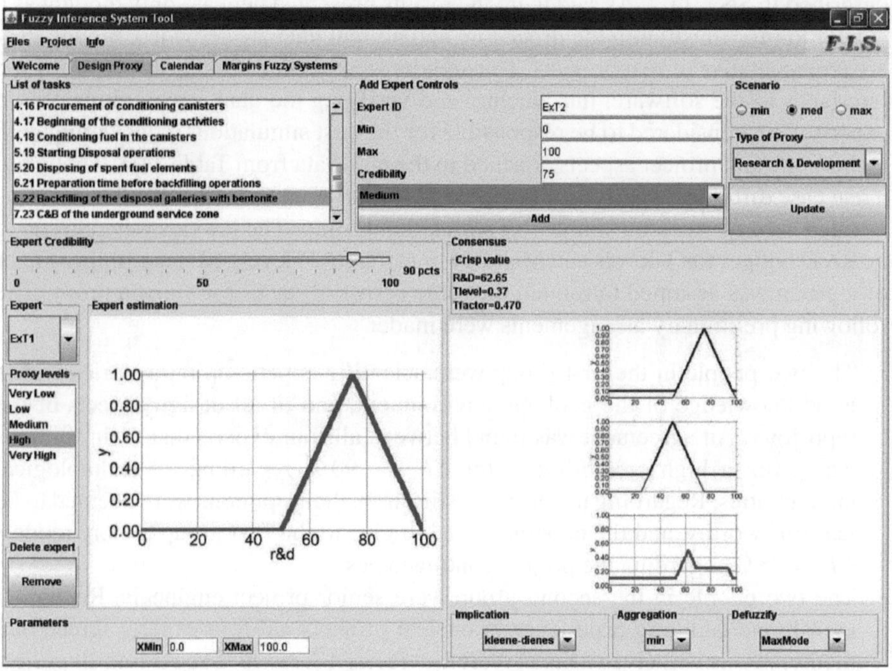

Fig. 11.5 The '*Proxy*' panels used for the experts' interrogation about the '*Proxy R&D budget*'

betonite' is selected from the list of tasks displayed in the upper left part of the screen. The R&D budget is selected from the menu '*Type of Proxy*' on the right. In this example, two experts, called respectively ExT_1 and ExT_2, are interviewed for the task. Both experts first introduce their universe of discourse for the R&D budget, here they are the same, i.e., $[XMin = 0, XMax = 100]$ in arbitrary units. Further they introduce their respective credibility factor, here 90 % for ExT_1, and 75 % for ExT_2. This is done by filling in the fields on top of the form. The median duration scenario for the schedule is chosen from the radio-button on top right. The proxy levels are introduced by means of a roll-down menu on the left, here '*High*' for ExT_1 and '*Medium*' for ExT_2. A window on the right shows the resulting aggregation of both opinions and displays the resulting R&D budget value on the [0, 100] scale, and the obtained T-level and T-factor for the task.

11.4 Procedure and Results of the Repository Case Study

11.4.1 The Preliminary Settings and the Expert Elicitation Process

The fuzzy approach has been used for assessing the costs of the repository project described in Sect. 11.2. As said there the results presented here are only thought as a simulation for illustrating the procedure and no real data are provided, though they are representative of real projects. The authors were acting as analysts preparing the interfaces to the software, introducing, and verifying the data. Two groups of two experts were considered to be responsible for the cost simulations, considering both technology and project aspects attached to the task data from Table 11.1. Though in a real case different experts may be called in for different tasks and proxies, this was avoided here for keeping simple this simulation testing. The proxies were chosen to be R&D budget for T-levels and Man Power (*MP*) for P-levels. The credibility factor of a group was assumed to remain the same across all tasks for a given proxy. The following preliminary arrangements were made:

- The two people in the first group were scientific experts on repositories with a good knowledge of the geologic environment, and of all design aspects of the repository. An agreement was found between all four experts that their opinions was given a high credibility factor $CF = 90\,\%$ regarding all technological uncertainties. Regarding the project realisation, their opinions were deemed to be less trustworthy, and the experts agreed to give to the first group a more modest $CF = 75\,\%$ regarding the project contingencies.
- The two people in the second group were senior project engineers. Regarding their broad and long experience in nuclear projects, all four experts agreed that their opinions was given a high credibility factor $CF = 90\,\%$ regarding all project contingencies. Regarding the technological aspects, their opinions were deemed

to be less trustworthy, and all experts agreed to give to the second group a more modest $CF = 75\,\%$ regarding technological uncertainties.

For preparing the data to be introduced into the software each expert group was requested to fill up an external template file, containing two parts, one for each proxy (R&D budget, or *MP*). The objective of the template is to ease the experts' elicitation of membership functions (*MF*'s) representing the proxies for all project tasks. The data to be introduced in *FIS*(1) are described in the last part of Sect. 11.3.5, and Fig. 11.5. The following fields in the template file, common to all tasks have first to be filled by each expert group by proxy:

- An identifier for the group and the proxy;
- The credibility factor regarding the proxy determined in the preliminary arrangements;
- A maximum value in suitable units (currency units for the R&D budget; Man-years for *MP*) representing the absolute maximum for the proxy considering all tasks in the project. By comparison between all experts a rescaling of the highest value is made to 100 for the absolute proxy maximum. The minimum proxy value being assumed to be zero, the largest relative universe of discourse for all experts and the given proxy is [0, 100]. Though in a real case, the universe of discourse of groups for a given proxy could be different, it was agreed to adopt in this case the common [0, 100] scale for both groups, and each proxy. Further on a list of all project tasks is provided by proxy. Each group is committed to introduce in front of each task a relative proxy value in the scale [0, 100]. The proxy's *MF* with a membership grade $MG > 0.5$ is selected among the sets:

$$\text{R\&D Budget} : \text{Very low}(VL);\ \text{Low}(L);\ \text{Medium}(M);\text{High}(H);\text{Very high}(VH) \qquad (11.29)$$

$$MP : \text{Low}(L);\ \text{Rather low}(RL);\ \text{Rather high}(RH);\ \text{High}(H) \qquad (11.30)$$

The selected *MF* is displayed to the experts when they pick up some value, along with the *MG* of the selected *MF*. If the *MG* is close by, or equal to 0.5, the experts in the group may reconsider, or decide to perform a sensitivity analysis on two neighbouring *MF*'s with $MG \approx 0.5$. After the elicitation process has been completed, the data are exported from the template files to the software for performing the three-tiered *FIS* evaluations in an automated way.

11.4.2 Results

The results of the experts' elicitation for all tasks are given in Table 11.3 providing the T- and P-factors per task. The credibility factors are indicated in the headings, i.e., for technology experts (ExT_1 90 %; ExT_2 75 %), and for project experts (ExP_1 75 %; ExP_2 90 %). The final valuations of the discounted costs are provided in Table 11.4 for the average time schedule, by combining the inputs in Table 11.1, on nominal costs and mean schedule, with the T-factors and P-factors in Table 11.3. It is clear from these results that the technology factor has the lion share in the uncertainties, because many task costs are characterised by large uncertainties,

Table 11.3 This table gives the results of the consultation of two expert groups for the T-factors and P-factors of the tasks in the repository projects ($R\&D$ = Research and development budget; MP = Manpower)

Task-ID	Tasks	ExT_1 R&D 90%	ExT_2 R&D 75%	ExP_1 MP 75%	ExP_2 MP 90%	$T_f - 1$	$P_f - 1$
1	Siting	VL	VL	VL	VL	0.08	0.13
2	Qualification of site	L	L	VL	VL	0.21	0.13
3	Construction of surface infrastructure	L	VL	L	L	0.21	0.18
4	Local infrastructure of the disposal site	VL	VL	L	L	0.08	0.18
5	Construction of wells and ramps	M	M	L	H	0.36	0.26
6	Construction of the disposal zone	H	M	H	H	0.47	0.37
7	Construction of the underground service zone	M	M	H	H	0.36	0.37
8	Preparation time before underground operations						
9	Construction of the fuel conditioning facility	L	L	L	VL	0.21	0.20
10	Procurement of conditioning canisters	VL	VL	VL	VL	0.08	0.13
11	Conditioning fuel in the canisters	M	M	H	L	0.36	0.26
12	Disposing of spent fuel elements	VH	H	VH	VH	0.64	0.48
13	Preparation time before backfilling operations						
14	Backfilling of the disposal galleries with bentonite	H	M	H	H	0.47	0.37
15	C&B of the underground service zone	H	H	H	H	0.60	0.37
16	C&B of wells and ramps	H	H	H	VH	0.60	0.39
17	C&B of the conditioning facility	M	M	L	L	0.36	0.18
18	Preparation time before decommissioning surface facilities						
19	Decommissioning of the surface facilities	M	L	L	L	0.32	0.18

This application is only valid for illustrating the methodology

due to the limited knowledge available today for the finalised repository project. The global P-factor (P_f) is calculated from Eq. (11.18) using the global standard deviation from Eq. (11.16).

Table 11.4 The final valuation of undiscounted costs (normalised nominal cost value=1,000) and contingency factors

Normalized costs		Contingency factors	
Nominal cost	1,000	Global T_f	1.290
Minimum cost $C_T(project)$	1,290	Global P_f	1.193
Average cost $M(project)$	1,463	Global $T_f \cdot P_f$	1.539
Maximum cost $C_{Max}(project)$	1,539	$\Sigma(project)$	44

11.5 Experience Gathered Through Practical Use

As said before in this article the first author has gathered some practical experience at the occasion of his work on financing radioactive-waste management (Kunsch, 2003, 2008). In this way he could appreciate difficulties of implementation, and deal with robustness and sensitivity issues of the proposed FIS approach. In particular the spent-fuel repository, serving for the case study presented in this chapter, brought interesting findings regarding the methodology use. In this sub-section aspects related to this specific experience are shortly reported. Of course, in other specific cases these conclusions may have to be reconsidered. The calibration of any *FIS* system includes the choice of many data, *MF*'s, rules, etc., and it is usually a rather strenuous and long-lasting task (see Passino and Yurkovich 1997 for a discussion on the calibration issues in engineering applications of fuzzy control). The present *FIS* analysis relies on existing EPRI rules and values in (11.1) and (11.6). It has been assumed that all experts in technology and project management agree upon these rules, and the choice of associated parameters. Therefore the calibration effort is limited. Some more difficult aspects have been discussed in Kunsch et al. (1999) regarding the choice of output *MF*'s for the Goguen implication in *FIS*(3).

The designation of experts has also been a relatively easy part in the process, as few really competent experts are generally available from the radioactive-waste agency, or other organisations involved with the repository project. Nevertheless, the choice of two important parameters may be an issue:

1. The number of experts participating in the elicitation;
2. The experts' respective credibility factors.

Regarding the number of experts, or expert groups, in which aggregated opinions are to be elicited, a specific panel of experts has to be designated in principle for each task, and each T-factor, or P-factor in the repository case study. In practice, however, the same experts will serve for multiple task valuations, as also assumed here. It appeared very soon that for evaluating each task a too large number of experts (above four) would be useless, due to the very mechanism of noise-filtering with the *KD* implication in *FIS*(1) (see Sect. 11.3.2) for the '*Proxy*' assessment. The choice of the *KD* implication and the 'min' operator eliminates opinions with a significantly lower credibility factor (*CF*). For that reason two to maximum four experts with quite '*comparable*' *CF*'s would give most of the time a sufficient picture.

The concept of '*comparable*' comes under the second topic. Sometimes a single expert opinion on the '*Proxy*' has to be split for performing sensitivity analyses, e.g., in case of an hesitation between a '*Low*' or '*Medium*' *MF* for the R&D budget in *FIS*(1), as discussed in Sect. 11.4.1. Also multiple runs are recommended to check the validity and robustness of the FIS Tool answers in function of the panel composition and *CF*'s. The second aspect is intertwined with the first one. It should be noted that the *CF* is not a label given to a particular expert in general, but it is only applicable to a particular task, and it measures the strength of conviction of some expert's arguments in favour of his or her answer. It is important that the experts recognise their own strengths and weaknesses before agreeing about the attribution of *CF*'s. As it has been shown in the case study a complete agreement was achieved beforehand between all experts regarding with *CF*'s that should be attributed. The role of the analyst as a mediator is here an important one.

Sensitivity analyses on values for *CF*'s showed that absolute values are not primordial, but rather the relative credibility positions of the experts. On one hand, because no opinion is certain, the authors consider that even the most credible opinions should be given a *CF* lower than 100 %: it is usual to keep a '*noisy background*' in the opinions, which are always subjective, depending on the assessment difficulties. On the other hand, opinions with a too low CF should not be considered, because they will not contribute to the final conclusions. The tests showed that a reasonable CF-interval would be [65 %; 90 %]. Therefore the following recommendations are given on the way for determining relative CF for the different opinions:

Most trustworthy	0.86–0.90
Trustworthy	0.81–0.85
Reliable	0.71–0.80
Least reliable	0.65–0.70

Of course several opinions may share the same *CF* value. This may require some sensitivity analyses in case a strong disagreement would appear between more or less equally credible experts. A problem may in fact arise when a flat *MF* is produced by *FIS*(1), so that no really valid crisp conclusion can be obtained on the '*Proxy*'. In this case a second round of discussion should take place to have opposing experts reconsider, or finding new arguments giving an advantage of credibility to one of the options. In any case it is recommended to test the robustness of the rule conclusions in the provided *CF* intervals.

11.6 Conclusions

In this chapter a three-tiered fuzzy inference system (*FIS*) has been presented for aggregating experts' opinions in the valuation of criteria for which limited, or no information is available. This approach has been developed and used for economic and financial assessments on future projects related to radioactive-waste management. A software called FIS Tool has been developed for such analyses. A simplified case study on a nuclear-fuel repository has been presented. The proposed methodological framework seems to be well adapted to this and similar complex decision problems. Many processes related to environmental preservation are thought to belong to this category of problems. Firstly, most of them deal with multiple dimensions, and therefore demand MCDA approaches. Secondly, there is a need for an experts' elicitation process for compensating the lack of knowledge.

A third aspect is the evolving knowledge level obtained by gathering observations, making experiments, or learning by doing and realising projects, etc. The dynamic learning process is very important. It is in complete agreement with the general philosophy of the EPRI approach, as formulated in (11.1) and (11.6). The cost assessment must be periodically revisited in the long life-time of project preparation and R&D programmes, as increasing knowledge and experience are being gathered. It is why it is definitely possible to combine the proposed fuzzy approach with probabilistic elements resulting from available data and experience, as proposed in Meyer et al. 2002). It has also been mentioned in Sect. 11.2 that past project experience provides information on existing statistical correlations between some tasks, influencing the global-project P-factor. Also progressive fuzzy rules, based on the Goguen implication used in *FIS*(3) (Kunsch et al., 1999), have been shown to be best adapted for capturing improvements in experience and learning.

References

Biewald, B., & Bernow, S. (1991). Confronting uncertainty: Contingency planning for decommissioning. *The Energy Journal, 12*, 233–246.

Bouyssou, D., Marchant, Th., Pirlot, M., Tsoukiàs, A., & Vincke, Ph. (2006). *Evaluation and decision models with multiple criteria: Stepping stones for the analyst*. New York: Springer.

Buckley, J., Eslami, E., & Feuring, Th. (2002). *Fuzzy mathematics in economics and engineering*. Heidelberg: Physica-Verlag(Springer).

European Commission. (1996). *Schemes for financing radioactive waste storage and disposal*. Technical Report. EUR 81185 Report, Luxembourg.

Fiordaliso, A., & Kunsch, P. (2005). A decision supported system based on the combination of fuzzy expert estimates to assess the financial risks in high-level radioactive waste projects. *Progress in Nuclear Energy, 46*(3–4), 374–387.

Kunsch, P. (2003). A framework for assessing the cost and financing uncertainties of the Belgian high level-waste repository. In *Doc. ICEM'03-4336, Proceedings of ICEM'03 Conference on Radioactive Waste Management and Environmental Remediation*. Oxford, England.

Kunsch, P. (2007). A financial option procedure for determining a fuzzy discount rate in radioactive waste management. *International Journal of Nuclear Knowledge Management, 2*(4), 363–374.

Kunsch, P. (2008). Robust and efficient funding of radioactive waste management. In J. Lavelle (Ed.), *Waste management: Research, technology, and developments* (pp. 235–258). Dewey: Nova Science Publishers.

Kunsch, P., Fiordaliso, A., & Fortemps, Ph. (1999). A fuzzy inference system for the economic calculus in radioactive waste management. In D. Ruan (Ed.), *Fuzzy systems and soft computing in nuclear engineering* (pp. 153–171). Heidelberg: Physica-Verlag(Springer).

Kunsch, P., & Fortemps, Ph. (2002). A fuzzy decision support system for the economic calculus in radioactive waste management. *Information Sciences, 142*, 103–116.

Kunsch, P., Ruttiens, A., & Chevalier, A. (2008). A methodology using option pricing to determine a suitable discount rate in environmental management. *European Journal of Operational Research, 185*(3), 1674–1679.

Kunsch, P., & Springael, J. (2005). A fuzzy methodology for evaluating a market of tradable CO2-permits. In R. Loulou, J.-Ph. Waaub, & G. Zaccour (Eds.), *Energy and environment*. Gerad 25th Anniversary Series (pp. 149–173). New York: Springer.

Kunsch, P., & Springael, J. (2008). Simulation with system dynamics and fuzzy reasoning of a tax policy to reduce CO2 emissions in the residential sector. *European Journal of Operational Research, 185*(3), 1285–1299.

Lootsma, F. (1989). Stochastic and fuzzy PERT. *European Journal of Operational Research, 43*(2), 174–183.

McCarthy, M. (2007). *Bayesian methods for ecology*. Cambridge: Cambridge University Press.

Meyer, M., & Booker, J. (2001). *Eliciting and analyzing expert judgment: A practical guide*. Cambridge: ASA-SIAM.

Meyer, M., Butterfield, K., Murray, W., Smith, R., & Booker, J. (2002). Guidelines for eliciting expert judgment as probabilities or fuzzy logic. In T. Ross, J. Booker, & W. Parkinson (Eds.), *Fuzzy logic and probability applications: Bridging the gap* (pp. 105–123). Philadelphia: ASA-SIAM.

Moder, J., Phillips, C., & Davis, E. (1983). *Project Management with CPM, PERT and precedence diagramming*, 3rd ed. New York: Van Nostrand Reinhold.

ONDRAF/NIRAS. (2001). *SAFIR-2, Report on the high-level-waste repository*. Technical Report. Nirond 2001-068 (Available from www.nirond.be).

Passino, K., & Yurkovich, S. (1997). *Fuzzy control*. Melo Park, CA: Addison-Wesley.

Editors' Comments on "The Cost of a Nuclear-Fuel Repository"

Pierre L. Kunsch and Mathieu Vander Straeten present in their text a detailed account of an often underestimated stage in a multicriteria decision aiding process: the task of assessing how good an alternative is according to each attribute. This is a stage that follows the problem definition and formulation stages (recall Sects. 2.2.1 and 2.3 in Chap. 2). This criterion by criterion assessment results in a performance tableau, which precedes the stage of multicriteria aggregation discussed at length in Chaps. 3 and 4. Even when considering a single criterion, aggregation models may play a role in the decision process, namely to take into account the opinions of multiple actors, as is the case in this application, which illustrates models based on fuzzy sets theory.

This application concerns project budgeting. The **objective of the intervention** consists in elaborating a methodology for assessing the cost of a very long term project, namely, the building of a geological repository for disposal of spent nuclear fuel. Although for understandable reasons the real data are not revealed, the authors have based their text on their experience as **analysts** for their **client**, the Belgian agency for radioactive waste management (ONDRAF/NIRAS). A specific software named FIS Tool has been built to be used by this client in addressing this type of problems.

The problem of assessing the cost of a project such as the building of a geological repository for spent nuclear fuel epitomizes the complexity of evaluating the performance of an alternative on a given criterion, since the complexity and uncertainties involved do require a lot of effort (dozens of tasks, high uncertainty, not only of probabilistic nature, aggregation of experts opinions) to obtain a performance value. The overarching goal of a decision process in which the methodology proposed in this chapter could be used is for instance to allow comparing different ways of disposing of used nuclear fuel or different disposal sites in terms of multiple criteria, one of which is cost. Let us note that the disposal of nuclear waste is a well-known example of a difficult problem in which multicriteria decision aiding methods have been used, see for instance Merkhofer and Keeney (1987), Briggs et al. (1990), Dyer et al. (1998), Wheeler et al. (1999) and, recently, Pierpoint (2011).

This chapter focusses on obtaining a cost estimate, which can be considered as a decision process itself, aiming at choosing the most appropriate value (a choice **problem statement**). The **set of alternatives** for this latter decision process is thus continuous, consisting in the set of nonnegative real values $\mathbb{R}_0^+$. To find cost values for each task a set of guidelines proposed by the Electric Power Research Institute (EPRI) helped **structuring** the (sub) **criteria** that would be used: a "no contingencies" base value, a technology factor (to take into account the maturity of the technology), and a project factor (to take into account contingencies during the construction work). These are elements to be aggregated according to a multiplicative **aggregation** formula.

There are many **stages** in this methodology. The values for the technology and project factors are elicited from teams of experts, in the form of fuzzy linguistic variables to model **uncertainty**. Moreover, the uncertainty about these estimates is complemented by a credibility degree associated to each statement. A parallel can be established between performing a multi-criteria aggregation of evaluations by different criteria and a multi-actor aggregation of evaluations by different actors in **group decision** aiding. Therefore, on another level of aggregation, the estimates from the different experts need to be combined. The authors propose using methods able to take into account the credibility of each expert concerning each task. This **aggregation** is performed using a three-tier fuzzy inference system, using different operators for each tier (KD implication, Mamdani inference, and Goguen implication). Cost schedules can be computed using fuzzy PERT to take into account the different scenarios relative to tasks durations. This also allows to compute discounted future costs based on different task schedules and arrive at global figures for the discounted cost of the project.

As an illustration, the authors present a case in which a group of **actors**, two scientific experts and a group of two senior project engineers, participate with their knowledge to indicate their opinion concerning the technology maturity and project contingencies. This **elicitation** was carried out using a questionnaire. The credibility of these experts is supposed to result from a self-assessment (another possibility would have been using cross-assessment, as suggested by Nakayama et al. 1979). The authors recognize that setting these credibility values might be a problem in some cases, in which the analyst would need to play an important role as a mediator. The authors also note that such credibility values should be subject to a sensitivity analysis. Alternatively, methods based on partial information might be useful (Salo, 1995), particularly when integrated in interactive approaches in which actors can change their minds based on what they learn from the inputs of other actors (Dias and Clímaco, 2005).

As **tangible results**, the work reported in this chapter has been used to assess the cost of alternatives in several projects and resulted in the production of the FIS Tool software tool. For the analysts, it also resulted in important **intangible results**, namely the lessons they report in Sect. 11.5. For us, readers, this chapter provides a rich set of suggestions on how to use knowledge of experts when assessing uncertain factors, how to deal with semantic non-numerical evaluations, and how to aggregate different opinions. Sometimes, as this problem exemplified, assessing the value of a single alternative on a single criterion can demand a lot of work.

The complexity of the problem tackled in this paper has warranted a very sophisticated approach. The methodology proposed in this work clearly is intended for being used by experts. The goal is to assess the cost of the project as reliably as possible. It is not designed for being discussed by the public. In general, however, in problems involving ethics and sustainable development stakeholders should be involved (Brans and Kunsch, 2010). This requires being able to let non-technical audiences participate in the decision process and understand the results. In such a case—and we emphasize that it is not the purpose of the authors here to allow involving non-technical audiences—a challenging issue is to find a good balance between the sophistication required by the nature of the problem and the simplicity and transparency needed to communicate with the general public.

References

Brans, J. -P., & Kunsch, P. L. (2010). Ethics in operations research and sustainable development. *International Transactions in Operational Research, 17*(4), 427–444. ISSN 1475-3995.

Briggs, Th., Kunsch, P., Mareschal, B. (1990). Nuclear waste management: An application of the multicriteria PROMETHEE methods, *European Journal of Operational Research, 44*(1), 1–10.

Dias, L. C., & Clímaco, J. N. (2005). Dealing with imprecise information in group multicriteria decisions: A methodology and a GDSS architecture. *European Journal of Operational Research, 160*(2), 291–307.

Dyer, J. S., Edmunds, T., Butler, J. C., & Jia, J. (1998). A multiattribute utility analysis of alternatives for the disposition of surplus weapons-grade plutonium. *Operations Research, 46*(6), 749–762.

Merkhofer, M. W., & Keeney, R. L. (1987). A multiattribute utility analysis of alternative sites for the disposal of nuclear waste. *Risk Analysis, 7*(2), 173–194.

Nakayama, H., Tanino, T., Matsumoto, K., Matsuo, H., Inoue, K., & Sawaragi, Y. (1979). Methodology for group decision support with an application to assessment of residential environment. *IEEE Transactions on Systems, Man and Cybernetics, 9*(9), 477–485.

Pierpoint, L. M. (2011). *A decision analysis framework for the U.S. nuclear fuel cycle*. Ph.D. Thesis. Cambridge (MA): Massachusetts Institute of Technology, Engineering Systems Division.

Salo, A. A. (1995). Interactive decision aiding for group decision support. *European Journal of Operational Research, 84*(1), 134–149.

Wheeler, T., Weiner, R., Davis, F., & Sorenson, K. (1999). A multi-attribute utility decision analysis for treatment alternatives for the DOE-SR aluminum-based spent nuclear fuel. In *WM'99 Conference*, February 28–March 4, 1999. Tucson, AZ.

Chapter 12
Assessing the Response to Land Degradation Risk: The Case of the Loulouka Catchment Basin in Burkina Faso

Stéphane Aimé Metchebon Takougang, Marc Pirlot, Samuel Yonkeu, and Blaise Some

Abstract This work is concerned with land use assessment in a region of Burkina Faso, Western Africa. It can help to support the definition of politics promoting a sustainable development of the region. A spatial decision support model is built, based on a coupling of Multi-Criteria Decision Analysis (MCDA) on the one hand and a Geographic Information System (GIS) on the other hand. The ELECTRE TRI method is used to sort the spatial units to ordered categories corresponding to various levels of response to the risk of landscape degradation. The model allows to aggregate physical, economical, socio-cultural and environmental aspects interpreted in terms of their impact on landscape preservation or degradation. Such a categorization leads to the determination of homogeneous zones in the region under study. It can possibly serve as a basis for allocating resources to the most promising sub-regions or the zones needing an urgent intervention.

12.1 Introduction

Because of its spatial character, the management of land (soil, vegetation) degradation of a given area involves the use of Geographic Information Systems (GIS). GIS are designed to manage spatial data and incorporate functionalities that allow to do so. However, land degradation is, most of the time, the result of the impact on the

S.A. Metchebon Takougang • M. Pirlot (✉)
Université de Mons, Faculté Polytechnique, 9, Rue de Houdain, 7000 Mons, Belgium
e-mail: aime.metchebon@u-auben.org; marc.pirlot@umons.ac.be

S. Yonkeu
Institut Supérieur d'Informatique et de Gestion, 06 BP 9283 Ouagadougou 06, Burkina Faso
e-mail: syonkeu@yahoo.fr

B. Some
Université de Ouagadoudou, Laboratoire LANIBIO, 03 BP 7021 Ouagadougou 03, Burkina Faso
e-mail: some@univ-ouaga.bf

R. Bisdorff et al. (eds.), *Evaluation and Decision Models with Multiple Criteria*, International Handbooks on Information Systems,
DOI 10.1007/978-3-662-46816-6_12

soil and the vegetation of a series of complex and conflicting factors resulting from the pressure of human activities and/or climatic pejoration. Operational research disciplines such as MultiCriteria Decision Analysis (MCDA) are dedicated to handle complex and conflicting aspects in general. In spite of their complementarity, the literature shows few examples in which MCDA methods are associated with GIS for tackling the land degradation problem. In contrast, the present work is an example of how both GIS and MCDA methods can be used, in synergy, for structuring the problem and assessing land degradation. The region of interest, the Loulouka catchment basin, is located in the Center North of Burkina Faso. Assessing the degradation of such a territory amounts to decompose it in spatial units (SU) and categorize them according to the quality or level of their response to the risk of degradation. Our goal is to produce a *decisional map* (Chakhar, 2006) representing the state of all SU composing the Loulouka Basin w.r.t. the land degradation problem. Based on such a map, it is possible, for instance, to prioritize zones on which actions should be undertaken and design such actions in the most efficient way, in view of guaranteeing a sustainable development of the region.

This chapter is organized as follows. Section 12.2 describes the context of the case study, including its aims in terms of fighting the land degradation problem. We propose a decisional aiding process scheme, called DAPDIMR, which we apply to the case study in Sects. 12.3–12.5. More precisely, Sect. 12.3 is devoted to the structuring of the problem, including the identification of the actors and their roles, the definition of the alternatives (zones or spatial units) and the relevant criteria. In Sect. 12.4, we select a model for assigning SU to categories, we set the model parameters and we obtain a first version of an assignment of SU to categories reflecting the level of response to degradation risk of the units. Validating the model, including robustness and sensitivity analysis, is the main concern of Sect. 12.5, which ends up with recommendations derived from the decisional map representing the SU assignments to categories according with the model. Some conclusions and perspectives are presented in Sect. 12.6. The appendix details the construction of the assessments of SU on each criterion on the basis of indicators reflecting partial aspects of this criterion.

12.2 Context of the Case Study and Decisional Approach

12.2.1 The Context

The Loulouka catchment basin[1] lies in the Center North of Burkina Faso, a country located in western Africa. This region is submitted to a Sudanese-Sahelian climate characterized by a weak rainfall and subject to an intense anthropogenic activity which causes land degradation. The choice of this catchment basin is motivated

[1]Area of land draining into a river.

by the fact that previous research (see, e.g., Taupin et al., 1998; Mahaman, 2001; Ibrahim, 2002; Iwaco, 1990a,b; Roose and Sarrailh, 1989; Karimou Ambouta et al., 1996; Diallo et al., 2002; Diello, 2002; Yacouba et al., 2002; Yonkeu and Kiniffo, 2004) has pointed out some causes of the degradation and the complexity of a sustainable management approach to solve this problem. These studies have generated actions proposals in view of restoring degraded parts of the land but the actions implemented did not lead to sustainable results (Ouedraogo et al., 2008). The degradation problem currently persists particularly in the catchment basin under study. Some limitations of the actions undertaken originate from the fact that previous studies only addressed particular aspects of the problem; they failed to propose global systemic remedies. Indeed, actions were undertaken to fight the impact of each degradation factor in an isolated way instead of a global way. Moreover, the solutions proposed in previous studies were mostly focused on physical (i.e. soil and vegetation) and technical aspects; they didn't take into account the economic, social and cultural dimensions of the local population who is principally concerned. It has become clear that the fundamental problem with the previous studies lies in the difficulty involved in integrating multidimensional information of heterogenous nature (erosion, loss of biodiversity, soil fertility, soil characteristics, agricultural practices, biologic, technical, economic, social aspects) and, consequently, in the unappropriate character of the means proposed to solve the degradation problem.

12.2.2 Decisional Approach

In recent works dealing with land degradation, e.g. the LADA project[2] (Brabant, 2009), the generally acknowledged approach can be summarized as follows. The solution to the degradation problem in a given physical environment passes through the assessment of its factual state as the seat of different pressures resulting from climate and anthropogenic actions; this assessment must take into consideration the capacity of reaction (intrinsic and/or due to remediation actions) of this environment. Indeed, knowing the factual degradation state of a region allows to target preferential intervention zones (i.e. zones presenting a poor level of response to the degradation risk) and also, as we shall see in Sect. 12.5, to prioritize remediation actions to be undertaken. Practically, for a given area, our approach's output will consist in a "decisional map" (Chakhar and Mousseau, 2007, 2008) representing the "response to the degradation risk" which, in addition to reflecting an assessment of the degradation state of the territory, will also constitute the basis

[2]Land Degradation Assessment in Drylands, current project for fighting desertification initiated since 2003 jointly by Food and Agriculture Organization (FAO), Global Environment Facility (GEF), United Nation Environment Programme (UNEP) and United Nation Convention to Combat Desertification (UNCCD).

for the exploration of sustainable and appropriate managerial policies for fighting against land degradation. This approach is *structured* and *participative*:

- *structured*: the assessment of the state of degradation relies on the elaboration of a model, involving a hierarchy of criteria, associated to indicators which reflect the relevant aspects of the criteria and allow for their assessment;
- *participative*: all the concerned parties (local population, authorities, experts) are associated to the assessment and their point of view is taken into account.

The problem of assessing land degradation hence appears as a spatial decision problem in which intervene many criteria reflecting different aspects to be taken into account. The main difficulty consists in balancing two antagonistic aspects, namely:

- on the one hand, the soil and the biodiversity which are limited resources and, consequently, need to be exploited in a rational and sustainable way,
- on the other hand, the population, which is continuously growing, and whose activities have prejudicial consequences on erosion, soil fertility and biodiversity.

The efficiency of remedying actions can only be guaranteed if both aspects are taken into account. In particular, feasible strategies must aim at improving the quality of life of local populations and should build on cultural traits, educational and training characteristics of these populations. Revisiting in depth the system of criteria that describe not only the physical state of the territory but also the human factor and have an impact on the response to the degradation risk is thus a fundamental initial step in our study. In our way of thinking about it, we wanted also to make sure that the elaborated system be transferable to different regions and contexts. In view of this, we have gained inspiration from work done in the framework of impact studies on the environment, such as Pictet (1996). The latter work has the specificity of being based on the principles of MCDA (see Vincke, 1989, 1992; Belton and Stewart, 2003), which views evaluation and decision making as the result of a process called "decision aiding".

The other specificity of the present case is its spatial character. GIS are particularly well suited to provide spatialized representation of indicators or criteria throughout the area of interest. They also possess built in capabilities for manipulating, combining and analyzing such data. However, the current GIS software packages, do not integrate, at least in their standard versions, sufficiently developed multicriteria treatment functionalities, which would allow to rank or select geographic units, or assign them to categories taking into account objective criteria (economic, for instance) and/or subjective criteria (social and cultural, for instance). Though they have not been initially conceived for being used in a spatial context, MCDA methods are made for dealing with multiple, generally conflicting, criteria, with the aim of ranking or selecting alternatives, or assigning them to categories. In our case study, we will be especially interested in MCDA methods for assigning alternatives, i.e. spatial units, to ordered categories. These categories represent the degree of quality of the response to the risk of degradation of a SU. Among the relevant MCDA methods, let us mention for instance ELECTRE TRI (Yu,

1992a,b; Mousseau and Slowinski, 1998; Roy, 2002; Bouyssou and Marchant, 2007a,b) and a method based on additive value functions, a learning version of which is implemented as UTADIS (Doumpos and Zopounidis, 2002).

Most of the works dealing with the assessment of land degradation only use a GIS without coupling it with a MCDA method. Some decisional problems relative to land management but not specifically to the assessment of land degradation, were dealt with thanks to some sort of conjoint use or integration of a GIS and MCDA methods (see, e.g. Jankowski, 2001; Laaribi, 2000; Joerin and Musy, 2000; Joerin et al., 2001; Previl et al., 2003; Malczewski, 2006; Chakhar, 2006). Our own research follows this path (Metchebon Takougang et al., 2008).

12.2.3 Decision Aiding Process Scheme in the Context of Territorial Management

Besides developing multicriteria aggregation methods, MCDA has a strong methodological dimension, providing guidelines for structuring the decision aiding process (see Chap. 2 of this book). Due to the specificity of decision making in the context of territorial management, this section will propose a scheme for a decision aiding process adapted to such a context. This scheme, referred to as DAPDIMR (Decision Aiding Process for the Development and the Integrated Management of Resources) and represented on Fig. 12.1, describes the integration of a GIS in the decision aiding process. Dark grey rectangles correspond to elements pertaining to GIS aided spatial management while light grey rectangles correspond to elements of the general multiple criteria decision aiding process.

We first emphasize that, as for Joerin's model (Joerin, 1998), the intervention of a person, "the analyst", who masters both the GIS and the MCDA methods is highly desirable. This person who normally conducts the decision aiding process, is generally qualified for explaining the different actors the representation(s) of the territory that can be provided by the GIS; he/she can show the incidence of the actors' options and choices by simulating their consequences, exploiting the functionalities of the GIS. The result of such simulations will generally result in a map.

Let us now briefly browse through the decision aiding process scheme as represented on Fig. 12.1. A basic component input to the process is a geographic data base (GDB), which structures a system of data describing or evaluating the area under study, which is generally decomposed in spatial units. This data base is usually linked with a GIS. The GIS functionalities allows the user to manipulate, transform and display the data, simulate evolution scenarii, etc.

In our application the area under investigation was decomposed in regular square spatial units or "meshes" as represented on Fig. 12.2. Information relative to each SU is stored in the GDB. For example, each SU is assessed w.r.t. a criterion labeled

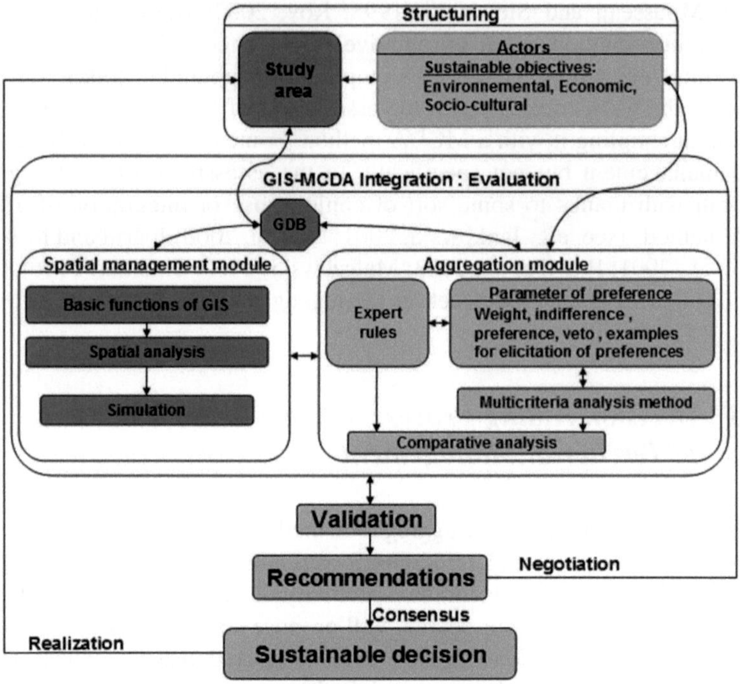

Fig. 12.1 The decisional process DAPDIMR

"Adequate application of Water and Soil Conservation techniques (WSC)", and their assessments can be represented on a "criterion map" as illustrated on Fig. 12.3.

The assessments of each SU w.r.t. the different criteria, i.e. the performance vector associated to a SU, can be aggregated using an appropriate MCDA method, which generally requires the elicitation of a number of parameters reflecting the preferences or the system of values of a decision maker. The obtained model should then be validated by confronting its consequences to the actors' judgment. If aggregation results in assigning the SU to categories, such an assignment can be represented on a map, which will be called a *decisional map*. The latter can then be used as a basis for building *recommendations*. If there are several actors who have a decisional power, for instance because their agreement on the conclusions of the study is required, a negotiation process can engage, which might lead to revising the model, hence iterating the decision aiding process until a consensus on the diagnosis made is reached. Putting the recommendations into application may then be envisaged.

Sections 12.3 and 12.4, which follow, describe the application of the decision aiding process DAPDIMR to the assessment of the land degradation risk in the Loulouka basin, in view of proposing policies to fight against this risk.

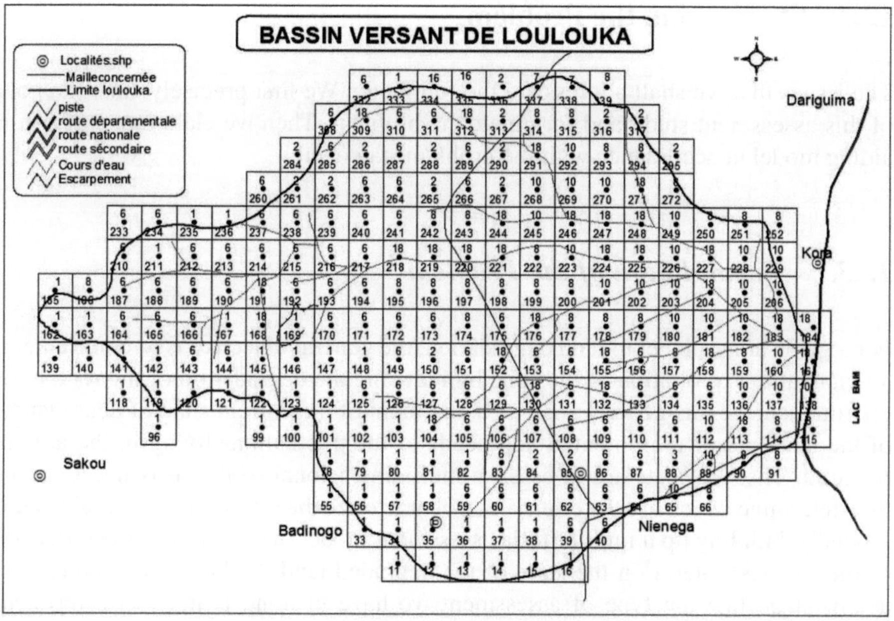

Fig. 12.2 Square lattice division of Loulouka basin. Source: BNDT

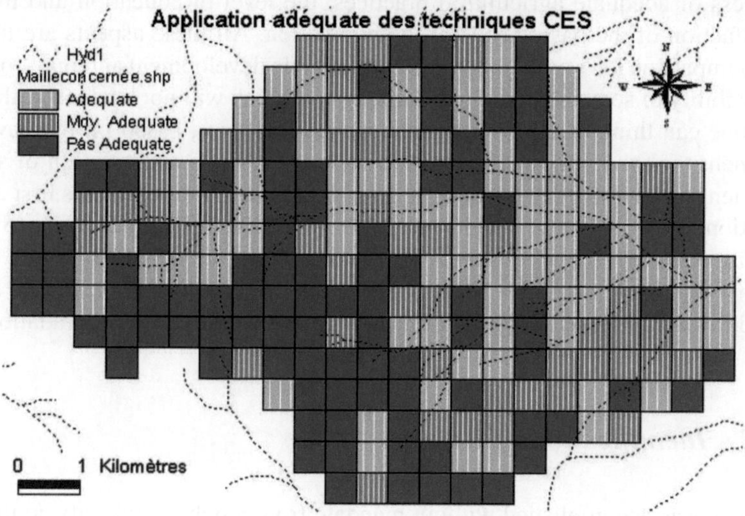

Fig. 12.3 Example of criterion map: adequate application of WSC techniques

12.3 Structuring the Problem

The issues that we shall address are the following. We first precisely state the goal of this assessment study and formulate the problem. Then we elaborate a decision aiding model in accordance with the problem statement.

12.3.1 Formulation of the Problem

For a given area subject to land degradation, the general objective is to contribute to a sustainable exploitation of the soils by reducing the degradation of the region. In order to achieve this general goal, an assessment of the current state of degradation of the land and of the potential and needs of the populations living in the area is required. These aspects are in essence multidimensional so that it is necessary to first determine which are the criteria that characterize the situation of the region and, secondly, building up a multicriteria assessment model that integrates the influence of the various criteria on the state of the degraded land. It should be emphasized at this stage that the type of assessment we have in mind is not just a physical evaluation of the state of degradation of the soils. In our assessment, we intend to take the human factor into account, especially elements such as the level of awareness of adequate agricultural practices, the level of education and the level of satisfaction of the basic needs of the population. All these aspects are likely to have an impact on the region in terms of sustainable development and may condition the possibility of some actions. In a further step (which will not be dealt with in this work) one can think of elaborating management policies, based on the developed assessment tool and negotiated with the populations. The construction of such an assessment tool is the main purpose of the present contribution. It goes first through a partitioning of the region under study in homogeneous *spatial units* (SU) and assigning each SU a level or category of response to the degradation risk. Hence our goal will be to elaborate a partitioning of the Loulouka basin in SU and apply a method for assigning these SU to levels of response to the risk of degradation.

12.3.2 Identification of Actors

This work was accomplished without mandate from a public authority so that, in a sense, it could be seen as purely academic. However, one of the authors (S. Yonkeu) was involved as an expert and an environmentalist in several studies related to the region of Loulouka (Yacouba et al., 2002; Yonkeu and Kiniffo, 2004); he has also witnessed the results of actions that were previously undertaken, aiming at reducing the land degradation (Ouedraogo et al., 2008). S. Yonkeu was thus quite naturally in the position of the expert in the present study and he is referred to as the environmentalist expert (EE) in the sequel. As this work was more a matter of evaluation than decision, no decision maker was really available, and the expert has very much played the role of the Decision Maker (DM): for instance, the EE provided information on the weighting of criteria, and on the preference parameters in the aggregation model.

The target part, that is to say the group who benefits from the action, are the local farmers and the territorial administration authorities. Recommendations issued from the evaluation process could be the basis of further action to be undertaken by the public authority in these regions.

12.3.3 Construction of the Set of Alternatives

In the perspective of providing the public authority with an assessment tool on which sustainable policy making can be based, we have to associate each SU of the Loulouka basin a level of response to the degradation risk. This level will be determined by pressure, state and response indicators associated to each SU. A preliminary issue consists in determining the size and shape of the SU forming a partition of the map. When associating each SU a level of response to the degradation risk to, one assumes that the size of these units is such that the level of response to the risk can be considered as constant on it.

As we are in a rural area and considering the final objective of preparing public authority's policy making, the idea of working with farms as SU naturally came to the mind. Unfortunately a cadastral map of the Loulouka basin was not available. The average size of a farm household being approximately 1 ha, we envisaged a regular division of the area in squares of 100 m side, hence 1 ha surface. In view of the catchment basin size, approximately 57.7 km^2, this would lead to approximately 5,750 square SU. In view of the limited human resources and financial support, it could not be envisaged to collect the necessary data for such a large number of SU. We thus opted for a regular square lattice division of the catchment basin area in 229 SU of 25 ha each. One SU represents 25 times the mean size of a farm. Such a rough subdivision finally proved realistic. Indeed, geomorphological characteristics, farming practices and socioeconomic conditions do not change so quickly that a finer grained subdivision would be required (Yonkeu and Kiniffo, 2004). Our assessment methodology has thus been applied to the 229 SU, each with a surface of twenty five hectares, which is the set of alternatives (or actions) we shall evaluate (see Sect. 12.4).

The chosen subdivision in SU of 25 ha each is represented on Fig. 12.2. Two numbers appear in each square: the number in the bottom is the SU label. The other above gives the pedo-geomorphologic[3] type (see Table 12.22) of the SU;

12.3.4 Identification of Criteria and Indicators

The retained criteria and indicators were organized in a hierarchical structure. In order to define the viewpoints to be taken into account and the indicators that assess the main aspects relevant to these viewpoints, we first adopted a *top-down* approach followed by *bottom-up* checking.

The top-down approach is inspired by Keeney's "value-focused thinking" concept (Keeney, 1992), which recommends that the DM first focuses on the definition of "fundamental objectives"[4] to achieve w.r.t the problem. In our case, five "No-Degradation" principles (see Sect. 12.3.5) were identified. They constitute our set of fundamental objectives. These "No-Degradation" principles encompass all aspects that were recognized as being relevant for the land degradation problem in similar contexts. Then we build the chain *Principles-Criteria-Indicators* (Schlaepfer, 2003). The criteria allow to appreciate to which extent principles are satisfied. In practice, they are related to factors which concur to land degradation or preservation, including human aspects. For each criterion, one or several indicators reflect the response to the degradation risk of the evaluated alternative w.r.t. this criterion. Note that using such an approach, we have built a hierarchy of criteria and indicators that is valid in a wide variety of situations, not for the sole Loulouka basin. Applying the same evaluation scheme to other regions of Burkina Faso for instance, would require no additional effort.

The bottom-up validation aims at checking the operational nature of the indicators which were proposed in the top-down scheme. Indeed, in each particular situation the value of some indicators may be unavailable or the resources needed for obtaining them may be lacking. In such a case, the construction of some indicators requires re-examination or, even, other elements of the assessment model must be revised. In our case, collecting the value of indicators for each farm household, as initially suggested, was not possible for practical reasons, which resulted in revising the size of the SU, keeping unchanged the definition of the indicators.

For criteria that are related to more than one indicator, we devised expert rules that aggregate the values of these indicators. These rules were built with the help of the EE. Expert rules are especially adequate for aggregating indicators assessed

[3]Geomorphology is the science of landforms and of the processes that shape them, while Pedology studies the soils. Both disciplines are important for determining the potential usage of the soils in a sustainable development perspective.

[4]Also called final objectives (Beaumont et al., 2006).

on qualitative scales (van der Werf and Zimmer, 1999; Jallas and Cretenet, 2002), which is the case in our work (see Sect. 12.3.6).

12.3.5 Construction of Principles and Criteria

The construction started with the formulation of fundamental objectives, the satisfaction of which leads to consider that the degradation is limited, in a framework of sustainable development and management of the area. These objectives constitute "the principles of the limitation of land degradation". Five of them were identified:

- *Principle 1: The soils EROsion is limited (ERO)*
- *Principle 2: The BIOdiversity lost is limited (BIO)*
- *Principle 3: The soil FERtility is preserved (FER)*
- *Principle 4: A good level of agricultural PROductivity is favored (PRO)*
- *Principle 5: The Elementary Needs, which are necessary conditions for the population welfare, are satisfied (EN).*

The potential causes of non-satisfaction of these principles were subdivided in two categories of factors that are:

- *Climatic factors* on which humans have little possible action: rainfall shortage, high diurnal temperature (causing high *evapotranspiration*,[5] dryness and soil desiccation, etc.), wind.
- *Anthropogenic factors* on which it is possible to act by establishing scenarios and developing managerial strategies: traditions, practices and usage of the populations (agriculture, cattle breeding, sheep and goat farming, commerce, bush fire, etc.) viewed under the angle of their impact on soil aptitude w.r.t envisaged activity in the concerned area, practices (operating method of the activity inside the area), socio-economic and cultural context.

From these factors undermining the "No-degradation" principles, we have derived evaluation criteria for the alternatives. Practically, criteria encompass the factors having an incidence on land degradation from the point of view of one of the fundamental principles. Table 12.1 gathers the five principles together with the criteria derived from them. The criteria are identified by two indices. Index i in the label Cr_{ij} of a criterion varies from 1 to 5 and refers to the ith principle. The second index (j) is the criterion number. We have listed 15 criteria (j varies from 1 to 15). For instance, Cr_{310} indicates the tenth criterion, which belongs to the 3rd principle (FER). The meaning of the criteria will be detailed below.

[5]Evaporation from land and water surfaces and transpiration of vegetation.

Table 12.1 No-degradation principles and associated criteria (WSC stands for Water and Soil Conservation, SP, for Soils Preservation)

Principles	Criteria
ERO: The soils erosion is limited (P_1)	Adequate pedo-geomorphologic choice (Cr_{11})
	Adequate application of WSC techniques (Cr_{12})
	Adequate application of SP techniques (Cr_{13})
	Limitation of soil compaction (Cr_{14})
BIO: The biodiversity loss is limited (P_2)	Limited Extension of cultivated soils (Cr_{25})
	Adequate pesticide usage (Cr_{26})
	Preservation of ecosystem integrity (Cr_{27})
	Bush fire limitation (Cr_{28})
FER: The soil fertility is preserved (P_3)	Adequate application of cultivation techniques (Cr_{39})
	Adequate practice of soil fertilization (Cr_{310})
PRO: A good agricultural productivity is favored (P_4)	Technical training of farmers (Cr_{411})
	Improvement of agricultural production (Cr_{412})
EN: The elementary needs required for populations welfare are satisfied (P_5)	Respect of sociocultural areas (Cr_{513})
	Improvement in training standards (Cr_{514})
	Improvement in socioeconomic conditions (Cr_{515})

12.3.6 *Construction of Indicators*

12.3.6.1 Preliminaries

In this work, the fifth principle (EN) will not be taken into account. The degree of satisfaction of population's needs is a global characteristic of a region of the size of the whole area under study. The criteria that can be derived from the fifth principle cannot be used to differentiate small 25 ha SU. Such characteristics could be assessed at the level of the whole region and be used to differentiate several regions of the size of the Loulouka basin (see Metchebon Takougang 2010 for more explanation on the use the fifth principle).

As is customary in the assessment of sustainable development, we have considered three types of indicators:

- *Pressure indicators*: express the level of anthropogenic or natural pressure imposed on each SU. For example: "Cultivation on marginal grounds";
- *State indicators*: express the capacity of the SU to resist some anthropogenic or natural pressures. For example: "Presence of nude soil";
- *Response indicators*: reflect remediation actions undertaken to resist pressures. For example: "Fertilizer use".

Due to the lack of reliable information allowing to assess criterion Cr_{26} ("Adequate pesticide usage"), we were forced not to take this criterion into consideration. For the remaining 11 criteria, we defined 23 indicators associated with them in order

Table 12.2 Criteria and indicators choice

Max or *Min*	Criteria	Indicators
Max	Cr_{11}	Comparison with agricultural aptitude map (i_{111})
Max	Cr_{12}	Presence of bund (i_{121})
		Presence of stony cordon (i_{122})
		Presence of zaï (i_{123})
Max	Cr_{13}	Fallow practice (i_{131})
		Ploughing technique (i_{132})
Min	Cr_{14}	Presence of nude soil (i_{141})
		Animals overstamping (i_{142})
Min	Cr_{25}	Cultivation on marginal lands (i_{251})
Max	Cr_{26}	Appropriate matching of pesticide and type of cultivation (i_{261})
		Pesticide usage frequency (i_{262})
Max	Cr_{27}	Presence of a sacred grove (i_{271})
		Reforestation zone (i_{272})
		Protected forest (i_{273})
		Presence of trees stump (i_{274})
Min	Cr_{28}	Presence of bush fire (i_{281})
Max	Cr_{39}	Practice of crop rotation (i_{391})
		Practice of crop association (i_{392})
Max	Cr_{310}	Presence of manure (i_{3101})
		Use of chemical fertilizer (i_{3102})
Max	Cr_{411}	Presence of trained farmers (i_{4111})
Max	Cr_{412}	Excess production (i_{4121})
		Practice of an activity, which is source of income (i_{4122})

to evaluate and compare SU w.r.t. degradation limitation (see Table 12.2). These indicators were chosen in order to reflect all relevant aspects for the assessment and the follow-up of degradation limitation.

For all criteria encompassing more than one indicator, expert rules were used, after having been validated by the EE.

In practice, each SU was visited and surveyed. A survey report sheet was filled in for each SU. For data collection, field work was performed in the periods from the 25th of September 2006 to the 6th of October 2006, from the 29th of July 2007 to the 4th of August 2007 and from the 30th of September 2007 to the 13th of October 2007. The field work required usage of a GPS.[6] The team responsible for the field work was composed of at least eight persons. During the sojourns on the field, interview meetings with public territorial authorities, governmental officers and village chiefs, were held as well as individual interviews and focus groups with local farmers. A first set of indicators was set up together with the EE. A first field

[6]Global Positioning System.

mission in the study area was mostly devoted to test the operational character of the indicators (which were fewer, about 15, in their initial version). Having noticed that some indicators were too complex, these were split in more elementary aspects in the final version. After a second round of consultation with the EE, the present set of 23 indicators was retained. It allowed us to give an account of the performance of each SU w.r.t. the considered criteria.

12.3.6.2 Setting Evaluation Scales for Indicators

For each indicator, we adopted a three levels evaluation scale. These levels received the following labels: Adequate (*A*), Moderately Adequate (*MA*), Not Adequate (*NA*), and this, for all indicators. The meaning of the different levels is detailed in appendix. The choice of a rather rough evaluation scale, distinguishing only three levels, is justified, on the one hand, by the weak differentiation of:

- farming practices of local populations,
- agricultural aptitude in the area, from a pedo-geomorphological point of view,

and by the search for simple indicators, on the other hand. Table 12.2 gives an overview of all the criteria and the associated indicators, which are described in detail in the appendix.

12.4 Sorting the Spatial Units in Categories

At this stage, a performance tableau (i.e. a matrix) was built in which each of the 229 SU is associated a vector of evaluations on 11 criteria. These are qualitative evaluations expressed on a scale that has at most three levels. In view of this, we decided to use the ELECTRE TRI method (see Yu, 1992a,b; Mousseau and Slowinski, 1998; Roy, 2002; Bouyssou and Marchant, 2007a,b) for sorting the alternatives into ordered categories. The choice of this method is dictated by the following facts.

First, let us recall that we need an "absolute" evaluation of the alternatives, rather than a ranking (which would be called "relative evaluation"). Indeed, the state of each SU, i.e. the level of response to the risk of degradation it belongs to, is supposed to govern actions to be applied to it in view of improving sustainability of management and development of the region.

Second, in view of the quite qualitative nature of the assessments, the somewhat ad hoc character of the expert rules and the rough categorization of the scales used, it seemed difficult to envisage to use a sorting method based on the construction of an additive value function (Zopounidis and Doumpos, 2001, 1999). In particular, obtaining reliable responses to questions aiming at eliciting tradeoffs seemed to be unrealistic. This is all the more true that the scales of the criteria are poorly detailed. In contrast, the ELECTRE TRI method is well-suited to qualitative descriptions on rough scales.

12.4.1 Requirements for the Application of ELECTRE TRI

For the reader's convenience, we briefly recall the principle of ELECTRE TRI. Categories are determined by means of limit profiles, which are special alternatives (real or fictitious). The assignment rule of an alternative to a category relies on the outranking relation between this alternative and the various profiles. There are two variants of the assignment rule: the pessimistic and the optimistic. With the pessimistic rule, an alternative is assigned to one of the categories above a profile if this alternative outranks the profile. Hence the alternative is assigned to the category whose "lower limit" is the last profile outranked by the alternative and its "upper limit" is the first profile that the alternative does not outrank. The optimistic rule assigns each alternative to the same or a higher category as compared to the pessimistic rule. To determine the category assigned by the optimistic rule, we look at the highest profile that does not strictly outrank the alternative (i.e. the alternative either is indifferent or outranks this profile) and we assign it to the category immediately above this profile.

An alternative outranks a profile if a *concordance-non-discordance* condition is fulfilled. The latter occurs whenever a certain mathematical expression passes a threshold, denoted λ, which can be interpreted as a generalized majority condition. The expression compared to threshold λ essentially measures the strength of the coalition of criteria on which the alternative is at least as good as the profile; it is modulated by the possible existence of vetoes, i.e. by criteria on which the alternative is exceedingly worse than the profile. We do not state here the precise expression since we will not use it for reasons to be explained later (see Sect. 12.4.2.3). The interested reader is referred to Roy and Bouyssou (1993), Yu (1992b) for further details on the original ELECTRE TRI rules. In this application, again due to the rough character of the criteria scales, we use a simplified version of the classical expression, which amounts to a qualified majority rule, possibly modulated by a binary non-veto condition. The concordance-non-discordance condition hence amounts to the following: an alternative outranks a profile if the sum of the weights of the criteria on which the alternative is at least as good as the profile passes a threshold λ and there is no criterion on which the performance of the alternative is exceedingly bad as compared with that of the profile.[7] The same rule applies *mutatis mutandis* to determine whether a profile outranks an alternative (used in the optimistic version).

[7]Note that this condition corresponds to the classical one, provided the indifference and the preference thresholds are appropriately set, i.e. set to 0, and there are no vetoes. Setting the indifference and the preference threshold to 0 is reasonable since the criteria scales have few levels; passing from a level to the next one is an improvement that leads to a strictly preferred level. In case there are vetoes, the rule we use here–which is essentially the ELECTRE I rule–differs only from the classical ELECTRE III rule by the fact that there is no zone between the preference and the veto thresholds in which the influence of the veto is gradual. With the ELECTRE I rule, the veto forbids all outranking as soon as the deficit of performance of an alternative w.r.t. a profile on some criterion becomes unacceptably large.

To be able to use ELECTRE TRI (with the ELECTRE I version of the concordance-non-discordance rule) we need to set the following parameters:

- the weights or importance coefficients of the criteria;
- the categories and their limiting profiles;
- threshold λ which determines the majority level required;
- the criteria subject to veto and the pairs of levels on these criteria which lead to a veto.

The process of setting these parameters in collaboration with the EE is described in the next subsection.

Note that this elicitation process, as well as the validation of the ensuing SU category assignments obtained by means of applying the model, have been facilitated by using visualization tools offered by the GIS ArcView3.2a. For illustration, Fig. 12.3 shows a *criterion map* representing the assessment of the SU w.r.t. criterion Cr_{12} ("adequate application of Water and Soils Conservation (WSC) techniques"). This figure represents the more or less appropriate character of the response of each SU w.r.t. the application of WSC techniques. The degrees of appropriateness (*A*, *MA* or *NA*) displayed on the map result from the application of expert rules (see Table 12.24) for aggregating the three indicators associated to this criterion. Similar maps have been obtained for all criteria. The result of the assignment to categories by using the ELECTRE TRI method can also be displayed on such a map, which greatly helps the decision maker or the EE in the validation of the results.

12.4.2 Setting the Parameters of the ELECTRE TRI *Method*

We successively assign values to criteria weights, categories limiting profiles, vetoes, and finally, the majority level λ.

12.4.2.1 Criteria Weights

We have used Simos' method (see Simos, 1990a,b) in its revised version by Figueira and Roy (2002). With this method, it is first asked the EE to rank cards on which the name of the criteria is written in increasing order of their importance. The expert can insert blank cards to emphasize the difference of importance between two criteria.

Figure 12.4 represents the result of applying this method to our case. The least important criterion is Cr_{11}. Between Cr_{11} and Cr_{412}, the expert has inserted two blank cards, whereas between Cr_{412} and Cr_{310} he did not insert any blank card. This results in a weight difference between Cr_{11} and Cr_{412} that will be three times as large as the one between Cr_{412} and Cr_{310}. Criteria appearing at the same level in Fig. 12.4, such as Cr_{310} and Cr_{411} are considered as equally important and will be associated the same weight value.

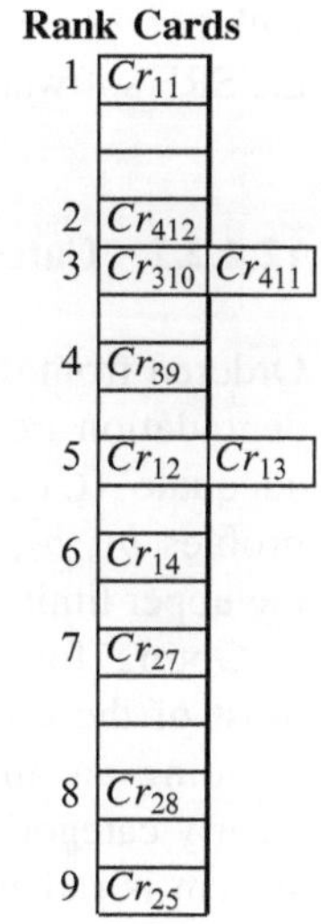

Fig. 12.4 Ranking of cards representing criteria in the application of the revised Simos' method

Table 12.3 Criteria weights obtained using the revised Simos' method

Criteria	Weights (%)
Adequate crops from pedo-geomorphologic viewpoint (Cr_{11})	2
Improvement of agricultural production (Cr_{412})	5
Adequate practice of soil fertilization (Cr_{310})	6
Technical training of farmers (Cr_{411})	6
Adequate application of cultivation techniques (Cr_{39})	7
Adequate application of WSC techniques (Cr_{12})	9
Adequate application of SP techniques (Cr_{13})	9
Limitation of soil compaction (C_{14})	11
Preservation of ecosystem integrity (Cr_{27})	13
Bush fire limitation (Cr_{28})	15
Limitation of cultivated soils extension (Cr_{25})	17

The final step in the interactive questioning process about weights consists in asking the EE to estimate the ratio z of the weights of the most important criterion ("Limitation of cultivated soils extension" Cr_{25}) and the least important criterion ("Adequate crops from pedo-geomorphologic viewpoint" Cr_{11}). This was the most difficult question in the whole process. As previously observed in the literature (see André, 2006, in the framework of environmental assessment of industrial sites), much explanation was required to make the expert accept to propose a value for this ratio, which he considered as rather arbitrary. The value finally proposed for z was lying between 8 and 10. Table 12.3 shows the values computed for the criteria weights by using the procedure described in Figueira and Roy (2002). The computations were performed using the value $z = 8$ and zero order rounding (see Figueira and Roy, 2002). The criteria weights, shown in Table 12.3, are displayed with two decimal figures (percentage). These values can also be obtained by using the SRF software package developed at the LAMSADE, University Paris Dauphine.

12.4.2.2 Categories Limiting Profiles

Ordered from the worse to the better, the four categories of response to the risk of degradation are the following: not adequate (C_1), weakly adequate (C_2), moderately adequate (C_3), adequate (C_4). These categories are respectively separated by profiles b_1, b_2, and b_3. For $i \in \{1, 2, 3\}$, profile b_i represents at the same time the upper limit of category C_i and the lower limit of category C_{i+1}.

Opting for a categorization in four classes instead of three classes (while most of the criteria are assessed on a three levels scale) stems from the will of avoiding an ambiguous median class, which would consist of SU that are not clearly categorized as good or bad. In contrast, the interpretation of our four class system is rather clear and operational. Through the definition of the profiles, that are viewed as environmental norms, the EE considers that the SU belonging to categories C_3 ("moderately adequate") and C_4 ("adequate") are not degraded, while those belonging to categories C_1 ("not adequate") and C_2 ("weakly adequate") are degraded.

In the process of determining the category limit profiles or norms, the most important criterion (having the largest weight), namely "Limitation of cultivated soils extension (Cr_{25})", has been the focal point. This is because all other criteria have a direct relationship with Cr_{25}. Indeed, when the anthropogenic or the natural pressures are strong, when the intrinsic capacity of the system to resist such pressures is weak, and when the development and management actions are not sufficient or not well oriented, the main consequence is that local populations start to cultivate additional surfaces, contributing to erosion or other forms of degradation.

In the region under study, the extension of cultivated surface can only be limited by the reduction of exerted pressure, by the intrinsic resistance capacity of the system, or by development plans and management measures; these effects or actions are reflected in the ten other criteria. Keeping these elements in mind, we have questioned the EE in the following way in order to determine the three required profiles:

- Profile b_3 (lower limit of the best category C_4) requires the highest scale level (A) of criterion Cr_{25}. For the other ten criteria, the expert was asked to state a level on each of them, which separates values typical of alternatives assigned to category C_4 from those typical of alternatives assigned to C_3. Notice that the ELECTRE I assignment rule allows an alternative to be assigned to category C_4 while some of its evaluations lie below the profile on some criteria: in order to be assigned to C_4 an alternative has to be above profile b_3 on a qualified majority of criteria . This remark is also valid for the assignment to the other categories.
- Profile b_1 (upper limit of the worst category C_1): the value of this profile regarding criterion Cr_{25} was set to the lowest scale level of this criterion (NA);

the ten others evaluations of b_1 constitute the EE's answers when asked for a level on each criterion separating the values typical of alternative assigned to the lowest category C_1 from those of alternatives assigned to C_2.

- Profile b_2 is not only the upper limit of category C_2 and the lower limit of category C_3; it also represents the norm separating SU considered as degraded from those considered as non-degraded. Therefore, profile b_2 was assigned the value corresponding to the intermediate level (*MA*) on the scale of criterion Cr_{25}. For each of the other ten criteria, the value assigned to b_2 is the one that separates the typical performance of degraded SU from those of non-degraded ones, according to the EE.

The levels obtained from the expert as describing the three profiles are displayed in Table 12.4 and illustrated in Fig. 12.5.

Table 12.4 Initial parameters setting: profiles and criteria weighting

Criteria	b_1	b_2	b_3	Weights (%)
Adequate pedo-geomorphologic choice (Cr_{11})	*NA*	*MA*	*MA*	2
Improvement of the agricultural production (Cr_{412})	*MA*	*MA*	*A*	5
Adequate practice of soil fertilization (Cr_{310})	*NA*	*MA*	*A*	6
Technical training of farmers (Cr_{411})	*NA*	*A*	*A*	6
Adequate application of cultivation techniques (Cr_{39})	*NA*	*MA*	*MA*	7
Adequate application of WSC techniques (Cr_{12})	*NA*	*NA*	*NA*	9
Adequate application of SP techniques (Cr_{13})	*MA*	*A*	*A*	9
Limitation of soil compaction (Cr_{14})	*MA*	*MA*	*A*	11
Preservation of the ecosystem integrity (Cr_{27})	*NA*	*MA*	*A*	13
Bush fire limitation (Cr_{28})	*NA*	*NA*	*A*	15
Extension limitation of the cultivated soils (Cr_{25})	*NA*	*MA*	*A*	17

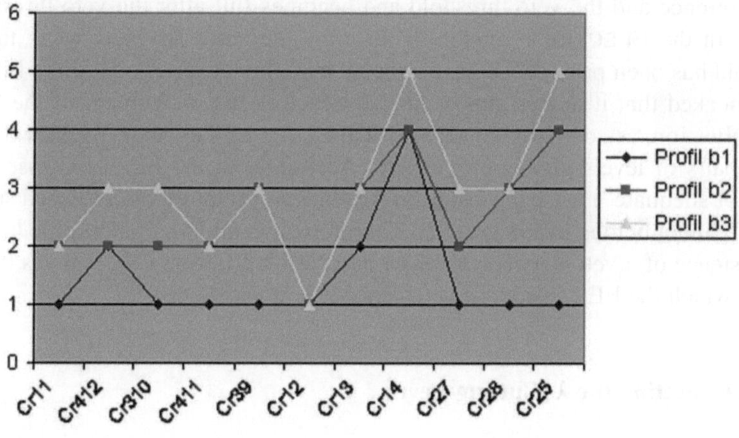

Fig. 12.5 Graphic representation of profiles

Comments

- Each profile is strictly dominated by the next one.
- The three profiles are assigned the same level (*NA*) on criterion Cr_{12}. This is due to the fact that the EE considers profiles as norms. Any performance improvement of a SU on criterion Cr_{12} will have positive consequences (at more or less long-term) on criteria such as Cr_{412}, Cr_{14}, Cr_{27}, Cr_{25}. Therefore, the EE considers that no minimal requirement should be imposed on this criterion. One might consequently think that criterion Cr_{12} plays no role and could be neglected. As will be discussed in Sect. 12.5.6, dropping criterion Cr_{12} has different consequences depending on whether the pessimistic or the optimistic version of the ELECTRE TRI method is used.

12.4.2.3 Specification of Vetoes

We are now ready to explicit the reasons why we have adopted the simpler concordance-non-discordance rule as in the ELECTRE I method instead of the classical ELECTRE TRI rule. The latter requires to determining indifference and preference thresholds for each criterion. In our case, the criteria scales distinguish very few levels (never more than three). Since the scale levels for each criterion represent neatly differentiated states of a dimension of reality that has an impact on the evaluation of a SU, the indifference thresholds can all be set to zero, each change making a difference. It is even the case that a difference of one level entails full preference, as confirmed by the EE. This means that also the preference threshold should be set to zero, in case we were in the process of eliciting the parameters of the classical ELECTRE TRI rule. With these values of the indifference and the preference thresholds, the ELECTRE TRI and the ELECTRE I outranking rules only differ w.r.t vetoes. With ELECTRE TRI, the veto is gradual in the interval separating the preference and the veto threshold and becomes full after the veto threshold is passed. In the ELECTRE I version of the rule, the veto only acts when the veto threshold has been passed. We have adopted here the latter version of the rule (and have checked that it makes almost no difference in the assignment of the SU for our application, as compared to the classical ELECTRE TRI rule). We now describe which pairs of levels give rise to a veto. According to the EE, a SU assessed as *NA* ("not adequate") w.r.t. the criterion "extension limitation of cultivated surfaces (Cr_{25})" cannot belong to category C_4. Therefore, it cannot outrank profile b_3 due to the existence of a veto between levels *A* and *NA* on criterion Cr_{25}. This is the only case in which the EE considers a veto is needed.

12.4.2.4 Setting the λ-Cutting Level

The level of qualified majority required in order to declare that an alternative outranks a profile (or the other way around) is represented by a parameter that we denote by λ. In our application, this cutting level was determined by examining some SU for which the EE a priori knew that they should be assigned to category C_1. From Table 12.4, we observe that profile b_1 is assigned the lowest possible value on a set of criteria whose sum of the weights reaches 0.75. Hence, any SU, even one that has the lowest possible evaluation on *all* criteria, will outrank profile b_1 and be assigned to category C_2 or higher as long as the cutting level λ is not greater than 0.75. For the EE, it was clear that a SU having the poorest possible evaluations on all criteria should be assigned to the worst category C_1. Therefore λ had to be assigned a value at least equal to 0.76. Since reaching the level of b_1 on any criterion on which it is higher than *NA* (i.e. Cr_{412}, Cr_{13} or Cr_{14}) could justify the assignment to category C_2 or higher, it was decided to set λ to 0.76.

12.5 Validation and Exploitation of the Results

Applying the pessimistic (resp. optimistic) ELECTRE TRI method with the parameters setting described in Sect. 12.4.2 (and using the ELECTRE I rule) results in assignments that can be represented on a decisional map of response to the degradation risk. We have implemented the ELECTRE TRI procedure (pessimistic and optimistic) in Visual Basic 6, a language that is compatible with ArcGis9. However, for practical reasons (most of the time we had only ArcView3.2a at our disposal), we did not implement ELECTRE TRI directly into ArcGis9. In other words, we have opted for an indirect integration in the sense of Chakhar (2006), but there should be no difficulty for moving to full integration in a recent version of ArcGis.

Using ArcView3.2a, we have produced two maps tentatively representing the response to the degradation risk. Figure 12.6 represents the assignments obtained with the pessimistic version of ELECTRE TRI while Fig. 12.7 represents those obtained with the optimistic version. We emphasize that these maps are not just like criteria maps: they aggregate the information conveyed in 11 criteria maps and—more importantly—integrate in addition preferential information provided by the EE. This section is dedicated to the validation of a model of assessment of the response to the degradation risk for the Loulouka basin and to the formulation of recommendations derived from the assignment results.

12.5.1 First Validation Round

The maps in Figs. 12.6 and 12.7 have first been carefully examined with the EE. To ease the comparison of the assignments made by the pessimistic and optimistic versions of ELECTRE TRI, a cross tabulation of these two classifications has been produced in Table 12.5.

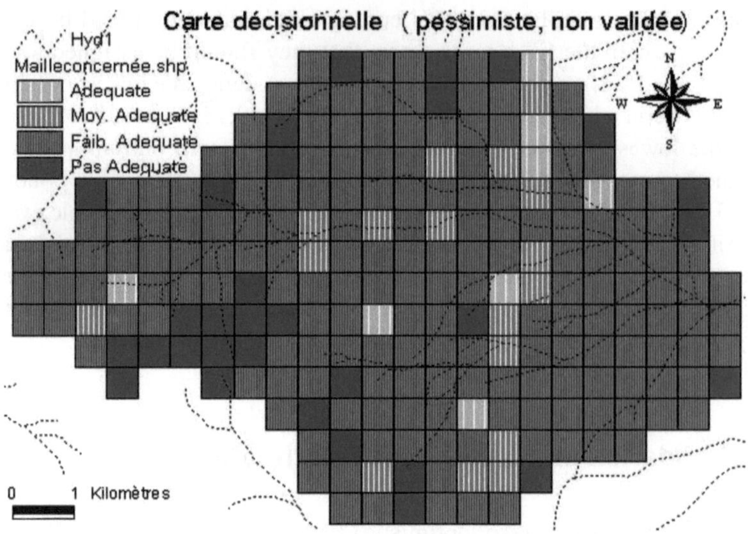

Fig. 12.6 Initial decisional map of response to the degradation risk (pessimistic) with cutting level $\lambda = 0.76$

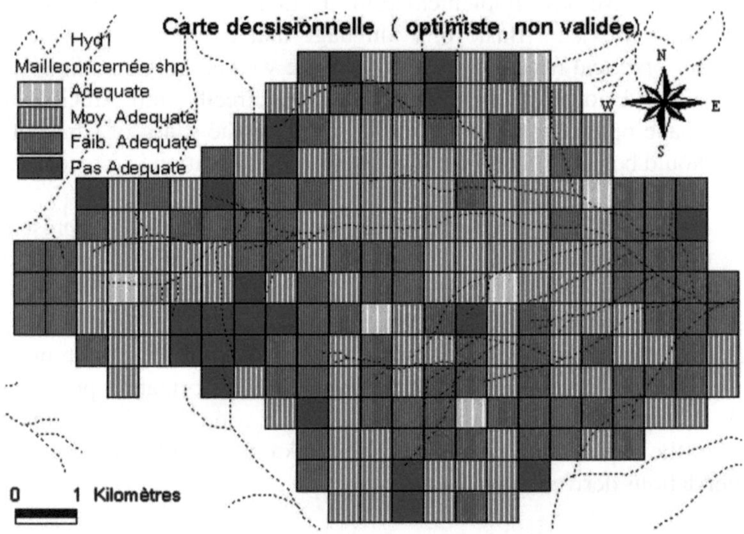

Fig. 12.7 Initial decisional map of response to the degradation risk (optimistic) with cutting level $\lambda = 0.76$

Examining Table 12.5 prompts the following comments:

- according to the pessimistic assignment procedure, the study area is overall strongly degraded with around 90 % (204 over 229) of degraded SU (belonging either to the C_1 or C_2 categories);

Table 12.5 Cross tabulation of the pessimistic vs. optimistic assignments of 229 spatial units to four categories of response to the degradation risk

		Optimistic					
		C_1	C_2	C_3	C_4	Total	%
Pessimistic	C_1	22	2	7		31	14
	C_2		87	86		173	76
	C_3			17		17	7
	C_4				8	8	3
	Total	22	89	110	8	229	100
	%	10	39	48	3	100	

Table 12.6 Revised definition of profile b_2 on criterion Cr_{28}

Criteria	b_1	b_2	b_3	Weights (%)
Bush fire limitation (Cr_{28})	*NA*	*A*	*A*	15

- according to the optimistic assignment procedure, the region is overall moderately non-degraded with around 51 % (118 of 229) of non-degraded SU (belonging either to the C_3 or C_4 categories);
- 41 % (95 out of 229) of SU are not assigned to the same class by the pessimistic and optimistic procedures. This implies (see Bouyssou et al. 2006, p. 382) that these SU are indifferent or incomparable to at least one of the three profiles. A SU in such a situation is assigned its worse (resp. best) possible classification by the pessimistic (resp. optimistic) version of the ELECTRE TRI procedure. For such SU, the EE opinion is required regarding the proper category the unit should be assigned to.

After having examined the maps, the EE considers that none of the classifications obtained correctly represents the state of the area. On the one hand, based on previous studies, the area is mostly in a degraded state, which disqualifies the classification stemming from the optimistic procedure. On the other hand, in the vicinity of the hydrographic network, one should find some SU that are ranked as "moderately adequate" or "adequate" w.r.t their response to the degradation risk, i.e. SU that are non-degraded. Indeed, these zones are low points (water course bank, outlet) whereto eroded soil particles converge from the top of the Loulouka basin. In contrast, according to the pessimistic procedure, all the zones around the hydrographic network are considered degraded, which disqualifies this classification too.

We have thus been led to revise some elements of our initial models with the help of the EE. We have concentrated on the definition of the profiles and especially of profile b_2. For the criterion "bush fire limitation" (Cr_{28}), which is a binary criterion, we observe that 66 % (151 out of 229) of the SU have a good performance (*A*) on this criterion. Cr_{28} is the second most important criterion. Among these 151 SU, 86 are indifferent or incomparable to the second profile b_2 (see Table 12.5), which has value *NA* on criterion Cr_{28}. Therefore we drew the conclusion that b_2 is not sufficiently discriminating and we have revised the value assigned to b_2 on criterion Cr_{28}, raising it to *A* (see Table 12.6). This modification has the following effect (see Table 12.7). Most SU (56 out of 86) that were assigned to category C_3 by the

Table 12.7 Cross tabulation of the pessimistic vs. optimistic assignments after profile b_2 has been modified

		Optimistic					
		C_1	C_2	C_3	C_4	Total	%
Pessimistic	C_1	22	9			31	13
	C_2		143	30		173	76
	C_3			17		17	8
	C_4				8	8	3
	Total	22	152	47	8	229	100
	%	10	66	21	3	100	

optimistic procedure and to C_2 by the pessimistic procedure are now assigned to C_2 by both procedures. This change is considered as absolutely realistic by the EE.

Using the revised definition of profile b_2, we find only 17 % (39 out of 229) of SU that are assigned differently by the pessimistic and the optimistic procedures versus 41 % (95 out of 229) with the first version of b_2. This reduction in assignment differences between the two procedures is the sign that the profiles are now better calibrated, the revised profile b_2 producing less indifference and incomparability.

12.5.2 *Second Validation Round*

The new results of both procedures were submitted to the EE. The decisional map stemming from the optimistic assignment procedure (Fig. 12.9) immediately received complete approval by the EE. According to the administrative authorities in charge of the territorial management of the area under study, the globally degraded state of the Loulouka basin is a fact. However, management efforts were brought to this region since more than two decades and these development policies have left some positive traces in spite of the fact that they have not been sufficiently successful. The decisional map stemming from the optimistic assignment procedure shows 76 % (vs. 90 % for the decisional map stemming from the pessimistic assignment procedure) of degraded SU, and 24 % (vs. only 10 % for the decisional map stemming from the pessimistic procedure) of non-degraded SU (see Table 12.7). Moreover, the non-degraded SU are located all around the hydrographic network as shown on the optimistic decisional map (Fig. 12.9), while the pessimistic decisional map (Fig. 12.8) presents uniformly degraded SU at the same location. This has contributed to consolidate the adoption of the optimistic assignment model by the EE. In particular, according to the EE, the 24 % of non-degraded SU as displayed on the optimistic decisional map seem to better reflect the insufficient impact of development efforts previously brought to the study area. The EE hence considers that the optimistic assignment model (with the revised choice of parameters) correctly reflects the response to the risk of degradation in the area.

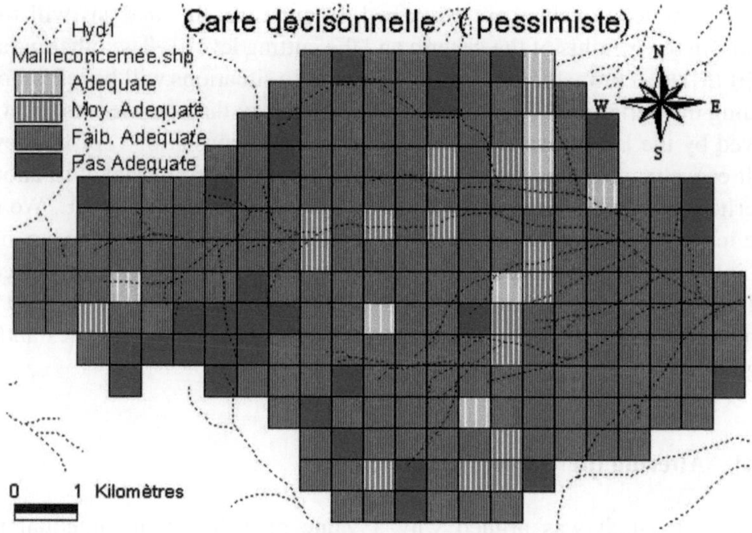

Fig. 12.8 Revised decisional map of response to the degradation risk (pessimistic) with cutting level $\lambda = 0.76$

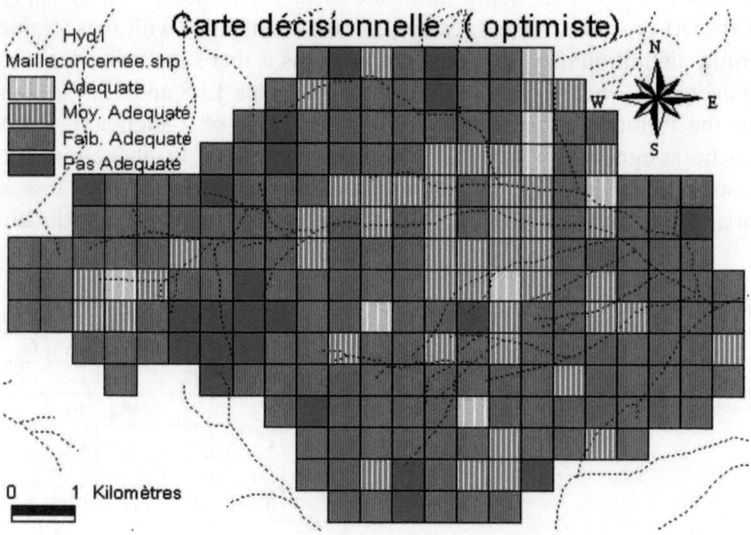

Fig. 12.9 Revised decisional map of response to the degradation risk (optimistic) with cutting level $\lambda = 0.76$

12.5.3 Robustness of the Assignments

Since the values of the model parameters are imprecisely determined, it is important to verify whether the assignment of SU to categories do not change dramatically when the parameters values are perturbed. In our case, the analysis will focus on variations in the weights of the criteria and the cutting level λ. The other parameters of the ELECTRE TRI method, i.e. profiles, and veto situations will be left untouched. Regarding the definition of the profiles, we would say that they represent norms as perceived by the EE. Since the scales of our criteria consist of very few levels (at most three), changing the value of a profile by passing from a level to another on some criterion would significantly alter the statement made by the EE. We did not engage in such modifications. Regarding the vetoes, only one single veto situation was pointed out in the analysis. It makes little sense to arbitrarily introduce other veto situations or remove the one that was explicitly identified. In the rest of this section, we examine the consequences of modifications of the profiles and of the cutting level.

12.5.3.1 Altering the Cutting Level

In Sect. 12.4.2.4, it was argued why a value of λ less than or equal to 0.75 could not be considered (considering that the criteria weights remain unchanged). We have thus given λ two other values, both larger than 0.76, namely 0.79 and 0.81. Tables 12.8 and 12.9 below show the assignments computed by applying the ELECTRE TRI procedure (both pessimistic and optimistic) with these values of λ. The profiles definition used in these computations is that summarized in Table 12.4 revised according with Table 12.6. Comparing Tables 12.8 and 12.9 to Table 12.7 prompts the following observations. When the value of λ increases, a given SU tends to be assigned to a better (resp. worse) category by the optimistic (resp. pessimistic) procedure. This is easy to understand since it becomes less and less easy for an alternative to outrank a profile and conversely. Since the optimistic (resp.

Table 12.8 ELECTRE TRI with $\lambda = 0.79$

		Optimistic				
		C_1	C_2	C_3	C_4	Total
Pessimistic	C_1	22	9			31
	C_2		138	46		184
	C_3			11		11
	C_4				3	3
	Total	22	147	57	3	229

Table 12.9 ELECTRE TRI with $\lambda = 0.81$

		Optimistic				
		C_1	C_2	C_3	C_4	Total
Pessimistic	C_1	24	17	5		46
	C_2		112	60		172
	C_3			8		8
	C_4				3	3
	Total	24	129	73	3	229

Table 12.10 Alternative sets of weights used in analysis

Criteria	Basic set of weights (%)	1st set of weights (%)	2nd set of weights (%)	3rd set of weights (%)	4th set of weights (%)	5th set of weights (%)
C_{11}	2	2	4	4	2	4
C_{412}	5	5	5	4	3	5
C_{310}	6	5	6	6	6	5
C_{411}	6	5	6	6	6	5
C_{39}	7	7	9	7	8	7
C_{12}	9	10	9	9	9	10
C_{13}	9	10	9	9	9	10
C_{14}	11	11	11	9	11	9
C_{27}	13	13	13	14	12	13
C_{28}	15	15	13	15	15	15
C_{25}	17	17	15	17	19	17

pessimistic) procedure assigns SU in categories below a profile that outranks them (resp. above profiles that they outrank), SU tend to be assigned to higher (resp. lower) categories. We correlatively observe an increasing number of incomparability cases with profile b_2; this number passes from 13 % (30 out of 229) to 26 % (60 out of 229). This is an indication that the definition of this profile could be further revised in order to reduce the difference between the optimistic and pessimistic procedures. However, upon presentation of these results, the EE confirmed that the optimistic assignments, obtained with the various values of λ (0.76; 0.79; 0.81), seem relatively similar and acceptable. The value 0.76 for λ received his preference.

12.5.3.2 Robustness w.r.t. the Weights

The five sets of weights displayed in Table 12.10 have been used to test the robustness w.r.t. the setting of the weights. The EE was reasonably sure about the order on the criteria weights while his assessment of the differences between successive weights might be more subject to errors. Therefore, we decided that the ordering should, most of the time, remain unchanged, while we introduced slight perturbations in the weight differences. The results of the experimentation with the five alternative sets of weights is summarized in Tables 12.12, 12.13, 12.14, 12.15, and 12.16; for facilitating the comparison with the assignments validated during the second round, we have reproduced Table 12.6 as Table 12.11 below. In Table 12.10, a weight value is underlined if and only if it differs from the value it takes in the initial setting of the weights. The perturbed values differ from the initial ones by at most 2 %.

Comparing Tables 12.12, 12.13, 12.14, 12.15, and 12.16 with Table 12.11 yields the following results:

Table 12.11 ELECTRE TRI results: basic weights, $\lambda = 0.76$, profiles read from Table 12.6

		Optimistic				
		C_1	C_2	C_3	C_4	Total
Pessimistic	C_1	22	9			31
	C_2		143	30		173
	C_3			17		17
	C_4				8	8
	Total	22	152	47	8	229

Table 12.12 ELECTRE TRI results: first set of weights, $\lambda = 0.76$, profiles read from Table 12.6

		Optimistic				
		C_1	C_2	C_3	C_4	Total
Pessimistic	C_1	22	9			31
	C_2		143	32		175
	C_3			15		15
	C_4				8	8
	Total	22	152	47	8	229

Table 12.13 ELECTRE TRI results: second set of weights, $\lambda = 0.76$, profiles read from Table 12.6

		Optimistic				
		C_1	C_2	C_3	C_4	Total
Pessimistic	C_1	22	9			31
	C_2		146	28		174
	C_3			16		16
	C_4				8	8
	Total	22	155	44	8	229

Table 12.14 ELECTRE TRI results: third set of weights, $\lambda = 0.76$, profiles read from Table 12.6

		Optimistic				
		C_1	C_2	C_3	C_4	Total
Pessimistic	C_1					
	C_2		178	28		206
	C_3			15		15
	C_4				8	8
	Total		178	43	8	229

Table 12.15 ELECTRE TRI result: fourth set of weights, $\lambda = 0.76$, profiles read from Table 12.6

		Optimistic				
		C_1	C_2	C_3	C_4	Total
Pessimistic	C_1					
	C_2		177	27		204
	C_3			17		17
	C_4				8	8
	Total		177	44	8	229

1. According to the optimistic classification (respectively pessimistic), the percentage of non-degraded SU lies between 24 % (55 out of 229) and 24.5 % (56 out of 229) [respectively 10 % (23 out of 229) and 11 % (25 out of 229)], which is

Table 12.16 ELECTRE TRI results: fifth set of weights, $\lambda = 0.76$, profiles read from Table 12.6

		Optimistic				
		C_1	C_2	C_3	C_4	Total
Pessimistic	C_1					
	C_2		178	28		206
	C_3			15		15
	C_4				8	8
	Total		178	48	8	229

not much different from the percentage observed for the reference solution that is 24 % (55 out of 229) [respectively 11 % (25 out of 229)]. The most important distinction, between degraded and non-degraded SU is well preserved.

2. Within the class of non-degraded SU, the distinction between categories C_3 ("moderately adequate") and C_4 ("adequate") is relatively robust. Category C_4 is totally stable (8 SU for all sets of weights). The number of SU assigned to C_3 varies from 15 to 17 (resp. 43 to 48) for the pessimistic (resp. optimistic) procedure.
3. There is much less stability in the distinction between categories C_1 and C_2. The number of SU categorized as C_1 remains the same for the original set of weights and the first two alternative sets (both in the pessimistic and the optimistic procedures), then this category vanishes for the last three sets of weights. The number of SU assigned to C_2 varies from 173 to 206 (pessimistic) and from 152 to 178 (optimistic).

These computations confirm that the main distinction between degraded and non degraded SU is robust, as well as the discrimination between C_3 and C_4. On the opposite, there appears to be no clear distinction between categories C_1 and C_2. As already observed, this is probably due to the insufficiently careful definition of profile b_1. Since the EE does not put much emphasis on discriminating C_1 from C_2, we have not devoted more time to improving the definition of b_1.

12.5.4 Assignment to Categories by Means of a Value Function Model

In this section, we build a model based on an additive value function for assigning SU to categories. Our goal is to check, in a rough manner, whether such a model assigns SU in a way that is not radically different from the ELECTRE TRI model. Provided it is eventually the case, this will increase our confidence in the results of our study using ELECTRE TRI. We start by briefly describing the additive value function based assignment model.

12.5.4.1 The Additive Value Function Assignment Model

This model is based on the construction of an additive value function (Keeney and Raiffa, 1976), which allows to attach a value to each SU; a SU is assigned to the hth category C_h if its value passes some threshold u^h but not the threshold u^{h+1} attached to the next category C_{h+1}. More precisely, let $(s_1, s_2, \ldots, s_n)$ denote the vector of assessments attached to the SU. The value $u(s)$ of s has the following form:

$$u(s) = \sum_{j=1}^{n} k_j u_j(s_j), \tag{12.1}$$

where the k_j's are tradeoffs attached to the criteria ($k_j \geq 0$ and $\sum_{j=1}^{n} k_j = 1$) and the u_j's are marginal value functions.

In order to use such a model in our case, we need to go through the following steps:

- build marginal value functions u_j on each dimension j;
- elicit the tradeoffs k_j;
- elicit the threshold value u^h associated with category C_h.

We will achieve this in the next section, leaning heavily on the work done for applying ELECTRE TRI. Note that a method for learning the parameters of an assignment model based on additive value functions was proposed by Zopounidis and Doumpos (1999, 2001) as the *UTADIS method.*

12.5.4.2 Eliciting the Parameters of the Additive Value Function Assignment Model

Building Marginal Value Functions

According with Keeney and Raiffa (1976); von Winterfeldt and Edwards (1986), we tried to assign numerical values to levels *A*, *MA*, *NA* of the scale associated with each criterion. Such values were attached in such a way that differences between them aim at being proportional to the difference of preference between the corresponding level on each criterion, as they are perceived by the EE. For instance regarding criterion Cr_{11} ("Adequate crops from pedo-geomorphologic viewpoint"), levels *A*, *MA* and *NA* were respectively assigned the values 3, 2, 1. The difference between the values "2" and "1" is perceived as equal (in terms of preference) to the difference between the values "3" and "2". In other words, for a given SU, the value improvement obtained from passing from level *NA* (corresponding to a given agricultural reality) to level *MA* (corresponding to a better agricultural reality) is perceived by the EE as practically the same as the value improvement corresponding to passing from level *MA* to level *A* (corresponding to an agricultural reality better than the second one). In the case of criterion Cr_{13} ("Adequate application of soil

Table 12.17 Attaching values to the ordinal scales of the criteria

Criteria	*A*	*MA*	*NA*
Adequate crops from pedo-geomorphologic viewpoint (Cr_{11})	3	2	1
Adequate application of WSC techniques (Cr_{12})	4	3	1
Adequate application of SP techniques (Cr_{13})	3	2	1
Limitation of soil compaction (Cr_{14})	5	4	1
Limitation of cultivated soils extension (Cr_{25})	5	4	1
Preservation of ecosystem integrity (Cr_{27})	3	2	1
Bush fire limitation (Cr_{28})	3		1
Adequate application of cultivation techniques ((Cr_{39})	4	3	1
Adequate practice of soil fertilization (Cr_{310})	3	2	1
Technical training of farmers (Cr_{411})	2		1
Improvement of agricultural production (Cr_{412})	3	2	1

preparation techniques"), the value improvement involved in passing from level *NA* to level *MA* is more important than that involved in passing from level *MA* to level *A*; it is estimated as twice as important, hence the values 4, 3 and 1 respectively assigned to levels *A*, *MA* and *NA*. Table 12.17 displays the values assigned to each level of the scale associated with each criterion. These values were obtained through a discussion with the EE.

We henceforth consider that the values in Table 12.17 are marginal value functions and we shall use them as the $u_j(s_j)$ in formula (12.1).

Setting the Tradeoffs and Categories Thresholds

In order to avoid a lengthy questioning of the EE to assess the tradeoffs associated with the eleven criteria, we simply use the weights displayed in Table 12.3. These weights were obtained, as described in Sect. 12.4.2.1, by using the revised Simos' method, which proceeds by questioning the decision maker (here the EE) on the relative importance of the criteria. It seems to us that this way of questioning is not radically different from "direct rating", a method that is rather commonly used to assess the tradeoffs in an additive value function model (see von Winterfeldt and Edwards 1986, p. 226 and p. 281).

With the marginal value functions determined in Sect. 12.5.4.2 and the tradeoffs in Table 12.3, we can now compute the value $u(s)$ of any SU using formula (12.1). We can also compute the value of a profile b_h by applying the same formula to the vector of evaluations of the profile.

To set the values of the categories thresholds, we use the profiles b_1, b_2, b_3 determined in the application of the ELECTRE TRI method (Table 12.6). We simply take as the lower threshold u^h of category C_h, the value $u(b_h)$ of the lower profile delimiting category C_h. The values computed for the three profiles form the vector $V_0 = (1.47; 2.78; 3.3)$.

Table 12.18 Comparing assignments obtained using value function and pessimistic ELECTRE TRI

		Value function (V_0)				
		C_1	C_2	C_3	C_4	Total
Pessimistic	C_1	23	8	0	0	31
	C_2	38	129	6	0	173
	C_3	0	3	14	0	17
	C_4	0	0	6	2	8
	Total	61	140	26	2	229

Table 12.19 Comparing assignments made using value function and optimistic ELECTRE TRI

		Value function (V_0)				
		C_1	C_2	C_3	C_4	Total
Optimistic	C_1	22	0	0	0	22
	C_2	39	113	0	0	152
	C_3	0	27	20	0	47
	C_4	0	0	6	2	8
	Total	61	140	26	2	229

12.5.4.3 Comparing the Assignments

Table 12.18 (resp. Table 12.19) is a cross tabulation that allows to compare the assignments made using the additive value function model and those obtained through the pessimistic (resp. optimistic) version of ELECTRE TRI.

We make the following two main observations:

- Regarding the distribution in the four categories, the method based on a value function assigns more SU in the worst category (C_1) than either versions of ELECTRE TRI. About the same number of SU are ranked in the two degraded categories (C_1 and C_2) as by the pessimistic version of ELECTRE TRI. Only two SU are assigned to the best category C_4. With the chosen categories thresholds (and the other parameters choice), the method based on a value function appears as even stricter than pessimistic ELECTRE TRI.
- Regarding the dichotomy degraded vs. non-degraded (C_1 or C_2 vs. C_3 or C_4), the method based on a value function and pessimistic ELECTRE TRI have a similar behavior. It is not only the case that the frequencies are similar but also the SU that are labeled as degraded (resp. non-degraded) are almost the same ones (6 SU are considered as degraded by ELECTRE TRI while they are considered as non-degraded by the value function method; 3 SU are in the opposite situation).

Since nothing forces us in using the values of the ELECTRE TRI profiles as categories thresholds, we have tried to see whether it is possible to make the value function assignments closer to the optimistic ELECTRE TRI assignments by selecting other values for the category thresholds. In order to obtain such a result, the categories thresholds must obviously be lowered. The values of these thresholds

Table 12.20 Comparing assignments obtained using value function (V_1) and optimistic ELECTRE TRI

		Value function (V_1)				
		C_1	C_2	C_3	C_4	Total
Optimistic	C_1	15	7	0	0	22
	C_2	2	138	12	0	152
	C_3	0	7	35	5	47
	C_4	0	0	0	8	8
	Total	17	152	47	13	229

Table 12.21 Comparing assignments obtained using value function (V_2) and optimistic ELECTRE TRI

		Value function (V_2)				
		C_1	C_2	C_3	C_4	Total
Optimistic	C_1	15	7	0	0	22
	C_2	17	127	8	0	152
	C_3	0	8	34	5	47
	C_4	0	0	0	8	8
	Total	32	142	42	13	229

for which the assignment frequencies are most similar to those obtained by the optimistic version of ELECTRE TRI are the following:

$V_1 = (1.09; 2.44; 3.04)$
or $V_2 = (1.1; 2.48; 3.04)$

instead of $V_0 = (1.47; 2.78; 3.3)$, the vector of categories thresholds used for obtaining Tables 12.18 and 12.19. Using categories thresholds V_1 (resp. V_2), we obtain the cross tabulations displayed in Table 12.20 (resp. Table 12.21). Examining Tables 12.20 and 12.21 prompts the following comments. While both methods yield similar assignments (both for V_1 and V_2), there are a number of SU that are not assigned to the same groups of categories (degraded vs. non-degraded). Using the thresholds V_1, there are 12 SU that are assigned to C_3 by the value function method while the optimistic ELECTRE TRI considers them as degraded; conversely, 7 SU are considered as degraded (C_2) using the value function method while the optimistic ELECTRE TRI places them in C_3. The picture is analogous in case we use V_2 instead of V_1 (8/8 instead of 12/7).

12.5.4.4 Concluding Remark

Summarizing, we can say that, for the essential, either type of method can produce similar assignments in our case. However some SU (around 10 %) are assigned to significantly different categories.

A more extensive and deeper experimental comparison of the two types of methods certainly constitute an appealing research topic. Among the most interesting issues, let us mention the following ones:

- characterize the alternatives (SU) that tend not to be assigned to the same category according to the method that is used;

- to which extent is it possible to reproduce the assignments of ELECTRE TRI (either the pessimistic or optimistic version) by means of a value function based assignment method? One may consider changing not only the categories thresholds but also the marginal value functions and the tradeoffs.

Obviously, exploring these questions goes beyond the scope of the present case study. We now turn to the recommendation phase, on the basis of the validated version of the ELECTRE TRI method.

12.5.5 Formulating Conclusions and Recommendations

At the end of the second validation round and after the robustness analysis has been performed, the EE is convinced that the decisional map issued from the optimistic assignment procedure using the revised profile b_2 reflects the current response to degradation risk of the region. In his view, the picture is correct enough to allow elaborating conclusions and recommendations on this basis.

Here are the main observations that we can make at this stage.

- The main fact that results from our analysis is that the region is degraded, to a large extent. The attention of the authorities in charge of territorial management, but also that of the peasants and farmers, can be drawn to the 76 % (174 out of 229) of degraded SU, and chiefly the 10 % (22 out of 229, see Table 12.7) most degraded among them. These SU should be the main target of future action that could be taken against the state of degradation of the region. In the same way, the SU that are categorized as non degraded should be protected against undesirable evolution.
- The map in Fig. 12.9 provides a tool for helping to conceive an appropriate intervention policy. Such a policy will be composed of strategies of action adequate to each SU (or homogeneous groups of them). More precisely, for each degraded SU, the actions to undertake depend on the identified weak points of this SU, that should be remedied to, and of its strong points that should be preserved and consolidated. In a similar way, for non-degraded SU, the focus should be on the protection of their strong points and their weak points should be cured. In view of identifying the weak and strong points of each SU, it is important to have easy access to its evaluation table. This evaluation table is accessible through the GIS as the table to associated to the intersection of all criteria maps (see Fig. 12.10). It is thus possible to compare the evaluation table of each SU to the profiles limiting (from below and from above) the category to which it was assigned. The criteria or factors of limitation of the degradation whereby the SU would be failing or would have a weak performance, can be identified and actions against degradation can accordingly be programmed. Similarly, the factors of limitation of the degradation on which a SU does well can be identified and protective actions can be undertaken.

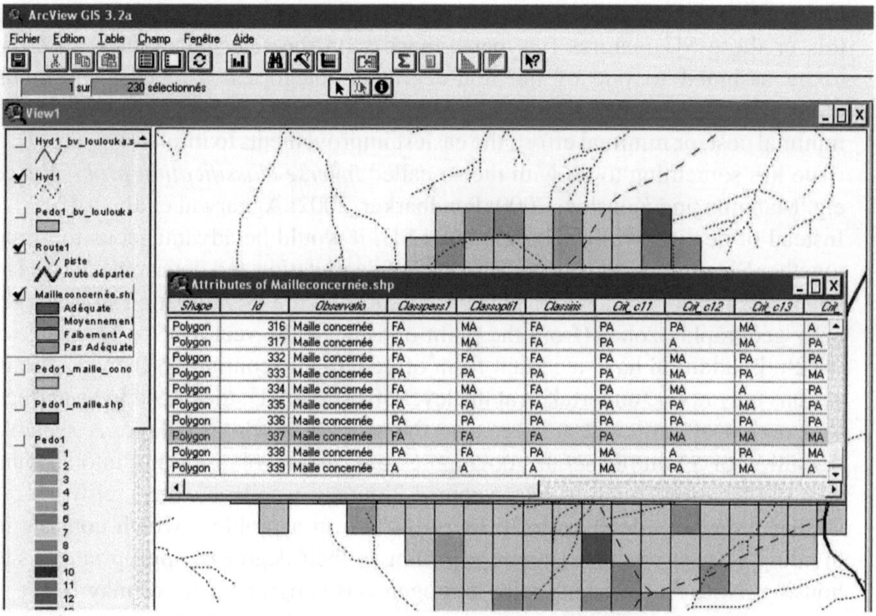

Fig. 12.10 Example of SU evaluation table available from a GIS interface

Consequently, the assignment of the SU to categories of response level to the degradation risk allows us to give appropriate degree of priority to the conservation, development and management actions to be undertaken; it also gives a hint on which factors it is most advisable to act in view of improving the global state of the territory.

At this stage, since we have no mandate for proposing policies, it does not make sense to go much further. Our main contribution is to have shown that the model we have developed (and which needs being maintained, improved and refined) can be useful to design territorial management policies. It is quite clear also that some additional tools are needed to further aid designing such policies. A brief description of these tools follows.

12.5.5.1 Further Needs for Supporting Regional Management Decision Making

Without pretending to be exhaustive, we list a number of questions raised by the exploitation of maps representing the response level to the risk of degradation in a region in view of establishing sustainable development policies to be applied to this region.

- For a given degraded SU identify the minimal improvements to be brought to this or these SU features (i.e. performances on the selected criteria) in order to be assigned to one of the non-degraded categories. The term "minimal improvements" can be understood in various ways: e.g. improvements requiring minimal cost, or minimal effort; the easiest improvements to implement; etc. This issue has something to do with the so-called *inverse classification problem* (see e.g. Mannino and Koushik, 2000; Pendharkar, 2002; Aggarwal et al., 2010).
- Instead of dealing with each individual SU, it would be advantageous to group together SU presenting similar situations of degradation and determine actions to undertake for all similar SU. This passes through the identification of homogenous geographic zones (from the point of view of the vector of performances), which, in addition have a certain form of geographic continuity. Indeed, certain actions may not be undertaken at the level of a single SU; they need to be applied to a region of sufficient area, e.g. on the scale of a whole village. A sensible definition of a homogeneous geographic zone also involves taking into account "natural frontiers" such as water course, limits of a village, forest, cliff, ... A similar issue was dealt with by Joerin (1998) in a problem which consists in dividing a Swiss canton in zones according to their degree of appropriateness to housing. Note that working with homogeneous geographic zones may result in including non-degraded SU into a degraded area and conversely.
- More ambitiously, one may aim at foreseeing the effect of actions on a homogeneous region in view of selecting the best possible actions. To this end, a model for the evolution of the degradation state must be postulated further to the realization of a given action or set of actions. Such an evolution model necessarily involves a large amount of uncertainty since the human as well as the natural factors (e.g. drought, rain, climate change, natural disasters, ...) have a huge influence on the effects of undertaken actions. Developing simulation tools of the zone evolution in reaction to some policy while also taking into account natural evolution factors would obviously be extremely useful. Used together with a tool for comparing decisional maps, it would allow to assess the effect of several policies *ex ante* and would help to argue in favor of a particular policy.
- In order to select the best possible policy, there is a need to develop a tool allowing us to compare decisional maps. Such a tool is also required for comparing maps representing the response to the degradation risk at different periods of time, perhaps before and after some policy has been applied on the territory. This should not be considered a trivial task. Indeed, as the result of the application of a management policy, it can be expected that the state of some SU will improve. On the other hand, some SU can see their state worsen due to uncontrolled natural or human factors. Hence we need a (multi-criteria) model allowing to compare two maps, e.g. the old and the new one, in order to be able to tell whether the overall situation has improved or worsened. In this way, we will also be able to assess the efficiency of implemented corrective measures. Two models for comparing maps were proposed in Metchebon Takougang (2010), Metchebon Takougang and Pirlot (2010) and further models, in Brison and Pirlot (2011).

We can see from this list that the questions raised by territorial management to the decision analysis community are both numerous and stimulating!

12.5.6 Taking into Account the "Elementary Needs" Principle

In our assignment model, we have not taken into account the three criteria that constitute the EN principle ("Elementary Needs", which are necessary conditions for the population welfare) for reasons explained in Sect. 12.3.6.1: the criteria pertaining to the EN principle (respect of socio-cultural spaces, improvement in training standards, improvement in socio-economic conditions) take constant values over all SU of the region. Although the criteria pertaining to the EN principle are not discriminating for assigning SU to categories, they may however play an important role in the determination of efficient actions to be undertaken to fight land degradation. Indeed, the possibility and efficiency of certain actions may depend e.g. on the training level of the local population (as reflected in criterion Cr_{514} "improvement of training standards") or on their socio-economic conditions (as reflected in criterion Cr_{515} "improvement of socioeconomic conditions").

We recall that the EN principle is relevant for discriminating between different catchment basins when evaluating the response to the land degradation risk of a set of catchment basins such as, for instance, the six ones that constitute the Upper Nakambe basin (and include the Loulouka basin). In such a case, two SU belonging to different catchment basins could be assigned to different categories on the basis of the criteria reflecting the EN principle. In the assignment model that we have developed in this study, it is likely that the EE has taken into account his implicit knowledge of the state of the Loulouka basin w.r.t. the criteria of the EN principle while answering questions about the parameters of the model.

A similar remark, yet not identical, can be made about criterion Cr_{12}, which takes the same value in all limiting profiles but not for all SU. We have indeed observed in Sect. 12.4.2.2, page 360, that the level assigned to all profiles on criterion Cr_{12} (Adequate application of WSC techniques) is the worst one, i.e. "Not Adequate" (*NA*). One might be tempted to infer that criterion Cr_{12} plays no role whatsoever, including for the assignment of the alternatives to categories, and might hence be dropped. This is not exactly true. Since for all profiles, criterion Cr_{12} is set to its minimal value, this criterion intervenes in the coalition of criteria that are in favor of any SU w.r.t any profile. Conversely, but not symmetrically, this criterion intervenes in the coalition of criteria that are in favor of any profile w.r.t. an SU if and only if the value of the SU on criterion $Cr12$ is "NA"; in all other cases, Cr_{12} does not belong in such a coalition. This means that criterion Cr_{12} does not differentiate SU in the pessimistic assignment procedure indeed, while, in the optimistic procedure, it makes a difference between SU assessed on Cr_{12} as *NA* on the one hand and *MA* or *A* on the other hand. Besides, this criterion may also play a role for the determination of appropriate actions to be undertaken, just as mentioned above for the criteria pertaining to the EN principle.

12.6 Conclusion

12.6.1 Putting the Case Study in Perspective

At the end of this study, we can see that we have actually followed the main steps of the decision-aiding process scheme DAPDIMR, presented in Sect. 12.2.3. We would like to emphasize the following aspects.

- The interaction between the analyst on the one hand, and different actors, especially the EE, on the other hand, has had a crucial importance, not only for determining the values of the model's parameters but also in the validation phase. Considerable effort has been required on behalf of the EE to understand the proposed model and get confident that it is able to provide a picture of the response to the degradation risk in the region, which does not clash with his expertise. As soon as the EE has gained intuition on the model, he has been able to give relevant assignment examples, propose parameters values and, in the validation phase, drive the analysis to the adoption of the optimistic version of the procedure. We have noted that the main factor that has generated confidence in the model is the results that it has been able to produce, i.e. the map representing the assignments of the SU to categories. Not unexpectedly, experts and decision makers usually leave the responsibility of choosing an appropriate model to the analyst and they assess the relevance of the choice a posteriori, on the basis of the quality of the description provided by the model output. Our experience in this case study illustrates and confirms this general statement.
- Choosing ELECTRE TRI instead of some sort of utility model seems fully justified by the relatively rough character of the assessment scales attached to the criteria. Using ELECTRE TRI is at advantage in such cases even though an additive utility model could give similar results (as we could see in Sect. 12.5.4). The latter model requires however the additional effort of building marginal value functions (Table 12.17).
- Certain steps of the DAPDIMR decisional aiding scheme have not been activated in our study. For instance, this scheme considers the possibility of returning to the structuring phase while it has reached the recommendation stage. If the model was to be put into practice, it might occur that the actors realize that an aspect relative to some planned managerial action has not been considered. This would justify the introduction of additional criteria that allow to assess the effects of the action. A new iteration of the process would then be needed. Since decision makers, i.e. public authorities have not been involved in the present work, the assignment map that constitutes its main result cannot be directly used as the basis for deciding actions. Involving the authorities will imply revisiting the model with them and possibly integrating additional concerns, which may result in incorporating additional criteria, hence forcing a new iteration of the entire model building process.

- The decisional map of response to the degradation risk, produced for the recommendation phase, appears as a most important tool that can serve several purposes. Its most obvious function is to offer a global way of appreciating the degradation risk in the whole region of interest. This is an important element to support decision making at the strategic level when elaborating policies for development and fighting land degradation. At the local level too, the decisional map can be used as a management tool for the implementation of sustainable measures for fighting degradation due to local farmers. When searching to set up measures at the strategic level, the GIS spatial functionalities can help a great deal. Even though some new specific tools would be welcome (see Sect. 12.5.5.1), the generic functionalities of a GIS already enable, for instance, to group together contiguous zones having similar weaknesses in such a way to launch specific actions in an efficient way.

12.6.2 Facilitating the Decision Aiding Process

Conducting a decision aiding process scheme such as DAPDIMR to a conclusion is no easy venture. Let us mention the following pitfalls and—existing or to be developed—remedies.

- The acceptance of a decisional model by the decision maker, experts and stakeholders is a delicate point by itself. Actors in the field of environmental management are not accustomed to use formal methods as, for instance, multi-criteria decision analysis models or expert rules. Therefore, they can exhibit a certain scepticism, or even resistance. Against such reactions, the analyst has to deploy an adequate pedagogy. The most efficient medicine is certainly producing convincing results but this requires that the interaction process with the experts and decision makers is not interrupted before the latter have provided enough reliable information to feed the model. In our application case, the EE's doubts were perceptible in the course of the process, but they faded out and muted into trust upon production of the first reasonable version of a map representing the response to the degradation risk.
- The multicriteria methods which are used for supporting and structuring the decisional process usually are far from being understandable by the decision maker or the expert. Though, the analyst must obtain information from them in order to set the model's parameters. The ability of the analyst to formulate his demands in the language of the expert or the decision maker is an important asset. In particular, a delicate step in the present application was the determination of the "z ratio" (the ratio of the weights of the most important and the least important criteria) in the method we used for eliciting criteria weights (Sect. 12.4.2.1). Avoiding answering complicate questions is possible to some extent and in certain cases. One may resort to learning methods, i.e., inferring the method's parameters by means of assignment examples. In our case, this was not an option,

since too few assignment examples were available. Methods were developed for inferring for instance the parameters of the pessimistic version of ELECTRE TRI (Mousseau and Slowinski, 1998; Mousseau et al., 2000, 2001; Dias et al., 2002; Ngo The and Mousseau, 2002; Mousseau and Dias, 2004). For the optimistic version, a specific method was recently proposed (Metchebon Takougang et al., 2010).

- Another opportunity for facilitating the communication between the analyst, on the one hand, and the decision maker and experts, on the other hand, is through using GIS's and developing specific functionalities within them. Geographic information systems such as ArcGIS9.X or ArcMAP8, incorporate compilers for advanced languages (Visual Basic, Python), which allows to enhance their spatial analysis and management capabilities via the incorporation of new modules such as for instance ELECTRE TRI, possibly with parameters learning tools, and simulation modules. Such an implementation, including parameters learning modules has recently be developed for the open source geographic information system QGIS (Sobrie et al., 2012). At certain stages of the interaction process with experts or decision makers, such modules would allow to work in "what if" mode, i.e. to directly see on the map the consequences of setting some parameter to a specific value.

Appendix: Description of Criteria and Indicators

Criteria and Indicators for Assessing the ERO Principle (P_1)

Four criteria were defined to account for Principle 1, i.e. erosion limitation

Adequate Pedo-Geomorphologic Choice (Cr_{11})

The soil texture or pedology (examples: sandy soil, clayey soil) and the geomorphology [example: slope, plain, plateau, shoal ("bas fond")] must be in close relation with the type of cultivation. If cultivated in a poor soil, a cultivation requiring soils that are rich in nutritive elements will impoverish the poor soil even more until it may become inappropriate to any vegetation, while vegetation can protect soils against rains and winds. Such a situation triggers soil erosion. This criterion has only one indicator:

i_{111}: *comparison with agricultural aptitude map.*

A pedo-geomorphologic map describing the agricultural aptitude of the area under study was obtained from BUNASOL.[8] This map allowed us to assign a class of agricultural aptitude to each spatial unit. Table 12.22 shows the list of

[8]National Office of Soils of Burkina Faso.

Table 12.22 Legend of agricultural aptitude of Loulouka watershed (source: BUNASOL)

Pedo-geo-morphologic type	Soils aptitude	
1, 2, 3	Unsuited	To pluvial cultivations of cereals (maize, sorghum, millet), to rent cultivations (groundnut, cotton), to fodder plant (dolichos biflorus, stylasanthes humulis, andropogon gayanus), to reafforestation, market gardening
	Good aptitude	To extensive cattle breeding, goat and sheep farming
6, 12, 8, 13	Weak aptitude	To pluvial cultivations of cereals (maize, sorghum, millet), to rent cultivations (groundnut, cotton), market gardening, to fodder plant (dolichos biflorus, stylasanthes humulis, andropogon gayanus)
	Good aptitude	To reafforestation (acacia albida, acacia senegal, eucalyptus camaldulensis), to extensive cattle breeding, goat and sheep farming
16, 4, 14, 10	Moderate aptitude	To pluvial cultivations of cereals (maize, sorghum, millet), to reafforestation of ligneous species (acacia senegal, eucalyptus camaldulensis), to intensive cattle breeding, goat and sheep farming, to fodder plant (dolichos biflorus, stylasanthes humulis, andropogon gayanus), to rent cultivations (groundnut, cotton)
7, 11, 5, 15, 17, 9	Moderate aptitude	To rent cultivations (groundnut, cotton), to fodder plant, to intensive cattle breeding, goat and sheep farming, to reafforestation (acacia albida, acacia senegal), to fruit tree plantation (mango, citrus fruits, guava, etc.)
18	Moderate to weak aptitude	To pluvial cultivations of cereals (maize, sorghum, millet), to market gardening (tomato, onion, potato), to fodder plant (dolichos biflorus, stylasanthes humulis, andropogon gayanus), to reafforestation (acacia albida, acacia senegal, prosopis juliflora, eucalyptus camaldulensis)
19	Moderate aptitude	To irrigated cultivations (rice), to market gardening (tomato, oignon, potato), to fruit tree plantation (mango, citrus fruits, guava, etc.), to fodder plant (dolichos biflorus, stylasanthes humulis, andropogon gayanus)

pedo-geomorphological categories on the BUNASOL map and the corresponding soils aptitudes. In each spatial unit represented on the map in Fig. 12.2, the type of pedo-geomorphologic zone which it belongs to is indicated in the upper part of each square. Hence, referring to Table 12.22, we know the degree with which each type of vegetation or cultivation is suitable to each spatial unit.

Assessment w.r.t. indicator i_{111} is qualitative (ordinal). It consists, through field observations, of comparing actual cultivations (farmlands) made by the farmer on each spatial unit to those recommended by the agricultural aptitude map provided by BUNASOL. Such comparison results in a degree of appropriateness of the response of each SU w.r.t. the type of cultivation. This response is assessed on a three level scale of appropriateness (*A*, *MA*, *NA*) as announced above. Note that the pedo-geomorphologic map and Table 12.22 actually distinguish five levels of agricultural aptitude. We have merged "moderate aptitude", "weak aptitude" and "moderate to weak aptitude" classes in Table 12.22 in one class that we label "moderate or weak aptitude".

The rule used for assessing SU's w.r.t indicator i_{111} reads as follows:

- Category *A* is for spatial units that belong to the "good aptitude" or "moderate or weak aptitude" class for a cultivation and on which this cultivation is actually present on more than $\frac{3}{4}$ of the surface of the spatial unit.
- A SU is assigned to category *MA* if less than $\frac{3}{4}$ and more than half of the spatial unit is occupied by a cultivation for which the SU has "good aptitude" or "moderate or weak aptitude" according with the BUNASOL map.
- A SU receives the *NA* mark in the following cases:
  - if the spatial unit belongs to the "good aptitude" or "moderate or weak aptitude" class for a cultivation practice and that less than half of the spatial unit is occupied by such a cultivation,
  - in case of agricultural unfitness of the spatial unit according with the BUNASOL map.

Table 12.23 summarizes the rule designed for assessing indicator i_{111}.

Table 12.23 Evaluation rule for indicator i_{111}

		Occupied surface S		
		$S \geq \frac{3}{4}$	$\frac{1}{2} \leq S < \frac{3}{4}$	$S < \frac{1}{2}$
Aptitude	Good	*A*	*MA*	*NA*
	Moderate or weak	*A*	*MA*	*NA*
	Unsuited	*NA*	*NA*	*NA*

Adequate Application of Water and Soils Conservation Techniques (WSC) (Cr_{12})

Some WSC techniques (bund[9]—in French, *diguette*, stony cordon—in French, *cordon pierreux*) are used to brake the water run-off which carries away land, thus leading to erosion. Other WSC techniques (micro water harvesting or zaï,[10] mulching[11]—in French "paillage") favor the fertilization of the soil on which a vegetation could then grow and ensure a form of protection against wind erosion and erosion due to water run-off. Mulching is no longer applied due to the scarcity of crop waste. Indeed, crop waste is used as animals fodder and also as energy source because of heating wood shortage. Hence, criterion Cr_{12} can be evaluated using the following three indicators:

i_{121} : *presence of bund,*
i_{122} : *presence of stony cordon,*
i_{123} : *presence of zaï.*

The evaluation of spatial units w.r.t. each of these three indicators is qualitative (ordinal):

- For indicator i_{121} (resp. i_{122}), the evaluation results from observing the presence or absence of bunds (resp. stony cordons) and, in case of their presence, from evaluating their state and, also, the distance between two bunds (resp. stony cordons) according to whether they lie on a slope, a plateau or a shoal. For these indicators, the assessment rules are the following. In case there are no bunds (resp. stony cordons) on a given SU, this is assigned to level *NA* on the scale of indicator i_{121} (resp. i_{122}). In case bunds (resp. stony cordons) are present in a SU, we value as level *A* the situation in which bunds (resp. stony cordons) are in good state and they are regularly spaced; if one of these conditions is not fulfilled, the value assigned to the SU is *MA*.
- Indicator i_{123} is related to the presence of zaï in SU's subject to zipella.[12] A SU subject to zipella receives the following marks on the scale of indicator i_{123}:
  - mark *A* if zaï is present on a surface *S* that represents at least $\frac{3}{4}$ of the zipella surface;
  - mark *MA* when this surface *S* lies between $\frac{1}{2}$ and $\frac{3}{4}$ of the zipella surface;
  - mark *NA* if *S* is smaller than $\frac{1}{2}$ of the zipella surface .

[9]Bund: a system which slows down the run-off and allows a better water infiltration in the soil while leaving excess water flow.

[10]Zaï: a soil conservation technique consisting of digging holes in the direction perpendicular to the run-off, then putting manure inside those holes before sowing seeds.

[11]Mulching: a soil conservation and protection technique consisting of cutting grass or using crop waste to treat nude soils.

[12]Zipella: Nude soils.

Table 12.24 Expert rules used for aggregating indicators in the case of criterion Cr_{12}

Adequate application of WSC techniques (Cr_{12})		
Zipella or nude soil absence		
Bund presence (i_{121})	Stony cordons presence (i_{122})	Aggregation 1 (i_{121}, i_{122})
A	*A*	*A*
A	*MA*	*A*
A	*NA*	*A*
MA	*A*	*A*
MA	*MA*	*MA*
MA	*NA*	*MA*
NA	*A*	*A*
NA	*MA*	*MA*
NA	*NA*	*NA*
Zipella or nude soil presence		
Aggregation 1 (i_{121}, i_{122})	Zaï presence (i_{123})	Aggregation 2 ($i_{121}, i_{122}, i_{123}$)
A	*A*	*A*
A	*MA*	*A*
A	*NA*	*MA*
MA	*A*	*A*
MA	*MA*	*MA*
MA	*NA*	*NA*
NA	*A*	*A*
NA	*MA*	*MA*
NA	*NA*	*NA*

If there is no zipella on the SU, only indicators i_{121} and i_{122} are assessed for that SU.

These three indicators are aggregated using expert rules, yielding an assessment of each SU on criterion Cr_{12}. The rules used are described in Table 12.24. The upper part of the table is used for SU's in which no zipella shows up: only indicators i_{121} and i_{122} intervene (Aggregation 1). In case of presence of zipella in a SU, then the result of Aggregation 1 is aggregated with indicator i_{123} yielding the rule called "Aggregation 2".

Adequate Application of Soils Preparation Techniques (SP) (Cr_{13})

Ploughing, by loosening the soil, favors erosion. Hence it is important to plough perpendicularly to the direction of water flow. The *fallow* practice allows the soil to

Table 12.25 Expert rules used for aggregating indicators in the case of criterion Cr_{13}

Fallow practice (i_{131})	Ploughing technique (i_{132})	Aggregation Cr_{13}
A	*A*	*A*
A	*NA*	*NA*
MA	*A*	*A*
MA	*NA*	*NA*
NA	*A*	*MA*
NA	*NA*	*NA*

rest. This favors vegetation growing in the long-term, which helps reducing erosion. Criterion Cr_{13} has two indicators:

i_{131} : *fallow practice,*
i_{132} : *ploughing technique.*

The evaluations of SU's w.r.t. indicators i_{131} and i_{132} are qualitative. For i_{131} (resp. i_{132}), the evaluation results from the observation of the fallow practice (resp. the ploughing technique) used on each SU. The appropriateness of the response of each SU w.r.t. fallow practice and ploughing technique is assessed on the three levels scale (*A*, *MA*, *NA*) of each indicator. The expert rule used for aggregating indicators i_{131} and i_{132} into criterion Cr_{13} is displayed in Table 12.25.

Soil Compaction Limitation (Cr_{14})

Compact nude soil forbids water infiltration. This induces run-off which takes away all solid particles from the ground surface. On the other hand, the soil overstamping by animals, either in habitual penning places (penning for the night), or due to seasonal move to summer pastures, or in watering places, has an impact on soil compaction. Cr_{14} has two indicators:

i_{141} : *presence of nude soil,*
i_{142} : *animals overstamping.*

The evaluation of SU's w.r.t. i_{141} and i_{142} was performed as follows:

- For i_{141}, mark *A* is assigned if less than a quarter of the SU is nude; mark *MA* is for SU's in which more than a quarter and less than half the surface is nude, *NA* is given when more than half the spatial unit is nude;
- i_{142} is a binary indicator noting the presence (mark *A*) or absence (mark *NA*) of animals overstamping on the SU.

The results of theses evaluations obtained by means of indicators i_{141} and i_{142} were aggregated following three classes (*A*, *MA*, *NA*) of appropriateness response of the spatial unit w.r.t. the soil compaction limitation (see Table 12.26).

Table 12.26 Expert rules used for aggregating indicators in the case of criterion Cr_{14}

Presence of nude soil (i_{141})	Animals over-stamping (i_{142})	Aggregation Cr_{14}
A	*A*	*A*
A	*NA*	*MA*
MA	*A*	*MA*
MA	*NA*	*NA*
NA	*A*	*NA*
NA	*NA*	*NA*

Criteria and Evaluation Indicators of BIO Principle (P_2)

Four criteria were identified to assess the limitation of biodiversity loss.

Limitation of Cultivated Surfaces Extension (Cr_{25})

Increasing the cultivated surface reduces biodiversity. In particular, it eliminates plants which are essential to soil reconstitution. Cultivated surface extension is most of the time made by using inapt soils left fallow. Historical data related to the extension of cultivated surface is not available. Therefore, we have opted for the quantification of cultivated marginal land. Criterion Cr_{25} has only one indicator:

i_{251} : *cultivation on marginal lands.*

The evaluation w.r.t. i_{251} is qualitative. It rests on the observation of the percentage of marginal lands cultivation in each SU. Mark *A* is attributed if there is no marginal land cultivation, *MA* results when cultivation on marginal land remains below one third of the SU surface, while *NA* is attributed if at least one third of the SU surface consists of cultivated marginal lands.

Adequate Pesticide Usage (Cr_{26})

Each type of crop is associated a particular type of pesticide which protects it by taking on its enemies (vegetal or animal). Using pesticides that attack other organisms is not adequate since, sooner or later, it will have a negative influence on some plants which are sensitive to these pesticides. Moreover, the right matching between the type of pesticide and the type of cultivation is not sufficient. Also the quantity of pesticide used and the moment at which it is spilled may be more or less appropriate.

Remark 12.1 Pesticide usage is not easily observable unless the team in charge of the survey remains on the field during all the cultivation period. Obtaining precise and reliable information on pesticide usage from the population is not easy either.

Table 12.27 Expert rules used for aggregating indicators in the case of criterion Cr_{26}

Appropriate matching of pesticide and type of cultivation (i_{261})	Pesticide usage frequency (i_{262})	Aggregation Cr_{26}
A	*MA*	*A*
A	*NA*	*A*
MA	*MA*	*MA*
MA	*NA*	*MA*
NA	*MA*	*NA*
NA	*NA*	*NA*

In our case we have not been able to gather the required information so that this criterion could not be taken into account.

Nonetheless this criterion Cr_{26} was analyzed; it has two indicators:

i_{261} : *appropriate matching pesticide-cultivation,*
i_{262} : *frequency of pesticide usage.*

These indicators are assessed on a qualitative scale. For indicator i_{261}, mark *A* is attributed in the case where no pesticide is used, *MA* is for the case where the pesticide appropriate for the type of cultivation is used, while *NA* results if the pesticide used is not adequate to the type of cultivation. For indicator i_{262}, mark *A* is assigned whenever no pesticide is used; the assessment of a SU is *MA* if the pesticide adequate for the crop is used once. For more than one use of pesticide per crop or in case of inadequate pesticide usage, we attribute mark *NA*. The expert rule designed for aggregating these two indicators is displayed in Table 12.27, using three classes (*A*, *MA*, *NA*) of appropriateness of response of SU's w.r.t. pesticide usage.

Preservation of Ecosystem Integrity (Cr_{27})

The presence of trees and forests has a positive impact on the preservation of the biodiversity. Criterion Cr_{27} has four indicators:

i_{271} : *presence of sacred grove (or copse),*
i_{272} : *reforestation zone,*
i_{273} : *protected forest,*
i_{274} : *presence of trees stump.*

For assessing a SU w.r.t each of the indicators i_{271}, i_{272} and i_{273}, we observe the surface percentage of the SU occupied either by a sacred grove, a reforestation zone, or a protected forest. The rule is the same for all three indicators. We attribute mark *A* (resp. *MA*, *NA*) if at least $\frac{2}{3}$ (resp. between $\frac{1}{3}$ and $\frac{2}{3}$, at least $\frac{1}{3}$) of the SU surface is occupied by a sacred grove, a reforestation zone, or a protected forest. The expert rule used for aggregating the indicators i_{271}, i_{272} and i_{273} in order to assess the degree

Table 12.28 Expert rules used for aggregating indicators in the case of criterion Cr_{27}

Presence of sacred grove (i_{271})	Reforestation zone (i_{272})	Protected forest (i_{273})	Aggregation Cr_{27}
A	*A*	*A*	*A*
A	*A*	*MA*	*A*
A	*A*	*NA*	*A*
A	*MA*	*A*	*A*
A	*MA*	*MA*	*A*
A	*MA*	*NA*	*A*
A	*NA*	*A*	*A*
A	*NA*	*MA*	*A*
A	*NA*	*NA*	*A*
MA	*A*	*A*	*A*
MA	*A*	*MA*	*A*
MA	*A*	*NA*	*A*
MA	*MA*	*A*	*A*
MA	*MA*	*MA*	*A*
MA	*MA*	*NA*	*A*
MA	*NA*	*A*	*A*
MA	*NA*	*MA*	*A*
MA	*NA*	*NA*	*MA*
NA	*A*	*A*	*A*
NA	*A*	*MA*	*A*
NA	*A*	*NA*	*A*
NA	*MA*	*A*	*A*
NA	*MA*	*MA*	*A*
NA	*MA*	*NA*	*MA*
NA	*NA*	*A*	*A*
NA	*NA*	*MA*	*MA*
NA	*NA*	*NA*	*NA*

of appropriateness of the response of each SU w.r.t. the preservation of ecosystem integrity is given in Table 12.28.

Remark 12.2 Indicator i_{274} could not be taken into account in the assessment of SU's w.r.t. criterion Cr_{27}. Assessing a SU w.r.t. this indicator, requires information about plants regeneration capacity as well as about the cutting technique applied to the plants. Some cutting techniques favor regeneration while others do not. In our case, these data on the vegetation of the area were not available so that we could not assess SU's w.r.t. indicator i_{274}.

Bush Fire Limitation (Cr_{28})

Bush fire is often practiced by farmers to clear land before cultivation by removing vegetation, or by animals farmers to eliminate straw and favor vegetation growth in view of feeding the animals in the beginning of the dry season. Bush fires have undesirable consequences such as the destruction of the vegetation, of animals, particularly the micro-fauna, and animals habitat. Bush fires also lead to soil erosion by the loss of vegetal coverage. Criterion Cr_{28} has only one indicator:

i_{281} : *presence of bush fire.*

Indicator i_{281} has only two modalities; it encodes the absence of bush fire (mark A) or, on the contrary, the practice of bush fire (NA) on each SU.

Criteria and Evaluation Indicators of FER Principle (P_3)

Criteria Cr_{39} and Cr_{40} represent the relevant aspects of the preservation of soil fertility:

Adequate Application of Cultivation Techniques (Cr_{39})

Crop rotation consists in varying the cultivations in a given field, alternating those which impoverish the soil and those which enrich it in some nutritive elements (for example, nitrogen). Crop rotation practice allows the soil to reconstitute. Likewise, choosing an adequate association of cultivations on the same SU (leguminous plants, bean, groundnut or others, on the one hand, and gramineae, maize, millet, sorghum or others, on the other hand) have a beneficial effect on the preservation of nutritive elements in the soil (nitrogen, organic matter, etc.). Two indicators account for criterion Cr_{39}:

i_{391} : *practice of crop rotation* ,
i_{392} : *practice of crop association*.

Indicators i_{391} and i_{392} are qualitative and binary. Regarding i_{391}, mark A is attributed when crop rotation is applied, mark NA, otherwise. Regarding indicator i_{392}, mark A is attributed when crop association is practised, mark NA, otherwise. Table 12.29 shows the aggregation rule used for assessing SU's on criterion Cr_{39} by aggregating indicators i_{391} and i_{392}. Criterion Cr_{39} is evaluated on a three classes (A, MA, NA) scale assessing the appropriateness of the response of the spatial unit w.r.t. the application of cultivation techniques.

Table 12.29 Expert rules used for aggregating indicators in the case of criterion Cr_{39}

Practice of crop rotation (i_{391})	Practice of crop association i_{392})	Aggregation Cr_{39}
A	*A*	*A*
A	*NA*	*MA*
NA	*A*	*MA*
NA	*NA*	*NA*

Table 12.30 Expert rules used for aggregating indicators in the case of criterion Cr_{310}

Presence of manure (i_{3101})	Use of chemical fertilizer (i_{3102})	Aggregation Cr_{310}
A	*A*	*A*
A	*NA*	*MA*
MA	*A*	*MA*
MA	*NA*	*NA*
NA	*A*	*MA*
NA	*NA*	*NA*

Adequate Practice of Soil Fertilization (Cr_{310})

The chemical fertilizer must be used in such a way to allow its absorption by the cultivated plants and to attenuate the risk of discharge in the environment. Organic manuring is recommended in association with NPK fertilizer [nitrogen (N), phosphorus (P), potassium (K)]. Two indicators are associated with criterion Cr_{310}:

i_{3101} : *presence of manure*,
i_{3102} : *use of chemical fertilizer*.

Indicator i_{3101} is assessed on a three degrees qualitative scale. The part of each SU surface enriched with organic manuring was observed. Mark *A* (resp. *MA*) is assigned if at least three quarters (resp. between half and three quarters) of the SU is enriched with manure; mark *NA* results otherwise. Regarding indicator i_{3102}, we have observed the quantity of chemical fertilizer used and compared it with the recommended norms. It appears that the norms for usage of chemical fertilizers are not respected in the region. Consequently, the evaluation w.r.t. i_{3102} was brought back to a binary scale. Mark *A* is attributed if chemical fertilizer is used, mark *NA* results otherwise. The evaluation results w.r.t. indicators i_{3101} and i_{3102} are aggregated using a three classes (*A*, *MA*, *NA*) scale assessing the appropriateness of the response of each SU w.r.t. the practice of soil fertilization. The aggregation rule is displayed in Table 12.30.

Criteria and Indicators of PRO Principle (P_4)

The agricultural productivity is measured by the quantity of cultivation produced per hectare during a given period. Two criteria were identified to evaluate the presence of a good potential of agricultural productivity.

Technical Training of Farmers (Cr_{411})

It is necessary to train the farmers to good cultivation techniques. A single indicator is used to evaluate a SU w.r.t. criterion Cr_{411}:

i_{4111} : *presence of trained farmers.*

Indicator i_{4111} is binary. The evaluation of a SU results from enquiry about the proportion of farmers having received a training in cultivation techniques and in water and soils conservation techniques. Mark *A* is assigned if at least half the farmers on the spatial unit were trained, otherwise mark *NA* is attributed. The choice of an evaluation of binary type is justified by the "spread effect": farmers generally imitate their neighbors' behavior if their results are better than theirs.

Improvement of the Agricultural Production (Cr_{412})

If the farmer has at disposal sufficient financial means in order to buy products or rent equipment (manure, fertilizer, ameliorated seeds, tractor and plough rental, etc.) for exploiting his field, he can improve his production; his family can live on the harvest in a satisfactory way; a part of this harvest can be sold and the profit used to satisfy other needs. In this way, the farmer can dispense from practising extensive agriculture, which would push him to exploit marginal or lying fallow soil. On the other hand, if the farmer has at disposal other sources of financial income (market-gardening, gold washing, cattle sale, etc.), the need to practise extensive agriculture will disappear, helping to install an intensive sustainable agriculture which requires purchasing seeds and fertilizer. To evaluate a SU w.r.t. criterion Cr_{412}, we use two indicators:

i_{4121} : *excess production,*
i_{4122} : *practice of an activity constituting a source of income.*

Indicators i_{4121} and i_{4122} are assessed on the three levels (*A*, *MA*, *NA*) scale. Regarding i_{4121} (resp. i_{4122}), mark *A* is attributed if at least three quarters of the farmers in the SU have an excess production (resp. another profitable activity); mark *MA* is assigned when this fraction lies between half and three quarters of the farmers and mark *NA* results otherwise. The evaluation results w.r.t. indicators i_{4121} and i_{4122} were aggregated on a three classes (*A*, *MA*, *NA*) scale assessing the appropriateness

Table 12.31 Expert rules used for aggregating indicators in the case of criterion Cr_{412}

Excess production (i_{4121})	Practice of activity source of income (i_{4122})	Aggregation Cr_{412}
A	*A*	*A*
A	*MA*	*A*
A	*NA*	*MA*
MA	*A*	*A*
MA	*MA*	*MA*
MA	*NA*	*NA*
NA	*A*	*MA*
NA	*MA*	*NA*
NA	*NA*	*NA*

of the response of the SU w.r.t. the improvement of the production. The aggregation rule used is displayed in Table 12.31.

Criteria and Indicators of EN Principle (P_5)

If the elementary needs of populations are satisfied, they will not need to overexploit and degrade their land. We have identified three criteria allowing to evaluate the intensity of satisfaction of the population's elementary needs. In contrast with those described above, these criteria do not vary from a SU to another. They can be assessed at the level of the whole region, namely the Loulouka watershed. These criteria would be needed for comparing two different regions. Since we are concerned with a single region, we do not use and assess them. Nevertheless, for the sake of completeness, we give below a short description of the three criteria accounting for the satisfaction of population's elementary needs and we try to propose some indicators that help to assess them.

Respect of Socio-Cultural Spaces (Cr_{513})

It is important to take into account populations' cultural practice. Let us mention for example the preservation of sacred groves (or copses) which represent particular spaces for the farmer in our study area. Actions to undertake for fighting against land degradation need to preserve these cultural spaces. More generally, recommended actions should not go against populations' cultural values, otherwise they will hardly be sustainable.

Improvement of Education Level (Cr_{514})

Education helps populations to become more aware of the problem of land degradation. It makes them able to understand what is at stake and helps to convince them to act according with the principles of degradation limitation. Moreover, education allows the populations to diversify their professional abilities. In this way, agricultural activities will cease to be the only professional perspective, and this will help to avoid over-exploiting the land. Two indicators account for criterion Cr_{514}:

i_{5141} : *percentage of children in full-time education,*
i_{5142} : *presence of school infrastructures*

Improvement of Socio-Economic Conditions (Cr_{515})

The farmers population need to attain food self-sufficiency in order to be able to draw financial income from their work. They also need to feel materially able to start actions or projects which will go along the lines of improvement of their social condition (e.g. by selling excess food). Two indicators can be proposed to account for criterion Cr_{515}:

i_{5151} : *living conditions,*
i_{5152} : *populations' health level.*

References

Aggarwal, C. C., Chen, C., & Han, J. (2010). The inverse classification problem. *Journal of Computer Science and Technology, 25*(3), 458–468.

André, S. (2006). Évaluation de synthèse ex post de la performance environnementale pour des sites industriels: cas des sites de l'entité raffinage de la société Total. Cahier du LAMSADE 241, Université Paris Dauphine.

Beaumont, J., Joumard, R., Maurin, M., Goger, T., Adolphe, L., & Rousval, B. (2006). Projet PIE Agrégation: L'aide à l'évaluation environnementale des systèmes de transport: Propositions. Rapport final-Tome 2, INRETS-LTE.

Belton, V., & Stewart, T. J. (2003). *Multiple criteria decision analysis: An integrated approach.* Dordrecht: Kluwer Academic.

Bouyssou, D., & Marchant, T. (2007a). An axiomatic approach to noncompensatory sorting methods in MCDM, I: The case of two categories. *European Journal of Operational Research, 178*(1), 217–245.

Bouyssou, D., & Marchant, T. (2007b). An axiomatic approach to noncompensatory sorting methods in MCDM, II: More than two categories. *European Journal of Operational Research, 178*(1), 246–276.

Bouyssou, D., Marchant, T., Pirlot, M., Tsoukiàs, A., & Vincke, P. (2006). *Evaluation and decision models with multiple criteria: Stepping stones for the analyst.* International series in operations research and management science (vol. 86). Boston: Springer.

Brabant, P. (2009). Une méthode d'évaluation et de cartographie de terres dans le monde: Proposition de directives normalisées. Fiche thématique no 8, Comité Scientifique Français de la Désertification, Montpellier.
Brison, V., & Pirlot, M. (2011, October 6–7). Comparing decisional maps. In *74th meeting of the european working group "multiple criteria decision aiding"*. Yverdon-les-Bains: HEIG-VD.
Chakhar, S. (2006). *Cartographie décisionnelle multicritère: Formalisation et implémentation informatique*. PhD thesis, Université Paris Dauphine.
Chakhar, S., & Mousseau, V. (2007). An algebra for multicriteria spatial modelling. *Computers, Environment and Urban Systems, 31*(5), 572–593.
Chakhar, S., & Mousseau, V. (2008). GIS-based multicriteria spatial modeling generic framework. *International Journal of Geographical Information Science, 22*(11–12), 1159–1196.
Diallo, D., Roose, E., Orange, D., & Morel, A. (2002). Influence des pratiques agricoles sur le ruissellement et l'érosion des sols en zone soudanienne du Mali. In *Proceedings envirowater conference*, Ouagadougou (pp. 326–334).
Dias, L., Mousseau, V., Figueira, J., & Clímaco, J. (2002, April). An aggregation/disaggregation approach to obtain robust conclusions with ELECTRE TRI. *European Journal of Operational Research, 138*(2), 332–348.
Diello, P. (2002). Relations entre indices de végétation, pluie et états de surface au Burkina Faso: Cas du bassin versant du Nakambé. Mémoire de DEA, Université Montpellier II.
Doumpos, M., & Zopounidis, C. (2002). Preference disaggregation classification methods. In *Multicriteria decision aid classification methods*. Applied optimization (vol. 73, pp. 77–122). New York: Springer.
Figueira, J., & Roy, B. (2002). Determining the weights of criteria in the ELECTRE type methods with a revised Simos' procedure. *European Journal of Operational Research, 139*, 317–326.
Ibrahim, B. (2002). Analyse de la variabilité climatique au Burkina Faso au cours de la seconde moitié du *XX*^{e} siècle. Mémoire de fin d'études, Ecole Inter Etats d'Ingénieurs de l'équipement Rural.
Iwaco (1990a). Etude du bilan d'eau au Burkina Faso: Etudes de quatre bassins versants expérimentaux au Burkina Faso. Volume II, bassin de Tougou. Rapport d'étude, Ministère de l'eau du Burkina Faso, Direction des études et de la planification.
Iwaco (1990b). Etude du bilan d'eau au Burkina Faso: Les aspects environnementaux du projet bilan d'eau. Rapport d'étude, Ministère de l'eau du Burkina Faso, Direction des études et de la planification.
Jallas, E., & Cretenet, M. (2002, May 27–31). Aide à la décision en agriculture et gestion des ressources naturelles: Note introductive. In *Actes du colloque Savanes africaines : des espaces en mutation, des acteurs face à de nouveaux défis*, Garoua.
Jankowski, P. (2001). Integrating geographical information systems and multiple criteria decision-making methods. *International Journal of Geographical Information Systems, 9*, 251–273.
Joerin, F. (1998). *Dćider sur le territoire. Proposition d'une approche par utilisation du SIG et de méthodes d'analyse multicritère*. PhD thesis, Ecole Polytechnique Fédérale de Lausanne.
Joerin, F., & Musy, A. (2000). Land management with GIS and multicriteria analysis. *International Transactions on Operational Research, 7*, 67–78
Joerin, F., Thériault, M., Musy, A. (2001). Using GIS and outranking multicriteria analysis. *International Transactions on Operational Research, 15*, 153–174.
Karimou Ambouta, J. M., Valentin, C., & Laverdière, M. R. (1996). Jachères et croûtes d'érosion au Sahel. *Sécheresse, 7*(4), 269–275.
Keeney, R. L. (1992). *Value-focused thinking : A path to creative decision making*. Cambridge, MA: Harvard University Press.
Keeney, R. L., & Raiffa, H. (1976). *Decision with multiple objectives: Preferences and value trade-offs*. New York: Wiley.
Laaribi, A. (2000). *SIG et analyse multicritère*. Paris: Hermes Science.
Mahaman, O. (2001). *Contribution à l'étude de l'impact de la variabilité climatique sur les ressources en eau en Afrique de l'Ouest. Analyse des conséquences d'une sécheresse*

persistante: normes hydrologiques et modélisation régionale. PhD thesis, Université de Montpellier II.
Malczewski, J. (2006). GIS-based multicriteria decision analysis: a survey of the literature. *International Journal of Geographical Information System/Science, 20*(7), 703–7264.
Mannino, M., & Koushik, M. (2000). The cost-minimizing inverse classification problem: a genetic algorithm approach. *Decision Support Systems, 29*(3), 283–300.
Metchebon Takougang, S. A. (2010). *Contribution à l'aide à la décison en matière de gestion spatialisée. Etude de cas en management environnemental et développement de nouveaux outils*. PhD thesis, Université de Mons, Faculté polytechnique
Metchebon Takougang, S. A., & Pirlot, M. (2010, April 15–17). Comparing decisional maps. In *Proceedings of the 25th mini EURO conference on uncertainty and robustness in planning and decision making (URPDM2010)*, University of Coimbra, ISBN: 978-989-95055-3-7.
Metchebon Takougang, S. A., Pirlot, M., Yonkeu, S., & Some, B. (2008, September 9–11). Towards a decision aid for sustainable management of landscape degradation: The case of Loulouka basin (Burkina Faso). In *Proceedings OR50 conference*, York.
Metchebon Takougang, S. A., Mousseau, V., & Zheng, J. (2010, April 15–17). Computing Robust Assignments for the ELECTRE TRI Optimistic Rule. In *Proceedings of the 25th mini EURO conference on uncertainty and robustness in planning and decision making (URPDM2010)*, University of Coimbra, ISBN: 978-989-95055-3-7.
Mousseau, V., & Dias, L. (2004). Valued outranking relations in ELECTRE providing manageable disaggregation procedures. *European Journal of Operational Research, 156*(2), 467–482.
Mousseau, V., & Slowinski, R. (1998). Inferring an ELECTRE TRI Model from Assignment Examples. *Journal of Global Optimization, 12*, 157–174.
Mousseau, V., Figueira, J., & Naux, J.-P. (2001). Using assigment examples to infer weights for ELECTRE TRI method: Some experimental results. *European Journal of Operational Research, 147*, 263–275.
Mousseau, V., Slowinski, R., & Zielniewicz, P. (2000). A user-oriented implementation of the ELECTRE TRI method integrating preference elicitation support. *Computers & Operations Research, 27*(7–8), 757–777.
Ngo The, A., & Mousseau, V. (2002). Using assignment examples to infer category limits for the ELECTRE TRI method. *Journal of Multi-Criteria Decision Analysis, 11*(1), 29–43.
Ouedraogo, S., Belemvire, A., Maiga, A., Savadogo, M., & Sawadogo, H. (2008). Évaluation des impacts biophysiques et socioéconomiques des investissements dans les actions de gestion des ressources naturelles au Nord plateau central du Burkina Faso. Rapport de synthèse, Comité permanent Inter-états de Lutte contre la sécheresse au Sahel.
Pendharkar, P. C. (2002). A potential use of data envelopment analysis for the inverse classification problem. *Omega, 30*(3), 243–248.
Pictet, J. (1996) *Dépasser l'Evaluation Environnementale*. Lausanne: Presses Polytechniques et Universitaires Romandes.
Previl, F., Thériault, M., & Rouffignat, J. (2003). Analyse multicritère et SIG pour faciliter la concertation en aménagement du territoire: vers une amélioration du processus décisionnel? *Cahiers de géographie du Québec, 47*(130), 153–174.
Roose, E., & Sarrailh, J. M. (1989). Erodibilité de quelques sols tropicaux: Vingt années de mesure en parcelles d'érosion sous pluies naturelles. In: Spécial Erosion. *Cahiers ORSTOM. Série Pédologie, 25*(1–2), 7–30.
Roy, B. (2002). Présentation et interprétation de la méthode ELECTRE TRI pour affecter des zones dans des catégories de risque. Document du LAMSADE no 124, Université Paris-Dauphine.
Roy, B., & Bouyssou, D. (1993). *Aide Multicritère à la Décision: Méthodes et Cas*. Paris: Economica.
Schlaepfer, R. (2003). Écologie du paysage, surveillance et gestion des écosystèmes. Cours de DESS 2003 en systématique et gestion de la biodiversité, EPFL, Laboratoire de Gestion des Ecosystèmes GECOS, Lausanne.
Simos, J. (1990a). *Evaluer l'impact sur l'environnement: Une approche originale par l'analyse multicritère et la négociation*. Lausanne: Presses Polytechniques et Universitaires Romandes.

Simos, J. (1990b) *L'évaluation environnementale: Un processus cognitif négocié.* PhD thesis, Ecole Polytechnique Fédérale de Lausanne.
Sobrie, O., Pirlot, M., & Joerin, F. (2012). Intégration de la méthode d'aide à la décision ELECTRE TRI dans un système d'information géographique open source. *Revue Internationale de Géomatique, 23*(1), 13–28.
Taupin, J. D., Amani, A., & Lebel, T. (1998). Variabilité spatiale des pluies au Sahel: une question d'échelles. Approche expérimentale. In *Water ressources variability in Africa during the XXth century*. Wallingford: IAHS Publication.
van der Werf, H. M. G., & Zimmer, C. (1999). Un indicateur d'impact environnemental de pesticides basé sur un système expert à logique floue. Courrier de l'environnement de l'INRA, no 34, Institut National de la Recherche Agronomique.
Vincke, P. (1989). *L'Aide Multicritère à la Décision.* Editions de l'Université de Bruxelles, Belgique.
Vincke, P. (1992). *Multicriteria decision-aid.* Chichester: Wiley.
von Winterfeldt, D., & Edwards, W. (1986). *Decison analysis and behavioral research.* Cambridge: Cambridge University Press.
Yacouba, H., Da, D. E. C., Yonkeu, S., Zombré, P., & Soulé, M. (2002). Caractérisation du ruissellement et de l'érosion hydrique dans le bassin supérieur du Nakambé (Burkina Faso). In *Proceedings envirowater conference*, Ouagadougou (pp. 318–325).
Yonkeu, S., & Kiniffo, G. F. (2004). Étude de la dégradation dans le bassin supérieur du fleuve Nakambé au Burkina Faso. Rapport de synthèse, EIER.
Yu, W. (1992a). *Aide multicritère à la décision dans le cadre de la problématique du tri: concepts, méthodes et applications*. PhD thesis, Université Paris-Dauphine.
Yu, W. (1992b). ELECTRE TRI: Aspects méthodologiques et manuel d'utilisation. Document du LAMSADE no 74, Université Paris-Dauphine.
Zopounidis, C., & Doumpos, M. (1999). A multicriteria decision aid methodology for sorting decision problems: The case of financial distress. *Computational Economics, 272*(20), 197–218.
Zopounidis, C., & Doumpos, M. (2001). A preference disaggregation decision support system for financial classification problems. *European Journal of Operational Research, 130*(20), 402–413.

Editors' Comments on "Assessing the Response to Land Degradation Risk in the Loulouka Basin"

Metchebon, Pirlot, Yonkeu and Some present in their study case a fully worked out example of what they call a *decisional map*—the association of MCDA methods with a GIS—in order to structure and assess land degradation risks in Africa. This chapter presents thus a thorough discussion on how to, both, formally model *and* visually illustrate a decision problem in order to achieve an effective decision aiding for all stakeholders in a territorial management problem.

Main aspects relevant for the purpose of this handbook are, on the one hand, the detailed analysis of the modelling process of the decision alternatives, the evaluation criteria and the performance evaluations (see Sect. 2.2). On the other hand, the decision **problem statement** illustrated here consists in sorting into a predefined set of ordered categories following an ELECTRE Tri approach (see Chap. 4, Sect. 4.2.3). As such, this study relates especially to the chapter by Mercat-Rommens, Chakhar, Chojnacki and Mousseau (Chap. 13) presenting a similar approach for building and evaluating a geographical nuclear risk map, and to the chapter by Lué and Colorni (Chap. 14).

Without a public mandate, this assessment study of the land degradation observed in the Loulouka catchment basin (Center North of Burkina Faso in Western Africa) does not directly imply any institutional and/or public decision makers. Instead, one of the authors of the study is a recognized **environmentalist expert**, who actively contributed to previous land degradation studies concerning the region under review (Yacouba et al., 2002; Yonkeu and Kiniffo, 2004). Here he acts as factual **decision maker** for providing all required preferential information such as the assessment criteria weights for instance. The **target group** for the decision recommendations are, in this case, local farmers and public authorities who will have to plan and undertake adequate land conservation actions.

The claimed specific **objective of the case study**, by the way appearing genuinely in many spatial decision problems (see Mercat-Rommens et al., Chap. 13, and Luè and Colorni, Chap. 14), is essentially to elaborate a *structured and participative assessment* of the land degradation state via a hierarchy of evaluation criteria based on relevant environmental indicators and taking into account all **stakeholders**—local population, authorities and experts—points of view.

The natural decision **problem statement** appearing in this kind of geographical decision aid problems consists, in a first **problem structuring** step, in describing geographical spatial units with respect to multiple evaluation criteria, and, in a second **aggregation** step, in sorting these spatial units, once assessed on all the relevant criteria, into four ordered categories assessing the degree of ability of each unit to respond to the risk of land degradation: inadequate, weakly adequate, moderately adequate, adequate.

As so often in a GIS integrated multiple criteria decision analysis, **decision alternatives** correspond to 229 identified contiguous spatial units—25 ha squares—that cover the region under review. These spatial units are, for the MCDA purpose, evaluated on a complex set of criteria in order to judge their response level to the land degradation risk they present. This part certainly represents the most specific and interesting aspect of this case study.

Five fundamental **objectives** for limiting land degradation within a framework of sustainable development and management of the region are here considered: limit soils erosion, preserve biodiversity, preserve soils fertility, favour a good level of agricultural productivity, satisfy elementary needs for social welfare. From climatic, as well as anthropogenic factors, undermining theses objectives, are derived 12 **criteria** like limited extension of cultivated soils, bush fire limitation, and technical training of farmers for instance. The response level to land degradation risk in each spatial unit is eventually assessed via the observation of 23 **performance indicators** like presence of nude soil, practice of crop rotation and appropriate matching of pesticide and type of cultivation for instance. Considering the large part of **imprecision** of these indicators, only three ordinal response levels:—not adequate, moderately adequate, adequate—are used as **measurement scale** on all the criteria.

The usage of the ELECTRE Tri method for multiple criteria based **sorting** of the spatial units is a rather natural application in a GIS application. One of the most critical aspect in using this method concerns setting adequate **criteria weights**. The authors have, similar to the Mercat-Rommens et al. approach (see Chap. 13), used Simos' method (Simos, 1997), not without practical difficulties. Why not simply start by default with considering the decision objectives as more or less equally important? This way, each criterion affecting a specific objective may be again considered as equi-significant contribution within the importance of the relevant objective. If the corresponding sorting result is not convincing the decision maker, differentiating the importance of the objectives, or the significance of some of the criteria may become useful. A similar comment may be addressed to the criteria weights used in the chapter on *Choosing a cooling system for a nuclear power plant in Belgium* (Chap. 8).

One may **question** at this point that, a sorting problem into $k = 4$ categories, when only $d = 3$ performance levels are discriminated on each criteria, is indeed well conditioned. Normally the marginal performance discrimination should allow to clearly map the global ordered outcome categories on each criterion's measurement scale. Indeed, how will it be possible to construct consistent majority sorting situations—the ground statements of the ELECTRE Tri method—if not all the outcome categories may be actually discriminated? With $k = 4 > d = 3$, this study shows here a rather special application context of the ELECTRE Tri method; an application needing both the category limiting profiles as well as the majority cut level, to be handled in a non standard way. It appears by the way that the final discussion of the results actually concentrates more or less on solely two global sorting categories: *not adequate* or *adequate*, regarding the response to the risk of degradation, such that we anyhow come back to a sounder situation where $k = 2 < d = 3$.

Due to the unusual mapping of three marginal ordered categories onto four global categories, the **validation** process of the ELECTRE Tri exhibits specific practical difficulties. This fact adds on to the impression that in this case study, the ELECTRE Tri method is somehow used outside of its genuine usage. In the absence of an explicit decision, as is in this application the case, a multiple criteria descriptive decision aid approach, instead of the classic prescriptive decision aid approach, would perhaps provide even more convincing and **tangible results**.

Finally, this application illustrates again the great **relevance** and usefulness of integrating MCDA approaches into a GIS systems. Especially, in the context of a territorial management problem, such systems may well provide a very useful and effective decision aid for all private and/or public stakeholders.

References

Simos, J. (1997). *Evaluer l'impact sur l'environnement*. Lausanne: Presses Polytechniques et Universitaires Romandes.

Yacouba, H., Da, D. E. C., Yonkeu, S., Zombré, P., & Soulé, M. (2002). Caractérisation du ruissellement et de l'érosion hydrique dans le bassin supérieur du Nakambé (Burkina Faso). In *Proceedings envirowater conference*, Ouagadougou (pp. 318–325).

Yonkeu, S., & Kiniffo, G. F. (2004). Étude de la dégradation dans le bassin supérieur du fleuve Nakambé au Burkina Faso. Rapport de synthèse, EIER.

Chapter 13
Coupling GIS and Multi-Criteria Modeling to Support Post-Accident Nuclear Risk Evaluation

Catherine Mercat-Rommens, Salem Chakhar, Eric Chojnacki, and Vincent Mousseau

Abstract In case of an accident concerning a nuclear installation, two intervention phases are distinguished: an *emergency phase* which calls for a rapid and organized response through intervention plans, and a *post-accidental phase* in which postponed actions are carried out on medium and/or long-term so that the situation comes back to a state judged as acceptable by stakeholders. The PRIME project has developed a decision aiding tool for risk managers involved in an industrial accident involving radioactive substances, through the evaluation of radio-ecological sensitivity of a territory in a post-accidental phase. The proposed decision aiding tool is grounded on the integration of Multiple Criteria Decision Aid (MCDA) and a Geographical Information System (GIS). The proposed methodology relies on the concept of decision map which corresponds to a planar subdivision of the territory in which each subdivision is evaluated on the basis of several criterion maps. This results in a set of disjoint spatial units evaluated on an ordinal scale using the ELECTRE TRI method. Hence, the result is a decision map representing the radio-ecological sensitivity of the territory; such maps prove to be very useful for stakeholders to design relevant post-accidental strategies.

C. Mercat-Rommens • E. Chojnacki
IRSN - Institut de Radioprotection et de Sûreté Nucléaire, Centre d'études de Cadarache, 13105 Saint Paul Lez Durance, France
e-mail: catherine.mercat-rommens@irsn.fr; eric.chojnacki@irsn.fr

S. Chakhar
Portsmouth Business School, University of Portsmouth, Portland Building, Portland Street, Portsmouth, PO1 3AH, UK
e-mail: salem.chakhar@port.ac.uk

V. Mousseau (✉)
Laboratoire Génie Industriel, Ecole Centrale Paris, Grande Voie des Vignes, 92295 Châtenay Malabry, France
e-mail: vincent.mousseau@exp.fr

R. Bisdorff et al. (eds.), *Evaluation and Decision Models with Multiple Criteria*, International Handbooks on Information Systems,
DOI 10.1007/978-3-662-46816-6_13

13.1 Nuclear Risk Management and the PRIME Project Context

Preparing for how to manage the consequences of a major nuclear accident necessarily involves the consideration of multiple criteria in order to ensure sustainable development in areas that might be affected. This often requires a multidisciplinary approach to produce a sustainable response to the environmental, economic and social problems linked to the various local intricacies. Moreover, the multiplicity of stakeholders produces multiple, often contradictory, objectives, which need to be taken into account and prioritized in order to facilitate decision-making. So that the decision-making process is transparent, properly recorded and reproducible, systems need to be developed to aid the process.

In cooperation with experts, decision-makers and local authorities, the objective of the PRIME project is to develop a multi-criteria method of analysis for use in characterizing an area contaminated after an industrial accident involving radioactive substances, see Mercat-Rommens et al. (2008). The main basis of the method used is the ranking of the vulnerability factors to a radioactive pollution. The ranking is established jointly by the various PRIME project participants in order to arrive at a shared vision, an essential prerequisite in devising an appropriate management strategy. This method is intended for the use of those managing risks. It should therefore meet two objectives: one being the protection of individual inhabitants, their personal property and their living conditions, and the other its general acceptability to people affected by living in a contaminated area.

The concept behind PRIME's research—which is participative, involving experts and also leading local figures—is to anticipate in a wide study area what the consequences of a nuclear accident will be. The aim is ambitious as it involves a large range of concerns which, moreover, are subject to local stakeholders' widely varying perceptions and interests, but the subject necessitates that these complexities are tackled head on. This requires, therefore, assembling as wide a cross-sectional panel of interests as possible to be able to appreciate the full range of consequences on the one hand and, on the other, engaging in a jointly agreed process with the panel to develop a rigorous method of classifying risks in the areas.

The study zone covers a radius of some 50 km around three nuclear sites in the lower Rhône valley (the Cruas, Tricastin-Pierrelatte, and Marcoule sites, see Fig. 13.1). To the south, the zone extends along the Rhône to the Mediterranean coastal area in order to take into account the possibility of radioactivity being carried into catchments basins.

The choice of this vast zone corresponds to a scenario where a major accident involves the release of radioactivity into the atmosphere. Such a choice means taking into account a large number of factors: high population density along the Rhône corridor, very diverse environments (natural, agricultural, built-up areas, river and coastal zones), demographic, economic and tourist factors, and wealth (personal and environmental) and property issues. With such a multiplicity of factors, it would

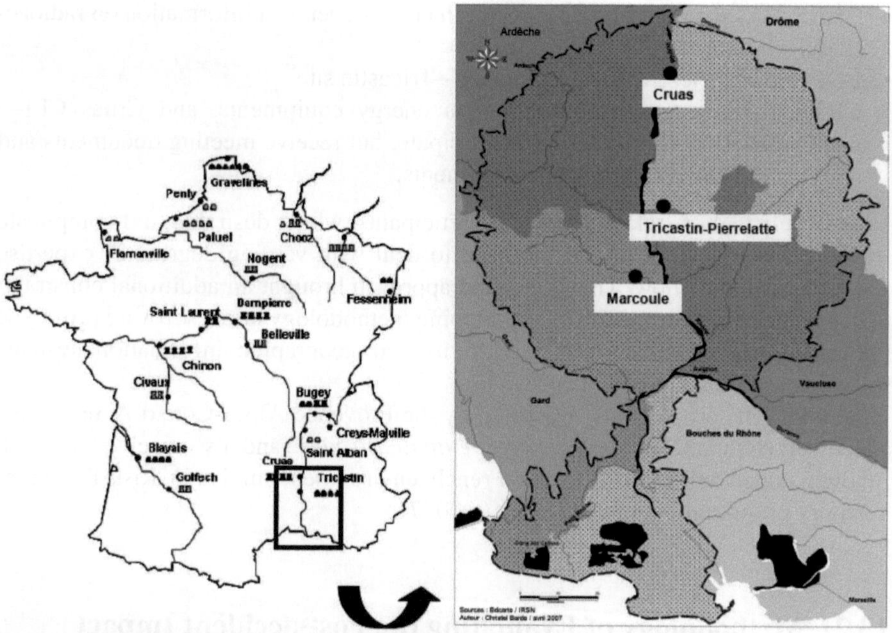

Fig. 13.1 The study area: Cruas/Tricastin-Pierrelatte/Marcoule

seem to be potentially worth exploring the tools that can result from a multi-criteria analysis for use in the preparation of decisions.

To carry out this research with multiple participants, a group of local stakeholders was approached to make up the PRIME working group (PRIME WG). The participants, in chronological order of becoming involved in the project) are:

- IRSN (French Institute for Radioprotection and Nuclear Safety),
- the Gard CLI (local information committee),
- ASN (Nuclear Safety Authority), Lyon Division,
- LAMSADE Laboratory, Paris-Dauphine University,
- INERIS, a public research institute on industrial chemical risks,
- the Prefecture of the Drôme and related government services (agriculture and forest services, social and health services, and veterinary control services),
- AREVA NC (state energy transmission and distribution company)—Pierrelatte site,
- a local wine producer from the Gard area,
- the Chairman of the Scientific Council of the Committee of the Bay of Toulon,
- the Director of "*Another Provence*",
- the Chairman of the Development Agency for the "*Gard rhodanien*",
- two representatives of the French Nuclear Safety Authority, and the Ministry of Agriculture),

- CRIIRAD,[1] the committee for research and independent information on radioactivity,
- EDF, the electrical services company—Tricastin site,
- CIGEET—information committee on energy equipments, and Cruas CLI—nuclear safety authority, do not participate, but receive meeting documents and are kept informed of project developments.

A large panel of stakeholders and participants, whilst desirable, did complicate working arrangements, as did the need to deal with varying degrees of expertise and technical knowhow. This concerted approach brought an additional constraint which is the need to integrate the developing methodology into a software prototype linking multi-criteria analysis algorithms and geographic information systems software, see Chakhar et al. (2008).

The PRIME project was supported by the Provence-Alpes-Côte d'Azur project agency on risks labeled "*pôle de compétitivité Risques*" and also received research funding under MEEDDAT's (the French environment ministry) Risk-Decision-Territory programme (convention no 0000771).

13.2 Methodology of Evaluating the Post-accident Impact on the Area

13.2.1 Managing the Consequences of a Nuclear Accident

Three phases are usually identified during the process of a nuclear accident, see Niel and Godet (2008):

- the *urgent phase*,
- the *transitional phase* (short-term post-accident phase), and
- the *long-term post-accident phase*.

The *urgent phase* covers the risk phase, which precedes the occurrence of the first releases into the environment, and the accidental release phase which produces a radioactive plume dispersing into the environment. It ceases when there are no further deposits, when the installation at the origin of the accident is made safe with no subsequent risk of producing fresh radioactive releases into the environment. The work of PRIME WG is not concerned with this first phase but needs to take into account the action taken during this phase for reasons of continuity and consistency.

The post-accident phase starts from the termination of deposits, and concerns the treatment of the consequences resulting from the event, especially those that result

[1]CRIRAD participates in GT PRIME's work as a consultant in order to express its vision of the contaminated areas and what needs to be protected. However CRIRAD's participation does not include approving the methodological software that implements the results of this consultation.

from the deposit of radioactive substances. This phase involves a survey of urgent protective action needed, the characterizing of the contamination and the introduction of the first protective measures in contaminated areas, as well as the preparation of long-term action. The *transitional phase* may last for several months or years, depending on the extent and the persistence of the radioactive contamination in the area. The *long-term post-accident phase* managing the long-term consequences is then begun, which leads to the implementation of a management plan for the long-lasting consequences of the event, worked out with all those involved in the transition phase. The PRIME project is concerned with the *transitional phase* that lasts for about 1 year and that takes into account local factors during this period, especially agricultural timetables.

The consequences of an accident on an area are reflected in the negative impact, shorter/longer-lasting and minor/major on people, assets and the economy in general. The classification of the geographical districts in an area affected by the fall-out from an accident means being able to take account of the radiological consequences on inhabitants as well as negative economic and environmental impacts. The problem lies in finding a method of classification, grounded on the characterization of the state of the area, shared by the various stakeholders. The approach taken within the PRIME project to construct a method is based on the successive stages described below. Through this approach, each district can be classified according to the degree to which it is at risk of a nuclear accident resulting in releases into the atmosphere. This risk scale has six levels, from 0 for a situation described as normal to 5 in the event of a major and long lasting negative impact (see Sect. 13.3.1).

13.2.2 Methodology for Supporting Post-Accidental Decisions

The first stage aims to identify, in a concerted manner, the stakes involved, meaning everything that is of fundamental importance to an area and which can be adversely affected by an accident (such as zones that are densely inhabited, business activities, and cultural and environmental assets). This stage requires as accurate a knowledge of the area as possible, provided both by local stakeholders and also by researching all the information available from those holding local data, such as INSEE, (the French National Institute for Statistics and Economic Studies), Agreste (which produces Ministry of Agriculture statistics) and CCI (the Chamber of Commerce and Industry). Then one or more adverse effects (such as radiological contamination, destruction or drop in sales of agricultural products, a drop in company turnover, and the impact on asset values or on tourist numbers) has to be linked to each stake so that they represent the consequences of an accident in various sectors.

Once the various factors and adverse effects have been selected, the criteria that characterize them have to be identified. The radiological impact on people can be characterized by the dosage expressed in millisievert (mSv). The economic impact can be characterized by the loss (in €) linked to the destruction or a drop in product sales, or again by the percentage drop in a company's turnover.

Specific benchmark values are assigned for each criterion. They correspond to the threshold values that make up the degrees of scale of gravity of the event. For example, below 10 μSv (microsievert = 10^{-6} Sievert) the negative impact is minor (below 1 on the scale), above 10 mSv, the impact can be major (up to 5 on the scale).

Once the first two steps have permitted the construction of a scale of gravity to measure the various detrimental impacts, how they work and how consistent they are can be tested in a trial run. For a simulated accident, this therefore involves evaluating the consequences on each district, that means how the criterion or criteria for each negative impact is measured, in order to position them on the scales of gravity (see Fig. 13.2). This stage is completed when the evaluation matrix is achieved, i.e. when a table of data is available, in which the lines represent the districts within the study zone and the columns represent the classification criteria. Each box then contains the corresponding value of the criterion for the district in question.

Once the multi-criteria evaluation matrix is designed, the information for a specific district then has to be aggregated in order to obtain a global indicator of the gravity for the district according to an accident scenario. The ranking criterion is inevitably seen differently from various stakeholders' points of view. It was therefore necessary to develop software able to capture the differences and to represent them. Multi-criteria tools were explored within the PRIME project and the development of software coupling GIS functions and multi-criteria modeling made it possible to draw up maps showing the gravity of a nuclear accident and the importance of each criterion for the various stakeholders.

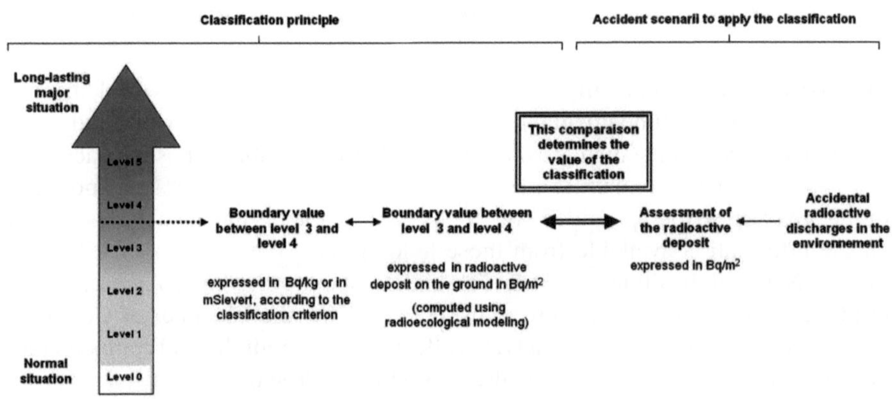

Fig. 13.2 The PRIME method classification principle

13.3 Application and Results: Using the Data and Results Obtained

The PRIME project's success depends on completing two successive phases:

1. the collection and organisation of relevant databases to show the state of an area contaminated by a nuclear accident,
2. the use of this database in one or more possible scenarios corresponding to nuclear accidents, to rank the most affected districts and, in these districts, to identify the areas most affected by the accident.

13.3.1 Elaborating the Multi-criteria Evaluation Matrix

In the first phase of the project, a database was developed for the PRIME study zone, gathering information a priori useful in a post-accident context. It is felt that this ad-hoc database can be relevant for decision-making processes if it gathers all the information necessary for classifying the area, in integrating the points of view of all the area's stakeholders. The database's architecture was therefore designed so that area stakes, as expressed by the panel of local representatives (PRIME WG) independently of administrative barriers, were taken into account, in order to permit the construction of classification criteria shared by everyone in the study zone. Moreover, the database structure allows easy access to data and will later facilitate their updating.

In the PRIME project, by taking into account the stakes identified by PRIME WG and/or expressed by other local stakeholders (local diagnostic phase, see Barde et al. 2007), various kinds of data are collected and analyzed: radio-ecological (linked to radioactive contamination in the area), economic and social (see Fig. 13.3).

13.3.1.1 Radio-Ecological Stakes

In the case of radio-ecological stakes, it has been possible through detailed analysis to propose indicators for the state of the area (known as radio-ecological criteria) and to link them to a classification system representing the scale of damage to a contaminated area.

Six levels of classification have been decided on, to indicate the radio-ecological vulnerability of the various media, with the following significance for each point on the scale:

0 "Normal situation": The view will be that, for districts at this level, no particular surveillance or remedial works will be necessary.

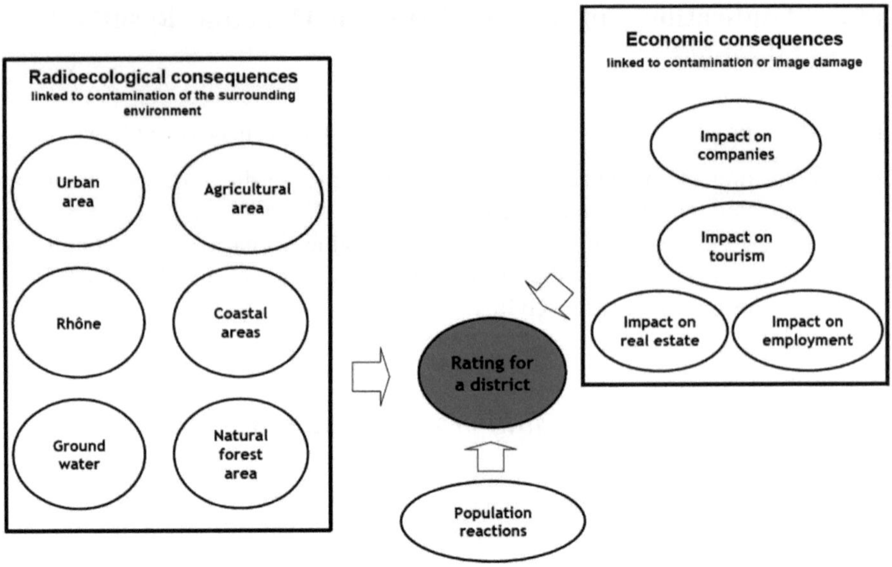

Fig. 13.3 Selected stakes

1 "Very minor": Typically this will be districts where there is only very slight contamination, difficult to measure with current means of assessment. For such districts, light monitoring measures could be proposed.
2 "Minor": A sector where there is measurable contamination but still slight. There will be stronger monitoring measures than for level 1.
3 "Moderate": Preventive action may be recommended (for example, a ban on the sale of agricultural produce, a ban on using food from the wild or a ban on certain foodstuffs).
4 "Major": The contamination of a sector has reached a predetermined normative value (NMA2 for agricultural produce, for example).
5 "Major and long-lasting": Contamination in a medium exceeds a predetermined normative value with effects lasting for more than 1 year.

The terms proposed for the radio-ecological classification scale were discussed at length by those who took part in the second PRIME WG meeting and were reviewed in subsequent meetings, as the choice of terms is of great importance in communication terms. Thus the term "negligible", originally suggested for level 1, was felt by a number of participants to be problematic. Because of this, it was decided to use the term "very minor". Similarly, the initial choice of the term "serious" for level 4 was questioned during the project, because it might suggest an impact on health, whereas this point on the scale is reached when a specific normative value for food contamination is exceeded, which does not necessarily imply a health risk for people consuming such food.

In choosing terms for the scale, the aim is both to be easily understood by people but also to be precise, so that the reasons for this or that classification decision made by the authorities can be explained. This is a difficult aim and it is probable that, at the end of the project, the choice of terms may have to be further adapted for communication purposes. It is also worth noting that the choice of terms is linked to the action strategies implicit at each point on the scale (monitoring or remedial strategies). The relationship between classifications and action strategies has particular relevance as a research field, with a view to the practical implementation of the PRIME approach.

There are two types of radio-ecological criteria used: food contamination criteria (such as agricultural produce, produce gathered from the wild, groundwater, river water, and seafood) and dosage of radiation criteria linked to the varying exposure of people by sector. These criteria are defined by the six sectors that make up the study area: the agricultural sector, built-up areas, natural forest areas, water tables, the River Rhône and the coastal zone. Moreover, the process of evaluating radio-ecological criteria was debated at PRIME WG and in particular the calibration of radio-ecological calculation formulae which make it possible to evaluate the dispersion and movement of radioactive contaminants within the various sectors of the environment.

The agricultural medium was particularly closely studied as it will be affected in the very short term after an accident and the associated economic factors could very rapidly become of major importance. For this sector, 15 agricultural products, specific to the study zone, have been considered—tomatoes, melons, apricots and peaches, wine, cherries, olives, aromatic plants, early new potatoes, hard wheat, rice, goat's milk, chicken, chicken egg production and lamb. These products were chosen to represent a cross-section of how radioactivity is spread in relation to time of year and farming techniques. This was not an attempt to include all forms of agricultural production (as would be in preparing an impact study) but to put together a group of agricultural products that would indicate a variety of effects. 2 Niveau Maximum Admissible (maximum permitted level) (Euratom regulation no 3954/87 of 22 December 1987 and CEE no 2219/89 of 18 July 1989)

For a given district, therefore, 15 classification ratings were obtained corresponding to each agricultural product. The 15 ratings therefore make up the classification criteria for the agricultural medium. For the agricultural medium (through ingesting foodstuffs) the classification scale is defined as in Fig. 13.4.

Two kinds of criteria have been proposed to define the thresholds between 0 and 5. For the levels of greater gravity (3 to 5), the proposal is to use the current norms for the sale of agricultural produce, the "NMA". For slighter levels (0 to 2), the proposal is to use the minimum detectable amounts (DL = detection limits) and the differentiation made between low-level metrology instrument DL readings (measured in becquerels) and DL using actual regular metrology instruments. These choices come from an analysis of the elements in current regulations concerning foodstuff. This means that there could be debatable elements in the current set of guidelines but, in the context of the PRIME project, the approach was to imagine

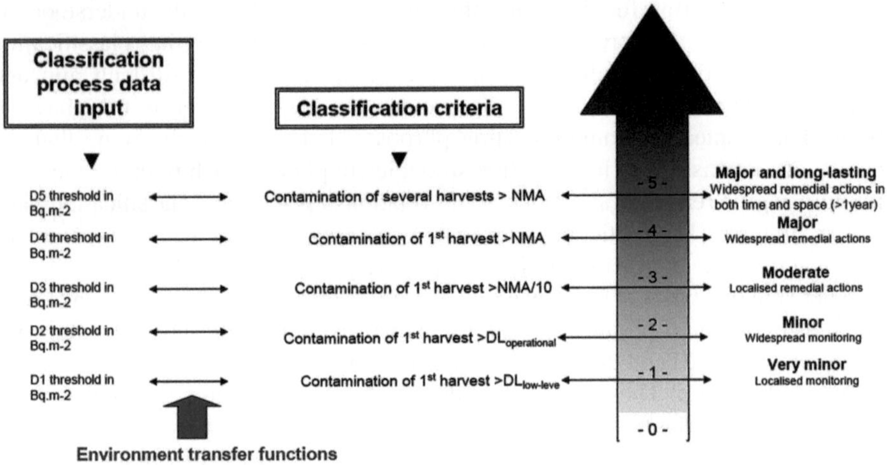

Fig. 13.4 Example of how the radio-ecological criteria on the agricultural medium are structured

how the regulation values would be used in post-accident management and not to discuss the precise amounts.

13.3.1.2 Economic Stakes

In taking into account, using the PRIME project method, the consequences of a nuclear accident on economic activity, the concept used is that of the damage function. It is an instrument taken from socioeconomic assessments and used for flood purposes, see MEDAD (2007). A variety of thinking has been expressed on how to assess these functions for flood-related damage and which can be transposed to a context of radioactive contamination: a damage chart for a given physical asset relating to the level of surface contamination and the percentage of damage to a given business activity, a damage function by homogeneous zone (a principle equating to the previous one but applied to a space and not a physical asset) and an approach based on average cost. So far as flooding is concerned, damage functions are calculated either in line with expert opinion or based on using statistics from observations gathered after actual disasters. In the nuclear field, there has been no major nuclear disaster in France which allows for an empirical approach and therefore the approach used by the PRIME project is an approach using expertise, whilst remaining conscious of the limits of this type of approach.

However, these limits are reduced within the PRIME project by the fact that, as for radiological consequences, the object of economic analysis for PRIME is not to quantify all the damage, but to provide overall simple and consistent economic criteria to show all the economic stakes in the area.

The economic stakes chosen for PRIME's classification approach are linked to companies' vulnerability, real estate vulnerability, employment vulnerability and the vulnerability of tourist activity. A theoretical study undertaken by one of the PRIME project's partners (see Genty and Brignon 2008) has made it possible to propose representative criteria for each of these four kinds of stakes. The financial vulnerability of companies is represented by the damage (called afterwards economic damage) to the added value that each business economic category produces. Real estate vulnerability is represented by the loss in value of surfaces according to their kind of use (built-up, agricultural or natural/forest area). Employment vulnerability is represented by the tendency to relocate jobs according to business category. Finally, the vulnerability of tourism activity is represented by the negative impact on tourism room capacity/occupancy in each district, see Venzal-Barde (2008).

To evaluate the economic impact, PRIME WG considered that knowledge about the consequences of a nuclear accident on activities is not sufficiently precise to justify many classes of effect. The classification of consequences has therefore been simplified and these simplifications have been made in various ways depending on whether or not the business consequences are linked to the contamination of a specific medium in the area. For example, for agricultural activities, the economic impact will be linked to the degree of contamination of the agricultural medium and the simplification proposed is consistent with the fact that the effects on image will increase the consequences of contamination, even when the level is minor, and thus lead to serious consequences from an economic point of view. The number of classes has therefore been reduced from 5 (major and long-lasting, major, moderate, minor and very minor) to 3 (major and long-lasting, major and minor), and the economic impact corresponding to each category has been determined through consultation. Thus, if after an accident, radioactive contamination in a district's agricultural medium reaches level 2, the loss to the added value of businesses in the agricultural sector and agricultural land values are rated as major and can have a total (100 %) effect on the values before the accident.

This *modus operandi* (Fig. 13.5), valid in the case of agricultural activity, is also used in the case of forestry in connection with contamination of the forest environment, for fishing in connection with the contamination of the River Rhône, for sea fishing in connection with contamination of the marine environment, for food in connection with contamination of the agricultural environment and for water distribution activity in connection with the Rhône and underground water sources (whichever is more contaminated).

In the case of economic activity not directly concerned with the radioactive contamination of a specific medium (trades, the construction sector and industries other than the food industry), it was felt that the overall economic consequences would be of minor importance and therefore the proposed simplification retains only the first points on the scale (Fig. 13.6).

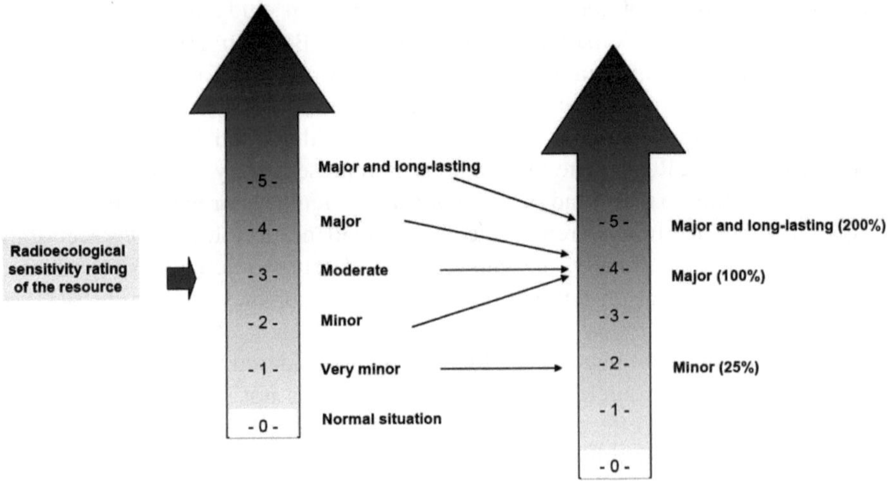

Fig. 13.5 Example of the relationship between radio-ecological and economic criteria for activities linked to the various media

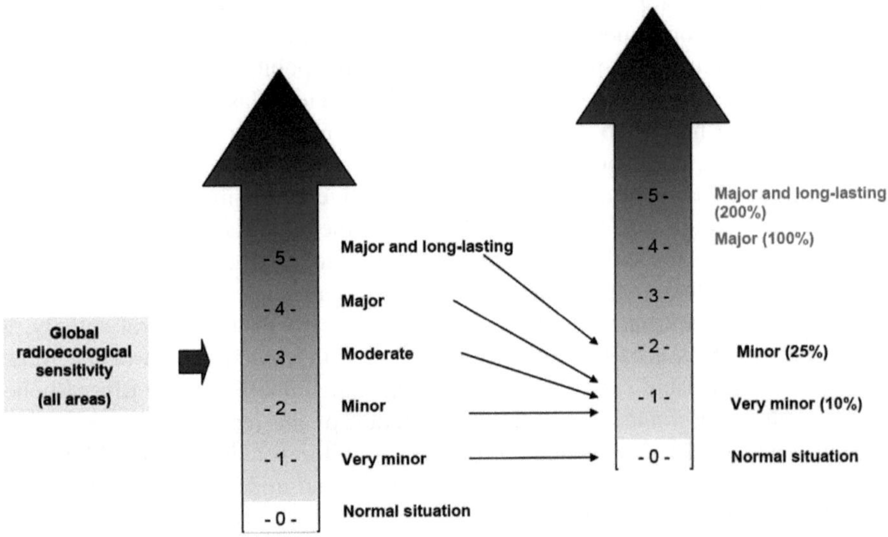

Fig. 13.6 Example of the relationships between radio-ecological and economic criteria in sectors not linked to a specific medium

13.3.1.3 Societal Stakes

In the PRIME project, the approach to social aspects of post-accident management is based on the concept of resilience. Determining resilience criteria thus means assessing the capacity of a district's population to react following an accident. This is a relatively innovative subject which is currently an area for research.

The variability criteria of this type of trauma are numerous. Research on risk perception (IRSN 2007) reveals criteria linked to the individual faced with risk: accustomed to risk, incomprehension, uncertainty, tacit acceptance, controllability, ethics. . . The French are particularly reluctant to trust the authorities with respect to pollution risks since they consider that risk management in this area is not easy to monitor. Certain other criteria with an influence on risk perception are linked to the social management of risk: identifying victims, trusting institutions, media coverage, advantage, equity. Other surveys show that in the population at large, different groups are characterized by their differences in approach to life (everyone has a perception of the world, imagining how best to make his way through life along paths defined by the values, beliefs and social networks which contribute to making a person who he or she is). And so resilience capacities will depend on social fabric, customs, experience and factors linked to collective behavior. Depending on the group, the people who count will be different: influence of celebrities, imitation, influence of prominent citizens, of those close to us, influence of experts and administrators. . .

Depending on the geographical district, the average age, depending on the weight of associations and their activeness, the reactions will be different. Even though the existing bibliography has been studied in depth, current knowledge of societal reaction following a nuclear crisis is not sufficient to identify sound theoretical criteria for ranking the resilience capacities of populations.

13.3.1.4 Summary of PRIME Method Classification Criteria

We summarize hereafter the criteria for vulnerability assessment recommended for assessing a district's global vulnerability to the consequences of radioactive contamination of the environment. All the information necessary for computing these criteria for each of the 491 geographical districts in the zone under study has been collected in a software prototype displaying the criteria values as a map and processing them using multi-criteria aggregation algorithms.

- District's global vulnerability for one radionuclide
  - Economic vulnerability of companies
  - Employment vulnerability
  - Real estate vulnerability
  - Tourism vulnerability
  - Global radio-ecological vulnerability for one radionuclide
    - Radio-ecological vulnerability of urban area
    - Radio-ecological vulnerability of coastal area
    - Radio-ecological vulnerability of River Rhône
    - Radio-ecological vulnerability of groundwater

- Radio-ecological vulnerability of forest area
- Radio-ecological vulnerability of agricultural area
    - Radio-ecological vulnerability of lettuce crop
    - Radio-ecological vulnerability of thyme crop
    - Radio-ecological vulnerability of olive crop
    - Radio-ecological vulnerability of melon crop
    - Radio-ecological vulnerability of peach crop
    - Radio-ecological vulnerability of potato crop
    - Radio-ecological vulnerability of rice crop
    - Radio-ecological vulnerability of tomato crop
    - Radio-ecological vulnerability of wine production
    - Radio-ecological vulnerability of durum wheat production
    - Radio-ecological vulnerability of goat's milk production
    - Radio-ecological vulnerability of egg production
    - Radio-ecological vulnerability of lamb meat production
    - Radio-ecological vulnerability of chicken meat production
    - Vulnerability due to presence in the area (irradiation)

13.3.1.5 Implementing the Multicriteria Analysis Core

Once the regional database has been completed (this being the matrix for the multicriteria assessment), it is then a question of understanding how each stakeholder uses this information to prioritize, from his perspective, the global gravity of the impact on each district in addition to the districts with respect to each other. This phase of assembling the ratings is done together with the various members of the PRIME WG in order to validate the coherence of the resulting database and also to note similarities or differences in the way the stakeholders prioritize elements. To support this second phase of the PRIME project, the GIS/multi-criteria prototype tool was used both for obtaining a map representation of criteria assessment and collecting stakeholders' various points of view and to illustrate in real time any substantial modifications to this or that criterion.

Stakeholders' preferences were collected during one-to-one interviews between the project team and each stakeholder. The idea was to place each stakeholder in an imaginary post-accident management situation in a given region after providing them with the keys to understanding obtained by the PRIME method. The points tested during these working sessions concerned use of the vulnerability criteria set up by the PRIME WG to establish priorities. Are these criteria sufficient? What's missing? Based on this information, how are vulnerabilities prioritized?

These sessions lasted for about 3 h. When stakeholders gave their permission, they were recorded to facilitate digital processing of the information they each provided. Interview guidelines were established to organise the dialogue so that overall homogeneity of the different interviews was ensured. The points addressed consecutively during the interview are:

1. The goal of the work session. The aim is to rank each geographical district in the zone surveyed in the context of PRIME on a vulnerability scale from level 0 to

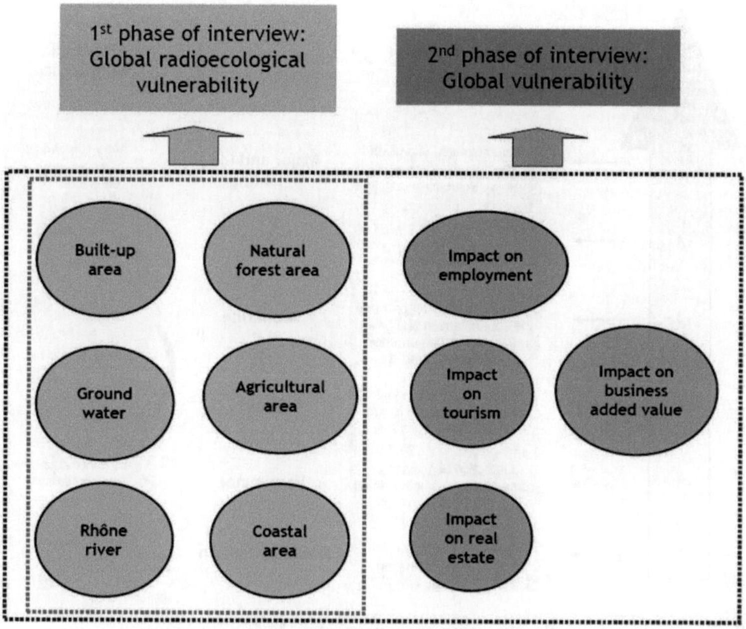

Fig. 13.7 Classification process presented during interviews

level 5, for an imaginary accident scenario. This ranking is done twice during the interview (Fig. 13.7): the first time on the basis of the contamination criteria of the district's various environments and the second time, integrating the economic consequences resulting from contamination of these environments.

2. General presentation of the surveyed zone (Fig. 13.7).
3. The classification scale and its interpretation (Fig. 13.8). This phase of the interview is crucial since it entails providing the stakeholder with sufficient understanding of the PRIME classification method for him to assimilate it and apply it later on.
4. The fictional accident scenario: 10GBq (=10 billion becquerels) cesium-137 are released non-stop into the atmosphere for 24 h on 1st July 2008. Weather conditions during this 24-h period remain constant: light rain and wind resulting in a substantial deposit of radioactive pollutants in the immediate vicinity of the site. The exercise begins on 10th July. The cesium-137 deposits are supposedly known and the experts have therefore been able to implement the PRIME method for computing criteria concerning the various environments in addition to the economic consequence criteria. Figure 13.9 illustrates the environment classification ratings in a map format as a result of applying the software prototype. This phase preparing for the simulation ends with the sentence "*Now, you rate the global vulnerability of each district with a view to establishing action priorities…*".

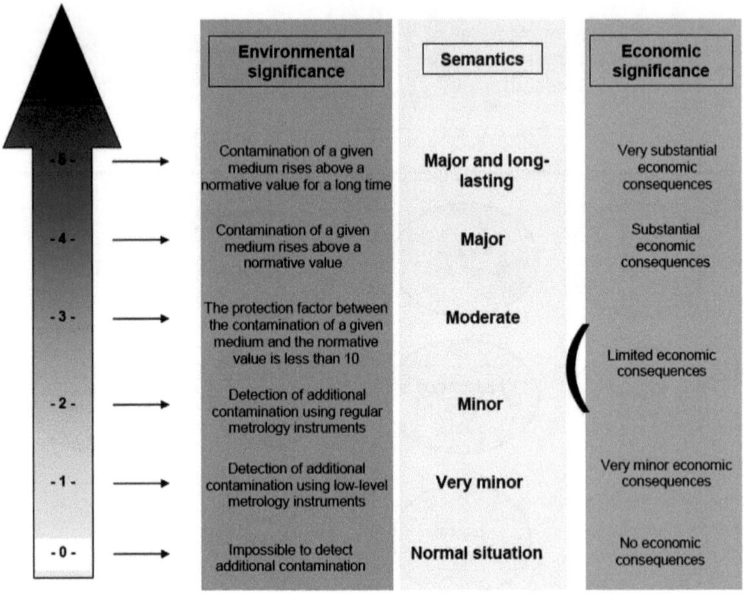

Fig. 13.8 Semantics of the classification scale presented during interviews

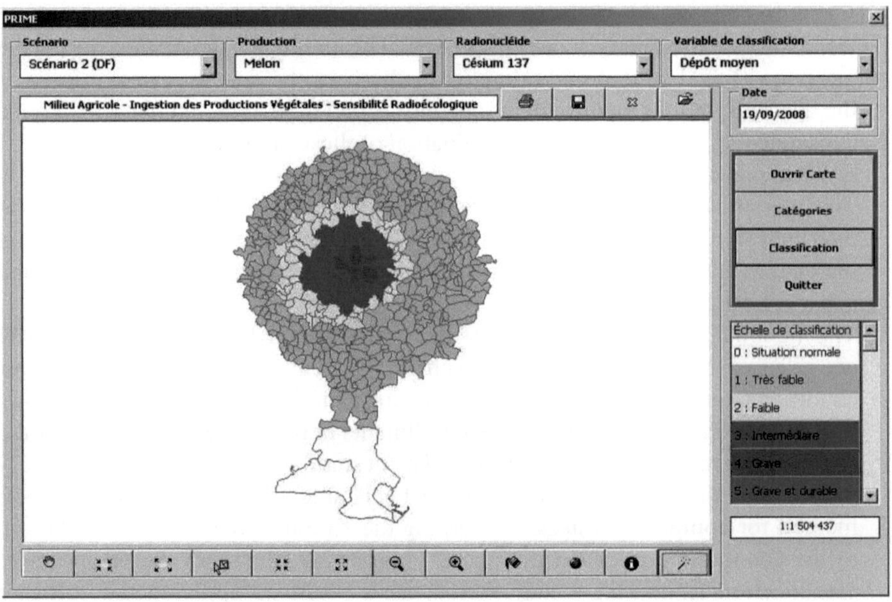

Fig. 13.9 Example of how environment classification criteria are presented

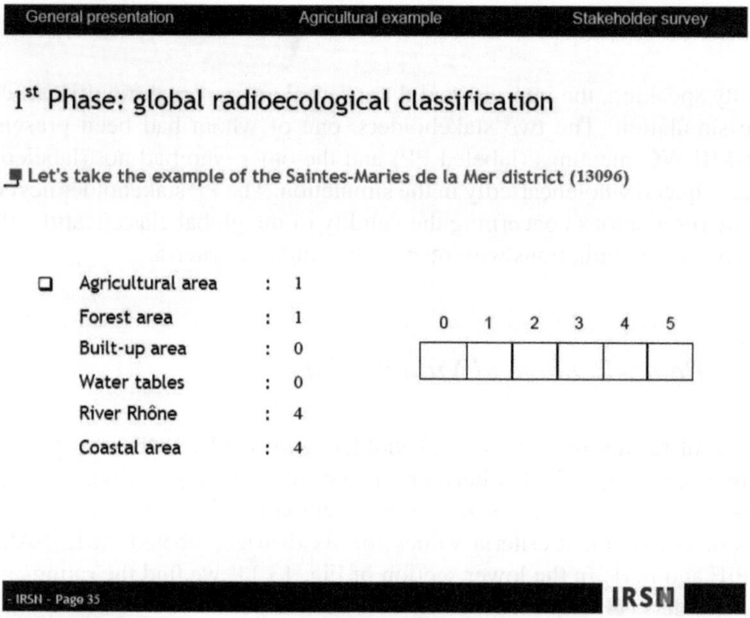

Fig. 13.10 Information is presented during interviews

5. This is followed by the enumeration of 18 examples of districts presenting various combinations of classification ratings for each of the six environments (agricultural, built-up area, Rhône river, underground water supplies and coastal area). An example of how criteria are presented to stakeholders is given in Fig. 13.10. For each geographical district, the stakeholder is then asked to define the value of the global rating of radio-ecological vulnerability or a range of values for this rating and then to distribute eight counters along a cardboard ruler calibrated from 0 to 5 to illustrate his preference for one level of the classification scale rather than another.
6. Once presentation of the 18 examples is over, the specific question of ranking the criteria linked to environment contamination by order of importance is addressed based on the Simos method, see Simos (1997).
7. The method is then reapplied from point 5 onwards to include the economic criteria. The stakeholder has to propose a rating for each district based on the six criteria ratings relative to environment contamination plus the four criteria ratings relative to economic factors (real estate value, tourism, added value business and employment). He then uses the Simos method for the ten criteria.

Five interviews have been carried out with stakeholders. To endorse the interview guidelines, the exercise was carried out by an engineer in the IRSN team on his own before tackling the interviews. There are currently three sets of data to illustrate the future potential for using the method once all the different points of view have been collected.

13.4 Results

Generally speaking, the interviews did not reveal any major difficulties in carrying out the simulation. The two stakeholders, one of whom had been present at all the PRIME WG meetings (labeled PP) and the other who had not (labeled CAL), both participated wholeheartedly in the simulation. The PP stakeholder nevertheless had some reservations concerning the validity of the global classification given the approach's many limitations with respect to economic criteria.

13.4.1 Radio-Ecological Vulnerability

Examples of results for the two stakeholders and for the IRSN engineer (labeled CM) are given in Fig. 13.11, where a rating or range of ratings is assigned to sample districts and in Fig. 13.12, for the Simos method results. Figure 13.11 shows the profiles of environment criteria values for six districts labeled ARL, SAU, SAO, BSA, PIE and LAP. In the lower section of Fig. 13.11, we find the ratings given by the stakeholders (■) and occasionally the range of possible ratings (← →).

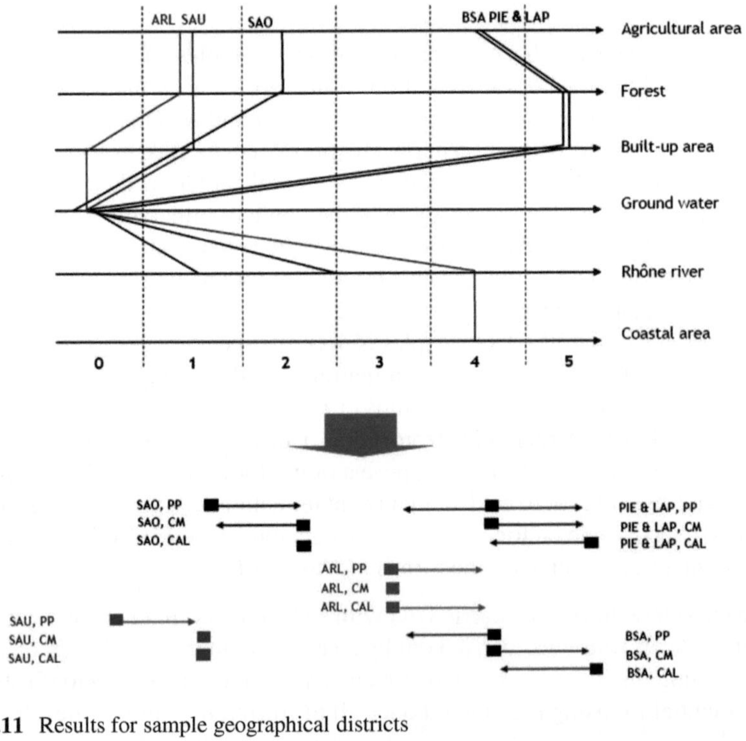

Fig. 13.11 Results for sample geographical districts

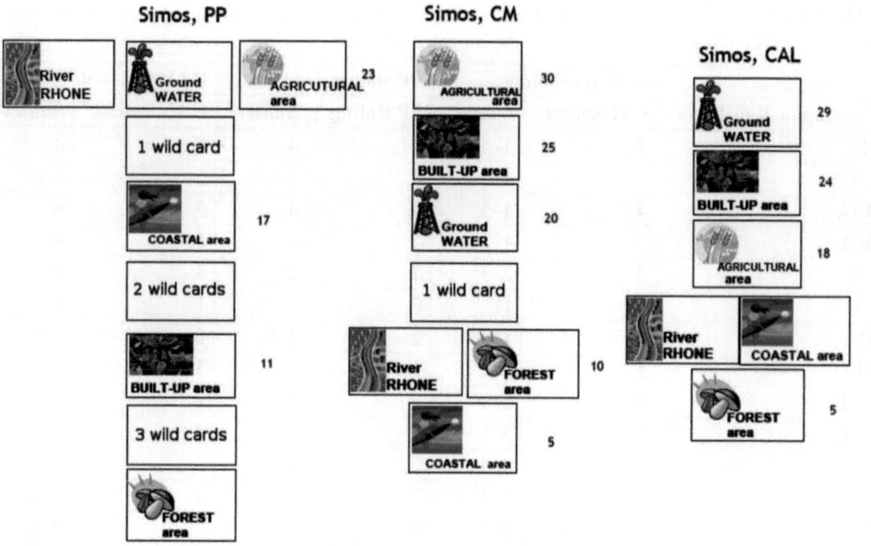

Fig. 13.12 Results of the Simos method for radio-ecological vulnerability (to the *right* of the cards, the weighted values when all media are represented

The results obtained by the Simos method were used to establish the weighted values for each criterion and for each stakeholder, distributing a global weight of 100 % among the various criteria in the order provided by the stakeholders. Since the number of radio-ecological criteria is variable depending on the district (some districts in the survey zone have no shoreline and therefore, no coastal area, and the River Rhône does not flow through others), the distribution of the global weight takes the unrepresented media into consideration by distributing their weight over the other media in the proportions determined by the Simos method. Thus, for the PIE district with no shoreline, the weight of 17 allocated by PP is redistributed among all the other media resulting in the following weighted values: 28 for the River Rhône, the water tables and the agricultural areas, 13 for the built-up and 4 for the forest areas.

These weighted values are then used as input parameters for the IRSN Sunset software which applies the ELECTRE TRI multi-criteria analysis method, see Roy (1996); Mousseau et al. (2000); Dias et al. (2002). The calculations are then used to define the possible range of ratings for each geographical district setting the majority threshold at 55 %. The variability in ratings proposed by the Sunset software corresponds to the hypotheses considered to handle situations of indifference or incomparability. If these situations are processed from either a systematically pessimistic or systematically optimistic perspective, we obtain a possible range of ratings for each district in line with the order obtained by the Simos method.

Table 13.1 Comparison of the stakeholders' direct ratings for environment contaminations with the Simos method results, processed by the Sunset software

	CM stakeholder		PP stakeholder		CAL stakeholder	
Geographical districts	CM Rating	Sunset	PP Rating	Sunset	CAL Rating	Sunset
PIE	4	4–5	4	4	5	4
LAP	4	4–5	4	4	5	4
BSA	4	4–5	4	4	5	4
BOL	5	4–5	4	4	5	4
VIC	3	2–3	2	2–3	3	2
SAU	1	1	0	0–1	1	1
AVI	3	1–2	2	1–2	2	1-2
BED	1	1	1	1	1	1
AUB	3	2–3	2	2–3	2	2–3
VAL	3	3	2	2–3	3	3
GRA	3	3–4	2	2–4	3	3–4
LUS	3	2–3	2	2–3	3	2–3
BEA	2	2–3	2	2–3	3	2–3
MON	2	2	1	1–2	2	2
VES	2	1–2	1	1–2	2	1–2
SAO	2	1–2	1	1–2	2	1–2
ARL	3	1	3	1–2	4	2
STE	3	0–1	3	1	3	1-2

On the whole, the three stakeholders applied the same reasoning to prioritizing environments: "*people first, then the environments*" (quote from one of the interviews). The first resources needing protection are therefore water (underground water supplies and in some cases the Rhône), foodstuffs (agricultural areas and maybe the sea) and/or housing (built-up areas). One of the stakeholders recognized that he was "*particularly fond of the coast, a fact which could lead him to considering coastal areas as the equivalent of agricultural areas if there were an accident in a coastal zone*". The other stakeholders consider the coast, and also forest areas, as leisure areas. Table 13.1 shows that examples of stakeholders' ratings are sometimes at odds with results processed using the Simos method.

The systematic disagreement for the AVI, ARL and STE districts is due to the minority criteria for the River Rhône and the sea which do not have enough influence on the ELECTRE method result to move the rating up the scale to another category, being blocked by the other criteria globally in majority. A solution for compensating this drawback would be to lower the majority threshold to 35 that the method could be adapted to the stakeholders' reasoning according to which when there are enough criteria with the same value (even if this does not represent the majority of criteria in the voting sense), then this vulnerability rating value could be assigned to the district as a whole.

For the CAL stakeholder, disagreement concerning the districts rated 5 (PIE, LAP, BSA and BOL) can be explained by the fact that CAL gives a 5 rating as soon as any major criterion is rated 5. According to this stakeholder, "*there is a major difference between the levels 1-3 and the levels 4-5; for levels 1-3, we're talking about monitoring and we are going to establish averages; for levels 4-5, we enter the sphere of health impact and here we're going to be dealing with extremes, we're talking about actual figures and no longer about averages*". From a formal point of view, we could take this reasoning into consideration by applying a veto process to the environment contamination criteria as soon as one of them is subject to major and lasting impact.

Finally, if we aggregate the Simos method results for the three stakeholders, we obtain the following sequence (the sum of weighted values for the three stakeholders appears between parentheses):

Groundwater (72) $\sim$ Agricultural area (71) > Built-up (60) > Rhône (45) > Sea (64) > Forest (18)

13.4.2 Global Vulnerability

The results for global vulnerability (criteria linked to environment contamination plus economic criteria) were processed in the same way as for radio-ecological vulnerability. Figure 13.13 shows the Simos method results for all ten criteria.

On the whole, the stakeholders feel that economic criteria are less important than criteria linked to environment contamination. This is particularly the case for the stakeholders PP and CM who give economic criteria a total weighted value of 17 and 16 respectively. For these two stakeholders, awareness of the numerous limitations encountered when creating the economic criteria probably has an influence on the way they use them. These two stakeholders believe that there are two groups of criteria: those linked to environments and those linked to economic factors. The third stakeholder makes finer distinctions in his reasoning and believes the criteria fall into three groups: the water tables and built-up areas (protection of man), agricultural areas, employment and added value (protection of human activities perceived as fundamental), the Rhône river, coastal areas, forests, tourism and real estate (protection of human activities perceived as secondary). This stakeholder nevertheless recognizes that with respect to "groundwater, built-up and agricultural areas, we can be proactive and make decisions. With respect to the added value of businesses and employment, the State will be reduced to providing support in the light of consequences". The issue of differences in temporality was also raised by the stakeholders during the various interviews: "action kinetics differ depending on the environment", which leads to ranking agricultural and built-up areas as being more vulnerable whereas they will probably be less lastingly affected than forest areas. Table 13.2 shows that examples of stakeholders' ratings are sometimes at odds with the Simos method of processing results. In particular, we see the effects of minority criteria and veto mentioned in the previous paragraph.

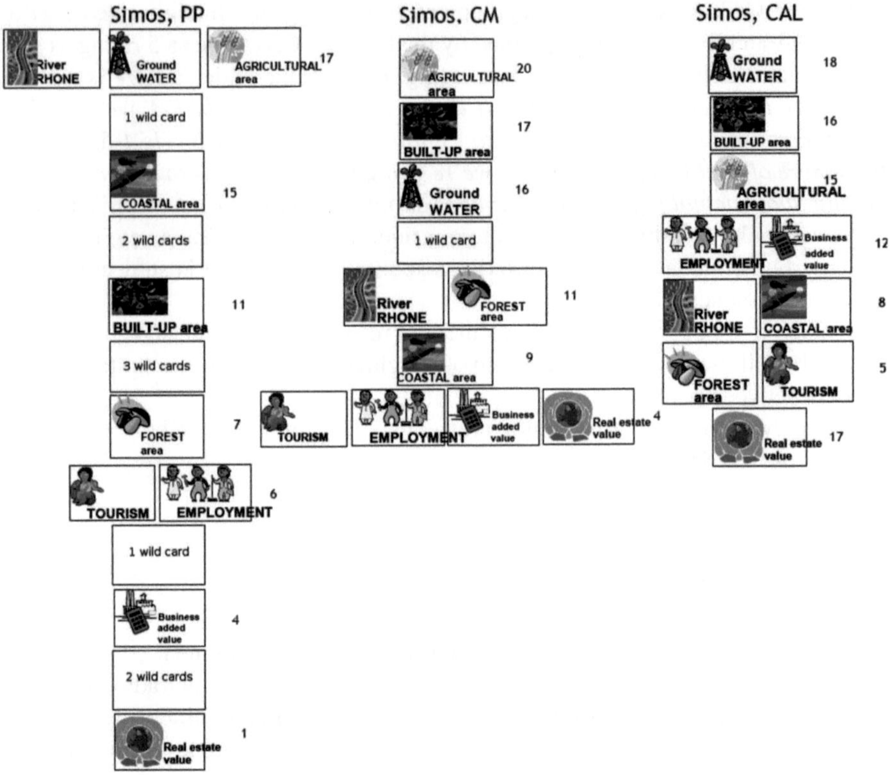

Fig. 13.13 Simos method results for global vulnerability

For CM stakeholder, the economy has little influence on the global ranking of districts. Information on economic criteria leads the PP stakeholder to give quite a surprising rating to SAU and BED which should perhaps be checked with this stakeholder. For CAL, the order of criteria proposed by the Simos method should lead to changing the ranking of the LUS, BEA, VES and SAO districts whereas the stakeholder maintains his rating.

Finally, if we aggregate the Simos method results for the three stakeholders, we obtain the following sequence (the sum of weighted values for the three stakeholders is displayed between parentheses):

Groundtables (51) ~ Agricultural area (52) > Built-up (44) > Rhône (36) > Sea (31) > Forest (23) > Employment (22) ~ Added value (20) > Tourism (15) > Real estate (6)

The two economic criteria in top position are the impact on employment and the added value produced by businesses. This indicates that stakeholders first consider the consequences on economic activity generated by the geographical districts. Tourism is however close behind because in this region, tourism is also one of the main sources of income and the existence of strong links between these three criteria

Table 13.2 Comparison of the stakeholders' direct ratings for global vulnerability with the Simos method results processed by the Sunset software

	CM stakeholder		PP stakeholder		CAL stakeholder	
Geographical districts	CM Rating	Sunset	PP Rating	Sunset	CAL Rating	Sunset
PIE	4	4–5	4	4	5	4
LAP	4	4–5	4	4	5	4
BSA	4	4–5	4	4	5	4
BOL	5	4–5	4	4	5	4–5
VIC	3	2–3	2	2–3	3	2–3
SAU	0	1	0	1	1	0–1
AVI	3	1–2	2	1–2	2	1–2
BED	0	1	0	1	1	1
AUB	3	2–3	2	2–3	2	2–3
VAL	3	3	2	2–3	3	2–3
GRA	3	3	2	2–3	3	2–3
LUS	3	2–3	2	2–3	3	2
BEA	2	2	2	2–3	3	2
MON	2	2	1	1–2	2	1–2
VES	2	1–2	1	1–2	2	1
SAO	2	1–2	1	1–2	2	1
ARL	3	1	3	1–2	4	1
STE	3	1	3	1–2	3	1

is mentioned during the interviews. The stakeholders also link economic criteria to the environment contamination criteria (for instance, employment and added value are linked to the agricultural area, real estate and tourism are linked to the forest area), thus confirming the relationships computed by the PRIME WG between the ratings for environment contamination and the ratings for economic consequences.

13.4.3 The Approach's Advantages and Limitations and Prospects

The PRIME project is based on an operational method which is somewhat innovative in the world of nuclear applications. The innovation lies mainly in the process of developing the method on the basis of dialogue, a process which allowed plenty of room for debate. Throughout the PRIME project, the traditional methods of assessing risks linked to the release of radioactive substances into the environment have been confronted with the region's perceptions of the event as expressed by the decision-makers (prefecture, mayor, safety authority) and by civil society representatives (associations, information centres). This desire to include a wide range of participants nevertheless came up against the practicalities of establishing a working group which necessarily limits the number of participants. To offset this difficulty, interviews with stakeholders other than those comprising the PRIME WG were carried out in parallel to the WG meetings.

The PRIME project enabled the creation of a database mapping the pertinent indicators for prioritizing a region's vulnerability in the event of a nuclear accident. Research focused mainly on building a tool (coupling GIS software with a multicriteria aggregation algorithm) and searching for available data to feed into it and also discussion on the limitations of this data. It is obvious that expectations in terms of decision-making tools go well beyond the mere characterization of regions' vulnerabilities. During interviews, some stakeholders were clearly frustrated in not being asked the question "*what decision would you make here?*". One stakeholder suggested applying the ranking method to a scenario, deciding on a course of action and then determining if this action was really pertinent and applicable in view of the foreseeable consequences on both environment contamination and the economy. The stakeholders nevertheless recognize that characterizing vulnerabilities is a fundamental prerequisite before contemplating action but determining strategies to reduce vulnerability could be considered a necessary extension to the PRIME project.

13.5 Conclusion

The use of multi-criteria analysis methods in the PRIME project has two advantages. On the one hand, building the multi-criteria analysis method (discussing the pertinence of criteria, deciding on criteria assessment methods, identifying the limits of shared knowledge) leads to structuring information exchanges between participants and establishing a trusting relationship among them. During development of the methodology, relationships were undeniably established between experts in the technical fields of radioecology and radiation protection and regional stakeholders who generally have little experience in these fields but who are well-placed for contributing information on how things work in their region. The evaluation tools and in particular, the computer codes used for assessing environmental consequences were therefore improved thanks to information contributed by the regional stakeholders, which led to modifying the generic data sets to adjust them to the local context of the PRIME survey zone. At the same time, regional stakeholders improve their understanding of how the regions are represented on the administrative level and how this information is used to prepare management decisions.

On the other hand, with multi-criteria analysis methods it becomes possible to express the perspectives of the various participants, identify common practices in prioritizing a region's vulnerabilities and characterize the differences. The PRIME exercise thus aims to make progress towards achieving a "differentiated consensus", see Noucher (2007). In point of fact, the wide variety of participants in the PRIME WG makes it impossible to come to a compromise as the ideological gap between the organisations consulted reveals substantial limits to their cooperation. However, revealing differences in values attributed to this or that criteria or factor facilitates mutual understanding of the different ways of prioritizing a region's vulnerabilities and results in a more global vision without concealing the particularities of the various participants. Ultimately, decisions concerning the management of contaminated regions will remain the prerogative of State departments but the information made available to them will portray these contrasting views with respect to local vulnerabilities.

References

Barde, C., Mercat-Rommens, C., Baumont, G., & Bachimon, P. (2007). Une construction concertée d'indicateurs spatiaux pour la gestion d'un territoire accidenté. In M. Batton-Hubert, T. Joliveau, & S. Lardon (Eds.), *SAGEO'2007, Colloque International de Géomatique et d'Analyse Spatiale*. Clermont-Ferrand: Saint-Etienne.

Chakhar, S., Mercat-Rommens, C., & Mousseau, V. (2008). Cartographie multicritère de la sensibilité radioécologique : projet PRIME. In *Conférence OPDE'2008 "Les nouveaux Outils Pour Décider Ensemble"*, Québec.

Dias, L., Mousseau, V., Figueira, J., & Clímaco, J. (2002). An aggregation/disaggregation approach to obtain robust conclusions with ELECTRE TRI. *European Journal of Operational Research, 138*(2), 332–348.

Genty, A., & Brignon, J. (2008). Caractérisation des critères socio-économiques dans le cadre de l'analyse multicritère du projet PRIME. Rapport d'étude INERIS no DRC-08-91439-11003A, Verneuil-en-Halatte, France, 31 pp.

MEDAD. (2007). Evaluations socio-économiques des instruments de prévention des inondations. Collection "Etudes et synthèses" du Ministère de l'Environnement, Paris.

Mercat-Rommens, C., Chakhar, S., Barde, C., Roussel-Debet, S., & Mousseau, V. (2008). Towards a shared method to classify contaminated territories in the case of an accidental nuclear event: the PRIME Project. In *SRA2008 conference. Risk analysis VI. WIT transactions on information and communication* (vol. 39).

Mousseau, V., Slowinski, R., & Zielniewicz, P. (2000). A user-oriented implementation of the ELECTRE TRI method integrating preference elicitation support. *Computers & Operations Research, 27*(7–8), 757–777.

Niel, J.-C., & Godet, J.-L. (2008). Development of a national doctrin for the management of the post-accident phase of a radiological emergency situation. *Revue Contrôle, Autorité de Sûreté Nucléaire*, Paris (pp. 2–8)

Noucher, M. (2007). Coproduction de données géographiques : pourquoi, comment et avec qui? In M. Batton-Hubert, T. Joliveau, and S. Lardon, editors, *SAGEO'2007, Colloque International de Géomatique et d'Analyse Spatiale*. Clermont-Ferrand: Saint-Etienne.

Roy, B. (1996). *Multicriteria methodology for decision aiding*. Dordrecht: Kluwer Academic.

Simos, J. (1997). *Evaluer l'impact sur l'environnement* (261 pp). Lausanne: Presses Polytechniques et Universitaires Romandes.

Venzal-Barde, C. (2008). Les outils SIG au service de la gestion d'un territoire contaminé. In *Conférence SIG 2008*, Versailles.

Editor's Comments on "Coupling GIS and Multi-Criteria Modeling to Support Post-Accident Nuclear Risk Evaluation"

Mercat-Rommens, Chakhar, Chojnacki and Mousseau present an application concerned with the evaluation of risk and the building a *geographical risk map*. This **case study** presents both the problem formulation stage (see Chap. 2) and the application of a risk aggregation procedure. The case illustrates the use of the ELECTRE TRI method (see Chap. 4, Sect. 4.4.4). It thus relates to Chaps. 16, 12 and 10 in the use of the same aggregation method (although other chapters use slight variations of it). It also relates to the chapter by Kunsch and Vander Straeten (Chap. 11) in the application industry: *nuclear energy*. Noteworthy is furthermore the coupling between MCDA and GIS, observed also in the applications reported by Metchebon et al. (Chap. 12) and Lué and Colorni (Chap. 14).

The authors studied a large area in the South of France, involving a working group representing over a dozen different local and national **stakeholders**; the objective of the application being to develop an MCDA model for assessing the risk upon geographical regions—the decision **alternatives**—in the event of a an accident involving the dissemination of radioactive substances. This was already considered to be an important concern, even though the application occurred before the Fukujima accident in Japan. The decision problem was framed as a the sorting **problem statement**: each geographical area (district, corresponding to the decision alternatives to be evaluated), has to be assigned a risk degree category, based on the perspectives of the stakeholders.

A **client** for the application is not explicitly identified. One may consider that the primary clients (to use Schein's taxonomy Schein, 1999) were the project sponsors: a project agency and the French environment ministry. However, these being public entities, it is also reasonable to consider civil society as the ultimate client. The involved **stakeholders** themselves can be regarded as intermediate clients in this perspective, i.e. as actors involved by representing their constituencies. The authors acted as **analysts**.

The decision aiding process encompassed several **stages**. First, the working group identified the stakes that would be affected in case of an accident. A second step was devoted to building a set of criteria to characterize those potential effects and identify values that could be used as benchmarks for those criteria. A third step concerned the construction of scales of gravity. Finally, an aggregation step yielded a global risk category.

The top-level **risk criteria** considered were divided in two groups. One initial group consisted of six sectors of concern in connection with radio-ecological vulnerability: agriculture, forest, built environment, ground water and, depending on the district, also coastal areas and Rhone river. An assessment of risk was made considering only these criteria, which encompassed many detailed indicators. A second assessment added four top-level criteria concerning economic impact on employment, tourism, business and real estate. Although the authors consider social stakes ("resilience") should be appraised, they did not have enough data to include them.

The **evaluations** of the stakeholders were collected by means of individual interviews, which were previously structured. A qualitative semantic scale with six levels was used to assess the potential impacts in the event of an accident, using the GIS as a visual aid. The authors comment of the careful choice of words used for the semantic levels, after discovering that some words might have different connotations and interpretations. This aspect, often neglected, is known to occur frequently in risk assessment (e.g., see Beyth-Marom 1982).

The elicitation of **criteria weights** was done using Simos's method (Simos, 1997). The case study illustrates the preferences of three stakeholders, presenting their inputs for Simos's method. One difficulty faced by the analysts was that not all criteria were applicable to all the districts (e.g., coastal area impact). For such districts, the weight of the missing criteria was proportionally distributed by the remaining criteria. An **alternative approach** would have been to repeat Simos's elicitation procedure for these specific cases, which would probably lead to slightly different weight vectors. It would also have been interesting to discuss the elicited information as a group, in a decision conference (Phillips and Bana e Costa, 2007) of stakeholders, rather than isolated interviews.

ELECTRE TRI was used for **sorting** districts into risk categories taking this information into account. Results were then compared with the global perception indicated by each stakeholder, in order to discuss how well the method was able to match the stakeholder's view. A view of the group is not presented, but the authors suggest a sum (or average) of the individual weights could be used. Another potentially more interesting way of discussing the preferences of the group could be the discussion of some outputs as suggested by Damart et al. (2007).

The **tangible** outcomes of this decision process are a set of criteria and scales, and a tool to support the dialogue with stakeholders concerning the risk assessment of districts to make a classification. This tool is implemented as a software coupling a GIS with the ELEDCTRE Tri aggregation algorithm. As **intangible** outcomes, the authors emphasize the establishment of relationships between experts in different fields, contributing to improve communication and mutual understanding.

This case study illustrates how a large group of stakeholders/experts can be involved in risk assessment involving technical and economical aspects. It emphasizes mainly the elicitation of information from these actors in an easy to understand but not always easy to implement format: qualitative information about performance and criteria importance. While it was developed for a particular application, the same methodology can be applied in other territorial risk assessment problems.

References

Beyth-Marom, R. (1982). How probable is probable? a numerical translation of verbal probability expressions. *Journal of Forecasting, 1*, 257–269.

Damart, S., Dias, L., & Mousseau, V. (2007). Supporting groups in sorting decisions: Methodology and use of a multi-criteria aggregation/disaggregation DSS. *Decision Support Systems, 43*(4), 1464–1475.

Phillips, L., & Bana e Costa, C. (2007). Transparent prioritisation, budgeting and resource allocation with multi-criteria decision analysis and decision conferencing. *Annals of Operations Research, 154*(1), 51–68.

Schein, E. (1999). *Process consultation revisited: Building the helping relationship.* Reading: Addison Wesley.

Simos, J. (1997). *Evaluer l'impact sur l'environnement.* Lausanne: Presses Polytechniques et Universitaires Romandes.

Chapter 14
A Multicriteria Spatial Decision Support System for Hazardous Material Transport

A. Luè and A. Colorni

Abstract The local public administrations of the Italian cities are responsible for the hazardous material transport within the municipality boundaries. The city of Milan is interested in implementing a system to support the municipal transport department in planning the shipments and control their positions. The paper presents an ongoing project to design and develop a spatial multicriteria decision support system (DSS) based on a Geographical Information System for hazardous material transport in the city of Milan. The DSS considers both the problems of routing and scheduling the shipments in urban and suburban road networks, taking into account the viewpoints of the interested parties (e.g. population, shipping company, vehicle driver, environment agency). We use a risk assessment model that considers the consequences of an accident for each road segment on population, territorial infrastructures, natural elements, critical areas (e.g. areas which may be a target for a terrorist attack). The DSS is in a prototype phase and has been tested on Niguarda, an area of the city of Milan characterized by the presence of an important hospital. The prototype considers the position and time of activities of schools, railways, park and agricultural areas, and hospital buildings that are located in the area. The DSS has been applied to an exemplificative shipment in the area, and the results are presented.

14.1 Introduction

There are many schemes for the classification of hazardous material (hazmat), formulated in various countries and for different scopes. The United Nations

---

A. Luè (✉)
Poliedra, via G. Colombo 40, 20133, Milano, Italy

Dipartimento Design, Politecnico di Milano, via Durando 38/A, 20158, Milano, Italy
e-mail: alessandro.lue@polimi.it

A. Colorni
Dipartimento Design, Politecnico di Milano, via Durando 38/A, 20158, Milano, Italy
e-mail: alberto.colorni@polimi.it

R. Bisdorff et al. (eds.), *Evaluation and Decision Models with Multiple Criteria*, International Handbooks on Information Systems,
DOI 10.1007/978-3-662-46816-6_14

Organization categorizes hazmats in nine categories (UNECE, 2007), with some subcategories, and specifying packaging requirements for some of them.

Quantitative risk analysis techniques were first developed with the purpose of assessing the risk in nuclear processes, and then widely applied to process industry (Center for Chemical Process Safety, 2000). The methodological approach to the problem of risk management in hazmat shipments derives from such techniques (Bubbico et al., 2004). In particular, the literature refers to industrial plants presenting a relevant risk of accidents, i.e. characterized by the presence of *point sources* of risk. There are some technical difficulties in extending such approach to cover mobile risk sources along *linear* routes, such as the vehicles transporting hazmat on the roads (*active risk*) and even more so when it is applied to the study of events that see the transportation system as the victim of externally originated disastrous events, e.g. in case of floods, landslides, earthquakes (*passive risk*) (Bruglieri et al., 2008).

There are two approaches to the analysis of hazmat shipments, as proposed by Waters (2003):

- aggregated analyses, which focus on aggregate statistics of hazmat movements to calculate the frequency of incidents, and to measure the total exposure of the population to hazmat movements, e.g. Dennis (1996);
- studies that evaluate specific hazmat shipments or proposed regulatory changes. This approach is intended for decision-making, e.g. Carotenuto et al. (2007b). The case study described in this paper follows such approach.

What differentiates hazardous materials shipments from the transport of other materials is the risk associated with an accidental release of hazardous materials. The danger associated with hazmat shipments may differ significantly depending on the situations. The degree of harm is not exclusively a function of the physical properties of the hazmat, but also of the amount that is released and, especially, of the circumstances (location, wind, etc.) (Dennis, 1996). Moreover, the danger of terrorist attacks has increased the concerns regarding the secure transport of hazardous materials (Field, 2004) .

Usually, in a freight transport problem, travel time is minimized in order to satisfy the time-windows requirements of the client. However, in the case of hazmat transport, minimizing travel time can put a large population at risk: dense-populated areas should be avoided by using slower and less direct roads (Zhang et al., 2000; Huang et al., 2003). For instance, Erkut and Glickman (1997) shows that rerouting may lead to significant risk reductions. On the other hand, sparse-populated areas in Italy are often environmentally vulnerable (e.g. because of the presence of natural parks or agricultural fields). Moreover, a truck driver would like to avoid the less safe roads for his/her own safety. This problem therefore involves conflicting objectives among interested parties: population, shipping company, vehicle driver, environment agency. In presence of conflicting interests, the improvement of one objective typically conflicts with the improvement of other objectives, and automatic technical search for the optimum becomes meaningless. In these situations, the use of a decision support system (DSS) is recommended (Guariso and Werthner, 1989; Colorni et al., 1999).

The present work concerns a particular problem: hazmat transport in urban areas. We outline an ongoing work to develop a DSS based on a Geographical Information System (GIS) for hazmat transport in the city of Milan. The GIS-DSS is designed to perform a risk analysis for hazmat road and rail transport, during all the necessary steps (from the initial route selection to risk assessment and dynamic route guidance). So far, the GIS-DSS is in a prototype phase, which has been developed within a commercial GIS and has been tested on Niguarda, an area of the city of Milan characterized by the presence of an important hospital.

The paper is organized as follows. In Sect. 14.2, an overview on the philosophy and the structure of the proposed GIS-DSS is presented. In Sect. 14.3, the mathematical model to calculate the risk associated to hazmat transport is described in detail. In Sect. 14.4, the multi-objective problem of hazmat routing is discussed. Section 14.5 explains the implementation of the DSS within the GIS and presents the results for an exemplificative hazmat shipment. Section 14.6 concludes the paper with a summary of the main properties of the proposed planner and with indications of future challenges.

14.2 Philosophy and Structure of the DSS

A comprehensive literature review on risk assessment, location, and routing of hazmat is presented in List et al. (1991), Erkut et al. (2006), and Centrone et al. (2008). Minor attention has been devoted to the problem, addressed to our knowledge for the first time in Cox and Turnquist (1986), of combining routing and scheduling of hazmat.

Possible goals and elements of a DSS for routing and scheduling of hazmat transport are described for instance in Baaj et al. (1990) and Frank et al. (2000). We do not consider the problem of locating the facilities that generate and attract hazmat, such as in Alumur and Kara (2007), where the authors propose a large-scale multiobjective location-routing model.

There are some aspects of the problem that the planning public authority has to take into account when implementing a DSS related with hazmat transport:

- goal of the system;
- tracking technology.

As regards the goal of the system, we can identify two situations: the public authority is interested just in tracking the vehicles or it is also interested in planning the hazmat shipment. The latter implies that the public authority decides a set of possible paths that the driver is authorized to take and/or a set of time-slots of the day (or days of the week) when the driver is allowed to enter certain areas.

Vehicle tracking can be implemented using two technology types:

- fixed infrastructures (e.g. gates with cameras that use automated plate number recognition);

- on-board devices.

Combining in different ways such aspects, different DSSs may be implemented based on the type of problem, on budget and legislative constraints, and on political choices.

As regards the vehicle driver, the first scope of the system is the a priori route and scheduling guidance, as explained as follows. The driver has to provide the system with the following information about the hazmat shipment: origin, destination, preferred time-slot and day, material, plate number and type of the vehicle. The system estimates the risks and travel time associated with the possible paths and time-slots, and proposes the "best-compromise" solution (or a set of solutions, among which the driver has to choose one). In Sect. 14.3, the meaning of "best-compromise" will be explained. The driver will have to follow the instructions, otherwise he/she will be spotted by the municipality tracking system and will be fined.

In addition to assisting the driver in selecting an optimal route, the system should also support dynamic route guidance. A combination of ICT, including GPS and wireless communications, make it possible to use real-time information. A range of dynamic information can potentially be incorporated, such as near real-time traffic information, roadworks, actual travel speeds, weather conditions (Sussman, 2005). For a review of real-time routing models see Ghiani et al. (2003).

The Municipality of Milan is interested in implementing a system that will track the vehicles' position, and will assist the city transport department in planning the paths and the day time-slots of each shipment within the municipality boundaries. At the moment, there are restrictions on single roads on the transport of freight and hazmat. The office responsible of the mobility management within the city transport department decided to study how to introduce a DSS for the hazmat transport. Note that the objectives and the issues of this problem could be different from those related with hazmat transport in regional areas. The Municipality of Milan decided to use a tracking technology based on gates with cameras that use automated plate number recognition (see Fig. 14.1), because it does not have the power (either legislative or operative) to force all the trucks to have an on-board device. Moreover, some of the gates are already used for the management of *Ecopass*, a road pricing system for the center of the city.

For the Department Transport and Mobility of the Municipality (the *client*), the authors (the *analysts*) have been designing the structure of a spatial DSS and implementing a prototype in a GIS. In addition to risk assessment and selection of the safest routes, the objective of the DSS is to schedule hazmat shipments, especially when there are many at the same time in the network. To integrate routing and scheduling decisions, the DSS has a two-stage structure (Fig. 14.2) (Carotenuto et al., 2007b). In the first stage, a set of alternative routes with a good combination of travel time and risk is generated for each hazmat shipment request. In a second stage, a departure time and a route, among those generated in the first stage, are assigned to each request. For example, given two materials A and B that are particularly

Fig. 14.1 One of the gates equipped with cameras for vehicle plate number recognition

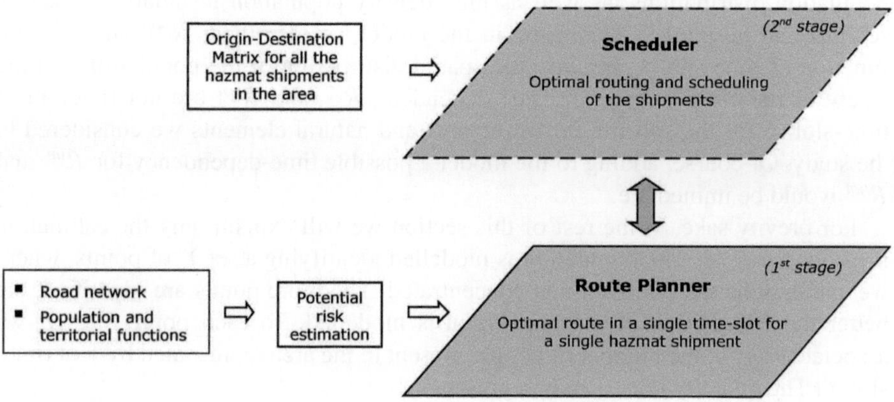

Fig. 14.2 The two stage GIS-DSS structure

dangerous when combined together, an hazmat shipment schedule should avoid two vehicles transporting A and B at the same time in the same area.

So far, the GIS-DSS is in a prototype phase and only the *route planner* module has been implemented (Luè et al., 2008).

14.3 The Risk Assessment Model

Let $G = (N, A)$ be a directed graph representing the transport network, with N and A being, respectively, the set of nodes and the set of directed links of the network. Each link $h \in A$ corresponds to a road segment of the network, and each node $i \in N$

corresponds to a road intersection. Some link attributes (e.g. speed, traffic density, ...) are assumed to be a function of the time-slot f of the day.

We consider the following risks associated with the transport of a hazmat m during time-slot f:

- $R^{pop}(h, f, m)$: risk on population (e.g. residents, workers);
- $R^{inf}(h, m)$: risk on territorial infrastructures (e.g. railways, electric lines);
- $R^{nat}(h, m)$: risk on natural elements (e.g. water bodies, green areas, ...);
- $R^{cri}(h, f, m)$: risk on critical areas (e.g. areas which may be a target for a terrorist attack).

The choice of consider such elements was taken through an interaction between the client and the analysts. Starting from an initial need description of the Municipality, we produced the set of risks to be taken into account, depending on the impacts, the available data and the dangerousness level.

Centrone et al. (2008) pointed out that "most residents are not at home during the day. Researchers need to take the next step and incorporate day versus night population distributions, as well as high-density population installations such as schools and hospitals". Therefore, in the model we identified, R^{pop} and R^{cri} are function of time-slot f, because the spatial distribution of the population and the safety of the critical areas are time-dependent. R^{inf} and R^{nat} are not function of time-slot f for the specific infrastructures and natural elements we considered in the study. Of course, adding to the model a possible time-dependency for R^{inf} and R^{nat} would be immediate.

For brevity sake, in the rest of this section we will explain only the estimation methods for R^{pop}. The population is modelled identifying a set Y of points, where we can assume the population is concentrated. The more points are identified, the better the distribution of the population is modelled. To each point $y \in Y$ we associate $pop_{y,f}$, the number of people present in the area represented by y at time-slot f. The quantity $pop_{y,f}$ may represent:

- the population living in the area;
- employees working in the area;
- people present in facilities (schools, stores, ...);
- people crossing the area (identified by the traffic flows).

The variable $pop_{y,f}$ is clearly time-dependent, and is a function of the trips to and from the considered area. Figure 14.3 depicts an exemplification.

For the estimation of the risk on the population, we used a method derived by Carotenuto et al. (2007a). An incident on a link may affect not only the people who live in that link, but also persons living and working in areas that are close to the incident. The entity of the effect of the incident decreases with the spatial distance from the point where the incident occurs. To model the risk appropriately, we consider the risk of a hazmat transport on a unit-length segment of the network. Given that each street link h is partitioned into a sequence of unit-length segments, the risk $\sigma^{pop}_{x,y}$ associated to the hazmat travelling on a segment x for the population living in the proximity of point y is calculated as in Eq. (14.1).

Fig. 14.3 An exemplification of the dependence of $pop_{y,f}$ on time-slot f. The presence of a school increases the population of y_3 during a particular time-slot, because some people from y_1 and y_2 reach the school

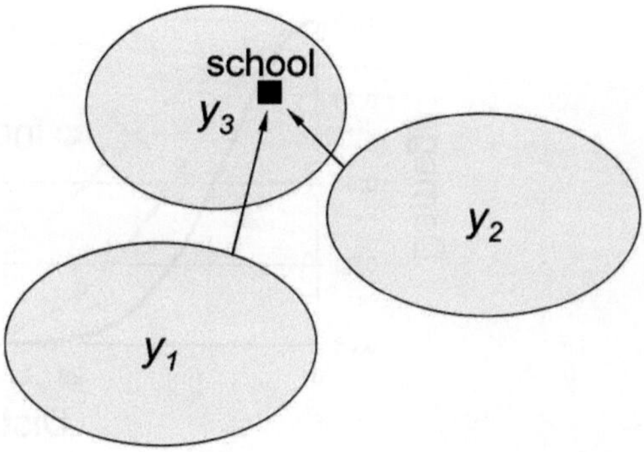

$$\sigma_{x,y}^{pop} = p_x^{inc} \times pop_{y,f} \times e^{-\varphi[L(x,y)]^\eta} \tag{14.1}$$

where:

- p_x^{inc} is the probability per unit-length of an accident occurring on x;
- $e^{-\varphi[L(x,y)]^\eta}$ is the estimated damage on population $pop_{y,f}$.

The damage decreases exponentially with a power of the Euclidean distance $L(x, y)$ between the centers of segment x and point y, where φ and η depend on the hazardous material m under consideration. Figure 14.4 shows qualitatively the shape of the damage function and, hence, the size of the impacted zone.

The risk on the population $R^{pop}(h, f, m)$ is calculated as sum of the contributes of all the unit-length segments of link h on all the points of the set Y, as in Eq. (14.2). Figure 14.5 depicts a graphical exemplification of the calculation.

$$R^{pop}(h, f, m) = \sum_{x \in h} \sum_{y \in Y} \sigma_{x,y}^{pop} \tag{14.2}$$

14.4 The Route Selection Model: A Multi-Objective Problem

Given an origin $o \in N$, a destination $d \in N$, and an hazardous material m, the problem we consider is to find the path (route) from o to d that minimizes the total cost induced by travelling on this path. The total cost is a function of five attributes: travel time, risk on population, risk on territorial infrastructures, risk on natural elements and risk on critical areas. Therefore, this is a multi-objective problem.

Many techniques have been proposed for solving multi-objective vehicle routing and scheduling problems. Jozefowiez et al. (2008) divides them into three general categories:

- *Scalar methods*. These methods use mathematical transformations, like weighted linear aggregation. They have some disadvantages, like the difficulty of eliciting

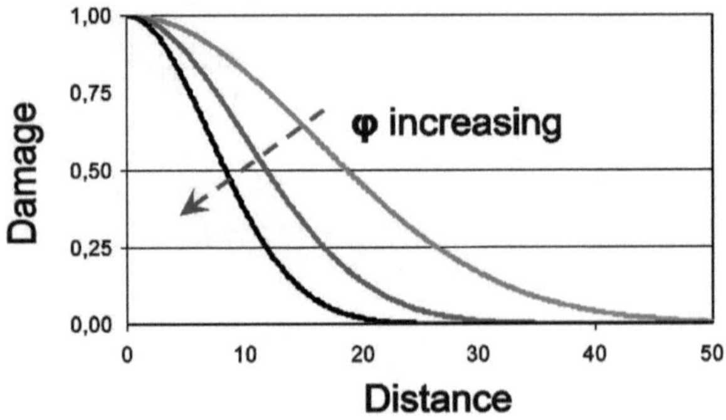

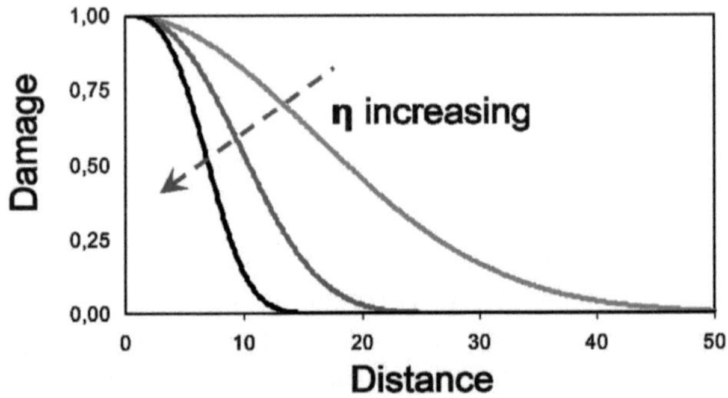

Fig. 14.4 Shape of the damage function varying the φ (on the *left*) and η (on the *right*) parameters

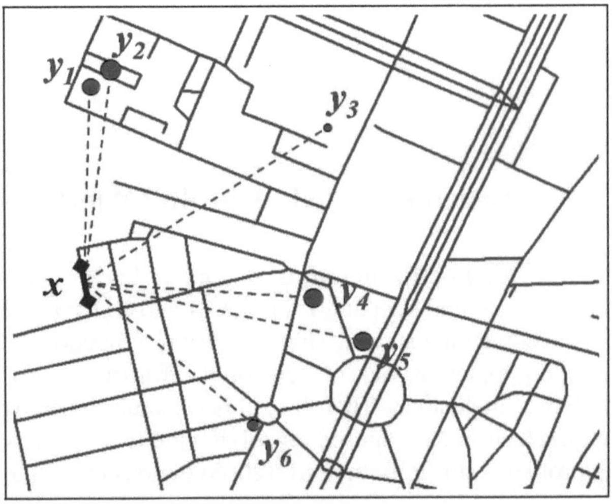

Fig. 14.5 Potential damage of an accident occurring in the unit-length segment x on the points $y_1, \ldots, y_6$, (identified by a *circle* whose area is proportional to the population)

the weights and the fact that they may not be able to find all the Pareto optimal solutions. However, these techniques are quite simple to implement and can be used with any of the single-objective heuristics described in literature.

- *Pareto methods.* These methods apply the notion of Pareto dominance to evaluate a solution or to compare solutions. This concept is frequently used within evolutionary algorithms, and is becoming more popular (Deb, 2001).
- *Non-scalar and non-Pareto algorithms.* These methods, which often consider the different objectives separately, are based on genetic algorithms (e.g. vector evaluated genetic algorithm), lexicographic strategies, ant colony mechanisms, or specific heuristics. See for instance Coutinho-Rodrigues et al. (1999).

So far, we implemented a simple scalar method, similarly to what was done in Huang and Fery (2005), where the authors considered the following conflicting objectives: travel cost, population exposure, environmental risk and security concerns.

Due to the wide variation of measurement scales, each type of link attribute (travel time and risk on population, territorial infrastructures, natural elements, and critical areas) is normalized using linear functions.

Note that the level of traffic congestion affects link travel time and is affected by the time of day. Therefore, link travel time is one of the time-dependent link attributes.

The total cost $C(h, f, m)$ on a link h in a time-slot f for the transport of a material m is calculated as a weighted sum of the attributes, as in Eq. (14.3)

$$C(h, f, m) = \alpha.\tilde{T}(h, f) + \beta\tilde{R}^{pop}(h, f, m) + \gamma\tilde{R}^{inf}(h, m) + \theta\tilde{R}^{nat}(h, m) + \epsilon\tilde{R}^{cri}(h, f, m) \tag{14.3}$$

where:

- $\tilde{T}(h, f)$ is the normalized link travel time;
- $\tilde{R}^{pop}$, $\tilde{R}^{inf}$, $\tilde{R}^{nat}$, $\tilde{R}^{cri}$ are the normalized link risks associated, respectively, to population, territorial infrastructures, natural elements, and critical areas;
- α, β, γ, θ, and ϵ are the relative weights to combine the link attributes into a single cost.

Note that Eq. (14.3) assumes that the shipment occurs within a certain time-slot f. This assumption is made because taking into account the time-dependency of the link attributes increases substantially the computational time of the problem (Malandraki and Daskin, 1992). Once the total cost attribute is calculated for each link of the network, a simple Dijkstra algorithm is used to calculate the minimal cost path and the corresponding route is selected. By varying the relative weights α, β, γ, θ, and ϵ, different routes can be created. Starting from the values chosen by the decision maker, weights can be slightly varied in order to measure the sensitivity on route selection and the robustness of the found solution.

The principal problem is related with the elicitation of the weights. For the decision-maker, the weights' estimation is a difficult task, because not all the attribute values have a physical meaning. Moreover, even if the decision-maker is able to determine the weights, there would be a problem associated with the automatism of the normalization. Because the maximum value may be different from situation to situation, the corresponding normalization will have a different meaning. So, the decision-maker cannot choose the weights once for all, but he/she should adapt the weights to every situation.

The method described above has been already implemented. So far, we are designing a different method where the focus is not on the single links, but on the possible paths. This method considers the following steps:

1. definition of a set of paths from the origin to destination. This concerns the problem of finding dissimilar Pareto-optimal paths. In order to solve this problem, several methods have been proposed, also for the transport of non hazardous material; see for instance Lombard and Church (1993), Dell'Olmo et al. (2005), and Dadkar et al. (2008);
2. interactive editing of generated and displayed paths: the analyst may wish to create a detour around a sensitive location, or to remove some links from the network and have a new path generated;
3. association to the paths of a "satisfaction" using utility functions;
4. comparison of the paths using a multi-criteria decision method (Figueira et al., 2005; Dias and Clímaco, 2000; Coutinho-Rodrigues et al., 1997). This step may also involve the definition of a measure from ideal solutions, as described for instance by Ehrgott and Wiecek (2005);
5. selection of the "best compromise" solution.

As already stated, this problem involves conflicting objectives among the interested parties. In presence of conflicting interests, the improvement of one objective typically conflicts with the improvement of another one, and automatic technical search for the optimum is assumed to be meaningless. The philosophy here is to give all the necessary information to the decision maker, and to eliminate successively all the alternatives that are inferior because they are Pareto-dominated or too conflicting, or because they have critical impacts on a particular attribute. The final decision will be political, but the underlying procedure can be made rational and transparent (Colorni et al., 1999). By an iterative process of displaying paths, using different solution methods and creating detours, a compromise path can be developed (Frank et al., 2000).

14.5 The Case Study

The GIS-DSS we are developing requires specific data structures to represent the complexities of road networks and to perform routing and scheduling algorithms (Fischer, 2004). We used the geo-relational model, which is the most widely used logical data model for networks (Miller and Shaw, 2001). The model has been implemented using ESRI ArcGIS 8.1. A toolbox was implemented using the module

ModelBuilder, which links together different predefined and ad-hoc developed tools. Using parameters as input/output of the tools, we created a set of tools in Python, an high-level programming language (van Rossum and Drake, 2006), using the geo-processing libraries. Each tool works in synergy with the others, generating reference tables, database tables and setting configuration parameters. The result of the toolbox is a geo-referenced map of the cost, where a cost $C(h, f, m)$ is assigned to each link $h \in A$. Once the cost attribute is assigned to each link of the network, a simple Dijkstra method is used to calculate the minimal cost path and the corresponding path is selected on the GIS application.

As regards the case study, the Municipality chose as test site the Niguarda area, characterized by the presence of one of the largest hospitals in Milan. The Niguarda hospital is built on a 322,000 m^2 site and hosts more than 9,000 people every day, including employees, patients, relatives, suppliers, etc. Moreover, the hospital buildings, located in the northern part of Milan, are protected by the Ministry of Fine Arts, because of their artistic and architectural importance.

The Municipality began to test the DSS in the Niguarda area, calibrating the model parameters and identifying the link attribute weights. We received comments and indications from the technical staff of the Municipality. In particular, they judged positively the possibility of giving weights to the different criteria. Moreover, they appreciated the possibility of re-assessing the alternatives and the solution found in function of changes of the parameters (e.g. indicators' values and criteria weights).

However, there has been a lack of strategic indications for the future development of the DSS. In fact, within the Municipality there has been a reorganization of the responsibilities and competences among departments and councillors. Moreover, the Municipality is waiting for integrative funding from the State Department of Infrastructures in order to develop the DSS, localize and implement additional gates, implement the IT infrastructure and set up of the bureaucratic procedures. These two elements brought to a stall of the process, and no strategic decisions have been made for the future of the system. Figure 14.6 depicts the Niguarda area, identifying the elements taken into account for the risk analysis: the schools (risk on population), the railway lines (risk on the infrastructures), a park area (risk on natural elements), and the Niguarda hospital (risk on critical areas). The Niguarda hospital has been chosen as a possible target for a terrorist attack, because it is the coordination structure of the Regional Emergency Unit in case of nuclear, biological, chemical and radiological incidents and attacks. Figures 14.7, 14.8, 14.9, and 14.10 illustrate the maps of the risk on, respectively, railway lines, schools, park areas, and the Niguarda hospital buildings.

In the following, the DSS is applied to a possible exemplificative hazmat shipment. Figure 14.6 shows the origin of the shipment (point 1), an intermediate destination (point 2), and the final destination (point 3). As already stated in the previous paragraph, the path at minimum cost depends on the weights $(\alpha, \beta, \gamma, \theta, \epsilon)$ given to the link attributes. Table 14.1 presents seven sets of values of the weights. The first five sets correspond to minimizing the cost associated with each of the elements: time, risk on population, risk on infrastructures, risk on natural elements,

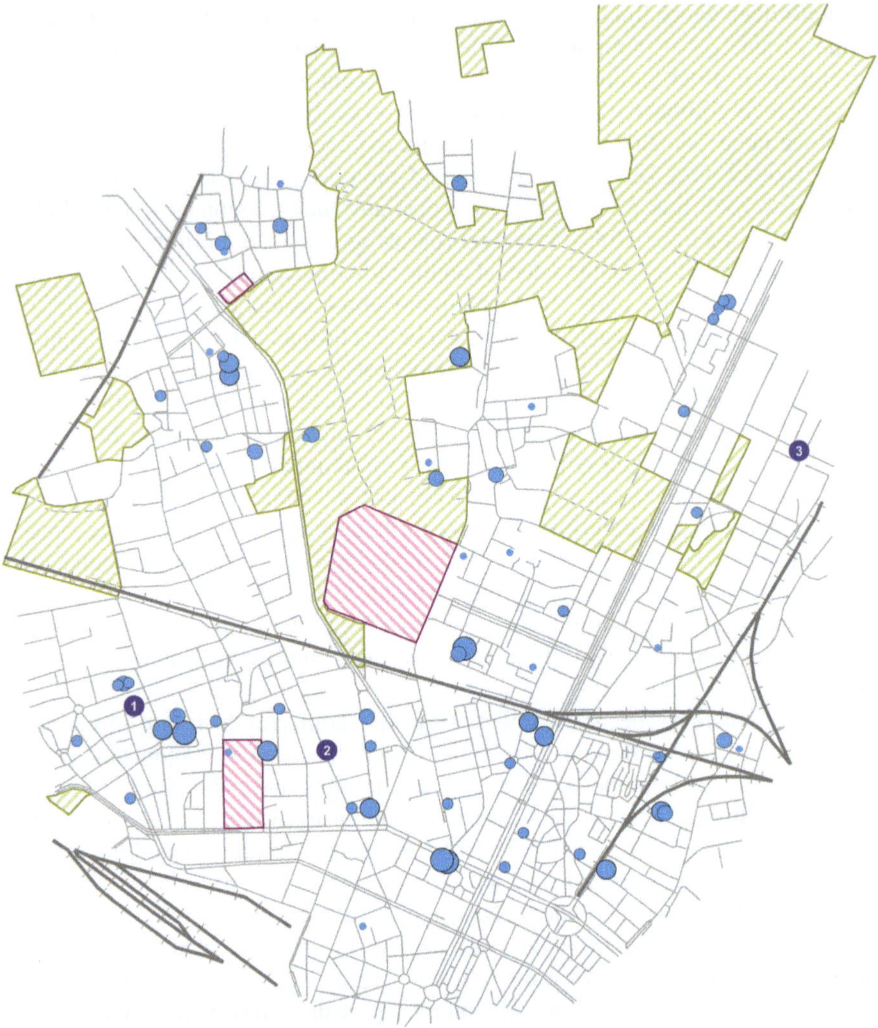

Fig. 14.6 The Niguarda area, where the following elements are identified: schools (*circles*, where the area is proportional to the number of students), railways (*hash lines*), urban parks and periurban agricultural fields (*bottom-left top-right diagonal pattern*; *green areas*), and the hospital buildings (*bottom-right top-left diagonal pattern*; *purple areas*)

and risk on critical areas. Set 6 assigns to each attribute the same importance, while for Set 7 the risk on population is the most important element. In Set 2, 3, 4, 5, a small weight is given also to the Time attribute, in order to choose—among the paths that minimise the corresponding risks—the one that is at minimum time. Table 14.1 indicates also the name given to the path that minimizes the total costs for each weights set. Such paths are represented in Figs. 14.7, 14.8, 14.9, 14.10, and 14.11. Note that Route A minimizes both travel time and risk on infrastructures. Because

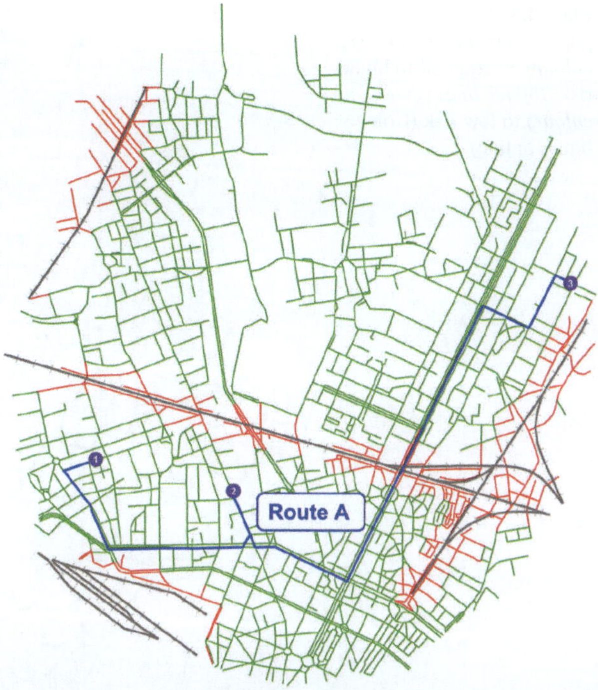

Fig. 14.7 Risk on infrastructures. *Darker lines* (*red colour*) correspond to higher risk; *lighter lines* (*green colour*) to low risk

the intermediate and the final destinations are separated by the main railway, all the paths connecting the two points have at least the same risk corresponding to cross such infrastructure.

14.6 Conclusions and Future Challenges

The paper presents an ongoing work to develop a DSS for the multi-objective problem of routing and scheduling hazmat in the city of Milan. We used a probabilistic risk assessment model, which takes into account, as route selection parameters, the probability of accidents and the consequences of an accident for each road segment. The model considers population, territorial infrastructures, natural elements, and critical areas. The planner has been developed within a GIS and has been tested on a road network in Niguarda, an area of the city of Milan. So far, the GIS-DSS is in a prototype phase and only one element has been implemented. We are working on the design of the second element of the DSS and of the second multi-criteria approach described in Sect. 14.3. At the moment, for bureaucratic and funding reasons, the process of designing and implementing the DSS has been slowed down, and no strategic decisions have been made yet on the future of the system. However, the objective is to have the system set up before the operational phase of the World

Fig. 14.8 Risk on population. *Darker lines* (*red colour*) correspond to higher risk; *lighter lines* (*green colour*) to low risk (Color figure online)

Exposition, that will take place in Milan in 2015. The complete DSS will allow risk assessment not only for road transport, but also for rail transport and for intermodal shipments, and will permit to efficiently investigate in an interactive way possible benefits deriving from changes of paths, time-slots, etc. The idea is to develop a comprehensive risk management tool. The benefits of such an approach are not limited to the possibility of associating the risk estimation to the links, but they include the possibility of visualizing the impact areas for the incident scenarios directly on the map of the zone, as well as the possibility of viewing, selecting or changing the routes or parts of them. Moreover, by combining the information on the area (population, weather, etc.) and the characteristics of shipped hazardous material, the system will also be able to support real-time emergency management, should a road or rail accident take place. Moreover, the fastest route from emergency centers (fire and police stations, hospitals, etc.) to the accident location can be also determined. The procedure described in the paper derives from a "command-and-control" approach: the municipality set the rules and the possible paths, and the vehicle driver has to comply with these requirements. This procedure is compatible with the legislative Italian framework, where the municipality has the responsibility for the hazmat transport, and reflects also the different importance between the municipality and the vehicle driver. Of course, in the real implementation of such DSS, the interaction rules and the route and schedule selection parameters (e.g. the weights) have to be discussed also with the associations of drivers and shipping

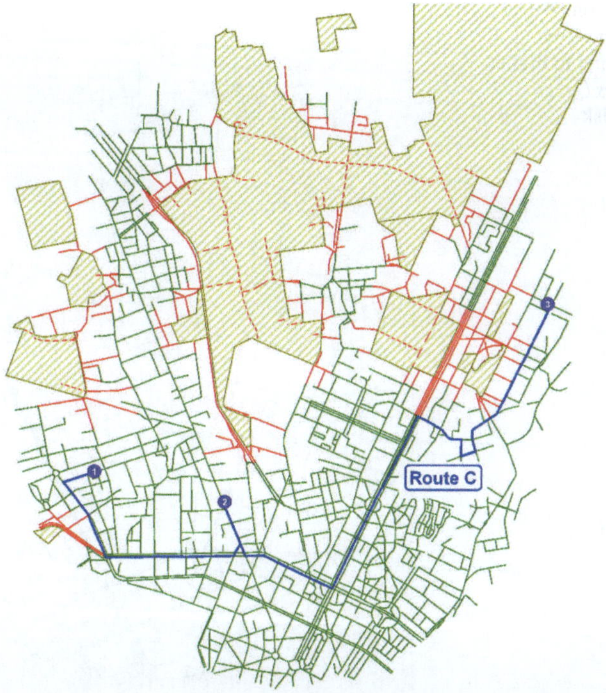

Fig. 14.9 Risk on natural elements. *Darker lines* (*red colour*) correspond to higher risk; *lighter lines* (*green colour*) to low risk

companies. Moreover, a participatory approach is suggested in order to minimize the possible conflict between the stakeholders. Besides the implementation of the DSS for the Municipality of Milan, more work needs to be done, both in the fields of theoretical and applied research. A first issue concerns the availability of reliable and real-time data. Dynamic route guidance systems offer the potential to provide significant benefits to both individual drivers and the overall transportation system (Nelson and Tarnoff, 2001). The realization of this potential requires a fully integrated infrastructure system that includes comprehensive surveillance of roadway conditions and coordinated dissemination of this information through travel information systems (see for instance Ciccarelli et al. 2006). This will require the establishment of a close partnership between the public and private sectors, as well as improving the mapping accuracy. Moreover, it also requires the development of new analytical tools for traffic congestion forecast (see for instance Ben-Akiva et al. 2001; Wang and Papageorgiou 2005, for a general description of the problem, and Dominioni et al. 2008 for a description of the work in progress in Milano). This process will be helped by the fact that wireless Internet is becoming increasingly popular among drivers and many handheld and in-vehicle products for localization and navigation are becoming available to the general public. An important extension would be consider uncertainty about the model parameters. Chang et al. (2005) for

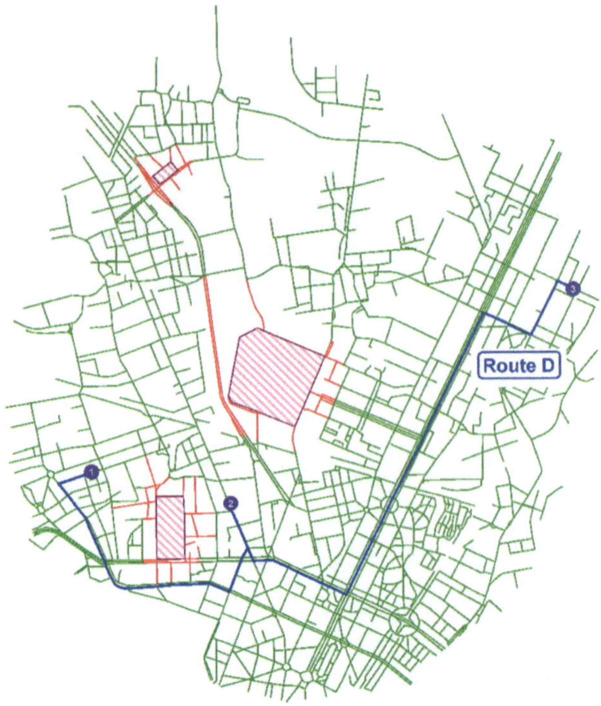

Fig. 14.10 Risk on critical areas. *Darker lines* (*red colour*) correspond to higher risk; *lighter lines* (*green colour*) to low risk

instance describe a method for finding non-dominated paths for multiple routing objectives in networks where the routing attributes are uncertain, and the probability distributions that describe those attributes vary by the time of day. Another issue concerns the equity of decision-making. Whenever several hazmat shipments occur in a certain area, the DSS should not only minimize the travel time and the risk, but also distribute the risk uniformly over different zones of the area. This issue is well defined in Keeney (1980), where a measure of a collective risk is determined with explicit reference to equity. The risk perception is an important aspect to be taken into consideration (Dennis, 1996). We can technically measure the probabilities and objective risks associated with an event such as a hazmat accident, but the DSS has to represent also the subjective preferences of the decision makers and stakeholders. Should we assume people are risk-neutral or willing to accept higher/lower degrees of risk? The theory provides that people "favour risk aversion in the domain of gains and risk seeking in the domain of losses" (Kahneman and Tversky, 1979), but how does this apply to the hazmat transport problem? The last issue involves the concept of risk communication (Dennis, 1996; Tversky and Kahneman, 1981), which is strongly related with the previous issue. Public fears, even if unjustified, there may be an opposition to hazmat transport. Risk communication has the important role of informing the public of the best estimates of the actual risks involved. This would improve the level of debate and facilitate better decisions.

Table 14.1 Set of weights values used for the estimation of the total cost for the exemplificative shipment

	Time (α)	Population (β)	Infrastructures (γ)	Natural elements (θ)	Critical areas (ϵ)	Path minimizing the total cost	Length of the path (m)
Set 1	1	0	0	0	0	Route A	8,339
Set 2	0.000001	0.999999	0	0	0	Route B	9,758
Set 3	0.000001	0	0.999999	0	0	Route A	8,339
Set 4	0.000001	0	0	0.999999	0	Route C	8,644
Set 5	0.000001	0	0	0	0.999999	Route D	8,621
Set 6	0.2	0.2	0.2	0.2	0.2	Route E	8,859
Set 7	0.1	0.6	0.1	0.1	0.1	Route F	9,104

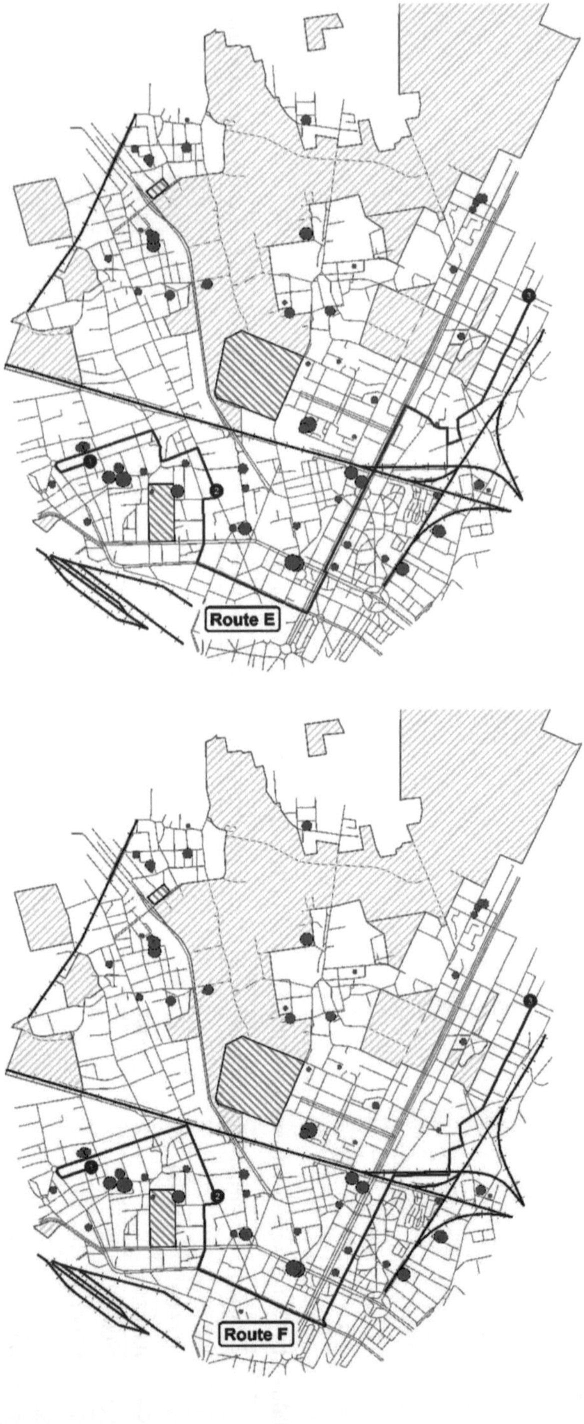

Fig. 14.11 Route E and Route F minimize the cost for the exemplificative shipment considering two different combinations of attribute weights

References

Alumur, S., & Kara, B. Y. (2007). A new model for the hazardous waste location-routing problem. *Computers and Operations Research, 34*(5), 1406–1423.

Baaj, M., Ashur, S., Chaparrofarina, M., & Pijawka, K. (1990). Design of routing networks using geographic information systems: Applications to solid and hazardous waste transportation planning. *Transportation Research Record, 1497*, 140–144.

Ben-Akiva, M., Bierlaire, M., Burton, D., Koutsopoulos, H. N., & Mishalani, R. (2001). Network state estimation and prediction for real-time traffic management. *Networks and Spatial Economics, 1*, 293–318.

Bruglieri, M., Maja, R., Marchionni, G., & Rainoldi, G. (2008). Safety in hazardous material road transportation: State of the art and emerging problems. In C. Bersani, A. Boulmakoul, E. Garbolino, & R. Sacile (Eds.), *Advanced technologies and methodologies for risk management in the global transport of dangerous goods* (pp. 88–129). Amsterdam: IOS NATO Science Series.

Bubbico, R., Cave, S. D., & Mazzarotta, B. (2004). Risk analysis for road and rail transport of hazardous materials: A GIS approach. *Journal of Loss Prevention in the Process Industries, 17*, 483–488.

Carotenuto, P., Giordani, S., & Ricciardelli, S. (2007a). Finding minimum and equitable risk routes for hazmat shipments. *Computers and Operations Research, 34*(5), 1304–1327.

Carotenuto, P., Giordani, S., Ricciardelli, S., & Rismondo, S. (2007b). A tabu search approach for scheduling hazmat shipments. *Computers and Operations Research, 34*(5), 1328–1350.

Center for Chemical Process Safety. (2000). *Guidelines for chemical process quantitative risk analysis*. New York: AIChE.

Centrone, G., Pesenti, R., & Ukovich, W. (2008). Hazardous materials transportation: a literature review and an annotated bibliography. In C. Bersani, A. Boulmakoul, E. Garbolino, & R. Sacile (Eds.), *Advanced technologies and methodologies for risk management in the global transport of dangerous goods* (pp. 33–62). Amsterdam: IOS NATO Science Series.

Chang, T. -S., Nozick, L. K., & Turnquist, M. A. (2005). Multiobjective path finding in stochastic dynamic networks, with application to routing hazardous materials shipments. *Transportation Science, 39*(3), 383–399.

Ciccarelli, D., Colorni, A., Luè, A., & Rossi, D. (2006). An integrated information and management system for traditional and demand-responsive mobility services in the city of Milan. In *Proceedings of the 85th TRB Annual Meeting*. Washington, DC.

Colorni, A., Laniado, E., & Muratori, S. (1999). Decision support systems for environmental impact assessment of transport infrastructures. *Transportation Research Part D: Transport and Environment, 4*(1), 1–11.

Coutinho-Rodrigues, J., Clímaco, J., & Current, J. (1999). An interactive bi-objective shortest path approach: Searching for unsupported nondominated solutions. *Computers and Operations Research, 26*(8), 789–798.

Coutinho-Rodrigues, J., Current, J., Clímaco, J., & Ratick, S. (1997). Interactive spatial decision-support system for multiobjective hazardous materials location-routing problems. *Transportation Research Record, 1602*, 101–109.

Cox, R., & Turnquist, M. (1986). Scheduling truck shipments of hazardous materials in the presence of curfews. *Transportation Research Record, 1603*, 21–26.

Dadkar, Y., Jones, D., & Nozick, L. (2008). Identifying geographically diverse routes for the transportation of hazardous materials. *Transportation Research Part E: Logistics and Transportation Review, 44*(3), 333–349.

Deb, K. (2001). *Multi-objective optimization using evolutionary algorithms*. Chichester: Wiley.

Dell'Olmo, P., Gentili, M., & Scozzari, A. (2005). On finding dissimilar Pareto-optimal paths. *European Journal of Operational Research, 162*(1), 70–82.

Dennis, S. (1996). Estimating risk costs per unit of exposure for hazardous materials transported by rail. *The Logistics and Transportation Review, 32*(4), 351–375.

Dias, L., & Clímaco, J. (2000). Shortest path problems with partial information: Models and algorithms for detecting dominance. *European Journal of Operational Research, 121*(1), 16–31.
Dominioni, O. C., Ciccarelli, D., Colorni, A., & Luè, A. (2008). A traffic estimation model based on inductive loops and floating car data for the city of Milano: a work in progress. In *Proceedings of the 12th Meeting of the EURO Working Group on Transportation*, Ischia, Italy.
Ehrgott, M., & Wiecek, M. (2005). Multiobjective programming. In J. Figueira, S. Greco, & M. Ehrgott (Eds.), *Multiple criteria decision analysis: State of the art surveys* (pp. 667–722). Boston/Dordrecht/London: Springer.
Erkut, E., & Glickman, T. (1997). Minimax population exposure in routing highway shipments of hazardous materials. *Transportation Research Record, 1602*, 93–100.
Erkut, E., Tjandra, S., & Verter, V. (2006). Hazardous materials transportation. In C. Barnhart & G. Laporte (Eds.), *Handbooks in operations research and management science: Transportation* (vol. 14, pp. 539–621). Amsterdam: Elsevier.
Field, M. A. (2004). Highway security and terrorism. *Review of Policy Research, 21*(3), 317–328.
Figueira, J., Greco, S., & Ehrgott, M. (2005). *Multiple criteria decision analysis: State of the art surveys*. Boston/Dordrecht/London: Springer.
Fischer, M. M. (2004). GIS and network analysis. In D. Hensher, K. Button, K. Haynes, & P. Stopher (Eds.), *Handbook of transport geography and spatial systems* (pp. 391–408). Amsterdam: Elsevier.
Frank, W. C., Thill, J. -C., & Batta, R. (2000). Spatial decision support system for hazardous material truck routing. *Transportation Research Part C: Emerging Technologies, 8*(1-6), 337–359.
Ghiani, G., Guerriero, F., Laporte, G., & Musmanno, R. (2003). Real-time vehicle routing: Solution concepts, algorithms and parallel computing strategies. *European Journal of Operational Research, 151*(1), 1–11.
Guariso, G., & Werthner, H. (1989). *Environmental decision support systems*. New York: Ellis Horwood-Wiley.
Huang, B., & Fery, P. (2005). Aiding route decision for hazardous material transportation. In *Proceedings of the 84th TRB Annual Meeting*. Washington, DC.
Huang, B., Long, C., & Liew, Y. (2003). GIS-AHP model for HAZMAT routing with security consideration. In *Proceeding of the IEEE 6th International Conference on Intelligent Transportation Systems* (vol. 2, pp. 1644–1649). Shanghai, China. IEEE. DOI: 10.1109/ITSC.2003.1252762.
Jozefowiez, N., Semet, F., & Talbi, E. -G. (2008). Multi-objective vehicle routing problems. *European Journal of Operational Research, 189*(2), 293–309.
Kahneman, D., & Tversky, A. (1979). Prospect theory: An analysis of decision under risk. *Econometrica, 47*(2), 263–291.
Keeney, R. L. (1980). Equity and public risk. *Operations Research, 28*(3-Part-I), 527–534.
List, G. F., Mirchandani, P. B., Turnquist, M. A., & Zografos, K. G. (1991). Modeling and analysis for hazardous materials transportation: Risk analysis, routing/scheduling and facility location. *Transportation Science, 25*(2), 100–114.
Lombard, K., & Church, R. (1993). The gateway shortest path problem: Generating alternative routes for a corridor routing problem. *Geographical Systems, 1*, 25–45.
Luè, A., Ciccarelli, D., & Colorni, A. (2008). A GIS-based multi-objective travel planner for hazardous material transport in the urban area of Milan. In C. Bersani, A. Boulmakoul, E. Garbolino, R. Sacile (Eds.), *Advanced technologies and methodologies for risk management in the global transport of dangerous goods* (pp. 217 – 236). Amsterdam: IOS NATO Science Series.
Malandraki, C., & Daskin, M. S. (1992). Time dependent vehicle routing problems: Formulations, properties and heuristic algorithms. *Transportation Science, 26*(3), 185–200.
Miller, H., & Shaw, S. (2001). *Geographic information systems for transportation. Principles and applications*. Oxford: Oxford University Press.
Nelson, D., & Tarnoff, P. (2001). Route guidance systems. In K. Button & D. Hensher (Eds.), *Handbook of transport systems and traffic control* (pp. 707–725). Amsterdam, Pergamon.

Sussman, J. (2005). *Perspectives on intelligent transportation systems*. New York, NY: Springer.
Tversky, A., & Kahneman, D. (1981). The framing of decisions and the psychology of choice. *Science, 211*, 453–458.
UNECE. (2007). *European agreement concerning the international carriage of dangerous goods by road (ADR)*. Technical Report. United Nations Economic Commission for Europe.
van Rossum, G., & Drake, F. (2006). *The python language reference manual*. Bristol: Network Theory.
Wang, Y., & Papageorgiou, M. (2005). Real-time freeway traffic state estimation based on extended Kalman filter: A general approach. *Transportation Research Part B: Methodological, 39*(2), 141–167.
Waters, W. (2003). Transportation of hazardous goods and materials. In D. Hensher & K. Button (Eds.), *Handbook of transport and the environment* (pp. 707–725). Amsterdam: Elsevier.
Zhang, J., Hodgson, J., & Erkut, E. (2000). Using GIS to assess the risks of hazardous materials transport in networks. *European Journal of Operational Research, 121*(2), 316–329.

Editors' Comments on "A Multi-Criteria Decision Support System for Hazardous Material Transport in Milan"

Alberto Colorni and Alessandro Luè present in their text an application of what is probably the most used (and abused) MCDA method: the simple weighted sum. It is therefore an application that illustrates the aggregation of multiple performance dimensions into a single scale of value, which was the subject of Sect. 3.2 of Chap. 3 "Modelling Preferences" and Sect. 4.2 of Chap. 4 in this book.

This application's **relevance** concerns the use of MCDA to support public policy, namely the definition of routes and schedules for hazardous material transportation taking into account risks for the environment and people. For this purpose a Decision Support System is being developed (see Burstein and Holsapple 2008 for a comprehensive panorama of DSS, computer-based tools for decision aiding). The basis for the DSS is a Geographical Information System, hence this is capable of providing spatial decision support (Chakhar and Mousseau, 2008). This system is partly built and is being tested on a pilot area in Milan.

The authors of the chapter acted as **the analysts** for the Municipality of Milan (**the client**), represented by members of its technical staff. There is no mention to intervention of elected officers that might have concerns of a more political nature or that might hinder the dialogue between analysts and client due to a possible lack of familiarity of the latter with the models used. Nevertheless, the authors would be interested in tuning their model in interaction with stakeholders, suggesting a participatory process could be promoted.

The ambitious **objective** set for the system is to allow what Colorni and Luè call a "command-and-control" approach in which the system would select the possible paths and schedules for trucks loaded with hazardous materials. A monitoring system would verify compliance by the truck drivers. The system would also be able to access real-time data that it would be able to take into account. It is not clear if the system would act as an expert system making autonomous decisions or a human decision maker would have to be available all the time. At this stage it also seems undefined how much decision power the truck drivers would be granted, namely whether they would be able to choose among several pre-approved routes or they would be directed to a route indicated by the system. The implemented part of the system addresses a more static type of problem. It considers a given network of nodes and arcs corresponding to a network of streets that exist in reality. Such a network allows a potentially large (but finite) number of alternative routes for a load that needs to be transported. It is therefore a combinatorial type of **decision problem**. The **problem statement** is one of selection of the best route or routes among two given nodes.

The analysts have defined a **criteria set** of four risk-related criteria and a fifth criterion reflecting travel time, without mentioning the need to use any **problem structuring** methodologies. Although the set of criteria is apparently simple, the computation of the impact of each possible arc in terms of the four **risk criteria** took quite sophisticated computations, taking into account the distances between the routes and the affected entities (population, nature, infrastructures and critical areas). The model is very detailed in order to take into account changes in population over the hours of a day and breaking each arc into smaller segments. **Modelling of uncertainties** is performed in terms of probabilities of accident per unit-length, which need to be elicited.

The evaluation of the alternatives (the possible routes between two given nodes) is based in three models. For each risk criterion and for each unit-length the risk is computed as the sum of the risks associated with potentially affected entities (e.g. different population agglomerates). Then, for each risk criterion the risks of all unit-length parts of an arc are summed (and the aggregation of the arcs composing a route is again a sum of the partial risks). Thus, on each risk criterion risks accumulate throughout the length of a route as a function of its nearby entities. One can note, however, that the result of the sum of unit-lengths risks for a given arc can hide the existence of a particular part of the arc that is extremely risky for some entity.

The **aggregation** of the four risk criteria plus travel time into a single measure is again obtained by using a sum operator, but using weights. As Luè and Colorni note, this type of aggregation may not be able to identify all the Pareto optimal solutions, as it is not able to choose the so-called unsupported solutions (see Coutinho-Rodrigues et al. 1999). Another concern is that this type of aggregation does not reflect the importance of the criteria in a direct way, independently of scale transformations (see Keeney 1992; Billaut et al. 2009). Indeed, the same weights can lead to different results depending on the normalization method (the authors used linear functions). In this work this does not appear to be problematic, since Luè and Colorni suggest that the weights from this **elicitation process** are used by the client mainly as a means to create different routes and need to be adapted for each situation.

Having defined a set of weights associated with the five criteria, an overall "cost" is computed for each arc in the network. Then, the problem becomes classical a network optimization formulation: to find the shortest path problem. This is solved using Dijkstra's well-known algorithm (Dijkstra, 1959).

At the time this chapter is written, there are already many tangible and intangible results of the decision aiding intervention. The most **tangible result** is a GIS-based decision support tool that contains detailed data about the alternatives (the network arcs) and the evaluation criteria, as well as the optimization tool and additive aggregation formula allowing obtaining different routes as a function of the chosen parameter values. **Intangible results** include the learning that has occurred within the client organization. Feedback has been positive, namely on the ability to 'play' with the parameter values as a means to obtain different solutions in an interactive way.

Concerning the **impact** of this study, the continuation of the development of the DSS is pending the approval of funding and other strategic decisions. The authors have shown how MCDA can be combined with optimization methods and risk assessment models within a sophisticated DSS integrated within a GIS. Despite the use of a simple method, this was a **success factor**: the clients have found it to be useful since it allows them to assess what routes would be better depending on the weight they place on each criterion. A future evolution of the DSS meant to be autonomously used (i.e., without the help of the analysts) should however provide much orientation concerning the role and meaning of the weights used in the model.

Although one cannot be sure about what would be different, it is possible to speculate that the simplicity of the method contributed to its acceptance by the client. Nevertheless, the use of other aggregation methods (the reader may recall Sect. 3.2 of Chap. 3) could introduce further refinements to the model or the ability of tailoring the model for each specific situation. This would on the other hand make the integration with a network optimization algorithm more difficult.

By using MCDA it will also be possible, if the client wishes so, to include other criteria such as monetary costs or greenhouse gas emissions. Another important concern that can potentially be taken into account is the equity of the chosen routes with respect to different population aggregates. A participatory process involving also the affected population might lead to a negotiation able to compensate those citizens more at risk. The integration of MCDA into a participatory GIS (e.g., Simao et al. 2009) would be an interesting avenue for the continuation of this work.

References

Billaut, J. -C., Bouyssou, D., & Vincke, P. (2009). Should you believe in the Shanghai ranking? An MCDM view. *Scientometrics, 1*(72), 25–32.

Burstein, F., & Holsapple, C. W. (Eds.). (2008). *Handbook on decision support systems 1: Basic themes*. Berlin: Springer.

Chakhar, S., & Mousseau, V. (2008). Spatial multicriteria decision making. In S. Shekhar & H. Xiong (Eds.), *Encyclopedia of GIS* (pp. 753–758). New York: Springer.

Coutinho-Rodrigues, J., Current, J., & Climaco, J. (1999). An interactive bi-objective shortest path approach: Searching for unsupported nondominated solutions. *Computers & Operations Research, 26*, 789–798.

Dijkstra, E. W. (1959). A note on two problems in connection with graphs. *Numerische Mathematik, 1*, 269–271.
Keeney, R. L. (1992). *Value-focused thinking: A path to creative decision making*. Cambridge, MA: Harvard University Press.
Simão, A., Densham, P. J., & Haklay, M. (2009). Web-based GIS for collaborative planning and public participation: An application to the strategic planning of wind farm sites. *Journal of Environmental Management, 90*(6), 2027–2040.

Chapter 15
Rural Road Maintenance in Madagascar the GENIS Project

Alexis Tsoukiàs and Herimandimbiniaina Ralijaona

Abstract The paper reports a real world decision aiding process concerning rural road maintenance in Madagascar. The issue arises within AGETIPA, the National Agency in charge of conducting Public Works in Madagascar, and can be summarised as a problem of resource allocation to a number of competitive projects. The problem has been modeled using multiple criteria and a classification procedure under two objectives: make the most rational use of the limited available resources and promote participation and commitment of the local actors in the maintenance process. The project is part of an on-going partnership between the LAMSADE and AGETIPA aiming to enhance Decision Support Capacity within AGETIPA.

15.1 Introduction

This is a paper on a real case study concerning decision support issues arising from the problem of improving the rural road maintenance activity in Madagascar. This is one among the regular activities of AGETIPA and the occasion to focus the attention on it was given within the GENIS project.

AGETIPA (Agence d'Execution des Travaux d'Intérêt Public) is a non profit Agency established in 1993 by the Government of Madagascar and the consulting and executive companies working in the sector of the public work in Madagascar. Since 1994 it is responsible for the executive follow up of most of the public works taking place in Madagascar, the development projects as well as in charge of capacity building in this sector. It is a member of AFRICATIP the African Association of Public Work Agencies (there are 18 such agencies over the continent). Besides its activities in executive support, AGETIPA provides technical support to other

A. Tsoukiàs (✉)
CNRS - LAMSADE, UMR 7243, Université Paris Dauphine, Paris, France
e-mail: tsoukias@lamsade.dauphine.fr

H. Ralijaona
AGETIPA, Antananarivo, Madagascar
e-mail: herimandimbiniaina@agetipa.mg

R. Bisdorff et al. (eds.), *Evaluation and Decision Models with Multiple Criteria*, International Handbooks on Information Systems,
DOI 10.1007/978-3-662-46816-6_15

Institutions and Government bodies, training for the staff of the consulting and construction companies and recently develops also Decision Support Activities.

The GENIS project (Gestion des Routes par Niveau de Service) has been proposed by the Transportation Minister in collaboration with the World Bank in order to improve rural road maintenance. A pilot study area has been selected, the greater Antananarivo urban and peri-urban area. The principal aim of the project is to contribute, to the improvement of accessibility from rural areas to markets, social services and economic activities, thus increasing income for rural population, improving their life conditions and ultimately reducing poverty. The implementation of the GENIS project should:

- satisfy the needs of the users in terms of necessary physical conditions of the roads to be maintained;
- the service level of the roads to be considered should be maintained or improved.

The principal decision problem within the GENIS project is to establish which roads should be considered first, in order to maximise the positive economic, social and environmental impact.

While trying to formalise the problem on how to make any decisions concerning priorities in rural road maintenance the CEO of AGETIPA realised that:

1. there were no internal resources (at that time) able to follow a decision support problem (not only the specific one);
2. there was a clear necessity to re-think the whole evaluation model as far as public works financing was concerned, at least in the case of rural roads in Madagascar.

Although evaluating public projects in economical mature societies can be considered as a typical cost-benefit analysis (the reader should note that this is an approach strongly argued in the literature; see Boardman 1996; Bouyssou et al. 2000; Dasgupta and Heal 1979; Dinwiddy and Teal 1996; Keeney 1992; Kulkarni et al. 2004; Liesiö et al. 2007; Mild and Salo 2009; Roy and Damart 2002), this is much more difficult in the case of countries under development. Deciding to fund a rural road maintenance project can be of vital importance for a local community and is basically a **political** decision which needs to be legitimated, explained and possibly negotiated. Behind such decisions there is a whole formal or informal process involving the participation of the local community and thus influencing also the future of this young democracy.

On that basis AGETIPA considered the hypothesis of involving a Decision Analysis expert with the aim: on the one hand to help conducting the GENIS project and on the other hand to introduce and enhance within AGETIPA a Decision Support capacity. This is how the first author has been involved in the project.

The presentation of this case study will follow the scheme presented in Tsoukiàs (2007) in order to emphasise in a structured way the different cognitive artifacts produced in the decision aiding process. More precisely we will try to describe the:

- *problem situation*; who are the actors involved, what are their concerns and what are their commitments?

- *problem formulation*; on what the decision process focusses, under which points of view (available and/or requested knowledge) and for what precise purpose?
- *evaluation model*; what are the elements composing such a model (set of alternatives, attributes and their scales, criteria, uncertainties and procedures to be used)?

There will be no final recommendation to talk about, since the study concerned the construction of a method to apply in several different problem situations repeatedly. There has been a pilot study though for which recommendations have been formulated, but this was basically a validation activity.

The objectives of this study can be thus summarised.

- provide a methodology for handling the rural road network maintenance problem;
- develop a decision aiding methodology for similar problems;
- create decision support capacity within AGETIPA with respect both to "internal" and "external" clients.

The paper is thus organised as follows. In Sect. 15.2 we present the Problem Situation. In Sect. 15.3 we present the Problem Formulation, while in Sect. 15.4 we present the Evaluation Model(s) used in order to handle the problem as formulated in Sect. 15.3. In Sect. 15.5 we present the pilot study conducted in order to validate the method suggested. In Sect. 15.6 we present the feedback obtained after 2 years of using this method in rural road maintenance in Madagascar. Section 15.7 concludes the paper.

15.2 Problem Situation

The maintenance and improvement of the rural road network in Madagascar is a vital project for the population living in these areas both for economic reasons (improve accessibility to land and markets) and social ones (improve accessibility to schools and health centres as well as improve communication among remotely located communities).

The result is an extremely high demand for rural road maintenance. In front of that the availability of funds to dedicate to this purpose is rather limited and largely depending from external donors and financial institutions such as the World Bank. The basic problem arises from this scarce availability of funds: given the annual spending of the national government for rural road maintenance where should be given the priority?

The demand for maintenance generates locally from communities and their local government which for simplicity we are going to represent by the local mayor. At the national level the management of the process is delegated by the government to AGETIPA who is expected to establish within the GENIS project the priorities and thus decide every year which are the projects that can be satisfied. However, in managing this problem AGETIPA is expected to pursue a precise policy:

- on the one hand maximise the positive impact of the policy in terms of benefiting population, economic activities impacted and general improvement of the whole road network of the island in terms of "level of service" guaranteed;
- on the other hand promote the participation and active implication of the local communities and their representatives as well as of possibly existing economic actors both to the decision and to the implementation process.

Under such a perspective, the accountability of the decision process is extremely important. It is important to explain why a project has been rejected AND under which conditions would have been accepted (or could actually be accepted).

The traditional approach used until the time of this study aiming at calculating the overall economic return of each project (seen as a public investment) seems inadequate with respect to the above policy for essentially two reasons:

- the difficulty to take into account qualitative information in order to establish an economic return (not all impacts of such projects have a clear economic dimension);
- the impossibility to establish a negotiation table with the local actors: indeed the accountability of decisions based on purely economic reasons is extremely difficult (at least with respect to precisely the local actors which are expected to be implied).

It should also be emphasised that the "client" (the government) considers very important to allow transparent negotiations with the local actors where the reasons for which projects submitted were rejected should be clear. A rural road can be of vital importance for a local community and rejecting its maintenance project can induce severe consequences.

We can summarise the problem situation as follows.

- The actors involved in the decision process (the stakeholders) are the National Government, AGETIPA, the local actors (economic, social and political), the population itself, fund raising institutions, international donors and financial institutions.
- The objects/concerns of such actors include: the rural roads network and the specific maintenance projects for given segments of the network, the funds available for maintenance at the National level, any local funds available, the decision process itself, the negotiation capacity, the local actors implication and commitment, the long term evolution of the whole road network of the island, the long term impact of this process on regional planning at the National level.
- The resources committed in the decision process include the maintenance funds, the local knowledge of the rural road network and the social and economic needs of the local communities, the satellite images of the rural areas, other information (statistics) about the areas crossed by the rural roads network, the technical knowledge about planning and road maintenance.

Decision Aiding is thus expected to:

- convince AGETIPA that the projects chosen will have the maximum positive impact;
- be inserted within a long term effort of improving regional planning and more precisely road maintenance;
- be accountable with respect to the National government, the local actors and the international donors and financial institutions;
- allow a transparent decision process enabling negotiations with the local actors.

15.3 Problem Formulation

The problem situation as previously described has been discussed within AGETIPA together with their advisor (the first author). Several hypotheses have been considered. In order to establish a precise problem formulation the following points have been fixed:

- the results of the model have to be easily explainable and give an immediate intuitive idea of the decision;
- the results of the model have to be consistent with the long term government policy in road network improvement;
- the model has to take into account the local actors' commitment.

On this basis the following problem formulation has been adopted: *Classify the submitted projects into three classes: accepted, rejected, negotiable, taking into account the social-economic impact of the projects, the local actors' commitment and the cost.* More precisely the problem formulation contains the following elements.

$\mathbb{A}$ The actions to be considered by the decision aiding process should be the precise rural road maintenance projects expressed and submitted by the local communities. More precisely the projects are established through a consultation process organised by FIFTAMA (the Association of the mayors of the towns surrounding Antananarivo). Some basic conditions are expected to be met in order to be eligible to apply:

  - the roads to be maintained need to be already inserted within the Provincial Transportation Plan established in 2004;
  - the roads need to already exist in "acceptable" physical conditions and to mobilise local resources;
  - the roads need to be part of transportation axes linking the communities between them, axes identified in local development plans and have to intersect the national road network.

$\mathbb{V}$ There are basically three points of view to take into account for assessing the various projects:

- the first one concerns the "commitment" of the local actors to the maintenance effort. The idea here is that the local actors should consider the rural road maintenance as one of their major commitments and that they should feel responsible for such a resource;
- the second one concerns the "social-economic" impact of each project for the local community. As already mentioned the rural road maintenance is considered as a key element of an overall policy aiming to sustain local development, reduce isolation, increase the economic, social and cultural exchanges and integrate the whole road network of the island. Proposed projects therefore need to demonstrate that they improve both internal accessibility (to key areas of the community) and external accessibility (to the national road network, both in quantity and in quality. Besides, priority should be given to areas with high population and/or economic density (priority expressed by the national government).
- the third one is the "cost", including both short term and long term financial costs as well as negative environmental and social impacts.

Π The problem statement adopted in this case is to classify the projects in three ordered categories:

- *accepted*, the ones that meet all requirements and result at the top of all priorities in "all" dimensions (the ones for which the positive decision appears fully legitimate);
- *rejected*, the ones that definitely cannot be accepted resulting at the bottom of the priorities in "all" dimensions (the ones for which the negative decision appears fully legitimate);
- *negotiable*, the ones who could be accepted in case one or more dimensions could be improved.

15.4 Evaluation Model

The evaluation model has been conceived in a straightforward implementation of the problem formulation. It has been constructed in two steps. The first has been a generic model suggested by AGETIPA which has been refined after discussion with the advisor in order to fulfill basic conditions of coherence of the model (for a discussion about the coherence of a model the reader can see Bouyssou et al. (2000) and Vincke (1992)). The second has been a more precise version adapted to the precise issues raised by the GENIS project. The presentation which follows concerns the model as conceived before the first round of applications (there is no mention to uncertainty issues since it was considered that there was no such problem presently). In the feedback section we present how the model has been modified.

15.4.1 Alternatives

The alternatives to be evaluated are considered to be the projects submitted by the local communities. Such projects concern precise segments of the rural roads network which can normally be identified on the satellite images of the whole island (data to which AGETIPA has access). Such projects concern already existing segments of the network and not new connections to build. It is assumed that for each project presented it is possible to identify the local community submitting it (a single administration or a group of administrations).

15.4.2 Dimensions and Measurement Scales

The structure of dimensions results from the analysis of the three points of view introduced in the problem formulation.

1. The "Local Commitment" dimension decomposes to two attributes: public and private participation and is measured considering the level of financial involvement of the local community and/or the private actors to both the immediate costs of the project as well as the subsequent maintenance costs. Practically we get two figures expressed in percentages.
2. The "social-economic impact" dimension decomposes to four attributes:
   - Internal accessibility. On its turn this attribute results taking into account four sub-attributes:
     - the number of social, cultural and administrative centres served by the project (schools, churches, townhalls etc.);
     - the agricultural area served by the project (measured in ha);
     - the number of "economic activities centres" served (such as markets, industries etc.);
     - the "level of service" presently offered by the road under consideration. The "level of service" is established considering three types of data:
     - seasonal availability;
     - maximum speed;
     - traveling comfort;
   - External accessibility. On its turn this attribute results taking into account four sub-attributes:
     - number of intersections of the proposed road maintenance project with the national road network;
     - state of the above intersections;
     - volume of traffic on the road (including the transit traffic);
     - existence of alternatives and/or shortcuts in case of major impediments.

- Population density. Measured by number of people living in the area by square km.
- Economic density. Measured by the average taxes perceived in the area by the number of people living in the area.

3. The "cost" dimension is represented by a single attribute representing the cost of the project submitted taken into account both the immediate costs and the subsequent maintenance costs. No further environmental or social costs have been considered at this level of the study.

The information concerning the above attributes have been collected from the satellite images to whom AGETIPA has access, from the census information of Madagascar and finally from direct visits in the interested area in order to double check doubtful information.

15.4.3 Criteria

The set of criteria results in an hierarchy as can be shown in Fig. 15.1. Leaves have simple preference models resulting from the client's values. Intermediate "parent" nodes have preference models resulting from aggregating the preferences expressed on the "son" nodes.

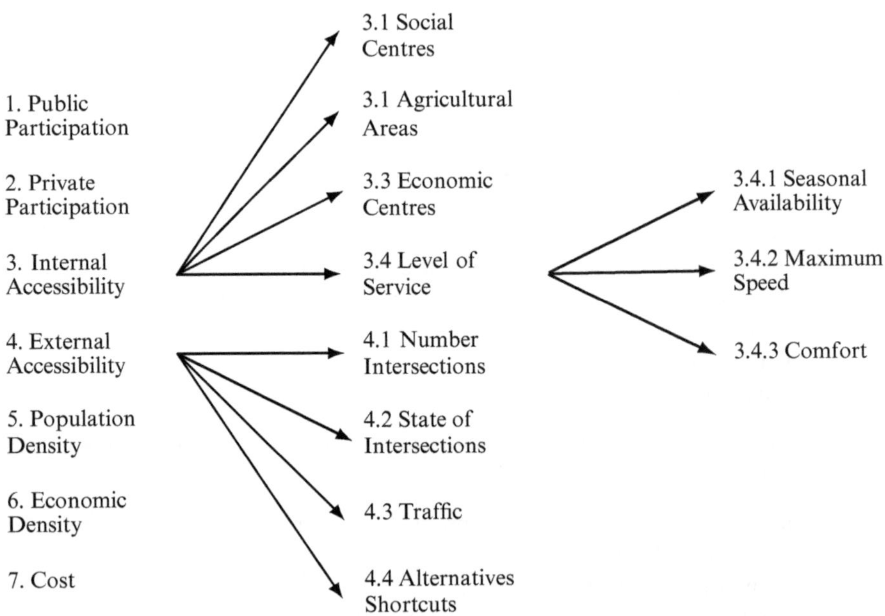

Fig. 15.1 The set of criteria

In the following we are going to present the preference models starting from the leaves of the criteria tree (the ones which have no "son" nodes).

1. Public Participation will be represented through a simple model, such that $x \succeq y$ iff $pu(x) \geq pu(y)$, where $pu(x)$ is the percentage of funds contributed by the local community to the project.
2. Private Participation will be represented through a simple model, such that $x \succeq y$ iff $pr(x) \geq pr(y)$, where $pr(x)$ is the percentage of funds contributed by private actors, possibly interested within the local community, to the project.
5. Population Density will be represented through a simple model, such that $x \succeq y$ iff $d(x) \geq d(y)$, where $d(x)$ is the number of habitants by square km in the area interested by the project.
6. Economic Density will be represented through a simple model, such that $x \succeq y$ iff $e(x) \geq e(y)$, where $e(x)$ is the average taxes perceived for each inhabitant in the area interested by the project.
7. Cost will be represented through a simple model such that $x \succeq y$ iff $c(x) \leq c(y)$ where $c(x)$ is the cost (immediate and subsequent maintenance) of the project.

In order to present the model of criterion 4 we need to present the preference models of nodes 4.1–4.4.

4.1 Number of Intersections simply takes into account how many intersections the project has with the national road network. There are three possible states (1, 2 or 3 intersections) and the more intersections the better it is (the case of no intersection is not considered since it is a reason of exclusion).
4.2 State of Intersections is a qualitative judgement: 0 for a bad condition, 1 for acceptable condition and 2 for good condition.
4.3 Traffic measures the volume of traffic as resulting from the official statistics (considering a market day and using the usual coefficients for "homogeneous vehicles", HV). Three levels are considered: less than 500 HV daily, less than 1,000 HV daily and more than 1,000 HV daily. The more traffic registered the more important is the project.
4.4 Alternatives and/or Shortcuts takes into account the presence of such routes. Three possible values are considered: no alternatives and shortcuts, either an alternative or a shortcut, both alternatives and shortcuts.

Criterion 4 is thus established on a discrete scale with values 1 (bad), 2 (acceptable), 3 (good). The procedure for assigning a value to a precise alternative is based on an ordered classification procedure of the type ELECTRE TRI (a simplified version based only on simple majority rules, for more details see for instance Dias and Mousseau (2003) and Mousseau et al. (2000)). The model is presented in Fig. 15.2. Projects whose profile is (by majority) on the left of the frontier $\langle 1, 1, 500, NN \rangle$ get the value 1, projects whose profile is (by majority) on the right of the frontier $\langle 2, 2, 1000, YY \rangle$ get the value 3, the rest get the value 2.

In order to establish the model of criterion 3 we first need to establish the model of node 3.4. This is shown in Fig. 15.3. Projects are noted on a four valued scale (1–4) resulting from an explicit enumeration of the 48 combinations of the 11

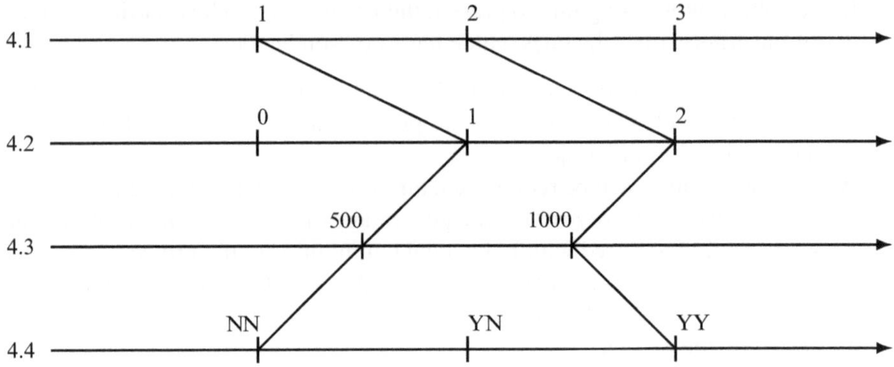

Fig. 15.2 Model of criterion 4

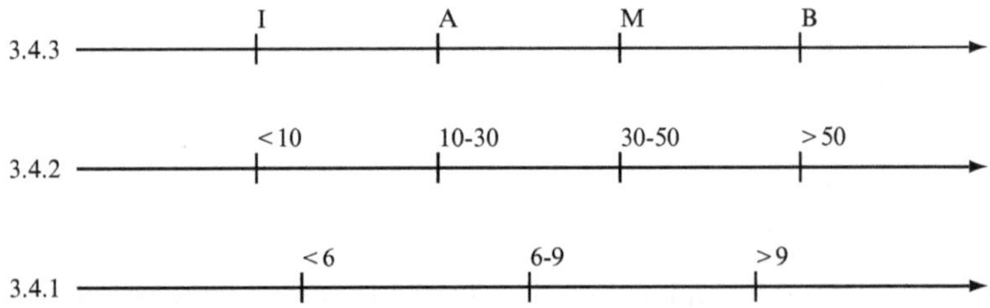

Fig. 15.3 Model of node 3.4

values on the nodes 3.4.3 (comfort I: unacceptable, A: acceptable, M: medium, B: good), 3.4.2 (maximum speed, less than 10 km/h, 10–30 km/h, 30–50 km/h, more than 50 km/h), 3.4.1 (seasonal availability: less than 6 months annually, from 6 to 9 months annually, more than 9 months annually).

Criterion 3 is also constructed putting together the four assessments expressed on nodes 3.1–3.4. The model of node 3.4 has been presented previously. We now present the models of nodes 3.1, 3.2 and 3.3.

3.1 There are three possible values: less than five social centres served, five to ten and more than ten social centres served. In counting such social centres we count principally schools, hospitals (and other health centres) churches and administration centres.
3.2 We take into account the land used (or potentially used) for agricultural purposes. This is measured in hectares.
3.3 There are three possible values: less than five economic centres served, five to ten and more than ten economic centres served. In counting such centres we count principally markets and any other economic activity which may attract mobility within the community.

Criterion 3 is thus established on a discrete scale with values M (bad), L (borderline), A (acceptable), B (good). The procedure for assigning a value to

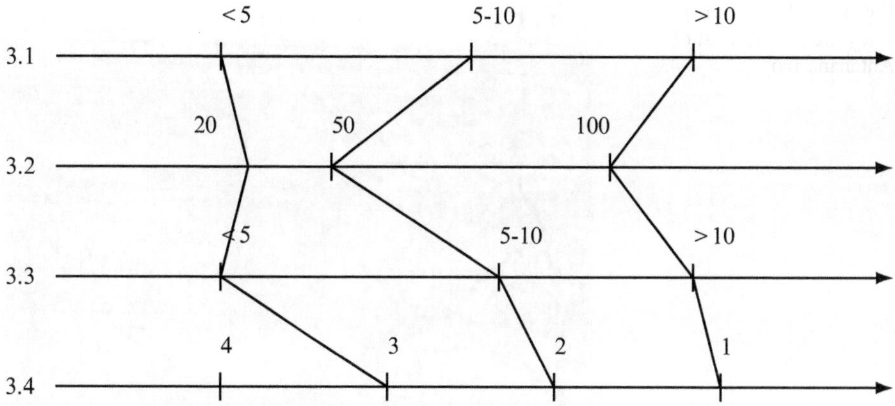

Fig. 15.4 Model of criterion 3

a precise alternative is based on an ordered classification procedure of the type ELECTRE TRI (a simplified version based only on simple majority rules, as for criterion 4). The model is presented in Fig. 15.4. Projects whose profile is (by majority) on the left of the frontier $\langle < 5, 20, < 5, 3\rangle$ get the value M, projects whose profile is (by majority) on the right of the frontier $\langle > 10, 100, > 10, 1\rangle$ get the value B. Projects who are on the right of the lowest profile, but lower than the profile $\langle 5\text{–}10, 50, 5\text{–}10, 2\rangle$ get the value L, the rest get the value A.

15.4.4 Aggregation Procedure

The overall aggregation procedure was aimed at assigning each project to one among the following classes: accepted, negotiable, rejected. The procedure once again is a simplified version of the ELECTRE TRI method. The final model can be seen in Fig. 15.8. A brief description of the method is provided in the Appendix. In the pilot study a "pessimistic" assignment procedure has been adopted. Generally speaking we adopted a very simple ordinal sorting procedure mostly in order to ease the explanations for each assignment decision and thus the discussion which followed.

15.5 Pilot Study

The proposed method has been tested in a pilot study concerning an area at the Nord East of the Great Antananarivo Metropolitan Area. This area can be seen in Fig. 15.5.

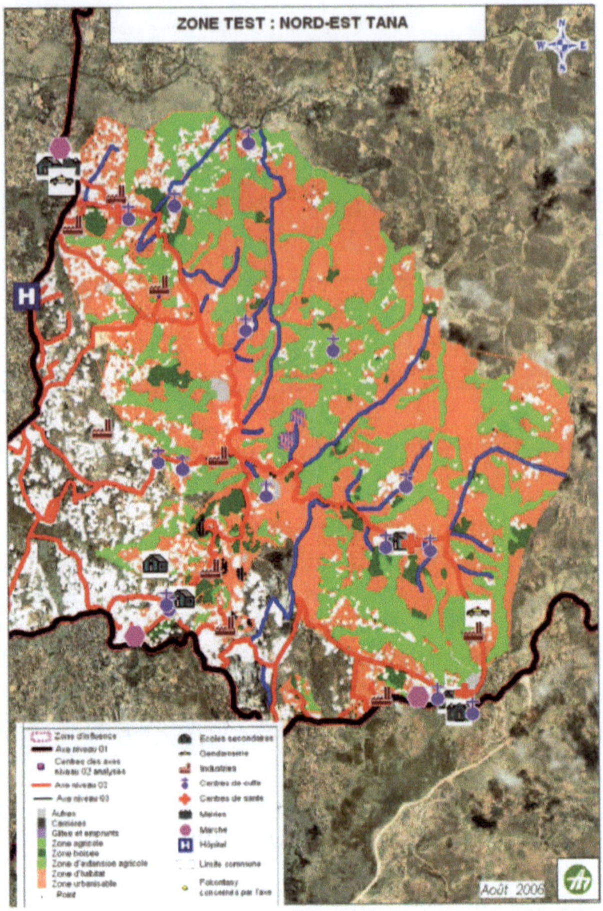

Fig. 15.5 Map of the pilot study area: Nord East of Antananarivo

Data have been collected from satellite images (to which AGETIPA has access), from the National Statistics office and from direct visits in the area under study. A data base with all relevant information has been thus established. A typical record of this data base can be seen in Fig. 15.6.

Four maintenance projects have been selected in order to be evaluated as a test for the method. These were at the moment of the study under discussion, but a basic consensus was already reached, although not using a formal evaluation tool. For this reason they seemed to be an interesting benchmark. The values of the four alternatives together with the chosen profiles for the three categories (to finance, to negotiate, to reject) can be seen in Fig. 15.7.

The classification model specifying the shape of the three categories can be seen in Fig. 15.8

In order to complete the model we need to establish the "importance parameters", that is the importance of each criterion for establishing the class of each alternative.

Fig. 15.6 Extract of the data base information

ID:	1
Nom:	Ambohimangakely-Ankadikely
Longueur_Km:	9
Linéaire_bitumé:	0
Linéaire_pavé:	0
Linéaire_terre:	9
Zone_influence_km2:	20
Nb_Fokontany:	11
Nombre_habitants:	27 700
Densité_hab_km:	3 078
Densité_hab_km2:	1 385
Nb_hôpitaux:	1
Nb_CSB:	3
Nb_écoles_secondaires:	3
Nb_mairies:	2
Centres_de_culte:	13
Nb_marchés:	3
Nb_industries:	7
Surface_agricole_ha:	266
S_zone_ext_agricole_ha:	323
Surface_boisée_ha:	70
Surface_urbanisée_ha:	287
Surface_urbanisable_ha_:	1 000
Pôle_de_croissance:	non
Nb_Carrières:	2

While in the intermediate nodes of the hierarchy a simple majority rule has been adopted, the final model needs to take more precisely into account the importance that the decision maker desires to associate to each criterion (as a manifestation of a certain policy).

Since the comparison between alternatives and profiles is based on a "weighted majority" rule the procedure for constructing such "weights" is the following (considering a set H of m criteria):

1. We first check if any majority of $m-1, m-2\ldots$ criteria is sufficient to establish a preference relation (winning coalitions).
2. If all coalitions with $m/2+1$ criteria are "winning" then we stop and consider that all criteria have the same importance and the rule is a simple majority rule.
3. If it is not the case we identify the first k such that not all coalitions with $m-k$ criteria are winning (obviously $k < m/2$) and we ask which among these ones are winning and which not.
4. For each winning coalition $W \subset H$ we can write $\sum_{j \in W} w_j \geq \delta$ (δ being the majority threshold, unknown).
5. We repeat the same procedure for $k+1, k+2$ until for some $k+l$ all coalitions are not winning.

Tableau de performance

CRITERES	Axe 1	Axe 2	Axe 3	Axe 4	Seuil Profil : axe à financer H1	Seuil Profil : axe à négocier H2
C1	90	90	90	90	50	0 - 50
C2	10	10	10	30	40	0 - 40
C3	B	A	A	M	A	L
C4	2	2	1	1	1	1
C5	2500	5200	7000	2000	3000	2000 - 3000
C6	6	6	6	6	6	4 - 6
C7	15	4	3	2	14	14-20

Fig. 15.7 Data concerning the four alternatives and the profiles

6. At this point we have a set of linear inequalities, the variables being the different w_j and δ.
7. We fix an arbitrary value K such that $\sum_{j \in H} w_j = K$.
8. We solve a linear programme minimising or maximising δ and we submit the result to the decision maker. In reality any feasible solution of the linear programme will fit, but the use of extreme solutions helps the decision maker to better discriminate among the values. For instance maximising δ we obtain a result which appears "highly confident" due to the qualified majority thus imposed. The reader should note that the arbitrary value K is irrelevant for the model and only allows to find a numerical representation.
9. In case the decision maker is able to establish a partial order among the criteria this will translate in some further inequalities in the linear programme. It is also interesting to note that in case the decision maker makes any inconsistent statements these will result in an unfeasible linear programme.

The four alternatives have been compared to the two profiles. The first three have been classified as "to be financed", while the fourth one as "to be negotiated". The result has been discussed and validated with the public authorities concerned. The successful application of the procedure to the pilot study has been thus followed by introducing the method in the regular business conducted by AGETIPA.

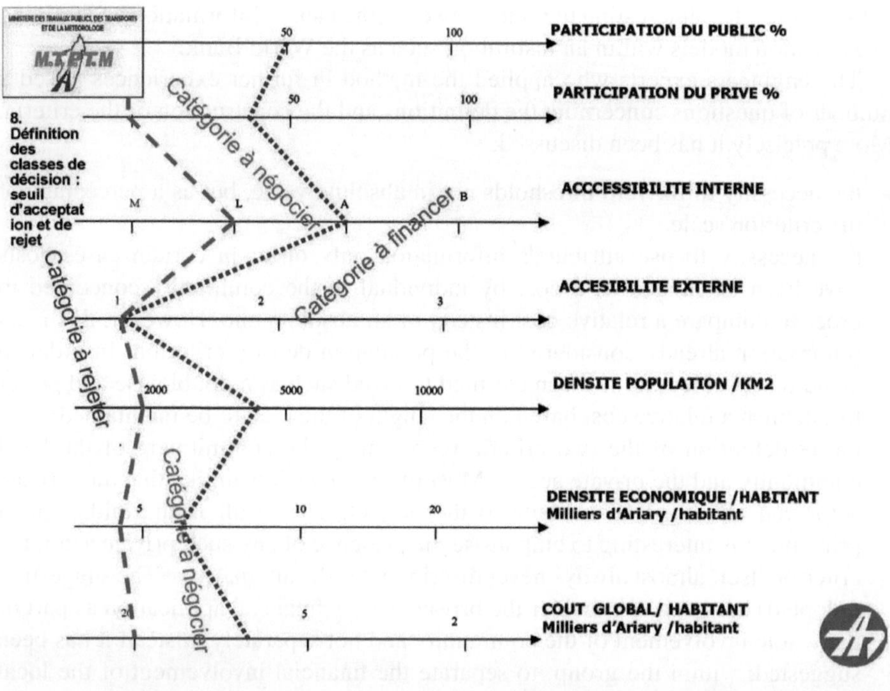

Fig. 15.8 Classification model

15.6 Feedback

The method suggested in this document has been conceived in September 2006 and since then applied by AGETIPA together with the "engineering" teams working in rural road maintenance and other public works under the supervision of the World Bank and the government. In September 2008 there has been a follow up meeting involving expert engineers, the Public Work Minister and the World Bank.

An issue raised by the World Bank concerned the legitimation of the precise method adopted. Basically two questions have been raised:

- are we sure about the "correctness" of the results?
- why not using a "weighted sum" as any other does?

On the first question we offered the necessary literature references (such as Bouyssou et al. 2000; Keeney and Raiffa 1976; Maystre et al. 1994; Pictet and Bollinger 2003). On the second question we emphasized the reasons for which the choice of establishing a single value function has been rejected: (1) the presence of information for which it is not immediate establishing a trade-off among the criteria and (2) the necessity to have clear the reasons for which a project is not chosen (rejected or to negotiate) in order to pursue further participation of the local communities. It is interesting to notice however, the lack of information and training in evaluation models within an institution such as the World Bank.

The engineers experts who applied the method in further experiences raised a number of questions concerning the definitions and the construction of the criteria. More precisely it has been discussed:

- the necessity to fix veto thresholds not in absolute value, but as a percentage of the criterion scale.
- the necessity to use attribute's information only once: in certain cases costs have been calculated as a cost by individual in the community concerned in order to compare a relative cost instead of an absolute one. However, this is an information already considered in the population density criterion. In order to avoid this problem it has been clarified to avoid such as a double use and prefer to establish a relative cost based on the length of the road to be maintained.
- the re-definition of the two criteria representing the commitment of the local community and the private actors. Most of the times it is unlike that any private actor can effectively contribute to the project. The result is that although in principle it is interesting to emphasise the presence of any such private actor, the criterion itself almost always never discriminates the alternatives. The suggestion (adopted) has been to consider the private actor's financial application as part of the whole involvement of the community and not separately. Instead it has been suggested, within the group, to separate the financial involvement of the local community to the short term direct costs of the project, from the further medium term maintenance costs.

A further element the discussion emphasised, was the necessity to establish a formal procedure, not only in order to apply, but also in order to further negotiate the application. The method as it is established today requires a procedure in order to formulate an application. Once the applicant knows that the proposal has been "approved" or "rejected" or that it is "negotiable", it is necessary to fix a procedure describing how these decisions are going to be implemented. For instance it is necessary to fix how the commitment of the local community to participate to the costs will be maintained after the decision to start the project has been taken (and the national financial commitment has been decided).

The overall assessment of the method has been positive. The projects handled using this approach show a better understanding, a major commitment of the local communities, while introducing accountability and elements of rationality in handling the road maintenance priorities.

15.7 Conclusions

In this chapter we present a real world decision support case: aiding AGETIPA (the operational agency of the Minister of Public Works in Madagascar) to handle the problem of "improving the rural road maintenance in Madagascar". As often happens behind the verbal presentation of the "problem" there exist multiple problem situations and problem formulations. In the document we present the ones fixed in this study and the reasons for doing so:

- take into account the qualitative information without necessarily transforming it in monetary consequences (not always feasible or accepted);
- allow and help to conduct negotiations with the local actors given the **political** nature of such decisions.

Technically the problem can be seen as an "ordinal measurement" problem where to each object to be measured is associated a label from an ordinal scale (in other terms a class among a set of ordered classes; in this case *accepted, negotiable, rejected*). A further specificity results from the existence of a hierarchy of similar evaluation models where once again the objects to be evaluated must be classified in ordered classes (for instance *level of service 1, 2, 3*). The overall assessment resulting from the hierarchical aggregation of the values (assignment to ordered classes) obtained on the nodes of the evaluation tree.

The model has been first applied with a pilot case study (in the Metropolitan Area of the Great Antananarivo, reported in this document) and then used for the last 2 years. We briefly report the feedback received from this experience. AGETIPA and the teams of engineers working in this area are satisfied with the methodology. Presently AGETIPA is considering the extension of the use of decision aiding methodology in other case studies including the location of a new port, the construction of new schools and the renovation of the "pedestrian path network" within Antananarivo.

Appendix

The basic concepts adopted in the procedure used (based on ELECTRE TRI) are the following.

- A set A of alternatives $a_i, i = 1 \cdots m$.
- A set G of criteria $g_j, j = 1 \cdots n$. A relative importance w_j (usually normalised in the interval [0, 1]) is attributed to each criterion g_j.
- Each criterion g_j is equipped with an ordinal scale $\mathscr{E}_j$ with degrees e^l_j, $l = 1 \cdots k$.
- A set $\mathscr{P}$ of profiles p_h, $h = 1 \cdots t$, p_h being a collection of degrees, $p_h = \langle e^h_1 \cdots e^h_n \rangle$, such that if e^h_j belongs to profile p_h, e^{h+1}_j cannot belong to profile p_{h-1}.
- A set $\mathscr{C}$ of categories c_λ, $\lambda = 1 \cdots t + 1$, such that the profile p_h is the upper bound of category c_h and the lower bound of category c_{h+1}.
- An outranking relation $S \subset (A \times \mathscr{P}) \cup (\mathscr{P} \times A)$, where $s(x, y)$ should be read as "x is at least as good as y".
- A set of preference relations $\langle P_j, I_j \rangle$ for each criterion g_j such that:

- $\forall x \in A \;\; P_j(x, e_j^h) \Leftrightarrow g_j(x) \succ e_j^h$
- $\forall x \in A \;\; P_j(e_j^h, x) \Leftrightarrow g_j(x) \prec e_j^h$
- $\forall x \in A \;\; I_j(x, e_j^h) \Leftrightarrow g_j(x) \approx e_j^h$

$\prec, \approx$ induced by the ordinal scale associated to criterion g_j.

The procedure works in two basic steps.

1. Establish the outranking relation on the basis of the following rule:

$$s(x, y) \Leftrightarrow C(x, y) \textbf{ and not } D(x, y)$$

where

$$\forall x \in A,\; y \in \mathscr{P} : C(x, y) \Leftrightarrow \sum_{j \in G^{\pm}} w_j \geq c \textbf{ and } \Big(\sum_{j \in G^{+}} w_j \geq \sum_{j \in G^{-}} w_j\Big)$$

$$\forall y \in A,\; x \in \mathscr{P} : C(x, y) \Leftrightarrow$$
$$\Big(\sum_{j \in G^{\pm}} w_j \geq c \textbf{ and } \sum_{j \in G^{+}} w_j \geq \sum_{j \in G^{-}} w_j\Big) \textbf{ or } \Big(\sum_{j \in G^{+}} w_j > \sum_{j \in G^{-}} w_j\Big)$$

$$\forall (x, y) \in (A \times \mathscr{P}) \cup (\mathscr{P} \times A) : \textbf{not } D(x, y) \Leftrightarrow$$
$$\sum_{j \in G^{-}} w_j \leq d \textbf{ and } \forall g_j \textbf{ not } v_j(x, y)$$

where

- $G^{+} = \{g_j \in G : P_j(x, y)\}$
- $G^{-} = \{g_j \in G : P_j(y, x)\}$
- $G^{=} = \{g_j \in G : I_j(x, y)\}$
- $G^{\pm} = G^{+} \cup G^{=}$
- c: the concordance threshold $c \in [0.5, 1]$
- d: the discordance threshold $d \in [0, 1]$
- $v_j(x, y)$: veto, expressed on criterion g_j, of y on x

2. When the relation S is established, assign any element a_i on the basis of the following rules.

2.1 pessimistic assignment

- a_i is iteratively compared with $p_t \cdots p_1$,
- as soon as $s(a_i, p_h)$ is established, assign a_i to category c_h.

2.2 optimistic assignment

– a_i is iteratively compared with $p_1 \cdots p_t$,
– as soon as is established $s(p_h, a_i) \wedge \neg s(a_i, p_h)$ then assign a_i to category c_{h-1}.

The pessimistic procedure finds the highest profile for which the element is not worse. The optimistic procedure finds the lowest profile against which the element is surely worse. If the optimistic and pessimistic assignments coincide, then no uncertainty exists for the assignment. Otherwise, an uncertainty exists and should be considered by the user.

References

Boardman, A. (1996). *Cost benefit analysis: Concepts and practices*. New York: Prentice-Hall.

Bouyssou, D., Marchant, T., Pirlot, M., Perny, P., Tsoukiàs, A., & Vincke, P. (2000). *Evaluation and decision models: A critical perspective*. Dordrecht: Kluwer Academic.

Dasgupta, P., & Heal, D. (1979). *Economic theory and exhaustible resources*. Cambridge: Cambridge University Press.

Dias, L., & Mousseau, V. (2003). IRIS: A DSS for multiple criteria sorting problems. *Journal of Multi-Criteria Decision Analysis, 12*, 285–298.

Dinwiddy, C., & Teal, F. (1996). *Principles of cost-benefit analysis for developing countries*. Cambridge: Cambridge University Press.

Keeney, R. (1992). *Value-focused thinking. A path to creative decision making*. Cambridge: Harvard University Press.

Keeney, R., & Raiffa, H. (1976). *Decisions with multiple objectives: Preferences and value tradeoffs*. New York: Wiley.

Kulkarni, R., Miller, D., Ingram, R., Wong, C., & Lorenz, J. (2004). Need-based project prioritization: Alternative to cost-benefit analysis. *Journal of Transportation Engineering, 130*, 150–158.

Liesiö, J., Mild, P., & Salo, A. (2007). Preference programming for robust portfolio modeling and project selection. *European Journal of Operational Research, 181*, 1488–1505.

Maystre, L., Pictet, J., & Simos, J. (1994). *Méthodes multicritères ELECTRE. Description, conseils pratiques et cas d'application à la gestion environnementale*. Lausanne: Presses Polytechniques et Universitaires Romandes.

Mild, P., & Salo, A. (2009). Combining a multiattribute value function with an optimization model: An application to dynamic resource allocation for infrastructure maintenance. *Decision Analysis, 6*, 139–152.

Mousseau, V., Slowinski, R., & Zielniewicz, P. (2000). A user-oriented implementation of the ELECTRE TRI method integrating preference elicitation support. *Computers & Operations Research, 27*(7–8), 757–777.

Pictet, J., & Bollinger, D. (2003). *Adjuger un marché au mieux-disant. Analyse multicritère, pratique et droit des marchés publics*. Lausanne: Presses Polytechniques et Universitaires Romandes.

Roy, B., & Damart, S. (2002). L'analyse coûts-avantages, outil de concertation et de légitimation? *Metropolis, 108–109*, 7–16.

Tsoukiàs, A. (2007). On the concept of decision aiding process. *Annals of Operations Research, 154*, 3–27.

Vincke, P. (1992). *Multicriteria decision-aid*. New York: Wiley.

Editors' Comments on "Rural Road Maintenance in Madagascar"

Tsoukiàs and Ralijaona address a common problem in many public and private organizations: to decide which projects are approved among a set of proposals. It encompasses the problem definition and formulation stages (see Chap. 2), the definition of an aggregation procedure and its application on a pilot case. This chapter illustrates the sorting problematic based on a variant of the ELECTRE TRI method (see Chap. 4, Sect. 4.4.4) in a case of public decision-making. It is also, in this book, one of the two applications taking place in the African continent (together with Chap. 12).

The **objective of the intervention** was to provide decision-aiding concerning resource allocation to projects, promoting public participation and commitment of local actors. A pilot study was carried out not only to demonstrate the usefulness of MCDA, but also to transfer knowledge to the client organization. The pilot study was intended to validate the MCDA approach and to be reproducible in the future by the client independently.

The **client** organization was AGETIPA, an agency established by the Government of Madagascar and several companies for the area of Public Work. The intervention was sponsored by a project proposed by the Transportation Minister in collaboration with the World Bank, which can be seen as secondary clients. The **analysts** (the authors) were a member of the client organization and an external consultant who, as a Decision Aiding expert, would be the main source for the knowledge to be transferred. Local **actors** and the population in general from the Pilot Study area were also involved in the decision process. Other stakeholders included financial and fund raising institutions.

Several **stages** can be identified in this intervention: formulation, model building, setting parameter values, application of the model and refinement of the model. The objects under evaluation are projects submitted by local communities concerning road maintenance actions. During the problem definition stage, it was decided that the four alternatives under analysis at the time would be the **set of alternatives** for the pilot study. It was also defined that the evaluation **criteria** should take into account local commitment (two attributes), social-economic impact (four attributes, two of which further decomposed into sub-attributes), and cost. This resulted in an hierarchical criteria structure having ten attributes as leaf nodes. The idea of using criteria hierarchies is often used in MCDA (e.g. Keeney 1992; Saaty 1980), for it allows decision makers to focus on a few criteria at a time and thereby facilitates eliciting information about their relative importance.

Although the client's problem is eventually to choose which projects are approved on a given year, a sorting **problem statement** was adopted. Indeed, the actors involved saw the problem as being one of justifying which projects are not selected and under which conditions such projects might be reconsidered. Thus, a sorting model would be able to distinguish projects that meet all the requirements, projects that definitely cannot be accepted, and an intermediary category of projects that are negotiable (which might be accepted if some conditions are met). One can also note that a sorting problematic allows evaluating projects on continuous "as they appear" basis. This is possible unless there are synergistic benefits or losses among projects if implemented simultaneously. In this case, an approach based on portfolio optimization (e.g., Salo et al. 2011) might be called for.

Concerning **aggregation**, ELECTRE TRI's pessimistic variant was the chosen sorting method, using a simplified outranking relation (simple majority, without imprecision thresholds), but allowing for an hierarchical criteria structure. This method was chosen on the grounds that its results are easily explainable, although initially there was some resistance to accept it by one of the sponsors. The variant followed can be seen as a new method combining ideas of existing approaches and tailored to the client's needs. There was no **uncertainty modelling**: data values were not considered to be subject to uncertainty, which might warrant using imprecision thresholds or sensitivity analyses.

Setting the criteria weights followed two strategies. For less important hierarchy levels all subcriteria were considered to be equally important and a simple majority rule was used. For the top level of the hierarchy weights were chosen according to the client's preferences. The **elicitation process** was carried out by examining which coalitions of criteria would be strong enough to justify that an alternative outranks a category profile, and using linear programming to infer the weight values. This is an innovative elicitation approach when compared to inference based on result examples (Mousseau and Dias, 2004; Mousseau and Słowiński, 1998) or approximation methods (Figueira and Roy, 2002).

The **tangible results** of this decision process were the definition of a criteria hierarchy and the characterization of an ELECTRE TRI sorting model, tested in the pilot study, that can be used to sort road maintenance projects. More important, an **intangible result** was the capacity gained by the client to use and adapt the model in the future. The authors describe that the model has been refined due to user requests and there exist plans to apply it to different decision problems in Madagascar.

This chapter's main **relevance** concerns addressing public decision making with MCDA. This is a particularly difficult problem when the client, as it should do, wishes to model the values of the public involving stakeholders and the population in general, aiming for transparency and legitimacy (see also on these issues Keeney 2004; Gregory et al. 2005). This led not only to emphasize the problem structuring phase as the most crucial one, leading to the idea of sorting with one category representing a "negotiation area", but also led to the use of a method variant that would be more suited to this particular application.

References

Figueira, J., & Roy, B. (2002). Determining the weights of criteria in the ELECTRE type methods with a revised Simos' procedure. *European Journal of Operational Research, 139*(2), 317–326.

Gregory, R., Fischhoff, B., & McDaniels, T. (2005). Acceptable input: Using decision analysis to guide public policy deliberations. *Decision Analysis, 2*(1), 4–16.

Keeney, R. (1992). *Value-focused thinking. A path to creative decision making*. Cambridge: Harvard University Press.
Keeney, R. (2004). Framing public policy decisions. *International Journal of Technology, Policy and Management, 4*(2), 95–115.
Mousseau, V., & Dias, L. (2004). Valued outranking relations in ELECTRE providing manageable disaggregation procedures. *European Journal of Operational Research, 156*(2), 467–482.
Mousseau, V., & Słowiński, R. (1998). Inferring an ELECTRE TRI model from assignment examples. *Journal of Global Optimization, 12*(2), 157–174.
Saaty, T. (1980). *The analytic hierarchy process*. New York: McGraw-Hill.
Salo, A., Keisler, J., & Morton, A. (Eds.). (2011). *Advances in portfolio decision analysis - Methods for improved resource allocation*. New York: Springer.

Chapter 16
On the Use of a Multicriteria Decision Aiding Tool for the Evaluation of Comfort

Meltem Öztürk, Alexis Tsoukiàs, and Sylvie Guerrand

Abstract In this paper we present a real word application of multicriteria decision aiding for the evaluation of high speed trains comfort from passengers's point of view. Our study is used as a feasibility analysis for the introduction of multicriteria tools in the SNCF. Our approach concerns different steps of a decision aiding procedure. We firstly define the complex notion of comfort and propose to use a hierarchical model for its representation. We then present in more detail the *seating comfort* by assigning value scales to its components. Our problem being a sorting problem and our data being very heterogeneous, we decide to use the ELECTRE TRI method for the aggregation of the components. The article presents how the decision parameters, such as thresholds, weights and limit profiles, of ELECTRE TRI are selected and conclude with three fictitious assignment examples.

16.1 Problem Definition

In this study we are interested in defining and evaluating the comfort for the French national railways, SNCF. More precisely, we conducted a feasibility study about the use of a multicriteria decision aiding tool within the ACONIT project 1 assigning comfort in high speed passenger trains. The main idea of the projet consists in considering comfort as a judgment based on a set of complex elements by taking into account the traveller's point of view. This project is focused on two key points: (1) comfort is a notion integrating different concepts which may be objective or

M. Öztürk
Lamsade - Université Paris IX Dauphine, Place du Maréchal de Lattre de Tassigny, 75775 Paris Cedex 16, France
e-mail: ozturk@lamsade.dauphine.fr

A. Tsoukiàs (✉)
CNRS-LAMSADE, Université Paris Dauphine, 75016 Paris, France
e-mail: tsoukias@lamsade.dauphine.fr

S. Guerrand
SNCF, Paris, France
e-mail: sylvie.guerrand@sncf.fr

R. Bisdorff et al. (eds.), *Evaluation and Decision Models with Multiple Criteria*, International Handbooks on Information Systems,
DOI 10.1007/978-3-662-46816-6_16

subjective; (2) the perception of comfort by the travellers may be different from the definition of comfort given by SNCF experts. The first part of ACONIT focused on the comprehension of this complex notion of comfort and tried to define it from the travellers point of view. Before ACONIT, comfort was defined by experts of SNCF; for instance some experts have done experiments with robots making clear the influence of sensorial aspects (resonance, vibration, vision, etc.) on the perception of comfort. ACONIT is interested in a similar subject, definition of comfort, but under a different perspective: comfort must also be defined by travellers. During the first part of ACONIT, different surveys have been conducted with travellers by SNCF experts and a supporting team of psycholinguists in order to catch how travellers perceive and define comfort.

This study has been conducted at the last step of the ACONIT project which is focused on the structuring of the knowledge acquired in the preliminary steps. Such a structuring must put together different results and provide a global vision of comfort. Such a vision will then be used in order to improve the global comfort of trains. Results of the previous steps have shown that there are three main types of comfort: (1) comfort of the services proposed by the SNCF (internet service for reservations, service for disabled persons, service on the train, quality of train connections, etc.); (2) comfort on the train (seats, sensorial aspects like noise, vibrations etc., place for baggages, etc.); (3) comfort of the train stations (benches, cleanliness, bar, etc.). SNCF decided to center their efforts firstly on the comfort on the train. The issue was how to put together different aspects of rolling materials in order to build an overall assessment of comfort compatible with the travellers perception. Our contribution to the ACONIT project is an answer to this issue.

Before describing the model we have to fix the perspectives under which the model was expected to be used: why is evaluating comfort a problem and for whom and for what purpose? Naturally the comfort on passengers trains is strongly related to the quality and the description of the rolling stocks. The purchase of such stocks is done through call for tenders. For the purchase or renovation of a coach the acquisition department prepares a call for tenders by specifying some needs (dimensions of seats, material of seats, distance between foot-rest and the seat, etc.) and evaluate them from especially two points of view: the cost and the number of specifications satisfied by the supplier. This evaluation is done using a weighted sum.

Unfortunately, even if some specifications are directly related to the notion of comfort, the global evaluation of offers does not provide a view of the comfort level of each offer. On the other hand, the specifications of call for tenders related to the comfort are also defined by the acquisition department and the ACONIT project has shown that the vision of comfort of this department may be different from the vision of experts which may not be the same as the one of travellers. For all these reasons the department of comfort decided to develop a tool in order to propose an evaluation of suppliers' offers from the comfort point of view where the notion of comfort will be in coherence with the perception of the acquisition department but also of the experts and the travellers. Since there are a number of different components determining the comfort, it has been decided to do a feasibility analysis for the use of a multicriteria decision aiding tool where different components of comfort will play the role of criteria. The evaluation of offers from the comfort point of view will be in terms of a classification, i.e. each offer will be assigned to a class representing its comfort level such as class of very comfortable offer or poorly comfortable offer, etc. This choice is related to some semantical and two mathematical reasons that we will present in the rest of this article.

The feasibility analysis is done in four steps:

- comfort definition integrating the travellers perception through the previous steps of the ACONIT project;
- construction of a hierarchy of the comfort components;
- definition of the scales of values for the evaluation of the comfort components;
- proposition of a classification model.

We present in Sect. 16.2 different components of comfort and we propose a hierarchy of these components in Sect. 16.3. The fact that comfort components are of different nature imposes a detailed study of their value scales, Sect. 16.4 gives some details on this subject. Section 16.5 shows basic notions related to the classification method that we chose, Sect. 16.6 provides decision parameters related to comfort components and chosen classification methods and finally Sect. 16.7 presents some examples.

16.2 Comfort Components

In this first step we tried to give a definition of the comfort from the travellers point of view.

As mentioned before, the data which we deal with in this part arise from inquiries done within the framework of a thesis on psycholinguistics domain conducted on the survey used by the SNCF. A first inquiry, called *exploratory*, was used to build the *main* inquiry by enabling to clarify the shape of more relevant and more productive questions. The analysis of the answers of the travellers to the second inquiry led to the naming of various semantic categories defining the global comfort. Seventy-seven categories were defined from the answers of the questioned travellers. They were then classified in 12 meta-categories (Table 16.1). The basic levels of the hierarchical model of the comfort components proposed in this study is presented in Table 16.2. Five meta-categories are retained: sensorial comfort, seating comfort, stand up comfort, activity and services. These meta-categories have a number of categories which are also shown in Table 16.2. Some of these categories could be again divided in subcategories, because of space lake we only showed the sub-categories related to seating comfort in Table 16.2 since we will develop only the aggregation of seating comfort components in the rest of this paper shows these categories.

Our commitment being to implement a model of comfort to use in rolling stocks acquisition call for tenders, we analyze more in detail these semantic categories in

Table 16.1 Comfort model given by the SNCF

Comfort before and after the train	Access to the train, station, reservation, number of people waiting for the train
General aspect	Activity
Sensorial	Air, atmosphere, noise, train movement, color, space, light, material, carpet, landscape, cleanliness, toilet cleanliness, security, temperature, air-condition, visibility, smell
Seating comfort	Arm-rest, head-rest, back comfort, leg comfort, internet connection, garbage, back seat net, travellers movements, functionality, socket, foot-rest, train direction, table
Stand up comfort	Corridor, door
Relational	Crowd, other passengers, civism, shifting of travellers, efficiency of SNCF staff, intimacy, presence of non real travellers
Services	Bar, material disadvantages, information multi-media, personnalization catering, phone, toilets, animals, langerie
Train	Compartmentalization, number of places, location, functionality, condition of transportation, door, luggage places, maintenance, classes, material, train dimension, being soft
SNCF image	Modernity
Temporal aspect	Trip time, speed, punctuality
Emotional aspect	Travellers emotion, train level, experience, pleasure
Financial aspect	Restoration cost, ticket cost

order to be able to select those that seem relevant for the preparation of call for tenders.

It is necessary to clarify that even if the surveys were mainly related to the comfort on the train, travellers mentioned also issues related to other types of comfort (bookings, strikes, connecting trains, etc.). For that reason among such categories there are some which are not relevant for our study.

Hence we begin our analysis by a detailed study of these categories and subcategories. At this step the components of comfort were analyzed one by one from a team formed by sensorial experts of SNCF, people from the comfort and

Table 16.2 Hierarchy of comfort on the train

Comfort on the train					
Sensorial comfort	Sitting comfort		Stand up comfort	Activity comfort	Service ,comfort
Sound	Arm-rest		Corridor	Multimedia	Bar/restorant
Visual	Leg comfort		Access to the train	Socket	Information systems
Air-conditioning	Seat back net		Door	Internet connection	Toilet
Atmosphere	Direction		Train movement	Light	Lingerie
Security feeling	Train movement			Table	Phone
	Garbage	Size		Visibility	Luggage
		Ergonomy		Atmosphere	Disabled people
	Table	Volume		Sitting comfort	Pregnant woman
		Ergonomy			
	Headrest	Angle			
		Sensorial			
	Back Comfort	Width			
		Length			
		Hardness			
		Uniformity			
		Angle			
	Foot-rest	Width			
		Slippiness			
		Distance			

the acquisition departments and decision experts. Such an analysis led to dropping off some meta-categories or categories. We first present some examples of different dropping off reasons and then list the abandoned metacategories.

- Dropping off of meta-categories which are not related to the comfort on the train: The meta-category called *comfort before and after the train* which contains categories like *reservation facilities, access to the train, location of train stations*, etc. does not directly relate to the comfort on the train, hence it was abandoned. However the elimination of each category was discussed by the team participants (SNCF experts, people from comfort and acquisition department and decision aiding experts); such discussion provided a better understanding of categories and allowed some modifications or addition of new categories. For instance, the category *reservation facilities* has a number of sub-categories: the possibility to choose the direction of the seat (in the same direction of the train or not) is one of them. With the new technologies its is possible to have seats with a modifiable back (this option is generally not chosen because of its cost). Even if this notion is really related to reservation, it shows that people are sensitive to the direction of their seat. For that reason a new category is added into the meta-category *seating comfort* showing if the direction of seats is modifiable or not. Similarly, the category *access to the train* related to the equipment for disabled people or people having luggage is moved to the meta-category *service* with a restriction of its contents, naturally the presence of elevators etc is eliminated.

- Dropping off of some categories which are irrelevant to the rolling stocks quality even if they are related to the comfort on the train: After a discussion it is decided to abandon the categories *landscape, maintenance, punctuality, trip time, speed, efficiency of SNCF staff, ticket cost, presence of non real travellers* (beggars, etc.), *restoration cost*. Such a decision is also confirmed by the fact that these categories have been identified as *uncharacteristic* components of comfort in previous steps of ACONIT.
- Some other categories are also ignored for other reasons:
  - they are very general (for instance *condition of transportation*),
  - they are redundant with other categories (for instance *personal characteristics* and the categories of *disabled people, smokers*, etc.)
  - they are vague and/or not frequently expressed (for instance *being soft, train dimension, functionality*).

  These eliminations were also justified by the weak apparition of their quote in the answers directly related to the comfort on the train.

Globally after our analysis, seven meta-categories were dropped off, five were retained and a new one was added. Some more comments are given in the following for the reasons of abandon for each category:

- the meta-category *before-after the trip*: As it is mentioned before, this meta-category is not directly related to the comfort on the train. Only the category *access to the train* is retained and added to the meta-category *stand up comfort*
- the meta-category *generic aspect*: All its categories, except the *activity*, being too general were redundant with other categories. Answers to inquiries and other studies done by the SNCF have shown that the practice of an activity (reading, writing, working with PC, etc.) becomes more and more important for travellers. For that reason it is decided to create a new meta-category named *activity*.
- the meta-category *relational*: Some of its components being directly related to the personality of people are abandoned. The others, *number of travellers, shifting of travellers* and *intimacy* become sub-categories of the category *ambiance* which is in the meta-category called *sensorial*.
- the meta-category *train*: Some categories were rebuilt: *compartmentalization, localization, number of places, door* and *luggage places*. The *compartmentalization* (coaches for different types of people and their activities) is divided into two sub-categories: *disabled people, pregnant women*. These categories are then placed into the meta-category *services*. The *number of travellers*, influencing the perception of ambiance is placed into the category *ambiance*. The *door* appears

in the majority of answers related to the moving on the train and noise, hence is placed in two different meta-categories, *sensorial* and *stand up comfort*. Finally, the *luggage place* is placed into the meta-category *service*.

- the meta-category *temporal aspect*: Assuming that the speed of the train does not depend on suppliers (but depends on the railroad) all the components of this meta-category were abandoned.
- the meta-category *financial aspect*: Its components being not directly related to comfort on the train are abandoned.
- the meta-category *emotional feeling*: Its components *pleasure* and *experience*, the first one being redundant with other categories and the second one being not related to our framework were abandoned.

We give now some details about the five retained meta-categories.

- the meta-category *sensorial*: It is divided into five categories *sound, visual, air-conditioning, ambiance* and *security feeling*. An analysis of dependency showed that a majority of these categories are perceived simultaneously.
- the meta-category *seating comfort*: It is divided into ten categories *arm-rest, head-rest, back, leg comfort, net, garbage, foot-rest, direction, train movement* and *table*.
- the meta-category *stand up comfort*: It is divided into four categories *corridor, access to the train, door* and *movement of the train*.
- the meta-category *activity*: It is divided into eight categories *multimedia, socket, internet connection, light, table, visibility, ambiance* and *seating comfort*.
- the meta-category *service*: It is divided into nine categories *restaurant, information, toilet, langerie, phone, luggage, disabled people, pregnant women* and *animals*.

16.3 Model

This second stage consists of the construction of a hierarchy of the comfort components. This takes into account only the components retained in the first part of our study.

The nature of the comfort components and the results of the previous steps of ACONIT are the main reasons of the choice of a hierarchical model. A hierarchical model is defined from various levels, the highest level representing the global purpose. Within our framework, the highest level represents the comfort in the train which is decomposed in different parts named *meta-categories* which are decomposed in smaller parts, entitled *categories*, and so on. Such a model can be represented in a graphic way by a tree where the root represents the global purpose, nodes are the main components of the global purpose and leaves (nodes having no branches) are the components of the lowest level.

The choice of a hierarchy has certain advantages, interested readers may find some examples of such models in Bouyssou et al. (2000):

- We obtain a simple representation of our model.
- The decomposition at several levels facilitates the procedures of aggregation because within models having only a single level (thus not hierarchical) each leave must be analyzed at the same stage, whereas with the hierarchical models the procedure follows step by step, beginning from the lowest level towards the highest.
- The levels facilitate also the comprehension of the results and provide supplementary information (for example we could come to a point where in order to improve the global comfort; in order to improve the seating comfort and to improve the seating comfort, the seat being very satisfactory, it will be necessary to improve the arm-rest, etc.).

The construction of the hierarchy of comfort is done by the help of data of previous steps of ACONIT:

- We used basically the hierarchy determined by a PhD thesis Delepaut (2007).
- During the PhD research work a dependency analysis between different comfort components is also done. Some "father and son" and "brothers" dependencies are found during this analysis, which helped us to define the relations between some categories and meta-categories.
- Answers in inquiries to some questions which are directly related to one of the meta-categories showed also "father and son" relations.

The basic levels of the hierarchical model of the comfort components proposed in this study is presented in Table 16.2. Five meta-categories are retained: *sensorial comfort, seating comfort, stand up comfort, activity* and *services*. These meta-categories have a number of categories which are also shown in Table 16.2. Some of these categories could be again divided in subcategories, because of space lake we only showed the sub-categories related to seating comfort in Table 16.2 since we will develop only the aggregation of seating comfort components in the rest of this paper.

Briefly, we are interested in a feasibility analysis of a multicriteria decision aiding tool for the evaluation of the comfort for call for tenders. This evaluation aims to assign suppliers' offers into different categories representing the level of comfort of their proposition. Our feasibility analysis is limited to the case of second class coaches of high speed trains with only one level. Our model shows that global comfort can be divided into five meta-categories which are then divided into categories which are divided into sub-categories. For sake of places and in order to give some precision we will present in the rest of this article the evaluation of one of the meta-categories, seating comfort; the evaluation of the others being similar. The choice of seating comfort is related to its importance and its complexity. It has many categories with different nature and its categories are generally divided into sub-categories. These subcategories being not object of answers to the inquiries do not appear in the first part of our article. They were determined after some meetings between people from acquisition, sensorial and comfort departments. The majority of these sub-categories were already mentioned in old calls for tenders, they will be presented in detail in the next section.

16.4 Value Scales for Seating Comfort

Components of *seating comfort* have different nature, for instance qualitative or quantitative data may be used. Such a diversity may impose the use of different types of scale for different components. The construction of such scales being an important step of our analysis, we devote this section to this issue. The interested reader can find some details on different types of scales in Appendix 1.

Before giving more detail about different types of scales used in our analysis, we present first of all different categories (and their sub-categories) of *seating comfort*:

- *arm-rest:* Its evaluation is done by sensorial experts who classify it among five options: *bad, not bad, normal, good* and *very good*.
- *head-rest:* Its evaluation is the result of an aggregation of the evaluation of two sub-categories named *angle of head-rest* and *sensorial of head-rest*. Such an aggregation is used in order to class an object into three ordered categories: *bad head-rest comfort, normal head-rest comfort* and *good head-rest comfort*.
  i. *angle:* Its evaluation is done by binary data: 1 when travellers can change the angle of the head-rest and 0 otherwise.
  ii. *sensorial:* Its evaluation (integrating maximal acceptable pressure in the contact area, the repartition of soft material and resistance to damages) is done by sensorial experts who give scores between 0 and 10 (10 being the best score).
- *back comfort:* Its evaluation is the result of an aggregation of the evaluation of five sub-categories named *width, length, hardness, uniformity* and *angle*. Such an aggregation is used in order to have five ordered categories for *back comfort*:
  i. *width:* This is the width while seated its value is presented in *mm* and the minimum acceptable value for SNCF is 450mm.
  ii. *length:* This is the width while seated *en charge*, its value is presented in *mm*.
  iii. *hardness:* This is the hardness of the *dossier* and *fessier*. It is evaluated by sensorial experts and graded between 10 and 0 (10 being the best score).
  iv. *uniformity:* It shows the presence or absence of hard parts. It is evaluated by sensorial experts and graded between 10 and 0 (10 being the best score).
  v. *angle:* As the angle of head-rest, its evaluation is done by binary data: 1 when travellers can change the angle of the back of the seat and 0 otherwise
- *leg comfort:* Its evaluation is the distance between the seat and foot-rest (in *mm*).

- *back seat net:* Its evaluation is done by sensorial experts who give notes between 0 and 10 (10 being the best score).
- *garbage:* Its evaluation is the result of an aggregation of the evaluation of its two sub-categories named *size* and *ergonomics*. Such an aggregation is used in order to have three ordered categories for *garbage*.

  i. *size:* Its evaluation is qualitative but ordinal with three levels: *small, normal, big*.
  ii. *ergonomics:* Its evaluation is done by sensorial experts who give notes between 0 and 10 (10 being the best score).

- *foot-rest:* Its evaluation is the result of an aggregation of the evaluation of its three sub-categories named *width, slipperiness* and *distance*. Such an aggregation is used in order to have three ordered categories for *foot-rest*.

  i. *width:* Its evaluation is in *mm* and the minimum acceptable value for SNCF is *300* mm.
  ii. *slipperiness:* Its shows the quality of having a non skid surface. The experts evaluate it by three levels: *good, normal, bad*.
  iii. *distance:* This is the distance (in *mm*) between the surface of foot-rest and the sole of the seat.

- *direction:* It shows the presence or absence of double numbering of seats (double numbering enabling the choice of the direction during the reservation). It has a binary evaluation, 1 (resp. 0) representing the presence (resp. absence).
- *movement of train:* Its evaluation is done by sensorial experts who give notes between 0 and 10 (10 being the best score).
- *table:* Its evaluation (score between 0 and 10) is the result of an aggregation of the evaluation of its two sub-categories named *bulk* and *ergonomics*.

  i. *bulk:* Its evaluation is done by sensorial experts who give notes between 0 and 10 (10 being the best score).
  ii. *ergonomics:* Its evaluation is done by sensorial experts who give notes between 0 and 10 (10 being the best score).

Table 16.3 summarizes scales of categories and sub-categories of *seating comfort*.

In order to perform the measures on parent nodes of the hierarchy above presented we may use different procedures, not necessarily the same. The last level aggregation has been done using ELECTRE TRI method (we explain this choice in the following section). Other procedures have also been tested and used for simple aggregation issues.

Table 16.3 Scales of *seating comfort* components and sub-components

Category	Category scale	Sub-category	Sub-category scale
Arm-rest	Bad, not bad, normal, good, very good	–	–
Head-rest	Bad, normal, good	Angle	{0, 1}
		Sensorial	{0, ..., 10}
Back comfort	Bad, not bad, normal, good, very good	Width	[400, 650]
		Length	[500, 700]
		Hardness	{0, ..., 10}
		Uniformity	{0, ..., 10}
		Angle	{0, 1}
Leg comfort	[850, 980],	–	–
Net	{0, ..., 10}	–	–
Garbage	Bad, normal, good	Size	Bad, normal, good
		Ergonomics	{0, ..., 10}
Foot-rest	Bad, normal, good	Width	[200, 600]
		Slipperiness	Bad, normal, good
		Distance	[80, 200]
Direction	{0, 1}	–	–
Train movement	{0, ..., 10}	–	–
Table	{0, ..., 10}	Volume	{0, ..., 10}
		Ergonomics	{0, ..., 10}

16.5 ELECTRE TRI as the Evaluation Tool of Our Study

We are looking for intrinsic evaluation of the offers and not just a ranking. Even if within a ranking approach the comparison of each pair of objects is known, there is no information about the quality level of objects. For instance if a ranking approach provides the following ranking from the best to the worst: *Offer 1, Offer 2, Offer 4* and *Offer 3*, we know that *Offer 1* is at least as good as *Offer 2* but no one can guarantee that *Offer 1* has a "good comfort". The intrinsic evaluation has to be performed despite the presence of quantitative information. This practically amounts to classifying the offers in pre-defined ordered classes; such a problematic is called sorting in the literature.

We chose to work with five categories representing *very bad, bad, intermediate, comfortable, very comfortable* levels. Note that such a categorization is an ordered one by nature and the number of categories may be changed if one wants more or less detailed results. Since categories are ordered (category *comfortable* is at least as good as category *intermediate* etc.) one can separate them with some frontiers. This is what ELECTRE TRI method is doing for classification problem.

16.5.1 Why ELECTRE TRI?

ELECTRE TRI method is a special multicriteria decision aiding tool designed for sorting problems. Sorting problems consist in analyzing the intrinsic value of each object to be classified in order to propose an appropriate recommendation for each one. ELECTRE TRI consists in assigning each object into one class. Classes are ordered (good, intermediate, not good, etc.) and are defined by the decision maker. The characterization of classes is done by the help of frontiers between classes, such frontiers are called limit *limit profiles*.

The assignment of an object into a class is done by the help of the comparison of this object with limit profiles. Objects to be classified are not compared to each other, hence the assignment of one object to a class is completely independent from the evaluation of another object. The comparison between an object and a limit profile is done by a binary relation called *outranking relation*.

The use of the outranking relation, contrary to what happens with classical methods based on the weighted sum principle, rejects the possibility of compensation between different performances of the object according to different criteria (for instance a very good evaluation for *seating comfort* can not compensate for a bad evaluation on *stand up comfort*). Such a compensation interdiction may be important and necessary when a compensation may be related to a very bad evaluation of an important criterion.

On the other hand, compensatory methods need in general the use of the same value scale for all criteria since the decrease of one unit for a criterion may be compensated by the increase of x units of another criterion. In our framework there are different types of scales with different domains, hence such an approach will need supplementary studies in order to define a common scale for all the components. Such a study needs a very strong interaction between different agents of the problem (decision experts, sensorial experts, people from comfort and acquisition department, etc.), can take a long time and may be difficult (for instance we have to be capable to say how many centimeters we have to increase the distance between the foot-rest and the seat if the garbage looses 8 mm^3 of its volume). As in the previous example the compensation may be relatively difficult to be expressed in some cases. Such a task becomes more and more difficult in the presence of qualitative data.

Briefly, the definition of our problem (classification of offers into ordered categories), the nature of comfort components (presence of qualitative data, different value scales and different value domains), our preference to have a non compensatory method and our will to have a method where the classifications of objects are independent from each other are the main reasons of our choice of ELECTRE TRI for our problematic. However as it will be explained in the rest of the paper, the evaluation of offers according to some sub-categories may be done by other methods.

Interested reader can find more details on ELECTRE TRI in Appendix 2.

16.6 Decision Parameters

Let us remind that in this section we are only interested in *seating comfort*.

16.6.1 Importance Parameters

The construction of importance weights for *seating comfort* is based on an analysis done before our study. This analysis is done by the SNCF people and a PhD student on psycholinguistics domain. In their study, the SNCF people calculated the frequency of answers of travellers to some questions. Such frequencies are presented in their study in two parts: the ones related to a positive evaluation of comfort and the others related to a negative evaluation. We use the sum of these frequencies in order to get an idea of the importance of different categories. Table 16.4 shows this evaluation.

16.6.2 Thresholds

Concerning the majority threshold, we choose to make use of the default value of ELECTRE TRI software, 0.76. It means that in order to say that object x is at least as good as a limit profile, at least 76 % of criteria must be in concordance with this affirmation (naturally after the weighting).

Veto thresholds help us to give up an assignment into a class if the offer is not strong enough according to one or more important criteria even if the majority (more then 76 % of criteria) is for this assignment. We decided to define three veto thresholds for the most important criteria, *back comfort*, *leg comfort* and *train*

Table 16.4 Frequency of answers and weights

	Positive answers	Negative answers	Total answers	Weight
Arm-rest	1	2	3	3/176
Head-rest	0	5	5	5/176
Back comfort	37	25	62	62/176
Leg comfort	2	42	44	44/176
Net	0	3	3	3/176
Garbage	0	5	5	5/176
Foot-rest	3	2	5	5/176
Direction	1	7	8	8/176
Train movem.	4	27	31	31/176
Table	4	6	10	10/176
Total	52	124	176	1

movement. We set these thresholds to 1 for the two first components and to 3 for the last one. A veto threshold fixed to 1 represents a very strong demand for the evaluation of its criterion. For instance, concerning the *seating comfort*, if the limit profile between the classes *very good* and *good* requires a *very good* evaluation for *back comfort*, an offer having a *normal* evaluation for *back comfort*, it can never be classed into the *very good seating comfort* class. Note that the smaller is the veto threshold, the stronger is its power.

The introduction of indifference thresholds is not judged necessary because of the small number of levels of scales.

16.6.3 Limit Profiles

The limit profiles are imaginary objects representing the limit between two consecutive classes. Figure 16.1 shows a graphical representation of classes where g_i represents the ith criterion, C_k the kth class and a_j the limit profile between the classes C_{j-1} and C_j. The limit profiles a_0 and a_m are omitted in our study.

We define five ordered classes for *seating comfort* and call them *very bad, bad, normal, good* and *very good*. Four limit profiles, a_1, a_2, a_3 and a_4 are defined in order to separate these classes. The profile a_1 separates the class *very bad* from the class *bad*, the profile a_2 separates the class *bad* from the class *normal*, etc. The evaluation of profiles for *seating comfort* components is shown in Table 16.5. Naturally these evaluations depend on the value scales defined in Sect. 16.4. A graphical representation of classes can be found in Fig. 16.2.

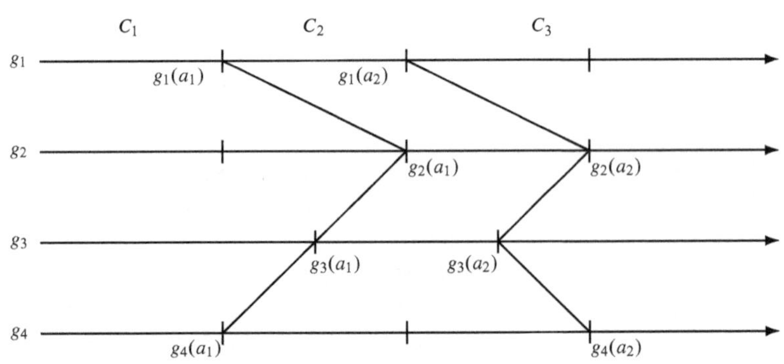

Fig. 16.1 General graphical representation of classes

Table 16.5 Presentation of limit profiles for *seating comfort*

	Frontier a_1	Frontier a_2	Frontier a_3	Frontier a_4
	Bad-not bad	Not bad-normal	Normal-good	Good-very good
Arm-rest	Not bad	Normal	Good	Very good
Head-rest	Normal	Normal	Good	Good
Back comfort	Not bad	Normal	Good	Very good
Leg comfort	Not bad	Normal	Good	Very good
Net	4	6	7	9
Garbage	Normal	Normal	Good	Good
Foot-rest	Normal	Normal	Good	Good
Direction	0	0	1	1
Train movem.	4	5	6	8
Table	4	5	6	8

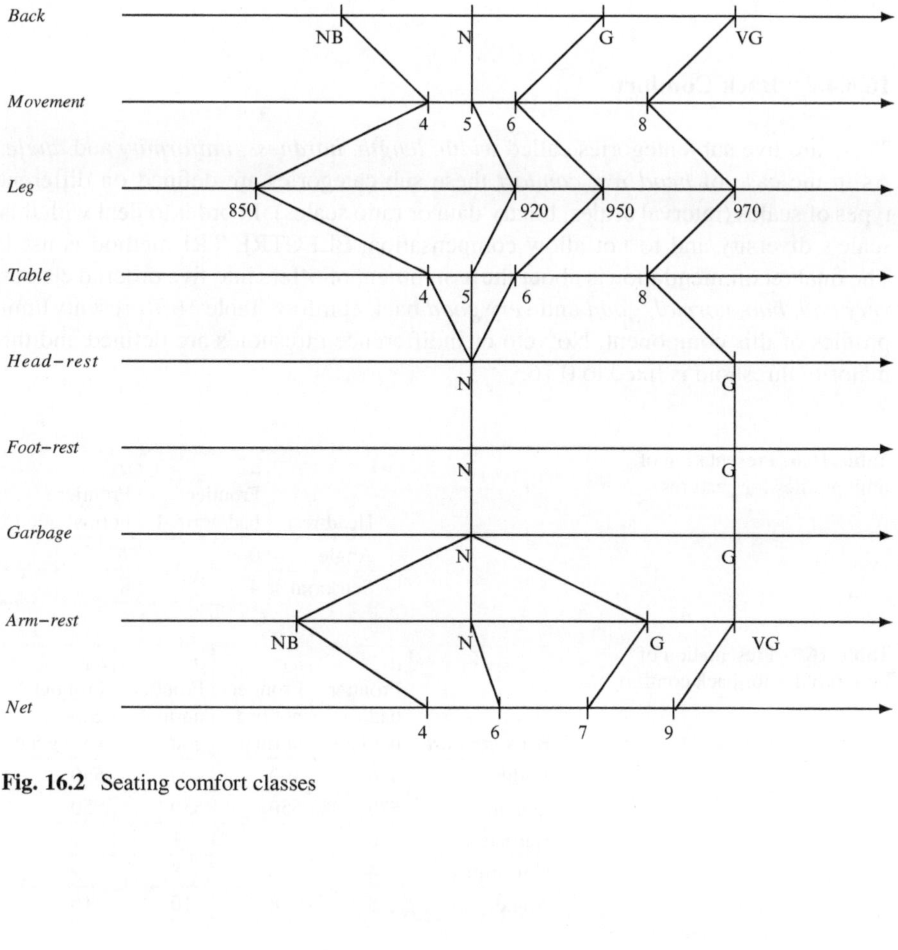

Fig. 16.2 Seating comfort classes

16.6.4 Aggregation of Sub-Categories

Some of *seating comfort* components have sub-components. The evaluation of these components may be done by different aggregation methods on their sub-components. We present in the following these aggregation methods.

16.6.4.1 Head-Rest Comfort

There are two sub-categories: *angle* and *sensorial*. These sub-categories are defined with different types of scales (binary data for *angle* and scores given by experts for *sensorial*) and the final recommendation on *head-rest comfort* is a classification in three ordered classes (*bad, normal* and *good*). The ELECTRE TRI method is used for the aggregation. Table 16.6 presents limit profiles of this component. No veto or indifference thresholds are defined and the majority threshold is fixed to 0.76.

16.6.4.2 Back Comfort

There are five sub-categories called *width, length, hardness, uniformity* and *angle*. As in the case of *head-rest comfort* these sub-categories are defined on different types of scales (interval scales, binary data or ratio scales). In order to deal with this scale's diversity and to not allow compensation, ELECTRE TRI method is used. The final recommendation is about the assignment of offers into five ordered classes *very bad, bad, normal, good* and *very good* back comfort. Table 16.7 presents limit profiles of this component. No veto or indifference thresholds are defined and the majority threshold is fixed to 0.76.

Table 16.6 Presentation of limit profiles for head-rest

Head-rest	a_1 Frontier bad/normal	a_2 Frontier normal/good
Angle	0	1
Sensorial	4	8

Table 16.7 Presentation of limit profiles for back comfort

Back comfort	a_1 Frontier bad not bad	a_2 Frontier not bad normal	a_3 Frontier normal good	a_4 Frontier good very good
Width	450	460	480	550
Length	530	550	550	550
Hardness	0	1	1	1
Uniformity	4	6	8	9
Angle	8	8	10	10

Table 16.8 Presentation of limit profiles for garbage

Garbage	a_1 Frontier bad/normal	a_2 Frontier normal/good
Size	Normal	Big
Ergonomics	5	8

Table 16.9 Presentation of limit profiles for foot-rest

Foot-rest	a_1 Frontier bad/normal	a_2 Frontier normal/good
Width (mm)	300	400
Slipperiness	Normal	Good
Distance (mm)	130	130

Table 16.10 Substitution rates for table

Table	Substitution rate (w_i)
Volume	0.5
Ergonomics	0.5

16.6.4.3 Foot-Rest and Garbage Comforts

There exist two sub-categories, *size* and *ergonomics*, for the component *garbage* and three sub-categories, *width, slipperiness* and *distance*, for the component *foot-rest*. Again for scale and non compensation reasons and the final recommendation being a classification, ELECTRE TRI method is used for these two components. Tables 16.8 and 16.9 present the limit profiles of classes.

16.6.4.4 Table Comfort

There are two sub-categories, *volume* and *ergonomics*, both of them defined on a ratio scale ($\{0, \ldots, 10\}$) representing the scores given by experts. The aggregation method must provide a score for *table comfort* as it is shown in Table 16.3. For this aggregation a weighted sum is used with the substitution rates presented in Table 16.10. The score of *table comfort* of an offer x, denoted for instance by $g(x)$ is calculated by $g(x) = \sum_i w_i g_i(x)$ where $g_i(x)$ presents the score of x for the sub-component i and w_i presents the substitution rate of the sub-component i.

16.7 Examples

In this section we present three imaginary offers and analyze their classification into different classes. These examples are prepared in order to illustrate and explain principles of ELECTRE TRI (veto threshold, incomparability, optimistic and pessimistic procedures, etc.). Table 16.11 represents evaluations of these three offers for *seating comfort* components and sub-components.

In the following we will focus on the aggregation of components, the aggregation of sub-components being easier a good comprehension of the one of components will be sufficient in order to master the aggregation of sub-components.

16.7.1 Assignment of Offer 1 to the Class Normal Seating Comfort

We analyse outranking relations between *Offer 1* and limit profiles for optimistic and pessimistic procedure:

- *Pessimistic procedure*: The procedure compares first of all the offer to the limit profile a_4 and then to a_3, a_2 etc. and stops when the offer outranks a limit profile. *Offer 1* does not outrank profiles a_4 and a_3 and is indifferent to profile a_2 (indifference being a part of the outranking relation—x outranks y if and only if x is preferred to y or x and y are indifferent—*Offer 1* outranks a_2). Hence the procedure stops and *Offer 1* is assigned to *normal seating comfort* class.
- *Optimistic procedure*: The procedure begins by comparing *Offer 1* to the limit profile a_1 (profile separating the lowest class C_1 from C_2), if limit profile is not preferred to *Offer 1*, the comparison procedure continues, *Offer 1* is compared to a_2, a_3, etc. limit profile a_1 is outranked by *Offer 1*, a_2 and *Offer 1* are indifferent and *Offer 1* is outranked from a_3; hence the procedure stops and *Offer 1* is assigned to *normal seating comfort* class.

Table 16.11 presents the evaluation of *Offer 1* for *seating comfort* components. This, together with Table 16.5, shows that the evaluation of *Offer 1* for *back comfort, train movement* and *leg comfort* are higher than the ones of limit profile existing between classes *not bad* and *normal*. Hence we conclude that if the supplier wants to improve his offer he must ameliorate his offer from the *table* point of view and reach 6 on the respective scale, *table* being one of the important *seating comfort* components.

16.7.2 Assignment of Offer 2 to the Class Good Seating Comfort

Table 16.11 presents the evaluation of *Offer 2* for *seating comfort* components. It is easy to remark that the veto threshold on *leg comfort* has a strong influence on the assignment of *Offer 2* to the *not bad seating comfort* class. The evaluations of *Offer 2* are at least as good as (better than or preferred to) all the evaluations of the limit profile a_4 except the one of *leg comfort*. Thank to these good evaluations *Offer 2*

Table 16.11 Evaluation of three offers as examples

		Offer 1		Offer 2	
		Sub-categories	Global	Sub-categories	Global
Arm-rest		–	Normal	–	Good
Head-rest	Angle	0	Normal	1	Good
	Sensorial	4		8	
Back comfort	Width	500	Normal	510	Good
	Length	540		550	
	Angle	1		1	
	Hardness	6		6	
	Uniformity	8		10	
Leg comfort		–	940	–	980
Net		–	2	–	8
Garbage	Size	Normal	Bad	Normal	Normal
Foot-rest	Ergonomie	4		9	
	Width	420	Good	422	Good
	Distance	125		130	
	Being slip	Good		Normal	
Direction		–	0	–	1
Train movement		–	5	–	8
Table	Bluck	5	4	6	8
	Ergonomie	5		10	

		Offer 3	
		Sub-categories	Global
Arm-rest		–	Normal
Head-rest	Angle	1	Normal
	Sensorial	7	
Back comfort	Width	560	Verygood
	Length	550	
	Angle	1	
	Hardness	9	
	Uniformity	10	
Leg comfort		–	930
Net		–	6
Garbage	Size	Bad	Bad
Foot-rest	Ergonomics	6	
	Width	430	Good
	Distance	131	
	Being slip	Good	
Direction		–	1
Train movement		–	5
Table	Bluck	7	7
	Ergonomie	7	

obtains a majority coalition in his favor against a_4 however the category *leg comfort* puts his veto to the outranking of a_4 by *Offer2*. Hence *Offer 2*, instead of being classified into the *very good seating comfort* class is classified only into the *good seating comfort* class. This example shows the importance of veto thresholds for imposing very good evaluations. In this example, if the supplier wants to ameliorate his offer he must improve his offer from *leg comfort* point of view.

16.7.3 Assignment of Offer 3 to Two Different Classes Not Bad Seating Comfort and Good Seating Comfort

We analyze outranking relations between *Offer 3* and limit profiles for optimistic and pessimistic procedure since these two procedures do not provide the same assignment. Table 16.11 presents the evaluation of *Offer 3* for *seating comfort* components.

- *Pessimistic procedure*: The procedure compares first of all the offer to the limit profile a_4, *Offer3* does not outrank a_4. Then for the comparison of *Offer3* and a_3 and a_2 we get incomparabilities. The procedure continues, *Offer3* outranks a_1, hence the procedure stops and *Offer3* is assigned to *not bad seating comfort* class.
- *Optimistic procedure*: The procedure begins by comparing *Offer 1* to the limit profile a_1 which does not outrank *Offer3*. Limit profiles a_2 and a_3 do not outrank *Offer 3* because of the incomparabilities. The profile a_4 is preferred to *Offer 3*, hence the procedure stops and *Offer3* is affected to *good seating comfort* class.

This example shows the role of incomparabilities in the assignment difference.

16.8 Conclusion

In this paper we presented a real word application of multicriteria decision aiding: Evaluating suppliers offers to call for tenders from the comfort point of view. Our study is used as a feasibility analysis for the introduction of multicriteria tools in the SNCF. The results found in our study are judged to be interesting by the SNCF who wants now to use similar approaches for the evaluation of other comfort aspect and/or other components of offers to call for tenders.

The complex nature of comfort is presented here by the help of a hierarchical model, in this paper we showed how and why to use such a model. The presence of different types of data,—qualitative, quantitative, binary, etc.—is handled by the use of different methods on different nodes of the comfort hierarchy, with a special interest on outranking methods. The overall assessment resulting from the hierarchical aggregation of the values helped the SNCF to classify the suppliers offers into five comfort categories. Such a classification gives information about the quality of offers and helps also to conduct negotiation with suppliers.

Appendix 1

For more details, see Roberts (1979).

A *scale* (or measurement scale) is a couple formed by a set of numbers, called *echelon*, used to code an information relative to objects. There exist different types of scales:

Ordinal scale: An ordinal scale is a measurement scale that assigns values to objects based on their ranking with respect to one another. It defines a total preorder of objects (objects are ranked from the worst one to the best one and there can be more than one objects in one ranking level). The scale values themselves have a total order; qualitative nouns may be used like "bad","medium","good", etc. If numbers are used they are only relevant up to strictly monotonically increasing transformations. For instance one can define an ordinal scale for global comfort with five echelons: very comfortable, comfortable, normal, not bad and very bad and put numbers like "5" for very comfortable, "3" for comfortable, etc.

Interval scale: On interval measurement scales, one unit on the scale represents the same magnitude on the trait or characteristic being measured across the whole range of the scale. For instance, if *pleasure* were measured on an interval scale, then a difference between a score of "10" and a score of "11" would represent the same difference in *pleasure* as would a difference between a score of "50" and a score of "51". Interval scales do not have a "true" zero point and therefore it is not possible to make statements about how many times higher one score is than another. For the *pleasure* scale, it would not be valid to say that a person with a score of "30" was twice as pleased as a person with a score of "15". Hence if f is a representation for an interval scale, all the other acceptable representations will be in form of $\alpha f + \beta$. A classical example of an interval scale is the Fahrenheit scale for temperature. Equal differences on this scale represent equal differences in temperature, but a temperature of 30° is not twice as warm as one of 15°.

Ratio scale: A ratio measurement scale is a scale in which a certain distance along the scale means the same thing no matter where on the scale you are, and where "0" on the scale represents the absence of the thing being measured. Thus a "4" on such a scale implies twice as much of the thing being measured as a "2." Hence if f is a representation of a ratio scale, all the other acceptable representations will be in form of αf. A classical example of a ratio scale is the metric scale for distance.

Appendix 2: General Presentation of Electre TRI

The general procedure of ELECTRE TRI has two consecutive steps:

- construction of a binary relation establishing how alternatives are compared to the boundaries of classes,
- exploitation (through assignment procedures) of the binary relation in order to assign each alternative to a specific class.

We present first of all the first step consisting in comparing alternatives to profiles representing the frontiers between ordered categories. We will note by X the set of objects to be classified (for instance suppliers' offers), $X = \{x_1, x_2, \ldots, x_n\}$, and by $A = \{a_0, a_2, \ldots, a_m\}$ the set of limit profiles. Let us denote by $C = \{C_1, C_2, \ldots, C_m\}$ the set of classes, the class C_1 being the worst one and C_m the best one etc. If we have m classes, we will have $m + 1$ limit profiles where a_0 (resp. a_m) represents a fictive profile having the worst (resp. the best) evaluation on each criterion while a limit profile a_i, $i \in \{1, 2, \ldots, m-1\}$, represents the frontier between the classes C_i and C_{i+1}. The comparison between two elements x and y (x may represent an object and y a limit profile or the inverse) is done by an outranking relation denoted by S. The affirmation xSy (or $S(x, y)$) means that "the element x is at least as good as the element y" and is calculated using two indices, the *Concordance* and the *Discordance* index. One can find different, more or less refined, definition of such indices in the literature but all of them are based on the same following idea:

- *Concordance index:* shows if there is a sufficiently strong majority of criteria in favor of the outranking relation;
- *Discordance index:* shows if there is at least one criterion "strongly opposed" to the outranking relation (in such a case we say that the criterion has a veto for the outranking relation).

In the following we note $C(S(x, y))$ (resp. $D(S(x, y))$) in order to say that there is a concordance (resp. discordance) for the outranking $S(x, y)$. Hence the relation $S(x, y)$ is verified if there is concordance but not discordance:

$$xSy \text{ if and only if } C(S(x, y)) \text{ and not } D(S(x, y))$$

We will present in the following a classical formula of concordance and discordance indices. An interested reader can find more detailed explanations on the subject in Roy (1996); Roy and Bouyssou (1993). The calculation of these indices makes use of different parameters such as importance weight of a criterion, indifference threshold, veto threshold and majority threshold.

$$C(x, y) \iff \frac{\sum_{j \in J_{xy}} w_j}{\sum_j w_j} \geq \gamma, \tag{16.1}$$

$$D(x, y) \iff \exists j : g_j(y) - g_j(x) > v_j \tag{16.2}$$

where:

- g_j is a real valued function representing the evaluation of alternatives with respect to the criterion c_j (to be maximized);
- w_j is a non negative coefficient which represents the importance of the criterion c_j;
- J_{xy} represents the set of criteria for which x is at least as good as y; more precisely, $J_{xy} = \{j : g_j(y) - g_j(x) \leq q_j\}$ where q_j is the indifference threshold associated to criterion c_j;
- γ is a majority threshold;
- v_j is a veto threshold on criterion c_j;

The majority threshold represents the minimum percentage of criteria (weighted according to their importance) needed in order to have a concordance. The veto threshold is used for the discordance index and represents for each criteria the threshold for which a difference of evaluation on this criterion becomes problematic for the construction of the outranking relation. The indifference threshold represents the maximum tolerated difference between evaluations of two objects x and y in order to say that x and y are indifferent. In what follows, we will assume, without any loss of generality, that preferences increase with the value on each criterion.

It is easy to see that comparing two objects x and y, four situations may appear:

- xSy and not ySx: we say that "x is preferred to y";
- not xSy and ySx: we say that "y is preferred to x";
- xSy and ySx: we say that "x and y are indifferent";
- not xSy and not ySx: we say that "x and y" can not be compared;

The last case shows that the outranking relation is not necessary a complete relation, this relation does not satisfy any special property other than reflexivity.

After the construction of all comparisons between alternatives and profiles, the exploitation procedure begins. The role of the exploitation procedure is to analyze the way which an alternative x compares to subsequent profiles in order to determine the class to which x should be assigned. ELECTRE TRI proposes two different assignment procedures:

- *the pessimistic assignment procedure*:

  i. compare x successively to limit profiles a_i, for $i \in \{p, p-1, \ldots, 0\}$,
  ii. a_h being the first profile such that xSa_h, assign x to class C_{h+1}.

  If a_{h-1} and a_h denote the lower and upper profile of the category C_h, the pessimistic procedure assigns alternative a to the highest class C_h such that x outranks a_{h-1}, i.e., xSa_{h-1}.
- *the optimistic assignment procedure* :

  i. compare x successively to a_i, for $i \in \{1, 2, \ldots, p\}$,
  ii. a_h being the first profile such that a_{hSx} and not xSa_h (i.e. x is preferred to a_h), assign x to class C_h.

  The optimistic procedure assigns x to the lowest class C_h for which the upper profile a_h is preferred to x.

The ideas that ground the two assignment procedures being different, these assignment procedures might assign some alternatives to different classes. The difference is basically related to the partial nature of the outranking relation, more precisely:

- when the evaluation of an alternative is between the two profiles of a class on each criterion, then both procedures assign this alternative to this class,
- a divergence exists among the results of the two assignment procedures only when an alternative is incomparable to one or several profiles; in such a case the pessimistic assignment rule assigns the alternative to a lower class than the optimistic one.

References

Bouyssou, D., Marchant, T., Pirlot, M., Perny, P., Tsoukiàs, A., & Vincke, P. (2000). *Evaluation and decision models: A critical perspective*. Dordrecht: Kluwer Academic.

Delepaut, G. (2007). *Contribution de la linguistique cognitive à l'identification du confort: analyse des discours des passagers sur le confort en train*. PhD thesis, 2007. Thèse de doctorat, Université Paris 3.

Roberts, F. S. (1979). *Measurement theory, with applications to decision making, utility and the social sciences*. Boston: Addison-Wesley.

Roy, B. (1996). *Multicriteria methodology for decision aiding*. Dordrecht: Kluwer Academic.

Roy, B., & Bouyssou, D. (1993). *Aide Multicritère à la Décision: Méthodes et Cas*. Paris: Economica.

Editors' Comments on "On the Use of a Multicriteria Decision Aiding Tool for the Evaluation of Comfort"

Özturk, Tsoukiàs, and Guerrand address an evaluation problem in the context of an important activity in many organizations: procurement. This chapter starts by presenting the problem definition and formulation stages (see Chap. 2), and then describes the definition and application of an aggregation procedure to a particular subproblem within a large project. This work illustrates the sorting problematic based on a variant of the ELECTRE TRI method (see Chap. 4, Sect. 4.4.4). In this case, ELECTRE TRI is used to evaluate alternatives according to a specific axis of evaluation, corresponding to one high-level criterion among other criteria. It therefore describes how the evaluation of a single (top-level) criterion can originate further aggregation problems concerning different aspects that need to be taken into account concerning that criterion, which in turn can be further decomposed in a hierarchical structure.

The French railways company SNCF, the **client** of this study, needs to evaluate the comfort of trains not only to select suppliers but also to define specifications in calls for tenders. The **objective of the intervention** was to improve a simplistic evaluation method used by the client, using comfort evaluation as a case study to demonstrate the value of a thorough MCDA study.

The decision process involved directly many **actors**: experts in decision aiding (**the analysts**), an expert in psycholinguistics, and company experts from the comfort and acquisition departments. Actors involved indirectly were the train passengers, whose voice was heard.

Several **stages** can be identified in this intervention: analysis of passenger survey data, definition of the evaluation criteria, definition of parameter values of the model, and application of the model. Among different dimensions of comfort, this chapter focusses on the passenger experience on the train. The hierarchy of **criteria** was developed based on a content analysis of passenger survey answers about what they value in terms of comfort, as well as on previous knowledge of the client organization. There were five top-level criteria which are subdivided into many more elementary attributes of the train. It is interesting to note that the same type of content analysis was used to define the criteria weights, under the assumption that aspects mentioned more often would correspond to higher importance for the passengers, instead of following a typical **elicitation process**. The analysts deemed these weights were acceptable and they set the remaining parameters of the evaluation model. This weight elicitation could be improved by performing new surveys based on the final list of criteria, possibly based on choosing among alternatives as often is the case in transportation research (Hensher 1994; Louviere 1988). Nevertheless, in their conclusions the authors warn that an implementation of this tool will require dealing with divergent opinions and performing sensitivity analysis.

The authors opted for a sorting **problem statement** because they intended to evaluate the intrinsic merit of potential offers in a call for tenders from the comfort viewpoint. This means they did not intend to select the most comfortable option, or to rank the options in terms of comfort. Actually, the chosen method, ELECTRE TRI, was used as a means to obtain a qualitative scale (this is a common use for ELECTRE TRI, see e.g., André and Roy 2007). ELECTRE TRI was the chosen **aggregation method**, using a simplified outranking relation which is slightly different from the one used in Chap. 15 in this book. The choice of ELECTRE TRI, besides fitting the sorting problem statement, is also justified for being a noncompensatory method, not requiring the definition of substitution rates among the criteria. ELECTRE TRI also presents the advantage of allowing the use of veto thresholds. Such thresholds can be used to prevent that an offer which is very bad in one of the subcriteria reaches a high category, which is a quite realistic requirement when we are dealing with comfort assessment. For most lower levels in the hierarchy, ELECTRE TRI was again used to aggregate subcriteria, but in some simpler cases a weighted sum was used.

As an illustration, the authors evaluate a **set of alternatives** consisting of three fictitious offers (confidentiality agreements do not allow presenting the true alternatives). These examples are characterized by a list of their characteristics in the comfort-related attributes, and are then sorted into their respective categories. Such categories correspond to qualitative grades that can be taken into account for a global evaluation of each offer considering other dimensions besides comfort.

The **tangible results** of this decision process were the definition of a criteria hierarchy and the characterization of an ELECTRE TRI sorting model—using inputs from the passengers—for building a global comfort scale. Concerning **intangible results**, the client understood the methodology as being useful, wishing to use it again in the future, and to extend it to other evaluation problems.

As for the **relevance** of this chapter, it demonstrates how the evaluation of alternatives under a single criterion (in this case comfort) can be in itself a complex MCDA problem. It also illustrates that the list of criteria does not necessarily have to be elicited from the client. Other stakeholders, in this case the train passengers, can be the source of the criteria list and contribute to the inclusion of aspects that might otherwise not be valued.

References

André, S., & Roy, B. (2007). Le cas des raffineries de la société Total. *Journal of Decision Systems, 16*(3), 335–367.

Hensher, D. (1994). Stated preference analysis of travel choices: The state of practice. *Transportation, 21*, 107–133.

Louviere, J. (1988). Conjoint analysis modelling of stated preferences: A review of theory, methods, recent developments and external validity. *Journal of Transport Economics and Policy, 22*, 93–119.

Chapter 17
An MCDA Approach for Evaluating Hydrogen Storage Systems for Future Vehicles

Florent Montignac, Vincent Mousseau, Denis Bouyssou, Mohamed Ali Aloulou, Benjamin Rousval, and Sébastien Damart

Abstract Hydrogen, a non carbonated energy carrier, is often considered as one possible solution to reduce greenhouse gas emissions from human activity. The use of hydrogen as a possible alternative fuel for automotive applications is envisaged by car manufacturers. However, before a large scale commercialization of hydrogen vehicles, numerous challenges have to be faced, among which the on-board storage of hydrogen. This paper provides a description of the implementation of an MCDA approach for evaluating various competing hydrogen storage technologies for future vehicles. This implementation has been conducted within the STORHY European research project. The MACBETH method has been identified as an appropriate approach for the evaluation and comparison of the technologies from a technical point of view. The evaluation process has been entirely implemented on one hand with several experts from CEA and on the other hand with one of the STORHY car manufacturers. The implementation within the project confirmed that this evaluation method could be used for "application-oriented" multicriteria evaluations. The advantages and drawbacks of the method are finally discussed.

F. Montignac
CEA, LITEN, 17 rue des Martyrs, Grenoble, France
e-mail: florent.montignac@cea.fr

V. Mousseau (✉)
Laboratoire Génie Industriel, Ecole Centrale Paris, Grande Voie des Vignes, 92295 Châtenay-Malabry Cedex, France
e-mail: vincent.mousseau@ecp.fr

D. Bouyssou • M.A. Aloulou • B. Rousval
LAMSADE, Université Paris Dauphine, Place De Lattre de Tassigny, 75775 Paris, France
e-mail: bouyssou@lamsade.dauphine.fr; aloulou@lamsade.dauphine.fr; rousval@lamsade.dauphine.fr

S. Damart
Département d'administration économique et sociale, Université de Rouen, 3, avenue Pasteur CS 46186, 76186 Rouen Cedex 1, France
e-mail: sebastien.damart@univ-rouen.fr

R. Bisdorff et al. (eds.), *Evaluation and Decision Models with Multiple Criteria*, International Handbooks on Information Systems,
DOI 10.1007/978-3-662-46816-6_17

17.1 Introduction

The intensive worldwide use of carbonated fossil fuels (oil, natural gas, coal) in human activities since the early twentieth century led to a remarkable increase of the CO_2 atmospheric concentration. This strong increase of the greenhouse gases emissions is considered to be responsible for the climate change phenomenon we are facing with (see IPCC 2007). In order to limit the intensity of this phenomenon and to protect the environment, the urgent development of new CO2-free energy technologies is required. Hydrogen energy is one possible alternative to the use of carbonated fossil fuels (see Goltsov and Veziroglu 2002; Goltsov et al. 2006; Cherry 2004; Dunn 2002; Ewan and Allen 2005). Hydrogen gas can be produced from various CO_2-free primary energy sources such as solar, wind or nuclear energies. It can be potentially used as a transportation fuel in hydrogen fuel cell cars; it can also be converted in fuel cell stationary systems for residential and industrial heat and electricity generation. Today transportation sector is the subject of intensive contribution to the CO_2 emissions from human activity and the implementation of hydrogen as a transportation fuel is the object of intensive research and development activities. One of the most crucial research topics in the field of automotive applications is the storage of hydrogen (Schlapbach and Zuttel, 2001). In ambient conditions, hydrogen, as a gas, is characterized by a particularly low volumetric energy density in comparison with conventional liquid carbonated fossil fuels such as gasoline. In order to increase the volumetric energy density, various hydrogen storage technologies are being investigated by car manufacturers: compressed gaseous hydrogen storage, liquid hydrogen storage and solid storage of hydrogen. Today, none of these three alternatives totally fulfils all the requirements specified by car manufacturers and a strong need of evaluation and comparison of the performance and potential of these technologies is expressed by stakeholders in the field of hydrogen technologies. Within this study, the three main hydrogen storage technologies (compressed, liquid and solid) were evaluated and compared using an MCDA approach. This study was achieved within the European research project "STORHY" (Hydrogen Storage Systems for Automotive Application). The general objectives of this project are presented in Sect. 17.2. The reasons for choosing MACBETH evaluation method for evaluating and comparing the technical performance of hydrogen storage systems are reported in Sect. 17.3 . The implementation of the method within the project is then discussed. Finally in Sect. 17.4 some comments on this case study and on the decision aiding process are formulated.

17.2 General Framework of the Study: The STORHY European Project

17.2.1 The STORHY European Project

The study described in this article has been conducted within the European research project "STORHY" (Hydrogen Storage Systems for Automotive Application). This project was an Integrated Project (IP) of the sixth Framework Programme involving thirty-four partners (private companies, public research centres and universities) from 13 European countries. It began in March 2004 and ended in August 2008. The central objective of the project was to develop hydrogen storage technologies for automotive application, focusing on (1) 70 MPa compressed hydrogen storage systems, (2) lightweight liquid hydrogen storage systems and (3) improved lightweight materials for solid storage of hydrogen. Complementary to these technological objectives, an evaluation of the performance and safety of these systems has been planned (see Strubel 2008). Thus, the STORHY integrated project has been organized in six sub-projects (Fig. 17.1):

- three of the six sub-projects (SP) dedicated to the technical development of hydrogen storage systems
  - SP Pressure: development of new 70 MPa compressed hydrogen storage systems
  - SP Cryogenic: development of new lightweight liquid hydrogen storage systems
  - SP Solid: development of improved lightweight materials for solid storage of hydrogen
- three sub-projects dedicated to transversal activities
  - SP Users: car manufacturers' requirements

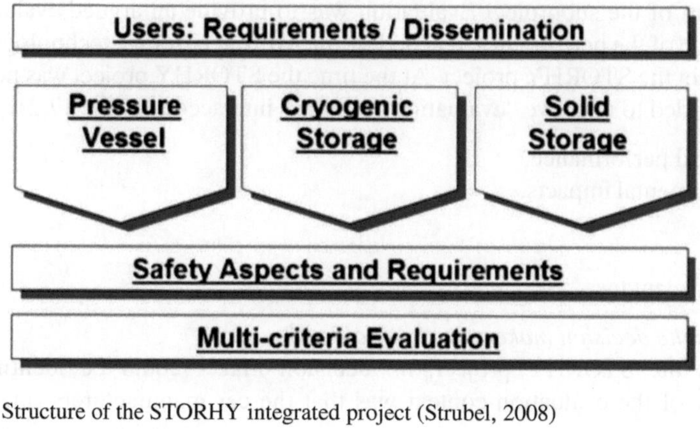

Fig. 17.1 Structure of the STORHY integrated project (Strubel, 2008)

- SP Safety: evaluation of the safety of the hydrogen storage systems
- SP Evaluation: multicriteria evaluation of the hydrogen storage systems

The study described in this article has been conducted within subproject Evaluation. The objectives of this subproject are presented in the following subsection.

17.2.2 The Subproject Evaluation

Why a "subproject Evaluation"?

The reason for involving a subproject dedicated to the multicriteria evaluation was the following: the European Commission asked for an evaluation and comparison of the performance of the hydrogen storage technologies developed within the STORHY project so that the results of such an evaluation could orientate the further financial support towards the remaining technological hurdles before commercialization. The client of the study conducted by the subproject Evaluation was then the European Commission. Using the MCDA terminology, the European Commission was the "client" of the study while the subproject Evaluation was the "analyst" (see Roy 1996).

Formally, the CEA was responsible for the SP evaluation. As the CEA did not have particular expertise in the field of multicriteria evaluation, a team from LAMSADE was hired to assist CEA in the conduct of this SP. This team therefore acted as the "analyst of the analyst". It had no direct access to the various stakeholders of the project. The LAMSADE team worked together with CEA on the SP evaluation for approximately 12 months. As this will be described in 3.3.1, the implementation of the MACBETH multicriteria evaluation method ("*Measuring Attractiveness by a Categorical Based Evaluation TecHnique*" (see Bana e Costa et al. 2005; Bana e Costa and Vansnick 1997a,b) has been conducted by the LAMSADE team on one hand with experts from CEA, and on the other hand with one STORHY car manufacturer.

What was the scope of the evaluation?

The aim of the subproject Evaluation was to provide an argued evaluation and comparison of the performance reached by the hydrogen storage technologies developed within the STORHY project. At the time the STORHY project was negotiated, it was decided to take five "evaluation domains" into account (Fig. 17.2):

- technical performance,
- environmental impacts,
- costs,
- safety,
- social acceptance.

Who were the decision makers or stakeholders?

Within the STORHY project, no decision maker could be identified. The specificity of the evaluation context was that the car manufacturers (identified as

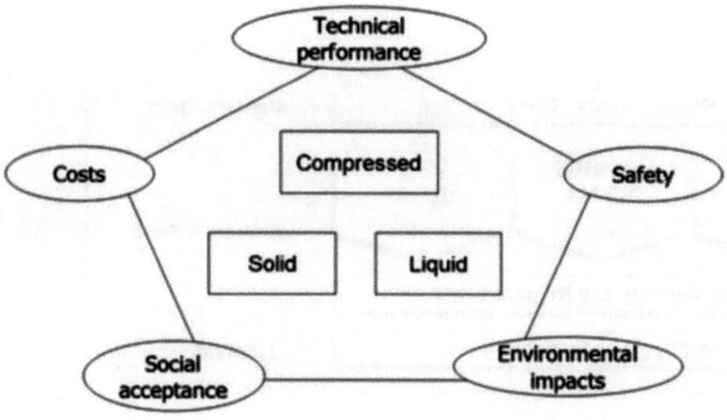

Fig. 17.2 Five evaluation domains taken into account for the evaluation of the H_2 storage technologies

the stakeholders) did not share a unique consensual vision of the requirements for hydrogen storage technologies. Car manufacturers were involved in the whole evaluation process in order to define appropriate evaluation criteria, appropriate final automotive applications and relevant performance targets for hydrogen storage systems. In such a context, the role of the analyst was not to conduct a "decision-aiding process" but rather an "evaluation-aiding process" aiming at providing objective elements of evaluation and comparison. Needless to say that behind STORHY there were huge industrial and commercial stakes. Although car manufacturers were involved in the project, they were comprehensibly reluctant, to openly share information with other members of the project. This explains why the delicate question of managing the multi-actor aspects involved in the SP evaluation could not be explicitly dealt with, within the period in which LAMSADE and CEA collaborated on the project.

What was the role of the other SP?

In addition to the state-of-the-art data found in the literature, the collection of data was carried out with experts from CEA. Moreover, the STORHY technical sub-projects dedicated to the development of the hydrogen storage technologies (sub-projects Pressure, Cryogenic and Solid) and to the study of safety aspects (subproject Safety) also did provide information and expertise.

Summary

Thus, to sum-up using the MCDA terminology, the actors involved in the overall evaluation process were the following (Fig. 17.3):

- the client was the European Commission,
- the stakeholders were the STORHY car manufacturers (subproject Users),
- the analyst of the project was the subproject Evaluation,
- the experts were the technical sub-projects developing the hydrogen storage technologies and providing raw data.

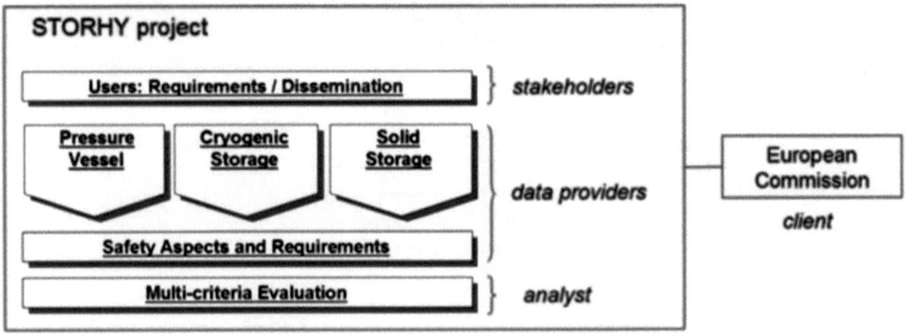

Fig. 17.3 Overview of the actors involved in the multicriteria evaluation study, using the MCDA terminology

17.2.3 Focus on the Evaluation of the Technical Performance

As a result of an early discussion in the project between the analyst (subproject Evaluation) and the stakeholders (subproject Users), it has been decided to emphasize the study on the technical performance of the hydrogen storage systems. The reason for this choice was that the assessment of the "technological feasibility" for hydrogen storage was considered by the stakeholders to be a priority before any other kind of evaluation. Thus, even if all of the evaluation domains specified in Fig. 17.2 have been explored by the SP Evaluation during the STORHY project, the method and results provided in the following sections are focusing especially on the technical performance evaluation domain. Moreover the technical evaluation domain was identified by the LAMSADE and the CEA as an appropriate evaluation domain for the "pilot" implementation of a multicriteria evaluation method provided that this was the most studied evaluation domain among the five envisaged.

In order to model and compare the technical performance of the assessed hydrogen storage technologies (pressure, liquid and solid), a set of five technical evaluation criteria has been defined at the beginning of the project:

- System volume (litres): volume of the whole hydrogen storage system included in the vehicle.
- System mass (kilograms): mass of the whole hydrogen storage system included in the vehicle.
- Refueling time (minutes): time spent by an end-user at the refueling station for a complete filling of the empty hydrogen storage system.
- Hydrogen loss rate (gram per hour per kilogram of hydrogen): amount of hydrogen lost by a filled hydrogen storage system while the vehicle is not used by the end-user.
- Conformability (qualitative criterion): ability of the hydrogen storage system to be shaped in various geometries so that it could be included in existing vehicle architecture.

These criteria, defined in cooperation between the SP Evaluation and the stakeholders, were quantified for various final automotive applications. In this study, we have decided to focus on a particular type of application, that of a "*private fuel cell vehicle application, with a range of 600 km, that is to say a storage capacity of 6 kg of hydrogen on-board*". This means that the evaluation and comparison between the three hydrogen storage technologies (pressure, liquid and solid) has been conducted taking into account a storage capacity of 6 kg of hydrogen.

The next section explains why MACBETH method has been identified as an appropriate approach for the modeling and evaluation of these criteria in the context of the STORHY project and provides an overview of the implementation process of this method.

17.3 MACBETH: Motivation and Brief Description

17.3.1 The Choice of MACBETH

As it has been presented in Sect. 17.2, focus has been made on five evaluation criteria: system volume (litres), system mass (kg), refueling time (min), hydrogen loss rate (g/h/kgH_2) and conformability (qualitative criterion). Three technologies had to be compared (pressure, liquid and solid). The final automotive application that has been chosen for this comparison was a "*private fuel cell vehicle application, with a range of 600 km, that is to say a storage capacity of 6 kg of hydrogen on-board*".

Due to the R&D context of this multicriteria evaluation, the requirements regarding the evaluation method were the following:

- to provide a relative comparison of the performances of the pressure, liquid and solid storage technologies (ranking and gaps of performance between the technologies),
- to provide an absolute assessment of these performances regarding the technical objectives of the car manufacturers (quantified targets),
- to model the notion of "remaining R&D needs",
- to model and process both quantitative (system volume, system mass, hydrogen loss rate, refueling time) and qualitative (conformability) criteria,
- to provide comparable individual formal outputs in situation with multiple stakeholders.

In that case, MACBETH method has been identified as an appropriate method for the evaluation:

- this method fulfils the requirements previously listed,
- the method can be easily implemented thanks to a user-friendly interface (the M-MACBETH software),
- several evaluation models can be built with different stakeholders,

- the questioning procedure in MACBETH is appropriate for taking into account the uncertainties of the raw performance data.

The LAMSADE team considered to use a more ordinal evaluation technique such as ELECTRE TRI (see Roy and Bouyssou 1993; Mousseau et al. 2000). However, it was felt that the people working in the other SP would not accept to work with an evaluation method that would not apparently take explicit advantage of the considerable data gathering that they were making. Hence, the choice of a more "cardinal" approach, such as MACBETH. The principles of this method are provided in the next subsection.

17.3.2 General Principles of MACBETH Method

The MACBETH method (see Bana e Costa et al. 2005; Bana e Costa and Vansnick 1997a,b) relies on a cardinal multicriteria aggregation procedure. Its specificity is that it requires only qualitative judgements about differences of attractiveness of value to help an individual or a group quantify the relative attractiveness of options. At first its aim is to translate the performances $g_i(a)$ of the alternative a regarding each criterion g_i into a new performance $v_i(g_i(a))$ representing the attractiveness of the alternative a on a normalized scale. Secondly "scaling constants" (weights) w_i are determined for each evaluation criterion in order to proceed to a weighted sum of the normalized scales. In other words, considering n evaluation criteria, the performance $v(a)$ of an alternative a can be modeled as:

$$v(a) = \sum_{i=1}^{n} w_i v_i(g_i(a)) \tag{17.1}$$

The implementation of MACBETH method is done interviewing a stakeholder and determining with him/her scales of attractiveness v_i and scaling constants w_i. In the example of the evaluation of hydrogen storage technologies for automotive applications, the interviewed stakeholders were experts from CEA and car manufacturers. The next subsections describe how MACBETH method was implemented in the specific case of the evaluation of hydrogen storage technologies for automotive applications, in the frame of the STORHY European project.

17.3.3 Implementation of the MACBETH Method for the Evaluation and Comparison of the Technical Performance of Hydrogen Storage Systems

17.3.3.1 Who Has Been Interviewed?

Within the project, the implementation of MACBETH method for the technical evaluation and comparison of the hydrogen storage technologies has been conducted with the following approach:

- internal implementation made by the analyst himself (in order to ensure that the MACBETH method is appropriate for the evaluation),
- implementation of the method with one of the STORHY car manufacturers (denoted *CM1* in the following subsections),
- extension of the approach with the other STORHY car manufacturers (details provided in Sect. 17.3.4).

The approach and results provided in the next subsections are corresponding to the implementation of the method with *CM1*.

A detailed overview of the input and output data that have been obtained during the implementation of MACBETH approach within STORHY project is provided in the Appendix.

17.3.3.2 Structuring the Context of the Evaluation

Let us recall that three alternatives (hydrogen storage systems) have been compared: a type IV 70 MPa hydrogen storage system (C-H_2), a cylindrical steel made liquid hydrogen storage system (L-H_2) and a solid storage system. The final automotive application that has been considered as a framework for the comparison was a fuel cell vehicle with 6 kg of hydrogen on-board. The evaluation was focused on five technical evaluation criteria: system volume (l), system mass (kg), refueling time (min), hydrogen loss rate (g/h/kgH_2) and conformability (constructed scale). Conformability was defined as the ability of the storage system to be shaped and included in an existing vehicle structure. The performances of these hydrogen storage technologies taken into account in this study are provided in Table 17.1.

Table 17.1 Performance of H_2 storage technologies (6 kg hydrogen fuel cell vehicle)

	System volume (l)	System mass (kg)	Refueling time (min)	H_2 loss rate (g/h/kg$_{H_2}$)	Conformability (constructed scale)
C-H_2	250	133	4	0	- -
L-H_2	167	100	2	1.3	- - -
Solid	250	500	1	0	-

17.3.3.3 Determining Two Reference Levels for Each Evaluation Criterion

One of the specificities of the MACBETH method is the possibility to introduce two reference levels that have to be defined for each evaluation criterion. Originally in MACBETH method, these two reference levels are called "*good*" and "*neutral*". These two levels are extensively used in the assessment procedure of value functions and scaling constants in MACBETH. The terminology of these reference levels has been modified and adapted to the R&D context of the evaluation in STORHY, in order to model the notion of R&D efforts. Thus the level "*neutral*" has been changed into "*acceptable*" and the level "*good*" has been changed into "*satisfying*". The following definitions have been chosen for these two levels (Fig. 17.4):

- "*acceptable level*": level below which a major R&D effort will be required to allow the adoption of the technology.
- "*satisfying level*": level above which the criterion is a strong point of the technology and R&D for improving the performance regarding the studied criterion is no more a priority.

In order to illustrate this concept, let us consider the criterion "system volume", quoted g_{vol} and expressed in litres. Car manufacturer *CM1* was asked to determine two values (expressed in litres), the one corresponding to a satisfying system volume and the other corresponding to an acceptable system volume, both in the case of the chosen final application. The values provided by CM1 were the following: "acceptable system volume" at 150 l, and the "satisfying system volume" at 80 l (Fig. 17.5).

CM1 was then asked to answer to the same question for the other technical evaluation criteria and in the case of the same final application. Table 17.2 provides the set of values that have been obtained from the interactive definition

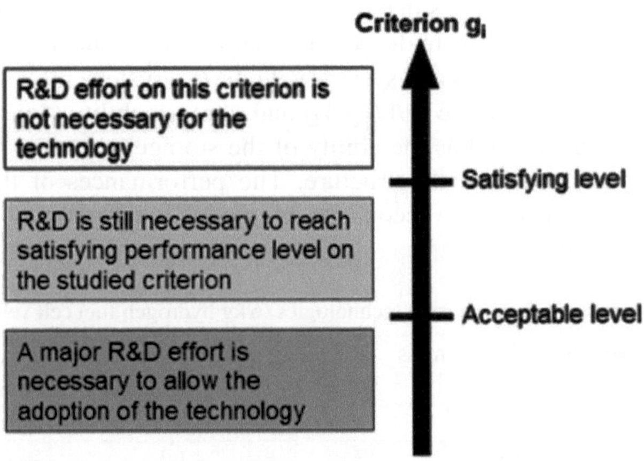

Fig. 17.4 Definition of the two reference levels used in MACBETH method for the evaluation of R& D

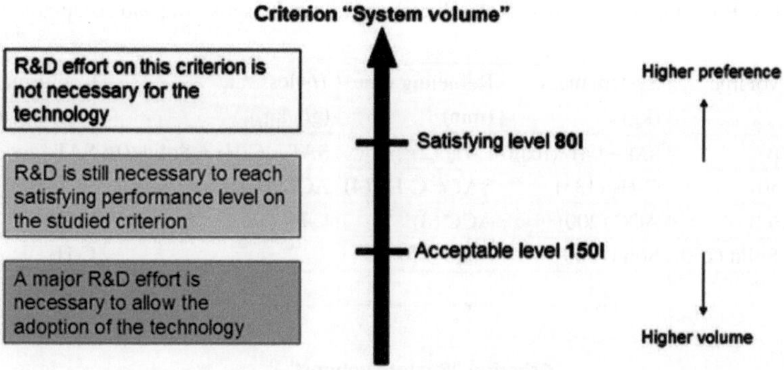

Fig. 17.5 Representation of the acceptable and satisfying storage system volumes expressed by the interviewed car manufacturer CM1 considering a fuel cell vehicle with 6 kg of hydrogen on-board

Table 17.2 Values obtained from car manufacturer CM1 concerning acceptable and satisfying reference levels, in the case of a fuel cell vehicle application)

	System volume (l)	System mass (kg)	Refueling time (min)	H_2 loss rate (g/h/kg$_{H_2}$)	Conformability (constructed scale)
Satisfying (SAT)	80	100	4	0	"*good*"
Acceptable (ACC)	150	200	8	0.04	"*low*"

of these reference levels. The participation of several car manufacturers for the implementation of this step was found to be difficult because of the strategic value of the information presented in Table 17.2.

In the above Table, "*good*" conformability means that the system could be easily shaped and included in an existing vehicle structure, and a "*low*" conformability means that the storage system was a constraint for the design of the vehicle.

17.3.3.4 Ranking of the Technologies

Knowing the performances of the technologies (Table 17.1) and the reference levels expressed by *CM1* (Table 17.2), the hydrogen storage technologies were then ranked, for each evaluation criterion, as shown in Table 17.3.

17.3.3.5 Differences of Attractiveness

The aim of this step is to translate the original numerical scales g_i into new scales v_i for each criterion, using the notion of "difference of attractiveness" between alternatives. In MACBETH, seven semantic categories are used for qualifying the differences of attractiveness between alternatives: "*extreme*", "*very strong*",

Table 17.3 Ranking of H_2 storage technologies regarding the satisfying and acceptable reference levels

System volume (l)	System mass (kg)	Refueling time (min)	H_2 loss rate (g/h/kg$_{H_2}$)	Conformability (constructed scale)
SAT (80)	SAT = L-H_2 (100)f	L-H_2 (2)	SAT = C-H_2 = Solid (0)	SAT (*good*)
ACC (150)	C-H_2 (133)	SAT = C-H_2 (4)	ACC (0,04)	ACC (*low*)
L-H_2 (167)	ACC (200)	ACC (8)	L-H_2 (1,3)	Solid
C-H_2 = Solid (250)	Solid (500)	Solid (15)		C-H_2
				L-H_2

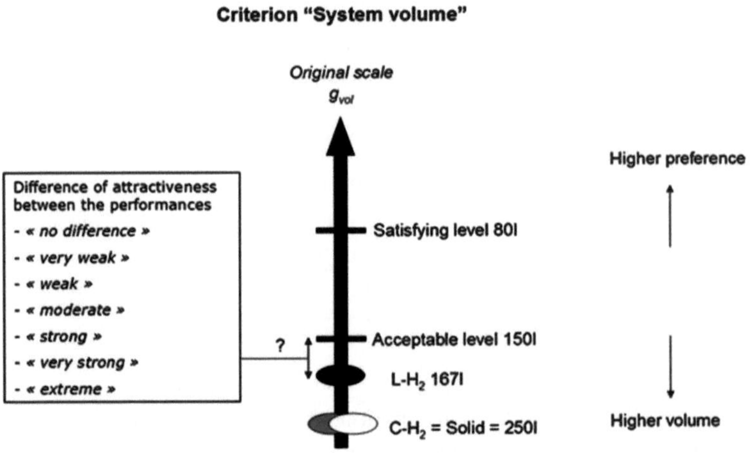

Fig. 17.6 Difference of attractiveness assessed by *CM1* between performances of the H_2 storage technologies

"*strong*", "*moderate*", "*weak*", "*very weak*", "*no difference*". This concept is illustrated in Fig. 17.6 in the case of the "system volume" criterion.

Using this semantic scale, the eventual non linearity of the judgment of car manufacturer *CM1* could be modeled. Indeed for example, in terms of interest in improving the system volume, a reduction of 10 l can have a different meaning at various places on the scale, e.g., between 90 l and 80 l and between 230 l and 220 l. Another advantage of this questioning procedure in MACBETH is that it is appropriate for taking into account the uncertainties of the raw performance data.

The information obtained at the end of this step was expressed by a dedicated matrix called "judgements matrix", for each evaluation criterion. Figure 17.7 provides the judgment matrix obtained for the "system volume" criterion. In this figure, "positive" means that the difference of attractiveness (for example between the acceptable level and C-H_2) has not been qualified specifically by CM1, but due to the original ranking of the technologies, this difference of attractiveness is automatically set "*positive*" by the M-MACBETH software.

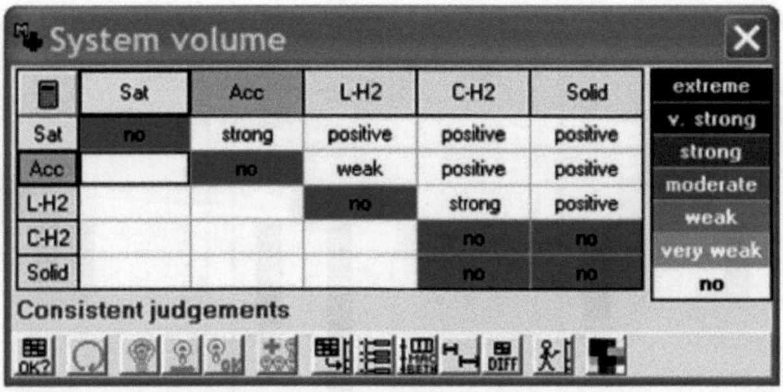

Fig. 17.7 Judgements matrix related to the system volume criterion, obtained with *CM1*

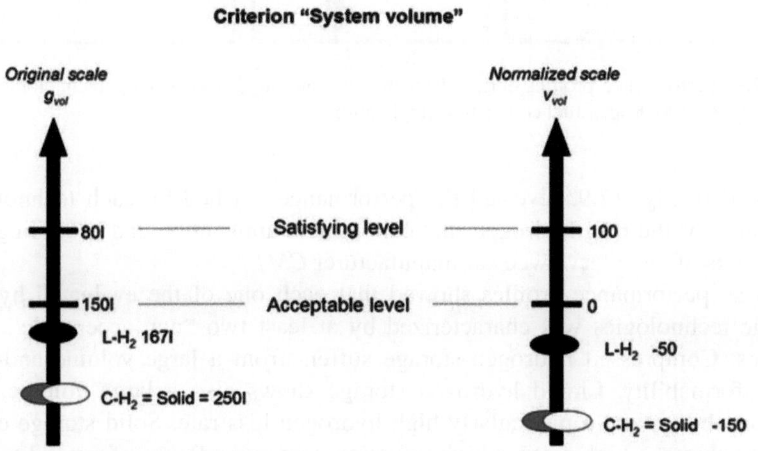

Fig. 17.8 Transformation of the original numerical scale g_{vol} into a normalized scale of attractiveness v_{vol}

These judgements were then processed by the M-MACBETH software using linear programming to build a scale of attractiveness reflecting these judgments. These scales were normalized with the acceptable reference level at 0 and the satisfying reference level at 100 (Fig. 17.8).

At the end of this step, five new numerical scales of attractiveness were then obtained (corresponding to the five technical evaluation criteria), each one being normalized with the acceptable reference level at 0 and the satisfying reference level at 100. These scales were extensively discussed with *CM1*, who finally approved the ones that we presented.

17.3.3.6 Performance Profiles

Thanks to the previously described evaluation process, the performance profile of each hydrogen storage technology could be obtained. These performance profiles,

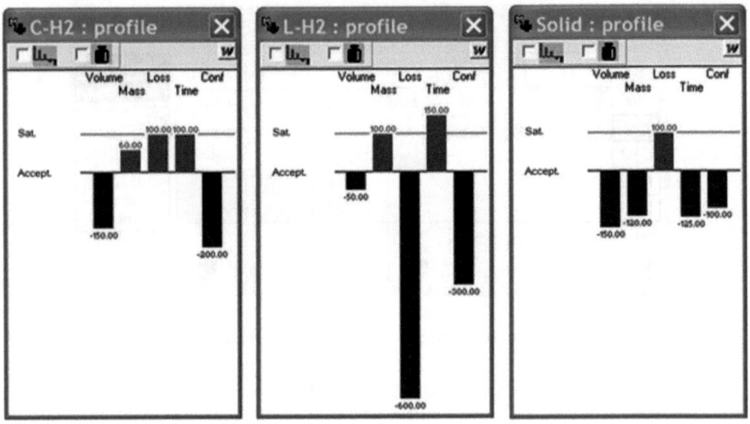

Fig. 17.9 Performance profiles obtained for the evaluated hydrogen storage technologies, in the frame of a 6 kg hydrogen fuel cell vehicle application

provided in Fig. 17.9, revealed the performance reached by each technology in the frame of the 6 kg hydrogen fuel cell vehicle application and according to the judgments of the interviewed car manufacturer *CM1*.

These performance profiles showed that each one of the evaluated hydrogen storage technologies was characterized by at least two "non acceptable" performances. Compressed hydrogen storage suffers from a large volume and a lack of conformability. Liquid hydrogen storage shows also a large volume, a low conformability, and a particularly high hydrogen loss rate. Solid storage exhibits a high volume, a high mass, a high refueling time and a low conformability. These results are representing the most important issues to be focused on in terms of R&D among the evaluation criteria that have been taken into account, and according to the vision of the interviewed car manufacturer *CM1*. The results show that in the frame of a fuel cell vehicle application, volume remains a critical issue for all of the evaluated hydrogen storage technologies. None of the compressed, liquid and solid storage methods is situated above the "acceptable" performance level defined by *CM1*. In the same way, conformability is considered to be an important issue for all of the evaluated hydrogen storage technologies. None of the hydrogen technologies is considered as "acceptable" on this criterion and in the frame of the studied final application. Concerning mass, according to *CM1*, none of the hydrogen storage technologies is situated above the "satisfying" reference level. However, compressed and liquid storage technologies are situated above the "acceptable" reference level defined by this end-user. Mass remains an issue especially for solid storage technology, for which the performance is evaluated below the "acceptable" reference level defined by *CM1* and for this specific final application. Concerning refueling time, compressed technology is considered "satisfying", liquid technology is "satisfying" and solid storage is positioned below the "acceptable" level. Finally, regarding hydrogen loss rate, the performance reached by compressed and solid storage technologies is satisfying, while the performance reached by liquid hydrogen storage technology is positioned far below the acceptable reference level, showing that this is the main critical issue of this technology, according to *CM1*, and in the frame of the studied final application.

In addition to the previous steps, the evaluation process can be completed by an aggregation phase. This phase consists in determining scaling constants (weights) and processing a weighted-sum of the normalized scales of attractiveness obtained for each criterion. Such aggregation leads to a final global ranking of the technologies. The next subsections provide a description of how the scaling constants have been determined and the result of the overall aggregation that has been obtained with *CM1*.

17.3.3.7 Determining Scaling Constants

Following the MACBETH method, scaling constants were determined through the definition of fictitious alternatives f_i. A fictitious alternative f_i is characterized by a satisfying performance for criterion g_i and acceptable performances for all other criteria. For example, the fictitious hydrogen storage technology f_{vol} is satisfying for system volume criterion (80 l), and acceptable for all other criteria. Table 17.4 summarizes the performances of the five fictitious hydrogen storage technologies corresponding to the reference levels that have been specified by *CM1*.

Then *CM1* was asked to rank these fictitious hydrogen technologies in terms of preferences by evaluating what would be the most interesting improvement, from acceptable level to satisfying level, among the five possibilities. *CM1* provided the following ranking (by order of preference):

$$f_{vol} > f_{mass} > f_{conf} > f_{ref} > f_{closs} \qquad (17.2)$$

Such ranking means the improvement from 150 to 80 l is considered by *CM1* as the most interesting improvement among the five possibilities of improvement.

Then in order to calculate scaling constants, *CM1* was asked to evaluate the difference of attractiveness between these fictitious alternatives, using the same

Table 17.4 Performances of the five fictitious hydrogen storage technologies related to the reference levels specified by *CM1*

	System volume (l)	System mass (kg)	Refueling time (min)	H_2 loss rate (g/h/kg$_{H_2}$)	Conformability (constructed scale)
f_{vol}	80	200	8	0.04	"*low*"
f_{mass}	150	100	8	0.04	"*low*"
f_{ref}	150	200	4	0.04	"*low*"
f_{loss}	150	200	8	0	"*low*"
f_{conf}	150	200	8	0.04	"*good*"

set of semantic categories as the one used in the previous phase, by answering questions such as "*How do you judge the difference of attractiveness between* f_{vol} *and* f_{mass}*?*" (in other words, "*how do you judge the difference of attractiveness between i) improving system volume from 150 l to 80 l and ii) reducing the system mass from 120 kg to 60 kg?*'"). As in the previous phase, the information obtained at the end of this step was expressed by a dedicated "judgements matrix" summarizing the ranking and the difference of attractiveness between the fictitious alternatives (Fig. 17.10).

These judgements were then processed by M-MACBETH software using linear programming, in order to calculate the scaling constants w_i in accordance with the preferences expressed in the judgements matrix (Fig. 17.11).

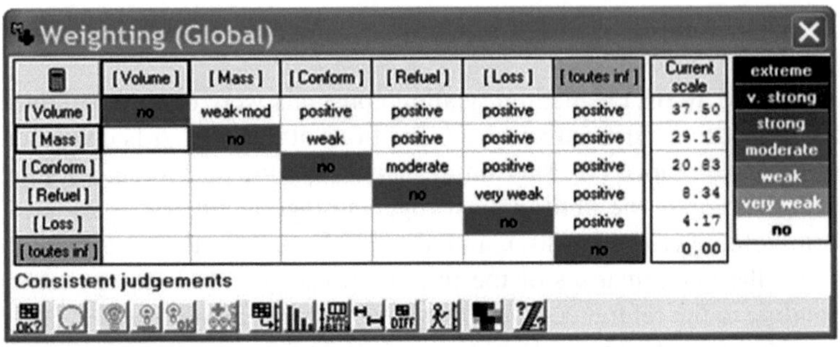

Fig. 17.10 Judgements matrix representing the differences of attractiveness between fictitious alternatives

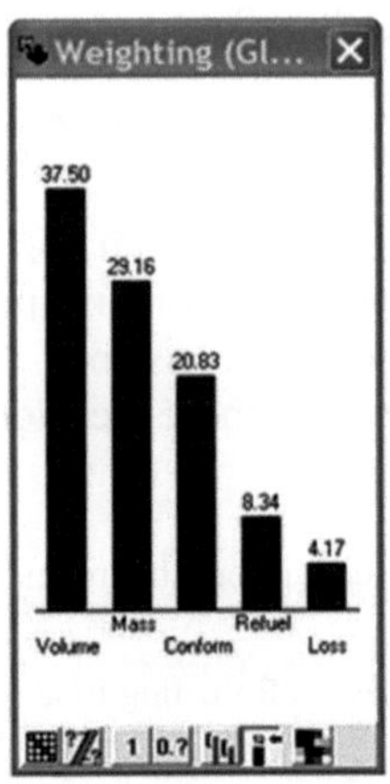

Fig. 17.11 Scaling constants w_i computed by M-MACBETH, based on the judgment matrix

17.3.3.8 Aggregation

Based on the five normalized scales of attractiveness and the scaling constants (weights) w_i, the global evaluation quote of each hydrogen storage technology was calculated using M-MACBETH software processing the weighted sum method:

$$v(CH_2) = \sum_{i=1}^{5} w_i v_i(g_i(CH_2)) \tag{17.3}$$

$$v(LH_2) = \sum_{i=1}^{5} w_i v_i(g_i(LH_2)) \tag{17.4}$$

$$v(Solid) = \sum_{i=1}^{5} w_i v_i(g_i(Solid)) \tag{17.5}$$

Finally, the result of this aggregation phase could be represented using a single global scale of attractiveness (Fig. 17.12). This result showed that in the frame of the studied fuel cell vehicle application, none of the three evaluated hydrogen storage technologies reaches the "acceptable" reference level. That is to say that strong R&D efforts are still needed from a technical point of view, for each one of the evaluated technologies.

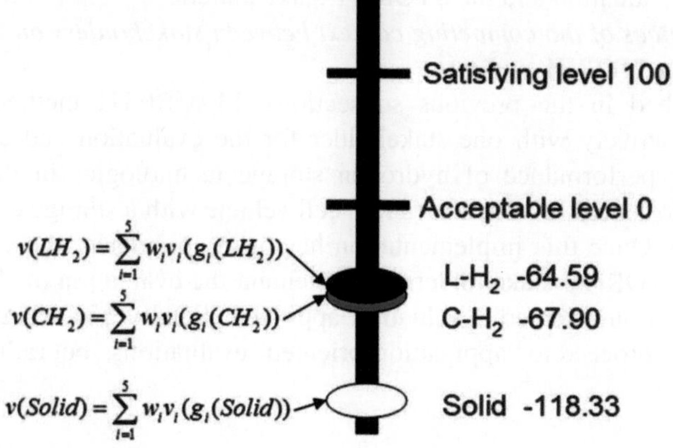

Fig. 17.12 Global attractiveness scale obtained with *CM1*

To conclude, the implementation process conducted with *CM1* and presented in the previous subsections revealed the added-value of MACBETH approach in the case of an "application-oriented" evaluation. Relying on (1) the performance of the storage technologies, (2) the reference levels and (3) the judgements formulated by *CM1*, performance profiles of the hydrogen storage technologies were obtained, showing the remaining R&D efforts that should be made, for each technology, in order to reach the targets settled by *CM1*. The use of MACBETH with CEA experts and *CM1* showed the added value of this method in particular for comparing the points of view of multiple actors.

However, within STORHY project, the conclusions obtained from the implementation of MACBETH method with *CM1* could not be considered as "STORHY conclusions". Indeed, global STORHY conclusions could have been drawn only if the whole stakeholders of the study could provide their reference levels and judgements; in such case the consensual results between the implementations could have been identified and could have been considered as STORHY conclusions. Many tasks of the MACBETH methodology process lead to provide representations of strategic visions. For instance, giving precise numerical value to the two reference levels described above is a strategic signal of what is considered by the car manufacturer as an internal admitted target.

The next subsection describes how the extension of the evaluation approach has been conducted with the other STORHY car manufacturers.

17.3.4 Extension of the Approach Within STORHY Project: Towards an "Improved Performance Table"

The work described in this subsection has been conducted by the CEA after the end of the collaboration with the LAMSADE team. The following paragraphs are showing that the use of "reference levels" allowed structuring the discussion between SP Evaluation and the STORHY stakeholders.

Consequences of the competing context between stakeholders on the evaluation process within STORHY project

As described in the previous subsections, MACBETH method was implemented interactively with one stakeholder for the evaluation and comparison of the technical performance of hydrogen storage technologies in the case of an "application-oriented" evaluation (a fuel cell vehicle with a storage capacity of 6 kg of hydrogen). Once this implementation has been completed, the CEA proposed to the other STORHY stakeholders to implement the evaluation method using this same "application-oriented" evaluation approach. Finally STORHY stakeholders decided not to proceed to "application-oriented" evaluations, but rather evaluations relying on relative parameters independently from any specific final application. This change was the consequence of the fact that STORHY stakeholders are in competition on the automotive market and each car manufacturer gets his own specific final applications and does not necessarily want to share his targets and visions with competing companies even when working in the same EU Research project.

New set of evaluation criteria using relative parameters instead of absolute ones

In this context, the proposal of the analyst was to take into account new evaluation criteria for the evaluation and comparison of the hydrogen storage technologies, in accordance with the wish of the stakeholders: system volumetric energy density (instead of system volume), system gravimetric energy density (instead of system mass), system refueling rate (instead of system refueling time), hydrogen loss rate was kept the same, as well as conformability. The objective of the analyst was then to identify the whole stakeholders' consensual vision of the performance of the technologies using the newly defined evaluation criteria and to collect their judgements on the remaining R&D needs for each technology.

Building a consensual "improved performance table"

In this context, it was agreed between STORHY stakeholders and the analyst to establish an "improved performance table" which could represent both performance of the technologies and qualitative evaluation of the remaining R&D efforts. To do so, the analyst proposed that car manufacturers could provide acceptable and satisfying reference levels for these new evaluation criteria. The definition of the reference levels was kept unchanged as in MACBETH procedure (strong remaining research efforts below the acceptable level, moderate research efforts between acceptable and satisfying reference levels, slight/no more research efforts above the satisfying reference level). Once these reference levels data were obtained, the "improved performance table" could be built by the analyst and was then validated by STORHY stakeholders. Table 17.5 provides such synthetic information in which dark gray cells correspond to items (below acceptable level) for which strong remaining research efforts are recommended, and light gray cells correspond to items (below satisfying level) for which remaining research efforts are recommended (for white cells slight/no more research efforts are recommended). In addition to hydrogen storage technologies, STORHY stakeholders proposed to show also the performance of a competing energy storage technology (Li-Ion battery) and the performance of reference gasoline tank.

Table 17.5 Final STORHY performance table built in cooperation between SP Evaluation and SP Users

	Volumetric energy density (kWh/l)	Gravimetric energy density (kWh/kg)	Refueling rate (kWh/min)	H_2 loss rate (g/h/kg$_{H_2}$)	Conformability 1 = cylindrical, 5 = complex
C-H_2 350 bar	0.5	1.3	50	0	2
STORHY C-H_2 700 bar Type III	0.8	1.3	50	0	2
STORHY C-H_2 700 bar Type IV	0.8	1.5	50	0.002	2
L-H_2 conventional	1.2	2.0	100	1.3	1
STORHY L-H_2 cylindrical	1.3	5.0	100	1.0	1
STORHY L-H_2 free-form demonstrator	1.2	5.9	100	0.8	4
Solid storage low temp. hydrides	0.8	0.4	13	0	3
STORHY solid storage $NaAlH_4$ pilot tank	0.7	0.3	25	0	3
STORHY solid storage $NaAlH_4$ forecast	1.2	0.7	25	0	3
Li ion battery	0.2	0.1	0.5	0	4
Gasoline tank	7.0	8.0	> 200	0	5

17.4 Comments on the Case and on the Decision Aiding Process

17.4.1 The Specific Context of an Integrated European Research Project: A Multi-Actor Context, No Single Decision Maker, Several Stakeholders in Competition

The STORHY project was an integrated European research project aiming at developing three competing hydrogen storage technologies. A subproject Evaluation has been created so that the results of the STORHY project could be assessed and the remaining R&D efforts for each technology could be identified. The specificities of the context in which the evaluation had to be achieved were the following:

- the client of the project was the European Commission,
- thirty-four academic and industrial partners were involved in the project,
- the aim of the project was to investigate the three main competing hydrogen storage technologies under development (pressure, liquid and solid),

- among these actors, there was no single decision maker but several stakeholders in competition,
- the mission of the subproject Evaluation (analyst) was then to conduct an objective and consensual evaluation and comparison of the technologies. Thus the terminology used for this study was not "decision aid" but "evaluation aid".

The support of the LAMSADE laboratory occurred about 2 years after the beginning of the STORHY project; at this time the problematic of the evaluation of the storage systems was already structured and the LAMSADE team did not participate to the structuring step and the definition of appropriate evaluation criteria. The support of LAMSADE team was conducted in an already structured context in which the evaluation criteria had been chosen before having studied deeply the whole evaluation problematic. From this experience within STORHY European project, the LAMSADE team recommends strongly to focus extensively on the structuring step for the future evaluations in further European projects.

17.4.2 The Interest of MACBETH Approach for the "Application-Oriented" Multicriteria Evaluation of H_2 Storage Technologies

From an early discussion between the stakeholders and the analyst, focus has been made on the technical performance of the hydrogen storage technologies. At first, five technical evaluation criteria were taken into account (system volume, system mass, refueling time, hydrogen loss rate and conformability). The analyst identified MACBETH approach as a potentially appropriate method for evaluating and comparing technical performance of hydrogen storage technologies conducting "application-oriented" multicriteria evaluations with the STORHY car manufacturers. The approach has been implemented successfully with one of the STORHY car manufacturers. The results of this implementation showed that MACBETH approach seemed adapted for evaluating technologies that are under development and for comparing their performance to the targets of the end-users or stakeholders when a final application is well identified and specified (Sect. 17.3.3).

In particular, the definition of "acceptable" and "satisfying" reference levels appeared to be helpful for the stakeholder. The performance profiles obtained at the end of the implementation process were showing clearly the strong and weak points, the remaining research efforts that have to be performed in order to bring the technologies above the acceptable level.

17.4.3 Multicriteria Evaluation in a Multi-Actor R&D Context: The Central Role of the Performance Table

The reluctance of the stakeholders for "black boxes" and data aggregation
Despite the interesting outcomes of the implementation of MACBETH approach for application-oriented evaluation, some limits in the interpretation and use of the results could be identified. In particular, the notion of criteria aggregation was sometimes considered as a "loss of information". In general, within the whole duration of the project, STORHY stakeholders considered that criteria aggregation would be too much subjective and not appropriate for the evaluation in such a competing context. As a consequence, the possibilities of "local evaluation domain aggregation" and "global inter-domain aggregation" were set aside.
An improved performance table
Despite the differences between the visions of the stakeholders, the consensual evaluation of the technical performance of the hydrogen storage technologies could be achieved thanks to an "improved performance table" (Table 17.5). The analyst focused on the validation of the raw performance data of the state-of-the-art and STORHY prototypes. The stakeholders agreed about the use of relative parameters instead of absolute parameters. Once these data were validated by STORHY stakeholders, the analyst asked the stakeholders to provide their judgement on the acceptable and satisfying reference levels for these criteria, using the same definition as for the MACBETH procedure. Thus an improved performance table could be obtained, showing both the raw performance of the technologies and the remaining R&D efforts that have been consensually identified by the stakeholders. For more detailed information on STORHY project evaluation and technical results, the reader can refer to STORHY final event presentations available in Strubel (2008).

Acknowledgements The authors wish to thank the European Commission for financial support of the Integrated Project STORHY Hydrogen Storage Systems for Automotive Application (Contract No SES6-CT-2004-502667) within the sixth RTD Framework Programme.

Appendix: Detailed Input and Output Data Obtained During the Implementation Process of MACBETH Method Within STORHY Project

In the following appendix, the detailed input and output data obtained during the implementation process of MACBETH method within STORHY project is provided.

1. Interviewed actors: the MACBETH method has been implemented with three experts. These experts are referenced as "expert 1", "expert 2" and "expert 3" in the following paragraphs.

2. Final application: for each one of these experts, the considered final application was a "*fuel cell private car, with a storage capacity of 6 kg of hydrogen and a corresponding autonomy of 600 km*".
3. Alternatives to be studied: the hydrogen storage technologies that have been compared were: (1) compressed hydrogen storage at 700 bar, (2) liquid hydrogen storage, and (3) solid storage using alanates materials.
   In addition to these hydrogen storage technologies, expert 2 considered that it would be useful to take into account another solid storage technology, i.e. solid storage using low temperature metal hydrides.
   To complete the evaluation, two reference storage technologies have also been taken into account: compressed natural gas storage, and gasoline storage.
4. Evaluation criteria: the evaluation criteria that have been considered were: system mass (kg), system volume (l), refueling time (min), hydrogen loss rate (g/h/kgH_2), and conformability (qualitative criterion).
5. Reference levels chosen by the interviewed experts: as described previously in the article, the evaluation model is built relying on two reference levels for each criterion (Table 17.6 provides the values chosen by the interviewed experts for these reference levels):
   - acceptable level (ACC): below this level of performance, a strong technological improvement is necessary from the point of view of the interviewed expert and for the assessed final application
   - satisfying level (SAT): above this level, the research for improving the performance on this criterion is no more a priority
6. Performance tables: Tables 17.7, 17.8, and 17.9 provide the raw physical data that have been used by the interviewed experts for the elaboration of the evaluation models.
7. Judgment matrices for each expert: the following figures are providing the judgement matrices obtained from the interviewed experts. These matrices are showing the positioning of the technologies in terms of differences of

Table 17.6 Reference levels defined by the interviewed experts

		Expert 1	Expert 2	Expert 3
Volume	ACC	255 l	250 l	150 l
	SAT	74 l	120 l	80 l
Mass	ACC	142 kg	150 kg	200 kg
	SAT	100 kg	80 kg	100 kg
Conformability	ACC	Non quantified	Non quantified	Non quantified
	SAT	Non quantified	Non quantified	Non quantified
H_2 loss rate	ACC	0.1 g/h/kg	0.5 %	0.1 %
	SAT	0.05 g/h/kg	0 %	0 %
Refueling time	ACC	6 min	10 min	8 min
	SAT	3 min	3 min	4 min

Table 17.7 Performance table for criteria "*Volume*" and "*Mass*"

	"*Volume*" (expressed in litres)			"*Mass*" (expressed in kg)		
	Expert 1	Expert 2	Expert 3	Expert 1	Expert 2	Expert 3
LIQ	205	210–220	260	117.5	110–120	117.5
PRE	255	240	326	142	142	142
SOLA	300	250–300	370	500	500	500
SOLH	175	150–200	–	175	500	–
GAZ	220	210–220	280	142	142	142
ESS	60	60	60	51.5	51.5	51.5
SAT	74	120	80	100	80	100
ACC	255	250	150	142	150	200

Table 17.8 Performance table for criteria "*Conformability*" and "H_2 *loss rate*"

	"*Conformability*" (constructed scale)			"H_2 *loss rate*" (g/h/kg, or % per day)		
	Expert 1	Expert 2	Expert 3	Expert 1	Expert 2	Expert 3
LIQ	–	–	4	1.25	1.25	1.25
PRE	–	–	7	0.0001	5ε	0.0001
SOLA	–	–	5	0	ε	0
SOLH	–	–	–	–	ε	–
GAZ	–	–	6	0	0	0
ESS	–	–	1	0	0	0
SAT	BC	BC	2	0.05	0	0
ACC	MC	MC	3	0.1	0.5 %	0.1 %

Table 17.9 Performance table for criterion "*Refueling time*"

	"*Refueling time*" (min)		
	Expert 1	Expert 2	Expert 3
LIQ	1.7	6	1.7
PRE	6	6	6
SOLA	30	15	30
SOLH	–	15	–
GAZ	3	3	3
ESS	2	3-2	2
SAT	3	3	4
ACC	6	10	8

attractiveness. These differences of attractiveness have been expressed thanks to the MACBETH qualitative scale as described in the article (see Figs. 17.13, 17.14, 17.15, 17.16, 17.17, 17.18, 17.19, 17.20, 17.21).

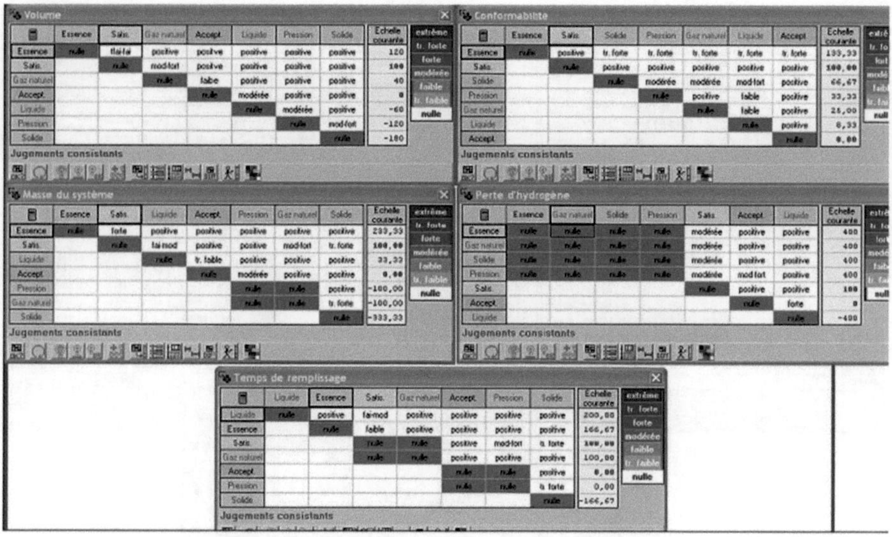

Fig. 17.13 Matrices of attractiveness obtained from Expert 1

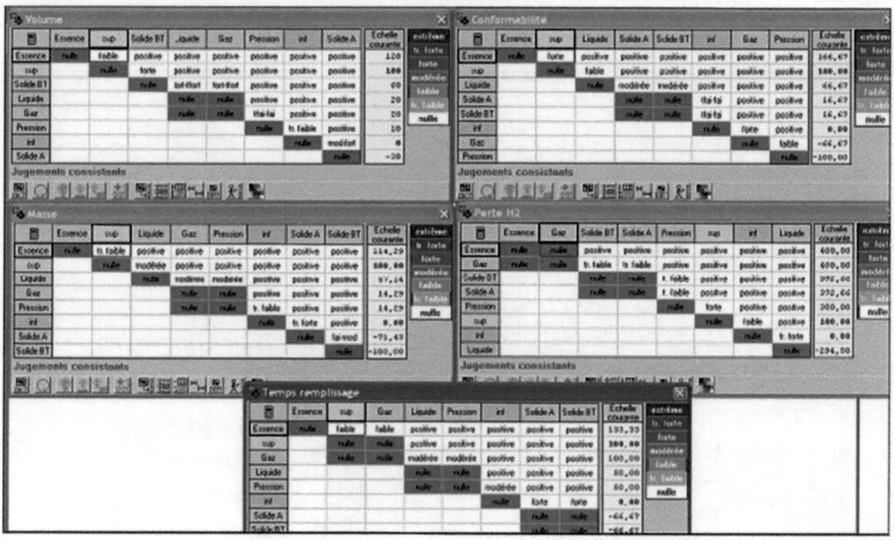

Fig. 17.14 Matrices of attractiveness obtained from Expert 2

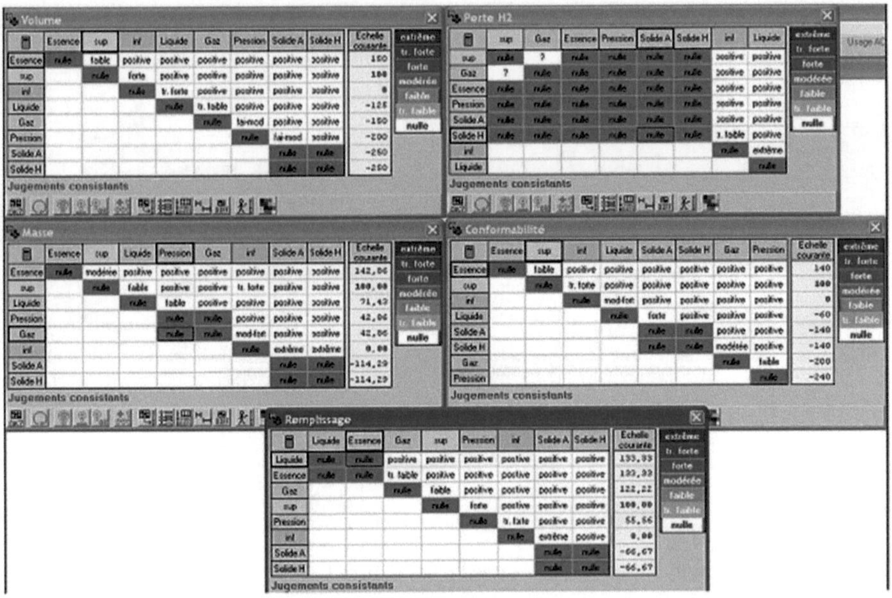

Fig. 17.15 Matrices of attractiveness obtained from Expert 3

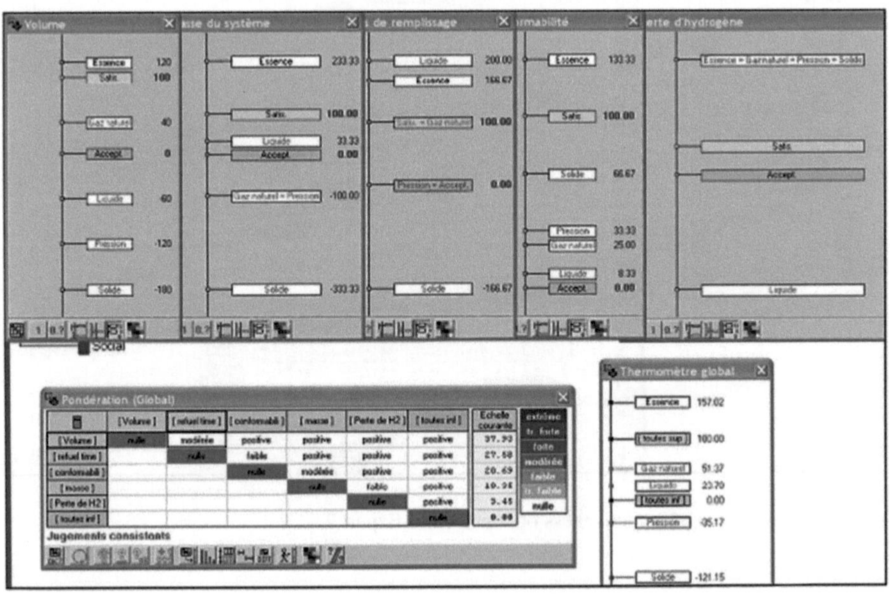

Fig. 17.16 Judgement matrix, scaling constants and evaluations for Expert 1

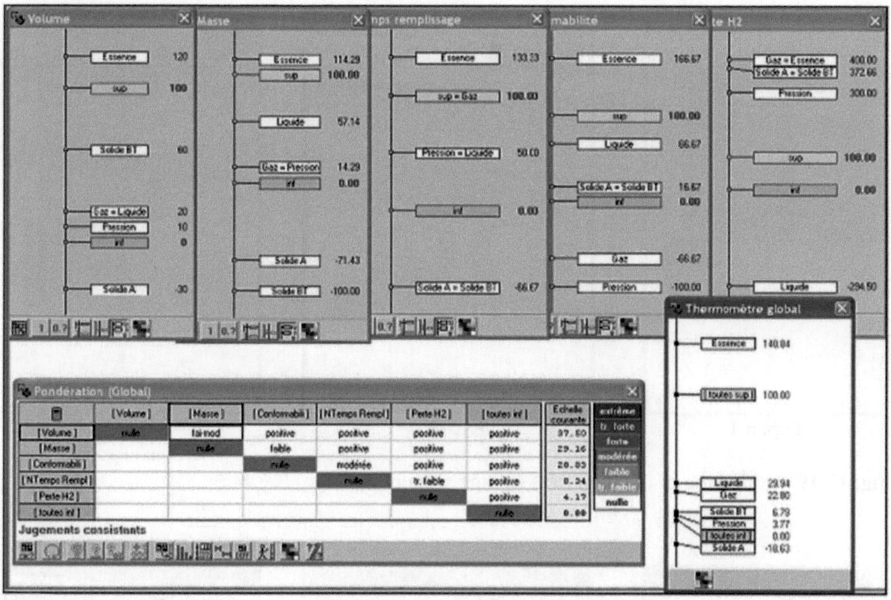

Fig. 17.17 Judgement matrix, scaling constants and evaluations for Expert 2

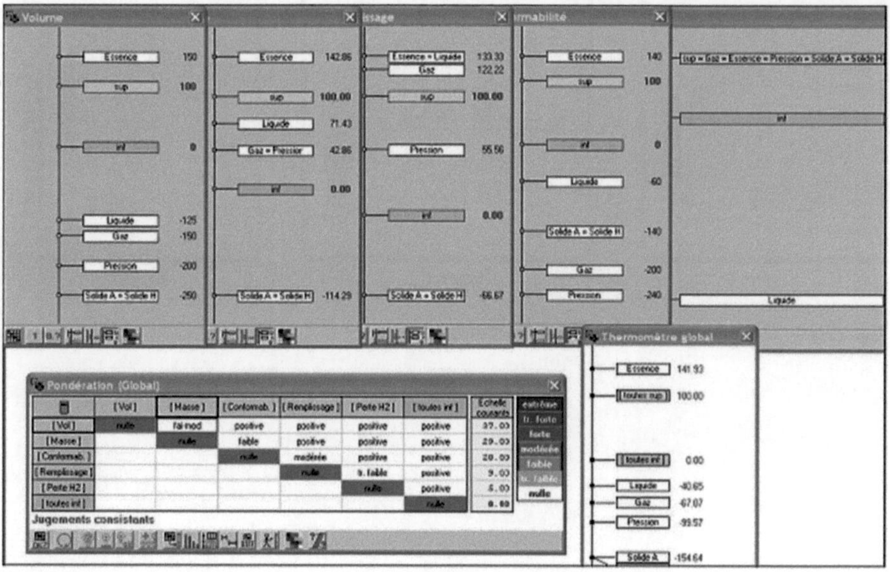

Fig. 17.18 Judgement matrix, scaling constants and evaluations for Expert 3

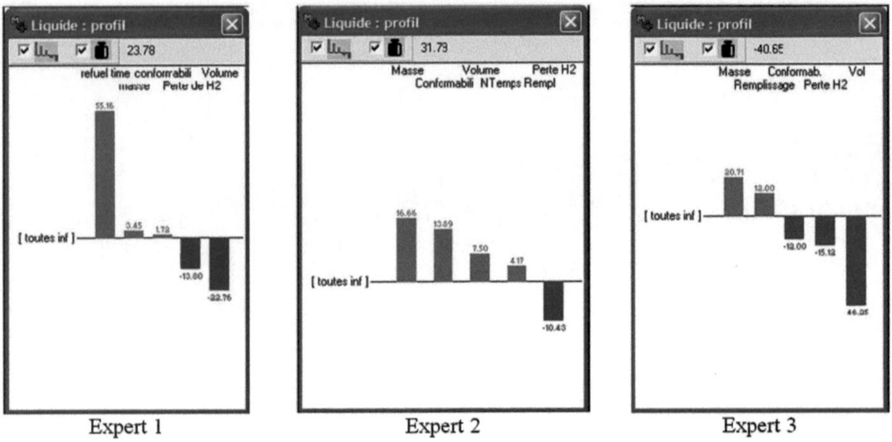

Fig. 17.19 Evaluation of the liquid H_2 storage system

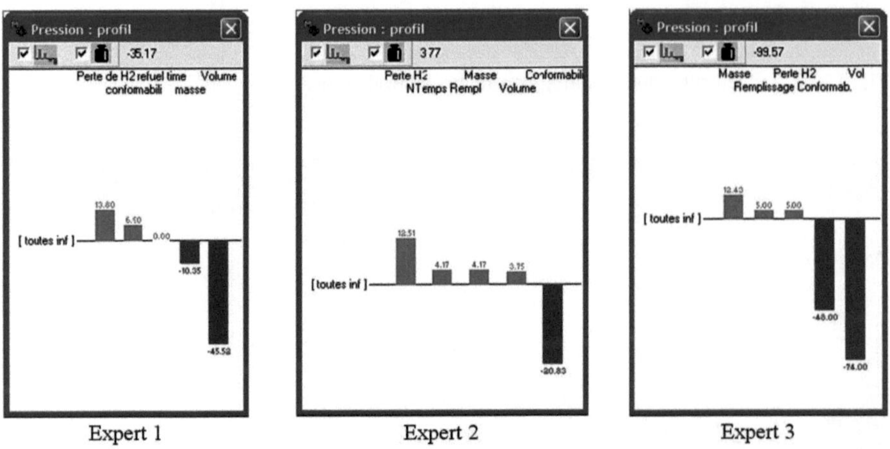

Fig. 17.20 Evaluation of the pressure H_2 storage system

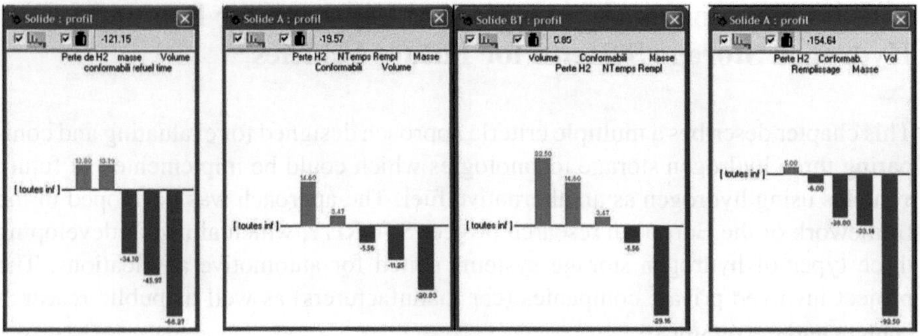

Fig. 17.21 Evaluation of the solid H_2 storage system

References

Bana e Costa, C., De Corte, J., & Vansnick, J. (2005). On the mathematical foundation of MACBETH. In J. Figueira, S. Greco, & M. Ehrgott (Eds.), *Multiple criteria decision analysis: State of the art surveys* (pp. 409–443). Boston: Springer.

Bana e Costa, C., & Vansnick, J. (1997a). Applications of the MACBETH approach in the framework of an additive aggregation model. *Journal of Multi-Criteria Decision Analysis, 6*, 107–114.

Bana e Costa, C., & Vansnick, J. (1997b). A theoretical framework for measuring attractiveness by a categorical based evaluation technique (MACBETH). In J. Climaco (Ed.), *Multicriteria Analysis. Proceedings of the XIth International Conference on MCDM* (pp. 15–24). Berlin: Springer.

Cherry, R. (2004). A hydrogen utopia? *International Journal of Hydrogen Energy, 29*, 124–129.

Dunn, S. (2002). Hydrogen futures: Toward a sustainable energy system. *International Journal of Hydrogen Energy, 27*, 235–264.

Ewan, B., & Allen, R. (2005). A figure of merit assessment of the routes to hydrogen. *International Journal of Hydrogen Energy, 30*, 809–819.

Goltsov, V., & Veziroglu, T. (2002). A step on the road to hydrogen civilization. *International Journal of Hydrogen Energy, 27*, 719–723.

Goltsov, V., Veziroglu, T., & Goltsova, L. (2006). Hydrogen civilization of the future - A new conception of the IAHE. *International Journal of Hydrogen Energy, 31*, 153–159.

IPCC. (2007). Climate change 2007: Synthesis report. Contribution of working groups I, II and III to the fourth assessment report of the intergovernmental panel on climate change. In Core Writing Team, R. K. Pachauri, & A. Reisinger (Eds.), IPCC, Geneva (104 pp.)

Mousseau, V., Slowinski, R., & Zielniewicz, P. (2000). A user-oriented implementation of the ELECTRE TRI method integrating preference elicitation support. *Computers & Operations Research, 27*(7–8), 757–777.

Roy, B. (1996). *Multicriteria methodology for decision aiding*. Dordrecht: Kluwer Academic.

Roy, B., & Bouyssou, D. (1993). *Aide Multicritère à la Décision: Méthodes et Cas*. Paris: Economica.

Schlapbach, L., & Zuttel, A. (2001). Hydrogen storage materials for mobile applications. *Nature, 414*, 353–358.

Strubel, V. (2008). STORHY objectives and results. Final event presentation. Available at www.storhy.net.

Editors' Comments on "An MCDA Approach for Evaluating Hydrogen Storage Systems for Future Vehicles"

This chapter describes a multiple criteria approach designed for evaluating and comparing three hydrogen storage technologies which could be implemented in future vehicles using hydrogen as an alternative fuel. The approach was developed in the framework of the European research project STORHY, which aimed at developing three types of hydrogen storage systems suited for automotive applications. The project involved private companies (car manufacturers) as well as public research centers and universities.

The **application** described here took place in the sub-project "Evaluation". The existence of this sub-project was required by the European Commission who wanted a comparison and an assessment of the different technologies in order to orientate further financial support from its part. The **case study** mainly describes a methodological approach for in depth comparison of a very small number of alternatives (three). The methodology is chosen, developed and applied with great care since the decision of promoting one of the three technologies is likely to have huge and complex impacts (financial impacts but also impacts on the environment, the competitiveness of European car manufacturers, etc.).

The **methodology** was focused on the evaluation of a single aspect (among five), namely the *technical performance*, which was considered crucial by the stakeholders (i.e. the car manufacturers involved in the project). The application did not provide a final recommendation concerning the choice of an hydrogen storage technology, since the evaluation of the three alternatives on all relevant aspects could not be completed during the course of the project. The case study's contribution should be understood as illustration of an **evaluation aiding** process rather than a multiple criteria decision aiding process.

The analysis of the stakeholders positions is of crucial interest since it had a strong influence on the process. The **client** can be identified with the European Commission, but this client had no influence on the evaluation process. The main **stakeholders** were the car manufacturers who are reluctant to openly share information due to huge industrial and commercial stakes. This led the process to focus mainly on methodological issues.

The application's **output** may be interpreted as an evaluation methodology that could be used by each car manufacturer to assess the three technologies for its own usage, while incorporating in the model its own strategic options and preferences. The present analysis can be considered a proof of concept for the attention of the European Commission (the client) and the car manufacturers.

The body responsible for the sub-project "Evaluation" was the CEA, the French *Commssariat à l'Énergie Atomique et aux Énergies Alternatives*, which acted in the role of the **analyst**. But, the CEA felt the need to hire a team from LAMSADE at University Paris Dauphine as experts in multiple criteria analysis.

The assessment of the three hydrogen storage technologies on the relevant aspects was performed by the partners in the project, who acted as **experts**.

The **timespan** of the Evaluation sub-project in which the LAMSADE team intervened covered 1 year while the whole STORHY projected extended over a period of 4 years.

There are only three **alternatives**, i.e., three technologies for storing hydrogen on board of vehicles. It was the main goal of the whole project to develop these technologies in three separate technical sub-projects.

Among the five "evaluation domains" (**points of view**) that were defined only one was the object of a multicriteria evaluation method. The evaluation of the technical performance was indeed considered a priority, before other domains such as the evaluation of the environmental impacts or the costs. Five **criteria** were identified in view of assessing the systems technical performance.

The selection of MACBETH as the **aggregation method** was motivated by explicit requirements, including the need for an absolute assessment of the performance of the three systems and the necessity of obtaining outputs, for each individual stakeholder, that are expressed on a common scale.

The **elicitation** of the model's parameters (comparison of the differences of attractiveness on each criterion and tradeoffs) was performed through interaction between the analyst (the CEA and the LAMSADE team) and *one* of the cars manufacturers. As the authors call it, this process was "application-oriented". This means that the comparisons of attractiveness and the tradeoffs required by MACBETH were assessed having in mind a particular application of the three technologies, i.e. a fuel cell for a private vehicle having an autonomy of 600 km. Presumably, the model elicited in this application is not only an evaluation of the three technologies but represents also the preferences of the involved car manufacturer.

The **evaluation** exercise of this particular application was not performed by the other cars manufacturers. Instead, in a further step, the analyst (after the end of the collaboration with the LAMSADE team) and all the car manufacturers involved in the STORHY project decided to work with relative criteria instead of absolute ones. For instance, the *system volume* criterion was substituted by the *system volumetric energy density*. This was motivated by the fact that the stakeholders are in competition on the automotive market. They have their own specific applications in view and they don't want to reveal their targets and visions to their competitors. As a consequence, the STORHY stakeholders built an "improved performance table" that not only represents the performance of the systems produced in the project but allows to evaluate the remaining research and development efforts. The evaluation in this table are formulated in terms of the relative criteria. On each criterion, the stakeholders consensually identified the levels for which strong additional (resp. additional) R&D efforts are recommended. This was done using the reference levels established in the application of the MACBETH procedure in the "application oriented" phase.

The **main characteristic** of this MCDA application is that it is an evaluation exercise rather than a decision aiding process. The second main aspect is related to the competing context of the stakeholders relationship. This strongly limited information sharing and, consequently, the scope of the evaluation exercise. Within this scope, the aspects on which further research and development efforts are required have been identified for each of the three storage technologies. Furthermore, an "application-oriented" evaluation method was set up. Each stakeholder can make use of it, for his own sake, to determine the most appropriate technology for the type of application targeted. In addition, the application of the MACBETH methodology enables to compare the system's performance to the end-users targets. In this view the definition of "acceptable" and "satisfying" reference levels has proved useful.

Chapter 18
An MCDA Approach for Personal Financial Planning

Oliver Braun and Marco Spohn

Abstract Personal Financial Planning (PFP) is the preparation of target-oriented decisions concerning assets, incomes, and expenses. As people have different preferences for different financial goals, and the goals are flexible, PFP is a Multicriteria Decision Analysis (MCDA) problem that is often addressed by trial calculations under different scenarios. We provide an MCDA model to derive a financial plan that maximizes the value of the expenses for a decision maker with respect to height, time, and type preferences. Specifically, we show how the problem can be solved through a mixed integer programming approach where the weights for the mathematical program are determined with the help of the Analytic Hierarchy Process.

18.1 Overview

A careful and target-oriented planning of financial decisions is one of the most urgent economic questions at the beginning of the twenty-first century. However, a quantitative approach to personal financial decision making is not generally accepted yet in Europe, whereas the USA have a quite long tradition of quantitative personal financial planning (PFP). PFP, in general, is about the management of all money activities during a person's lifetime, including satisfying financial life goals, maximizing wealth, and managing risks (Braun, 2009; ChiangLin and Lin, 2008; Madura, 2006).

More formally, PFP can be defined as the preparation of target-oriented decisions concerning *(1) assets*, and *(2) incomes and expenses*. The *assets view* on PFP investigates the problem of determining an optimal structure of the assets of a decision maker. This problem is known as portfolio optimization and well supplied with a lot of research contributions. To the best of our knowledge, there is only one mathematical optimization model for the *incomes and expenses view* on

O. Braun (✉) • M. Spohn
Department of Quantitative Methods for Business and Management, Trier University of Applied Sciences, Environmental Campus Birkenfeld, P.O. Box 1380, 55761 Birkenfeld, Germany
e-mail: o.braun@umwelt-campus.de

R. Bisdorff et al. (eds.), *Evaluation and Decision Models with Multiple Criteria*, International Handbooks on Information Systems,
DOI 10.1007/978-3-662-46816-6_18

PFP, namely described in the article of ChiangLin and Lin (2008). We base our investigation on the results of this article and develop an MCDA model for solving the expenses problem of personal financial planning to derive a financial plan that maximizes the value of the expenses for a decision maker with respect to height, time, and type preferences. Decision makers can be any persons who are developing a financial plan, i.e. financial planner from banks and insurances, freelancer, and individuals who do financial planning on their own. In more detail, we understand the expenses problem of personal financial planning as the complex and dynamic process of meeting financial life goals through the proper management of finances. Financial life goals can include buying a home, saving for children's education, or planning for retirement. Hereby, the decision maker might have various preferences for his or her different financial goals and these goals might be contrary in the sense that more realization of one goal means less realization of another goal. As a result, we have a multicriteria decision analysis (MCDA) problem, and mathematical programming appears as an appropriate method for formulating and solving this problem.

The paper is organized as follows. In the rest of this section, we give a literature review to the field of personal financial planning. Section 18.2 identifies the AHP and MILP framework. Section 18.3 describes the MCDA model for the expenses problem of personal financial planning. We show how height, type and time preferences of the decision maker can be derived. In Sect. 18.4, an illustrative example of how to apply the developed model is given. The model was evaluated by actors from banks and insurances, freelancers, and master students of information systems, operational research and management science. Finally, the results of the investigation are summarized in Sect. 18.5.

The PFP related literature is vast and originates a number of disciplines that investigate specific topics of importance for PFP, among them economics, psychology, and medicine. Bodie et al. (1992) investigate consumption and savings decisions as labour-leisure choice. Wittmüß (2006) investigates optimal consumption strategies with respect to different risk attitudes of a decision maker. Results concerning the optimization in models of dynamic consumption under uncertainty and (robust) expected utilities include risk aversion (Karatzas and Zitkovic, 2003; Kreps and Porteus, 1978), ambiguity (Epstein and Schneider, 2003; Gilboa and Schmeidler, 1989), and loss aversion (Siegmann and Lucas, 2006; Tversky and Kahneman, 1992). Ethical preferences and taxpayer behaviour (tax evasion) is investigated by Eisenhauer (2008). Other PFP-related models investigate models of spending and financing, and determinants of credit decisions in the private household (Kirchler et al., 2008), psychological cost of credit (Brown et al., 2005), mental accounting in consumer credit decision processes (Ranyard et al., 2006), liquidity constraints and consumer behaviour (Gross and Souleles, 2002), and mental accounting of delayed consumption (Shafir and Thaler, 2006). Brulde (2007) investigates reasons for the quality of a person's life (happiness theories). Tobler et al. (2007) investigate human brain activities reflecting individual finances.

A review of the use of OR in financial management is given in Ashford et al. (1988). The authors state that recent years have seen the development of numerous applications for OR models and algorithms in the financial world, as computer capacity and power were growing exponentially. In addition, financial institutions, large corporations and research centers are increasingly devoting important resources to research and development in financial modeling and optimization. Within the field of OR, multicriteria decision analysis (MCDA) has evolved as one important discipline. The development of MCDA is based on the finding that a single objective, goal, criterion or point of view is rarely used to make real-world decisions. State-of-the-art reviews (Steuer and Na, 2003; Spronk et al., 2005; Zopounidis and Doumpos, 2002) of the research made on the application of the techniques of MCDA to problems and issues in finance show that the multidimensional nature of financial decisions has already motivated researchers to explore the potential of MCDA in addressing financial decision-making problems because the necessity to address financial problems in a broader and more realistic context has been noted.

Especially the *assets view* on PFP is well supplied with a lot of research contributions. MCDA models for the asset's view on PFP are presented by Puelz and Puelz (1992) and Ehrgott et al. (2004). For further references on the use of optimization models for portfolio selection, the reader is referred to Pardalos et al. (1994). Gao et al. (2005, 2007) develop an agent-assisted decision support system for mainly the asset's view on family financial planning. Samaras et al. (2005) present an intelligent decision support system for portfolio management. In addition, the field is well supplied with a lot of Textbooks (Kapoor et al., 2007; Garman and Forgue, 2006; Madura, 2006). Most books can be used as guides to handle personal financial problems on a trial-and error-basis, e.g. how to come to wealth, achieving various financial goals, determining emergency savings and retirement plan contributions.

We base our contribution on the paper of ChiangLin and Lin (2008). They describe the first PFP model with the incomes and expenses view based on fuzzy multiple objective programming. They argue that solving the financial planning problem by trial-and-error gives a satisfying suggestion, but not necessarily the (concerning the preferences of the decision maker) best solution that can be found. Their approach with fuzzy goal programming is motivated by the fact that financial goals set by the decision maker or by the financial planner might be flexible. So it seems to be preferable to provide an acceptable range for a goal instead of an exact value. They close their motivation for their study by the conclusion that in view of the above difficulties, mathematical programming appears a promising approach for PFP. In more detail, ChiangLin and Lin (2008) formulate a decision model for PFP that considers the incomes from salary and investment and the expenses for living, purchasing a house and raising children. Four objectives are considered, including the level of living expense, the time to buy a house, the value of the house, and the pension available at retirement. All the objectives that contribute to one's life quality before and after retirement are to be maximized except the time to buy a house. Numerical examples are provided to show the effectiveness of their approach to PFP.

Vahidov and He (2009) describe the design and implementation of a situated decision support system (SDSS) for PFP. The SDSS model is a type of DSS that maintains close links with the target environment and has capabilities for sensing, monitoring, decision support, and limited decision making, action generation, and implementation. The authors perform experiments using human subjects to test their prototype. The experiments involve subjects who carry out their normal shopping tasks in a simulated setup. One group of subjects were provided with SDSS support, while the others used a traditional decision support model. The results show the superiority of the SDSS model over the traditional DSS in terms of key decision performance variables.

To deal with the complexities of the financial decision-making process, often an integration of Saaty's analytic hierarchy process (AHP) (Saaty, 1980, 1990) is proposed. The AHP is a multi-attribute decision-making approach based on the reasoning, knowledge, experience, and perceptions of the decision maker. Steuer and Na (2003) give a literature review on the AHP combined with finance. Besides applying to the finance sector the AHP was adopted in education, engineering, government, industry, management, manufacturing, personal, political, social, and sports (Vaidya and Kumar, 2006). An overview of the current state-of-the-art in the AHP is given in Ho (2008). Ho surveys the applications of the integrated AHPs through a literature review and classification of the international journal articles from 1997 to 2006. The study of Ho (2008) is different from the studies of Steuer and Na (2003) and Vaidya and Kumar (2006), in which the applications of the stand-alone AHP were mainly reviewed. The tools integrated with the AHP include (mixed integer) linear programming (Crary et al., 2002; Ozdemir and Gasimov, 2004), goal programming (Schniederjans and Garvin, 1997; Kwak and Lee, 1998, 2002; Kwak et al., 2005), QFD (Oboulhas et al., 2004; Partovi and Corredoira, 2002), genetic algorithms and artificial neural networks, SWOT analysis, and DEA (Yang and Kuo, 2003). It is observed that the applicability of the integrated AHPs is wide. They can be applied to more than a dozen different fields. Among these fields, logistics has attracted the most attention, followed by manufacturing, government, higher education, business, environment, military, agriculture, healthcare, marketing, industry, service, sports, and tourism.

As we are doing in this contribution, in the combined AHP–MILP approach, the AHP is used to measure the relative importance weightings of the evaluation criteria, which were then incorporated into the MILP model. As an example, Crary et al. (2002) applied the AHP to evaluate the relative importance weightings of alternative ships with respect to various missions in the US Navy. A MILP incorporating with the AHP weightings was formulated to select the best combination of ships for a particular mission, and determine the optimal number of ships for the missions. The objective of the MILP model is to maximize the fleet effectiveness or the probability of winning the wars. Other examples using an AHP–MILP combination include Tyagi and Das (1997), Korpela and Lehmusvaara (1999), Korpela et al. (2001a,b), and Korpela et al. (2002).

18.2 Problem Structuring

The main planning and control instrument of personal financial planning is the finance plan, i.e. a listing of all expected future incomes and expenses. We consider $n + 1$ time points $t = 0, \ldots, n$. The difference between two time points t and $t + 1$ corresponds to one time period. Without loss of generality there are $n + 1$ sums of incomes and $n + 1$ sums of expenses with quantities $I_t > 0$ (incomes) and $E_t > 0$ (expenses) for $t = 0, \ldots, n$. Let $I_0 > 0$ be the current liquidated wealth and $E_0 = 0$. In more detail, we define

$$I_t = \sum_{j=1}^{i_t} I_{tj}$$

the sum of incomes in period t and i_t declares the maximum number of incomes in period t. Furthermore

$$E_t = \sum_{j=1}^{e_t^{Fix}} E_{tj}^{Fix} + \sum_{j=1}^{e_t^{Var}} E_{tj}^{Var}$$

represents the sum of fixed and variable expenses where e_t^{fix} defines the maximum number of fixed expenses and e_t^{Var} the maximum number of variable expenses. We consider fixed expenses as exogenous variables which are determined by the decision maker.

In the expenses problem of personal financial planning, the decision maker has to decide about the quantities and realization timepoints of specific variable expenses reflecting his personal goals or wishes (e.g. buying a car or a house, raising children, saving for retirement). Therefore we have to consider only some classes of variable expenses and do not need to consider each expense separately. As a result, we introduce e classes of expenses $\overline{E}_1, \ldots, \overline{E}_e$ that occur repeatedly over the planning horizon.

We define a finance plan as *feasible* if all planned future expenses can be financed by current liquidated wealth and future incomes. A finance plan is *optimal* if it is feasible and if the utility of the planned variable expenses is maximized. In most cases, an approach by trial calculations under different scenarios is done to reach an acceptable finance plan satisfying most of the decision maker's requirements. This approach is not necessarily optimal and does not necessarily lead to an optimal finance plan as conflicting objectives with different goals of varying levels of importance for the decision maker might be involved in our decision problem. As a result, we have a multi-objective decision problem, and mathematical programming appears as an appropriate method for formulating and solving that problem (ChiangLin and Lin, 2008).

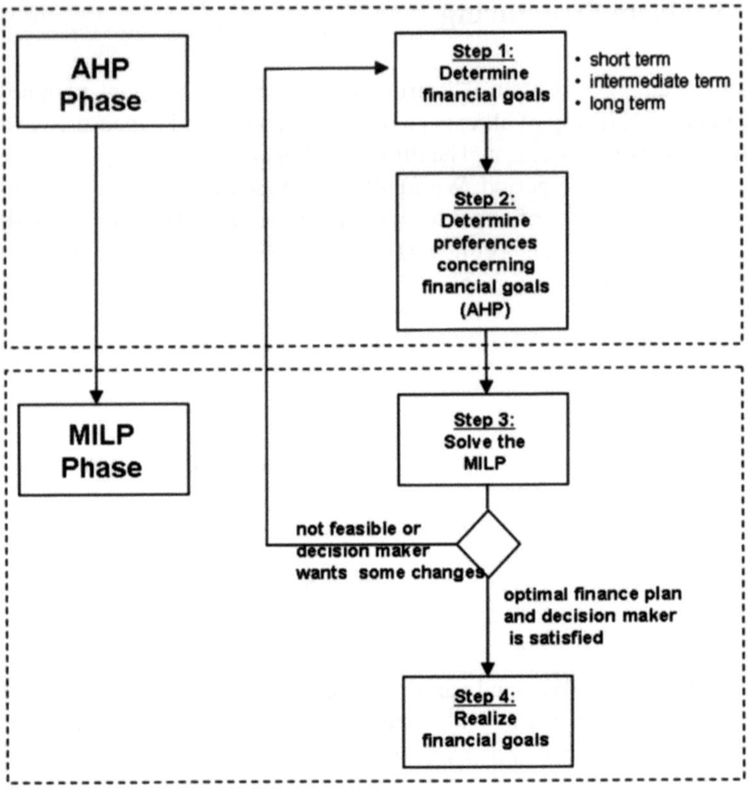

Fig. 18.1 Conceptual model

The conceptual model of the planning process for variable expenses is shown in Fig. 18.1.

The *AHP phase* is marked by identifying variable financial goals and structuring preference criteria concerning financial goals. The *MILP phase* determines an optimal solution of the financial planning problem and relaizes the financial goals.

In Step 1, financial goals and corresponding criteria are requested from the decision maker and a complete finance plan is developed. This plan contains all future incomes and expenses and is derived from the financial goals of the decision maker. Determining variable financial goals can be done with the help of individualized life-cycle scenarios. Examples of typical variable financial goals are purchasing a house or a car, raising children, saving for retirement, improving standard of living or accomplishing a world trip. Objectives might be the value of the house, car or world trip, the level of living expenses and the level of annuity. Goals can be short term, intermediate term and long term. Short term goals refer to the next 12 months (e.g. buying a computer or a car), intermediate goals often address where one wants to be in 5–20 years (e.g. buying a house). For most people, long-term goals include their date of retirement and their accumulated wealth at retirement. In Step 2, one determines the decision maker's preferences concerning her or his financial goals with the help of the analytic hierarchy process (AHP). AHP is a multi-attribute decision-making approach based on the reasoning, knowledge, experience, and perceptions of the decision maker. Over the last years, research focus has changed to the applications of the integrated AHP rather than the stand-alone AHP. Among the tools commonly combined with the AHP are mathematical programming including goal programming and mixed integer linear programming (MILP). In this line, we investigate the application of AHP combined with MILP for the solution of the expenses problem of personal financial planning.

With the parameters derived from the AHP, we build and solve in Step 3 a mixed integer linear program to determine the amount and timeframe of the variable financial goals. In this step also a *Financial Health-Check* is performed by comparing current achieved ratios to given benchmarks. Financial ratios combine numbers from the financial statements to measure a specific aspect of the personal financial situation of a client. Financial ratios are used to measure changes in the quality of the financial situation over time, to measure the absolute quality of the current financial situation, and as guidelines for how to improve the financial situation (DeVaney, 1994). The ratios are grouped into the following eight categories: liquidity, solvency, savings, asset allocation, inflation protection, tax burden, housing expenses and insolvency/credit. Even if it turns out that the finance plan is optimal with respect to the given goals and constraints, the decision maker might not be satisfied with the proposed structure of her or his financial affairs. Therefore we might jump back to Step 1 and re-formulate the variable financial goals to get a new structure. In Step 4, the decision maker chooses the (according to his or her preferences) best alternative that meets the criteria, and makes the final decision. New financial situations will make it necessary to start again with Step 1 developing a new finance plan.

18.3 Evaluation

The MCDA model choice for aggregating criteria advances the use of the AHP as an effective, realistic and new modeling approach for determining the type preferences concerning financial goals in the personal financial planning process. AHP consists of electing pairwise comparisons from the decision maker and then applying the Eigenvector theory in order to obtain the set of weights most consistent with the pairwise comparisons. The greater the AHP weight, the greater the relative importance of that criterion. In this scale, a value of "1" implies that the two criteria or expenses are of equal importance, a value of "5" implies that one criterion/expense is strongly more important than the other, and a value of "9" implies absolute importance. Assuming k criteria/expenses, we get a $k \times k$ matrix

$$M = \begin{pmatrix} a_{11} = \frac{c_1}{c_1} & a_{12} = \frac{c_1}{c_2} & \dots & a_{1k} = \frac{c_1}{c_k} \\ a_{21} = \frac{c_2}{c_1} & a_{22} = \frac{c_2}{c_2} & \dots & a_{2k} = \frac{c_2}{c_k} \\ \vdots & \vdots & \vdots & \vdots \\ a_{k1} = \frac{c_k}{c_1} & a_{k2} = \frac{c_k}{c_2} & \dots & a_{kk} = \frac{c_k}{c_k} \end{pmatrix}. \tag{18.1}$$

a_{ij} represent the number of times more important of criterion/expense i than criterion/expense j. $a_{12} = C_1/C_2 = 3$ means that criterion/expense 1 is three times more important than criterion/expense 2. In total we have $k \cdot (k-1)/2$ comparisons needed for a problem with k criteria/expenses. Because all possible pairs are compared, redundant information is obtained. This redundant information adds to the robustness of the priority weights and is used to assess consistency of judgments. The resulting matrix of preferences is evaluated by using Eigenvalues to check the consistency of the responses. Consistency can be measured by the *Consistency Ratio CR* which is the quotient of a the *Consistency Index CI* of M and a random *Consistency Value RI*, i.e. $CR := \frac{CI}{RI}$. The consistency index is obtained through

$$CI := \frac{\lambda_{max} - k}{k-1} \tag{18.2}$$

where λ_{max} defines the maximum Eigenvalue of M and k is the number of the criteria/expenses. The values of the random consistency can be calculated as

$$RI := 1.98 \cdot \frac{k-2}{k} \quad \text{(Saaty, 1980).} \tag{18.3}$$

For the consistency ratio there is a value of less than 0.05 for 3×3 matrices sought, a value of less than 0.09 for 4×4 matrices and a value of less than 0.10 for larger matrices. For the cases where one has to face a problem of incomplete pairwise comparisons, e.g. if the number of alternatives is large or if it is convenient to skip some directal comparisons, there exist approaches which try to compute the missing elements (Carmone et al., 1997; Fedrizzi and Giove, 2006; Kwiesielewicz, 1996).

Type preferences represent the decision maker's appreciation to the type of the variable expenses among each other. Therefore the decision maker has to determine values w_a^{Tpe} $(a = 1, \dots, e)$ reflecting his type preferences for each of the variable expenses. This can be accomplished by the following two steps:

1. In a first step, the decision maker has to determine criteria with which the classes of expenses can be made comparable.
2. In a second step, the values of the classes of expenses with respect to each of the criteria have to be compared.

The criteria with which the expenses can be made comparable have to be derived from objectives of the decision maker. Keeney (1992) describes an objective as a statement of something that one desires to achieve. It is characterized by three features: a decision context, an object, and a direction of preference. For the objective maximizing fortune the decision context is personal financial planning, the objective is wealth, and more wealth is preferred to less wealth. There are two types of objective: Fundamental objectives characterize an essential reason for interest in a decision situation. Means objectives are of interest in the decision context because of their implications for the degree to which a more fundamental objective can be achieved. As an example, maximizing the time that a person is working is a means objective, because of its implications for the objective of maximizing fortune.

For an individual, the strategic decision context is managing one's life. The fundamental and overall strategic objective in this decision context is to maximize the quality of life, a notion closely related to self-actualizations described in Maslow (1968). Maximizing the quality of life as strategic objective is shared by most, if not all, individuals. What differs from one individual to another is the definition of quality of life. Major objectives in this context may be to enjoy life, to be intellectually fulfilled, to enhance the lives of family and friends, and to contribute to society. In our framework, we propose the following three categories of strategic objectives:

1. economical (fortune, prestige),
2. social (family, friends, society), and
3. personal (health, mind).

Other categories of strategic objectives are also possible and have to be defined together with the decision maker. This is one of the most important steps in personal financial planning as categories of strategic objectives are essential to guide all the effort in decision situations and in the evaluation of means objectives. Those means objectives are necessary for analyzing the decision problem of choosing between a set of variable financial goals. As stated above, one means objective may be maximizing fortune. Other means objectives that are commonly named are to manage property and liability risk, to manage retirement planning, to provide children a good education, to manage health expenses, to manage life insurance planning, to manage vehicle and other major purchases, to manage buying a home, to manage estate planning, and to manage investments (Kapoor et al., 2007). In either case, strategic and means objectives have to be defined together with the person who has to choose between the expenses. What is important is that all of the means objectives have to be set in relationship to the strategic objectives in a central relationship matrix (a similar concept has been realized in the quality function deployment process (QFD) for supplier criteria (Oboulhas et al., 2004; Akao, 1990)). As a result, the weights $w_a^{Tpe}, a = 1, \ldots, e$, that reflect the type preferences concerning variable financial goals of the decision maker can then be determined with the following algorithm.

1. In the first step, the overall importance weighting of the strategic objectives is computed by using the AHP technique. The resulting vector records the relative degree of importance for each strategic objective. In this stage, the decision maker makes pair wise comparisons of the m strategic objectives using the nine-point scale of AHP to construct the column vector $s_i, i = 1, 2, \ldots, m$, of importance weighting of strategic objectives.
2. In the second step, a central relationship matrix is established that determines the degree of relationship between each pair of strategic and means objective.
   a. In this matrix a scale of 9, 6, 3, 0 denoting a strong, moderate, weak and no relationship is used in each cell that reflects the extent to which the means objective contributes to meeting the corresponding strategic objective.
   b. The degree of importance of each means objective is computed from the weighted column sum of the importance weighting of each strategic objective multiplied by the AHP-relationship value of the corresponding means objective in the central evaluation matrix. That is, if n means objectives and m strategic objectives are considered, the degree of importance of each means objective is computed by the following equation.

$$t_j = \sum_{i=1}^{m} R_{ij} s_i \tag{18.4}$$

   where s_i = importance weighting of the ith strategic objective ($i = 1, 2, \ldots, m$), t_j = importance degree of the jth means objective ($j = 1, 2, \ldots, n$), R_{ij} = quantified relationship value between the ith strategic objective and the jth means objective in the central relationship matrix.
   c. The degree of importance of each means objective is then normalized to a total of 100 to represent the weight of each means objective in the PFP model:

$$tN_j = \frac{t_j}{\sum_{j=1}^{n} t_j} \cdot 100. \tag{18.5}$$

3. For all of the means objectives, AHP is used to make pair wise comparisons of the expenses to indicate how much more satisfactory one candidate of each pair is than the other one. The pair wise comparison is used to compute the evaluating score for each expense for each of the means objectives. As we consider e classes of expenses, this step requires $m\ e\ (e-1)/2$ comparisons.
4. In the final step, an overall score for each of the expenses is computed by the following equation:

$$w_a^{Tpe} = \sum_{i=1}^{n} tN_j e_{ja}/100 \tag{18.6}$$

where w_a^{Tpe} = weight of ath expense ($a = 1, 2, \ldots, e$), tN_j = normalized importance degree of the jth means objective, e_{ja} = evaluating score of the ath expense on the jth means objective computed with AHP.

The higher the overall score of an expense the more useful is this expense to the decision maker.

In the following we describe the mixed integer linear program. We use the notation of Table 18.1.

It is easy to see that the feasibility of a finance plan can be checked in (in the number of periods) linear time as the condition $S_t > 0$ must hold in every single period t. Thereby the income surplus S_t can be iteratively computed as

$$S_t := S_{t-1} \cdot (1 + r) + I_t - E_t \tag{18.7}$$

with r the average inflation-adjusted interest rate per period. In this case, all future expenses can be financed by current wealth and future incomes. Furthermore people often feel more safe if they have a certain amount of money that is available at any time, i.e. a liquidity reserve. Let this liquidity reserve be a constant value L. Therewith we can formulate the liquidity constraints as follows where $q = 1 + r$.

$$\sum_{s=1}^{t} \left(\sum_{j=1}^{e_s} E_{sj}^{Fix} + \sum_{j=1}^{e_s^{Var}} E_{sj}^{Var} \right) q^{t-s} \leq \sum_{s=0}^{t} \sum_{j=1}^{i_s} I_{sj} q^{t-s} - L \tag{18.8}$$

If an expense, such as the purchase of a car or house, cannot be financed by current wealth and current income, our model allows the raising of a credit. For ease of use we regard only one credit per period. Furthermore we assume a certain credit limit K_t^+ for period t. The amount of the credit is defined by K_t. As a consequence we need additional constraints $K_t \leq K_t^+$ for each period $t = 1, \ldots, n$ in order to assure that the credit limit is not exceeded. With respect to our model we distinguish two forms of debt capital: short and long term debt capital. We want to examine three examples which show the application of these credit forms.

The first one (short term credit) implies for instance an overdraft credit that can be seen as additional income which has to repaid in the following period together with the overdraft interest. We consider again a liquidity reserve L that may be hold in an investment, c defines the lending rate. Then, the liquidity constraint for a single period t can be described as:

$$\sum_{s=1}^{t} \left(\sum_{j=1}^{e_s^{Fix}} E_{sj}^{Fix} + \sum_{j=1}^{e_s^{Var}} E_{sj}^{Var} + cK_{s-1} \right) q^{t-s} \leq \sum_{s=0}^{t} \left(\sum_{j=1}^{i_s} I_{sj} + K_s \right) \cdot q^{t-s} - L \tag{18.9}$$

The second possibility (long term credit) depicts an installment credit, for example. In this form of credit, the annual payment rate consists of a constant

Table 18.1 Notation

E_t	Sum of fixed and variable expenses in period t
E_{tj}^{Fix}	Amount of fixed expense j in period t
E_{tj}^{Var}	Amount of variable expense j in period t
E_{tj}^{RC}	Sum of resulting costs belonging to variable expense E_{tj}
E_{tj}^{DP}	Amount of a single consumer debt payment j in period t
E_{tj}^{GDP}	Amount of a single gross annual debt payment j in period t
E_{tj}^{SC}	Amount of a single shelter payment j in period t
E_t^{Deb}	Amount of a single loan repayment in period t
E_{tj}^{+}	Desired amount of expense j in period t
E_{tj}^{-}	Minimum amount of expense j in period t
e_t^{Fix}	Maximum number of fixed expenses in period t
e_t^{Var}	Maximum number of variable expenses in period t
e_t^{DP}	Maximum number of consumer debt payments in period t
e_t^{GDP}	Maximum number of gross annual debt payments in period t
e_t^{SC}	Maximum number of shelter payments in period t
e	Number of classes of variable expenses to be considered
$\overline{E}_1, \ldots, \overline{E}_e$	Classes of variable expenses to be considered
I_t	Sum of incomes in period t
I_{tj}	Feasible amount of income j in period t
I_0	Current liquidated wealth
i_t	Maximum number of incomes in period t
r	Average inflation adapted interest rate per period
q	1+r
c	Average lending rate per period
S_t	Income surplus in period t
L	Liquidity reserve
K_t	Required amount of loan in period t
K_t^{+}	Credit limit
K_{tf}^{Ins}	Annual installment of an installment credit which was granted in period t and has to be repaid in period f
K_{tf}^{Ann}	Annuity of an annuity loan that was raised in period t and has to be repaid in period f
$w_{lm}^{Hgt}, w_{tjk}^{Hgt}$	Height preferences: weights for $\overline{E}_l$ and E_{tj}^{Var} respectively regarding the realized quantity
w_{tj}^{Tpe}	Type preferences: weight for expense E_{tj}^{Var} in comparison to all other expenses
w_{tjk}^{Tme}	Time preferences: weight for E_{tj} if it is realized in period k
p_l	Number of intervals in which the height preference function of expense class $\overline{E}_l$ can be split up

(continued)

Table 18.1 (continued)

v_l^{Hgt}, v_{tj}^{Hgt}	Value functions that describe height preferences of class $\overline{E}_l$ and a single expense E_{tj} respectively
v_l^{Tme}, v_{tj}^{Tme}	Value functions that describe time preferences of class $\overline{E}_l$ and a single expense E_{tj} respectively
E_{tji}^{+}	Upper bound of interval i belonging to the height preference function of expense tj
n	Number of periods in the planning horizon

repayment and an interest payment which is based on the remaining debt. Hence we obtain the liquidity constraint for a certain period t as follows:

$$\sum_{s=1}^{t}\left(\sum_{j=1}^{e_s^{Fix}} E_{sj}^{Fix} + \sum_{j=1}^{e_s^{Var}} E_{sj}^{Var} + \frac{f-t+1}{f-s}\cdot cK_{sf}^{Ins} + \frac{K_{sf}^{Ins}}{f-s}\right) q^{t-s}$$

$$\leq \sum_{s=0}^{t}\left(\sum_{j=1}^{i_s} I_{sj} + K_s\right)\cdot q^{t-s} - L \tag{18.10}$$

In this example c determines the lending rate of the credit and the variable K_s defines the amount of credit a consumer should borrow in period s. Consequently we can establish

$$K_{sf}^{Ins} = \begin{cases} K_s & \text{if } 1 < s \leq f \\ 0 & \text{otherwise} \end{cases}$$

where the index f indicates the period the credit has to be repaid. The third possibility (long term credit) displays an annuity loan (redemption at the end of duration). Therefore we can express the liquidity constraints as:

$$\sum_{s=1}^{t}\left(E_s + K_{s-1,f}^{Ann}\right)\cdot q^{t-s} \leq \sum_{s=0}^{t}\left(\sum_{j=1}^{i_s} I_{sj} + K_s\right)\cdot q^{t-s} - L \tag{18.11}$$

where

$$K_{sf}^{Ann} = \begin{cases} \frac{K_s}{\sum_{t=1}^{f-s}(1+c)^{-t}} = \frac{(1+c)^{f-s}c}{(1+c)^{f-s}-1}\cdot K_s & \text{if } s \leq f \\ 0 & \text{otherwise.} \end{cases} \tag{18.12}$$

K_{sf}^{Ann} implies the annuity of a credit that was raised in period s and has to be repaid in period f.

Financial ratios combine numbers from the financial statements to measure a specific aspect of the personal financial situation. They are used to measure changes in the quality of the financial situation over time, to measure the absolute quality of the current financial situation, and as guidelines for how to improve the financial situation or predict a households insolvency (Mason and Griffith, 1988). In order to ensure a household's financial health we consider the following ratios according to DeVaney (1994).

Gross Annual Debt Payments/Income < 0.35*:* This ratio indicates the portion of income going towards debt payment. The *Gross Annual Debt Payments* consist of the household's debt payments and its shelter costs. This leads to

$$\frac{\sum_{j=1}^{e_t^{GDP}} E_{tj}^{GDP}}{\sum_{j=1}^{i_t} I_{tj}} < 0.35 \tag{18.13}$$

where E_{tj}^{GDP} determines a single debt payment and e_t^{GDP} the number of *Gross Annual Debt Payments* in period t.

Annual Consumer Debt Payments/Income < 0.15*:* This *consumer debt ratio* examines the portion of disposable income committed to the payment of debt. With regard to our model we can formulate the constraint for a certain period t:

$$\frac{\sum_{j=1}^{e_t^{DP}} E_{tj}^{DP}}{\sum_{j=1}^{i_t} I_{tj}} < 0.15 \tag{18.14}$$

At this, E_{tj}^{DP} determines a single consumer debt payment and e_t^{DP} the number of consumer debt payments in period t. In case of an installment credit amounting to K_s which was granted in period s and has to be repaid in period f (with $s \leq t \leq f$) the loan repayment E_{tj}^{DP} can be assessed as

$$E_t^{DP} = \frac{f - t + 1}{f - s} \cdot cK_s + \frac{K_s}{f - s} \quad . \tag{18.15}$$

Annual Shelter Costs/Income < 0.28*:* This ratio indicates the portion of income going to housing. We can formulate this constraint for period t as follows:

$$\frac{\sum_{j=1}^{e_t^{SC}} E_{tj}^{SC}}{\sum_{j=1}^{i_t} I_{tj}} < 0.28 \tag{18.16}$$

E_{tj}^{SC} defines a single shelter payment. Shelter costs include rent or mortgage and a maintenance fee for homeowners where the maintenance fee can be calculated by multiplying the current market value of the home by 3 %.

Note that we consider in the following only e classes of variable expenses $\overline{E}_1, \ldots, \overline{E}_l, \ldots, \overline{E}_e$. It is not necessary to determine preferences for every single expense but only for the classes. Height preferences reflect the decision maker's ideals concerning each of his financial goals and can be illustrated by value functions. Therefore it is necessary to ask for a lower bound $\overline{E}_l^-$ and an upper bound $\overline{E}_l^+$ for each of the variable expenses classes $\overline{E}_l$. In general there exist different types of value functions which correspond to the microeconomical view of consumption preferences. In our case we assume a *concave* height preference in the interval from $\overline{E}_l^-$ to $\overline{E}_l^+$ which is or can be approximated by a piecewise linear function. Concave height preferences imply the more of a certain financial goal can be realized the better. Each of the value functions v_l^{Hgt} that belong to a certain class of expenses $\overline{E}_l$ can be split into p_l ranges $[u_{l,m-1}, u_{l,m}]$ with $m = 1, \ldots, p_l$ and we have $v_l^{Hgt}(x) = \sum_{i=1}^{p_l} v_{li}^{Hgt}(x)$ with linear functions v_{li}^{Hgt}. From a practical standpoint, these intervals are often determined by model types. Furthermore the value function v_l^{Hgt} is usually normalized to the interval [0, 1] and can be written as $v_l = \sum_{m=1}^{p_l} w_{lm}^{Hgt} \overline{E}_{lm}$ where $0 \leq \overline{E}_{lm} \leq u_{lm} - u_{l,m-1}$ and w_{lm}^{Hgt} defines the gradient of the corresponding line segment between $u_{l,m-1}$ and u_{lm}. The gradient itself can be computed as

$$w_{lm}^{Hgt} = \frac{v(u_{lm}) - v(u_{l,m-1})}{u_{lm} - u_{l,m-1}}. \tag{18.17}$$

The height preferences for each of the variable expenses can then be derived from the height preferences of the corresponding classes of expenses.

We assume the existence of an additive intertemporal value function for each class of variable expenses $\overline{E}_l$ that can be generally written as $\sum_{t=1}^{n} w_{lt}^{Tme} v_{lt}^{Tme}(\overline{E}_l^+)$ where $\overline{E}_l^+$ determines the desired value for a certain class of expenses $\overline{E}_l$ and v_{lt}^{Tme} defines the associated single value function of a certain period t. As we imply the same value function for all periods we want to write v_l instead of v_{lt} from now on. Furthermore we assume a decreasing run of the value curve in the interval [0, 1], i.e. the earlier an expense can be realized the better. Therefore time preferences sometimes allow a time shift of particular expenses. If it is for example not possible to afford two expenses of the same amount in period one, it is maybe possible to realize one in the first and one in the second period. Which of them should be realized in the first and the second period depends on the decision maker's time preference. Again we can derive the time preferences for a single expense E_{tj}^{Var} from the corresponding class of expenses.

The liquidity constraint for a particular period t can be displayed as

$$\sum_{s=1}^{t} \sum_{j=1}^{e_s} \sum_{k=s}^{t} E_{sj}^{+} y_{sjk} \leq I_0 q^t + \sum_{s=1}^{t} \sum_{j=1}^{i_s} I_{sj} q^{t-s} - L \tag{18.18}$$

where

$$y_{sjk} = \begin{cases} 1 & \text{if expense } E_{sj} \text{ can be realized in period } k, \\ 0 & \text{otherwise} \end{cases} \tag{18.19}$$

Sometimes there is also a need to consider resulting costs that are connected to acquisitions. As an example, in case of purchasing a car, these costs might be insurances or gasoline. If we want to take this possibility into account we can add the term $y_{tjk} E_{tj}^{RC}$ to the yearly expenses where E_{tj}^{RC} defines the sum of resulting costs of expense E_{tj}^{Var} in period t.

In order to ascertain that a particular expense E_{tj}^{Var} is only realized once we have to add the constraint $\sum_{k=s}^{n} y_{sjk} \leq 1$ to the model.

As mentioned above, the weights for the periods w_{sj}^{Tme} can be obtained through interaction with the decision maker. If we assume a linear run where t_{sj}^{-} defines the earliest and t_{sj}^{+} the latest possible realization period, the points $(t_{sj}^{-}, 1)$ and $(t_{sj}^{+}, 0)$ define a straight line. Therewith the weights can be derived as $w_{sj}^{Tme} = \frac{t_{sj}^{-} - t}{t_{sj}^{+} - t_{sj}^{-}} + 1$. A probably more realistic way to determine the value function exists in splitting the period under consideration into several parts and defining values for the corresponding interval borders. Within the intervals a linear run of the value function can be assumed. This approach is e.g. used by the *Direct-Rating-Method*, *Difference Standard Sequence Method* or the *Bisection Method*.

Summing up the results of the preceding sections, we come to the optimization model displayed in Fig. 18.2. We assume that all time preferences w_{sjk}^{Tme}, type preferences w_{sj}^{Tpe}, height preferences w_{sji}^{Hgt} and incomes I_{sj} as well as the inflation rate r and $q = 1 + r$ are previously known or defined by the decision maker, i.e. exogenously determined whereas the expenses E_{sji}^{Var} are endogenous. All variables y_{sjk} and y_{tjk}, respectively, are of type boolean and indicate whether an variable expense E_{tjk}^{Var} can be realized in the desired period k or not.

$$\begin{aligned}
&Max \sum_{s=1}^{n} \sum_{j=1}^{e_s} w_{sj}^{Tpe} \left(\sum_{k=s}^{n} w_{sjk}^{Tme} y_{sjk} + \sum_{i=1}^{p_{sj}} m_{sji} E_{sji}^{Var} \right) \\
&s.t. \quad \text{(liquidity constraints)} \\
&\qquad \sum_{s=1}^{t} \sum_{j=1}^{e_s^{Var}} \sum_{i=1}^{p_{sj}} E_{sji}^{Var} q^{t-s} \qquad \leq \sum_{s=0}^{t} \sum_{j=1}^{i_s} I_{sj} q^{t-s} \\
&\qquad \qquad \qquad \qquad \qquad \qquad \qquad -L \forall t = 1, \ldots, n \\
&\qquad \text{(realize goals not more than once)} \\
&\qquad \sum_{k=s}^{n} y_{tjk} \qquad \leq 1 \qquad \forall t = 1, \ldots, n \\
&\qquad \qquad \qquad \qquad \qquad \qquad \forall j = 1, \ldots, e_t^{Var}
\end{aligned}$$

Fig. 18.2 Linear programming model for the expenses problem for personal financial planning

(upper bounds)

$$\sum_{i=1}^{p_{tj}} E^{Var}_{tji} \leq E^{+}_{tj} \quad \forall t = 1,\dots,n \quad \forall j = 1,\dots,e^{Var}_t$$

(lower bounds)

$$\sum_{i=1}^{p_{tj}} E^{Var}_{tji} \geq E^{-}_{tj} \quad \forall t = 1,\dots,n \quad \forall j = 1,\dots,e^{Var}_t$$

(interval constraints)

$$E^{Var}_{tji} \leq E^{+}_{tji} \quad \forall t = 1,\dots,n \quad \forall j = 1,\dots,e^{Var}_t$$

(credit restrictions)

$$K_t \leq K^{+}_t y_t$$

(financial ratios)

$$\frac{\sum_{j=1}^{e^{GDP}_t} E^{GDP}_{tj}}{\sum_{j=1}^{i_t} I_{tj}} < 0,35 \quad \forall t = 1,\dots,n$$

$$\frac{\sum_{j=1}^{e^{DP}_t} E^{DP}_{tj}}{\sum_{j=1}^{i_t} I_{tj}} < 0,15 \quad \forall t = 1,\dots,n$$

$$\frac{\sum_{j=1}^{e^{SC}_t} E^{SC}_{tj}}{\sum_{j=1}^{i_t} I_{tj}} < 0,28 \quad \forall t = 1,\dots,n$$

$$y_t, y_{tjk} \in \{0,1\} \quad \forall t = 1,\dots,n \quad \forall j = 1,\dots,e_t \quad \forall k = t,\dots,n$$

18.4 Process-Related Aspects

In general, the decision making process concerning personal financial planning is an iterative process which requires the interaction of client and analyst. In our case we want to assume that the client can be any single person that wants to perform an analysis of her or his personal financial affairs. This person can be a banker, an insurance specialist, or a student. The underlying software which was built to assist these people managing their personal financial affairs can be seen as the analyst (maybe supported by a financial planning analyst).

From time to time there might be some changes necessary to the financial plan which is the result of every planning process as described. These changes can be caused by new wishes which come up at a later stage, changes of the personal situation, e.g. marriage, modifications in the underlying priorities or changes in outer circumstances, e.g. a significant pay raise, adaptations in interest rates etc. Therefore, the overall financial planning process should be rather seen as an iterative process between client and analyst than as one time activity. Doing this, it is the best way to ensure that the client's personal financial goals and all her or his preferences are correctly incorporated and handled by the model. In this context it should be underlined that the purpose of our model is not the determination of an objective optimum.

We implemented the proposed framework and presented the software to financial planners from banks and insurances, and to master students with a financial planning and information management background. The feedback shows that the software is meaningful to use. One of the most important points is that the software helps people to clarify and rank wishes on future variable incomes and expenses much more better than a trial-and-error approach. The software allows people to come to personal financial plans that fit their personal preferences in an optimal way.

In the following we present a small illustration of the developed model. For demonstration purposes we restrict to an artificial problem setting with only three variable expenses. All incomes and expenses are expected to increase with the inflation rate which is estimated to be 3 %.

A couple has regular incomes of 60,000 EUR per year and their regular expenses amount is 40,000 EUR per year including 12,000 EUR rent for their apartment.. The couple currently has 200,000 EUR in investment with an annual inflation-adjusted rate of return of 3%. All surplus incomes will be reinvested in the same investment. Both partners plan to retire at the age of 60, after their retirement their income comes down to 40,000 EUR per year, the expenses to 30,000 EUR per year. Overall their finance plan should cover the next 35 years and their liquidity reserve should be 10,000 EUR. The couple plans to buy their own house within the next five years. They prefer a price range from 300,000 to 400,000 EUR. They are able to use an installment credit up to the amount of 120,000 EUR in order to finance their house. The credit period would be 15 years. They also want to spend money every five years in the category of 50,000 to 60,000 EUR (for cars and travelling) until their retirement. This goal should be handled flexible. For the university attendance of their son in 10 years, their expenses will increase by 8,000 to 10,000 EUR per year for a period of approximately five years.

In case we consider a house of 400,000 EUR, a new car of 60,000 EUR every 5 years and an additional amount of 10,000 EUR for the university attendance, the resulting finance plan is not feasible as the investments are steadily lower than 0. However, if we regard the minimum amount there is still money available which could be invested into one of the financial goals to improve the couple's quality of life.

Now, the questions are

- how much money should be spend for which financial goal,
- when should which financial goal be realized, and
- to what amount should a credit be raised.

In order to answer the questions we need to determine the corresponding preferences of the couple. The weights derived from these preferences are then used as parameters for the MILP.

18.4.1 AHP Phase

In the AHP phase, the type preferences can be defined in dialogue with the couple. Therefore the couple have to determine criteria with which the expenses can be made comparable. They might come to $k = 3$ criteria:

- C_1 = *economical (fortune, prestige)*,
- C_2 = *social (family, friends)*, and
- C_3 = *personal (health, mind)*.

In our example, the couple assigns a value of $a_{12} = 7$ in comparing C_1 to C_2 (i.e. C_1 is very strongly more important than C_2) and assigns a value of $a_{23} = 1/5$ (i.e. C_3 is strongly more important than C_2) in comparing C_2 to C_3. Assuming perfect consistency, a value of $a_{13} = 7/5$ would be assigned in comparing C_1 to C_3. Although this might be calculated in such using this method, the couple also directly compares C_1 to C_3, thus providing redundant information, e. g. $a_{13} = 1/2$ (i.e. C_3 is slightly more important than C_1).

In this example, the resulting AHP-matrix is not consistent, and such inconsistencies are typical. The Eigenvalue of M is $\mathbf{g} = (0.379, 0.072, 0.549)^T$. The second iteration leads to an Eigenvalue of $\mathbf{g} = (0.382, 0.077,\ 0.541)^T$ and the iteration terminates as the difference between the Eigenvalues is smaller than a prescribed value (in our case e.g. 0.01). The consistency index is $CI = (\lambda_{max} - k)/(k-1) = 0.12$. As the result, the couple gives criterion C_3 = *personal (health, mind)* the highest value ($g_3 = 0.541$), criterion C_1 = *economical (fortune, prestige)* the second highest value ($g_1 = 0.382$), and criterion C_2 = *social (family, friends)* the lowest value ($g_2 = 0.077$).

In the second step, the value of each of the financial goals *House*, *Education*, and *Cars* is compared in respect to the three criteria C_1, C_2 and C_3.

Let's assume a questioning of the couple's preferences yields to the following matrices (with respect to the three criteria):

$$M(C_1) = \begin{pmatrix} 1 & 1/9 & 1 \\ 9 & 1 & 9 \\ 1 & 1/9 & 1 \end{pmatrix},\ M(C_2) = \begin{pmatrix} 1 & 1/5 & 1/9 \\ 5 & 1 & 1/7 \\ 9 & 7 & 1 \end{pmatrix},\ M(C_3) = \begin{pmatrix} 1 & 7 & 6 \\ 1/7 & 1 & 1/3 \\ 1/6 & 3 & 1 \end{pmatrix}.$$

The Eigenvalues are $\mathbf{h_1} = (0.091, 0.818, 0.091)^T$, $\mathbf{h_2} = (0.055, 0.173, 0.772)^T$, and $\mathbf{h_3} = (0.750, 0.078, 0.172)^T$. The consistency indexes are $CI(\mathbf{h}_1) = 0.00$, $CI(\mathbf{h}_2) = 0.11$ and $CI(\mathbf{h}_3) = 0.05$. Therewith the type preferences $w_t^{Tpe} = \sum_{j=1}^{k} h_{t,j} \cdot g_j$ for the MILP are then $w_1 = 0.445$, $w_2 = 0.368$, and $w_3 = 0.187$.

18.4.2 MILP Phase

The couple's height preferences for their financial goals *House*, *Education* and *Cars* are displayed in Fig. 18.3 where e.g. 10' represents 10,000 EUR.

As we can see, the height preference curve for *House* can be split into four intervals with piecewise linear segments. The slope of the curve decreases in every interval, the greatest utility increase shows therefore in the first segment. The height

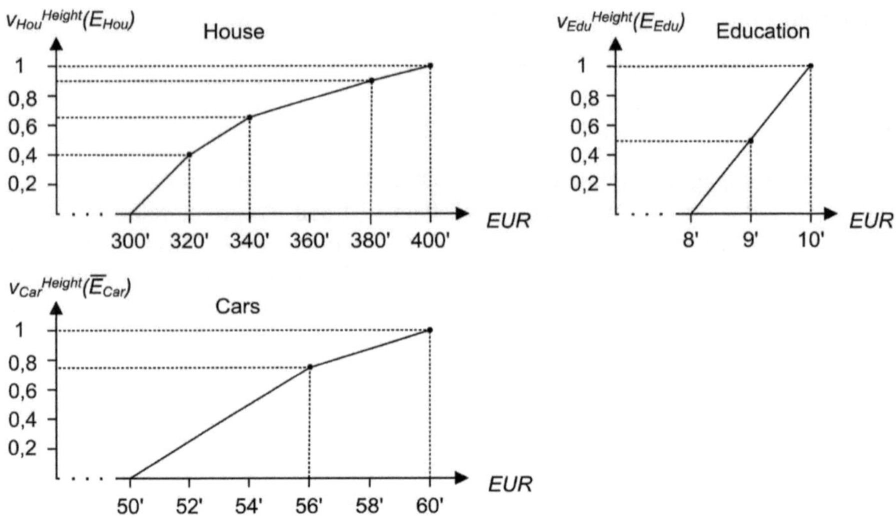

Fig. 18.3 Height preferences: house, education and cars

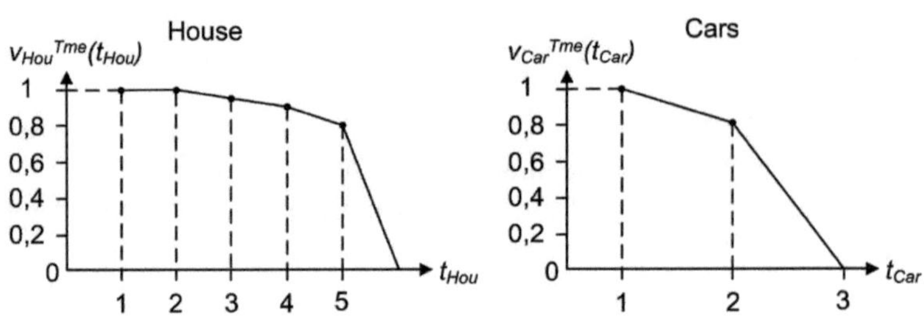

Fig. 18.4 Time preferences: *house* and *cars*

preference curve of *Education* has its greatest slope in the interval from 50,000 EUR to 56,000 EUR where it reaches a preference value of 0.75. The height preference for *Cars* is a straight line, i.e. the utility increases continuously from 8,000 EUR to 10,000 EUR.

We need to know how flexible the goals are in time, i.e. the time preferences have to be determined. We could imagine that the couple defined them as follows.

Figure 18.4 shows that the couple is indifferent about the realization point of their *House* within the first two periods. Each of these time points leads to a maximum utility of 1. In the following periods the utility decreases slightly until it falls down to 0 in period 5. From Fig. 18.4 we can also see that utility of the realization of the *Cars* decreases from 1 in period 1 to 0.8 in period 2 which means should take place within the first 2 years since the value function reaches its minimum value of 0 in period 3. Since there is no flexibility in time for *Education* a time preference function does not need to be explicitly determined. Nevertheless, if we would do so we had value 1 in period 1 and 0 for all other periods.

The resulting mixed integer linear program is described in the following. In order to better distinguish goals we want to write E_{111}^{Hou} instead of just E_{111}^{Var} as proposed in the general model. In the same way we also want to display all other goals. Therefore let E_{sji}^{Hou} be the amount of money that could be spent for the financial goal *House*, E_{sji}^{Edu} the amount of money for *Education*, and $E_{sji}^{Car_o}$ the amount of money for the financial goal *Cars*. Thereby s defines the realization period relatively to the planned realization time point (1 means the expense is realized in the same period, 2 means the expense is postponed one period) and i the interval according to the height preferences. Furthermore y_s^{Hou} indicates whether the house can be realized in period s or not—just as y_{ts}^{Edu} for *Education* and $y_{ts}^{Car_o}$ for the goal *Cars*. y_t^K indicates whether the loan should be taken out in period t or not.

$$
\begin{aligned}
Max\ & 0.445 \cdot (y_1^{Hou} + y_2^{Hou} + 0.95y_3^{Hou} + 0.9y_4^{Hou} + 0.8y_5^{Hou} + 0.0002 \\
& \cdot (E_{111}^{Hou} + E_{112}^{Hou} + E_{113}^{Hou} + E_{114}^{Hou}) + \ldots + 0.000005 \cdot (E_{511}^{Hou} + E_{512}^{Hou} + E_{513}^{Hou} + E_{514}^{Hou}) \\
& + 0.000184 \cdot E_{10,1,1}^{Edu} + 0.187 \cdot \left(y_1^{Car_1} + 0.8y_2^{Car_1} + 0.000125 \cdot (E_{521}^{Car_1} + E_{522}^{Car_1})\right. \\
& + 0.0000625 \cdot (E_{611}^{Car_1} + E_{612}^{Car_1}) + \ldots + y_1^{Car_4} + 0.8y_2^{Car_4} + 0.000125 \\
& \left. \cdot (E_{20,1,1}^{Car_4} + E_{20,1,2}^{Car_4}) + 0.0000625 \cdot (E_{21,1,1}^{Car_4} + E_{21,1,2}^{Car_4})\right)
\end{aligned}
$$

$$
\begin{array}{lll}
s.t. & \text{(liquidity constraints)} & \\
(1) & 40{,}000 + E_{111}^{Hou} + E_{112}^{Hou} & \\
 & + E_{113}^{Hou} + E_{114}^{Hou} & \leq 200{,}000q + 60{,}000 + K_1 - 10{,}000 \\
(2) & (40{,}000 + E_{111}^{Hou} + E_{112}^{Hou} + E_{113}^{Hou} + E_{114}^{Hou}) \cdot q + & \leq 200{,}000q^2 + (60{,}000 + K_1) \cdot q + \\
 & 40{,}000 + E_{211}^{Hou} + E_{212}^{Hou} & \\
 & + E_{213}^{Hou} + E_{214}^{Hou} + cK_1 + \frac{K_1}{15} & 60{,}000 + K_2 - 10{,}000 \\
(3) & (40{,}000 + E_{111}^{Hou} + E_{112}^{Hou} + E_{113}^{Hou} + E_{114}^{Hou}) \cdot q^2 + & \leq 200{,}000q^3 + (60{,}000 + K_1) \cdot q^2 + \\
 & (40{,}000 + E_{211}^{Hou} + E_{212}^{Hou} + E_{213}^{Hou} & \\
 & + E_{214}^{Hou} + cK_1 + \frac{K_1}{15}) \cdot q + & (60{,}000 + K_2) \cdot q + \\
 & 40{,}000 + E_{311}^{Hou} + E_{312}^{Hou} + E_{313}^{Hou} + E_{314}^{Hou} & \\
 & + \frac{14cK_1}{15} + \frac{K_1}{15} + cK_2 + \frac{K_2}{15} & 60{,}000 + K_3 - 10{,}000 \\
\vdots & \text{(realize goals not more than once)} & \\
(36) & y_1^{Hou} + y_2^{Hou} + y_3^{Hou} + y_4^{Hou} + y_5^{Hou} & \leq 1 \\
(37) & y_1^{Car_1} + y_2^{Car_1} & \leq 1 \\
\vdots & \text{(upper bounds)} & \\
(41) & E_{111}^{Hou} + E_{112}^{Hou} + E_{113}^{Hou} + E_{114}^{Hou} & \leq 400{,}000y_1^{Hou} \\
(42) & E_{211}^{Hou} + E_{212}^{Hou} + E_{213}^{Hou} + E_{214}^{Hou} & \leq 400{,}000y_2^{Hou} \\
\vdots & & \\
(46) & E_{10,2,1}^{T} & \leq 10{,}000 \\
(47) & E_{521}^{Car_1} + E_{522}^{Car_1} & \leq 60{,}000y_1^{Car_1} \\
(48) & E_{611}^{Car_1} + E_{612}^{Car_1} & \leq 60{,}000y_2^{Car_1} \\
\vdots & \text{(lower bounds)} & \\
(55) & E_{111}^{Hou} + E_{112}^{Hou} + E_{113}^{Hou} + E_{114}^{Hou} & \geq 300{,}000y_1^{Hou} \\
(56) & E_{211}^{Hou} + E_{212}^{Hou} + E_{213}^{Hou} + E_{214}^{Hou} & \geq 300{,}000y_2^{Hou} \\
\vdots & &
\end{array}
$$

$$
\begin{array}{lll}
(60) & E^{Edu}_{10,1,1} & \geq 8{,}000 \\
(61) & E^{Car_1}_{521} + E^{Car_1}_{522} & \geq 50{,}000 y^{Car_1}_1 \\
(62) & E^{Car_1}_{611} + E^{Car_1}_{612} & \geq 50{,}000 y^{Car_1}_2 \\
\vdots & \text{(interval constraints)} & \\
(69)-(73) & E^{Hou}_{111}, E^{Hou}_{211}, E^{Hou}_{311}, E^{Hou}_{411}, E^{Hou}_{511} & \leq 320{,}000 \\
(74)-(78) & E^{Hou}_{112}, E^{Hou}_{212}, E^{Hou}_{312}, E^{Hou}_{412}, E^{Hou}_{512} & \leq 20{,}000 \\
(79)-(83) & E^{Hou}_{113}, E^{Hou}_{213}, E^{Hou}_{313}, E^{Hou}_{413}, E^{Hou}_{513} & \leq 40{,}000 \\
(84)-(88) & E^{Hou}_{114}, E^{Hou}_{214}, E^{Hou}_{314}, E^{Hou}_{414}, E^{Hou}_{514} & \leq 20{,}000 \\
(89)-(93) & E^{Car_1}_{521}, E^{Car_1}_{611}, E^{Car_2}_{10,2,1}, E^{Car_2}_{11,1,1}, & \\
 & E^{Car_3}_{15,1,1}, E^{Car_3}_{16,1,1}, E^{Car_4}_{20,1,1}, E^{Car_4}_{21,1,1} & \leq 55{,}000 \\
(94)-(101) & E^{Car_1}_{522}, E^{Car_1}_{612}, E^{Car_2}_{10,2,2}, E^{Car_2}_{11,1,2}, & \\
 & E^{Car_3}_{15,1,2}, E^{Car_3}_{16,1,2}, E^{Car_4}_{20,1,2}, E^{Car_4}_{21,1,2} & \leq 5{,}000 \\
\vdots & \text{(credit restrictions)} & \\
(102) & K_1 & \leq 120{,}000 y^{Hou}_1 \\
(103) & K_2 & \leq 120{,}000 y^{Hou}_2 \\
\vdots & & \\
(107) & y^K_1 + y^K_2 + y^K_3 + y^K_4 + y^K_5 & \leq 1 \\
 & \text{(financial ratios: shelter costs / income)} & \\
(108) & \big(12{,}000 \cdot (1 - y^{Hou}_1) + 0.03 & \\
 & \cdot (E^{Hou}_{11} + E^{Hou}_{12} + E^{Hou}_{13} + E^{Hou}_{14})\big) \cdot \frac{1}{60{,}000} & < 0.28 \\
(109) & \big(120{,}000 \cdot (1 - y^{Hou}_1 - y^{Hou}_2) + 0.03 & \\
 & \cdot \big(E^{Hou}_{111} + E^{Hou}_{112} + E^{Hou}_{113} + E^{Hou}_{14} + E^{Hou}_{211} + E^{Hou}_{212} + E^{Hou}_{213} & \\
 & + E^{Hou}_{214} + E^{Hou}_{215}\big)\big) \cdot \frac{1}{60{,}000} & < 0.28 \\
\vdots & \text{(financial ratios: debt payments / income)} & \\
(114) & \left(cK_1 + \frac{K_1}{15}\right) \cdot \frac{1}{60{,}000} & < 0.15 \\
(115) & \left(\frac{14cK_1}{15} + \frac{K_1}{15} + cK_2 + \frac{K_2}{15}\right) \cdot \frac{1}{60{,}000} & < 0.15 \\
\vdots & & \\
(133)-(150) & y^{Hou}_1, y^{Hou}_2, y^{Hou}_3, y^{Hou}_4, y^{Hou}_5, y^{Car_1}_1, y^{Car_1}_2, y^{Car_2}_1, y^{Car_2}_2, y^{Car_3}_1, y^{Car_3}_2, y^{Car_4}_1, y^{Car_4}_2, & \\
 & y^K_1, y^K_1, y^K_2, y^K_3, y^K_4, y^K_5 \in \{0, 1\} &
\end{array}
$$

Solving the MILP leads to the cash flows shown in Table 18.2. Although the *House* is considered the most important expense, it only can be realized to the minimum desired amount and also has to be postponed to the fourth period. This is due to the fact that we consider financial ratios, especially the annual debt payments/income quota influences the model very strongly. However, *Education* can be realized as desired. The amounts that can be spend for *Car 1* needs to be reduced, additionally the purchase of *Car 3* has to be postponed one period. From the finance plan depicted in Table 18.2 we can see that the couple's investment never falls under the desired limit of 10,000 EUR (*** in years 5 and 16). But we get down to this level in periods 5 and 16 which means we could not have spent more money to increase the couple's satisfaction. Starting at period 20 the family's wealth increases again up to 279,733 EUR at the end of the planning period.

Table 18.2 Resulting finance plan

Year	Age	Income	Credit	Fixed expenses	House	Car	Education	Installment	Investment
0	35	200,000		0					200,000
1	36	60,000		40,000					226,000
2	37	60,000		40,000					252,780
3	38	60,000		40,000					280,363
4	39	60,000	46,756	40,000	300,000				55,530
5	40	60,000		40,000		59,404		7,793	***10,000
6	41	60,000		40,000				7,481	22,819
7	42	60,000		40,000				7,169	36,334
8	43	60,000		40,000				6,857	50,567
9	44	60,000		40,000				6,546	65,538
10	45	60,000		40,000		60,000	10,000	6,234	11,270
11	46	60,000		40,000			10,000	5,922	15,686
12	47	60,000		40,000			10,000	5,611	20,546
13	48	60,000		40,000			10,000	5,299	25,863
14	49	60,000		40,000			10,000	4,987	31,652
15	50	60,000		40,000				4,676	47,926
16	51	60,000		40,000		55,000		4,364	***10,000
17	52	60,000		40,000				4,052	26,248
18	53	60,000		40,000				3,740	43,295
19	54	60,000		40,000				3,429	61,165
20	55	60,000		40,000		60,000			23,000

(continued)

Table 18.2 (continued)

Year	Age	Income	Credit	Fixed expenses	House	Car	Education	Installment	Investment
21	56	60,000		40,000					43,690
22	57	60,000		40,000					65,001
23	58	60,000		40,000					86,951
24	59	60,000		40,000					109,559
25	60	40,000		30,000					122,846
26	61	40,000		30,000					136,531
27	62	40,000		30,000					150,627
28	63	40,000		30,000					165,146
29	64	40,000		30,000					180,100
30	65	40,000		30,000					195,503
31	66	40,000		30,000					211,369
32	67	40,000		30,000					227,710
33	68	40,000		30,000					244,541
34	69	40,000		30,000					261,877
35	70	40,000		30,000					279,733

Table 18.3 Optimal quantities and dates without considering financial ratios

	Desired amount (EUR)	Actual amount (EUR)	Desired time point	Time point of realization
House	400,000	300,000	1	4
Education	10,000	10,000	10–14	10–14
Car 1	60,000	59,404	5	5
Car 2	60,000	60,000	10	10
Car 3	60,000	55,000	15	16
Car 4	60,000	60,000	20	20

As already mentioned, it is important to note that the solution is strongly influenced by the financial ratio *Annual Consumer Debt Payments/Income*. If we had not considered this ratio, the resulting *Finance Plan* would have led to a higher decision maker's satisfaction, but also to a higher risk of a potential personal insolvency. The resulting scenario without considering the financial ratios is shown in Table 18.3.

In this scenario it is possible to take out a loan in the amount of 46,756 EUR. Therefore the couple can afford a *House* in the amount of 300,000 EUR in the fourth period and for *Education* are 10,000 EUR available as desired. Car 1 can be bought in period 5, up to 59,404 EUR are available to achieve this goal. Furthermore, Car 2 can be realized as desired, in period 10 the desired amount of 60,000 EUR is fully available for this financial goal. Whereas the amount of Car 3 has to be reduced to 55,000 EUR and the realization has to be postponed from period 15 to 16, Car 4 can be realized as desired.

18.5 Results

Personal financial planning investigates the question of how solid planning of financial affairs can contribute to our fundamental goals. Comprehensive personal financial planning consists of planning the investment of assets as well as planning incomes and expenses during a person's lifetime. We restrict ourselves in this paper to the view on the expenses and consider the expenses problem of personal financial planning which is to find a feasible financial plan with the value of planned expenses for a decision maker to be maximized. This expenses problem of personal financial planning can be considered as a multicriteria decision analysis problem as conflicting objectives with different goals of varying levels of importance for the decision maker are involved in the problem.

We propose a decision model for solving the problem based on a mixed integer program with the parameters for the program derived from the analytic hierarchy process. We assume the fully deterministic case, i.e. all data are given and risk or uncertainty are out of the scope of this model. It might be interesting to consider these cases in further research. We show the effectiveness of our approach by providing a numerical example that helps to compromise among the objectives and produces a feasible and (concerning the preferences of the decision maker) optimal personal finance plan. Our approach has the advantage to change trial calculations-based personal financial planning practices that are done to reach acceptable financial plans satisfying most of the decision maker's preferences by a line of action where the decision maker has to clearly define criteria based on his preferences concerning spending expenses.

The decision making process concerning personal financial affairs is an iterative process and is not finished until the intuitive mental image of a solution fits with the model's solution as far as possible. Doing this, consistency will be guaranteed and the decision maker can be of sure that his objectives and preferences are correctly handled by the model. In this context it should be underlined that the purpose of our model is not the determination of an objective optimum. The purpose of our model is rather the determination of an action alternative which is optimal with respect to subjective expectations and the personal objectives, criteria, and preferences of the decision maker. In this process the decision maker has to reflect about values and criteria underlying decisions about personal financial affairs. The proposed model does not make the independent reasoning person redundant, it is rather an assistance for the preparation of goal- and preferences-oriented decisions concerning personal financial affairs. In order to find a solution for the presented model, an optimization algorithm for mixed-integer programs, such as a Branch-and-Bound algorithm, has to be applied. Therefore most of the spreadsheet programs are not able to solve the proposed model.

Computational experiments were done on a Silicon Graphics SGI Origin200 computer with 16 GB main memory and 4 RISC processors R10000 width 195/250 MHz, 32 Mips, 64-Bit. Operating system is IRIX 6.5 with C++ compiler 7.3.1.1m. The tests show that we can handle problem settings with up to 200 constraints in less than 2 s (Table 18.4).

Our basic model of personal financial planning and can be enlarged in several ways. As an example, the decision maker might have risk preferences for specific expenses, or non-linear preferences might be of interest for consideration in the model. The preferences-oriented approach for solving the expenses problem of

Table 18.4 Solution times

	Total variables	Integer variables	Constraints	Iterations	Solution time (s)
1	30	5	50	12	< 0.1
2	40	10	70	20	< 0.3
3	50	15	100	37	< 0.6
4	64	18	114	48	< 1.0
4	100	25	152	68	< 1.3
5	150	30	200	104	< 2.0

personal financial planning in general is transferable from the expenses view to the incomes view and to the assets view. A general preferences-oriented personal financial planning in this sense can help clarify values that guide the decision-making process about proper planning of personal financial affairs, and can show the right direction for usage of the expenses, deriving the incomes, and investing the assets.

References

Akao, Y. (1990). *Quality function deployment: Integrating customer requirements into product design*. Cambridge: Productivity Press.

Ashford, R. W., Berry, R. H., & Dyson, R. G. (1988). Operational research and financial management. *European Journal of Operational Research, 36*, 143–152.

Bodie, Z., Merton, R. C., & Samuelson, W. F. (1992). Labor supply flexibility and portfolio choice in a life cycle model. *Journal of Economic Dynamics and Control, 16*, 427–449.

Braun, O. (2009). *Decision support for personal financial planning* (in German). Wiesbaden: Gabler.

Brown, S., Taylor, L., & Wheatley Price, S. (2005). Debt and distress: Evaluating the psychological cost of credit. *Journal of Economic Psychology, 26*, 642–663.

Brulde, B. (2007). Happiness theories of the good life. *Journal of Happiness Studies, 8*, 15–49.

Carmone, F. J., Kara, A., & Zanakis, S. H. (1997). A Monte Carlo investigation of incomplete pairwise comparison matrices in AHP. *European Journal of Operational Research, 102*, 538–553.

ChiangLin, C.-Y., & Lin, C.-C. (2008). Personal financial planning based on fuzzy multiple objective programming. *Expert Systems with Applications, 35*, 373–378.

Crary, M., Nozick, L. K., & Whitaker, L. R. (2002). Sizing the US destroyer fleet. *European Journal of Operational Research, 136*, 680–695.

DeVaney, S. A. (1994). The usefulness of financial ratios as predictors of household insolvency: Two perspectives. *Financial Counseling and Planning, 5*, 5–24.

Ehrgott, M., Klamroth, K., & Schwehm, C. (2004). An MCDM approach to portfolio optimization. *European Journal of Operational Research, 155*, 752–770.

Eisenhauer, J. G. (2008). Ethical preferences, risk aversion, and taxpayer behaviour. *The Journal of Socio-Economics, 37*, 45–63.

Epstein, L., & Schneider, M. (2003). Recursive multiple-priors. *Journal of Economic Theory, 113*, 1–31.

Fedrizzi, M., & Giove, S. (2006). Incomplete pairwise comparison and consistency optimization. *European Journal of Operational Research, 183*, 303–313.

Gao, S., Wang, H., Wang, Y., Shen, W., & Yeung, S. (2005). Web-service-agents-based family wealth management system. *Expert Systems with Applications, 29*, 219–228.

Gao, S., Wang, H., Xu, D., & Wang, Y. (2007). An intelligent agent-assisted decision support system for family financial planning. *Decision Support Systems, 44*, 60–78.

Garman, T., & Forgue, R. (2006). *Personal finance*. New York: Houghton Mifflin Company.

Gilboa, I., & Schmeidler, D. (1989). Maxmin expected utility with non-unique prior. *Journal of Mathematical Economics, 18*, 141–153.

Gross, D. B., & Souleles, N. S. (2002). Do liquidity constraints and interest rates matter for consumer behavior? *The Quaterly Journal of Economics, 117*, 149–185.

Ho, W. (2008). Integrated analytic hierarchy process and its applications - A literature review. *European Journal of Operational Research, 186*, 211–228.

Kapoor, J. R., Dlabay, L. R., & Hughes, R. J. (2007). *Personal finance* (8th ed.). New York: McGraw-Hill.

Karatzas, I., & Zitkovic, G. (2003). Optimal consumption from investment and random endowment in incomplete semimartingale markets. *The Annals of Probability, 31*, 1821–1858.
Keeney, R. L. (1992). *Value-focused thinking*. Cambridge: Harvard University Press.
Kirchler, E., Hoelzl, E., & Kamleitner, B. (2008). Spending and credit use in the private household. *Journal of Socio-Economics, 37*, 519–532.
Korpela, J., Kyläheiko, K., Lehmusvaara, A., & Tuominen, M. (2001). The effect of ecological factors on distribution network evaluation. *International Journal of Logistics: Research and Applications, 4*, 257–269.
Korpela, J., Kyläheiko, K., Lehmusvaara, A., & Tuominen, M. (2002). An analytic approach to production capacity allocation and supply chain design. *International Journal of Production Economics, 78*, 187–195.
Korpela, J., & Lehmusvaara, A. (1999). A customer oriented approach to warehouse network evaluation and design. *International Journal of Production Economics, 59*, 135–146.
Korpela, J., Lehmusvaara, A., & Tuominen, M. (2001). Customer service based design of the supply chain. *International Journal of Production Economics, 69*, 193–204.
Kreps, D., & Porteus, E. L. (1978). Temporal resolution of uncertainty and dynamic choice theory. *Econometrica, 46*, 185–200.
Kwak, N. K., & Lee, C. W. (1998). A multicriteria decision-making approach to university resource allocations and information infrastructure planning. *European Journal of Operational Research, 110*, 234–242.
Kwak, N. K., & Lee, C. W. (2002). Business process reengineering for health-care system using multicriteria mathematical programming. *European Journal of Operational Research, 140*, 447–458.
Kwak, N. K., Lee, C. W., & Kim, J. H. (2005). An MCDM model for media selection in the dual consumer/industrial market. *European Journal of Operational Research, 166*, 255–265.
Kwiesielewicz, M. (1996). The logarithmic least squares and the generalized pseudoinverse in estimating ratios. *European Journal of Operational Research, 93*, 611–619.
Madura, J. (2006). *Personal finance with financial planning software*. Boston: Addison Wesley.
Maslow, A. H. (1968). *Toward a psychology of being*. Princeton: Van Nostrand.
Mason, R., & Griffith, R. (1988). New ratios for analyzing and interpreting personal financial statements. *Journal of Financial Planning, 9*, 71–87.
Oboulhas, C. T. O., Xiaofei, X., & Zhan, D. (2004). A decision support system for supplier selection process. *International Journal of Information Technology & Decision Making, 3*, 453–470.
Ozdemir, M. S., & Gasimov, R. N. (2004). The analytic hierarchy process and multiobjective 0–1 faculty course assignment. *European Journal of Operational Research, 157*, 398–408.
Pardalos, P., Sandström, M., & Zopounidis, C. (1994). On the use of optimization models for portfolio selection: A review and some computational results. *Computational Economics, 7*, 227–244.
Partovi, F. Y., & Corredoira, R. A. (2002). Quality function deployment for the good of soccer. *European Journal of Operational Research, 137*, 642–656.
Puelz, A., & Puelz, R. (1992). Personal financial planning and the allocation of disposable wealth. *Financial Services Review, 1*, 87–99.
Ranyard, R., Hinkley, L., Williamson, J., & McHugh, S. (2006). The role of mental accounting in consumer credit decision processes. *Journal of Economic Psychology, 27*, 571–588.
Saaty, T. L. (1980). *The analytic hierarchy process*. New York: McGraw Hill.
Saaty, T. L. (1990). How to make a decision: The analytic hierarchy process. *European Journal of Operational Research, 48*, 9–26.
Samaras, G. D., Matsatsinis, N. F., & Zopounidis, C. (2005). Towards an intelligent decision support system for portfolio management. *Foundations of Computing and Decision Sciences, 2*, 141–162.
Schniederjans, M. J., & Garvin, T. (1997). Using the analytic hierarchy process and multi-objective programming for the selection of cost drivers in activity-based costing. *European Journal of Operational Research, 100*, 72–80.

Shafir, E., & Thaler, R. H. (2006). Invest now, drink later, spend never: On the mental accounting of delayed consumption. *Journal of Economic Psychology, 27*, 694–712.
Siegmann, A., & Lucas, A. (2006). Discrete-time financial planning models under loss-averse preferences. *Operations Research, 53*, 403–414.
Spronk, J., Steuer, R. E., & Zopounidis, C. (2005). Multicriteria decision aid/analysis in finance. In J. Figuera, S. Greco, & M. Ehrgott (Eds.), *Multiple criteria decision analysis: State of the art surveys*. Berlin: Springer.
Steuer, R. E., & Na, P. (2003). Multiple criteria decision making combined with finance: A categorized bibliographic study. *European Journal of Operational Research, 150*, 496–515.
Tobler, P. N., Fletcher, P. C., Bullmore, E. T., & Schultz, W. (2007). Learning-related human brain activations reflecting individual finances. *Neuron, 54*, 167–175.
Tversky, A., & Kahneman, D. (1992). Advances in the prospect theory: Cumulative representation of uncertainty. *Journal of Risk and Uncertainty, 5*, 297–323.
Tyagi, R., & Das, C. (1997). A methodology for cost versus service trade-offs in wholesale location-distribution using mathematical programming and analytic hierarchy process. *Journal of Business Logistics, 18*, 77–99.
Vahidov, R., & He, X. (2009). Situated DSS for personal finance management: Design and evaluation. *Information & Management, 46*(8), 78–86.
Vaidya, O. S., & Kumar, S. (2006). Analytic hierarchy process: An overview of applications. *European Journal of Operational Research, 169*, 1–29.
Wittmüß, W. (2006). Robust optimization of consumption with random endowment. SFB 649 Paper 2006–063 (urn:nbn:de:kobv:11-10068436).
Yang, T., & Kuo, C. (2003). A hierarchical AHP/DEA methodology for the facilities layout design problem. *European Journal of Operational Research, 147*, 128–136.
Zopounidis, C., & Doumpos, M. (2002). Multi-criteria decision aid in financial decision making: Methodologies and literature review. *Journal of Multi-criteria Decision Analysis, 11*, 167–186.

Editors' Comments on "An MCDA Approach for Personal Financial Planning"

The chapter by Braun and Spohn presents an innovative methodological contribution for adapting an optimal Personal Financial Planning (PFP) approach to specific personal preferences. The PFP optimization problem is modelled as a mixed integer linear programming (MILP) model where the parameters are proposed to be set in interaction with a potential decision maker via a classic Analytical Hierarchy Process (AHP) approach. In this sense, this chapter presents an interesting proposal for using a multiple criteria decision aid approach for setting model parameters when numerically solving a MILP problem.

Main aspect relevant for the purpose of this handbook is the detailed methodological illustration of how a structured and interactive multiple criteria decision analysis like the AHP approach, may indeed be used for adapting a complex generic multiobjective optimization model to individual needs and subjective preferences of an individual decision maker; the **objective of the case study** being to claim and illustrate feasibility and usefulness of the proposed methodological approach.

The authors do not explicitly give the methodological reasons for specifically using in their decision aid problem the AHP approach. But, one may guess that AHP's structured and interactive procedure for elaborating a weighted **hierarchy**

of strategic objectives and related performance measuring criteria and subcriteria fits well with the authors' intention to help a potential user setting correct **criteria weights** in their PFP multicriteria optimization model.

Other multiple criteria decision aid approaches like the ELECTRE outranking methods (Roy, 1991), do not explicitly provide such an interactive help for elaborating a set of weighted objectives and significant criteria. Only in a **value or scoring** approach, like in the APH method, may indeed weights of strategic objectives and performance criteria share the same semantics, namely **substitution rates**. With pairwise weighted majority confirmed preference situations, like the ones handled in an outranking approach (Bisdorff, 2002), the strategic importance of decision objectives and the preference validating significance of marginal performance criteria do not share at all the same semantics.

One may finally notice that the proposed **MCDA application** appears more scientific and academic than really practical. Only a small didactic PFP problem, with three genuine strategic objectives and/or criteria: economic, social or personal, illustrates a potential practical application. However, the authors have positively validated a **software implementation** of their MCDA enhanced PFP approach with actual planners from banks and insurance, and with master students knowledgeable in financial planning and information management.

References

Bisdorff, R. (2002). Logical foundation of multicriteria preference aggregation. In D. Bouyssou, E. Jacquet-Lagrèze, P. Perny, R. Słowiński, D. Vanderpooten, & P. Vincke (Eds.), *Aiding decisions with multiple criteria* (pp. 379–403). Dordrecht: Kluwer Academic.

Roy, B. (1991). The outranking approach and the foundations of ELECTRE methods. *Theory and Decision, 31*(1), 49–73.

Chapter 19
A Multicriteria Approach to Bank Rating

Michael Doumpos and Constantin Zopounidis

Abstract Bank rating refers to the analysis of a bank's overall viability, performance and risk exposure. Within the recent financial turmoil, bank rating has become extremely important. Typically, bank rating is performed through empirical procedures that combine financial and qualitative data into an overall performance index. This paper presents a case study on the implementation of a multicriteria approach to bank rating. The proposed methodology is based on the PROMETHEE II method. A rich set of evaluation criteria are used in the analysis, selected in accordance with widely accepted bank rating principals. Special emphasis is put on the sensitivity of the results with regard to the relative importance of the evaluation criteria and the parameters of the PROMETHEE method. Analytic and Monte Carlo simulation techniques are used for this purpose.

19.1 Introduction

Banks have a prominent role in the financial and business environment. The increasing risks that banks face, have led to the introduction of the new regulatory framework of Basel II, which defines the core principles for financial risk management in banking institutions. One of the pillars of this framework involves the banking supervision process. The central banks that are responsible for supervising the banks in each country use rating systems to assess the soundness of the banks. According to Sahajwala and Van den Bergh (2000), the emphasis is put on the development of formal, structured and quantified assessments taking into account the financial performance of banks as well as their underlying risk profile and risk management capabilities. Such assessments support the supervisors and examiners in identifying changes in banks' condition as early as possible.

M. Doumpos (✉) • C. Zopounidis
School of Production Engineering and Management, Financial Engineering Laboratory, Technical University of Crete, University Campus, 73100 Chania, Greece
e-mail: mdoumpos@dpem.tuc.gr; kostas@dpem.tuc.gr

R. Bisdorff et al. (eds.), *Evaluation and Decision Models with Multiple Criteria*, International Handbooks on Information Systems,
DOI 10.1007/978-3-662-46816-6_19

Due to lack of sufficient historical data about bank defaults, bank rating systems are usually based on empirical assessment techniques. Sahajwala and Van den Bergh (2000) provide an extensive overview of several systems, which are currently used in practice. The most popular approach is based on the CAMELS framework, which involves the consideration of six major factors: Capital, Assets, Management, Earnings, Liquidity, and Sensitivity to market risk. Specific criteria within these categories are usually aggregated in a simple weighted average model.

Several multicriteria techniques have also been used for the evaluation of bank performance. Mareschal and Brans (1991), Mareschal and Mertens (1992) as well as Kosmidou and Zopounidis (2008) used the PROMETHEE method, Zopounidis et al. (1995) and Spathis et al. (2002) used disaggregation techniques, Raveh (2000) used the Co-plot method, whereas Ho (2006) implemented the grey relational analysis. Several data envelopment analysis models have also been used (Parkan and Liu, 1999; Halkos and Salamouris, 2004; Kao and Liu, 2004).

This paper presents a case study on the development and implementation of a multicriteria bank rating approach. The proposed methodology is based on the PROMETHEE II method. The bank evaluation criteria are selected in cooperation with expert analysts from the Bank of Greece. The selected criteria comply with the CAMELS framework and include both qualitative and quantitative measures. Special emphasis is put on the sensitivity of the results with regard to the relative importance of the evaluation criteria and the parameters of the PROMETHEE method. Analytic sensitivity analysis techniques are used for this purpose, together with Monte Carlo simulation.

The rest of the paper is organized as follows. Section 19.2 describes the problem context and the details of the multicriteria methodology. Section 19.3 presents detailed results from the application on Greek banks. Finally, Sect. 19.4 concludes the paper and outlines some future research directions.

19.2 Problem Context and Multicriteria Methodology

The main output of bank rating models is an evaluation of the overall risk and performance of banks. In a supervisory context, expert analysts (supervisors of a central bank) gather detailed information that enables the evaluation of a bank's condition and the monitoring of its compliance with the regulatory framework. The result of this evaluation process is a rating (CAMELS rating), which provides a forward-looking approach of a bank's current overall condition and potential risk.

In common practice, the ratings are usually assigned in a scale of 1–5, which *resembles* an ordinal classification setting. Banks with ratings of 1 or 2 are considered to present few supervisory concerns, while banks with higher ratings present moderate to extreme degrees of supervisory concern. The definition of the grades in such a rating system, is based on the composite score of the banks obtained by aggregating their performance on all evaluation criteria. This score is expressed on a scale similar to the ratings (e.g., in [1, 5] or [0.5, 5.5]) so that each rating can be matched to a predefined score interval. Within this context, bank rating does not correspond to a "traditional" multicriteria classification problem, in the sense that the actual outcome of the evaluation process is a numerical evaluation score, which is matched to a risk grade at the final stage of the evaluation process, as a means of "defuzzification". This approach provides flexibility to the supervisory authorities, which may take similar actions for banks whose rating scores are very similar, even if they correspond to different ratings.

In accordance, with the CAMELS model which is currently in use by the Bank of Greece, a multicriteria methodology has been implemented that enables not only to define the required risk grades, but also to develop an overall performance index that permits comparisons on the relative performance of the banks. The methodology is based on the PROMETHEE II method (Brans and Vincke, 1985). The workflow of the methodology is given in Fig. 19.1.

The PROMETHEE method is widely used to rank a set of alternatives on the basis of pairwise comparisons. Except for this kind of analysis, the method was also used to perform an absolute evaluation in comparison to a pre-specified reference

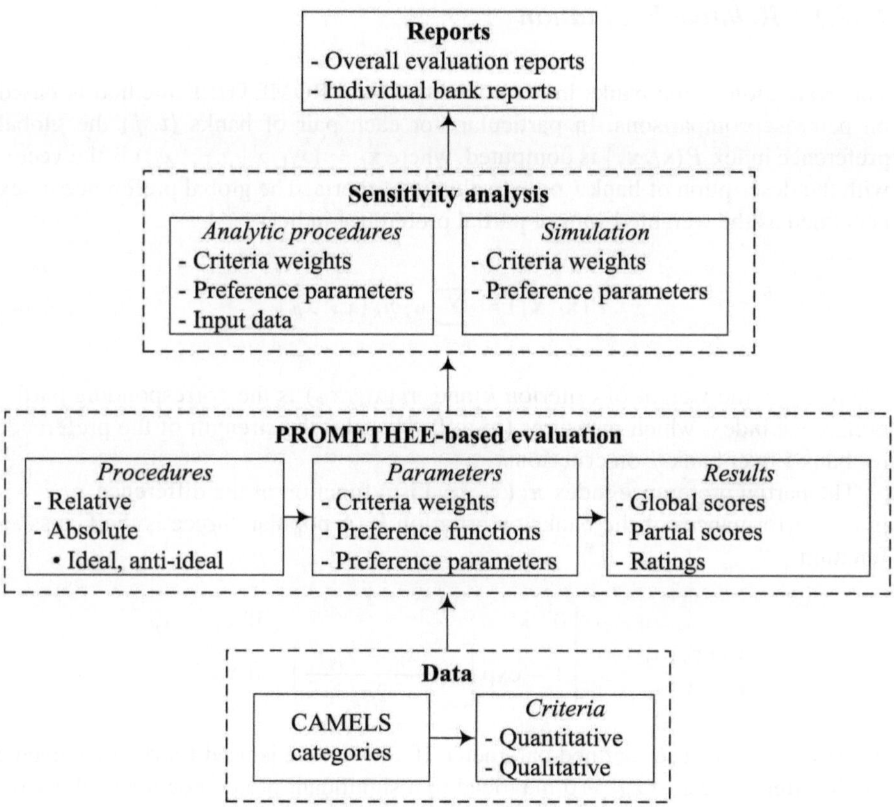

Fig. 19.1 The workflow of the methodology

point. Thus, the use of the PROMETHEE method enables the consideration of both the relative and absolute performance of the banks in a unified context. The relative evaluation enables the consideration of the strengths and weaknesses of a bank taking as opposed to other banks (i.e., on the basis of the conditions that prevail in the banking sector), whereas the absolute evaluation enables the analysis of the condition of a bank compared to predefined reference points representing specific risk profiles. The combination of these approaches provides supervisors an overall view of the risk faced by the banks, taking into account the characteristics of each individual bank, the interrelationships between the banks, and the overall condition of the banking sector. The consideration of these two issues in other MCDA models (e.g., a value function) would require the introduction of specific criteria, which were difficult to define and measure in this case.

The subsections below provide details on the implementation of the PROMETHEE method in both these contexts. Details on the evaluation criteria and the details of the evaluation process are given in Sect. 19.3.

19.2.1 Relative Evaluation

The evaluation of the banks in the context of the PROMETHEE method is based on pairwise comparisons. In particular, for each pair of banks (i, j) the global preference index $P(\mathbf{x}_i, \mathbf{x}_j)$ is computed, where $\mathbf{x}_i = (x_{i1}, x_{i2}, \ldots, x_{in})$ is the vector with the description of bank i on n evaluation criteria. The global preference index is defined as the weighted sum of partial preference indices:

$$P(\mathbf{x}_i, \mathbf{x}_j) = \sum_{k=1}^{n} w_k \pi_k(x_{ik}, x_{jk})$$

where w_k is the weight of criterion k and $\pi_k(x_{ik}, x_{jk})$ is the corresponding partial preference index, which measures (in a [0, 1] scale) the strength of the preference for bank i over bank j on criterion k.

The partial preference index $\pi_k(x_{ik}, x_{jk})$ is a function of the difference $x_{ik} - x_{jk}$ in the performances of the banks on criterion k. A popular choice is the Gaussian function:

$$\pi_k(x_{ik}, x_{jk}) = \begin{cases} 0 & \text{if } x_{ik} \leq x_{jk} \\ 1 - \exp\left[-\dfrac{(x_{ik} - x_{jk})^2}{2\sigma_k^2}\right] & \text{if } x_{ik} > x_{jk} \end{cases}$$

where $\sigma_k > 0$ is a user defined parameter. If a low value is used for σ_k, then even a small difference $x_{ik} - x_{jk} > 0$ may lead to a significant preference for bank i over bank j. On the contrary, for large values of σ_k, strict preference may only occur when $x_{ik} \gg x_{jk}$.

An alternative function for the definition of the partial preference index is the linear generalized criterion:

$$\pi_k(x_{ik}, x_{jk}) = \begin{cases} 0 & \text{if } x_{ik} - x_{jk} \leq 0 \\ \dfrac{x_{ik} - x_{jk}}{p_k} & \text{if } 0 < x_{ik} - x_{jk} \leq p_k \\ 1 & \text{if } x_{ik} - x_{jk} > p_k \end{cases}$$

where $p_k > 0$ is the preference threshold, which defines the minimum difference $x_{ik} - x_{jk}$ above which bank i is assumed to be strictly preferred over bank j on criterion k. Note that the above functions are only meaningful for quantitative data. Brans and Vincke (1985) present alternative options suitable for qualitative criteria.

Assuming a set of m banks under evaluation, the results of all the pairwise comparisons are aggregated into a global performance index (net flow) as follows:

$$\Phi(\mathbf{x}_i) = \frac{1}{m-1}\left[\phi^+(\mathbf{x}_i) - \phi^-(\mathbf{x}_i)\right] \tag{19.1}$$

where $\phi^+(\mathbf{x}_i) = \sum_{j \neq i} P(\mathbf{x}_i, \mathbf{x}_j)$ is the outgoing flow representing the outranking character of bank i over all the other banks and $\phi^-(\mathbf{x}_i) = \sum_{j \neq i} P(\mathbf{x}_j, \mathbf{x}_i)$ is the incoming flow representing the outranking character of all banks in the sample over bank i. Thus, the above net flow index combines the strengths and weaknesses of a bank compared to its competitors in an overall evaluation measure. The overall net flow index $\Phi(\mathbf{x}_i)$ ranges in $[-1, 1]$, with higher values associated with low risk/high performance banks.

The net flow index (19.1) can be alternatively written in additive form as:

$$\Phi(\mathbf{x}_i) = \sum_{k=1}^{n} w_k \phi_k(\mathbf{x}_i) \tag{19.2}$$

where $\phi_k(\mathbf{x}_i) = \varphi_k^+(\mathbf{x}_i) - \varphi_k^-(\mathbf{x}_i)$ is the partial evaluation score (uni-criterion net flow, see Mareschal and Brans 1991; Bouyssou et al. 2006) defined for criterion k, with

$$\varphi_k^+(x_{ik}) = \frac{1}{m-1}\sum_{j \neq i} \pi_k(x_{ik}, x_{jk}) \quad \text{and} \quad \varphi_k^-(x_{ik}) = \frac{1}{m-1}\sum_{j \neq i} \pi_k(x_{jk}, x_{ik})$$

representing, respectively, the advantages and disadvantages of bank i compared to the others with respect to criterion k.

The advantage of using the additive form (19.2) over (19.1) is that it provides the decomposition of the overall performance of a bank on each evaluation criterion through the corresponding uni-criterion flow. Thus, the strengths and weaknesses of the bank can be easily identified in terms of the criteria.

In order to build the required bank rating model, the evaluation scale for both the overall performance index, as well as for all the partial performance indices had to be modified in order to enable the definition of a five-point rating scale. In this model calibration step, the partial net flows $\phi_k(\mathbf{x}_i)$ were used to define a modified partial evaluation function as follows:

$$v_k(x_{ik}) = \begin{cases} 0.5 & \text{if } x_{ik} \geq x_k^* \\ 0.5 + 5\dfrac{\phi_k(x_{ik}) - \phi_k(x_k^*)}{\phi_k(x_{k*}) - \phi_k(x_k^*)} & \text{if } x_{k*} < x_{ik} < x_k^* \\ 5.5 & \text{if } x_{ik} \leq x_{k*} \end{cases} \tag{19.3}$$

where x_{k*} and x_k^* are the least and most preferred values of criterion k, respectively. With this normalization, the partial evaluation of the banks on a criterion k ranges in a scale from 0.5 (best performance) to 5.5 (worst performance), and the final evaluation model is just a modified version of the net flow model (19.2):

$$V(\mathbf{x}_i) = \sum_{k=1}^{n} w_k v_k(x_{ik}) \in [0.5, 5.5] \tag{19.4}$$

This model is then used to rank the banks in terms of their relative performance, thus providing insight into the strengths and weaknesses of each bank within the competitive market and the conditions that prevail. Given the overall score defined in this way, the associated relative rating is specified by defining the intervals [0.5, 1.5] for group 1, (1.5, 2.5] for group 2, (2.5, 3.5] for group 3, (3.5, 4.5] for group 4 and (4.5, 5.5] for group 5.

It should be noted, however, that while the net flow model (19.2) is purely relational (e.g., the evaluation of a bank is expressed solely in terms of the other banks in the sample), with the introduction of the transformation (19.3), the final evaluation model (19.4) incorporates both relational and absolute aspects. This is because the least and most preferred values of the criteria are not defined on the basis of the banks under consideration. Instead, they represent reference points corresponding to high and low risk bank profiles, defined on the basis of the risk analyst's attitude towards risk. In that respect, as the banking sector is improved, the differences $\phi_k(x_{ik}) - \phi_k(x_k^*)$ will decrease, thus leading to improved ratings. Similarly, as the sector deteriorates as a whole, the differences $\phi_k(x_k^*) - \phi_k(x_{ik})$ will increase, resulting in a deterioration of the ratings. Therefore, the rating score of a bank combines its relative performance as opposed to other banks, as well as the performance of the banking sector as a whole compared to predefined risk profiles. The relative evaluation enables the consideration of the interrelationships and interactions between the banks, which is related to systematic risk.

19.2.2 Absolute Evaluation

Except for the above "hybrid" evaluation process, which combines both relative and absolute elements, a purely absolute evaluation approach can also be realized within the context of the PROMETHEE methodology. In this case the results are based only on the comparison of the banks to a pre-specified reference point, whereas the relative performance of the banks is excluded from the analysis.

In cooperation with the analysts in the Bank of Greece, two options were defined for the specification of the reference point. In the first case the banks are compared to the ideal point (ideal bank). This kind of evaluation provides an assessment of the capability of the banks to perform as good as possible. The second option uses an anti-ideal point. Both the anti-ideal and the ideal point ($\mathbf{x}_*$ and $\mathbf{x}^*$, respectively) are defined by the analysts of the Bank of Greece, each consisting of the least and most preferred values of each criterion, i.e. $\mathbf{x}_* = (x_{1*}, x_{2*}, \ldots, x_{n*})$ and $\mathbf{x}^* = (x_1^*, x_2^*, \ldots, x_n^*)$.

In the case where the banks are compared to the ideal point, the partial evaluation function is adjusted as follows:

$$v_k(x_{ik}) = \begin{cases} 5.5 & \text{if } x_{ik} \leq x_{k*} \\ 0.5 + 5\dfrac{\pi_k(x_k^*, x_{ik})}{\pi_k(x_k^*, x_{k*})} & \text{if } x_{ik} > x_{k*} \end{cases}$$

On the other hand, when the anti-ideal point is used, the following partial evaluation function is used:

$$v_k(x_{ik}) = \begin{cases} 0.5 + 5\dfrac{\pi_k(x_k^*, x_{*k}) - \pi_k(x_{ik}, x_{*k})}{\pi_k(x_k^*, x_{*k})} & \text{if } x_{ik} < x_k^* \\ 0.5 & \text{if } x_{ik} \geq x_k^* \end{cases}$$

19.2.3 Sensitivity Analysis

Naturally, the multicriteria evaluations defined above incorporate some uncertainty and subjectivity, mainly with regard to the parameters of the PROMETHEE method, which include the criteria weights and the parameters σ_k and p_k of the partial preference functions. Furthermore, since banks operate in a dynamic environment, it is also important to identify changes in the input data that may lead to changes in the rating result. This analysis is performed both for the complete set of banks, as well as for each individual bank separately.

In a first stage, these issues are addressed by analytic sensitivity procedures. For the criteria weights, the objective of the analysis is to define a range of values for the weight of each criterion k for which the rating of the banks remains unchanged.

This can be easily done by imposing the condition that the global score $V(\mathbf{x}_i)$ of each bank i should remain within the score range associated with its rating, as defined with the pre-specified weights.

A similar process is also employed for the parameters of the criteria preference functions. However, with the pairwise relative evaluation scheme of the PROMETHEE method, the partial preference indices are generally non-monotone and non-convex functions of the corresponding parameters σ and p. Thus, in this case it is not possible to define specific bounds for these parameters within which the rating of the banks does not change. On the other hand, the bounds can be explicitly defined for the absolute evaluation process. In particular, let us assume a bank i which is assigned to the rating group ℓ, defined by a range of scores $(\alpha_\ell, \beta_\ell]$ and suppose that a range $[l_k, u_k]$ should be defined for the parameters of the preference function of a criterion k, such that the rating group of the bank does not change, i.e. $\alpha_\ell < V(\mathbf{x}_i) \leq \beta_\ell$. Then:

$$V(\mathbf{x}_i) > \alpha_\ell \Leftrightarrow v_k(x_{ik}) > \max\left\{0.5, \frac{\alpha_\ell - \sum_{j \neq k} w_j v_j(x_{ij})}{w_k}\right\} \tag{19.5}$$

For illustrative purposes, it can be assumed that: (1) the Gaussian preference function is used, (2) the absolute evaluation is performed in comparison to the ideal point, and (3) $x_{k*} < x_{ik} < x_k^*$. Then, taking into account that $v_k(x_{ik})$ decreases with the preference parameter, and denoting by z_{ik} the left-hand side of (19.5), the upper bound u_k is defined as follows:

$$0.5 + 5\frac{\pi_k(x_k^*, x_{ik})}{\pi_k(x_k^*, x_{k*})} > z_{ik} \Rightarrow$$

$$\pi_k(x_k^*, x_{ik}) > \frac{(z_{ik} - 0.5)\pi_k(x_k^*, x_{k*})}{5} \Rightarrow$$

$$1 - \exp\left[-\frac{(x_k^* - x_{ik})^2}{2u_k^2}\right] > \frac{(z_{ik} - 0.5)\pi_k(x_k^*, x_{k*})}{5} \Rightarrow$$

$$u_k < \sqrt{\frac{-(x_k^* - x_{ik})^2}{2\ln[1 - 0.2(z_{ik} - 0.5)\pi_k(x_k^*, x_{k*})]}}$$

Note that if $z_{ik} > 0.5 + 5/\pi_k(x_k^*, x_{k*})$, then $u_k = +\infty$. The same process is used to define the lower bound l_k:

$$V(\mathbf{x}_i) \leq \beta_\ell \Leftrightarrow v_k(x_{ik}) \leq \min\left\{5.5, \frac{\beta_\ell - \sum_{j \neq k} w_j v_j(x_{ij})}{w_k}\right\} = o_{ik} \Rightarrow$$

$$1 - \exp\left[-\frac{(x_k^* - x_{ik})^2}{2l_k^2}\right] \leq \frac{(o_{ik} - 0.5)\pi_k(x_k^*, x_{k*})}{5} \Rightarrow$$

$$l_k \geq \sqrt{\frac{-(x_k^* - x_{ik})^2}{2\ln[1 - 0.2(o_{ik} - 0.5)\pi_k(x_k^*, x_{k*})]}}$$

With $l_k = 0$ whenever $o_{ik} < 0.5$.

A similar procedure can also be applied with the linear preference function and the comparison to the anti-ideal point. In addition to the specification of bounds for the parameters of the preference functions, additional information can be obtained by observing the general impact of the preference parameters to the overall evaluation of the banks (as a whole and individually). This is done with the calculation of a sensitivity index Δ_k, which measures the mean maximum percentage change in the global evaluation of the banks due to a change in the preference parameter of criterion k. In particular, let $v_k(x_{ik}, a_k)$ denote the partial performance of bank i on criterion k, expressed as a function of x_{ik} and the criterion's preference parameter a_k. Then, two optimization problems are solved to find the parameter value a_{*ik} (a_{ik}^*) that minimize (maximize), the partial performance of bank i on criterion k, i.e.:

$$v_k^{\min}(x_{ik}, a_{*ik}) = \min_{a_{ik}>0} v_k(x_{ik}, a_{ik}) \quad \text{and} \quad v_k^{\max}(x_{ik}, a_{ik}^*) = \max_{a_{ik}>0} v_k(x_{ik}, a_{ik})$$

Then, the sensitivity index δ_{ik} measuring the impact of criterion's k preference parameter on the global performance of bank i is defined as follows:

$$\delta_{ik} = \max\left\{ w_k \frac{v_k^{\max}(x_{ik}, a_{ik}^*) - v_k(x_{ik})}{V(\mathbf{x}_i)},\ w_k \frac{v_k(x_{ik}) - v_k^{\min}(x_{ik}, a_{*ik})}{V(\mathbf{x}_i)} \right\} \tag{19.6}$$

where $V(\mathbf{x}_i)$ is the global performance of the bank obtained with criterion's k preference parameter defined by the decision-maker and $v_k(x_{ik})$ the corresponding partial score. For instance, a sensitivity index $\delta_{ik} = 0.3$ indicates that a change in the preference parameter of criterion k, may lead to a change of up to 30 % in the global performance of bank i. The direction of the change (decrease or increase) can be easily found by identifying which of the two arguments provides the maximum in (19.6).

The sensitivity index Δ_k is then calculated as:

$$\Delta_k = \frac{1}{m}\sum_{i=1}^{m} \delta_{ik}$$

In the case of absolute evaluation $v_k^{\min}(x_{ik}, a_{*ik})$ and $v_k^{\max}(x_{ik}, a_{ik}^*)$ are easy to find because $v_k(x_{ik}, a_k)$ is a monotone function of a_k, and the extremes are found by imposing a range of reasonable values for a_k (e.g., between 0.001 and 100). On the other hand, in the relative evaluation process, $v_k(x_{ik}, a_k)$ is generally a non-convex function of a_k. In this case, a simple genetic algorithm is employed in order to find $v_k^{\min}(x_{ik}, a_{*ik})$ and $v_k^{\max}(x_{ik}, a_{ik}^*)$.

19.2.4 Monte Carlo Simulation

The analytic procedures described in the previous section, provide useful local information about the sensitivity of the rating results. Further information is obtained with Monte Carlo simulation. In the proposed methodology, simulation is used to analyze the sensitivity of the ratings with respect to changes in the weights of the criteria, but the process can be easily extended to consider the parameters of the preference functions, too.

The simulation involves the generation of multiple scenarios regarding the weights of the criteria. Two options can be considered for the generation of the weights. In the first case, the weights are generated at random over the unit simplex (Butler et al., 1997). Alternatively, the decision maker can provide a ranking of the criteria according to their relative importance, and then random weights are generated, which are in accordance with the ordering of the criteria.

The results of the simulation are analyzed in terms of the mean and median of the global performance scores, their standard deviation and confidence intervals. Furthermore, for each individual bank useful conclusions can be drawn on the distribution of its rating under different weighting scenarios.

19.2.5 Implementation

The proposed multicriteria methodology has been implemented in an integrated decision support system (DSS). The system enables multiple users (senior or junior level analysts) to work simultaneously on a common data base. Senior bank analysts are responsible for setting the main parameters of the evaluation process, namely the criteria weights, the type of the corresponding preference function and the associated preference parameters. Lower level analysts have full access to all features of the multicriteria evaluation process, but they are not allowed to perform permanent changes in the evaluation parameters.

Except for data base management and the use of the multicriteria tools, the DSS includes a user-friendly interface that facilitates the preparation of several reports in graphical and tabular format. The system also includes some additional modules that support the analysts on the specification of the criteria weights using the rank-order centroid (ROCD) and rank-sum (RS) approaches (Jia et al., 1998), as well as multivariate statistical analysis techniques such as principal components analysis.

The system has been developed in Visual Basic 6 and runs on any MS Windows-based PC. The system is currently used by the Risk Analysis & Supervisory Techniques Division of the Bank of Greece for evaluating and monitoring the strengths and weaknesses of Greek banks, on the basis of the supervisory policy defined in accordance with the international regulatory framework.

The next section presents an illustrative application of the methodology on sample data for Greek commercial banks over the period 2001–2005.

19.3 Application

The proposed multicriteria methodology has been employed for the evaluation of Greek banks. The following subsections provide details on the data used and the obtained results.

19.3.1 Data and Evaluation Parameters

The data involve detailed information for all Greek banks during the period 2001–2005. Overall, 18 banks are considered. The banks are evaluated on a set of 31 criteria (Table 19.1). The criteria have been selected in close co-operation with expert analysts of the Bank of Greece, who are responsible for monitoring and evaluating the performance of the banks. The criteria are organized into six categories (capital, assets, management, earnings, liquidity, sensitivity to market risks), in accordance with the CAMELS framework. Overall, 17 quantitative and 14 qualitative criteria are used. By "quantitative"/"qualitative" criteria, we refer to criteria used to evaluate the financial and non-financial, respectively, aspects of the operation of a bank. All criteria are actually measured in numerical scales. For the qualitative criteria an interval 0.5–5.5 scale was used (with lower values indicating higher performance), in accordance with the existing practice followed by the risk analysts of the Bank of Greece, who are responsible for collecting and evaluating the corresponding information. The complete data table for the year 2005 is given in Appendix "Data Table for 2005".

The weights of each category of criteria and the criteria therein have been defined by the expert analysts of the Bank of Greece.[1] Table 19.2 presents the weights defined for each category of criteria along with the corresponding ROCD and RS estimates defined using the ordering of the criteria according to the expert's weights. It is interesting to note that the RS estimates are very close to the actual relative importance of each criteria group. The same was also observed at the individual criteria level. Overall, the quantitative criteria are assigned a weight of 70 %, with the remaining 30 % involving qualitative criteria. Appendix "Criteria Information" provides complete details on the relative weights of the criteria (normalized to sum

[1]The aggregation models with the procedures presented in Sect. 19.2, are built at the criteria level. The overall weight of each criterion is obtained by the product of its weight within the category where it belongs, with the weight of the corresponding category. In that regard, the criteria hierarchy is not used explicitly at the aggregation process; it is only used to facilitate the specification of the weights, because it is much easier for the experts to judge the relative important of the criteria in each category, than to define this information directly for a large set of criteria.

Table 19.1 Evaluation criteria

Categories	Abbr.	Criteria
Capital	Cap1	Capital adequacy ratio
	Cap2	TIER II capital/TIER I
	Cap3	Qualitative
Assets	Ass1	Risk-weighted assets/assets
	Ass2	Non performing loans—provisions/loans
	Ass3	Large exposures/(TIER I + TIER II capital)
	Ass4	[0.5(Non performing loans)—provisions]/equity
	Ass5	Qualitative
Management	Man1	Operating expenses/operating income
	Man2	Staff cost/assets
	Man3	Operating income/business units
	Man4	Top management competencies, qualifications and continuity
	Man5	Managers' experience and competence
	Man6	Resilience to change, strategy, long term horizon
	Man7	Management of information systems
	Man8	Internal control systems
	Man9	Financial risk management system
	Man10	Internal processes charter—implementation monitoring
	Man11	Timely and accurate data collection
	Man12	Information technology systems
Earnings	Ear1	Net income/assets
	Ear2	Net income/equity
	Ear3	Interest revenue/assets
	Ear4	Other operating revenue/assets
	Ear5	Qualitative
Liquidity	Liq1	Cash/assets
	Liq2	Loans—provisions/deposits
	Liq3	Real funding from credit institutions/assets
	Liq4	Qualitative
Market	Mar1	Risk-weighted assets II/risk-weighted assets (I & II)
	Mar2	Qualitative

Table 19.2 Weights of each category of criteria

Categories	Weight	ROCD weights	RS weights
Capital	30	47.92	30.77
Assets	20	22.92	23.08
Management	15	10.42	15.38
Earnings	15	10.42	15.38
Liquidity	10	4.17	7.69
Market	10	4.17	7.69

up to 100 for each criteria category), their type (minimization or maximization), the preference functions used in the PROMETHEE modeling process, the parameters of the preferences functions, as well as the ideal and anti-ideal points.

By default, all the quantitative criteria are evaluated using the Gaussian preference function, whereas a linear preference function is used for the qualitative criteria. Figure 19.2 illustrates the partial performance function for the capital adequacy ratio. The function decreases with the values of the criterion, thus indicating that higher capital adequacy values are associated with higher performance and lower risk. The least and most preferred values have been set by the expert analysts to 6.67 and 13.33, respectively. Thus, banks with capital adequacy ratio higher than 13.33 achieve a partial score of 0.5, whereas high risk bank with capital adequacy ratio below 6.67 have a partial score of 5.5. In all cases, the preference parameters have been set in such a way so as to ensure that the partial scores of the banks span, as much as possible, the whole range of values in the pre-specified score range [0.5, 5.5].

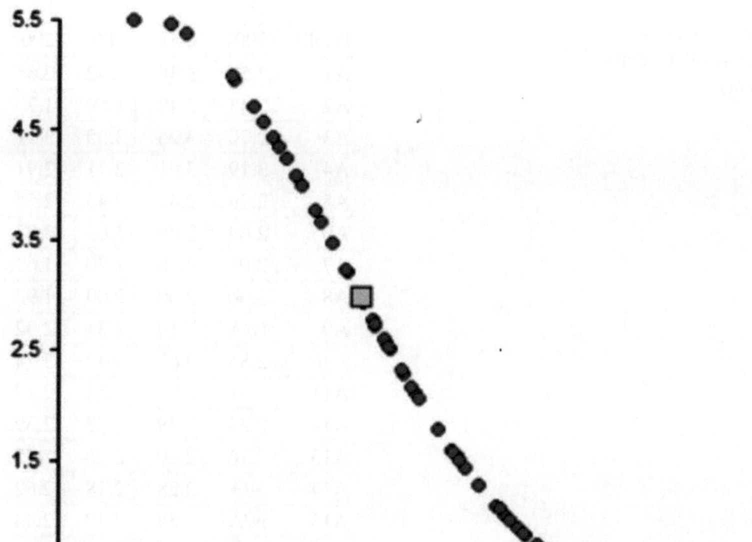

Fig. 19.2 The partial performance function for the capital adequacy ratio (absolute evaluation)

19.3.2 *Results*

Table 19.3 presents the overall evaluation results using the relative assessment procedure. Similar results are also obtained with the absolute evaluation process.[2] The results indicate that most banks achieve a rating grade of 2 or 3, each corresponding to performance scores in (1.5, 2.5] and (2.5, 3.5], respectively. There is no bank in the first (best) grade (score ≤ 1.5) nor in the highest (5th) risk grade (scores > 4.5).

The dynamics of the performance scores of the banks, indicate that no significant changes are observed between the 5 years of the analysis. Nevertheless, 2002 appears to have been the worst year; compared to 2001 only two banks managed to improve their performance. In 2003 most banks improved their performance (compared to 2002). In 2004 and 2005 no noticeable trend is observed. The highest performance improvements have been achieved by banks A7 (20.7 % improvement in 2005 compared to 2001) and A18 (21.4 % improvement in 2005 compared to

Table 19.3 Overall evaluation results (relative assessment)

Banks	2001	2002	2003	2004	2005
A1	2.59	3.38	2.82	2.65	2.33
A2	2.43	2.48	1.89	1.77	2.03
A3	2.70	3.26	3.35	3.21	3.04
A4	3.19	3.01	2.71	2.91	3.15
A5	2.29	2.45	2.43	2.54	2.52
A6	2.09	2.88	3.02	3.07	3.04
A7	2.03	2.18	1.70	1.63	1.61
A8	1.60	2.00	2.09	1.93	1.95
A9	N/A	2.10	2.31	2.32	2.59
A10	2.85	3.67	3.42	3.74	3.43
A11	2.31	2.82	2.52	2.17	2.52
A12	2.34	2.49	2.35	2.39	2.36
A13	2.16	2.20	2.26	2.75	2.13
A14	N/A	2.28	2.18	2.62	3.78
A15	N/A	2.58	2.40	2.44	2.50
A16	2.64	2.58	2.40	2.27	2.24
A17	N/A	2.18	2.40	1.98	2.03
A18	N/A	2.49	2.24	2.32	1.95

[2]On average, the rating scores with the absolute evaluation using the ideal reference point were lower (better) compared to the relative evaluation (average difference −0.064). Throughout the 5 years, the ratings were identical in 92 % of the cases with two downgrades and five upgrades. Similarly, the rating scores with the absolute evaluation using the anti-ideal reference point, were on average higher (worse) compared to the relative evaluation (average difference 0.06). Throughout the 5 years, the ratings were identical in 87 % of the cases with 13 downgrades and none upgrade.

Table 19.4 Sensitivity analysis results

Categories	Weight	2001	2002	2003	2004	2005
Capital	30	[21.9, 36.5]	[29.4, 31.8]	[25.3, 33.9]	[25.4, 34.8]	[29.9, 32]
Asset	20	[11.7, 29.1]	[17.8, 23]	[4.2, 24.5]	[13.4, 34.2]	[0, 20.5]
Management	15	[0.3, 29.6]	[12.2, 16]	[0.0, 23.1]	[0.9, 22.7]	[12.3, 15.4]
Earnings	15	[7.2, 23.4]	[11.3, 15.7]	[13.4, 20.1]	[5.9, 21.2]	[13.7, 15.2]
Liquidity	10	[4.2, 22.2]	[4.3, 11.6]	[8.9, 14.1]	[6.4, 14.4]	[8.4, 10.1]
Market risk	10	[0, 18.9]	[8.3, 10.9]	[5.3, 11.9]	[4.2, 13.1]	[9.8, 11.4]

2002). On the other hand, the highest decreases in performance involve banks A14 and A6. Bank A14 is the only bank that has been downgraded by more than one rating point during the examined time period. In 2002 (the first year being evaluated) bank A14 was assigned in the 2nd risk grade, deteriorated in the 3rd grade in 2004 and then in the 4th grade in 2005. This downgrade has been mainly due to the deterioration of the assets quality and the weakening of the earnings of the bank.

Table 19.4 provides some sensitivity analysis results for each category of criteria. The presented results involve the weight's range within which the rating of the banks remains unchanged in each year. When compared to the pre-specified weights of each category of criteria, it becomes apparent that the rating of the banks is most sensitive to changes in the relative importance of the capital dimension. The earnings dimension also seems to be critical (mainly in 2002 and 2003). On other hand, the relative importance of the management dimension is the least likely to alter the rating of the banks. Overall, the ratings in 2002 and 2005 seem to be the most sensitive to changes in the relative importance of the criteria categories, since the obtained bounds are generally closer to the pre-specified weights. As far as the individual criteria are concerned, the most critical ones (as far as their weighting is concerned) were found to be Cap1 (capital adequacy ratio) and Mar1 (risk-weighted assets II/risk-weighted assets I & II). The same two criteria were also found to have among the highest sensitivity indices, particularly in the most recent years (2004–2005). In general, the sensitivity indices were found to be limited (lower than 4 % in all cases). On the other hand, in the case of absolute evaluation the impact of the preference parameters was higher, with sensitivity indices up to 8.5 %.

Further results on the sensitivity of the ratings to the weighting of the criteria are obtained with Monte Carlo simulation. The simulation is based on 1,000 different weighting scenarios. In each simulation run, a weight vector is generated at random, but taking into account the ranking of the criteria according to their importance as defined by the expert analysts. Summary results for 2005 are presented in Table 19.5. The results involve statistics on the global performance score of the banks (mean, median 95 % confidence interval), as well as the distribution of the ratings for each bank. The obtained results are in accordance with the ones given earlier in Table 19.3. In most cases the rating of the banks is quite stable under different weighting scenarios. The most ambiguous cases involve banks A5, A9, A10, A11

Table 19.5 Simulation results for 2005

	Statistics				Rating distribution				
Banks	Mean	Median	95 % CI		1	2	3	4	5
A1	2.36	2.37	2.05	2.62	0.0	83.2	16.8	0.0	0.0
A2	2.02	2.03	1.57	2.39	0.7	99.1	0.2	0.0	0.0
A3	3.11	3.10	2.85	3.37	0.0	0.0	99.8	0.2	0.0
A4	3.17	3.17	2.86	3.45	0.0	0.0	98.6	1.4	0.0
A5	2.55	2.56	2.26	2.80	0.0	34.8	65.2	0.0	0.0
A6	3.00	3.00	2.73	3.29	0.0	0.0	100.0	0.0	0.0
A7	1.68	1.69	1.32	2.00	20.2	79.8	0.0	0.0	0.0
A8	1.91	1.92	1.48	2.29	2.9	97.1	0.0	0.0	0.0
A9	2.55	2.56	2.23	2.84	0.0	35.1	64.9	0.0	0.0
A10	3.48	3.48	3.17	3.78	0.0	0.0	56.1	43.9	0.0
A11	2.48	2.48	2.21	2.73	0.0	55.5	44.5	0.0	0.0
A12	2.38	2.37	2.15	2.64	0.0	82.1	17.9	0.0	0.0
A13	2.08	2.08	1.77	2.38	0.1	99.7	0.2	0.0	0.0
A14	3.75	3.74	3.39	4.16	0.0	0.0	11.0	89.0	0.0
A15	2.52	2.53	2.13	2.85	0.0	43.7	56.3	0.0	0.0
A16	2.18	2.18	1.93	2.42	0.0	99.6	0.4	0.0	0.0
A17	2.01	2.01	1.77	2.24	0.0	100.0	0.0	0.0	0.0
A18	1.91	1.91	1.54	2.27	1.6	98.4	0.0	0.0	0.0

Table 19.6 Correlations between the criteria weights and the performance of banks A10, A14

A10		A14	
Mar1	−52.2	Cap2	−56.6
Ass4	−40.4	Mar1	−48.1
Cap1	−33.0	Mar2	−26.6
Mar2	−26.9	Liq3	−13.4
Liq2	20.7	Ass3	−11.5
Liq3	24.6	Ear1	18.7
Ass2	32.1	Ear2	22.7
Ear1	32.2	Ass2	22.8
Liq1	32.6	Ass4	24.0
Ear2	34.5	Cap1	54.7

and A15. Future revisions of the rating process or changes in the input data for these banks are highly likely to affect their ratings.

Banks A10 and A14 are the only ones for which a high risk rating seems quite applicable. Further analysis for these two high risk banks is performed by examining the correlations between the randomly generated criteria weights and the global performance of the banks, throughout the simulation experiment. Table 19.6 summarizes the results for the most influential criteria, i.e., the ones whose weight has the highest absolute correlation with the performance of the banks. Criteria with negative correlations are associated with the points of strength for the banks, in the sense that an increase in the weight of these criteria leads to a decrease in the global performance score of the banks, thus to lower (better) rating. On the other hand, criteria with positive correlations indicate the weaknesses of the banks, in the sense that an increase in the weight of these criteria leads to an increase in the global performance score of the banks, thus to higher (worse) rating. The obtained results show that the major weaknesses of bank A10 involve its exposure to liquidity risk and its weak earnings. On the other hand, its exposure to market risk is limited, thus leading to an improvement of its overall performance. The exposure to market risk is also a strength for bank A14, which seems to suffer from poor earnings, low asset quality and low capital adequacy.

19.4 Conclusions

Bank performance monitoring and evaluation is gaining increasing interest within the context of the recent financial crisis. This paper presented a multicriteria methodology aiming towards providing comprehensive support to expert analysts. Special emphasis is put on the sensitivity of the results to the main evaluation parameters, which enables the derivation of useful conclusions on the strengths and weaknesses of the banks.

The methodology has been implemented in an integrated DSS, which is currently in use at the Bank of Greece. The DSS provides the users-analysts with enhanced data base management capabilities (including the modification of evaluation criteria), several analysis options and reporting tools. Actually, since the first installation of the system at the Bank of Greece in 2007, the expert analysts at the Risk Analysis and Supervisory Techniques Division have taken advantage of the flexibility that the DSS provides, proceeding with modifications in the set of criteria and their weighting to accommodate the changing economic conditions due to the recent crisis. Furthermore, the results of the DSS obtained with the proposed multicriteria methodology have been "validated" against the results of several stress testing scenarios and were found to be in agreement with the observed trends in key economic indicators (e.g., GDP growth, inflation rate, etc.). This successful "empirical" testing together with the flexibility of the DSS and the methodology, which enables the expert analysts to calibrate the parameters of the evaluation process in accordance with the Bank of Greece's supervisory guidelines and the prevailing economic conditions, were considered by the risk analysts at the Bank of Greece as important qualities before proceeding with the actual use of the system in practice.

The multicriteria methodology and the DSS can be used by expert bank analysts as supportive tools in their daily practice for monitoring and evaluating the performance of banks. At a further step, the aim would be to develop an early-warning system capable of identifying (as early as possible) banks which are likely to face problems. The consideration of macroeconomic factors would also enhance the analysis and enable the implementation of stress testing scenarios regarding the impact of external factors on the performance and viability of the banks.

Appendix 1: Data Table for 2005

	A1	A2	A3	A4	A5	A6	A7	A8	A9
Cap1	13.56	13.39	10.78	10.65	12.30	8.83	15.19	12.73	10.63
Cap2	31.04	88.94	41.79	46.96	53.90	3.75	81.35	79.31	0.00
Cap3	3.0	1.0	4.0	3.0	3.0	3.0	1.0	1.0	2.0
Ass1	41.46	60.84	66.01	80.81	75.67	77.25	49.19	63.56	72.92
Ass2	3.64	3.31	5.21	4.39	3.19	4.70	2.13	1.01	0.82
Ass3	0.71	0.96	1.11	0.72	0.85	1.92	1.05	1.46	5.21
Ass4	−47.91	−0.34	11.90	−8.84	−3.72	2.40	−6.05	−9.06	−3.89
Ass5	2.5	2.0	3.5	3.0	3.0	2.5	1.5	2.0	2.5
Man1	79.42	64.46	82.98	108.20	81.66	84.11	65.50	63.30	58.26
Man2	1.62	0.91	1.63	2.02	1.76	1.73	1.29	0.90	0.95
Man3	1.54	3.59	1.17	1.91	1.74	1.95	3.06	4.07	2.13
Man4	3.5	2.0	3.5	4.0	2.0	3.0	2.0	2.0	2.0
Man5	3.0	1.5	3.0	3.0	3.0	2.0	1.5	1.5	2.0
Man6	4.0	1.5	3.0	4.0	3.0	3.0	2.0	1.5	3.0
Man7	3.0	2.0	4.0	4.0	2.0	3.0	2.0	2.0	3.0
Man8	3.0	1.5	3.0	3.0	3.0	1.5	2.0	2.5	2.0
Man9	2.0	2.0	2.0	4.0	2.0	2.0	1.5	2.0	3.0
Man10	3.0	2.0	3.0	4.0	3.0	2.0	2.0	2.0	2.0
Man11	2.0	2.0	4.0	4.0	2.0	3.0	2.0	2.0	2.0
Man12	4.2	3.1	2.5	3.7	2.5	3.1	1.9	2.5	3.1
Ear1	0.74	1.27	0.69	−0.45	0.72	0.60	1.23	1.57	0.11
Ear2	13.24	21.01	10.06	−6.08	8.01	9.71	22.15	24.93	1.13
Ear3	3.00	2.66	2.34	3.11	2.91	3.04	2.63	3.20	2.10
Ear4	0.55	0.90	1.69	1.62	1.02	0.87	0.85	0.79	0.70
Ear5	4.0	1.5	3.0	3.0	3.0	4.0	1.5	1.5	2.0
Liq1	10.56	4.24	3.43	4.53	3.62	7.79	28.80	4.72	8.37
Liq2	62.79	121.16	86.54	83.04	82.63	95.35	63.91	88.20	102.96
Liq3	−10.73	6.99	−7.07	−6.97	−18.82	−1.22	1.58	15.30	2.88
Liq4	2.0	1.5	3.5	3.5	3.5	2.5	1.0	1.5	2.5
Mar1	10.17	2.18	1.25	1.66	0.25	2.37	3.74	1.46	6.19
Mar2	3.5	2.0	3.0	3.5	2.5	2.5	1.5	2.0	2.5

	A10	A11	A12	A13	A14	A15	A16	A17	A18
Cap1	10.36	10.42	9.78	12.42	7.03	13.44	10.89	12.52	45.28
Cap2	45.27	0.01	0.92	39.23	0.00	0.00	43.64	0.00	8.24
Cap3	4.0	2.0	3.0	2.0	3.0	3.0	2.0	2.0	3.0
Ass1	79.93	59.82	41.94	63.75	83.29	73.52	70.66	69.02	66.16
Ass2	6.28	1.49	0.98	0.61	5.79	3.16	1.33	1.85	−0.57
Ass3	3.87	2.58	6.44	0.70	2.26	1.65	1.95	1.34	0.99
Ass4	−24.80	−4.65	−1.48	−3.60	21.01	−0.11	−5.74	−0.18	−0.25
Ass5	3.0	3.0	2.5	1.5	3.0	3.0	2.5	2.5	3.0
Man1	109.94	91.93	54.88	82.20	206.47	58.46	64.60	55.81	27.62
Man2	2.44	0.87	0.78	1.73	1.45	1.20	1.08	1.54	0.74
Man3	1.42	1.36	2.52	1.10	0.83	0.90	2.69	1.09	31.59
Man4	3.0	2.0	3.5	3.0	3.0	3.5	2.0	2.0	3.0
Man5	3.5	2.0	3.0	2.5	3.0	3.0	1.5	2.0	2.0
Man6	3.0	2.0	3.5	3.0	3.0	4.0	2.0	2.0	3.0
Man7	3.0	2.0	3.0	2.0	3.0	3.5	2.0	3.0	2.0
Man8	3.0	3.0	3.0	2.0	3.5	3.0	2.0	2.0	2.5
Man9	3.0	3.0	4.0	2.0	3.5	3.5	2.0	3.0	3.0
Man10	3.0	2.0	2.0	2.0	3.0	3.0	2.0	3.0	3.0
Man11	3.0	2.0	2.0	3.0	3.5	3.0	3.0	1.5	4.0
Man12	3.7	2.5	3.7	3.7	2.5	4.5	2.5	2.5	2.5
Ear1	−0.50	0.22	1.27	1.05	−3.38	0.13	1.44	0.87	10.43
Ear2	−9.79	3.19	11.36	15.18	−43.86	1.29	19.29	8.75	16.68
Ear3	4.12	2.10	1.11	3.18	2.36	2.97	2.56	2.64	0.28
Ear4	0.87	0.68	1.72	1.26	−1.07	1.34	1.42	1.48	14.13
Ear5	3.0	2.5	3.0	3.0	3.0	3.0	2.5	2.0	3.0
Liq1	3.00	4.82	23.18	2.21	10.07	12.11	11.11	6.05	38.75
Liq2	93.63	90.20	37.74	112.94	83.11	109.77	124.23	72.36	157.50
Liq3	9.61	−7.42	−18.47	4.45	−6.94	8.82	6.07	−26.18	−14.40
Liq4	1.5	2.5	3.5	2.0	3.5	3.0	2.0	2.5	3.5
Mar1	0.00	1.95	12.44	1.77	2.43	1.49	3.37	0.11	47.08
Mar2	3.0	2.5	2.5	1.5	3.5	3.0	2.0	3.0	3.5

Appendix 2: Criteria Information

Criteria	Type	Weight	Preference function		Ideal	Anti-ideal
			Type	Parameter		
Cap1	Max	60	Gauss	3.00	13.33	6.67
Cap2	Min	20	Gauss	35.00	0.00	80.00
Cap3	Min	20	Linear	5.00	0.50	5.50
Ass1	Min	10	Gauss	22.00	35.00	85.00
Ass2	Min	20	Gauss	3.30	−1.50	6.00
Ass3	Min	20	Gauss	2.20	0.00	5.00
Ass4	Min	20	Gauss	2.20	−1.50	3.50
Ass5	Min	30	Linear	5.00	0.50	5.50
Man1	Min	20	Gauss	22.00	40.00	90.00
Man2	Min	15	Gauss	0.65	0.70	2.20
Man3	Max	5	Gauss	2.20	5.00	0.00
Man4	Min	5	Linear	5.00	0.50	5.50
Man5	Min	5	Linear	5.00	0.50	5.50
Man6	Min	5	Linear	5.00	0.50	5.50
Man7	Min	10	Linear	5.00	0.50	5.50
Man8	Min	10	Linear	5.00	0.50	5.50
Man9	Min	5	Linear	5.00	0.50	5.50
Man10	Min	5	Linear	5.00	0.50	5.50
Man11	Min	5	Linear	5.00	0.50	5.50
Man12	Min	10	Linear	5.00	0.50	5.50
Ear1	Max	30	Gauss	0.90	1.60	−0.40
Ear2	Max	30	Gauss	11.00	20.00	−5.00
Ear3	Max	10	Gauss	4.00	9.00	0.00
Ear4	Max	10	Gauss	0.95	2.00	0.00
Ear5	Min	20	Linear	5.00	0.50	5.50
Liq1	Max	40	Gauss	11.00	35.00	10.00
Liq2	Min	20	Gauss	33.00	45.00	120.00
Liq3	Min	20	Gauss	6.50	−3.00	12.00
Liq4	Min	20	Linear	5.00	0.50	5.50
Mar1	Min	60	Gauss	13.00	0.00	30.00
Mar2	Min	40	Linear	5.00	0.50	5.50

References

Bouyssou, D., Marchant, T., Pirlot, M., Tsoukias, A., & Vincke, P. (2006). *Evaluation and decision models with multiple criteria: Stepping stones for the analyst*. New York: Springer.

Brans, J., & Vincke, P. (1985). A preference ranking organization method. *Management Science, 31*(6), 647–656.

Butler, J., Jia, J., & Dyer, J. (1997). Simulation techniques for the sensitivity analysis of multi-criteria decision models. *European Journal of Operational Research, 103*, 531–546.

Halkos, G., & Salamouris, D. (2004). Efficiency measurement of Greek commercial banks with the use of financial ratios: A data envelopment analysis approach. *Management Account Research, 15*, 201–224.

Ho, C.-T. (2006). Measuring bank operations performance: An approach based on grey relation analysis. *Journal of the Operational Research Society, 57*(4), 337–349.

Jia, J., Fischer, G., & Dyer, J. (1998). Attribute weighting methods and decision quality in the presence of response error: A simulation study. *Journal of Behavioral Decision Making, 11*, 85–105.

Kao, C., & Liu, S.-T. (2004). Predicting bank performance with financial forecasts: A case of Taiwan commercial banks. *Journal of Banking and Finance, 28*(10), 2353–2368.

Kosmidou, K., & Zopounidis, C. (2008). Measurement of bank performance in Greece. *South-Eastern Europe Journal of Economics, 6*(1), 79–95.

Mareschal, B., & Brans, J. (1991). BANKADVISER: An industrial evaluation system. *European Journal of Operational Research, 54*, 318–324.

Mareschal, B., & Mertens, D. (1992). BANKS: A multicriteria decision support system for financial evaluation in the international banking sector. *Journal of Decision Systems, 1*(2–3), 175–189.

Parkan, C., & Liu, M.-L. (1999). Measurement of the performance of an investment bank using the operational competitiveness rating procedure. *Omega, 27*(2), 201–217.

Raveh, A. (2000). The Greek banking system: Reanalysis of performance. *European Journal of Operational Research, 120*(3), 525–534.

Sahajwala, R., & Van den Bergh, P. (2000, December). Supervisory risk assessment and early warning systems. Technical Report 4, Bank of International Settlements, Basel.

Spathis, C., Kosmidou, K., & Doumpos, M. (2002). Assessing profitability factors in the Greek banking system: A multicriteria approach. *International Transactions in Operational Research, 9*, 517–530.

Zopounidis, C., Despotis, D., & Stavropoulou, E. (1995). Multiattribute evaluation of Greek banking performance. *Applied Stochastic Models and Data Analysis, 11*(1), 97–107.

Editors' Comments on "A Multi-Criteria Approach to Bank Rating"

Michael Doumpos and Constantin Zopounidis propose a new method for evaluating the overall condition and potential risk of the banks established in a country. They describe how this method was applied and implemented in a Decision Support System (DSS) for the Bank of Greece. While there is no doubt that such a tool can be used for supporting decisions made by the Bank of Greece or the Greek government, the system presented here is mainly designed for **evaluation purposes**. The model and the DSS are not constructed to address a well-defined specific decision problem.

The proposed application aims at supporting a variety of decision processes in which an assessment of the performance and the exposition at risk of banks matters. Therefore, the preference models discussed in this case mainly concern **experts' judgments**.

Regarding the persons who participated in the elaboration of the DSS, we note that the **client** was the Bank of Greece and the **actors**, besides the authors, are senior analysts, who belong to the "Risk and Supervision Techniques" division in the Bank. These acted as experts, rather than as decision makers, by suggesting or validating the choice of indicators and providing values for the evaluation model's parameters. In the final stage of the project, they may also have acted as end users, specifying which parts of the DSS require improvement or tuning. The **analysts**, which are the authors, are members of the Financial Engineering Laboratory of the University of Crete. They are experts in the application of multicriteria methods to the finance domain.

The data used in the **validation phase** consist in the evaluations of 18 banks on 31 criteria or indicators, some relative to the assessment of financial aspects (17) and the others relative to non-financial aspects (14). All criteria scales are numerical. The available data are relative to the years 2001–2005. The DSS was installed at the Bank of Greece in 2007. Since then, some criteria and their weighting have been adapted to take into account the evolving economic conditions, in particular those resulting from the financial crisis in 2009. The DSS conception thus allows for adaptation and evolution.

No specific **problem structuring** methodology seems to have been applied. The elaboration of the evaluation model had to take into account international regulations. In particular, the 31 criteria used are grouped in the six categories of criteria specified in the CAMELS framework, a supervisory rating system used for assessing banks overall condition. Since the authors' aim is to propose a tool for supporting the **analysis and monitoring** of the bank sector in Greece rather than addressing a well-specified **decision problem**, it is not surprising that their system provides bank evaluations of different kinds, namely:

- it assigns a risk grade to each bank, using a five level scales, as required by the CAMELS framework; the banks that are not at risk are assigned to level 1 while level 5 corresponds to the banks most exposed to risk;
- it computes two scores, one allowing to rank the banks in terms of their relative performance (relative evaluation) and the other positioning each bank w.r.t. an ideal and an anti-ideal bank (absolute evaluation).

The scores also allow for comparing the evolution of the banks through time, as is done for the years 2001 to 2005 in the application (Sect. 19.3).

The **evaluation model** relies on the PROMETHEE II method (Brans and Vincke, 1985); see also Sect. 3.2.7 in Chap. 3, around formula (3.16). A net flow index is computed for each bank according to formula (19.2) and is used to **rank** the banks (relative evaluation). It is also used to assign them a risk grade on a five level scale. This is not a standard use of the **net flow score**, which has to be rescaled in order to vary in the range [0.5, 5.5]. This interval is then divided in five equal parts, each corresponding to a risk grade. The extreme values of the rescaled net flow index, namely 0.5 and 5.5, correspond to artificial banks the performance of which are, respectively, the most and the least preferred value on each criterion. This is a way of using the net flow score of the PROMETHEE method in view of assigning alternatives to ordered categories. A similar adaptation of the PROMETHEE method for **sorting** purposes was proposed in Nemery and Lamboray (2008), with the difference that the category limits are defined by the (net flow) value of limiting profiles. In the present work, it is thus implicitly assumed that the net flow value of the profiles separating the five categories of banks are equally spaced in the [0.5, 5.5] interval. This assumption is a strong one. One could alternatively have asked the risk analysts to elicit limiting bank profiles for each category of risk, i.e. typical performance vectors of artificial banks for which one would hesitate between assigning them to a category or the category just above.

The absolute evaluation of the banks also relies on tools borrowed from the PROMETHEE method. The experts form the Bank of Greece provide **ideal and anti-ideal evaluations** on each criterion (not necessarily the best and worst performance, respectively, observed on the 18 banks. Each bank is then positioned with respect to the ideal value (or the anti-ideal value), on each criterion.

Computing the net flow scores involves the **elicitation** of several parameters, including the weights of the criteria and the type of preference model on differences. Among the latter, the "linear generalized" and the Gaussian forms of preference models were the ones chosen by the experts. Both involve the elicitation of one parameter. The least and the most preferred value on each criterion must also be determined by the decision maker. Not much detail is given on the way this information (summarized in Appendix B) was obtained from the experts. In any case, the values provided by the experts most likely involve a great deal of **uncertainty**. That's why the authors developed an adapted methodology for analyzing the sensitivity of their conclusions w.r.t. the imprecision in the determination of the parameters. In particular, a range of the parameters values for which the rating of a bank remains unchanged is determined. These ranges are found by using optimization techniques as well as simulation. The part of the chapter devoted to explaining the design of the **sensitivity analysis** methodology, as well as the analysis of its results when applied to the set of 18 banks, is substantial and this is fully justified by the relatively large number of modeling options (such as selecting the type of preference model on differences) and parameters (weights, parameters of the preference model on differences). Since the precise implications of these choices are not easy to perceive, it is highly advisable to perform extensive sensitivity analysis and retain, as recommendations, only the conclusions that are insensitive to relatively large variations of the parameters.

Little detail is provided regarding the **process of elaboration** of the DSS except that the criteria have been selected in close cooperation with expert analysts from the Bank of Greece. The performance of the 18 banks on these criteria, for the period

2001–2005, were provided by them as well as the criteria weights. It is likely that the results of the analysis of the 18 banks, using the model, presented in Sect. 19.3.2, was an important step in the decision made by the Bank of implementing the model in a DSS at the disposal of the analysts of the Risk Analysis and Supervisory Techniques division. The model's conclusions were found in agreement with stress tests and the evolution of economic indicators.

The **main result** of this project is that the DSS is used at the Bank of Greece for monitoring and evaluating the performance of the commercial banks. Future developments are envisaged, especially regarding predictive aspects (early identification of banks at risk). **Key success** features of the implemented DSS are:

1. the flexibility of the underlying model and of its implementation that allow to modify the criteria and the model's parameters in order to adapt to the changing economic conditions (in particular, after the 2009 crisis);
2. the enhanced analysis capabilities it provides, together with a user-friendly interface that allows the generation of reports in graphic and tabular formats.

From a **methodological perspective**, the choice of PROMETHEE raises some questions. In this application, PROMETHEE is basically used to score the banks (by means of the net flow). When a score is needed in MCDM for evaluating an alternative x_i, the first idea is to build an additive value function $u(x_i) = \sum_{k=1}^{n} u_k(x_{ik})$. If, in addition, we want to compare preference differences, under some conditions (see e.g. Dyer and Sarin 1979), we can think of ranking them using the associated value difference. More precisely, the value difference $u(x_i) - u(x_j)$ is an assessment of the difference of preference between the pair of alternatives (x_i, x_j). This model is at the root of the MACBETH method (Bana e Costa and Vansnick (1994); see also Chap. 17 where this method is used). It is also a particular case of the PROMETHEE model, corresponding to defining the "partial preference index" $\pi_k(x_{ik}, x_{jk})$ as $\max(u_k(x_{ik}) - u_k(x_{jk}), 0)$ (where u_k is any partial value function) instead of choosing the Gaussian or the linear generalized criterion as the authors do (see Sect. 19.2.1). With the former, the net flow $\Phi(x_i)$ is equal to $\frac{m}{m-1}u(x_i) - \frac{1}{m-1}\sum_{j=1}^{m} u(x_j)$, with $u(x_j) = \sum_{k=1}^{n} u_k(x_{jk})$. Using this net flow function for ranking alternatives yields the same order as the one obtained using the value function u (since the second term in the expression of $\Phi(x_i)$ is a constant, independent of i, it does not play any role when comparing two alternatives). Such a model thus cannot be used for *relative* evaluation of the banks, i.e. evaluating them in a way that takes into account the performance of the other banks. When the partial preference index π_{ik} is for instance Gaussian, the ranking obtained using PROMETHEE may vary when an alternative is removed from the set of considered alternatives or, on the opposite, when a new alternative is added. This behavior corresponds to *rank reversal*, i.e. the violation of a property known as the *independence of irrelevant alternatives* (see Example 3.4 in Chap. 3). Conditions for PROMETHEE *not* exhibiting rank reversal have been investigated in Roland et al. (2012); Verly and De Smet (2013). Usually rank reversal is considered a drawback, while here the authors are seeking an evaluation method that is sensitive to the whole set of alternatives under consideration. This is a quite original feature and also an interesting subject for future research. In particular, the following **research issues** deserve further investigation:

- Give a formal definition of "relative evaluation" in MCDM. What are the desired properties of relative evaluation methods?
- How does PROMETHEE (and other methods subject to rank reversal such as e.g. AHP) take into account the other alternatives when assessing one? Describe the properties of the method (depending in particular on the type of partial preference index chosen). Give an axiomatic characterization of PROMETHEE.

Another, not unrelated, research issue could address temporal aspects. How can we assess the evolution of a bank over time in relative terms, i.e. taking into account the changing economic environment, in particular, the evolution of the other banks in the country?

References

Bana e Costa, C., & Vansnick, J. (1994). MACBETH - An interactive path towards the construction of cardinal value functions. *International Transactions in Operational Research, 1*, 489–500.

Brans, J., & Vincke, P. (1985). A preference ranking organization method. *Management Science, 31*(6), 647–656.

Dyer, J., & Sarin, R. K. (1979). Measurable multiattribute value functions. *Operations Research, 27*, 810–822.

Nemery, P., & Lamboray, C. (2008). Flowsort: A flow-based sorting method with limiting or central profiles. *Top, 16*(1), 90–113.

Roland, J., De Smet, Y., & Verly, C. (2012). Rank reversal as a source of uncertainty and manipulation in the PROMETHEE II ranking: A first investigation. In *Advances in computational intelligence* (pp. 338–346). Heidelberg: Springer.

Verly, C., & De Smet, Y. (2013). Some considerations about rank reversal occurrences in the PROMETHEE methods. *International Journal of Multicriteria Decision Making, 3*(4), 325–345.

Part III
MCDA Process Support Tools

Chapter 20
XMCDA: An XML-Based Encoding Standard for MCDA Data

Sébastien Bigaret and Patrick Meyer

Abstract Up to recently, the processing of a decision problem via several Multiple Criteria Decision Aiding (MCDA) programs required to write the data in various formats. This chapter presents XMCDA, an initiative of the Decision Deck Consortium, which is a standard data model enabling to encode classical concepts from MCDA in XML. Among other things, it eases the analysis of a problem instance by various MCDA techniques compatible with XMCDA without requiring data conversions and it simplifies the sequencing of MCDA algorithms for the resolution of complex decision problems.

20.1 Introduction

Research activities in and around the field of Multiple Criteria Decision Aiding (MCDA) have developed quite rapidly over the past decades, and have resulted in various streams of thought and methodological formulations to solve complex decision problems. In particular, many so-called MCDA *methods* and have been proposed in the literature and are very often available as software programs, along with some programs implementing the algorithmic elements composing these methods.

Among the difficulties that arise when one wants to use these programs in practice, a major one is that they all use their own, distinct, data format to encode the MCDA problems (other difficulties exist, which are discussed in Chap. 21). Therefore, these data need to be re-encoded for every software application one wants to run. Moreover, this problem of the heterogeneous input and output data formats in MCDA software prevented users from combining existing algorithms, in order to create treatment chains involving multiple MCDA algorithms. Consequently, in

---

S. Bigaret • P. Meyer (✉)
Institut Mines-Télécom, Télécom Bretagne, UMR CNRS 6285 Lab-STICC, Technopôle Brest-Iroise CS 83818, 29238 Brest Cedex 3, France

Université européenne de Bretagne, Brest, France
e-mail: sebastien.bigaret@telecom-bretagne.eu; patrick.meyer@telecom-bretagne.eu

R. Bisdorff et al. (eds.), *Evaluation and Decision Models with Multiple Criteria*, International Handbooks on Information Systems,
DOI 10.1007/978-3-662-46816-6_20

such a situation, the resolution of a complex decision problem comes generally down to testing only one software and using various supplementary tools to analyze the results of the resolution. This can be frustrating for a lot of MCDA analysts who might like to test various algorithms on a given problem, without having to recode the instance in various data formats.

Given this situation, a group of researchers within the Decision Deck Consortium (see Decision Deck Consortium, 2009) decided to gather together to address this particular problem; the Consortium itself is presented in more details in Chap. 21.

To allow running a problem instance through multiple methods and to allow the chaining of various MCDA algorithms, this group of researchers suggested to define a data standard, called XMCDA, which could be adopted by programs to ease their interoperability.

In this chapter, we present the latest version of XMCDA, explain its construction and motivate the choices which have been made during the elaboration process. The chapter is structured as follows: first, in Sect. 20.2 we present the history of XMCDA and explain the general ideas which facilitate the understanding of the structure of XMCDA. Then, in Sect. 20.3 we present how a lot of common MCDA related concepts can be encoded in XMCDA. Finally, in Sect. 20.4 we present the use of XMCDA in practice, before concluding in Sect. 20.5.

20.2 A First Cup of XMCDA

The objective of this section is to ease the understanding of the standard by presenting a quick overview of its purpose and the philosophy which guided its construction. We therefore start by discussing the general principles of XMCDA and the course which has lead to the current version. Then, we present some general conventions that should guide the reader of the sequel. Finally, we present some atomic elements of XMCDA which underlie more general structures presented in Sect. 20.3.

20.2.1 Technical Aspects and Choices for XMCDA

The XMCDA markup language is an application of XML,[1] a general-purpose text format used to capture data and their structures. XML's purpose is to aid information systems in sharing structured data, especially via the Internet and to encode documents. XMCDA is defined by an XML Schema,[2] a set of syntax rules (together with a set of constraints) which define its content and its structure. An XML document that complies with the XMCDA Schema is said to be a *valid*

[1]http://www.w3.org/XML/.

[2]http://www.w3.org/XML/Schema.

XMCDA document. The XML Schema of the latest version of XMCDA is available via the XMCDA website at http://www.decision-deck.org/xmcda. At the time of writing, the official version approved by the Decision Deck Consortium is `3.0.0`.

A powerful feature of XML-based markup languages is the possibility to easily transform documents from one format into another. XSLT[3] is a language for such transformations and allows us to convert XMCDA documents into HTML pages for a convenient visualization of their content in any web browser. The website of XMCDA provides a basic XSLT file which can be adapted for various purposes. Note that this possibility to easily manipulate XMCDA documents gives the Decision Deck Consortium the possibility to propose converters for future versions of XMCDA which will allow to transform older XMCDA documents to the newer standards (and vice versa, under certain constraints).

Last, the order of the elements *is* significant in an XML document; XMCDA takes advantage of this to store the order of its elements when it matters (think values in a vector e.g.)

In order to understand the choices which have led to the current version of XMCDA and their consequences on its application domain, it is important to differentiate between two fundamental aspects of a multiple criteria decision aiding procedure. First, we consider the decision aiding process which consists in multiple stepping stones and the intervention of various stakeholders. This operation aims at easing a decision maker's decision and might require the use of one or more clearly identified calculation steps, often called MCDA methods. This leads to the second important aspect of a decision aiding procedure, which are the algorithmic elements underlying such MCDA methods. Such series of operations may consist of various elementary calculation steps requiring and providing specific input and output data elements.

XMCDA is clearly intended for this second type of procedures, and focuses on data structures and concepts originally from the field of multiple criteria decision aiding methods. As such, it does not provide means of representing the key moments or the various stakeholders of the decision aiding process.

The origin of XMCDA goes back to fall 2007, where a group of researchers of the Decision Deck Consortium gathered in Paris to think about and work on a data standard which could be used by various MCDA methods. This meeting gave birth to the Decision Deck Specification Committee whose task is, among other things, to maintain XMCDA and to propose future evolutions of the standard. This committee approved in Spring 2008 a first version of XMCDA, named `1.0`, which was used mainly by two MCDA libraries, KAPPALAB (by Grabisch et al., 2008) and DIGRAPH3 (by Bisdorff, 2014). Very quickly, the poor genericity of this version limited its practical use and its spreading. Therefore, 1 year later, in Spring 2009, the Decision Deck Consortium approved version `2.0.0` of XMCDA, which is a lot more generic and flexible than its predecessor and was used by multiple software pieces like RUBIS (Bisdorff, 2014) or J-MCDA (Cailloux, 2010). In Fall 2013, after

[3]http://www.w3.org/Style/XSL.

4 years of dedicated and distinguished service, the Consortium approved a deep-down cleaning of XMCDA which removes recurrent inconsistencies of the `2.2.0` version and consequently approved version `3.0.0`. Software using this version include *diviz* (Meyer and Bigaret, 2012) and the XMCDA web-services.

The releases of XMCDA are versioned `a.b.c`, where `a`, `b` and `c` are integers which are increased in case of a new release, according to the following rules:

- change from XMCDA `a.b.c` to XMCDA `a.b.(c+1)` for minor modifications on the standard, like, e.g., the addition of a new subtag in an XMCDA tag;
- change from XMCDA `a.b.c` to XMCDA `a.(b+1).0` for more substantial modifications on the standard, like, e.g., the addition of a new tag under the root tag;
- change from XMCDA `a.b.c` to XMCDA `(a+1).0.0` for modifications on the standard which do not allow full compatibility to earlier versions, like, e.g., the renaming of a fundamental XMCDA tag.

20.2.2 Conventions

After this short history of XMCDA, we now give further technical details on the standard. In order to avoid misunderstandings, let us first briefly introduce a few conventions used in this chapter:

- The term 'MCDA *concept*' describes a real or abstract construction related to the field of MCDA which needs to be stored in XMCDA (like, for example, an alternative, the importance of the criteria, an attribute, a criterion, etc.);
- An 'XMCDA *type*' corresponds to an XML data type defined by the XMCDA XML Schema (and which will be written as follows: `xmcda:typeName`);
- An 'XMCDA *tag*' is an XML tag which is defined by the XMCDA Schema. An XMCDA type may be instantiated as multiple XMCDA tags.

The name of an XMCDA tag is written in medial capitals, or *camel case*, i.e. it is composed of concatenated words beginning with a capital letter, with the exception of the first letter of the name which is lower case; example: `alternativesSetsMatrix`. This allows to easily read and understand the meaning of a tag, as we use whole words and avoid acronyms and abbreviations. Other examples are `performanceTable`, storing the performance table, and `criterionValue`, storing a value related to a criterion, as, e.g., its weight. Note that objects of the same XMCDA type are in general be gathered in a compound tag, represented by a single XML tag named after the plural form of its elements (e.g., `alternatives` is the *container* of `alternative` tags).

The following three XML attributes can be found in many XMCDA tags: `id`, `name` and `mcdaConcept`. They are in general optional, except for the `id` attribute in the definition of an alternative, a set of alternatives, a criterion, a set of criteria, a category, or a set of categories. Each of these three XML attributes has a particular purpose in XMCDA:

- The `id` XML attribute identifies an object with a *machine-readable* code or identifier. As an illustration consider the following alternative "a12" which is a Peugeot 309:

```
<alternative id="a12">
 <description>
  <comment>A red Peugeot 309 from 1986</comment>
 </description>
</alternative>
```

  The `id` attribute allows to distinguish between the various alternatives and identifies them unequivocally.

- The `name` attribute allows to give a *human-readable* name to a particular MCDA object. The previous example can therefore be completed as follows:

```
<alternative id="a12" name="Peugeot 309">
 <description>
  <comment>A red Peugeot 309 from 1986</comment>
 </description>
</alternative>
```

  In a software using the XMCDA standard, this name should be displayed to the user instead of (or at least next to) the id.

- The `mcdaConcept` XML attribute allows to specify the MCDA concept linked to a particular instance of an XMCDA tag. Some XMCDA tagnames are quite general and may not be directly related to a very specific MCDA concept. This XML attribute therefore allows to indicate more precisely what kind of information is contained in the related tag. To illustrate this, consider the following example, which presents how a ranking of alternatives could be stored by using the XMCDA tag `alternativesValues`. Alternative "a03" is ranked before "a11" and therefore has a lower rank.

```
<alternativesValues name="Ranks of the alternatives"
    mcdaConcept="ranks">
 <alternativeValue>
  <alternativeID>a03</alternativeID>
  <value>
   <integer>1</integer>
  </value>
 </alternativeValue>
 <alternativeValue>
  <alternativeID>a11</alternativeID>
  <value>
   <integer>2</integer>
  </value>
 </alternativeValue>
 <!-- ... -->
</alternativesValues>
```

In practice, the `mcdaConcept` should be used by algorithms to specify what content is produced or what type of data is required as input, in case of a possible ambiguity. No specific vocabulary is imposed for this XML attribute, which gives a great flexibility to XMCDA. A further example of its use is given by the following piece of code:

```
<criteriaThresholds>
 <criterionThreshold>
  <criterionID>g1</criterionID>
  <thresholds>
   <threshold id="g1i"
          name="indifference threshold"
          mcdaConcept="indifference">
    <constant><integer>3</integer></constant>
   </threshold>
   <threshold id="g1p"
          name="preference threshold"
          mcdaConcept="preference">
    <constant><integer>4</integer></constant>
   </threshold>
  </thresholds>
 </criterionThreshold>
 <!-- ... -->
</criteriaThresholds>
```

In this case, the authors of the algorithm which processes this data have specified that the discrimination thresholds have to be called “indifference” and “preference” in the `mcdaConcept` attribute so that the program can distinguish between the two `threshold` tags.

As a general rule, to leave the greatest possible flexibility to the MCDA algorithms, and in particular, to allow them to be combined with each other, the `mcdaConcept` attribute should be used with great parsimony, especially concerning the requirements on the inputs of the algorithms.

20.2.3 Three Essential XMCDA Types

The XML Schema which determines the structure of an XMCDA document defines among others three essential XMCDA types which appear in most of the XMCDA tags.

The first one is `xmcda:description`. It is intended to store meta-data on the information which is stored in an XMCDA tag. This type allows, among other things, to specify an author and a date of creation, to make a comment or to specify a bibliographical reference. In XMCDA the `xmcda:description` type is instantiated as the `description` tag which appears in all the XMCDA tags.

Hereafter we give a short excerpt of an XMCDA file showing such an instantiation of the `xmcda:description` type for a car selection problem.

```
<alternatives>
 <description>
  <author>Calvin Hobbes</author>
  <comment>Only European cars are considered.</comment>
  <keyword>cars</keyword>
  <keyword>choice</keyword>
  <creationDate>2010-06-02</creationDate>
  <!-- ... -->
 </description>
 [..]
<alternatives>
```

The second essential XMCDA type is `xmcda:value`. Its main purpose is to store numerical or literal values related to MCDA data. This type allows to store an integer, a real number (float), an interval, a rational, a nominal value, an ordinal value, a fuzzy number, etc. In XMCDA, this type is mainly instantiated as the `value` tag, which appears in a large number of XMCDA tags.

Hereafter we give an excerpt of an XMCDA file showing five different values. The bounds of an interval can be specified as open or not.

```
<value><integer>8</integer></value>

<value>
 <valuedLabel>
  <label>Good</label>
  <value>
   <integer>3</integer>
  </value>
 </valuedLabel>
</value>

<value>
 <rational>
  <numerator>10</numerator>
  <denominator>3</denominator>
 </rational>
</value>

<interval>
 <lowerBound open="true">
  <integer>4</integer>
 </lowerBound>
 <upperBound open="false">
  <integer>8</integer>
 </upperBound>
</interval>

<value><real>3.141526</real></value>
```

A third important XMCDA type is `xmcda:numericValue` which restricts `xmcda:value` to numeric values. This type is used in many XMCDA tags (minimum, maximum, `constant`, `coefficient`, ...) which exclusively require a numeric value.

20.2.4 Elementary XMCDA Tags

In this section we present some elementary tags which are used in many more complex XMCDA tags.

20.2.4.1 Value and Values

As already mentioned in Sect. 20.2.3, the `value` tag is an instance of the `xmcda:value` type and appears in many XMCDA tags. The `values` tag is a compound tag which contains a list of `value` tags. It can be used to represent a set or a sequence of values. As noted in Sect. 20.2.1, XMCDA uses the fact that elements are naturally ordered in an XML document to store the order of its values when it matters: that order obviously matters when storing a sequence of values.

20.2.4.2 Point and Points

Some more complex XMCDA tags, as, e.g., `function` (see hereafter), require the concept of *point*. The abscissa as well as the ordinate are of type `xmcda:value`. The following example shows a point whose coordinates are $(2.71, 23)$.

```
<point>
 <abscissa><real>2.71</real></abscissa>
 <ordinate><real>23</real></ordinate>
</point>
```

20.2.4.3 Function

Functions are used in complex tags related to criteria, as for example to specify a discrimination threshold or a value function. A `function` can either be a constant, an affine, a piecewise linear function or a discrete function. The following code shows a constant function, an affine function, and a discrete function described by a set of points.

```
<function>
 <constant><real>456.3847</real></constant>
</function>

<function>
 <affine>
  <slope><real>4.00</real></slope>
  <intercept><real>4.00</real></intercept>
 </affine>
</function>

<function>
```

```
 <discrete>
  <point>
   <abscissa><real>2.71</real></abscissa>
   <ordinate><real>23</real></ordinate>
  </point>
  <point>
   <abscissa><real>7</real></abscissa>
   <ordinate><real>45.23</real></ordinate>
  </point>
  <!-- etc. -->
 </discrete>
</function>
```

20.2.4.4 Scale

XMCDA allows to store the definition of evaluation scales, which may be *quantitative*, *qualitative* or *nominal*. The `scale` tag is in particular used to specify the evaluation scale of a criterion. The following example shows the description of a quantitative scale whose minimal value is 0 and whose maximal value is 100 and for which higher values are considered as better (the `minimum` and `maximum` tags are of type `xmcda:numericalValue`).

```
<scale>
 <quantitative>
  <preferenceDirection>max</preferenceDirection>
  <minimum><real>0</real></minimum>
  <maximum><real>100</real></maximum>
 </quantitative>
</scale>
```

20.2.4.5 References to Criteria, Alternatives, Categories, ...

In many XMCDA tags, a reference has to be made to a certain criterion, a set of criteria, an alternative, a set of alternatives, a category or a set of categories. This allows to specify which of these MCDA concepts the data stored in the tag is related to. To do so, we use tags named `criterionID`, `criteriaSetID`, `alternativeID`, `alternativesSetID`, `categoryID` or `categoriesSetID` which contain a string specifying the id of a criterion, set of criteria, alternative, set of alternatives, category, or set of categories defined elsewhere (see Sect. 20.3.1 on how such MCDA objects are defined). The following example shows the XMCDA encoding of the weights of the criteria “g01” and “g02” and the way a reference is made to these criteria.

```
<criteriaValues name="criteria weights">
 <criterionValue>
  <criterionID>g01</criterionID>
  <value>
```

```
   <real>0.4</real>
  </value>
 </criterionValue>
 <criterionValue>
  <criterionID>g02</criterionID>
  <value>
   <real>0.6</real>
  </value>
 </criterionValue>
</criteriaValues>
```

20.2.4.6 The `active` Attribute

In the tags defining criteria, alternatives or categories, an attribute named `active` (which accepts the boolean values `true` or `false`) can be used to activate or deactivate the concept it is related to. In practice, this can be very convenient if the user wishes to check the behavior of an algorithm on, e.g, a subset of criteria. Instead of deleting all the references to the unused criteria in the XMCDA file, he simply deactivates them in their definition by putting the `active` attribute to false. The standard requires programs to ignore deactivated MCDA concepts in the general case, and that exceptions to this rule, or options allowing the user to bypass it, must be clearly documented.

*

After this preliminary presentation of some concepts and rules underlying the standard, we present in the following section how main concepts from MCDA can be encoded in XMCDA.

20.3 XMCDA Encoding of MCDA Data

The root tag of XMCDA is named `XMCDA` and contains several sub-tags, each of them describing data related to a multicriteria decision aiding problem. To summarize, these tags can be put in four general categories:

- definitions of MCDA concepts like criteria, sets of criteria, alternatives, sets of alternatives, categories and sets of categories;
- the performance table;
- information on preferences related to criteria, sets of criteria, alternatives, sets of alternatives, categories or sets of categories (either provided as input by a decision maker or produced as the output of an algorithm);
- parameters for programs or algorithms that do not fall in any of the previous categories, and their execution status (success or failure).

Note that an XMCDA file does not require that all of these categories are present to be considered as valid. A valid XMCDA file may contain only one tag under the root element or even only the root tag.

In the following sections we describe each of these categories and the tags they contain.

20.3.1 Definition of Alternatives, Criteria, Categories and Performances

20.3.1.1 Alternatives/Sets of Alternatives

Alternatives are defined in the `alternatives` tag via the `alternative` tag. They can be either `active` or not and either be `real` or `fictive`. The XML attribute `id` of an alternative is mandatory. The following piece of code defines three alternatives related to a transportation means selection problem.

```
<alternatives>
 <description>
  <title>List of transportation means.</title>
  <author>Susie Derkins</author>
  <!-- ... -->
 </description>

 <alternative id="x1" name="Train"/>

 <alternative id="x2" name="Corvette">
  <type>real</type>
  <active>true</active>
 </alternative>

 <alternative id="x3" name="UFO">
  <description>
   <comment>Definitely not a real alternative.</comment>
   <!-- ... -->
  </description>
  <type>fictive</type>
 </alternative>
</alternatives>
```

Sets of alternatives can be defined via the `alternativesSets` tag. Again, the XML attribute `id` is mandatory for each set and defines it unequivocally. The following code shows a set of two alternatives, each element of the set being characterized by a membership degree.

```
<alternativesSets>
 <alternativesSet id="set1">
  <element>
   <alternativeID>a01</alternativeID>
   <values>
```

```
    <value mcdaConcept="membership">
     <real>0.8</real>
    </value>
   </values>
  </element>
  <element>
   <alternativeID>a02</alternativeID>
   <values>
    <value mcdaConcept="membership">
     <real>0.75</real>
    </value>
   </values>
  </element>
 </alternativesSet>
</alternativesSets>
```

20.3.1.2 Criteria/Sets of Criteria

Criteria are defined and described under the `criteria` tag. For each criterion, the XML attribute `id` has to be given. A criterion can be active or not. In the following example, the first criterion "g1" represents the power of a car. By default it is active (no `active` tag given).

```
<criteria>
 <criterion id="g1" name="horsepower">
  <description>
   <comment>Power in horsepower</comment>
  </description>
 </criterion>

 <criterion id="g2"/>
</criteria>
```

It is also possible to define sets of criteria under the `criteriaSets` tag similarly as for sets of alternatives.

20.3.1.3 Categories/Sets of Categories

Sorting procedures require the use of categories which can be defined under the `categories` tag. They can be active or not. The following example defines three categories of students, the second one being currently inactive.

```
<categories>
 <category id="g" name="good">
  <active>true</active>
 <category>

 <category id="m" name="medium">
  <active>false</active>
```

```
<category>

<category id="b" name="bad"/>
</categories>
```

Note that sets of categories can be defined by the categoriesSets tag similarly as for sets of alternatives.

20.3.1.4 The Performance Table

The table containing the evaluations of the alternatives on the various criteria is called performance table. It is defined by the tag performanceTable, and contains, for alternatives (given by a reference to its id), a sequence of performances, composed of a reference to a criterion id and a corresponding performance value. The following example shows part of such a performance table for two alternatives and two criteria.

```
<performanceTable>
 <alternativePerformances>
  <alternativeID>alt1</alternativeID>
  <performance>
   <criterionID>g1</criterionID>
   <values>
    <value>
     <real>72.10</real>
    </value>
   </values>
  </performance>
  <performance>
   <criterionID>g2</criterionID>
   <values>
    <value>
     <valuedLabel>
      <label>medium</label>
      <value>
       <integer>3</integer>
      </value>
     </valuedLabel>
    </value>
   </values>
  </performance>
 </alternativePerformances>

 <alternativePerformances>
  <alternativeID>alt2</alternativeID>
  [..]
 </alternativePerformances>
</performanceTable>
```

*

To fully specify criteria, it might be useful to define the evaluation scale for each of them, some discrimination thresholds which might have been expressed by a decision maker, or some value functions related to them. We describe in the sequel the XMCDA tag `criteriaScales`, `criteriaThresholds` and `criteriaFunctions`, which are placeholders designed for that use.

20.3.2 *Advanced Information and Preferences on Alternatives, Criteria and Categories*

In the previous section we have shown how the fundamental concepts from MCDA are defined in XMCDA. Here we present how supplementary data linked to these concepts is represented in the standard.

20.3.2.1 Evaluation Scales of Criteria

The `criteriaScale` tag associates a criterion `id` with a scale. This allows to specify on what scale the alternatives are evaluated and what preference direction should be used. In the following example, two scales are defined for two criteria. Criterion “g1” uses a quantitative one, where the higher values are preferred by the decision maker, whereas “g2” is evaluated through a qualitative scale with 3 levels. In the latter one, the definition and the ranks of the various levels of the scale are given in the `valuedLabel` tag.

```
<criteriaScales>
 <criterionScale>
  <criterionID>g1</criterionID>
  <scales>
   <scale>
    <quantitative>
     <preferenceDirection>max</preferenceDirection>
     <minimum><real>0</real></minimum>
     <maximum><real>100</real></maximum>
    </quantitative>
   </scale>
  </scales>
 </criterionScale>

 <criterionScale>
  <criterionID>g2</criterionID>
  <scales>
   <scale>
    <qualitative>
     <preferenceDirection>min</preferenceDirection>
     <valuedLabels>
      <valuedLabel>
       <label>bad</label>
```

```
      <value><integer>3</integer></value>
     </valuedLabel>
     <valuedLabel>
      <label>neutral</label>
      <value><integer>2</integer></value>
     </valuedLabel>
     <valuedLabel>
      <label>good</label>
      <value><integer>1</integer></value>
     </valuedLabel>
    </valuedLabels>
   </qualitative>
  </scale>
 </scales>
 </criterionScale>
</criteriaScales>
```

20.3.2.2 Discrimination Thresholds on Criteria

In outranking methods, the decision maker may specify some discrimination thresholds on each of the criteria. To do so in XMCDA, the `criteriaThresholds` tag should be used. In the example below, for criterion "g1" two thresholds have been defined : an indifference and a preference threshold.

```
<criteriaThresholds>
 <criterionThreshold>
  <criterionID>g1</criterionID>
  <thresholds>
   <threshold id="g1i" name="indifference threshold"
           mcdaConcept="indifference">
    <constant><integer>3</integer></constant>
   </threshold>

   <threshold id="g1p" name="preference threshold"
           mcdaConcept="preference">
    <constant><integer>4</integer></constant>
   </threshold>
  </thresholds>
 </criterionThreshold>
</criteriaThresholds>
```

It is important to notice the importance of the `mcdaConcept` attribute here, which allows to distinguish between the two discrimination thresholds. It can be assumed that the authors of the algorithm which will use this piece of XMCDA have specified how the discrimination thresholds should be labeled in order for the program to work properly.

20.3.2.3 Value Functions on Criteria

In the value functions paradigm, the preferences of a decision maker can be expressed by value functions associated with the criteria. In XMCDA, this kind of preferences is stored in the `criteriaFunctions` tag. In the following piece of code, two value functions are defined for criteria "g1" and "g2". The first one is a piecewise linear function, which is represented here through a sequence of two segments. Each of the linear segments is defined by a head and a tail, which are points. The attribute `open` indicates whether each end is included in the interval. The second value function associated with "g2" is a linear function defined by a slope and an intercept.

```
<criteriaFunctions>
 <criterionFunction>
  <criterionID>g1</criterionID>
  <functions>
   <function>
   <piecewiseLinear>
    &lt;segment&gt;
     <head>
      <abscissa><label>bad</label></abscissa>
      <ordinate><real>0</real></ordinate>
     </head>
     <tail>
      <abscissa><label>medium</label></abscissa>
      <ordinate><real>0.25</real></ordinate>
     </tail>
    &lt;/segment&gt;
    &lt;segment&gt;
     <head open="true">
      <abscissa><label>medium</label></abscissa>
      <ordinate><real>0.25</real></ordinate>
     </head>
     <tail>
      <abscissa><label>good</label></abscissa>
      <ordinate><real>1</real></ordinate>
     </tail>
    &lt;/segment&gt;
   </piecewiseLinear>
  </function>
 </functions>
</criterionFunction>

<criterionFunction>
 <criterionID>g2</criterionID>
 <functions>
  <function>
   <linear>
    <slope><real>0.1</real></slope>
    <intercept><real>0</real></intercept>
   </linear>
  </function>
```

```
  </functions>
 </criterionFunction>
</criteriaFunctions>
```

*

In the sequel we present generic structures which can be adapted for alternatives, criteria and categories, as well as sets of alternatives, sets of criteria and sets of categories. To avoid redundant explanations and notation, we write xValues for the generic structure related to the XMCDA tags `alternativesValues`, `alternativesSetsValues`, `criteriaValues`, `criteriaSetsValues`, `categoriesValues` and `categoriesSetsValues`. The same convention is used for the xLinearConstraints and xMatrix tags described hereafter.

20.3.2.4 Values Associated with MCDA Concepts

An xValue is a value associated with an element of type `x` (`x` being either alternatives, criteria or categories, or sets of them). This tag is found in compound tags called xValues. The following example shows a value associated with an alternative "alt1", and one associated with a set of criteria "cs3". In the first case, the stored information could be the overall value of alternative "alt1", whereas in the second case it could be the weight of the set of criteria "cs3".

```
<alternativeValue mcdaConcept="overallValue">
 <alternativeID>alt1</alternativeID>
 <values>
  <value><real>0.8</real></value>
 </values>
</alternativeValue>

<criteriaSetValue mcdaConcept="importance">
 <criteriaSetID>cs3</criteriaSetID>
 <values>
  <value><real>0.5</real></value>
 </values>
</criteriaSetValue>
```

For both values, we assume that the alternative and the set of criteria are defined elsewhere in an `alternative` and a `criteriaSet` tag. The `mcdaConcept` attributes are again not mandatory, and they depend on the specifications of the program which uses or produces the XMCDA file.

20.3.2.5 Linear Constraints Related to MCDA Concepts

XMCDA also allows to represent linear constraints related to alternatives, criteria and categories, or sets of them. The following example shows the representation of the constraint

$$2 \cdot \text{weight}(c_2) - 3 \cdot \text{weight}(c_4) \leq \varepsilon$$

in the standard:

```
<criteriaLinearConstraints>
 <variables>
  <variable id="epsilon"></variable>
 </variables>
 <constraint id="c1">
  <elements>
   <element mcdaConcept="weight">
    <criterionID>c2</criterionID>
    <coefficient>
     <real>2</real>
    </coefficient>
   </element>
   <element mcdaConcept="weight">
    <criterionID>c4</criterionID>
    <coefficient>
     <real>-3</real>
    </coefficient>
   </element>
   <element>
    <variableID>epsilon</variableID>
    <coefficient>
     <real>-1</real>
    </coefficient>
   </element>
  </elements>
  <operator>leq</operator>
  <rhs>
   <real>0</real>
  </rhs>
 </constraint>
</criteriaLinearConstraints>
```

ε is a variable which needs to be determined by the linear program. It is declared in the `variable` tag, and can then be referenced in the constraint. The `operator` tag can either be `eq` (=), `leq` ($\leq$) or `geq` ($\geq$). Linear constraints related to sets of `x` can similarly be represented in the `xSetsLinearConstraints` tags.

20.3.2.6 Matrices Related to MCDA Concepts

An xMatrix allows to represent matrices of values on criteria, alternatives and categories, or sets of them. The scale of the values can be specified in the valuation tag. The following example presents a short example of a correlation matrix between criteria, where criterion "g01" is positively correlated with "g02" and negatively correlated with "g03".

```
<criteriaMatrix mcdaConcept="correlation">
 <row>
  <criterionID>g01</criterionID>
  <!-- ... -->
  <column>
   <criterionID>g02</criterionID>
   <values>
    <value><real>0.9</real></value>
   </values>
  </column>
  <column>
   <criterionID>g03</criterionID>
   <values>
    <value><real>-0.8</real><value>
   </values>
  </column>
 </row>
 <!-- ... -->
</criteriaMatrix>
```

Among other things, this structure can also represent relations or graphs between MCDA concepts (like outranking relations for example or partial preorders on alternatives).

*

In the context of sorting or clustering techniques, two further concepts need to be representable in XMCDA : the description of categories in terms of profiles, and the assignments of the alternatives to the categories.

20.3.2.7 Profiles of Categories

The tag categoryProfile is used to describe the characteristics of a category via *central* or *limit* profiles. The following piece of code shows that the "medium" category is bounded by alternatives "p1" and "p2", whereas the "high" category has alternative "p3" as a central profile. The categoryProfile tags are grouped in a categoriesProfiles compound tag.

```
<categoriesProfiles>
 <categoryProfile>
  <categoryID>medium</categoryID>
```

```
  <bounding>
   <lowerBound>
    <alternativeID>p1</alternativeID>
   </lowerBound>
   <upperBound>
    <alternativeID>p2</alternativeID>
   </upperBound>
  </bounding>
 </categoryProfile>

 <categoryProfile>
  <categoryID>high</categoryID>
  <central>
   <alternativeID>p3</alternativeID>
  </central>
 </categoryProfile>
</categoriesProfiles>
```

Separation profiles are a special case of the bounding profiles, where the lower bound of a category corresponds to the upper bound of the category below.

20.3.2.8 Assignment of Alternatives

The tag `alternativesAssignments` allows to detail to which category or categories each of the alternatives is assigned. The following excerpt shows that alternative "alt2" is assigned to category "cat03" with a credibility of 0.8, the set of alternatives "alts3" belongs to the set of categories "catSet13" and alternative "alt4" is assigned to an interval of categories.

```
<alternativesAssignments>
 <alternativeAssignment>
  <alternativeID>alt2</alternativeID>
  <categoryID>cat03</categoryID>
  <values>
   <value mcdaConcept="credibility"><real>0.8</real></value>
  </values>
 </alternativeAssignment>

 <alternativeAssignment>
  <alternativesSetID>alts3</alternativesSetID>
  <categoriesSetID>catSet13</categoriesSetID>
 </alternativeAssignment>

 <alternativeAssignment>
  <alternativeID>alt4</alternativeID>
  <categoriesInterval>
   <lowerBound>
    <categoryID>medium</categoryID>
   </lowerBound>
   <upperBound>
    <categoryID>veryGood</categoryID>
```

```
   </upperBound>
  </categoriesInterval>
 </alternativeAssignment>
</alternativesAssignments>
```

20.3.3 Program Specific Data

20.3.3.1 Input Parameters for Programs

Programs or algorithms may require specific parameters in order to guide the resolution of a decision problem. Those parameters may not necessarily be linked to MCDA concepts, and they are specified within the dedicated tag `programParameters`, which consists in a list of `programParameter` tags. The following example presents a parameter specifying the maximal number of iterations of an algorithm and a parameter specifying a minimal separation threshold between the overall values of two consecutive alternatives in a ranking.

```
<programParameters>
 <programParameter id="nb_iter_max"
                   name="maximal number of iterations">
  <values>
   <value>
    <integer>1000</integer>
   </value>
  </values>
 </programParameter>
 <programParameter id="min_separation_threshold"
                   name="minimal separation threshold">
  <values>
   <value>
    <real>0.01</real>
   </value>
  </values>
 </programParameter>
</programParameters>
```

As expected, the attribute `id` should be reserved for automatic processing. Obviously, each program must describe in its documentation the different `id`s it expects, along with the domain of validity for their respective values.

20.3.3.2 Execution Results of Programs

Since one of the goals of XMCDA is inter-operability, we also have a standard way for programs to communicate their return status, i.e. to success or failure.

This status is stored in the dedicated `programExecutionResult` tag; it can be either `ok`, `warning`, `error` or `terminated`. Additionally, a program may produce some human-readable messages to provide further information on its execution status. The following example shows how a program will use this tag to signal that the execution of the algorithm has failed because one of its parameter had an invalid value.

```
<programExecutionResult>
 <status>error</status>
 <messages>
  <message>
   <text>Parameter nb_iter_max: invalid value 7.3 (real)
The value must be a positive integer</text>
  </message>
 </messages>
</programExecutionResult>
```

We recommend to keep the usage of messages focused on the explanation of the execution status; in particular, they are not intended to hold logging messages produced by a program, including debugging messages.

The semantics of the status is summarized here:

- `ok`: successful execution.
- `warning`: successful execution, but the results need to be validated. For example, this can be the case when the program has made some hypothesis which cannot be automatically validated.
- `error`: the program detected a problem and stopped its execution.
- `terminated`: the program was terminated by an external cause (a crash e.g.). This status may be used by the program itself if it is capable to handle such cases, or by its execution environment.

The full details about the semantics of the return status (including what can be inferred on the validity of a program's outputs) can be found in the XMCDA reference documentation.

*

This overview of XMCDA shows the great flexibility and versatility of this encoding. For further details on the XMCDA encoding, we recommend that the interested user refers to the full documentation of the XMCDA XML Schema which can be found on XMCDA's web site at http://www.decision-deck.org/xmcda.

20.4 Illustration of XMCDA in Practice

In order to illustrate the technical discourse of Sects. 20.2 and 20.3, we present in this section the XMCDA coding of a classical MCDA problem which has been widely discussed in the literature, namely the choice of a sports car (see Bouyssou et al. 2000, Chap. 6). Further illustrations of the use of XMCDA can be found in

Chap. 21 where we present the *diviz* workbench (Meyer and Bigaret, 2012) and the XMCDA web-services (http://www.decision-deck.org/ws) which both extensively make use of XMCDA.

20.4.1 XMCDA Encoding of Thierry's Car Selection Problem

Let us first briefly recall the main characteristics of this example and the underlying data. In 1993, Thierry, a 21 years old student, plans to buy a middle-range, second-hand car with a powerful engine. To help with its choice, he considers five viewpoints related to cost (criterion *g1*), performance of the engine (criteria *g2* and *g3*) and safety (criteria *g4* and *g5*). Table 20.1 summarizes the alternatives (the cars) and their evaluations on the five criteria he considers.

Two of these criteria have to be maximized, namely: the road-hold and the safety criteria; the remaining three criteria have to be minimized (cost, and performances of acceleration and pickup, both of which are measured in seconds).

The reader willing to get further details on these data will refer to Bouyssou et al. (2000).

As done in Bouyssou et al. (2006, Chap. 7), Thierry also has some knowledge about the 14 cars already, and he is able to express the following ranking on a few of them:

$$\text{P309-16} \succ \text{Sunny} \succ \text{Galant} \succ \text{Escort} \succ \text{R21t}.$$

Table 20.1 Data for Thierry's car selection problem

Car ID	Car name	Cost (*g1*, €)	Accel. (*g2*, s)	Pick up (*g3*, s)	Brakes (*g4*)	Road-hold (*g5*)
a01	Tipo	18,342	30.7	37.2	2.33	3
a02	Alfa	15,335	30.2	41.6	2	2.5
a03	Sunny	16,973	29	34.9	2.66	2.5
a04	Mazda	15,460	30.4	35.8	1.66	1.5
a05	Colt	15,131	29.7	35.6	1.66	1.75
a06	Corolla	13,841	30.8	36.5	1.33	2
a07	Civic	18,971	28	35.6	2.33	2
a08	Astra	18,319	28.9	35.3	1.66	2
a09	Escort	19,800	29.4	34.7	2	1.75
a10	R19	16,966	30	37.7	2.33	3.25
a11	P309-16	17,537	28.3	34.8	2.33	2.75
a12	P309	15,980	29.6	35.3	2.33	2.75
a13	Galant	17,219	30.2	36.9	1.66	1.25
a14	R21t	21,334	28.9	36.7	2	2.25

Let us now illustrate how this problem can be encoded using the XMCDA data format. First of all, the alternatives are defined as follows ("..." denotes an ellipsis in the examples, so that they remain compact):

```
<alternatives name="Thierry's potential cars">
 <alternative id="a12" name="P309">
  <description>
   <comment>Peugeot 309</comment>
  </description>
 </alternative>
 <!-- ... -->
 <alternative id="a14" name="R21t">
  <description>
   <comment>Renault 21</comment>
  </description>
 </alternative>
</alternatives>
```

Then, the criteria are defined by the following piece of code:

```
<criteria>
 <criterion id="g1" name="Cost">
  <description>
   <comment>Cost in Euros</comment>
  </description>
 </criterion>
 <!-- ... -->
 <criterion id="g5" name="Road-hold">
  <description>
   <comment>Road hold (0 is worst, 4 is best).</comment>
  </description>
 </criterion>
</criteria>
```

The evaluation scales of the various criteria are stored in the `criteriaScales` tag as follows:

```
<criteriaScales>
 <criterionScale>
  <criterionID>g1</criterionID>
  <scales>
   <scale>
    <quantitative>
     <preferenceDirection>min</preferenceDirection>
    </quantitative>
   </scale>
  </scales>
 </criterionScale>
 <!-- ... -->
 <criterionScale>
  <criterionID>g5</criterionID>
  <scales>
   <scale>
    <quantitative>
     <preferenceDirection>max</preferenceDirection>
```

```
    <minimum><real>0</real></minimum>
    <maximum><real>4</real></maximum>
   </quantitative>
  </scale>
 </scales>
 </criterionScale>
</criteriaScales>
```

The evaluations of the cars on the criteria are stored in the following performance table:

```
<performanceTable>
 <alternativePerformances>
  <alternativeID>a11</alternativeID>
  <performance>
   <criterionID>g1</criterionID>
   <values>
    <value><real>17537</real></value>
   </values>
  </performance>
  <!-- ... -->
  <performance>
   <criterionID>g5</criterionID>
   <values>
    <value><real>2.75</real></value>
   </values>
  </performance>
 </alternativePerformances>
 <!-- ... -->
 <alternativePerformances>
  <alternativeID>a14</alternativeID>
  <performance>
   <criterionID>g1</criterionID>
   <values>
    <value><real>21334</real></value>
   </values>
  </performance>
  <!-- ... -->
  <performance>
   <criterionID>g5</criterionID>
   <values>
    <value><real>2.25</real></value>
   </values>
  </performance>
 </alternativePerformances>
</performanceTable>
```

Finally, the ranking provided by Thierry can be stored as follows:

```
<alternativesValues name="ranks">
 <description>
      <comment>Thierry's a priori ranking of 5 cars.</comment>
 </description>
 <alternativeValue>
  <alternativeID>a11</alternativeID>
```

```
    <values>
     <value><integer>1</integer></value>
    </values>
   </alternativeValue>
   <!-- ... -->
   <alternativeValue>
    <alternativeID>a14</alternativeID>
    <values>
     <value><integer>5</integer></value>
    </values>
   </alternativeValue>
  </alternativesValues>
```

The interested reader will find this example in Chap. 21, where it serves as the material on which a decision aiding process is demonstrated through the use of the *diviz* workbench (a Decision Deck Consortium software).

20.5 Conclusion

At the time of writing, the official version of XMCDA approved by the Decision Deck Consortium is `3.0.0`. Regularly, the specifications committee receives suggestions for evolutions of XMCDA which can lead to a new release of the standard.

The work on XMCDA is clearly in an *ongoing* status. The standard is still young but it has already proven solid, operational and stable by being used by a hundred or so web-services; however, all aspects of MCDA found in the literature are not fully covered yet; the standard evolves and integrates new concepts when they are brought to our attention. Hence, any contribution, suggestion or help are welcome, and we invite you to contact the authors or the Decision Deck Consortium for anything related to this matter.

XMCDA is used by software pieces like *diviz* (Meyer and Bigaret, 2012) and the XMCDA web-services and MCDA calculation libraries like ws-RXMCDA (Bigaret and Meyer, 2009–2010), RUBIS (Bisdorff, 2014), J-MCDA (Cailloux, 2010) and ws-PyXMCDA (Veneziano, 2010).

A reference implementation in Java is provided by the Consortium and is available on its website (Decision Deck Consortium, 2014). This is a library which enables the reading and writing of XMCDA files, and the manipulation of the corresponding XMCDA objects. At the time of writing, this library is also available for Python and R; you'll find more on the current status on the XMCDA Home Page, plus tutorials and documentation on how to use these libraries.

References

Bigaret, S., & Meyer, P. (2009/2010). ws-RXMCDA. http://www.github.com/paterijk/ws-RXMCDA.

Bisdorff, R. (2014). The Python Digraph3 modules for Rubis. http://www.leopold-loewenheim.uni.lu/Digraph3/docSphinx/html/.

Bouyssou, D., Marchant, T., Pirlot, M., Perny, P., Tsoukias, A., & Vincke, P. (2000). *Evaluation and decision models: A critical Perspective*. Kluwer's International Series. Massachusetts: Kluwer.

Bouyssou, D., Marchant, T., Pirlot, M., Tsoukias, A., & Vincke, P. (2006). *Evaluation and decision models with multiple criteria: Stepping stones for the analyst*. Springer's International Series. New York: Springer.

Cailloux, O. (2010). J-MCDA. http://www.sourceforge.net/projects/j-mcda/.

Decision Deck Consortium. (2009). Strategic manifesto of the Decision Deck project. http://www.decision-deck.org/manifesto.html.

Decision Deck Consortium. (2014). XMCDA Home Page. http://www.decision-deck.org/xmcda.

Grabisch, M., Kojadinovic, I., & Meyer, P. (2008). A review of capacity identification methods for Choquet integral based multi-attribute utility theory: Applications of the Kappalab R package. *European Journal of Operational Research, 186*(2), 766–785. doi:10.1016/j.ejor.2007.02.025.

Meyer, P., & Bigaret, S. (2012). diviz: A software for modeling, processing and sharing algorithmic workflows in MCDA. *Intelligent Decision Technologies, 6*(4), 283–296. doi:10.3233/IDT-2012-0144.

Veneziano, T. (2010). ws-PyXMCDA. http://www.github.com/quiewbee/ws-PyXMCDA.

Chapter 21
Supporting the MCDA Process with the diviz workbench

Sébastien Bigaret and Patrick Meyer

Abstract In this chapter, we illustrate how the MCDA process can be supported by the use of a decision aiding software called *diviz*. The *diviz* workbench allows to build, execute and share complex *workflows* of MCDA algorithms, and as such, is a convenient tool to help the analyst in the decision aiding process. We start by a presentation of *diviz*, before switching to the detailed description of a didactic MCDA process, based on a classical example from the MCDA literature. We show how each major step of this process can be backed up by *diviz*, and how the software can help to build the final recommendation.

21.1 Introduction

The *diviz* workbench is one of the initiatives of the Decision Deck Consortium (2009). It facilitates the use of algorithmic resources from the field of Multicriteria Decision Aiding (MCDA). Before the birth of *diviz* and the tools it relies on, the analyst who had to perform a decision aiding process for the decision maker was regularly facing the following difficulties:

1. different MCDA techniques were generally implemented in separate software products, with *heterogeneous* user interfaces;
2. testing multiple MCDA algorithms on one problem instance was not easy, because of the various input *data formats* required by the software applications—this problem is specifically addressed in Chap. 20;
3. a lot of MCDA algorithms which were presented and published in scientific articles were not easily *available* and consequently often only used by their authors;

S. Bigaret • P. Meyer (✉)
Institut Mines-Télécom, Télécom Bretagne, UMR CNRS 6285 Lab-STICC, Technopôle Brest-Iroise CS 83818, 29238 Brest Cedex 3, France

Université européenne de Bretagne, Brest, France
e-mail: sebastien.bigaret@telecom-bretagne.eu; patrick.meyer@telecom-bretagne.eu

R. Bisdorff et al. (eds.), *Evaluation and Decision Models with Multiple Criteria*, International Handbooks on Information Systems,
DOI 10.1007/978-3-662-46816-6_21

4. several MCDA software products were not *free* (neither from a financial, nor from an open-source point of view), which can be considered as a weakness for their large dissemination.

In other scientific research fields, as, e.g., statistics or data mining, there exist software platforms which allow to easily compare different analysis methods and to test them on a given data set inside a common framework. Among the most famous ones, one can cite platforms such as the GNU R statistical system by the R Development Core Team (2005) or the Weka suite of machine learning software by Hall et al. (2009). Both of these suites are open-source and independent from the operating system, which has certainly contributed to their large dissemination and acceptance among many researchers and users.

In order to overcome the earlier mentioned difficulties linked to the software situation in the field of MCDA, a group of researchers have joined their efforts and created the Decision Deck Consortium (2009). Its objective is to collaboratively develop open-source software tools implementing MCDA techniques. As such, its purpose is to provide effective tools for at least three types of users:

- consultants (analysts) who use MCDA tools to support actual decision makers involved in real world decision problems;
- teachers who present MCDA algorithms in courses;
- researchers who want to test, share and compare algorithms or to develop new ones.

In this chapter we focus on *diviz*, one of the software initiatives of the Decision Deck project, which eases the use of algorithmic resources from the field of MCDA. The *diviz* tool is an easy to use software to build, execute and share complex workflows of MCDA algorithms. In the literature, such workflows are often called *methods* [consider, e.g., the ELECTRE method by Roy (1968), the UTA method by Jacquet-Lagrèze and Siskos (1982), etc.]. One of the main features of *diviz* is that it facilitates the construction of these classical MCDA *methods*, as well as variants, by combining various elementary calculation components via an intuitive graphical user interface.

The *diviz* tool uses extensively two other outcomes of the Decision Deck project, which we also present shortly in the sequel:

- XMCDA: a standardized XML recommendation to represent objects and data structures coming from the field of MCDA. Its main objective is to allow different MCDA algorithms to *interact* and to analyze a problem instance stored in XMCDA by various MCDA algorithms (see also Chap. 20 in this book);
- XMCDA web-services: distributed open-source computational MCDA resources.

The goal of this chapter is to show how *diviz* can be used to support the MCDA process. We therefore present in Sect. 21.2 the workbench together with the resources it relies on. Then, in Sect. 21.3 we illustrate the use of *diviz* to back up a didactic decision aiding process concerning a classical MCDA problem which deals with the choice of a sports car.

21.2 diviz for Dummies

In this section we present the main features of diviz, along with its practical usage, as well as the external resources it relies on.

21.2.1 Use of diviz

The *diviz* workbench allows to build, execute and share complex *workflows* of MCDA algorithms. The design of these workflows is done via an intuitive graphical user interface, where each algorithm is represented by a box which can be linked to data files or supplementary calculation elements by using connectors. Thus, the construction of complex sequences of algorithms does not require any programming skills, but only necessitates to understand the functioning of each calculation module.

Figure 21.1 shows the *diviz* workbench.

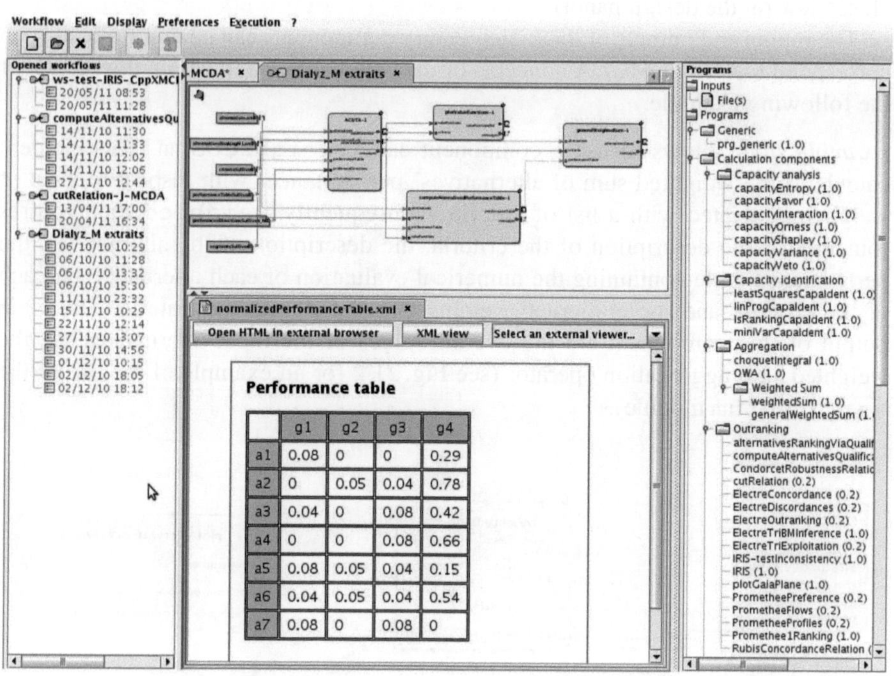

Fig. 21.1 A typical *diviz* workbench, here showing a workflow and one of its execution results

- On the left side, a tree presents the list of the opened workflows, along with their execution results.
- The upper-middle panel contains the currently selected workflow: it shows either the *design panel*, i.e. the workflow while it is designed with its input files and programs, or the workflow that has been executed when consulting an execution result.
- The lower-middle panel appears only when viewing an execution result, it shows the results of every program in the workflow.
- On the right side, all available programs are organized by theme (e.g. aggregation, outranking, elicitation).

The *diviz* software can be downloaded from http://www.diviz.org.

21.2.1.1 Workflow Design

The design of the MCDA workflows is performed via an intuitive graphical user interface, where each algorithm is represented by a box which can be linked to data files or supplementary calculation elements by using connectors (see Fig. 21.2 for a close view on the design panel).

The inputs and outputs of these elementary components can be manifold and can correspond to various MCDA concepts or data elements. To illustrate this, consider the following example.

Example diviz allows to use a component called `weightedSum`. This element calculates the weighted sum of alternatives' performances with respect to a set of weights associated with a list of criteria. Consequently, `weightedSum` requires four inputs: the description of the criteria, the description of the alternatives, the performance table containing the numerical evaluation of each alternative on each of the criteria, and the numerical weights associated with the criteria. The main output of this component are the overall values of the input alternatives via the weighted sum aggregation operator (see Fig. 21.2 for an example of the use of the `weightedSum` module).

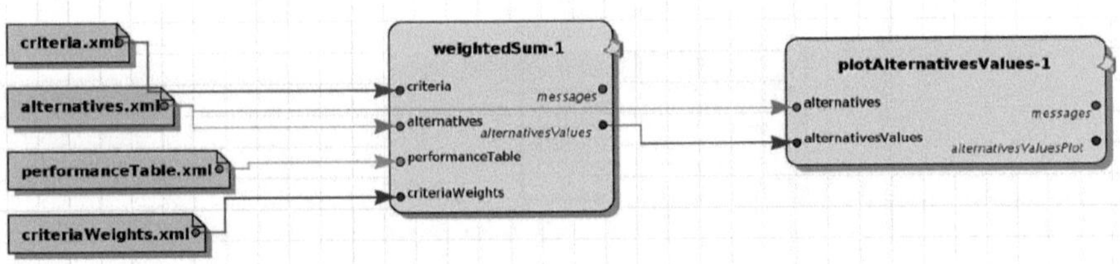

Fig. 21.2 An MCDA workflow representing the input data (*left*) and a weighted sum (*middle*) combined with a module which plots a graphical representation of the output (*right*)

To construct a new MCDA workflow, the user chooses the modules in the list of the available calculation elements and (s)he drags and drops them into the design panel. Then (s)he adds data files to the workspace and connects them appropriately to the inputs of the elements. Finally (s)he connects the inputs and outputs of the components to complete the structure of the workflow.

21.2.1.2 Execution and Results

Once the design of the MCDA workflow is finished, the user can execute it in order to obtain the possibly multiple outputs of the algorithms. These calculations are performed on high performance computing servers through the use of Decision Deck's XMCDA web-services (see Sect. 21.2.2 describing the external resources used by *diviz*). As a consequence, *diviz* does not *physically* contain any calculation modules, and requires a connection to the Internet to access these resources.

After the execution of the workflow, the outputs of each of the components can be viewed and analyzed by the user. Some of these outputs might represent intermediate results of the various calculation steps of the workflow. This feature helps tuning the parameters of the various algorithms of the workflow. We illustrate this in the following example.

Example Consider the following workflow (typically a UTA-like disaggregation method, see Sect. 4.3 in Chap. 4 of this book): a first module determines piecewise linear value functions on basis of a ranking of alternatives provided by the user; a second module transforms a performance table by applying these value functions on the performances of the alternatives; a third module calculates the sum of these performances for each of the alternatives; a fourth module draws a ranking of the alternatives on the basis of the overall values previously computed. The intermediary results are the value functions, the transformed performance table and the overall values of the alternatives. As each of these elements is explicitly available for the user, first (s)he can gain a deeper understanding of the decision aiding method which (s)he has constructed, and second, the fine-tuning of the input parameters (here, the number of segments of the value functions to be constructed, the ranking provided by the user, etc.) is facilitated.

In *diviz* the history of the past executions is kept in the software and can at any moment be viewed by the user. More precisely, if a workflow is modified, the former executions' results and their associated workflows are still available—this includes the values of the programs' parameters at the time the workflow was executed. This also contributes to the good understanding of the constructed chain of algorithms and helps calibrating the parameters of the workflow's elementary components.

21.2.1.3 Available Algorithmic Components

The algorithmic elements available in *diviz* are web-services proposed by the Decision Deck Consortium. At the time of writing, about 100 such components can be used, which can be divided into four main categories:

1. *calculation components* containing aggregation operators, disaggregation techniques, post-analysis elements, pre-processing tools, etc.;
2. *methods* containing full MCDA methods;
3. *visualization components* containing modules allowing to represent graphically certain input and output data elements;
4. *reporting components* containing techniques to create aggregated reports of multiple output data pieces.

These programs allow to reconstruct for example classical MCDA methods like the ELECTRE series by Roy (1968), the PROMETHEE series by Brans and Vincke (1985) or UTA-like techniques by Jacquet-Lagrèze and Siskos (1982). Next to that, more recent techniques linked to the elicitation of capacities in Choquet integral-based MCDA can also be used (see Grabisch et al., 2008), as well as some inverse analysis techniques by Bisdorff et al. (2009).

The complete list of the available calculation components is given on *diviz*'s website, where each of them is documented and details are given on their inputs, outputs and parameters.

21.2.1.4 Comparison of "Methods"

Next to designing and executing MCDA workflows, *diviz* can also be a convenient tool to compare the outputs of various methods and algorithms on the same input data.

Earlier, such a task has been far from easy, as no unified software platform for MCDA techniques existed. However, with *diviz* and its possibility to construct complex workflows, it is easy to connect a dataset of a specific decision problem to various workflows in a single workspace, each of them representing a different MCDA method, and to compare their outputs. This is clearly a very simple way to check the robustness of the output recommendation of an analysis with respect to the choice of the decision aiding technique. Note that in practice this possibility has to be used carefully, as the preferential parameters used by two MCDA methods may have very different meanings (for example, the tradeoff weights used by an additive model may not be compatible with an outranking-based technique. See Chap. 3.).

21.2.1.5 Workflow Sharing and Dissemination

The *diviz* software enables to export any workflow, with or without the data, as an archive. The latter can then be shared with any other *diviz* user, who can import it (by loading the archive) into the software and continue the development of the workflow or execute it on the original data.

Consequently, *diviz* can be used as a convenient dissemination tool: first, in combination with a research article, the authors of a new MCDA technique or an experiment could propose the corresponding *diviz* workflow together with an appropriate data set as supplementary electronic material with their article. Second, in a practical context, MCDA analysts could also be willing to share the algorithmic treatment they have performed with the various stakeholders of the process. This feature may contribute to a larger dissemination of new algorithms and might facilitate their acceptance among many researchers and users.

In this context, the examples which are presented in Sects. 21.3.1–21.3.4 are available as downloadable archives from the *diviz* website, and can be tested by any interested reader in their own copy of *diviz*.

21.2.2 Resources Used by diviz

We made mention earlier of the fact that *diviz* relies on further outcomes of the Decision Deck Consortium, as for example the XMCDA web-services, which are the calculation resources implementing MCDA algorithms. In this section we briefly recall the purpose of XMCDA, present the XMCDA web-services, and show how these two initiatives contribute to the *diviz* tool.

The XMCDA data format has been proposed by the Decision Deck Consortium to solve the problem of the heterogeneity of the data formats used by the available software programs. Indeed, this problem prevented existing tools to inter-operate, and it also made it necessary to re-encode all existing data each time one wants to use a new tool, so that they comply to the new expected data format.

The XMCDA markup language is written in XML (http://www.w3.org/XML/), a general-purpose syntax for defining markup languages. XMCDA allows to store data and concepts related to an MCDA problem, as for example descriptions of the criteria and alternatives, performances of alternatives on the criteria, preferences of decision makers, ... For further details on the use of XMCDA, we recommend that the reader refers to Chap. 20 of this book.

The various calculation modules which are available in *diviz* use the XMCDA standard to represent their input and output data. Consequently, they are interoperable, and they can be chained in complex workflows.

The XMCDA web-services are an initiative of the Decision Deck project and they are all available as calculation resources in *diviz*. From a general point of view, a web-service is an application which can be accessed via the Internet and is executed on a remote system. One of the great advantages of such online programs is their availability to anyone at any time and any place and on any computer which is connected to the Internet; they are accessible through the same mechanism, without requiring the (sometimes complicated) installation of each of them, and their dependencies, on the user's computer. Furthermore, the user of web-services is always sure to use the latest available version of the programs.

XMCDA web-services have furthermore the following properties:

- they are released under an open-source licence;
- they "speak" XMCDA: their inputs and outputs are formatted using this standard. This guarantees that all web-services are able to inter-operate with one another;
- they are asynchronous: each of them exposes a method for submitting a problem and an other one for retrieving the results. Consequently, one can submit long-running tasks (hours, or even days) and retrieve them afterwards, without having to stay connected in-between (in this case, the user regularly polls for available results until their are available);
- they can be made with any programming language, with the current limitation that the program should be runnable on a Linux machine, because they are deployed on Linux servers (we really mean *runnable* here: they can be developped on the user's favorite operating system as long as the language used is also available for Linux, which is in fact the case for most languages nowadays). This way everyone can participate to the web-services construction effort using their favorite language.

From an algorithmic point of view, the XMCDA web-services propose elementary calculation steps, which, if properly chained, can rebuild MCDA methods in complex workflows, as, for example, in the *diviz* workbench.

*

This introductory presentation of the *diviz* workbench and its underlying resources should show the coherence and the versatility of this ecosystem, which among other things simplifies the use of MCDA algorithms.

21.3 diviz to Support the MCDA Process

In this section we present the use of *diviz* on a didactic MCDA problem which has been widely discussed in the literature, namely the choice of a sports car (see Bouyssou et al. 2000, Chap. 6). We show how the workbench can be used in the various steps of the MCDA process. In a real-world decision aiding process, there might be round-trips between these different steps, in order, for example, to tune the input and output parameters of the various algorithms. The goal of this section being to highlight the advantages of using *diviz*, we will not discuss the decision aiding process and its variants here, which are thoroughly presented in Chap. 2.

We first present the context of the example and then illustrate the use of *diviz* in a fictitious decision aiding process involving four main phases: preparatory analysis of the problem, preference elicitation, aggregation, and finally analysis of the results. This process is inspired from Chap. 6 of Bouyssou et al. (2000), but in order to illustrate all the steps which we wish to highlight, we take the liberty of slightly modifying the original description.

Table 21.1 Data for Thierry's car selection problem

Car ID	Car name	Cost ($g1$, €)	Accel. ($g2$, s)	Pick up ($g3$, s)	Brakes ($g4$)	Road-holding ($g5$)
a01	Tipo	18,342	30.7	37.2	2.33	3
a02	Alfa	15,335	30.2	41.6	2	2.5
a03	Sunny	16,973	29	34.9	2.66	2.5
a04	Mazda	15,460	30.4	35.8	1.66	1.5
a05	Colt	15,131	29.7	35.6	1.66	1.75
a06	Corolla	13,841	30.8	36.5	1.33	2
a07	Civic	18,971	28	35.6	2.33	2
a08	Astra	18,319	28.9	35.3	1.66	2
a09	Escort	19,800	29.4	34.7	2	1.75
a10	R19	16,966	30	37.7	2.33	3.25
a11	P309-16	17,537	28.3	34.8	2.33	2.75
a12	P309	15,980	29.6	35.3	2.33	2.75
a13	Galant	17,219	30.2	36.9	1.66	1.25
a14	R21t	21,334	28.9	36.7	2	2.25

The problem we are dealing with here takes place in 1993, when Thierry, a student aged 21, is passionate about sports cars and wishes to buy a middle range, 4 years old car with a powerful engine. He selects five criteria related to: cost (criterion $g1$), performance of the engine (criteria $g2$ and $g3$) and safety (criteria $g4$ and $g5$). The list of alternatives and their evaluations on these five criteria is presented in Table 21.1. The "cost" criterion (€) and the performance criteria "acceleration" (seconds) and "pick up" (seconds) have to be minimized, whereas the safety criteria "brakes" and "road-hold" have to be maximized. Note that the values of the latter two criteria are average evaluations obtained from multiple qualitative evaluations which have been re-coded as integers between 0 and 4. Further details on these data can be found in Bouyssou et al. (2000), Chap. 6.

We will play the role of the analyst in this decision aiding process.

21.3.1 Analysis of the Problem and the Underlying Data

In this first step, Thierry wishes to set some rules on the evaluations in order to filter out certain cars. Consequently he asks that only cars respecting the following set of rules are kept:

$$\begin{aligned} \text{brakes } (g4) &\geq 2 \\ \text{road-hold } (g5) &\geq 2 \\ \text{acceleration } (g2) &< 30 \end{aligned}$$

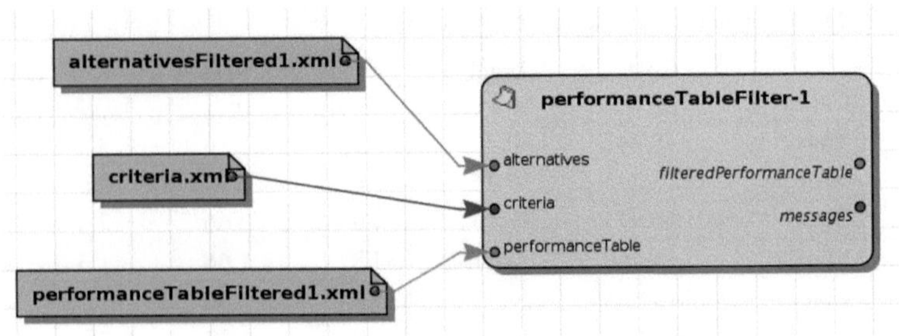

Fig. 21.3 The workflow representing the input data (*left*) and the module to filter out alternatives according Thierry's rules (*right*)

Filtered performance table

	g1	g2	g3	g4	g5
a11	17537	28.3	34.8	2.33	2.75
a03	16973	29	34.9	2.66	2.5
a07	18971	28	35.6	2.33	2
a12	15980	29.6	35.3	2.33	2.75

Fig. 21.4 The performance table resulting from the filtering step

Furthermore, Thierry notices that car a11 (P309-16) is at least as good as car a14 (R21t) on all the criteria, and thus he wishes to remove the latter.

To help Thierry, in *diviz*, we construct a simple workflow which only uses the calculation element `performanceTableFilter`, which is connected to the XMCDA files containing the definitions of the alternatives and the criteria and a file containing the performance table. The module `performanceTableFilter` allows to filter out alternatives which do not respect a set of conjunctive rules. Alternative a14 has been left out in this filtering. The workflow is represented on Fig. 21.3.

The resulting performance table is shown on Fig. 21.4.

Thierry now asks for a graphical representation of the data. We choose to show him first the performances of the remaining alternatives as star graphs. This allows him to compare their performances in a very synthetic way and to become aware of their conflicting evaluations.

In *diviz*, we complete the previous workflow with the calculation element `plotStarGraphPerformanceTable`, which is connected to the output of the filtering module and the definitions of the alternatives and criteria. In the XMCDA file containing the criteria, we furthermore specify the preference directions on the various criteria. This allows to put the preferred values in the star graphs on the

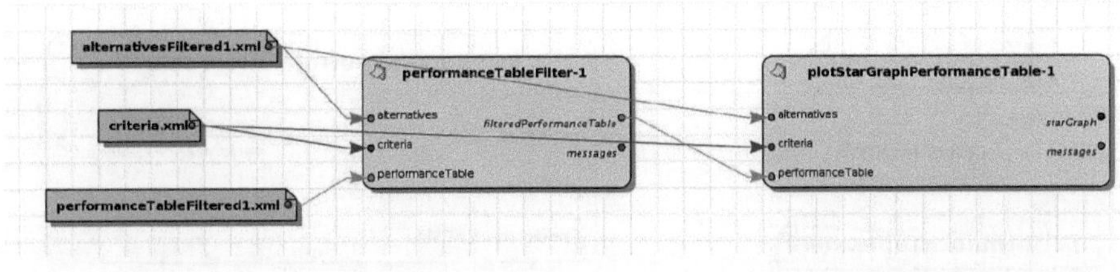

Fig. 21.5 The workflow representing the input data (*left*), the filtering module (*center*) and the module to plot star graphs of the alternatives (*right*)

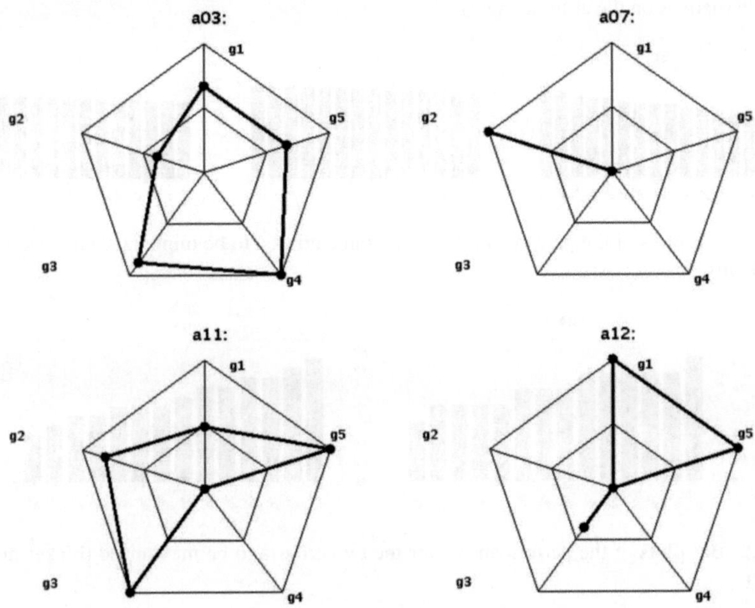

Fig. 21.6 Star graphs of alternatives a03 (Sunny), a07 (Civic), a11 (P309-16) and a12 (P309)

outside of the star, whereas the less preferred values are situated in the center of the graph. The workflow is represented on Fig. 21.5.

The resulting plots are shown to Thierry. On Fig. 21.6 we show these star graphs for the four remaining alternatives. Thierry can easily notice that a12 (P309) is the best car (among the four remaining cars) in terms of price and road-hold, but that it has quite bad evaluations for the acceleration, pick-up and brakes criteria. a03 (Sunny) and a11 (P309-16) seem to be much more well-balanced, whereas a07 (Civic) is only good on the acceleration criterion.

All in all, Thierry considers that his filtering rules have probably been too strict, and that he wishes to continue the analysis with all the initial alternatives. He now proposes to see how the alternatives compare one to another on each criterion. Among other things, he wishes to determine which alternatives have the best and worst evaluations on the criteria. We therefore construct him in *diviz* a new workflow

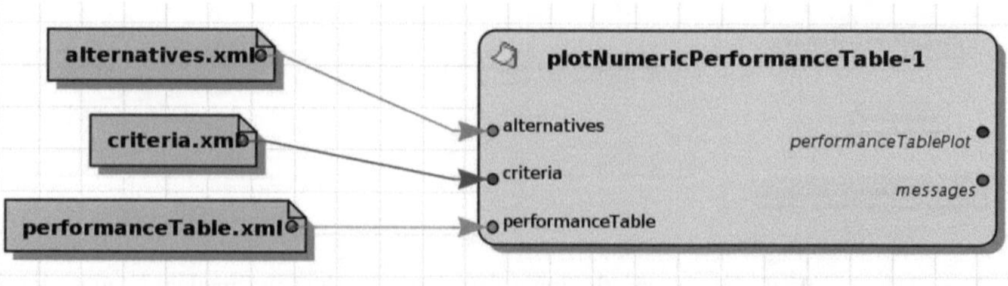

Fig. 21.7 The workflow representing the input data (*left*) and the module to plot the performances of the alternatives on the criteria (*right*)

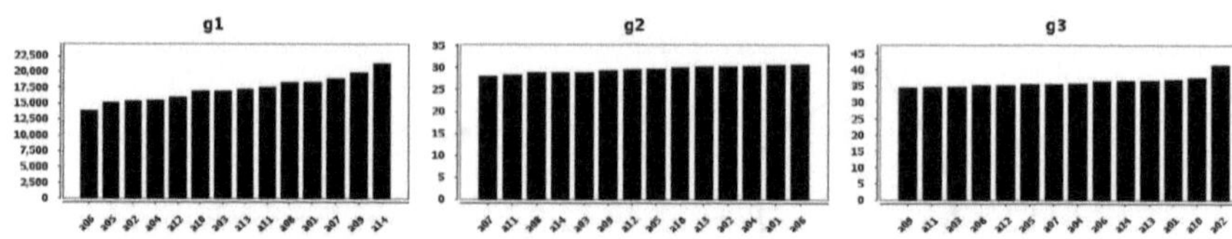

Fig. 21.8 Bar plots of the performances, for the three criteria to be minimized (cost, acceleration and pick up)

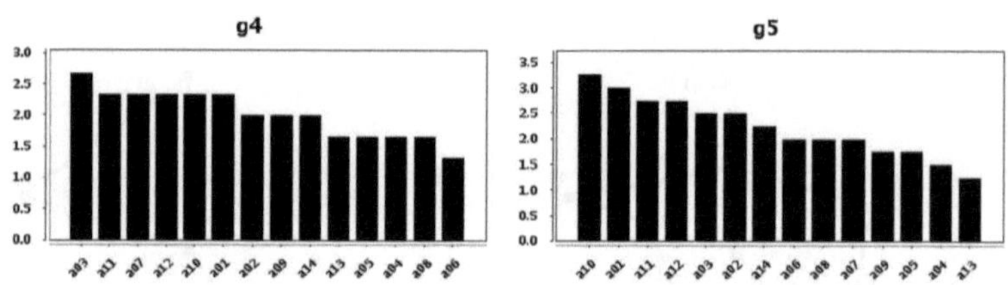

Fig. 21.9 Bar plots of the performances, for the two criteria to be maximized (brakes and road-holding)

which uses the whole performance table as input and plots the values taken by the alternatives in barcharts, for each of the criteria. The corresponding workflow is shown on Fig. 21.7.

Thierry analyzes the resulting plots. They are shown on Fig. 21.8 for the three criteria to be minimized, and on Fig. 21.9 for the two criteria to be maximized. The alternatives labeled on the horizontal axis are ordered from left to right according to the preferential direction.

Thierry observes, among other things, that alternative a11 (P309-16) seems to be a good alternative, as it has good values on a lot of criteria (except $g1$ (price)). He seems to be very interested by this alternative, and says that the rather bad performance on the price criterion could be compensated by the good performances on the other criteria.

We deduce from this first discussion with Thierry that he wishes to maximize a quantity which we could call the "value" of the cars. Consequently, our goal in the next steps of the decision aiding process will be to construct a single "super-scale" which reflects the value system of Thierry and his preferences. If we write $\succsim$ for the overall preference relation of Thierry on the set of cars, the goal will be to determine a value function u that allows to rank the alternatives and represent Thierry's preferences, i.e., which satisfies

$$a \succsim b \iff u(a) \geq u(b).$$

for all alternatives a and b.

The value $u(a)$ depends naturally on the evaluations $\{g_i(a), i = 1, \ldots n\}$ of alternative a (where n is the number of criteria), and we choose to construct a quite simple model of Thierry's preferences through an additive model, aggregating some marginal value functions on the original evaluations via a weighted sum (the weights representing trade-offs between the criteria).

21.3.2 Preference Elicitation

Now that a motivated choice has been made on the preference model, the next step of this decision aiding process is to elicit the preferences of Thierry (with respect to this additive value model). To determine the marginal value functions, a direct method could be used (by direct numerical estimations, or by indifference judgements, as described in Chap. 3, Sect. 3.2.6). However, as he seems to be quite an expert in sports cars, we decide to switch to an indirect elicitation method, where the shapes of the marginal value functions and the trade-offs are inferred from Thierry's overall preferences on some cars.

The chosen disaggregation method is UTA and was described by Jacquet-Lagrèze and Siskos (1982). It searches for piecewise linear marginal value functions which respect the input preferences expressed by the decision maker. In our case, these a priori preferences are represented by a preorder on a subset of cars, that Thierry knows quite well (the learning set). Thierry chooses to rank five cars as follows:

$$a11 \succ a03 \succ a13 \succ a09 \succ a14.$$

In order to identify his preferences in the chosen aggregation model, we construct a new workflow in *diviz*, by using the calculation module called `UTA`. The workflow is represented in Fig. 21.10. Next to the definitions of the alternatives and the criteria, and the performance table, it uses as input the ranking provided by Thierry, as well as the number of segments for each marginal value function which has to be determined. For arguments of parsimony, we decide to search for piecewise linear value functions with two segments. Thierry's input ranking is completed by two fictive alternatives (also sometimes called "ideal" and "anti-ideal" points), which simply are the best possible (ranked first) and the worst possible (ranked last) alternatives, given the ranges of values taken by the alternatives on the criteria.

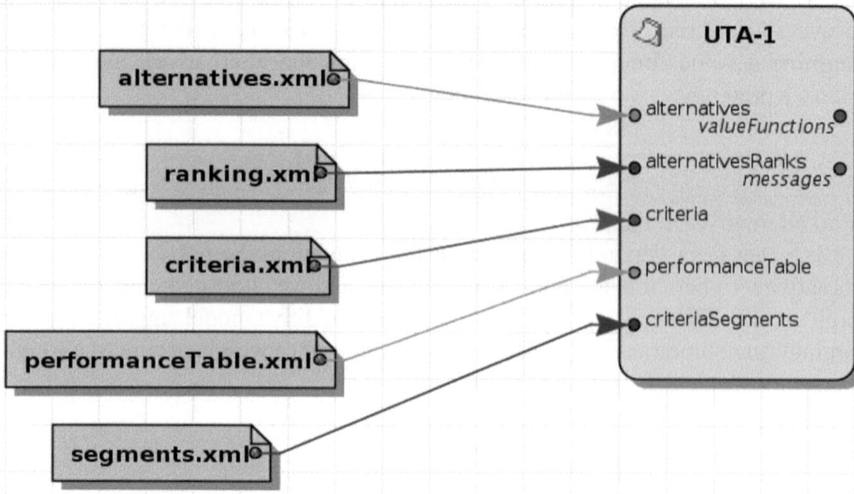

Fig. 21.10 The workflow representing the input data (*left*) and the UTA module to determine the piecewise linear value functions compliant with Thierry's input preferences (*right*)

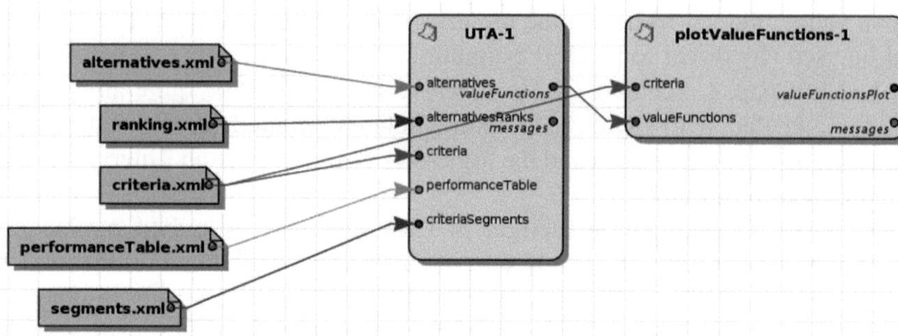

Fig. 21.11 The workflow representing the input data (*left*), the UTA module (*center*), and the plot module (*right*)

Thierry's ranking is compatible with the chosen model, and we plot the obtained value functions, by completing the previous workflow with the `plotValueFunctions` module (see Fig. 21.11).

The resulting marginal value functions are shown on Fig. 21.12. Only those for criteria g1, g2 and g5 are represented, as the ones for g3 and g4 do not intervene in the aggregation (the marginal value equals 0 for any evaluation on g3 and g4). The maximal value on the ordinate axis represents the trade-off weight in the aggregation.

Thierry is not totally convinced by this preference model. He agrees that the price is very important in the aggregation, but he considers that the pick up and

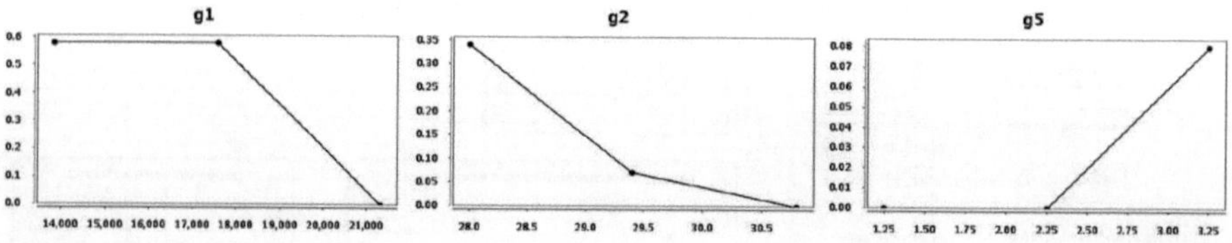

Fig. 21.12 Marginal value functions for criteria g1 (price), g2 (acceleration) and g5 (road-hold)

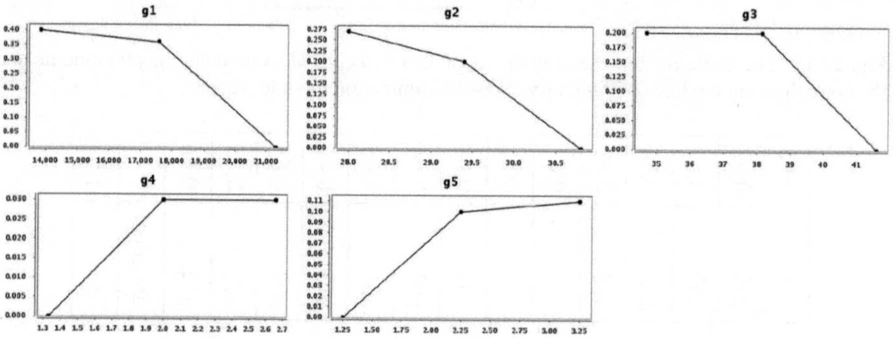

Fig. 21.13 The marginal value functions after the update of the a priori ranking of Thierry

brakes criteria should also be considered to discriminate between alternatives. He decides to modify his a priori ranking by adding two alternatives:

$$a11 \succ a03 \succ a08 \succ a04 \succ a13 \succ a09 \succ a14.$$

The new calculations generate the value functions represented on Fig. 21.13. This time Thierry validates the model, as at least the pick up criterion plays a significant role in the aggregation.

21.3.3 The Aggregation Phase

Now that a model of Thierry's preferences has been found, these marginal value functions can be used to rank all the cars. This is done by applying the value functions on the original performance table, and by performing an additive aggregation of the marginal values vector, for each alternative. In *diviz*, we therefore add the module `computeNormalizedPerformanceTable`, which takes as input the marginal value functions, the performance table, and the descriptions of the criteria and the alternatives. We then combine the result of this module with the `generalWeightedSum` one, to get the overall score of each car. This workflow is shown on Fig. 21.14.

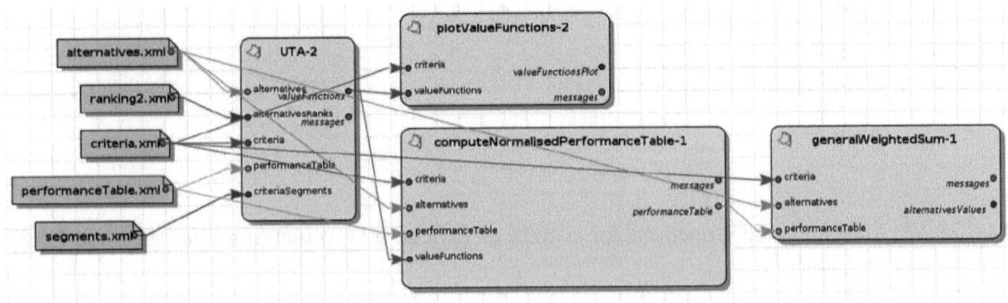

Fig. 21.14 The workflow representing the input data (*left*), the UTA module, the plot module and the normalization module (*center*), as well as the summation module (*right*)

a11	0.95
a03	0.92
a07	0.8
a12	0.88
a10	0.82
a08	0.8
a05	0.81
a04	0.68
a01	0.64
a06	0.68
a13	0.66
a02	0.6
a09	0.63
a14	0.56
antiIdeal	0
ideal	1.0

Fig. 21.15 The overall scores of the cars

The output of the `generalWeightedSum` module is the "super-scale" we were mentioning earlier. It indicates, provided it can be considered as accurate, the value of each car, according to Thierry's preference model. These overall scores are represented on Fig. 21.15.

We can observe that the car which obtains the highest score is a11 (P309-16) (after the fictive "ideal" car). This confirms Thierry's preliminary analysis.

Note here that after the confrontation of the decision maker to the overall scores, one could easily imagine that Thierry is not satisfied with the result, and that he wishes to update the preference model. To avoid adding complexity to this fictive process, we suppose that Thierry is satisfied with the scores.

21.3.4 Analysis of the Results

A last step of the decision aiding process could be to analyze the result, and to plot some graphical summaries of the outputs. In a more complex process, this phase could also be completed by a sensitivity or robustness analysis. It could also be the right place to compare the outputs of various aggregation models (for example, the ELECTRE methods, see Bouyssou et al. (2000), Chap. 6, or Meyer and Bigaret (2012) for the PROMETHEE methods).

We mainly confront Thierry to the ranking of the cars according to their overall scores, and compare the output obtained by his preference model to the

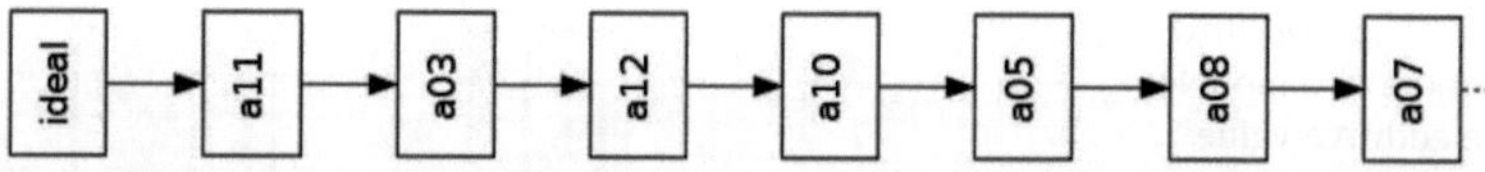

Fig. 21.16 The ranking obtained by the additive value model

Table 21.2 Thierry's naive weights for the weighted sum model

	Cost ($g1$, €)	Accel. ($g2$, s)	Pick up ($g3$, s)	Brakes ($g4$)	Road-hold ($g5$)
Weight	−1	−2	−1	0.5	0.5

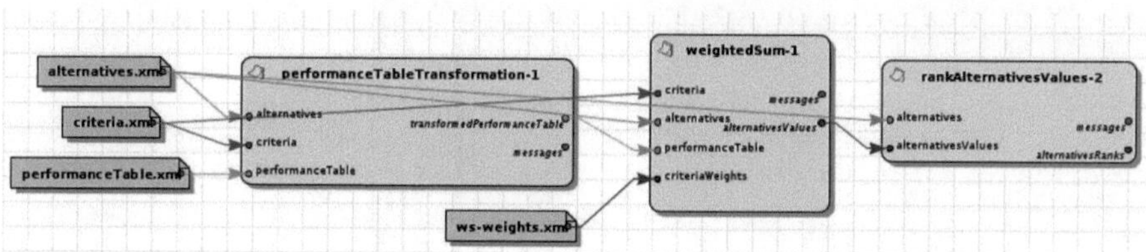

Fig. 21.17 The workflow representing the input data (*left*), data normalization module and the weighted sum module (*center*), and a module to obtain the ranks of the alternatives (*right*)

one calculated through a weighted sum (with more or less arbitrary weights and normalized data). This latter model is extensively discussed in Bouyssou et al. (2000) on pages 103–109.

In a first step, we complete the workflow of Fig. 21.14 by two elements: first a module to obtain the ranks of the alternatives according to their overall scores, and, second, a module to represent this ranking graphically. Figure 21.16 shows the first seven positions of this ranking (plus the "ideal" fictive car).

In a second step, Thierry wishes to see what would have happened if, instead of this preference elicitation phase, he had used a simpler weighted sum model. As described in Bouyssou et al. (2000), he chooses to normalize the data (each criterion at a time) by dividing each evaluation by the highest value obtained on the corresponding criterion. He then assigns weights to the criteria according to Table 21.2. The first three criteria receive negative weights since they have to be minimized.

The workflow corresponding to this aggregation in *diviz* is presented in Fig. 21.17. We first use the `performanceTableTransformation` module to normalize the data according to the method described above. Then we use the `weightedSum` module to calculate the weighted sum of each alternative, before deriving their ranks via `rankAlternativesValues`.

According to this model, car a03 is ranked first, before car a11 and a12. This is quite similar as compared to the model obtained by eliciting Thierry's preferences in an additive value model (compare to Fig. 21.16). This similarity (but not equality) is also confirmed by a rather high Kendall's rank correlation index (0.73) between the two rankings, obtained by adding the `alternativesValuesKendall` module in the end of the workflow, as shown on Fig. 21.18.

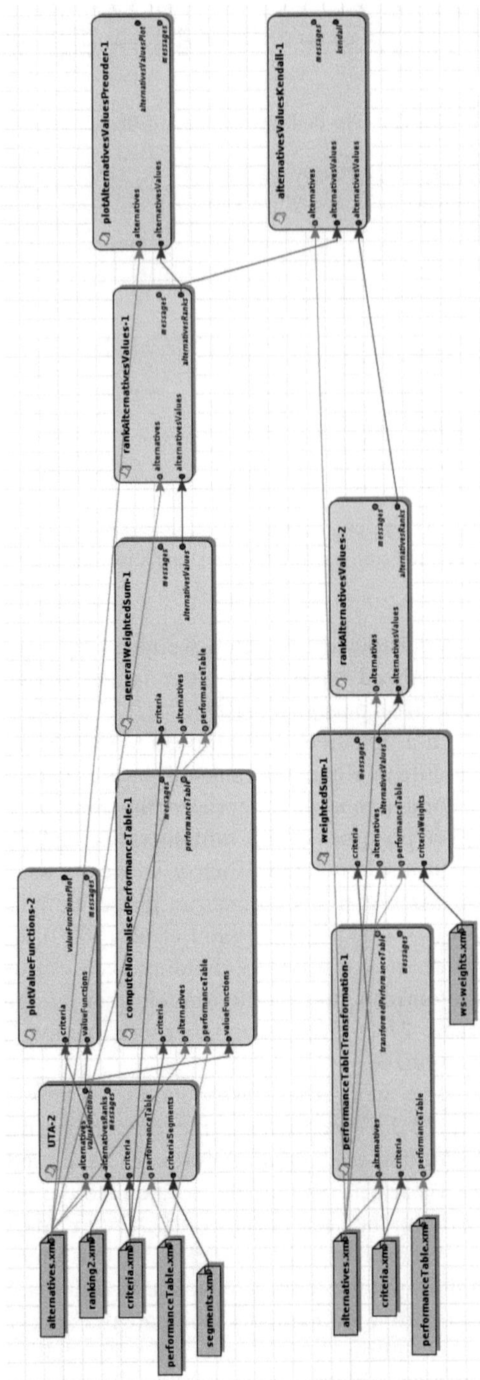

Fig. 21.18 The workflow comparing the two models: on top the additive value model, and in the bottom the weighted sum model. In the end, both rankings are compared by calculating their Kendall's rank correlation index (on the *right*)

Thierry however has a higher confidence in the output of the additive value function model, as it confirms his initial feeling about a11, and the determination of the parameters of the model seems less arbitrary to him.

21.4 Concluding Remarks

In this chapter we have shown the flexibility and the main advantages of the *diviz* workbench. We have highlighted how it can be used to design and execute algorithmic MCDA workflows and to disseminate research results. The *diviz* software is being constantly improved, and the number of available components is quickly growing.

The example detailed in Sect. 21.3 underlines the big potential of the software for the analyst, and shows how *diviz* can be adapted to various practical decision aiding situation. Next to that, *diviz* is also an easy-to-use pedagogical tool for teachers who need to present and compare classical MCDA methods.

All in all, *diviz* gives rise to an innovative working methodology in MCDA, which no longer considers the methods as static and immutable black boxes, but rather as dynamic workflows which can be changed and adapted for the current purpose.

Currently *diviz* is already used in MCDA courses in a lot of universities and engineering schools throughout Europe. It has clearly proven its great potential as a pedagogical tool via its large adoption by the students.

References

Bisdorff, R., Meyer, P., & Veneziano, T. (2009). Inverse analysis from a Condorcet robustness denotation of valued outranking relations. In F. Rossi, & A. Tsoukiàs (Eds.), *Algorithmic decision theory. Lecture notes in artificial intelligence* (Vol. 5783, pp. 180–191). Berlin: Springer.

Bouyssou, D., Marchant, T., Pirlot, M., Perny, P., Tsoukiàs, A., & Vincke, P. (2000). *Evaluation and decision models: A critical perspective*. Dordrecht: Kluwer.

Brans, J.-P., & Vincke, P. (1985). A preference ranking organization method. *Management Science, 31*(6), 647–656.

Decision Deck Consortium. (2009). *Strategic manifesto of the Decision Deck project*, http://www.decision-deck.org/manifesto.html.

Grabisch, M., Kojadinovic, I., & Meyer, P. (2008). A review of capacity identification methods for Choquet integral based multi-attribute utility theory; Applications of the Kappalab R package. *European Journal of Operational Research, 186*(2), 766–785. doi:10.1016/j.ejor.2007.02.025.

Hall, M., Frank, E., Holmes, G., Pfahringer, B., Reutemann, P., & Witten, I. H. (2009). The WEKA data mining software: An update. *SIGKDD Explorations, 11*(1), 10–18.

Jacquet-Lagrèze, E., & Siskos, Y. (1982). Assessing a set of additive utility functions for multicriteria decision making: The UTA method. *European Journal of Operational Research, 10*,151–164.

Meyer, P., & Bigaret, S. (2012). diviz: A software for modeling, processing and sharing algorithmic workflows in MCDA. *Intelligent Decision Technologies, 6*(4), 283–296. doi:10.3233/IDT-2012-0144.

R Development Core Team. (2005). *R: A language and environment for statistical computing.* Vienna: R Foundation for Statistical Computing, http://www.R-project.org [ISBN 3-900051-00-3].

Roy, B. (1968). Classement et choix en présence de points de vue multiples (la méthode ELECTRE). *Revue française d'informatique et de recherche opérationnelle (RIRO), 2*, 57–75.

Index

R. Bisdorff et al. (eds.), *Evaluation and Decision Models with Multiple Criteria*,
International Handbooks on Information Systems,
DOI 10.1007/978-3-662-46816-6

MIX
Papier aus verantwortungsvollen Quellen
Paper from responsible sources
FSC® C105338

If you have any concerns about our products,
you can contact us on
ProductSafety@springernature.com

In case Publisher is established outside the EU,
the EU authorized representative is:
Springer Nature Customer Service Center GmbH
Europaplatz 3, 69115 Heidelberg, Germany

Printed by Libri Plureos GmbH
in Hamburg, Germany